SQL Server 2012 Data Design and Retrieval

Author: Mike Hotek
Series Editor: Judith Hotek
Technical Editor: Daniel Swindle

SQL Server 2012 Data Design and Retrieval
Copyright © 2013 by Michael R Hotek

All rights reserved. No part of this work may be reproduced or transmitted in any form or by any means, mechanical, digital, electronic, or chemical, including copying, recording, or by any information storage or retrieval system without the express written consent of the copyright owner and publisher.

ISBN-13: 978-1482730067

Champion Valley Pens® and Champion Valley Press® are registered trademarks of Champion Valley Software, Inc. All other trademarks which are used in this book are owned by the registrant. Instead of using the registered trademark symbol following every occurrence of a trademark, the trademarks are used in an editorial fashion to the benefit of the trademark owner with no rights claimed nor any intention of infringement of the trademark.

Series Editor: Judith Hotek
Technical Editor: Daniel Swindle
Cover Design: Judith Hotek
Project Manager: Judith Hotek
All around support and encouragement: Judith Hotek

Distributed world-wide via CreateSpace.
For information on translations, please contact Champion Valley Software
e-mail: **admin@ChampionValleySoftware.com**
Web: **http://www.ChampionValleySoftware.com**
  http://www.ChampionValleyPress.com

The information in this book is distributed "as is", without warranty. While every precaution has been taken in preparing this book, neither the author, publisher, distributor, or any publisher's agent shall have any liability to any person or entity with respect to any loss or damage caused or alleged to be caused directly, indirectly, or inadvertently by the information contained within this book.

Source code and sample databases for this book are available at http://www.ChampionValleyPress.com.

For Judith,
I love you

To my wife, Stacey, and my children, Brandon, Ashley, Caleb, (and +1 on the way!) whom I love more than life itself. And to my Mother, Susan who taught me to keep my head down and work hard. - Daniel

Acknowledgements

Thank you to all of my readers over the past decade and a half. I can't believe that we're on our 9th SQL Server book. None of this would be possible without your support.

Judith, this book would have been impossible without you. This project started out as a single book, but turned into an entire publishing company as well as a series of books. You are responsible for all of the unseen things which make delivery of this book even possible. Your love and support has seen me through to the end of this book and kept me going through the entire process. You have supported me through all of the long weekends, late nights, and put up with a serious lack of attention all while keeping me sane with all of the walks, runs, bike rides, and trips to Yogurtland. I love you, could not do any of this without you, and it wouldn't be worth it without you.

Thank you to all of the developers who have worked on SQL Server across the years. Your patience with all of my questions….and comments, has been invaluable. Through working with, writing about, and teaching SQL Server, I've met many friends and SQL Server has given me more than I could ever possibly give back. There aren't many people who can say they met their spouse because of SQL Server, although she did have to get out a "club" and "smack me upside the head", after all I am still a guy who is a geek.

It has been my pleasure to know Daniel Swindle over many years. I initially met him at Sonic when I was working on a project there. I believe our first conversation was about a process he was running against one of my production servers that had the entire system so locked up nothing else could get done. I've watched him grow from a developer with a little database administration to one of the best DBAs I've had the pleasure of working with. Daniel and his family have also become very good friends of ours. His help on this book has been immeasurable and I always enjoy those times when he manages to "break" SQL Server in a completely impossible way.

I'd also like to thank Andy, Mary, and Joan for "are we there yet"? ☺ You've kept me focused knowing that there are at least 3 other people who will read this book. Thank you to the Fort Worth SQL Server User's Group. You've provided me with a venue to teach, but more importantly learn SQL Server to a level which made this book possible.

I'd also like to thank Microsoft Press. Writing on my own has been something I've wanted to do for a very long time. I can finally write books my way against software that is not still in a beta cycle. I've also been able to get out of the purely introductory books which had very little depth and write books that take my readers from the basics through all of the advanced topics.

Table of Contents

Chapter 1: Overview of Microsoft SQL Server 1
- Database Development 2
  - Storage Engine 2
  - Data Storage and Retrieval 3

Chapter 2: Installation and Configuration 4
- SQL Server 2012 Editions 4
- Service Accounts 5
- SQL Server Instances 6
- Collation Sequences 6
- Authentication Modes 6
- Summary 9

Chapter 3: SQL Server Tools 10
- Books Online 10
- SQL Server Configuration Manager 11
- SQL Server Management Studio 12
- SQL Server Profiler 15
- Distributed Replay 15
- Database Engine Tuning Advisor 16
- Summary 16

Chapter 4: Creating Databases 18
- Database Structure 18
  - Filegroups 18
  - Database Files 19
  - FILESTREAM 20
  - Transaction Log 20
  - Creating a Database 21
- System Databases 23
  - master 23
  - model 24
  - msdb 24
  - tempdb 24
  - mssqlsystemresource 25
- Database Context 25

- Modifying a Database 25
- Moving Databases 26
- Contained Databases 27
- Summary 28

Chapter 5: Designing Tables 29

- Database Design 29
- Data Modeling 32
- Naming Objects 34
  - Naming Conventions 34
- Schemas 34
- Data Structure 35
  - Character Data Types 36
    - Fixed vs. Variable Length Data Types 36
    - Unicode Data 37
    - Large Objects 37
  - Numeric Data Types 38
    - Exact and Approximate Numeric Data Types 38
    - Decimal and Numeric Data Types 39
    - Float vs. Decimal 39
  - Date and Time Data Types 40
  - Binary Data Types 42
  - Specialized Data Types 42
    - XML 42
    - HIERARCHYID 43
    - Spatial 45
    - ROWVERSION 46
    - UNIQUEIDENTIFIER 46
    - SQL_VARIANT 46
  - Data Types – Why Should You Care? 47
  - How to Store Nothing 47
- Creating Tables 48
- Constraints 49
  - Primary Keys 50
  - Foreign Keys 51
  - Check Constraints 55
  - Default Constraints 56

Unique Constraints	56
Many to Many Relationships	**57**
Special Column Properties	**58**
IDENTITY	58
FILESTREAM	59
FILESTREAM Considerations	62
ROWGUIDCOL	65
SPARSE	65
Computed Columns	66
Special Tables	**71**
Temporary Tables	71
FileTables	73
Pre-requisites	74
Restrictions	74
Summary	**75**
Chapter 6: Data Storage Structures	**77**
Database Allocation	**77**
Page Chains	**78**
Page Structure	80
Slots 81	
Row Structure	82
Fixed Length Rows	82
Variable Length Rows	83
Large Objects	84
Restricted Length Data	84
Unrestricted Length Data	85
MAX Length Data Types	85
Sparse Columns	86
Compression	86
Compressed Row Structure	87
Row Compression	88
Page Compression	88
Compression Considerations	89
Storage Metadata	**89**
Summary	**90**
Chapter 7: Data Manipulation	**91**

Retrieving Data 91
Adding Data 92
    Identities 93
    Hierarchies 96
        Variables 98
        Hierarchy Functions 99
    Default Constraints 102
    Mass Loading Data 103
        Recovery Models 105
        BCP 105
        BULK INSERT 108
    Loading FileTable Data 108
    SELECT INTO 109
Modifying Data 109
    Assign a Value While Updating 114
Removing Data 114
    Mass Removal of Data 116
Data Modification Tables 116
Multiple Modifications 117
    Foreign Keys 120
    Terminators 120
Tracking Changes 122
    Change Tracking 123
        Change Tracking Functions 125
    Change Data Capture 126
        Change Data Capture Functions 129
        CDC Capture and Cleanup 130
Summary 132

Chapter 8: Managing Concurrency 133
Concurrency Models 133
Transactions 134
    Types of Transactions 134
    ACID properties 136
Locking 137
    Lock Types 137
    Lock Structures 138

Static Allocation	139
Dynamic Allocation	139
Lock Escalation	140
Intent Locks	141
Lock Timeout	142
Transaction Behaviors	142
Dirty Reads	143
Lost Updates	143
Nonrepeatable Reads	143
Phantom Reads	144

Transaction Isolation Levels **144**
   Read Uncommitted 144
   Read Committed 145
   Repeatable Read 145
   Serializable 146
   Snapshot 146
   Key Locks 146
   View Lock Information 147

Deadlocks **149**

Row Versioning **152**
   Isolation Levels 153
   Version Store 153
   Version Store management 155
      Snapshot Conflicts 161

Summary **162**

Chapter 9: Data Retrieval 163

General Select Statement **163**

FROM Clause **165**

Aliasing **168**
   Alias Method 1 168
   Alias Method 2 168
   Alias Method 3 168
   Query Results 169

Data Manipulation **170**
   Determinism 170
   Built-in Functions 170

    Data Type Conversion 171

    Variables 173

    Handling NULLs 174

    Date and Time Data 176

    Calculations 180

    CASE 182

Sorting Data **183**

Returning a Subset of Rows **185**

    TOP 185

    TABLESAMPLE 186

    WHERE 186

        Comparison Operators 187

        Wildcards 188

        NULLs 190

        Operator Precedence 191

Multi-table queries **196**

    INNER JOIN 198

    OUTER JOIN 199

    CROSS JOIN 201

    Subqueries 202

        Non-Correlated Subqueries 202

        Correlated Subqueries 204

Unique Results **206**

Aggregation – GROUP BY Clause **207**

    OUTER JOINS 209

    NULLs 210

    Multi-Level Aggregates 210

        ROLLUP 210

        CUBE 212

    Multiple Groupings 212

Filtering Aggregates – HAVING clause **214**

Derived Tables **215**

Processing Order **216**

Summary **222**

Chapter 10: Advanced Data Retrieval **223**

    Set Operations **223**

UNION	224
INTERSECT	225
EXCEPT	226
Data Modification	**227**
Table Expressions	**228**
Row/Table Constructors	228
Common Table Expressions (CTEs)	228
Regular CTEs	229
Recursive CTEs	232
PIVOT	233
UNPIVOT	235
Set Operators	**237**
Window Functions	**240**
Aggregate Functions	241
Ranking Functions	249
ROW_NUMBER()	250
NTILE(n)	251
RANK() and DENSE_RANK()	254
Analytic Functions	255
FIRST_VALUE() and LAST_VALUE()	255
LEAD() and LAG()	256
PERCENTILE_CONT() and PERCENTILE_DISC()	257
CUME_DIST() and PERCENT_RANK()	258
Window Function Performance	258
Window Functions Reloaded	259
XML	**260**
Formatting Results as XML	261
Querying XML Data	265
Summary	**270**
Chapter 11: Spatial Queries	**271**
Overview of Spatial Data	**271**
Points	273
Lines	273
Polygons	273
Circular Strings	273
Compound Curves	274

    Curved Polygons 275

    GeometryCollection 275

    Boundaries 275

Defining Geometric Shapes **276**

Spatial Calculations **279**

    Retrieving Properties 280

    Modifying and Comparing Objects 283

Defining Geographic Shapes **290**

    Objects on a Globe 291

    Spatial Reference Systems 293

    Left Hand Rule 295

    Geography Methods 295

    Loading Real Geographic Objects 296

Summary **300**

Chapter 12: Designing Indexes 301

Index Structure **301**

    B-Trees 302

Clustered Indexes **304**

    Unique Clustered Indexes 304

    Creating an Index 306

        Page Splits 307

        Fill Factor 307

        PAD_INDEX 308

        Compression 308

        Index Options Affecting Creation 308

        Index Options Affecting Queries 309

        Duplicate Keys 309

    Non-Unique Clustered Indexes 311

Nonclustered Indexes **314**

    Heaps 314

    Non-Unique Nonclustered Indexes 315

    Unique Nonclustered Indexes 315

    Forwarding Pointers 316

    Nonclustered Indexes with a Clustered Index 319

        Uniqueness 319

        Designing an Index 320

| Computed Columns 324
| Filtered Indexes 324
| Covering Indexes 326
| Included columns 327

Hierarchies 328

XML Data 329
    Primary Index 329
    PATH Index 330
    VALUE Index 331
    PROPERTY Index 331

Selective XML Indexes 332
    Selective XML Index Storage 332
    Creating a Selective XML Index 334
    Typing XML 334
    Index Optimizations 335
    Enabling Selective XML Indexes 336

Spatial Indexes 338
    Tessellating Objects 340
        Cells Per Object 340
        Covering 341
        Deepest Cell 342
        Primary Key 342
    Geometry Indexes 342
    Supported Spatial Methods 342
        Filter() 343
        Geometry 343
        Geography 344

Indexes and the Optimizer 345
    Distribution Statistics 346
        Density 347
        Histograms 347
        Creating a Histogram 350
        Selectivity and Cardinality 354
    Creating Statistics 354
        Automatic Creation 356
        Filtered Statistics 357

- Correlated Columns 357
- String Statistics 359
- Updating Statistics 360

Data Modifications 364
- Inserts 365
  - Page Splits Revisited 365
- Deletes 366
- Updates 369
  - Unique Indexes 370
- Multiple Changes 373

Index Maintenance 374
- Fragmentation 376
- Rebuilding Indexes 376
  - Analysing Indexes 378
  - Removing Fragmentation 378

Disabling an Index 381

Designing Indexes Revisited 381
- Complementary indexes 383
- Monitor Index Usage 384
  - Missing Indexes 384
  - Evaluate Index Usage 389

Columnstore Indexes 390
- Columnstore Indexes Defined 394
  - Columnstore Index Structure 394
  - Columnstore Restrictions 395
  - Columnstore Index Processing 396
  - Processing Blocks 398
  - Character data 399
- Creating a Columnstore Index 399

Summary 399

Chapter 13: Full-Text Indexes 400

"Unstructured" Data 400

Full-text Catalogs 402

Full-text Indexes 403
- Parsers 403
- Helper Services 404

- Word Breaker 404
- Stemmer 404
- Stop Words 404
- Languages 405
- Creating a Full-Text Index 406
- Language, Word Breakers, and Stemmers 407
- Populate Full Text Indexes 408
  - Change Tracking 409
  - Build Process 410
- Custom Filters 410
- Property Lists 412

Querying Full-Text Indexes **414**
- FREETEXT 415
- CONTAINS 416
  - Exact Match Searches 417
  - Wildcard Searches 417
  - Word Forms 417
  - Thesaurus Files 417
  - Proximity Searches 420
  - Weighted Results 420

Monitoring Index Population **421**
Contents of a Full-Text Index **421**
Semantic Search **422**
- Configuring Semantic Search 423
- Semantic Searches 425

Summary **426**

Chapter 14: Partitioning..427

Partition Functions **427**
Partition Schemes **429**
Partitioning Tables and Indexes **430**
- Creating a Partitioned Table 430
- Creating a Partitioned Index 432

Querying Partitioned Tables **437**
Managing Partitions **438**
- Next Used 438
- Split and Merge 441

- Merge 442
  - Split 443
- Altering a Partition Scheme 444
- Index Alignment 446
- Switch Operator 446
  - Change Tracking 449
  - Columnstore Indexes 449

Summary **452**

About the Author and Editor

Mike Hotek is a SQL Server professional and best-selling author with a depth and breadth of experience few can match. He has over 30 years of experience developing application using a variety of programming languages and over 20 years of experience building database solutions. His solutions span virtually every business sector and are among the largest, most complex solutions ever deployed. In his more than 2 decades, he has built solutions encompassing every SQL Server feature and blending those with a variety of other platforms and services. He has been teaching and writing about SQL Server for more than 15 years and has been on the leading edge (and sometimes beyond the bleeding edge) of the processes and techniques used throughout the industry today. The book in your hands will be Mike's 9th SQL Server book

Daniel Swindle is the President and Data Savant of Syndrome Industries, Inc. With over 13 years as a SQL Server professional he has consulted on projects spanning every feature within SQL Server in Public, Private, Non-Profit, and Governmental sectors. Being highly proficient in data architecture, data security, ETL design/processing, database administration, and data driven application development, he is capable of solving the most complex data dilemmas in an expedient and cost efficient manner. First and foremost, he is a husband and father who loves his wife and children above all else.

Introduction

The book you hold in your hands started off with a very different design and for a different publisher. The project that started out as a single book that could only do a very superficial "fly-by" of SQL Server 2012 has turned into a series of books that will take quite a while to complete. I started this project trying to figure how to cover all of the features in a product which has exploded over the last 4 years and still fit everything into an 800 page book. What I would have wound up with is a book that only managed to get 1 – 2 pages for a major feature and only a handful of sentences for many others. It would have been a complete failure.

When I got the notice from Microsoft Press that I would no longer be writing books for them, it was a pretty big shock. But what grew out that decision were Champion Valley Press and this book.

I wasn't going to give up writing and Judith turned me on to CreateSpace. That was all it really took. Realizing that you couldn't possible cram useful information about every feature in SQL Server inside a single book, I started out by designing a 3 book series. Book 1 would cover database development, book 2 would cover database administration, and the 3rd book would cover the business intelligence stack. As I got into the first book, I finally realized the massive advantage I now had by writing and publishing on my own. I no longer had to hold back content or cut off a subject before we had covered every area, because my publisher wanted to put that information in another book. I was my own publisher and I could do whatever I wanted. As you can see, the database development book has now been split in half because it would have been impossible to get everything I wanted into a single 800 page book. This book covers the first half of the database development subject area while the next book in the series will be covering the other half of database development.

This book should get you from installing SQL Server to understanding the how and why of designing and querying databases. Along the way, you'll see topics that go all the way into the on disk storage structures to explain why SQL Server and queries behave the way they do. For those interested in certification, this book covers almost all of the information necessary to take and pass the 70-461 certification exam while going well beyond the exam topics to information you will find indispensable for your job.

While I have taken every effort to ensure that the exercises and all code run successfully and all information is accurate and up to date, it is inevitable that something has slipped through. All errors and omissions are my responsibility. But, this is your book. I strongly encourage you to send your comments and corrections and I will make every effort to accommodate them. You can send all feedback to feedback@ChampionValleyPress.com.

Downloading the Code

You can download all source code and sample databases at http://www.ChampionValleyPress.com.

Kindle Edition

This book will be published in both a paper and Kindle edition. I strongly encourage you to get the Kindle edition for more reasons than to save trees. As updates are made to this book, they will be loaded to Amazon as updates which you will automatically get when you synch, no need to go out and buy a second edition of the book to get any corrections or additional content.

Section One
Getting Started

In This Section:

Chapter 1: Introduction to Microsoft SQL Server

Chapter 2: Installation and Configuration

Chapter 3: SQL Server Tools

Chapter 1
Overview of Microsoft SQL Server

Over the last decade, there has been a major push in all organizations to outsource non-essential functions such as accounting, payroll, and customer support so all effort can be spent on core functions that drive profitability such as marketing and product development. Along with the out-sourcing, the entire interaction with the customer has been automated from the placement of an order to the delivery.

Customers browse online product catalogs, select products, and place orders 24 hours a day. Orders flow through a web application and are stored in a database. Payments are automatically routed to a clearinghouse, debited from the customer's account, deposited into the company's account, and the payment status is updated on the customer's order. Once the order is marked as paid, a smart warehouse receives the order and dispatches machines to locate and pull products from the shelf, combine into a box, add any necessary paperwork, seal the box, add the shipping label and send the package to the dock where another machine loads the packages into a truck for shipment. The tracking number for the label is automatically sent to the customer and logged with the order. The warehouse decrements the available inventory and may even automatically send orders out to suppliers to restock an item that is running low along with updating a purchase order system with each auto-generated order. The shipping company uses automated sorting and routing equipment which updates the package location information and routes the packages to the final destination, where a person finally delivers it to your door. In a process that might have taken dozens of people in the past, your order might have only been touched by two or three people from the warehouse to your door. Even when you call into an organization, you are met by a computer that routes your call and in many cases looks up your order, provides tracking information, and may even allow you to cancel, re-route, or modify an order.

While all of this activity is happening, employees within the organization are querying the database to determine how many orders are coming in, what products are being sold, what the inventory status is, or how much time it takes from an order being placed to when the order is delivered. Customer data needs to be secured to meet regulatory requirements as well as keep the organization out of the news with all of the data breaches being publicized. The IT department is monitoring the entire system, looking for bottlenecks or failures. Any performance issues need to be diagnosed and fixed in very short amounts of time, because an organization may only have a few seconds to capture a customer and keep them. Outages and performance issues have to be masked from the customer, because while people may have patiently waited in line to check out in the past, having to wait 5 seconds for a web page to load could have a large number of people flaming the company on multiple blogs. Even though the issue may have been fleeting, customers may go to competitors in droves thereby having a major impact on the organization's reputation or even ending months of carefully crafted work to roll out a new product or service.

Even when an organization has a physical presence for customers to visit, you will find far less staff and a push for customers to self-service. Banks have ATMs which allow you to perform most functions without ever interacting with a teller. Supermarkets and large retailers have self-service lanes where a customer might not ever have to speak to an employee. Even in stores without self-service checkouts, it is very common to find a single person managing the entire store.

Lost in this world of web-based ordering at all hours of the day, self-service checkouts, and very limited staffing is the personal interaction that businesses have always had with their customers. In simple conversations, organizations have gained insight into how their customers' preferences are changing as well as how they could better help them. A teller talking to a customer making a deposit might find out that they are thinking about starting a new business and can direct them to a variety of business services that the bank offers. A clerk at the checkout counter might learn that a customer has just gotten engaged and can offer a lot of tips since they just got married. These types of interactions, whether they directly sold products or not, build customer loyalty by showing that the people at the business listen, care about, and are willing to help their customers.

The cost of keeping an existing customer is far lower than acquiring a new customer. So, organizations are trying to bridge the gap in direct customer interactions by gaining deeper insight into customer behavior and customer trends. However, to gain insight, requires increasingly powerful IT systems along with ever increasing volumes of data.

As SQL Server passes 20 years old, the database of the past has evolved into an integrated data platform capable of securely processing the largest amounts of data in existence, maintaining 'round the clock availability, and delivering stunning visualizations that provide insight into the reams of data captured.

Database Development

While SQL Server has evolved into a complete data platform that spans multiple capabilities the core of the product, the relational engine, has largely remained the same. The relational engine is composed of what most people refer to as SQL Server. Responsible for managing the basic storage, security, availability, retrieval, and recoverability of your data, the relational engine sits at the heart of everything you will do with a SQL Server. The relational engine encompasses all of the features people typically attribute to a database like SQL Server.

Storage Engine

The storage engine lies at the heart of the relational engine. The entire purpose of a database is to store data. In chapters 4 and 5, you will learn how to store data in a logical and consistent format so that users can easily find the data they need. Chapter 6 will cover some of the relevant internal storage structures to help you understand how your design choices affect how much disk space, memory, and processing you need on your servers.

A database is worthless without data or users to retrieve and use the data. In chapters 7 and 8, you will learn how to store and manipulate data. In chapters 9 and 10 you will learn how to efficiently retrieve the data your users need. In chapter 11, you will learn how to leverage the spatial engine to find the location of the nearest Starbucks for when you need that extra caffeine jolt to get through the day. Of course, you'll also learn how to organize and retrieve data that has a spatial reference so your organization can put it to use.

In chapter 14, you will learn how to extend your data storage structures to rapidly load and archive data.

Data Storage and Retrieval

You may have stored all of your organization's data in a logical manner, but users need to quickly retrieve information. In chapter 10, you will learn how to improve your query performance by designing indexes. In chapter 13, you will learn how to build indexes and search large volumes of semi-structured data so that your users spend less time finding documents that they need and can get back to playing Angry Birds.

Chapter 2
Installation and Configuration

The first step in learning SQL Server is getting everything installed and configured. While installing SQL Server is a relatively straight forward task, you will need to understand all of the options available in order to make the proper choices.

> Note: You will need administrative authority on the machine where SQL Server will be installed to complete the exercises in this chapter.

SQL Server 2012 Editions

There are several editions of SQL Server 2012 which are designed to meet a variety of general needs. In addition to the monetary difference, the edition you choose will dictate the feature set available for your applications. Table 2.1 lists the available editions of SQL Server 2012.

Table 2-1 SQL Server 2012 Editions

SQL Server Edition	Purpose
Enterprise	Designed for the largest organizations to meet the most demanding applications. The Enterprise Edition contains all of the features available, but is limited to a maximum of 20 processor cores.
Enterprise Core	Contains the same feature set as Enterprise Edition, but allows you to unlock more than 20 cores.
Developer	Designed to allow organizations to develop applications with the same feature set as Enterprise Edition, but can only be used to develop and test applications. This is the edition that should be installed on all of your development, test, and QA servers.
Evaluation	The evaluation edition expires 180 days after installation and contains all of the features of Enterprise Edition. The Evaluation Edition cannot be deployed to a production environment.
Standard	Contains most of the SQL Server features needed by small and medium-sized businesses.
Business Intelligence	New in SQL Server 2012, this edition contains all of the features of the Standard edition and adds in the features for the SQL Server Business Intelligence stack.
Web	Contains the features needed to support web based applications with limited hardware.

SQL Server Edition	Purpose
Express	This comes in two different versions. Express with Advanced Services includes a Reporting Services engine while Express with Tools is the core relational engine with the development tools. Free and redistributable with applications to provide local data storage. Express Edition is commonly deployed as the backend for very small web sites or applications that need limited, local storage.
Azure	The cloud based version of SQL Server 2012

> Note: For a comparison of the features available in each edition, please go to http://www.microsoft.com/sql.

Service Accounts

All of the core SQL Server components, such as the Database Engine and SQL Server Agent run as services. Prior to installing SQL Server, you will need to create Windows accounts for:

- Database Engine
- SQL Server Agent
- Distributed Replay Controller

When we install SQL Server, we will be using the same service account for both the Database Engine and SQL Server Agent services.

Exercise 1: Creating Service Accounts

In the following exercise, you will create the two service accounts we will need to install SQL Server and the Distributed Replay Controller. The service account names are my choice. You can change these to anything you want.

1. Click Start, right-click My Computer, and select Manage.
2. Expand Local Users and Groups, right click Users and select New User.
3. Specify SQLEngine in the User Name field, supply a strong password, deselect User Must Change Password At Next Logon, select Password Never Expires, and click Create.
4. Repeat step 4 to create an account named SQLReplay for the Distributed Replay Controller.

> Tip: You always want to set service accounts to never expire.

Microsoft has recommended having a separate service account for SQL Server Agent and the Database Engine. Then they require both services accounts to have the same permission level within the SQL Server. Until they decide to change these requirements, I don't see any point in having two service accounts that have the same level of access to the instance.

SQL Server Instances

Each SQL Server installation defines an instance on the machine. Instances are the security containers for all of your databases. Each instance you create has its own set of databases, security credentials, configuration settings, Windows services, and other SQL Server objects. You can have 1 default instance and up to 49 named instances or 50 total instances on a single machine.

When you connect to a default instance of SQL Server, you use the name of the machine that the instance is installed on. When connecting to a named instance, you use the combination of the machine name and instance name, e.g. <machinename>\<instancename>.

Some of the reasons for installing more than one instance of SQL Server on a single machine are:

- Supporting QA and development
- Supporting multiple service packs or patch levels

Collation Sequences

Character based data is one of the most common types of data stored in a database. Not every language uses the same character set or even sorts data in the same way. A collation sequence is used to define the rules that SQL Server applies to storing, retrieving, and sorting character data. The rules define the character set that is supported along with how case, accent, and kana is handled. The last two parts of a collation sequence designate the case sensitivity and the accent sensitivity respectively. For example, if you use the default collation sequence of SQL_Latin1_General_CP1_CI_AI, you will get support for a Western European character set that is case insensitive and accent insensitive. SQL_Latin1_General_CP1_CI_AI will treat e, E, è, é, ê, and ë as the same character for sorting and comparison operations. However, if you a use SQL_Latin1_General_CP1_CS_AS collation sequence e, E, è, é, ê, and ë will be treated as a different character.

Authentication Modes

The authentication mode specifies the types of logins allowed to the instance. SQL Server supports the following authentication modes:

- Windows only (integrated security)
- Windows and SQL Server (mixed mode)

When the authentication mode is set to Windows only authentication, you will only be able to use Windows accounts to login to the instance. When the authentication mode is set to mixed, you can use either Windows accounts or SQL Server created accounts to login to the instance.

The Windows accounts can either be Active Directory domain accounts or local machine accounts;

although it is recommended that you use domain accounts for all access. By using domain accounts, you move the account management piece to your system administrators who already manage all of the login credentials in your organization allowing you to just focus on the access required for the accounts.

Exercise 2: SQL Server 2012 Installation

> **Note:** Make sure that you have .NET Framework 3.5 SP1 installed on the machine prior to starting the SQL Server 2012 installation. It is also very strongly recommended that you apply all Windows updates prior to installation and then apply any additional updates which may be necessary after install. Installing Windows patches on a regular basis, usually monthly, is one of the best preventative actions you can take.

1. Launch the SQL Server installation routine and click the Installation link in the left hand navigation bar. Select New SQL Server stand-alone installation or add features to an existing installation.

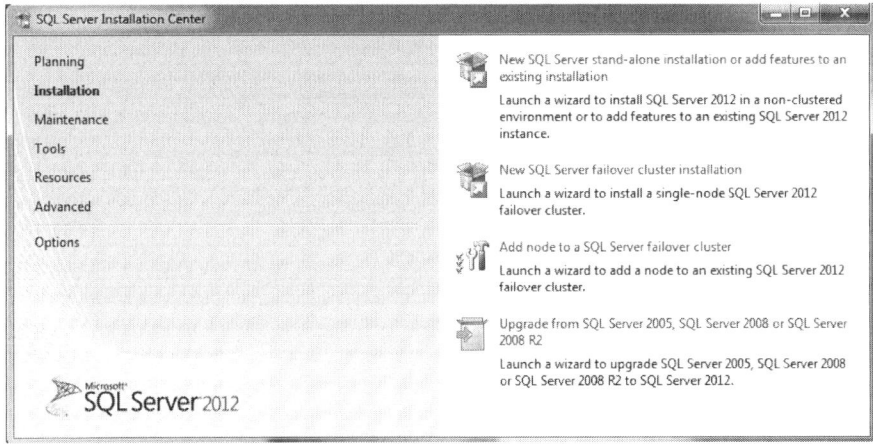

Figure 2-1 SQL Server installation options

2. Click OK when setup finishes checking the installation rules.

3. Specify the Edition you want to install or enter your product key and click Next.

4. Accept the license terms and click Next.

5. After installing the setup support files, setup rules will be checked again. Click Next.

6. Select SQL Server Feature Installation and click Next.

7. Select Database Engine Services, Full Text and Semantic Extractions, Client Tools Connectivity, Documentation Components, Management Tools Basic and Complete, Distributed Replay Controller, and Distributed Replay Client. Click Next.

> **Note:** There are a lot of features and options which can be installed. We are only installing the features which will be needed to complete all of the exercises in this book. You can always go back and install additional features.

8. Click Next when the Installation Rules finish.
9. Leave the option for Default instance selected and click Next.
10. Click Next on the disk space requirements screen.
11. Enter SQLEngine and your password for the SQL Server Agent and SQL Server Database Engine. Enter SQLReplay and your password for the SQL Server Distributed Replay Client and SQL Server Distributed Replay Controller as shown in Figure 2-3 below and click Next.

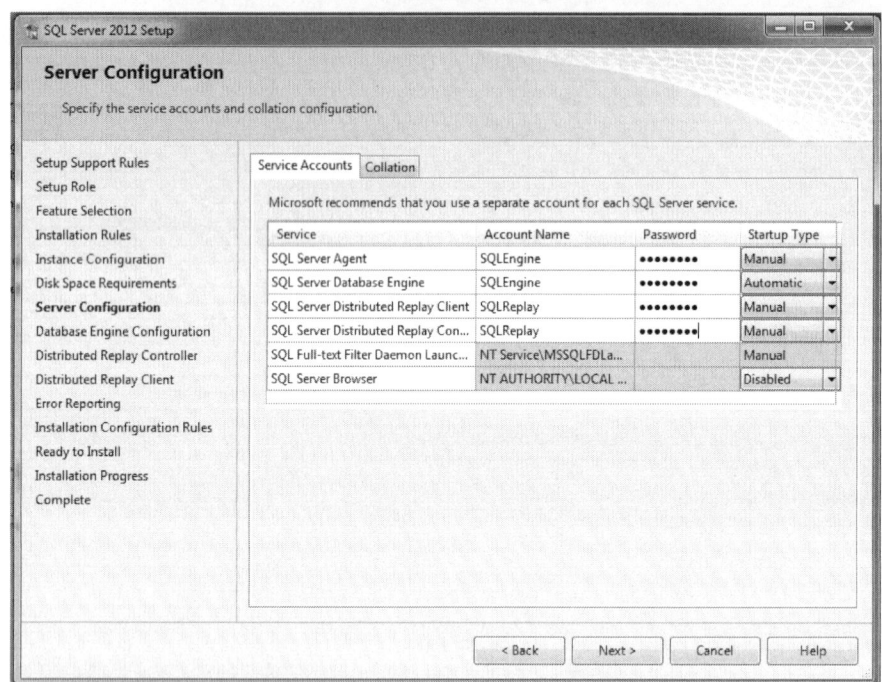

Figure 2-3 Service Accounts

12. Select Mixed Mode and enter a strong password for the sa account and click the Add Current User button.
13. Click the FILESTREAM tab and Enable FILESTREAM for Transact-SQL access. Click Next.
14. Click Add Current User to add your account for permissions to Distributed Replay and click Next.
15. Enter SQLReplay for the name of the replay controller and click Next.
16. Click Next on the Error Reporting screen.

> **Note:** It is recommended that you enable sending of error reports. Many of the bug fixes that are created for SQL Server occur because of automated error reporting.

17. After the configuration rules finish running, click Next.
18. Review your installation selections and click Install.

19. Go get a cup of coffee or go for lunch/dinner, the installation will take about 10 – 15 minutes to complete. When you return, your SQL Server will be ready to use.

Summary

Prior to installing SQL Server, you need to decide on the following factors:

- Edition that meets the feature set requirements of your applications
- Service accounts that will be used
- Collation sequence that defines the character set supported by default on the instance
- Authentication mode that governs which types of accounts can be used to connect to the instance

Chapter 3
SQL Server Tools

SQL Server ships with a large number of tools for development, management, and configuration of components. In this chapter, you will find a brief overview of each of the tools that are related to database development.

Books Online

The primary tool used with any product is information. Books Online contains tens of thousands of technical documents published by Microsoft with explanations of every feature within SQL Server, syntax on every command, and thousands of code samples. Integrated into Books Online are thousands of articles from over a dozen websites which Microsoft has integrated and made searchable through the interface. Instead of a static set of documents that you used to receive, Books Online is a living document that can be constantly updated as new information becomes available.

The content for Books Online no longer ships with SQL Server. Instead, the Microsoft Help Viewer was installed in Chapter 1. In order to get the Books Online content, you will need to download and install SQL Server Books Online into the Help Viewer.

I always load Books Online content locally even though I do reference the online version. The online version is updated as necessary to fix errors and add additional content while you have to explicitly download updates for the local content. I know some may find it shocking, but you don't always have internet access and at other times access to online content can be extremely slow. So, I prefer to utilize local help which is available even without an internet connection.

When using the help viewer, you also have to remember that means you are using a Microsoft product. I know that statement sounds dumb, but Microsoft assumes and builds all of their products to use their other products. The help viewer is displaying HTML. If you use a browser other than Internet Explorer as your default browser, you might get some really strange things like the help viewer starting and showing an error page, even though you are trying to access local content. If you don't want to use Internet Explorer as your default browser, the way to fix this problem is to launch Internet Explorer, select Tools | Internet Options, on the Connections tab click the LAN Setting button, and select the checkbox next to Automatically detect settings. You then have to stop and restart the Microsoft Help Viewer application before content will be displayed.

Exercise 1: Installing Books Online Content

1. Go to Start | All Programs | Microsoft SQL Server 2012 | Documentation & Community | Manage Help Settings.
2. Click the rightmost button on the help viewer to launch the Help Library Manager.

3. Click Install content from online.

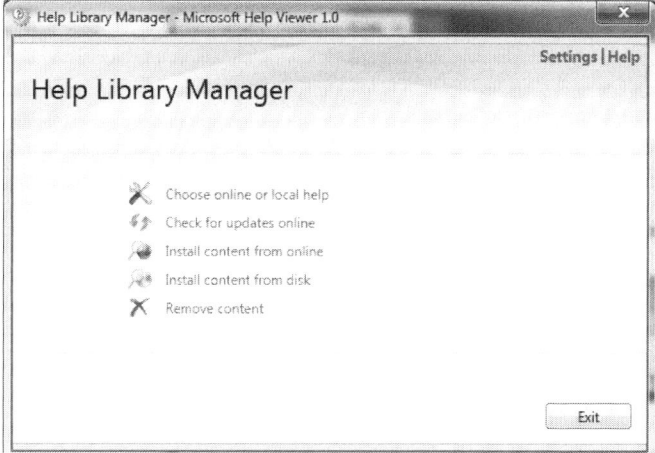

Figure 3-1 Help Library Manager

4. Scroll down and add Books Online, Developer Reference, and Installation underneath SQL Server 2012 and click Update.

5. Once everything has downloaded, click Finish, click Exit, and restart Help.

SQL Server Configuration Manager

Shown in Figure 3-2, SQL Server Configuration Manager manages SQL Server services, network protocols, and SQL Native client. From within SQL Server Configuration Manager, you can start/stop/pause/restart a service, change startup parameters, and change service accounts and passwords.

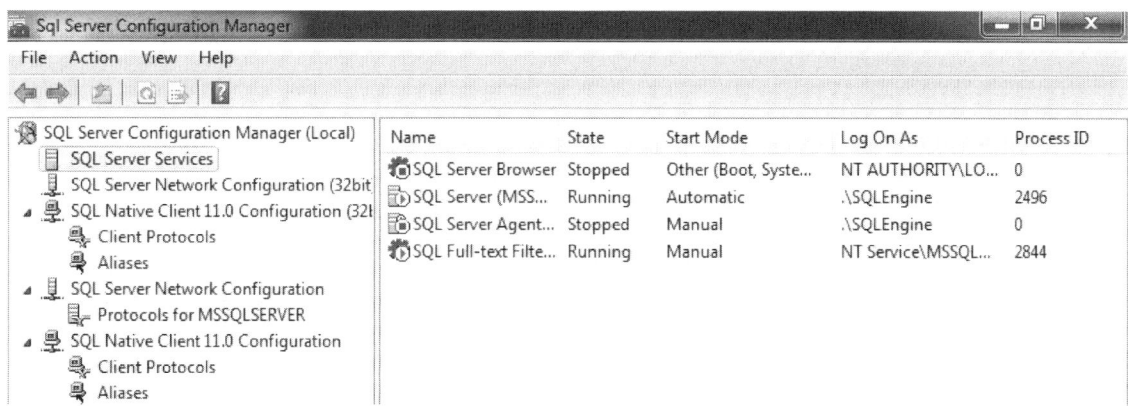

Figure 3-2 Services and Protocols in SQL Server Configuration Manager

Windows Service Control Applet provides the same capabilities as SQL Server Configuration Manager to manage service account settings. However, only the Configuration Manager has the code to properly decrypt and re-encrypt the service master key that each instance relies on. Therefore, you should only use the Configuration Manager to change service accounts and service account password to ensure a valid service master key.

> **Note:** While changing service accounts and password should only be done in the Configuration Manager, the Windows Service Control Applet can start, stop, pause, and restart service more quickly than the Configuration Manager.

In addition to service account management, SQL Server Configuration Manager also allows you to configure the server and client network protocols as shown in Figure 3-3.

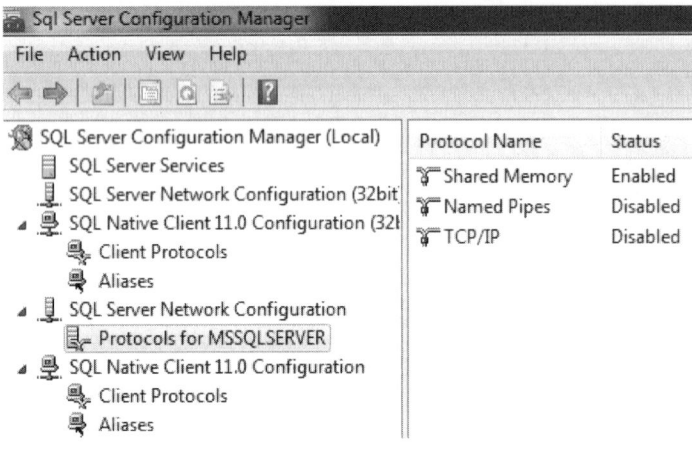

Figure 3-3 Server protocols

Several years ago, a virus called SQL Slammer was specifically written to take advantage of a particular vulnerability within the SQL Server platform. Since SQL Server was installed with hundreds of products as a local data store, this virus managed to infect and launch wide spread denial of service attacks, because all SQL Server instances were reachable on a network. Realizing that the vast majority of SQL Servers are used for local data storage and do not require clients external to the machine to connect, the way the network protocols operated was changed in SQL Server 2005.

You now have the option to configure a SQL Server instance to accept remote connections, i.e. connections from a machine other than the one hosting the SQL Server instance. By default, the Enterprise, Standard, Business Intelligence, and Web editions install with remote connections enabled. The Evaluation and Express editions install with remote connections disabled. You control where remote connections are enabled by enabling/disabling the TCP/IP protocol. If TCP/IP is disabled, you will not be able to remotely connect to the instance.

SQL Server Management Studio

SQL Server Management Studio (SSMS) is used to manage instances, run queries, execute commands, and develop objects that will be deployed to a database. Every action that can be performed in SQL Server can be executed from SSMS.

You can write code in four different languages:

- Transact-SQL (T-SQL) – command and query language used by the database engine
- MDX – Multidimensional Expressions used to query Analysis Services cubes
- XMLA – XML for Analysis used to execute commands against an Analysis Services cube
- DMX – Data Mining Extensions used to execute command and query data mining models

Exercise 2: Connecting to an instance

1. Launch SSMS by selecting Start | All Programs | Microsoft SQL Server 2012 | SQL Server Management Studio.
2. When the Connect To Server dialog is displayed, accept the default options and click Connect.

Figure 3-4 Connect to Server dialog

> **Note:** In chapter 2, you installed a default instance of SQL Server. The name of the computer that I installed to is MININT-SIPAOQV. The name of your computer will be different. The Connect dialog should default to the name of your computer. If the name of your computer is not shown, change the server name to your computer name. If you installed a named instance, then enter the instance name in the form <computer name>\<instance name>. One of the shortcuts to connect to the default instance running on the machine you are connected to is to use a single period ".". For example, if I'm on the desktop of MININT-SIPAOQV and I wanted to access the default instance I have installed, I can just specify "." for the Server name. This will route the connection through the Shared network library instead of the TCP/IP stack.

When you first open SSMS, you will see the Object Explorer on the left hand side. The View menu allows you to display additional windows such as registered servers, template explorer, and object explorer details. The Registered Servers window allows you to register a SQL Server instance and arrange instances in folders. An instance registration stores your connection information so that you can simply launch a connection from the Registered Servers window. The Template Explorer contains code templates for any object that you need to create in any of the four supported languages. You can create, delete, and edit templates to ensure standardized code within your environment. Object Explorer Details provides extended information about an object or folder that is selected in the Object Explorer.

> **Note:** Within the Object Explorer Details window, you can select and perform actions on multiple objects.

Each of the windows can float or dock in a variety of positions. Figure 3-5 shows SSMS with the Object Explorer, Registered Servers, Object Explorer Details, and Template Explorer all open.

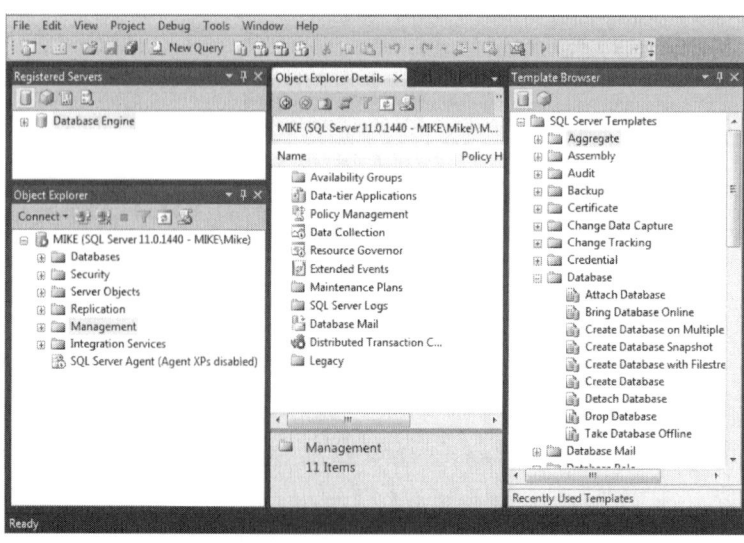

Figure 3-5 Windows in SSMS

> **Note:** You will have much more screen real estate than the image above shows. In order for images to render properly within this book, I have to use an 800x600 screen resolution, which does not leave much space for display.

Exercise 3: Configuring the TSQL code format

1. Select Tools | Options.
2. Expand Text Editor, All Languages and select Tabs.
3. Set the tab size to 4 and select the Insert spaces radio button. Click OK.

> **Tip:** Formatting your code so that it is readable and maintainable is just as important as the functionality provided. Replacing tabs with spaces allows your code to retain a stable format even when copied from SSMS to Notepad, Word, or any other program.

SQL Server Profiler

SQL Server Profiler is a graphical tool that allows you to capture any event that occurs on a SQL Server instance such as queries, object creation, auto creation of statistics, and query compilations. In prior versions of SQL Server, Profiler was a graphical interface to the SQL Trace API. SQL Server 2012 has deprecated the SQL Trace API and replaced it with a standardized event model. Extended Events are built on top of a core Windows service and allow a simplified approach to gathering and reporting on events.

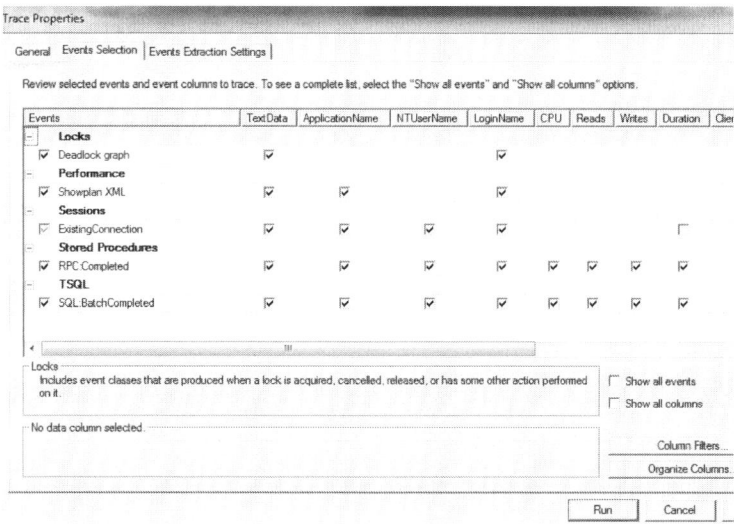

Figure 3-6 Configuring events to capture in SQL Server Profiler

Distributed Replay

When you build production systems, the initial code set that is deployed is extensively tested to ensure that the application functions properly against the database. Once deployed, your users will create reports, *ad hoc* queries, data warehouses, cubes, data mining algorithms, and additional applications against your database. You applications will undergo numerous enhancements and revisions. At some point in time, you will upgrade your databases to the next version of SQL Server. While all of this change is occurring, you need to ensure that any changes to the database structure do not break existing applications. While you could keep a library of every query, report, application, cube, data mining model, and ETL process that touches the database, in a complex system it becomes extremely time consuming to retest all of the various applications that touch your database server.

Instead of testing the actual applications that are running, you could simply test the interface with your database. In prior versions of SQL Server, you could use Profiler to capture a trace and then replay that trace against another system to simulate the same activity. However, Profiler was relatively limited in its replay capabilities and if you wanted to scale the load or vary the mix of queries to simulate interaction, you usually had to find another product to perform the task.

SQL Server 2012 now includes a separate tool to launch and manage the replay of a workload. Distributed Replay consists of two components: a central controller that can dispatch requests and monitor activity and a client that can execute a workload. Distributed Replay allows you to run multiple copies of a replay client in order to perform load tests as well as vary the mix of queries being executed against the test system.

Database Engine Tuning Advisor

Database Engine Tuning Advisor (DTA) is a graphical tool used to analyze query workloads and make recommendations that can improve the performance of your queries. In prior versions of SQL Server, you would use Profiler to capture a workload for analysis. In SQL Server 2012, you can analyze a workload captured by Profiler or you can analyze the existing query cache on a running server..

Summary

SQL Server ships with a variety of tools to develop, tune, and manage SQL Server instances, databases, objects, and queries. Books Online and SSMS are tools that you will use every day in your SQL Server career. Profiler, DTA, and Distributed Replay will be used extensively to improve performance and ensure compatibility with database enhancements or upgrades.

Section Two
Database Design

In This Section:

Chapter 4: Creating Databases

Chapter 5: Designing Tables

Chapter 6: Data Storage Structures

Chapter 4
Creating Databases

All data managed by SQL Server has to be stored within a database. Instances of SQL Server will contain at least 6 databases with a maximum limit of 32,767. In this chapter, you will learn about the structure of a database as well as how to create and manage a database. You will learn how to configure your database to utilize the different types of storage available and move databases between instances. You will also learn about the system databases that store all of the configuration and management data for the instance.

Database Structure

A SQL Server database is a logical structure that contains objects which are used to store, present, and manipulate data. A database also defines the logical boundary of all transactions that are executed.

A database can have multiple states that define its operational status. The most common state is ONLINE, which tells SQL Server that the database is accessible and can allow transactions. A database could be in a PENDING RECOVERY state when SQL Server is initially started or just after a restore operation has finished and SQL Server is making the database transactionally consistent.

Filegroups

A database is sub-divided into another logical structure called a filegroup. A database must contain at least 1 filegroup and can contain up to 32,766 user defined filegroups, for a total of 32,767 filegroups. Filegroups provide a logical storage structure for any objects that contain data such as tables and indexes. Filegroups mask the complexities of the underlying storage in order to simplify management activities.

One of the properties of a filegroup is the *DEFAULT* property. Only one filegroup can be the default filegroup. When you create objects such as tables, indexes, and indexed views, you need to specify the filegroup where the object should be stored. If you do not specify a filegroup for the object, the object is created on the filegroup that is marked with the *DEFAULT* property. The filegroup that contains the first file created in the database is called the primary filegroup and will initially be marked the DEFAULT filegroup. The primary filegroup contains the database catalog.

Each filegroup within a database also has a state. A database can have filegroups in various states, but the state of the database is the same as the state of the primary filegroup. In order to maximize the availability of a database, it is recommended that every database you create have a minimum of two filegroups – the primary filegroup containing the database catalog and at least 1 additional filegroup that is marked with the *DEFAULT* property. By marking another filegroup as the default, you ensure that objects are not placed on the primary filegroup by accident. By not placing any of your objects on the primary filegroup, you minimize the writes to the files containing the database catalog, thereby reducing the risk of corruption along with the amount of time it takes for the database to come online when the instance is started.

Database Files

Data is ultimately stored somewhere on disk. For SQL Server, all data is stored in a set of database files. Each filegroup is associated to one or more database files and a given database file can only be associated with a single filegroup. Database files are of three different types: primary, secondary, and log. A database will have 1 primary data file that is associated with the primary filegroup and contains at least the database catalog. A database can have 0 or more secondary data files and 1 or more log files. The simplest database that can be created will have a single filegroup and two data files – a primary data file and a log file. Log files are never associated to a filegroup and instead belong directly to the database.

Files on an operating system do not have to have file extensions and when present, a file extension does not convey any special properties to a file. When you double click a file with an extension of .docx, Windows will launch Microsoft Word and Word will load the file. This is a built-in behavior of Windows based on Microsoft Word registering the .docx file extension during installation. When the internal storage structures of SQL Server were changed with SQL Server 7.0, a set of naming conventions for the data files was adopted within the SQL Server community. By convention, the primary data file has an extension of .mdf, secondary data files have an extension of .ndf, and log files have an extension of .ldf.

When you create a data file, you will specify a logical name, physical name, initial file size, amount of space for the file to grow, and optionally whether the file size will be limited. When a database file fills to capacity, as long as the disk drive has sufficient space remaining and the file size has not reached the maximum limit, SQL Server will automatically increase the size of the file by the increment amount specified.

When SQL Server dynamically grows data files, it does so for all files associated to a filegroup. In order to minimize disruption due to file growth, the SQL Server storage engine utilizes a proportional fill algorithm that ensures that all files will reach capacity at the same time. For example, if you have File1 that is 1GB and one File2 that is 10GB, SQL Server will perform 10 writes to File2 for every 1 write to File1, thereby ensuring that both files reach capacity at the same time. Since you normally associate multiple data files to a filegroup in order to spread the disk I/O to multiple drives, having a large imbalance in the write operation can lead to unintended performance bottlenecks. In order to eliminate the need for proportional fill, all data files in a filegroup should have the same size.

> Tip: While SQL Server can dynamically grow files, file growth operations are very expensive and can lead to performance bottlenecks. It is recommended that you manually increase the size of data files as needed. However, you should leave the file properties set to automatically grow so that you don't accidentally run out of space and have the database stop accepting writes. It's preferable to occasionally have data files automatically grow so that you can go on vacation or have a quiet weekend.

FILESTREAM

Many applications are responsible for managing large volumes of semi-structured data along with discrete pieces of information about that data. Usually, the semi-structured data is stored in one or more files such as a collection of Word documents or Excel spread sheets. While SQL Server is very good at storing discrete pieces of information and allowing you to easily search for data that you need, the ability to associate discrete data with collections of documents was left to a variety of methods and application interfaces. To bridge this gap in organizations' expanding need to store and manage large collections of documents, SQL Server 2008 introduced a new option for a filegroup called *FILESTREAM*.

Transaction Log

The transaction log is analogous to a flight recorder. Every change that occurs within a database is recorded in the transaction log. Unlike data files where all changes occur on a copy stored in memory and are later flushed to disk by a background process, all records written to the transaction log go directly to disk. The reason everything written to the transaction log is persisted directly to disk is to ensure that a database will always be at a consistent state even in the event of a sudden disruption such as a power outage or server crash.

Every change to a database occurs within a transaction, which you will learn more about in chapter 8, "Managing Concurrency". Each transaction consists of one or more commands that are grouped together in the transaction log by a transaction ID. Every entry in the log has a log sequence number (LSN) that uniquely identifies the changes made, and the start/end times for the transaction .

The LSN for a database starts at 1 and increments to infinity. The LSN doesn't ever repeat values or start over. The SQL Server storage engine ensures that transactions are recorded in the order they are received and maintains the ordering through the LSN. As each change is written to the data files, the storage engine ensures that changes can only be written that are less than or equal to the maximum LSN in the transaction log. In this way, SQL Server uses the transaction log to ensure that all data files in the database are kept at a consistent state. In the event of a failure, when the database starts back up, SQL Server looks at each data file and writes any changes from the transaction log that had not been persisted to the data file before allowing access to the objects stored on those data files.

Since all changes are written to the transaction log on disk, the maximum write performance that can ever be achieved for a database corresponds to the maximum number of writes per unit time that can be written to the transaction log. While the code you utilize to make changes is the dominant factor in write performance, the upper bound that can be achieved will be governed by the write performance of the disks underneath the transaction log.

Chapter 4: Creating Databases   21

The storage structure of a database is shown in figure 4-1 below.

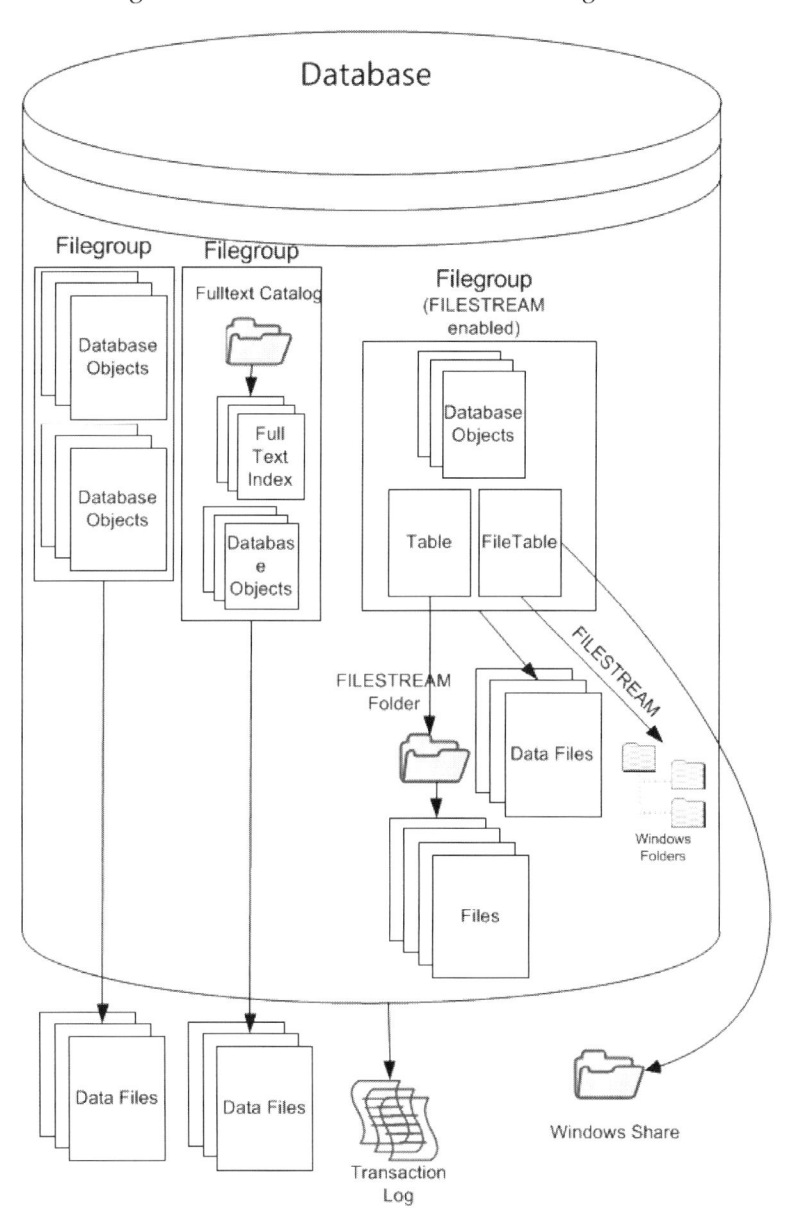

Figure 4-1 Structure of a database

Creating a Database

> **Note:** You can create a database using either SSMS or TSQL. Throughout all of my books, you will generally use TSQL, so that when you decide to use SSMS, you actually understand the command being executed when you click the OK button.

You create a database by executing the CREATE DATABASE statement. CREATE DATABASE has three requirements: a database name, at least one data file, and at least one transaction log file. Each file is required to have both a logical name and a physical name. The logical name is used within SQL Server and the physical name specifies the full file path and name on the operating system for the file. The simple syntax to create a database is:

```
CREATE DATABASE database_name
[ ON [ PRIMARY ] <filespec> [ ,...n ]  [ , <filegroup> [ ,...n ] ]
    [ LOG ON <filespec> [ ,...n ] ] ]
```

However, the simplest command that you can execute to create a database is:

```
CREATE DATABASE ChampionValleyPens
```

The code above will create a database named ChampionValleyPens that has one data file named ChampionValleyPens.mdf and one log file named ChampionValleyPens_log.ldf. When you installed SQL Server, you specified default data and log directories, which are used when you do not specify a location for the files. If a data and log file are not specified in the CREATE DATABASE command, SQL Server will create default names from the database name.

> **Warning:** It is generally discouraged to simply rely on default behavior since Microsoft can change the default behavior at any time, the simplest form of a CREATE DATABASE statement should always explicitly specify data/log file names and locations.

Exercise 1: Creating a Database

> Note: Throughout this book, we will use a consistent example, based on a real business, to build all of the objects that you will learn about. In the wood working industry, there is a skill called turning. Turning is a process where you load a piece of wood or some other soft material, spin it at several hundred RPMs, and use a tool to shape and carve the material. One piece of turning is pen making. Some people, me included, create pens as a hobby while others do so as a business. Champion Valley Pens is an online retailer that has both a website (http://www.championvalleypens.com) and an eBay presence. Champion Valley Pens sells kits and blanks that pen turners use to create custom made pens.

Champion Valley Pens needs a database to store product, customer, and order information. The product information is in Word documents and will be stored inside a database for retrieval by the website. We will be using a new feature called a FileTable, which will be covered in Chapter 5 "Designing Tables". Since this feature is incompatible with Database Mirroring, we will create two databases. One database to store product documents and one database to support the order functions of the website.

> Note: SSMS provides a graphical interface to perform almost every operation within a SQL Server. However, clicking through an interface doesn't explain very much about SQL Server and you can also make some bad decisions very easily. In almost every case, you will find the actions to perform in T-SQL commands so that when you select options and click buttons in SSMS, you actually understand the T-SQL commands that are going to be executed.

1. Open Windows Explorer and create the following folders C:\ChampionValleyPress\Data and C:\ChampionValleyPress\Log.

2. Launch SSMS and connect to your instance.

3. Open a new query window by clicking the New Query button.

4. Type in the following command and either press F5 or click the Execute button to run the command:

    ```
    CREATE DATABASE ChampionValleyPens
    ON PRIMARY
    (NAME = N'ChampionValleyPens', FILENAME =
    N'C:\ChampionValleyPress\Data\ChampionValleyPens.mdf')
    LOG ON
    (NAME = N'ChampionValleyPens_log', FILENAME =
    N'C:\ChampionValleyPress\Log\ChampionValleyPens.ldf')
    ```

5. Type the following command and press F5 to create the ChampionValleyPensDocs database:

    ```
    CREATE DATABASE ChampionValleyPensDocs
    ON PRIMARY
    (NAME = N'ChampionValleyPensDocs',
        FILENAME = N'C:\ChampionValleyPress\Data\ChampionValleyPensDocs.mdf'),
    FILEGROUP ProductDocuments CONTAINS FILESTREAM
        (NAME = ProductDocuments, FILENAME = 'C:\ChampionValleyPress\ProductDocs'),
    FILEGROUP EmployeeDocuments CONTAINS FILESTREAM
        (NAME = EmployeeDocuments, FILENAME = 'C:\ChampionValleyPress\EmployeeDocs')
    LOG ON
    (NAME = N'ChampionValleyPensDocs_log',
        FILENAME = N'C:\ChampionValleyPress\Log\ChampionValleyPensDocs.ldf')
    ```

    > Note: You only specify a folder for FILESTREAM and not a file name. The folder will be created automatically and cannot exist prior to creating the database.

6. Right click the Databases node in Object Explorer and select Refresh to see your newly created database

7. View the contents of the folders to verify the files that were created on the operating system.

System Databases

In addition to the databases that you create, SQL Server has five databases, called system databases, which exist on every instance of SQL Server. A sixth system database, distribution, is created when you enable replication.

master

The master database does exactly what the name implies, it contains all of the master data that is required to connect to and manage every other object within the instance.

At a very basic level, a SQL Server service is just a call to start up a program and pass in start-up parameters. When the service starts, Windows launches the SQL Server executable and one of the parameters that is passed to the executable is the location of the master database. Once SQL Server is running, the master database is loaded. Following the load of the master database, SQL Server reads the list of databases, which is stored in the master database, in order to determine the location of the files for all other databases in order to start each database that is valid for an instance.

In addition to the list of databases, which you can retrieve from the sys.databases view, some of the other lists which apply to the instance the master database contains are:

- Logins
- Linked Servers
- CLR Assemblies
- Cryptographic Providers

The collection of tables and views that contain the information about all of the instance level objects is referred to as the system catalog. Since master is also a database, it contains a second set of database objects you will find in every SQL Server database, which is referred to as the database catalog. The database catalog contains information about all of the objects contained within a specific database.

model

The model database is used as a template for all databases that you will create. When you create a new database, SQL Server makes a copy of the model database. If you have objects that you want created in every database, you should add them to the model database. Keep in mind that, the model database is copied when you create a new database, so anything added to the model database will only be added to the databases that you create following the addition of the object.

msdb

When you installed SQL Server, a service called SQL Server Agent was also installed. SQL Server Agent is the scheduling engine that ships with SQL Server. The msdb database contains all of the objects the scheduling engine needs to operate. In addition to all of the job related tables, views, and stored procedures, the msdb database also contains data and objects for:

- Audit data about all backups performed on the instance
- Data collector objects used by the Performance Data Warehouse

- Policy Based Management
- Database Mail

tempdb

The tempdb database is shared among all users and stores transient data and objects. When a SQL Server instance starts, all system and user databases are recovered to the last state prior to the shutdown, except tempdb. The tempdb database is recreated each time SQL Server starts, so information is never persisted. You can increase and decrease the size, but you cannot drop or backup the tempdb database.

The tempdb database contains user objects that are explicitly created, system objects such as work tables used for sort and grouping operations, and the version store used with snapshot isolation level.

mssqlsystemresource

The mssqlsystemresource database, commonly called the resource database, is a hidden database that contains the stored procedures, functions, and views that Microsoft ships with SQL Server. The resource database is inaccessible and not visible within SSMS or any catalog view. The purpose of the resource database was to separate the code for system objects from the master database in order to streamline the application of patches and service packs.

Database Context

Now that you have created a couple of databases you need to build the habit of making sure you execute the right statements against the right database. Unless you have rearranged your Management Studio tool bars already, the active database context is displayed in a drop down box in the top left corner. Each time you connect to an instance the default database context is set to the default database for the login, which is most cases will be the master database. Click the drop down menu to see that you can change to one of your newly created databases. Build this habit now, or you will end up with several objects scripted and created into the default database that should not be there. Later you will learn to specify which database to create your objects in with the USE statement.

Modifying a Database

By default, database files will automatically expand when more space is needed in the file. Depending upon the amount of additional space allocated, expanding a file can be a very expensive operation. In order to schedule the impact of a file grow operation, you can manually add space to a database. You expand the size of one or more files underneath a database with the ALTER DATABASE command.

Following the purge of a large amount of data from a database, you may find that the size of the data files is consuming more disk space than necessary. You can decrease the size of a database with the DBCC SHRINKDATABASE command. DBCC SHRINKDATABASE will shrink the entire database and DBCC SHRINKFILE will shrink a single data or log file.

Exercise 2: Expand a Database

1. Open a query window and execute the following command:
   ```
   ALTER DATABASE ChampionValleyPens
   MODIFY FILE (NAME = ChampionValleyPens, SIZE = 10MB)
   ```
2. Go to Windows Explorer and verify that the primary data file is now 10MB in size on disk.

Exercise 3: Shrink a Database

1. Open a query window and execute the following command:
   ```
   DBCC SHRINKDATABASE (ChampionValleyPens,10)
   ```
2. Go to Windows Explorer and verify that the primary data file is now less than 10MB in size on disk.

Moving Databases

There are times when you may want to move your databases between instances of SQL Server. You may also want to move your data files to another drive or folder.

SQL Server offers two methods to move the entire database – backup/restore and detach/attach. You can learn about backing up and restoring your databases in *SQL Server 2012: Database Administration*, Chapter 22 "Data Recovery". When you detach a database, by running the sp_detach_db stored procedure, SQL Server performs the following actions:

1. Flushing all changes to the data files for the database
2. Closing all data files for the database
3. Remove the entry for the database from the system catalog

Once the database is detached, you can then move the files to any location. Once the files have been moved, you can attach the database to the instance by running the CREATE DATABASE command using the FOR ATTACH option.

You can move data files for a database by detaching, moving the files, and reattaching. You can also move data or log files by performing a two-step operation:

1. Execute an ALTER DATABASE…MODIFY FILE command to change the path to the file in the database catalog.
2. Take the database offline and then bring it back online.

> **Caution:** Before you detach a database, make certain you have a valid, full backup of the database. While very uncommon, I have had databases become corrupted during the detach process. If you do not have a valid backup of the database to recover from, you will lose the entire database if it corrupts during a detach operation.

Exercise 2: Detach a Database

1. Make sure your database context is set to master.
2. Execute the following command:
   ```
   EXEC sp_detach_db 'ChampionValleyPens'
   ```
3. Refresh the Object Explorer and verify that the ChampionValleyPens database is no longer listed.

Exercise 3: Attach a Database

1. Execute the following command:
   ```
   CREATE DATABASE ChampionValleyPens ON
   ( FILENAME = N'C:\ChampionValleyPress\Data\ChampionValleyPens.mdf' ),
   ( FILENAME = N'C:\ChampionValleyPress\Log\ChampionValleyPens.ldf' )
    FOR ATTACH
   ```
2. Refresh the Object Explorer and verify that the ChampionValleyPens database is now listed.

Contained Databases

Any database you create will only contain information related to the database. However, a large number of features available to a database rely on objects stored in system databases. You gain access to a database by going through a login that is stored in the master database. You can encrypt a database by using a certificate stored in the master database. You can back up the database using a job that is stored in the msdb database.

When you move a database to another instance, none of the instance level objects move with the database. This can create a situation where you have moved the database to a new instance, but the database is not useable by an application without all of the supporting objects. To eliminate this problem, SQL Server 2012 added a new feature called contained databases.

A contained database is configured by setting the containment property. In SQL Server 2012, you can set the containment to NONE or PARTIAL with NONE being the default option when containment is not specified during the creation of the database. When a database is set to partial containment, if features are used which rely on objects outside of the database a warning event is generated.

> **Note:** The most useful option for containment would be FULL, which is not implemented in the first release of SQL Server 2012. A database set to full containment would not allow the use of any features which cross the database boundary, ensuring that you can move a database between instances and guarantee the database does not have any dependencies on instance level objects.

Exercise 4: Setting Containment on a Database

1. Execute the following command:
   ```
   EXEC sp_configure 'contained database authentication', 1
   GO
   RECONFIGURE WITH OVERRIDE
   GO
   ALTER DATABASE ChampionValleyPens
   SET CONTAINMENT = PARTIAL
   GO
   ```
2. Right click the ChampionValleyPens database in Object Explorer, select Properties, select Options, and verify that the containment setting is Partial.

Summary

Without a database, SQL Server does not provide any functionality to your environment since all data is stored within a database. Databases are logically divided into filegroups. Filegroups contain one or more data files which store all of your data on disk. Every database has one or more transaction log files responsible for logging every change that occurs within a database in order to ensure data consistency and integrity if the database server has to restart. SQL Server allows the storage and retrieval of documents and other unstructured data in a folder structure outside the database through the use of the FILESTREAM feature. You create a database with the CREATE DATABASE statement and make modifications using the ALTER DATABASE statement. SQL Server ships with a set of system databases responsible for storing the system catalog, mail settings and messages, policies, and other instance level objects. A new feature in SQL Server 2012 called contained databases will eventually allow you to ensure that a database can function as a standalone object, independent of any instance level objects.

Chapter 5
Designing Tables

> **Setup:** Please run the Chapter 5 Setup script in the companion files prior to starting the exercises in this chapter to ensure that your databases are at the correct starting point. Every exercise in this book assumes that you have created the c:\ChampionValleyPress\Data and c:\ChampionValleyPress\Log folders, contained databases are enabled, and this is the location of all of the data, log, and filestream files which will be used for this book. If you have chosen a different path, you will need to adjust the paths listed accordingly. Every setup script also assumes that you have enabled FILESTREAM access for the instance. When executing commands, it is assumed that you will change context to the appropriate database since understanding the contents of each database in this book is the same skill you will need for working with your databases. All scripts also assume you are using a default instance.

A database without tables is like a car without an engine. You can enjoy the look of the car sitting in your driveway, but you want to receive something useful for the money you are spending. Likewise, having a table without data is like owning a car without any fuel. The car needs fuel to perform any useful function.

The discipline of designing the tables for your database is referred to as database design, which is part of a slightly larger discipline called data modeling. You build models to represent the data you want to store in a database and then apply database design to create the table structures to store the data.

In this chapter you will learn how to design the tables for your database. You will also learn how to create all of the table elements which enforce business requirements and define how data is stored on disk.

Database Design

Hundreds of books have been written on database design, in fact, you might have one or more books on your bookshelf that are entirely devoted to database design. We have database design targeted specifically at a particular vendor database platform. We have database design books for transactional databases, data warehouses, data marts, operational data stores, cloud databases and any other kind of database that a vendor, consultant or author can dream up to sell you software, books or services. Throughout the IT world, people talk endlessly about data architecture, database design and data modeling. So, what is this stuff that has so much time and effort devoted to it?

Database design, as we know it in the computer world, is a relatively new concept. But, database design pre-dates computers by millennia. Database design is simply a method to organize data so that it can be easily found. Throughout the ancient world, scribes kept stacks of scrolls and later sets of ledger books in which a variety of information was recorded such as births/deaths, debts or the price of wheat/corn/silk/fava beans. While someone could simply start with the first page and record information as it either happened or was compiled, scribes quickly learned that it became exceedingly difficult to find the information you needed in such an unstructured pile of information. Individual scribes or groups of scribes devised methods for storing information in an organized fashion and taught these techniques to their apprentices. Such systems were localized and making sense of another scribe's organization wasn't always easy.

Another widespread issue was in dealing with changes to the data. You could cut out the old information, discard it, glue a piece of paper/hide/leaf over the hole in the page and record the new information. You could cross out the old information and write the new information above, below or to the side of the old information or you could write in a reference to another location that contains the updated information. You could erase the old information, using a variety of methods (liquid paper is only a recent invention) and write in the new information. Barring all of those methods, you could employ the methodology that monks used for centuries – whenever a piece of information changed, a scribe would re-copy the entire document and then discard the out-dated document.

As trade routes brought groups of people from far flung areas together, more ideas were intermingled and the process of organizing information started to become more standardized. As we moved from individual scrolls to groups of scrolls bound together into this new thing called a book, one of the first universal database design concepts was created. Any book that you pick up, including this one, is a physical example of database design. Everyone expects each page in the book to have a number, the book to be broken into chapters that are numbered and organized starting at 1, and a table of contents at the beginning of the book which tells the reader the page number each chapter starts on. By using this system of page numbers and table of contents, you can quickly jump to any location in the book to find the information you need.

A little while later, people devised a way to find information based on a word or phrase instead of the chapter titles that authors began to use. This structure was referred to as the index, placed at the back of a book, and contained alphabetical lists of words along with a reference to the page number(s) the word could be found on.

These structures helped publishers, because information could be written in smaller blocks and then assembled into a larger work with references to where each piece of information could be found. The structures weren't so helpful to the people responsible for storing large volumes of books. Libraries underwent the same problems with organizing information, which in this case was comprised of potentially thousands of volumes. The earliest system was alphabetical, but people quickly realized that someone looking for information wanted multiple books on a particular subject. So, libraries re-arranged books into subject areas and then placed those subject areas alphabetically within the library. Enter a new problem, shelf space. A popular subject would have large numbers of books written and eventually exceed the storage space on the shelf. So, libraries had to do one of three things:

1. Move all of the books in the library to make space for the new ones in their proper location
2. Insert a reference card to another location in the library where the books could be found
3. Leave empty space on the shelves to accommodate new volumes, hoping that enough free space always remained. If all the free space was used up, see 1 and 2 above.

Even with all of this organization, walking miles of aisles in a library, climbing up and down ladders in an attempt to locate the volumes you were after was very inefficient. If you were looking for a particular book, you wouldn't even know if the library had one unless you located the area where the book should be and scanned the shelves to see if the book was there. This issue was solved by creating a card catalog. A series of drawers could be found in a central location in the library with each drawer marked on the outside with the range of letters in the alphabet that corresponded to cards inside the drawer. The drawer marked A would only contain book titles starting with A. You could quickly scan the ends of the drawers to find the one that possibly contained the book you needed, then open the drawer and go through the cards. If the book existed, you would find a card with a small amount of information and directions to where the book was stored in the library. Based on the same organizational system, you would usually find one card catalog with books alphabetically and one card catalog with books alphabetically within alphabetical subjects. Also, since it would be inconvenient to move cards around, space was left inside drawers for additional cards to be added. The end result of the organization was the implementation of the first version of the Dewey Decimal System in 1876.

In fact, if you were to go through history, you would find that every feature in SQL Server existed as manual process millennia before the computer was invented. SQL Server is equivalent to the scribes from millennia ago tasked with organizing information. The tables within a database are equivalent to the scrolls and ledgers maintained by the scribes. The table of contents and card catalog in libraries are equivalent to the indexes that you will design in chapters 11 – 13. The commands that you use to store and retrieve information in chapters 6 – 10 are a computerized version of a manager telling a scribe what information to record or retrieve. The fill factors that are applied to indexes are SQL Server's implementation of leaving space on the shelf for new books. Prior to computers existing, information was secured with locks, guards, and individually designed cyphers. Information was protected by making multiple copies and storing those copies in different locations. The copies of the information could be used for research, which gave rise to the first implementations of scalability and availability.

You already possess all the knowledge that you need to design a database. Billions of people have been storing, managing, and retrieving information for millennia. You have learned pieces of that knowledge and lived in a world organized as a great, big database all your life. Database design is not an art form, it is not hard, and you do not need to hire some high priced consultant to do something you already know how to do. In fact, this chapter, along with the hundreds of books on the subject will not teach you database design. This chapter will explain to you the toolbox that is available in SQL Server for organizing your information the way you already know how to organize it.

At this point, there will be at least one reader who will have sent an e-mail to feedback@championvalleypress.com explaining how I don't have the slightest clue what I'm talking about and they are stupid to have published a book written by me. You've probably met them at some point in your IT career, the people that can't explain something or have a conversation without filling it full of acronyms and what I like to call technobabble. I grew up on a farm, am a Marine, majored in high energy physics, started on a career in the IT industry at a time when the IT industry was a "necessary evil" for businesses, and later specialized in databases. No one in my family had a clue what I did until I learned how to explain this technology stuff in plain words and neither did any of the business people whose databases I was designing and managing. Everything that we do in IT is to come up with ways to represent, mimic, and store things that happen in the real world. Therefore, you shouldn't be surprised none of the concepts are new.

At the risk of making these people even more upset, I'm going to boil the hundreds of thousands of pages that attempt to teach you "database design" into a single sentence that encompasses everything you need to know to design a database. You design a database by ***putting stuff where it belongs***. The rest of this chapter will be devoted to giving you an example of how to apply "put stuff where it belongs" to a SQL Server database and the rules that can be applied to ensure your information is consistent and predictable. When we finish, you will have designed a database and we didn't even have to go off into several hundred pages of technobabble.

Data Modeling

The first step in designing a database is to model your data. As described in chapter 4, "Creating Databases", Champion Valley Pens is a retail business that sells pen making supplies to wood turners. In more generic terms, Champion Valley Pens sells products to customers. Since everyone reading this book has purchased a product, you already know most of the objects that Champion Valley Pens needs to store information. Some of the objects are:

- Customers
- Products
- Orders

Congratulations, you now know what the first three tables in your database will be. Now, we need to understand the pieces of information that make up each business object and these will become columns in your tables.

A product has a name and a price. An order should contain the quantity of each product ordered and the price of the product. A customer should have a name. This gives us an initial table design as follows:

Product	Customer	Order
ProductName	LastName	Quantity
ProductPrice	FirstName	ProductName
		OrderAmount

We are going to ship products to a customer, so we need to store an address. So, the new database design now looks as follows:

Product	Customer	Order
ProductName	LastName	Quantity
ProductPrice	FirstName	ProductName
	CustomerAddress	OrderAmount

Congratulations, you just designed your first database. Champion Valley Pens now has everything it needs for customers to select products from a list, place an order, and get their order shipped to an address.

While the structure above isn't very friendly to the customer or someone at Champion Valley Pens tasked with managing orders, it does define the minimum pieces of data that are required for the business to function. The *Product* table only contains a name to describe the product, which isn't very user friendly, so we'll add a description and up to three pictures. It would be nice to search for customers based on a city or a state/province, so we'll break the *CustomerAddress* apart into components. We've decided that customers can store up to two addresses for quick recall during ordering, but can enter a new address at the time an order is placed. This will result in the following table structure:

Product	**Customer**	**Order**
ProductName	LastName	Quantity
ProductDescription	FirstName	ProductName
ProductPrice	CustomerAddress1	OrderAmount
ProductImage1	CustomerCity1	ShippingAddress
ProductImage2	CustomerState1	ShippingCity
ProductImage3	CustomerPostalCode1	ShippingState
	CustomerAddress2	ShippingPostalCode
	CustomerCity2	
	CustomerState2	
	CustomerPostalCode2	

You may have noticed a few issues at this point. What if I want to add another image or store more than two customer addresses? You would need to add more columns to your table to accommodate the additional information. While there isn't anything wrong with the structure above, it causes excessive administrative overhead to simply add more of a business item. We can solve this problem, by splitting the items that repeat into a separate table so that adding an additional one just becomes a data entry operation. This now produces the following table structure:

Product	**ProductImage**	**Customer**	**Address**	**Order**
ProductName	ProductImage	LastName	AddressType	Quantity
ProductDescription		FirstName	Address	ProductName
ProductPrice			City	OrderAmount
			State	
			PostalCode	

You continue to repeat this process until you have modelled all of the business objects that you need to flexibly store your information.

Naming Objects

In the previous section on data modeling, you were introduced to one of the first structural elements of a database. Every object in a database is required to have a name and the name must be unique within the database. The name of an object is generically referred to as an identifier.

Identifiers have a set of rules they must obey as follows:

- Maximum of 128 characters

- The first character must be a letter

- Cannot be a T-SQL reserved word

- Cannot contain spaces or special most characters. You can use #, $, @, and _.

While rules are established for identifiers, you can violate any of the naming rules for an identifier by enclosing the name in brackets, []. However, unless you want to spend a lot of time typing brackets around everything, I would strongly recommend that you obey the rules for identifiers.

Naming Conventions

If you want to start an immediate argument on any team in the IT industry, just say "naming conventions". It is interesting to note that very few people can clearly articulate a comprehensive set of naming conventions for all objects within a database, but they will have VERY strong opinions about how objects should be named, usually arguing against anything that anyone else proposes. Naming conventions exist for one reason – predictability. Naming conventions provide a structure for the identifiers of the hundreds or thousands of objects that may be defined in a single database while ensuring that the names are meaningful as well as unique.

I don't care what your naming conventions are. I only care that you have naming conventions. So, get the arguments out of the way at the very beginning of a project and realize that how you name objects does not matter as long as the names are understandable to a non-technical person. A database with several hundred objects with 4 – 6 character, cryptic abbreviations does not equate to understandable.

Schemas

All objects within SQL Server are contained in a namespace which provides a mechanism to group objects into logical units. For example, you might want to group all of the objects related to customer into a *Customers* container or all of the objects related to products into a *Products* container.

SQL Server uses a four part naming scheme to uniquely identify every object within an instance as follows: <instance name>.<database name>.<schema name>.<object name>. The only required portion of the naming scheme is the object name. While it is part of the naming scheme, the only time you will ever utilize an instance name is when writing queries that utilize linked servers.

You would only specify the database name when creating or referencing an object if you wanted to perform operations in another database. If you don't specify a schema name when creating an object, the default schema for the database user will be assigned to the object.

> **Note:** The best practice for naming and referring to objects is to always explicitly specify <schema name>.<object name>.

The general syntax for creating a schema is:

```
CREATE SCHEMA [schema_name] AUTHORIZATION [owner_name]
```

> **Note**: As I already said, if you want to start an immediate argument in almost any IT group all you have to do is say "naming conventions" or "coding standards". From my perspective, I don't care what your naming conventions and coding standards are. I only care that you have naming conventions and coding standards. Throughout this book, I will use what is referred to as camel case, first letter of each word capitalized and no spaces between words, for all names. Schema names will be plural and all other names will be singular. T-SQL keywords will be in all capital letters and code will be appropriately indented for readability.

Exercise 1: Creating Schemas

1. Execute the following code against the ChampionValleyPens database (remember to change your database context):

    ```
    CREATE SCHEMA Customers AUTHORIZATION dbo
    GO
    CREATE SCHEMA Products AUTHORIZATION dbo
    GO
    CREATE SCHEMA Orders AUTHORIZATION dbo
    GO
    CREATE SCHEMA HumanResources AUTHORIZATION dbo
    GO
    CREATE SCHEMA Lookups AUTHORIZATION dbo
    GO
    ```

2. Execute the following code against the ChampionValleyPensDocs database:

    ```
    CREATE SCHEMA Products AUTHORIZATION dbo
    GO
    ```

Data Structure

Databases are designed to not only store information, but also to enforce business rules that data must obey. Business rules can be simple or complicated, but it is impossible to design a database without embedding many business rules into the table structures. The business rules that are designed into the database ensure data is consistently stored and has a structure that can be easily communicated to anyone who needs to access the data.

The ledger books of ancient times were information stored on paper. You could also store your data in an Excel spread sheet or a Word document. However, each of these methods is incapable of enforcing a structure on the data and structured data is what makes databases useful. For example, you could type ProductPrice into a cell in Excel and then proceed to input currency values in the same column for multiple rows down the spread sheet. However, at any time, you could type in characters or a date value and Excel won't care. If someone were to pick up your spread sheet, they would be confused since the ProductPrice column doesn't always contain prices.

Enter the most fundamental business rule in a database, the type of data that can be stored in a column, also known as a data type. All columns in a table are required to have a name to identify the column and a data type to constrain the range of values that can be stored in the column. SQL Server ships with dozens of data types broken down into a few simple categories:

- Character
- Numeric
- Date and Time
- Binary
- Specialized

Character Data Types

Words and numbers make up more than 90% of the data stored in databases. SQL Server ships with four data types to handle character based data. The data types are specialized to handle either fixed length or variable length data and single byte (ANSI) or double byte(Unicode) characters. Unicode data types are prefixed with "n" and variable data types with "var". The available character data types and storage space requirements are listed below:

Data Type	Storage Space
CHAR(n)	ANSI – 1 byte per character defined by n up to a maximum of 8000 characters
VARCHAR(n)	ANSI – 1 byte per character stored up to a maximum of 8000 characters
NCHAR(n)	UNICODE – 2 bytes per character defined by n up to a maximum of 4000 characters
NVARCHAR(n)	UNICODE – 2 bytes per character stored up to a maximum of 4000 characters

Fixed vs. Variable Length Data Types

The fixed length data types – CHAR and NCHAR consume storage for every character they are defined to allow. If you define a column as CHAR (10), it will consume 10 bytes of storage regardless of whether you store 1 character or 10 characters in the column. The variable length columns will only consume space for the amount of characters that are actually stored in a column, so a VARCHAR(10) will consume 1 byte of storage if a single character is stored in the column and 10 bytes of storage if 10 characters are stored in the column.

Your first question might be, "Why don't I just define all of my character columns as

VARCHAR(8000) because it only consumes what I actually write to the column?" Your data types provide the first level of business rules inside your database and should reflect the allowed character data defined by the organization. If a product name is required to be 50 characters or less, your column should not allow more than 50 characters. A VARCHAR column requires slightly more storage than a char column. Since the size of the row is not fixed, SQL Server has to maintain a data structure in each row called the offset that defines the start location of each column in the row. With variable length rows, modifications to existing rows can cause fragmentation, which will be described in detail in chapter 11, "Designing Indexes". Also, the maximum size of any row of data is 8060 bytes, and if you exceed this limit an error will occur in your application and the transaction will be rejected. So, while it might seem like an easy way out to just define every character column as a VARCHAR(8000), you need to carefully consider the data storage needs of your application when you define how large each character column will be.

There is one more important, but subtle difference between fixed and variable length columns. A fixed length column always consumes the same amount of space, because SQL Server will pad any unused characters with spaces. For example, if you define a column as CHAR (10) and only write 1 character to the column, SQL Server will store the 1 character along with 9 spaces. If the same column were defined as VARCHAR(10), SQL Server would only store the single character. The biggest impact of the storage is when two character columns are concatenated together. A fixed length column could potentially introduce many spaces between the two values whereas the variable length column won't introduce any additional spaces.

Unicode Data

Character data can be stored using either an ANSI or Unicode character set. The ANSI character set allows 32,767 characters which is large enough to handle most of the world's languages. Several languages such as Arabic, Hebrew, and some Chinese dialects contain more than 32,767 characters. Instead of the single byte representation of an ANSI character, Unicode defines two bytes for character storage, which is more than enough to allow unique assignment to every character in all of the world's languages.

Both character schemes assign a number to each character, which is then stored by SQL Server in binary form. If you were to take all of the unique characters for all languages that by themselves can be represented by an ANSI language set, you would have more than 32,767 characters. Across languages, you can have different characters represented by the same number in the ANSI character scheme. This is where your selected collation sequence becomes very important since the collation sequence defines the character encoding scheme in addition to how SQL Server treats characters for searching and sorting operations. If you commonly move data between databases, you need to pay attention to the collation sequence for the columns in each database if you are using a CHAR/VARCHAR data type.

If you are using Unicode, each character receives a unique number, so you do not have any character translation issues when moving between databases with different collation sequences. However, Unicode does incur the penalty of an extra byte of storage for each character.

Large Objects

Only being able to store 8000 bytes of character data is limiting for some applications, so SQL

Server includes a special option for variable length columns. You can use the MAX keyword in place of a numeric value. VARCHAR(MAX) and NVARCHAR(MAX) allow you to store up to 2GB of data in the column. You may recall that I stated above a row cannot exceed 8060 bytes in length, so how can you store 2GB of data in a VARCHAR(MAX)/NVARCHAR(MAX) column? If the data stored in the column causes the row to be less than 8060 bytes, SQL Server stores the data with the rest of the row on a page. If the data in the column causes the row size to exceed 8060 bytes, then a 16 byte pointer is stored with the row and the remainder of the data is stored in a separate set of pages. Data pages and internal storage structures will be discussed in more detail in Chapter 14, "Page Structures".

Numeric Data Types

SQL Server ships with 10 data types to store numeric data – 4 for integers, 2 for monetary values, and 4 for decimals with varying accuracy. The available character data types and storage space requirements are listed below:

Data type	Range of Values	Storage Space
TINYINT	0 to 255	1 byte
SMALLINT	-32,768 to 32,767	2 bytes
INT	-2^{31} to $2^{31}-1$	4 bytes
BIGINT	-2^{63} to 2^{63-1}	8 bytes
DECIMAL(p,s)	$-10^{38}+1$ to $10^{38}-1$	5 to 17 bytes
NUMERIC(p,s)	$-10^{38}+1$ to $10^{38}-1$	5 to 17 bytes
SMALLMONEY	- 214,748.3648 to 214,748.3647	4 bytes
MONEY	-922,337,203,685,477.5808 to 922,337,203,685,477.5807	8 bytes
REAL	-3.4^{38} to -1.18^{38}, 0, and 1.18^{38} to 3.4^{38}	4 bytes
FLOAT(n)	-1.79^{308} to -2.23^{308}, 0, and 2.23^{308} to 1.79^{308}	4 bytes or 8 bytes

In SQL Server 2000, the definition of the numeric data type was modified to match the decimal data type. Due to backward compatibility issues, both data types were left in the product even though decimal and numeric are now equivalent to each other.

The optional parameter for the float data type designates the number of digits after the decimal. A value 1 and 24 will consume 4 bytes of storage while a value between 25 and 53 will consume 8 bytes of storage.

Exact and Approximate Numeric Data Types

Data types that store decimals can be either exact or approximate also referred to as floating point numbers. An exact numeric data type stores the data exactly as entered, with no rounding errors occurring in calculations. Approximate numeric data types, when rounded off, will return the value that was stored, but the actual storage value can vary. For example, if you stored 1.0 in an exact numeric data type, you would retrieve 1.0 and all calculations would be computed using 1.0. Storing 1.0 in an approximate numeric data type could have the value actually stored as 0.9999999…9 or 1.00000000…1 and this stored value would be used for any calculations, thereby introducing an accumulating error factor in any calculations.

The exact numeric data types are money, smallmoney, decimal, and numeric. The approximate numeric data types are float and real. You might be wondering why you would ever utilize an approximate numeric data type since it can introduce compounding error factors in calculations. Float and real are used for very large numbers that will not fit within the range available for any of the exact numeric data types.

Decimal and Numeric Data Types

Decimal and numeric data types have two parameters – precision and scale. Precision denotes the total number of digits that can be stored to the left and right of the decimal. Scale indicates the maximum number of digits allowed to the right of the decimal. For example, a decimal(10,3) would allow the storage of a total of 10 digits with 3 of the digits to the right of the decimal or values between -9,999,999.999 and 9,999,999.999. The storage space consumed by a decimal or numeric data type depends on the precision defined as shown below:

Precision	Storage Space
1 to 9	5 bytes
10 to 19	9 bytes
20 to 28	13 bytes
29 to 38	17 bytes

Float vs. Decimal

One of the most interesting debates is whether I should use a float or a decimal to store numeric data. Decimal is called an exact data type while float is called an approximate data type, so the answer should seem logical to use decimal instead of float, because we all want to have exact data along with exact calculations.

It turns out that FLOAT is actually a much better choice than DECIMAL for both storing and computing data. If you doubt that, open a query window and execute the following code (don't worry about the syntax, we'll cover syntax in a little while):

```
DECLARE @float    FLOAT = 1,
        @decimal  DECIMAL(5,4) = 1
SELECT (@float/3) * 3, (@decimal/3) * 3
```

What this code does is take 1 divide it by 3 and then multiply it by 3. Everyone knows that should produce a value exactly equal to 1. So, if decimal is an exact numeric data type, why does this calculation produce a value of 0.999999 when we use a DECIMAL and exactly 1 when we use a FLOAT? The simple answer is that DECIMAL isn't all that exact when we start doing calculations with it while FLOAT will always produce the correct answer to a calculation. If you want even more detail about the inexact nature of the DECIMAL data type, read some of the stuff published by Jeff Moden.

Date and Time Data Types

Prior to SQL Server 2008, there were only two data types to store date and time information DATETIME and SMALLDATETIME. Both data types stored both date and time. If you only wanted the date or the time portion, you either had to parse the value out of the data type or store the data in another data type, losing all of the temporal logic. The original date/time data types also suffered from a relatively restrictive range of dates allowed. Expanding on the original two data types, SQL Server 2012 supplies 6 data types to store temporal data as shown below:

Data Type	Range of Values	Accuracy	Storage Space
SMALLDATETIME	01/01/1900 to 06/06/2079	1 minute	4 bytes
DATETIME	01/01/1753 to 12/31/9999	0.00333 seconds	8 bytes
DATETIME2(s)	01/01/0001 to 12/31/9999	100 nanoseconds	6 to 8 bytes
DATETIMEOFFSET(s)	01/01/0001 to 12/31/9999	100 nanoseconds	8 to 10 bytes
DATE	01/01/0001 to 12/31/9999	1 day	3 bytes
TIME(s)	00:00:00.0000000 to 23:59:59.9999999	100 nanoseconds	3 to 5 bytes

TIME, DATETIMEOFFSET, and DATETIME2 have variable storage based on the optional precision defined for the time portion of the data type as shown below:

Digits of Precision for Milliseconds	Storage
0 – 2	6 bytes
3 – 4	7 bytes
5 – 7	8 bytes Scale = 7 is the default

The DATETIME2 data type covers the entire date/time range of both DATETIME and SMALLDATETIME, with better precision. I'd suggest starting the conversion process as soon as possible, because it is unlikely that Microsoft will retain multiple, overlapping data types for many more versions.

DATETIMEOFFSET allows you to store temporal data that is sensitive to time zone. The data type has two components: the date and time along with a UTC offset of +/- 14:00. The first two places represent the number of hours offset from UTC and the second two digits represent number of minutes offset. The plus or minus sign is mandatory to indicate whether the offset should be added or subtracted from UTC in order to obtain local time.

SQL Server has a default value for both dates and times. If you do not specify a time for a data type that has a time component, the default time of midnight will be used. If you do not specify a date, SQL Server will use January 1, 1900.

SQL Server stores the date and time values that you enter in an entirely different format, breaking the elements of the data into components. The DATE and TIME data types have the simplest storage structure. DATE is stored as the number of days since January 1, 0001. TIME is stored based on the precision specified using the following formula:

(((Hours * 60) + Minutes) * 60 + Seconds) * 10^{Scale} + Fractional Seconds

For example:

Time Value	Scale	Calculation	Stored Value
10:21:57.640	3	(((10 * 60) + 21) * 60 + 57) * 10^3 + 640	37317640
10:21:57.6400000	7	(((10 * 60) + 21) * 60 + 57) * 10^7 + 640	373170640
10:21:57.6400	4	(((10 * 60) + 21) * 60 + 57) * 10^4 + 640	373170000640

The DATETIME, SMALLDATETIME, and DATETIME2 data types store the data internally as two components. The first component is the number of days since the anchor date for the data type. The second component is the number of time accuracy increments since midnight. For example: DATETIME stores the first component as the number of days since January 1, 1753 and the second component as number of 0.00333 second increments since midnight while the SMALLDATETIME stores the first component as the number of days since January, 1 1900 and the second component as the number of minutes after midnight.

Understanding the internal storage format for DATETIME, SMALLDATETIME, and DATETIME2 provide an interesting optimization for those cases where you need to strip the time component from the data type. The internal storage appears to be a decimal number when you put the two components together, so, you can convert the value to a FLOAT data type, strip the decimal off, and then convert the result back to a date and time value. For example you could run the following code to view the separate components as well as strip the time from the value:

```
DECLARE @var   DATETIME
SET @var = GETDATE()
SELECT @var, CAST(@var AS FLOAT), CAST(FLOOR(CAST(@var AS FLOAT)) AS DATETIME)
```

> NOTE: You will learn more about SELECT statements in chapter 9:Data Retrieval.

DATETIMEOFFSET is stored as four components internally – number of days since January 1, 0001, amount of time from midnight based on the scale defined, the scale, and the offset. A value of 2011-09-29 21:19:23.153 +06:00 with the default scale of 7 would be stored as shown below.

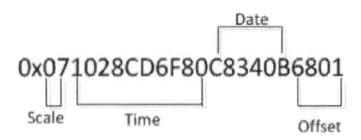

```
                    Date
                 ┌────┴────┐
0x071028CD6F80C8340B6801
  └┘└──────┘         └────┘
 Scale  Time          Offset
```

Figure 5.1 Internal storage structure of a DATETIMEOFFSET value

There are 21 different date/time formats used throughout the world, which poses a challenge of storing an unambiguous date. You might think that 8/6/1988 is a perfectly understandable date. If you are in the US, 8/6/1988 would mean August 6, 1988. However, in Europe, the same value would be June 8, 1988. The actual value interpreted and stored by SQL Server will depend upon the date format and language settings that were in effect when the value is written. To avoid ambiguity in dates, it is recommended that you utilize the ISO8601 format which specifies dates and times as yyyymmddThh:mi:ss.mmm. For example June 8, 1988 at 1:42 PM would be specified as 19880608T13:42.

Binary Data Types

Binary data is stored within three data types as shown below:

Data Type	Range of Values	Storage Space
BIT	Null, 0, and 1	1 bit
BINARY	Not applicable	Up to 8000 bytes
VARBINARY	Not applicable	Up to 8000 bytes

Just like the VARCHAR data type, you can apply the MAX keyword to the VARBINARY data type to allow for the storage of up to 2GB of data.

Specialized Data Types

In addition to the core data types, SQL Server ships with a group of specialized data types that enable new features and extend the functionality available to your applications.

XML

In order for applications to work with XML documents, the application has to load the document into an object model that parses the nodes and presents a programming interface to query the data contained within the document. The XML data type in SQL Server provides all of the API functionality allowing you to store and manipulate XML directly without any intermediate steps.

The only limitation on the XML data type is that you cannot store documents larger than 2GB or with more than 128 levels. XML documents are useful because both the data and structure are stored in a single text based file that allows for platform independent transfer of data.

Application developers like XML documents, because they think that XML will allow them to avoid having to deal with a database. Database administrators don't like XML, because there isn't any control or standardization over the data structure. Both groups of people are right and wrong at the same time. XML documents have their place when used to exchange data between applications where direct access to a database might not be possible. However, an XML document is not a substitute for a well-designed database.

You can get the best of both worlds by using XML documents for those cases where the data might have a general structure, but defining the tables to flexibly store the data can get extremely complicated. For example, you might have a set of products that can have one or more attributes. Not all products would have the same attributes or even the same number of attributes. While you could model a structure that allowed for an unlimited number of attributes for a product, the structure becomes extremely complicated when you want to restrict the list of attributes available on a product by product basis.

You can solve this problem very easily by storing the product attributes in an XML column. XML allows you to restrict the attributes available

by defining an XML schema for each product. SQL Server allows you to bundle one or more XML schemas together into an XML schema collection and then use that schema collection to restrict the XML documents that can be written to the column. When you type an XML column by associating an XML schema collection, SQL Server will only allow XML documents to be stored that meet one of the XML schemas in the collection.

In the following practice, you will create a schema collection for the products table which will allow for mandatory and optional information to be supplied depending upon the type of product.

Exercise 2: Creating an XML Schema Collection

In the following exercise, you will create an XML Schema Collection which will be used later in this chapter.

1. Execute the query in Exercise 2 Chapter 5.sql from the companion files against the ChampionValleyPens database.

2. Execute the following query to review the XML schema collection just created.
    ```
    SELECT * FROM sys.xml_schema_collections
    ```

HIERARCHYID

HIERARCHYID is a variable length data type that is designed to provide compact storage for a group of problems generally dealt with in the field of mathematics called graph theory. Graphs are composed of nodes and edges which connect the nodes together. Graphs break down into two types – directed or undirected. A directed graph allows a connection to be made in only one direction while an undirected graph allows connections between two nodes in both directions.

Two of the most easily recognizable examples of graphs are an organization chart and a bill of materials. However, any system where you need to model the connections between two or more objects falls into the field of graph theory e.g. the shortest route from your office to a tasty lunch, the interaction of a cloud bank with a mountain range, the connection from one web page to another, or the chain of links from one web page to another. An organization chart would be an example of a directed graph problem since organization relationships usually go in a single direction. The shortest route from your office could be an undirected, directed, or hybrid graph problem depending upon whether the roads are one way or two way.

Two additional terms that you will deal with in graph theory are indegree and outdegree. The indegree is the numbers of edges inbound to a node. The outdegree is the number of edges outbound from a node.

A specialized form of a graph that has its own area of study in mathematics is a tree. No, this isn't the tree that you have growing outside your house or apartment, but it is a fairly accurate representation of the implementation of a tree in mathematics as well as in databases (which is nothing more than applied mathematics anyway). A tree is a directed graph that has no cycles, which is a fancy way of saying that you are modelling a structure that starts with a single node, connections go in a single direction, and a connection cannot be created that points back up the chain. An organization chart is an example of a tree where authority starts with a single person and then moves down through the organization and never has a supervisor reporting to a subordinate.

In order to store a tree or any other graph, you need a way to represent the relationships between the nodes. One method is to traverse the tree and number each edge from top to bottom and left to right. You start at the left edge of the topmost node, the root, and continue around the tree until you end up back at the right edge of the root node. When drawing your graph, you could start with the root node on top and grow the tree downwards, the root on the bottom and grow the tree upwards, the root on the left and grow the tree to the right, or the root on the right and grow the tree to the left. The way you draw the tree is irrelevant, because if you obey the rules of the tree you are drawing, a simple rotation will change the visual representation with the information unaffected. In the US, we have been taught to grow trees upside down.

An example of a simple tree, represented as an organization chart, is shown below.

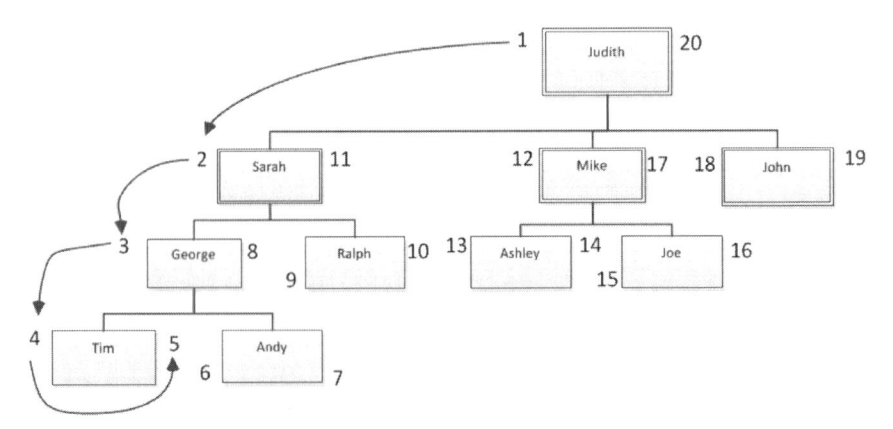

Figure 5.2 Numbering a tree

You'll note that I started at 1 and not 0. You can pick any numbering scheme you want as long as the numbers follow the pattern above. You'll note that I did not leave any gaps in my sequence when I numbered the tree. By eliminating the gaps, you can answer some simple questions about the graph.

- The root node has a 1 on the left edge.
- Nodes without any children are sequentially numbered (right – left = 1).
- The number of children of any node is (right - left - 1) / 2.
- You can retrieve all children of any node by finding all nodes with a left (or right) value between the left and right value of the node.
- You can retrieve all parents of a node by retrieve the nodes where the left value is less than left value of the node and the right value is greater than the right value of the node.

While this structure allows several questions to be answered very easily, the storage is extremely inflexible. If you need to add another node into the tree, you need to re-number nodes. This causes a single change to the graph to magnify into many changes in order to maintain the consistent numbering scheme. You could decrease the likelihood of renumbering by using an increment value greater than 1 such as 1000. You would then have gaps of 1000 for each edge on the initial numbering which would leave room to add nodes or entire sub-trees into the graph. However, by introducing gaps, you lose the ability to answer several questions based on some simple math rules. Unfortunately, there really is no solution to this problem. You can either renumber nodes when you change the graph structure or you leave gaps losing the ability to apply simple math rules to solve a few common questions.

The HIERARCHYID data type is built such that you can always add nodes or entire sub-trees into the graph, sacrificing the ability to answer questions by performing simple math operations. To deal with the fact that the numbering scheme within the graph is not necessarily sequential, the HIERARCHID ships with several functions to retrieve various pieces of information about the graph. We will cover manipulating data in a HIERARCHYID data type in chapter 7, "Data Manipulation" and retrieving information in Chapter 10, "Advanced Data Retrieval".

The space consumed by HIERARCHYID depends upon the length of the data required to represent the position on the graph for the node, but has a maximum size of 892 bytes.

Spatial

Prior to SQL Server 2008, in order to support geographic applications, developers would store longitude and latitude information as either numbers or strings in a table and then utilize various calculations such as the great circle approximation to return information such as distances between two points. Performing these calculations on large data sets could be cumbersome and extremely slow.

In addition storing geographic information, many applications existed that needed to store and manipulate shapes. While you could design database structures to store representations of shapes as a series of points, it required specialized applications to render and manipulate the objects as shapes with defined boundaries.

In SQL Server 2008, Microsoft leveraged the Common Language Runtime (CLR) capabilities and added GEOMETRY and GEOGRAPHY data types. SQL Server 2012 added significant capabilities to store and manipulate spatial data.

> When SQL Server first released the spatial data types, I found them potentially useful for a number of applications although I felt that spatial data types would need several years to begin to be used in applications. The feeling was strong enough that in my SQL Server 2008 books, I devoted exactly one paragraph to spatial data types. With the enhancements that have been added over the last two versions, the spatial data types coupled with data visualization which is finally going mainstream will become increasingly important to organizations. Instead of the one paragraph in previous books, Chapter 11, "Spatial Queries" will cover both GEOGRAPHY and GEOMETRY in detail.

ROWVERSION

ROWVERSION replaces the TIMESTAMP data type from previous versions of SQL Server and provides an 8 byte, unique, binary number that automatically changes anytime a value in the row changes. The most common use for the ROWVERSION data type is to provide version stamping of rows so that applications running in multi-user environments can determine if someone else has changed a row since it was retrieved. You can only have one column per table with a ROWVERSION data type.

Internally, each database maintains a counter value that is incremented every time a new row is added or an existing row is modified in any table that has a ROWVERSION data type. The last value of the counter is stored as the row version of the database, preserving the value between restarts of SQL Server. Since the database row version increments, you can generally use the value to determine which rows are more recent within the database, but you cannot associate the value to the actual time on a clock.

UNIQUEIDENTIFIER

The UNIQUEIDENTIFIER data type stores a 16 byte Globally Unique Identifier (GUID) that is generated using the NEWID() function. The value generated is normally considered to be unique, but is not guaranteed to be unique. It is possible for NEWID() to generate a duplicate GUID. An example of a GUID is 98A18E0C-DF21-43F1-878F-9E1D4CAD928B.

You will rarely use the UNIQUEIDENTIFIER data type simply because it is extremely rare to have to uniquely identify a row across databases or instances. The most common case for using a UNIQUEIDENTIFIER is when you are replicating databases to multiple instances and allowing changes to the data to be done on any instance.

SQL_VARIANT

One of the core requirements for designing any database is to be able to enforce a structure on the data being stored so that applications can reliably and predictably manipulate data. SQL_VARIANT has none of these characteristics and in my opinion does not have a place in SQL Server, any database system, or any application. SQL_VARIANT is no data type and most of the other data types at the same time. It provides a bucket to stuff in any type of data, but requires the application to convert the data into some consumable data type before it can be used.

A column defined with a SQL_VARIANT data type would allow you to store a date in one row, a time in another row, a character value in another row, and an integer in yet another row. In fact, you could store data of just about every data type available in SQL Server in a single column by using SQL_VARIANT. If you're going to bypass every reason that a database exists by using SQL_VARIANT, then you really should just stick your data into a spread sheet and query it from there. From this point forward, SQL_VARIANT will not be discussed and you will never find me using it.

Data Types – Why Should You Care?

We've spent a considerable amount of time and space covering the various data types available in SQL Server, so you should understand the data type selected for a column is extremely important. I encounter applications whose developers obviously didn't understand how critical selecting the appropriate data type would be to the proper function of the application. It should be obvious why you don't store numbers or dates as characters. Not as obvious is why you shouldn't just select the biggest data type available so that you never have to worry about not being able to store a piece of data. If you think you are only going to store values between 0 and 255, you could define the column using TINYINT, SMALLINT, INT, and BIGINT and accomplish your data storage needs. After all, disk space is cheap and you can always just slap more disk space underneath your database.

Your choice of data type actually has very little to do with the disk space required to store the row, because it is relatively easy to allocate extremely large amounts of disk space to a database if the data is important enough to your organization. The pieces of the equation that are missing are the memory and processor capacity on the server hosting your database. All of the data you manipulate has to go through your memory and be pushed through the processor. Servers have a very limited amount of memory available and an even more limited number of processors. Increasing the amount of memory or processors is several orders of magnitude more expensive than allocating disk space. So, wasting 7 bytes of space for every row in a table by using a BIGINT instead of a TINYINT will quickly add up to an application that performs poorly and wastes a large amount of very scarce machine resources.

While you may be able to move the database to a machine with more memory and processors to attempt to overcome a performance problem due to a poor database design decision, it is very uncommon to be able to re-design the database. Take your time during the design process and make sure you are using the smallest data type possible to store the range of data that is expected for the application. While this might sound difficult, remember, you are modelling the real world and there isn't anything in the real world that is infinite.

How to Store Nothing

Your database will have a design that allows you to capture all of the information required about a subject. But what do you do when there is no information to capture? It sounds pretty strange to build a system that allows you to store nothing. No, I didn't just fall down and hit my head. In the database we've designed for Champion Valley Pens, how do you capture information about a customer who doesn't have an address? The customer may live in a small village that doesn't have streets and therefore no address, but the city exists and you can ship a product to the customer in that city.

In a database, you store the non-existence of something as using the value of NULL. Saying that NULL is a value is a contradiction. After all, how can something that doesn't exist have a value that you can store in a table? Fortunately, you don't have to burst any brain cells figuring that out, because according to the SQL-92 standard, the accepted convention for data that is missing is to store a NULL. If you want to read a more detailed explanation of missing data, I'd recommend reading Joe Celko's "Data & Databases: Concepts in Practice".

A simpler way of looking at the problem is from an application perspective. Any property in an application that does not require a value to be entered, an optional value, will correspond to a column in a table that allows values to be NULL.

NULLs have three simple rules you need to remember:

1. A NULL does not equal another NULL or any other value. (Non-existence can't equal anything.)
2. A NULL in a function or computation will make the result NULL, except for the functions that explicitly convert NULLs to some other value.
3. When you are creating groups of data, all NULLs are combined into a single group.

Creating Tables

We now have all of the pieces required to be able to create definitions for the tables that Champion Valley Pens will need. Column definitions have three components – name, data type, and nullability. While the nullability is an optional parameter, you should always follow good programming practices and never leave set up to the default values.

The T-SQL language has two sections – Data Definition Language (DDL) and Data Manipulation Language (DML). DDL is the set of commands that are used to create, change, and remove objects. DML is the set of commands that are used to manipulate data. You'll learn about DML in Section 3, "Retrieving and Manipulating Data".

You create new objects with CREATE, modify object definitions with ALTER, and remove objects with DROP. The CREATE, ALTER, and DROP commands are followed by the type of object and the object name. The most basic form of a CREATE TABLE statement is:

CREATE TABLE <name>
(<ColumnName> <data type> <nullability>)

Our current table design for Champion Valley Pens is as follows:

Product	ProductImage	Customer	Address	Order
ProductName	ProductImage	LastName	AddressType	Quantity
ProductDescription		FirstName	Address	ProductName
ProductPrice			City	OrderAmount
			State	
			PostalCode	

The ProductPrice and OrderAmount are monetary columns and should use a MONEY data type. The ProductImage will be the contents of a file, which means VARBINARY (MAX). The Quantity column is a whole number and should be defined as an INT. While you could make an argument that Quantity could be TINYINT or SMALLINT, Champion Valley Pens wouldn't be very happy if a customer couldn't place an order for 50,000 units of a single product. All of the other columns should contain character data of various lengths. With the exception of the Address column, all other columns should be required (NOT NULL). Order is a reserved word, so we are going to change the name slightly to Orders so we don't have to enclose the table name in bracket even though this is a slight violation of our naming conventions. This design becomes the following DDL commands. (Do not run these commands against your database at this point; we will be creating all of these tables in a subsequent exercise.)

```
CREATE TABLE Products.Product
(ProductName         VARCHAR(75)     NOT NULL,
ProductDescription   VARCHAR(MAX)    NOT NULL,
ProductPrice         MONEY           NOT NULL)
```

```
CREATE TABLE Products.ProductImage
(ProductImage VARBINARY(MAX)   NOT NULL)
```

```
CREATE TABLE Customers.Customer
(FirstName    VARCHAR(75) NOT NULL,
LastName      VARCHAR(75) NOT NULL)
```

```
CREATE TABLE Orders.Orders
(Quantity       INT            NOT NULL,
ProductName     VARCHAR(75)    NOT NULL,
OrderAmount     MONEY          NOT NULL)
```

```
CREATE TABLE Customers.Address
(AddressType    CHAR(8)         NOT NULL,
Address         VARCHAR(75)     NOT NULL,
City            VARCHAR(100)    NOT NULL,
StateProvince   VARCHAR(75)     NOT NULL,
PostalCode      CHAR(10)        NOT NULL)
```

If you run the following commands against the Champion Valley Pens database, you will have implemented your first database design. However, if you try to use the table design to store and more importantly retrieve information for the business, you will find several problems.

Constraints

The first problem in your database design is an inability to retrieve the specific information that you need. The Customers.Customer table works until you have two customers with the same first and last name. You might be able to retrieve John Smith from the database, but you will never be able to distinguish between the 87 John Smiths that are your customers.

Constraints are a group of objects that are used to enforce rules on your data. There are five types of constraints that you can create: primary key, foreign key, check, default, and unique.

Primary Keys

A primary key is a column or columns in a table that are used to uniquely identify every row in the table. A NULL does not equal another NULL or any other value and is not allowed in a primary key. Therefore every column that makes up a primary key in a table is required to have the NOT NULL property.

A primary key constraint can be specified two different ways within the CREATE TABLE statement. You can either add the PRIMARY KEY keyword after the nullability property of the column or you can place the definition at the end of the CREATE TABLE statement. The two different syntax formats are as follows:

```
CREATE TABLE <schema>.<table name>
(PKColumn    INT    NOT NULL   PRIMARY KEY,
Column...)

CREATE TABLE <schema>.<table name>
(PKColumn    INT    NOT NULL,
Column...,
CONSTRAINT <name> PRIMARY KEY (<primary key column(s)>))
```

The first format only allows a single column to be designated as the primary key and SQL Server will auto generate a name for the primary key constraint. The second format allows you to specify multiple columns as the primary key and requires that you specify a name for the constraint.

It is with the second format that SQL Server has an extremely confusing behaviour which has existed since the product's roots in Sybase. Neither a primary key nor ANY other type of constraint can exist independently because it requires a column name or it has to be assigned directly to a column.

Because of that dependency, you would assume that the namespace for a constraint would be <schema>.**<table>**.<constraint>. You would be wrong in that assumption. Going back to the original Sybase roots, constraints are stored directly in sys.objects as independent objects, even though it is impossible to create a constraint without a table. So, the actual name space of a constraint is <schema>.<constraint>. This means that constraint names must be unique within each schema. You can reuse column names as you spread your foreign keys throughout your tables by specifying <table>.<column>, but you need to remember this quirk when you name your constraints.

The Customers, Orders, and Address tables all have the problem of not being able to distinguish one row from another when data values are duplicated. In order to solve this problem, we will need to add another column to the table and make it the primary key. So, we will add a CustomerID column to the Customers table, OrderID column to the Orders table, and AddressID column to the Address table. While we are adding columns, let's add columns to the Orders table so that Champion Valley Pens can track the date and time and order was placed.

The Product and ProductImage tables have enough information to uniquely identify each row since you shouldn't have two products with the same name and a product image shouldn't be loaded more than once. You can change the name of a product as well as change the product image. These changes would cause the primary key to be modified, which is a bad idea that will be explained in the next section. So, we will introduce a ProductID column to the Product table and a ProductImageID to the ProductImage table.

This produces the following table structure. (Do not run these commands against your database at this point; we will be creating all of these tables in a subsequent exercise.)

```
CREATE TABLE Products.Product
(ProductID           INT             NOT NULL,
ProductName          VARCHAR(75)     NOT NULL,
ProductDescription   VARCHAR(MAX)    NOT NULL,
ProductPrice         MONEY           NOT NULL,
CONSTRAINT pk_product PRIMARY KEY
(ProductID))
```

```
CREATE TABLE Products.ProductImage
(ProductImageID      INT             NOT NULL,
ProductImage         VARBINARY(MAX)  NOT NULL,
CONSTRAINT pk_productimage PRIMARY KEY
(ProductImageID))
```

```
CREATE TABLE Customers.Address
(AddressID           INT             NOT NULL,
AddressType          CHAR(8)         NOT NULL,
Address              VARCHAR(75)     NOT NULL,
City                 VARCHAR(100)    NOT NULL,
StateProvince        VARCHAR(75)     NOT NULL,
PostalCode           CHAR(10)        NOT NULL,
CONSTRAINT pk_address PRIMARY KEY
(AddressID))
```

```
CREATE TABLE Orders.Orders
(OrderID             INT             NOT NULL,
OrderDate            DATE            NOT NULL,
OrderTime            TIME            NOT NULL,
Quantity             INT             NOT NULL,
ProductName          VARCHAR(75)     NOT NULL,
OrderAmount          MONEY           NOT NULL,
CONSTRAINT pk_orders PRIMARY KEY
(OrderID))
```

```
CREATE TABLE Customers.Customer
(CustomerID     INT         NOT NULL,
FirstName       VARCHAR(75) NOT NULL,
LastName        VARCHAR(75) NOT NULL,
CONSTRAINT pk_customer PRIMARY KEY
(CustomerID))
```

Foreign Keys

Now that you can uniquely identify every row in your tables, there is a second issue that needs to be dealt with. A customer can have one or more addresses and can place one or more orders. However, you have no way of telling which address or order belongs to which customer. This is where relational databases get their name.

You can relate one table to another by adding the primary key of one table to another table. This is generally referred to as a parent – child relationship. For example, adding the parent CustomerID to the child Orders table allows you to associate orders to a customer.

This produces the following table structure. (Do not run these commands against your database at this point; we will be creating all of these tables in a subsequent exercise.)

```
CREATE TABLE Products.Product                          CREATE TABLE Products.ProductImage
(ProductID           INT              NOT NULL,        (ProductImageID      INT              NOT NULL,
 ProductName         VARCHAR(75)      NOT NULL,         ProductID           INT              NOT NULL,
 ProductDescription  VARCHAR(MAX)     NOT NULL,         ProductImage        VARBINARY(MAX)   NOT NULL,
 ProductPrice        MONEY            NOT NULL,         CONSTRAINT pk_productimage PRIMARY KEY
 CONSTRAINT pk_product PRIMARY KEY                      (ProductImageID))
 (ProductID))

CREATE TABLE Customers.Address                         CREATE TABLE Orders.Orders
(AddressID           INT              NOT NULL,        (OrderID             INT              NOT NULL,
 CustomerID          INT              NOT NULL,         CustomerID          INT              NOT NULL,
 AddressType         CHAR(8)          NOT NULL,         OrderDate           DATE             NOT NULL,
 Address             VARCHAR(75)      NOT NULL,         OrderTime           TIME             NOT NULL,
 City                VARCHAR(100)     NOT NULL,         Quantity            INT              NOT NULL,
 StateProvince       VARCHAR(75)      NOT NULL,         ProductID           INT              NOT NULL,
 PostalCode          CHAR(10)         NOT NULL,         OrderAmount         MONEY            NOT NULL,
 CONSTRAINT pk_address PRIMARY KEY                      CONSTRAINT pk_orders PRIMARY KEY
 (AddressID))                                           (OrderID))

CREATE TABLE Customers.Customer
(CustomerID   INT           NOT NULL,
 FirstName    VARCHAR(75)   NOT NULL,
 LastName     VARCHAR(75)   NOT NULL,
 CONSTRAINT pk_customer PRIMARY KEY
 (CustomerID))
```

While you are relating tables together, you also need to enforce business rules such as an address and an order cannot exist without a customer and a customer cannot order a product that does not exist. Contrary to popular belief, foreign keys are not used to relate two tables together. Foreign keys are used to enforce business rules in the relationship of two tables.

> The foreign key column in the child table can allow NULLs. This designates a column that is optional, however, if a value is specified, it must exist in the parent table.

It is the use of the primary key to relate tables together that drives the rule that your primary keys should never be a piece of business information that is changeable. If you define a primary key using business data that can change, then every time the value changes you also need to change all of the rows that reference the value. When the primary key changes, you will find yourself facing a very awkward requirement for changing the data. You can't change the value in the parent first without violating the foreign key, something that is not allowed. You can't change the value in the child first without also violating the foreign key. The only way around this problem is to create a new row in the parent table, change the values in the child table to point at the newly created row, and then delete the previous value from the parent table.

Foreign keys have a property defined in the ANSI standard called CASCADE. This allows you to cascade changes to a parent down through all tables that reference it. I've always thought this is an extremely bad idea since it makes it very easy to modify or remove large amounts of data by accident. Here's a scenario describing why I rarely use CASCADE: A representative at Champion Valley Pens is tasked with removing any customers who have not placed orders. The representative determines that Joe Johnson has not placed an order, looks up Joe's CustomerID, and goes to remove Joe from the database. As the representative was typing Joe's CustomerID, someone walked into her cube disrupting what she was doing and the only the first 2 numbers of Joe's CustomerID were typed in before she looked up to place her office fantasy football bets. The representative runs the query to remove Joe and because the foreign keys were defined with the CASCADE property, she removes Bill Jordan along with all 16 of Bill's addresses plus the 852 orders Bill placed. No one notices a problem until Bill, who happens to be the largest customer, calls in to find out why he hasn't received the order he placed a week ago and he can't even access his account. If the CASCADE property had been left off the foreign key definition, the representative would have received an error on trying to delete Bill and been able to correct her mistake without damaging data.

> Because the CASCADE property has the potential to affect large amounts of data spanning multiple tables, I very strongly discourage ever using it. I also strongly discourage using any piece of data that has a business meaning for your primary keys, thereby avoiding any need to even consider setting the CASCADE problem.

Being able to enforce an existence relationship between two tables allows you to impose even more structure on the data, avoiding data entry mistakes and providing consistency. The AddressType column will accept 8 characters and a user can put anything into the column that is 8 characters or less. One person might input Ship To, another SHIP TO, a 3rd person might call it SHIPPING, and a 4th would reference SHIP ADD. All 4 values designate a shipping address for the customer, but all of the permutations make it very difficult to retrieve the information you need. An application can standardize the data entry by providing a drop down list of accepted values, but those values need to come from somewhere. The application could simply hard code the list of values for the drop down list, but this doesn't help any data entry that is done outside of the application. A better solution is to store the list in a table, have the application retrieve the list for the drop down, and then create a foreign key to enforce the use of a specific set of values regardless of where the data originated from.

Standardizing input will add a table to store the possible types of addresses along with a table for the valid states and provinces. We'll also add a table of countries so that states/provinces can be grouped into their respective countries. The AddressType column will change to AddressTypeID and be related to the Lookups.AddressType table and the StateProvince column will change to a StateProvinceID and be related to the Lookups.StateProvince table as follows. (Do not run these commands against your database at this point; we will be creating all of these tables in a subsequent exercise.)

```
CREATE TABLE Customers.Address                      CREATE TABLE Lookups.Country
(AddressID       INT           NOT NULL,            (CountryID       INT              NOT NULL,
CustomerID       INT           NOT NULL,            Country          VARCHAR(75)      NOT NULL,
AddressTypeID    INT           NOT NULL,            CONSTRAINT pk_country PRIMARY KEY
Address          VARCHAR(75)   NOT NULL,            (CountryID))
City             VARCHAR(100)  NOT NULL,
StateProvinceID  INT           NOT NULL,            CREATE TABLE Lookups.StateProvince
PostalCode       CHAR(10)      NOT NULL,            (StateProvinceID    INT           NOT NULL,
CONSTRAINT pk_address PRIMARY KEY                   CountryID           INT           NOT NULL,
(AddressID))                                        StateProvince       VARCHAR(75)   NOT NULL,
                                                    StateProvinceCode   CHAR(5)       NOT NULL,
                                                    CONSTRAINT pk_stateprovince PRIMARY KEY
                                                    (StateProvinceID))

                                                    CREATE TABLE Lookups.AddressType
                                                    (AddressTypeID   INT       NOT NULL,
                                                    AddressType      CHAR(8)   NOT NULL,
                                                    CONSTRAINT pk_addresstype PRIMARY KEY
                                                    (AddressTypeID))
```

You can specify the foreign keys in the CREATE TABLE statement, but the parent table must already exist. SQL Server does not restrict how to define foreign keys, which does allow you to create references in both directions between tables. When you do this, it becomes impossible to specify the foreign key relationships inside the CREATE TABLE statement since both tables have to exist before either table can be created. It might be possible for an object to exist before it is created in some alternate reality, but since we are hopefully designing and implementing databases while sober, it is not a possibility. Because of the fact that you can create relationships in both directions between two tables, the common practice is to create all of your tables and then add the foreign keys once all of the tables are created.

You add the foreign keys by using an ALTER TABLE statement. The foreign keys for our database structure would be defined as follows:

```
ALTER TABLE Products.ProductImage
    ADD CONSTRAINT fk_ProductToProductImageOnProductID FOREIGN KEY (ProductID)
    REFERENCES Products.Product(ProductID)
GO
ALTER TABLE Customers.Address
    ADD CONSTRAINT fk_CustomerToAddressOnCustomerID FOREIGN KEY (CustomerID)
    REFERENCES Customers.Customer(CustomerID)
GO
ALTER TABLE Customers.Address
    ADD CONSTRAINT fk_StateProvinceToAddressOnStateProvinceID
        FOREIGN KEY (StateProvinceID)
    REFERENCES Lookups.StateProvince(StateProvinceID)
GO
ALTER TABLE Customers.Address
    ADD CONSTRAINT fk_AddressTypeToAddressOnAddressTypeID
        FOREIGN KEY (AddressTypeID)
    REFERENCES Lookups.AddressType(AddressTypeID)
GO
ALTER TABLE Orders.Orders
    ADD CONSTRAINT fk_CustomerToOrdersOnCustomerID FOREIGN KEY (CustomerID)
    REFERENCES Customers.Customer(CustomerID)
GO
```

```
ALTER TABLE Orders.Orders
    ADD CONSTRAINT fk_ProductToOrdersOnProductID FOREIGN KEY (ProductID)
    REFERENCES Products.Product(ProductID)
GO
ALTER TABLE Lookups.StateProvince
    ADD CONSTRAINT fk_CountryToStateProvinceOnCountryID FOREIGN KEY (CountryID)
    REFERENCES Lookups.Country(CountryID)
GO
```

Check Constraints

While you have carefully selected the data types defined for your columns, there are times when you need to restrict the range of values that can be stored in a column. For example, Champion Valley Pens can accept an order for products, but you want to make sure the quantity ordered is a positive number. Negative five (-5) pen kits as an order quantity doesn't make sense to the business. Check constraints are used to restrict the range of values that a column will accept.

Check constraints can be defined either within the CREATE TABLE statement or with an ALTER TABLE statement. In the Champion Valley Pens database, we should place check constraints on the ProductPrice, Quantity, and OrderAmount columns. This would modify the database structure to the following. (Do not run these commands against your database at this point; we will be creating all of these tables in a subsequent exercise.)

```
CREATE TABLE Products.Product                        CREATE TABLE Orders.Orders
(ProductID         INT           NOT NULL,           (OrderID          INT           NOT NULL,
ProductName        VARCHAR(75)   NOT NULL,           CustomerID        INT           NOT NULL,
ProductDescription VARCHAR(MAX)  NOT NULL,           OrderDate         DATE          NOT NULL,
ProductPrice       MONEY         NOT NULL            OrderTime         TIME          NOT NULL,
CONSTRAINT ck_PriceGreaterThanZero CHECK             Quantity          INT           NOT NULL
(ProductPrice > 0),                                  CONSTRAINT ck_QuantityGreaterThanZero
CONSTRAINT pk_product PRIMARY KEY                    CHECK (Quantity > 0),
(ProductID))                                         ProductID         INT           NOT NULL,
                                                     OrderAmount       MONEY         NOT NULL
                                                     CONSTRAINT ck_OrderAmountGreaterThanZero
                                                     CHECK (OrderAmount > 0),
                                                     CONSTRAINT pk_orders PRIMARY KEY
                                                     (OrderID))
```

You might have noticed something that doesn't look quite right about the Orders table. While a customer can place an order, each order only allows a single product to be ordered. Since you would want customers to order as many products as they want on a single order, let's break the Orders.Orders table apart into an OrderHeader with the basic details of the order and an OrderDetails with information about each product ordered. Since customers can have multiple addresses on file, we need to store the address the customer wants the order shipped with the order. This changes the table structure to the following. (Do not run these commands against your database at this point; we will be creating all of these tables in a subsequent exercise.)

```
CREATE TABLE Orders.OrderHeader                CREATE TABLE Orders.OrderDetail
(OrderID        INT         NOT NULL,          (OrderDetailID INT          NOT NULL,
CustomerID      INT         NOT NULL,          OrderID        INT          NOT NULL,
AddressID       INT         NOT NULL,          ProductID      INT          NOT NULL,
OrderDate       DATE        NOT NULL,          Quantity       INT          NOT NULL
OrderTime       TIME        NOT NULL,          CONSTRAINT ck_QuantityGreaterThanZero
OrderAmount     MONEY       NOT NULL           CHECK (Quantity > 0),
CONSTRAINT ck_OrderAmountGreaterThanZero       Price          MONEY        NOT NULL
CHECK (OrderAmount > 0),                       CONSTRAINT ck_PriceGreaterThanZero CHECK
CONSTRAINT pk_orderheader PRIMARY KEY          (Price > 0),
(OrderID))                                     CONSTRAINT pk_orderdetail PRIMARY KEY
                                               (OrderDetailID))
```

```
        ALTER TABLE Orders.OrderHeader
            ADD CONSTRAINT fk_CustomerToOrderHeaderOnCustomerID FOREIGN KEY (CustomerID)
            REFERENCES Customers.Customer(CustomerID)
        GO
        ALTER TABLE Orders.OrderDetail
            ADD CONSTRAINT fk_ProductToOrderDetailOnProductID FOREIGN KEY (ProductID)
            REFERENCES Products.Product(ProductID)
        GO
        ALTER TABLE Orders.OrderDetail
            ADD CONSTRAINT fk_OrderHeaderToOrderDetailOnOrderID FOREIGN KEY (OrderID)
            REFERENCES Orders.OrderHeader(OrderID)
        GO
```

Default Constraints

The final constraint gives you the ability to fill a value into a column when one is not specified as data is being added to the table. An order is considered to be placed when it is stored in the database. Instead of having an application generate the date and time of an order, we can add a default constraint which will automatically populate the OrderDate and OrderTime columns. This would modify the OrderHeader table to look like the following:

```
        CREATE TABLE Orders.OrderHeader
        (OrderID        INT         NOT NULL,
        CustomerID      INT         NOT NULL,
        OrderDate       DATE        NOT NULL
            CONSTRAINT df_CurrentDate DEFAULT (GETDATE()),
        OrderTime       TIME        NOT NULL
            CONSTRAINT df_CurrentTime DEFAULT (GETDATE()),
        OrderAmount     MONEY       NOT NULL
            CONSTRAINT ck_OrderAmountGreaterThanZero CHECK (OrderAmount > 0),
        CONSTRAINT pk_orderheader PRIMARY KEY (OrderID))
```

Unique Constraints

Primary keys are a subset of unique constraint that do not allow NULLs. Unique constraints ensure that all values are unique within the columns defined, but also allow NULLs. While unique constraints allow NULLs, it is not an unlimited number of NULLs. While the general rule that a NULL does not equal another NULL still applies, databases still have to evaluate everything that is stored (or not stored) when it comes to applying a constraint. So, for the purposes of a unique constraint, all NULLs are considered to be the same "value" in the evaluation.

What this means is that a single column, unique constraint will allow a single row to have a

NULL. A two column, unique constraint will allow multiple NULLs between the two columns as long as a pair of values, with NULL being treated as a value do not repeat.

Within the Champion Valley Pens database, we'll want to constrain the ProductName, AddressType, Country, and the combination of StateProvince and CountryID to be unique. The Product table definition below shows how to define a single column constraint in-line and the StateProvince table shows how to define a multi-column constraint.

```
CREATE TABLE Lookups.StateProvince       CREATE TABLE Products.Product
(StateProvinceID   INT        NOT NULL,  (ProductID          INT           NOT NULL,
CountryID          INT        NOT NULL,  ProductName         VARCHAR(75)   NOT NULL
StateProvince      VARCHAR(75) NOT NULL,    CONSTRAINT uc_ProductName UNIQUE,
StateProvinceCode  CHAR(5)    NOT NULL,  ProductDescription VARCHAR(MAX)   NOT NULL,
CONSTRAINT pk_stateprovince PRIMARY KEY  ProductPrice        MONEY         NOT NULL
(StateProvinceID),                         CONSTRAINT ck_PriceGreaterThanZero CHECK
CONSTRAINT uc_stateprovince UNIQUE         (ProductPrice > 0),
(CountryID,StateProvince))               CONSTRAINT pk_product PRIMARY KEY (ProductID))
```

Many to Many Relationships

At this point we've handled almost all of the guidelines for designing a database, you just didn't know we were following a set of guidelines which is exactly my point in designing databases based on ***put stuff where it belongs***. There is one additional rule that "database purists" will say must happen, while I'm of the belief that you stop when your database makes sense and if duplicating a little data keeps it simple, then take the simple approach.

The rule is that you shouldn't duplicate data within a table. In our database, we have one table where this can happen: Customers.Address. It is possible and very common to have multiple customers with the same address. Judith and I both have a Kindle, which you might be reading this book on; and we both are customers of Amazon. Amazon has separate customer accounts for us, but all of our orders ship to the same address. If we count our parent's house, where we've sent items, we also have multiple addresses. This is what is referred to as a many-to-many relationship: 1 address has multiple customers while at the same time 1 customer can have many addresses.

Amazon, like Champion Valley Pens, has two choices in designing this relationship. Option 1 is the table design that we currently have which simply adds the CustomerID to the Customers.Address table. Option 1 would mean that my CustomerID can appear in the Address table multiple times while at the same time our entire address row appears more than once with different CustomerIDs. Option 2 is to enforce that data cannot be duplicated in the table. To accomplish Option 2, you would remove the CustomerID from the Address table and introduce a third table as shown below that cross references CustomerIDs to AddressIDs.

```
CREATE TABLE Customers.Customer            CREATE TABLE Customers.Address
(CustomerID   INT          NOT NULL,       (AddressID        INT           NOT NULL,
FirstName     VARCHAR(75)  NOT NULL,       AddressTypeID     INT           NOT NULL,
LastName      VARCHAR(75)  NOT NULL,       Address           VARCHAR(75)   NOT NULL,
CONSTRAINT pk_customer PRIMARY KEY         City              VARCHAR(100)  NOT NULL,
(CustomerID))                              StateProvinceID   INT           NOT NULL,
                                           PostalCode        CHAR(10)      NOT NULL,
                                           CONSTRAINT pk_address PRIMARY KEY (AddressID))

CREATE TABLE Customers.CustomerXrefAddress
(CustomerID   INT          NOT NULL,
AddressID     INT          NOT NULL,
CONSTRAINT pk_customerxrefaddress PRIMARY KEY (CustomerID,AddressID))
```

With the structure above, you could allow a customer to have multiple addresses while at the same time a single address could belong to multiple customers. Either structure will work, but at the risk of angering the database purists, which I probably don't have to worry about anyway since they all stopped reading this book as soon as I said that you design databases by ***putting stuff where it belongs***, I would argue that the cross reference table will cause you more hassles (read phone calls from your users that your database is slow) by using a cross reference table. The reality is that while this situation exists, the overall amount of duplication of addresses is going to be reasonably low within the table, so the additional storage space required will be negligible. However, look at the opposite side of the argument. Before you added an address to the Customers.Address table, you would first have to read the table to determine if that address already existed and if so, use the AddressID of the row that already existed. Since we hope that Champion Valley Pens will have large numbers of customers, it could require a significant amount of machine resources to check if an address already exists, making the use of a small amount of extra disk space a much better choice. The techno-babble term for that simple redundancy choice is denormalization.

Special Column Properties

In addition to data types and nullability, you can specify additional properties for columns to provide special capabilities.

IDENTITY

Within our database design, we introduced ID columns to all of the tables that were an integer data type that did not allow nulls and we used these ID columns as the primary key of each of our tables. Neither of these choices was an accident and you may have wondered about the choice. After all, all of the ID columns were artificial and did not exist in the real world of our business application. The choice of an artificial value was explained within the foreign key section, the not null property was explained in the primary key section, but the choice of an integer seems completely arbitrary.

We could have used any data type for the ID columns, but numeric columns provide a very simple algorithm for uniquely setting the ID value, add 1 to the previous value. Since the simplest algorithm adds 1 to the previous value, we don't need any decimal places, so a choice of one of the integer data types is the most appropriate. TINYINT and SMALLINT only provide a range of values that is much smaller than Champion Valley Pens would want. Both an INT and a BIGINT will probably be large enough to store as many ID values as Champion Valley Pens would need, so the INT data type was chosen because it consumes half the storage space as a BIGINT. If Champion Valley Pens only uses the positive side of the INT data type and exceeds 2.14 billion customers or 2.14 billion orders, they would be very happy to have to modify the database structure at that point to accommodate larger values.

That explains the choice of an INT data type for all of the ID columns, but does not explain why we used half a page in this book to discuss why an INT data type was selected or why we waited so long to discuss it. The ID columns all require a unique, integer value for each row. Therefore you need a method to set the value of the ID column. SQL Server has a property that can be applied to a column named IDENTITY which will accomplish setting the value for you. The IDENTITY property has two parameters: seed and increment. The seed specifies the value to start with and the increment specifies the amount to add to the previous value e.g. IDENTITY (1, 3) starts with the value of 1 and increments by 3 for a sequence of 1, 4, 7, 10, etc. By applying the IDENTITY property to our ID columns, you get the following table structure:

```
CREATE TABLE Orders.OrderHeader
(OrderID       INT        NOT NULL IDENTITY (1, 1),
 CustomerID    INT        NOT NULL,
 OrderDate     DATE       NOT NULL CONSTRAINT df_CurrentDate DEFAULT (GETDATE()),
 OrderTime     TIME       NOT NULL CONSTRAINT df_CurrentTime DEFAULT (GETDATE()),
 OrderAmount   MONEY      NOT NULL CONSTRAINT ck_OrderAmountGreaterThanZero
                                            CHECK  (OrderAmount > 0),
 CONSTRAINT pk_orderheader PRIMARY KEY (OrderID))
```

A column with the IDENTITY property is not guaranteed to be unique. In order to make an identity column unique, you must apply a unique or primary key constraint.

FILESTREAM

A fraction of the world's data resides split out and ordered in a relational database. The rest of the ever growing mound of documents, emails and IMs might be spread over numerous data centers all over the world. That semi-structured data might come in hundreds of different formats, many of which require special software to read. There may be discrete attributes that describe basic characteristics of the information, but the core information follows either a user-defined format or no format at all. While databases are very good at storing and retrieving structured data, they are very bad with unstructured data. For example, it is very easy for Champion Valley Pens to store customer and order information as well as the product information necessary for customers to place order, but very difficult to store the product manuals each of which may have a completely different format in a useable way.

There were two methods to storing all of this semi-structured data:

1. Extract the contents of the file and store it in either a VARCHAR(MAX) or VARBINARY(MAX) column.
2. Store the file on the file system and store the location of the file inside the database.

VARCHAR(MAX) and VARBINARY(MAX) have a 2GB limit, so larger files could not be stored inside the database. If you stored the path to the file in the database, you were never guaranteed that the file was still in the same location when you went to retrieve it or that backups of the files and database would ever be in sync.

SQL Server introduced a new feature in SQL Server 2008 which has been extended and enhanced which allows discrete data stored within a database to be linked to one or more files stored outside of the database on the file system. The feature is enabled through the use of a VARBINARY(MAX) column with the FILESTREAM property enabled.

FILESTREAM does impose some limitations on features that can be used. You cannot enable Database Mirroring on a database that is using FILESTREAM. You can create a Database Snapshot against a database with FILESTREAM enabled, however, the FILESTREAM data will not be part of the Database Snapshot.

The CREATE TABLE statement has an ON clause that allows you to specify the filegroup to store the table. Similarly, you can designate the FILESTREAM filegroup to store the table's FILESTREAM data on by specifying the FILESTREAM_ON clause.

There are two access modes for FILESTREAM data, Transact-SQL and Win32 API (File I/O). When FILESTREAM is enabled for only Transact-SQL access the only way to read or write files is to stream the binary data through a T-SQL query. When the Win32 API is enabled, SQL Server still controls the files on the file system, but applications can utilize a Win32 API to directly stream the file to/from the file system.

You have to complete two steps before SQL Server will allow you to specify the FILESTREAM property for a column:

1. Enable FILESTREAM capabilities
2. Enable FILESTREAM access within the instance

Exercise 3: Enabling FILESTREAM

In the following exercise, you will enable FILESTREAM so that it can be used for the ProductDocuments tables in the ChampionValleyPensDocs database.

1. Click Start | All Programs | Microsoft SQL Server 2012 | Configuration Tools | SQL Server Configuration Manager.

2. Select the SQL Server Services node in the left hand pane and then right click the SQL Server service in the right hand pane and select Properties as shown below:

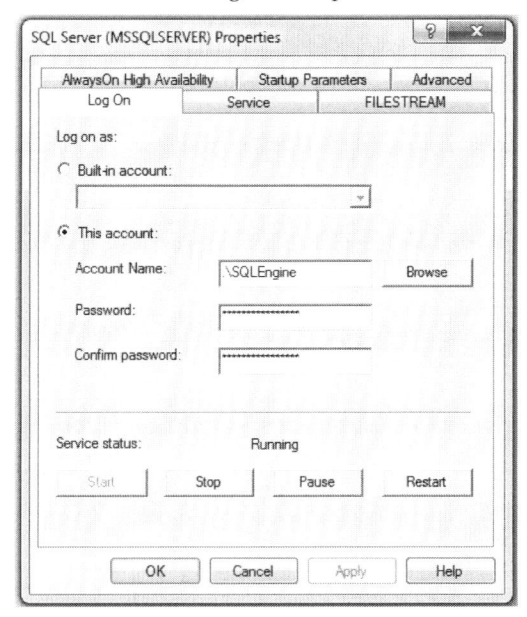

Figure 5-3 Service Properties

3. Set the FILESTREAM options as shown below and click OK.

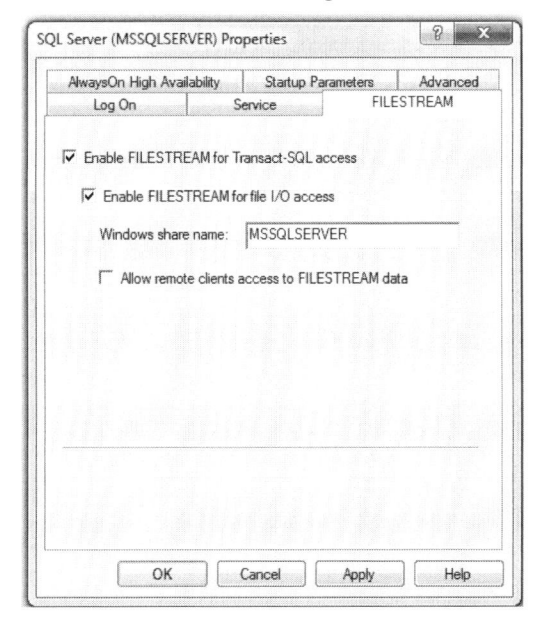

Figure 5-4 Setting FILESTREAM properties

4. Restart the SQL Server instance for the changes to take effect.

5. Open a new query window in SSMS and execute the following code to enable FILESTREAM within the instance:

```
EXEC sp_configure 'show advanced options',1
GO
RECONFIGURE WITH OVERRIDE
GO
EXEC sp_configure 'filestream access level',2
GO
RECONFIGURE WITH OVERRIDE
GO
```

FILESTREAM Considerations

There are several scenarios you will want to consider when determining whether to use FILESTREAM.

- While you could store a file of up to 2GB in size in a VARBINARY(MAX) column, once a file exceeds 900KB to 1MB, the read and write activity will be more efficient when stored in FILESTREAM.

- You could directly write the contents of a file using T-SQL, but having a large binary string inside a T-SQL statement would be very user unfriendly and prone to error. So, you will want to have an application that handles all of the logic of reading and writing files.

- You cannot nest directories at the FILESTREAM location.

- The table that is used to store the FILESTREAM data must have a unique row ID assigned to every row.

- The most efficient way to read and write FILESTREAM data is through the use of the Win32 API. As the size of the file increases the Win32 API increasingly outperforms T-SQL access.

> **Why should I care?**
>
> As a database professional, why should you even care about being able to store documents "in" your databases? The volume of unstructured data found in documents and e-mail far exceeds the structured data stored in current databases and the discrepancy is only increasing as you add in blogs, text messages, and an increasingly distributed work force.
>
> One of the challenges of having a large amount of structured data is an increasing amount of business knowledge is locked up in documents and e-mails. In order to be able to search all of the unstructured data to gather all information about a specific topic requires significant effort to consolidate and convert formats. These efforts are so time intensive most companies never consolidate information and usually re-create the same information multiple times, often with discrepancies between the versions, leading to confusion between what people think is happening and what is actually occurring. By leveraging FILESTREAM in conjunction with full-text indexing which you will learn about in chapter 14, you can simply load all of your documents in their current formats and leave it to SQL Server to index and make them searchable.
>
> Document management systems are built to attempt to alleviate the challenges of managing large volumes of documents. One of the downsides of a document management system is storing document metadata separately from the documents. Since documents and metadata are stored in different systems, it is very easy for the two to get out of synch, creating additional management overhead. By implementing FILESTREAM underneath a document management system, you can ensure that the documents and metadata remain synchronized.

For over a decade, Microsoft has had four database platforms with four separate teams doing development and significant duplication of features between platforms. JET Red, JET Blue, the extensible storage engine, and SQL Server have undergone parallel development tracks within the Windows, Office, Exchange, and SQL Server teams. Those who pay attention to Microsoft trivia would be able to tell you which JET version became the storage engine underneath Exchange and which JET version became Access. The extensible storage engine is the backbone of Windows and Active Directory. The SQL Server engine is obviously the commercial database platform that everyone reading this book will recognize. Each development team has had to tackle the problems of storage architecture, backup/restore, transaction handling, security, and a host of other problems.

For many versions, the Access database engine has had a tiny subset of functionality that the SQL Server engine possessed and since Access was introduced the only real selling point was all of the application development tools packaged with the product since from a database engine standpoint Access could only accomplish a fraction of the SQL Server features. The interesting database platforms are the Exchange storage engine and the extensible storage engine in Windows.

When you go past the functionality of e-mail, from a storage perspective, a mail server is really just a specialized implementation of a document management system. Within a mail store, you have contacts, tasks, calendar events, mail messages, mail attachments, and mail folders. Contacts, tasks, calendar events are well defined, discrete blocks of data as are pieces of a mail message – recipient list and subject line, which SQL Server has always been able to manage. The message body was a bit more challenging, but solved for every case except extreme examples by the implementation of a varchar(MAX). Mail folders are nothing more than a hierarchical list which has always been possible to define in SQL Server and made even easier with the inclusion of the HIERARCHYID data type introduced in SQL Server 2008. Mail attachments have always been the difficult part for SQL Server, but the inclusion of FILESTREAM capabilities now makes the storage of attachments trivial. So, if you really look at the data storage needs of a mail server, a barrier no longer exists in using SQL Server as the data store underneath Exchange. Such a move also makes a lot of sense in allowing the Exchange team to focus development efforts on mail routing and delivery capabilities while leaving all the details of data storage up to the team whose only purpose is to store and retrieve data. Only Microsoft knows whether they will take advantage of the SQL Server capabilities to change the data store underneath Exchange and get rid of one of the four database engines currently being developed.

The extensible storage engine underneath Windows has three main functions – storing data for Active Directory, storing the registry, and the file system. Active Directory is simply a hierarchical set of data with various properties assigned to nodes within the hierarchy. This type of structure can easily be managed in SQL Server using a HIERARCHYID data type. The properties for each node can vary depending upon the type of the node and can simply be encapsulated in an XML document and stored. The registry is a HIERARCHY with a single property assigned to each node which can have one of three different data types, a structure that is very easy to model in a database. A file system structure is composed of a nested list of folders and each folder can contain one of more files. Folders have a static set of properties such as the name and access rights while files also have a static set of properties such as the name, file size, creation/modified date, and access rights. By now, you should have realized that modeling the structure and properties of the entire file system can be accomplished in SQL Server. If you haven't heard about WinFS, I'd encourage you to do a little searching online and then consider why the WinFS initiative failed and how the story could have been very different if the feature set of SQL Server 2012 been available a decade ago. If you really want to twist your brain, consider the possibility of Windows running on top of SQL Server as the storage engine, but SQL Server needing the services of Windows to start up and function.

You might think that I'm just dreaming up possibilities, but consider the following:

1. Is it cheaper to have four teams developing four different storage engines or one team building a single, flexible storage engine?

> 2. SQL Server already has versioning built in through the transaction log with the capability for you to roll back to any change that occurred in the database.
>
>   a. Developers all over the world work with source control systems whose main feature is to track versions of files.
>
>   b. One of the features that continue to be requested for the registry and Active Directory is the ability to roll back to a previous point in time in order to correct corruption or other errors.
>
>   c. One of the features that continue to be requested for Exchange is the ability to roll back to a previous point in time in order to correct configuration issues or retrieve versions of mail messages.
>
> 3. People continue to request enhancements to search features in both Exchange and Windows, a problem that has already been solved by the SQL Server team for both discrete values as well as unstructured text.
>
> Why should you care about a tiny little feature called FILESTREAM and why will we spend about 30 pages in this book dealing with FILESTREAM? The very real possibility exists that SQL Server will start appearing underneath just about everything in one form or another.

ROWGUIDCOL

ROWGUIDCOL is a property that can be applied to a column with a UNIQUEIDENTIFIER data type. Only one UNIQUEIDENTFIER column in any table can have the ROWGUIDCOL property and allows the column to be referenced with the $ROWGUID function. You are still responsible for generating the GUID value using the NEWSEQUENTIALID() function. The ROWGUIDCOL property also will not enforce uniqueness within the column. The two places you will normally use the ROWGUIDCOL property is with FILESTREAM and merge replication.

SPARSE

Normally a table can contain up to 1024 columns and each column consumes storage space with the maximum size of a row being 8060 bytes. Some nullable columns in your tables could contain a large percentage of nulls, however each null will still consume storage space. With respect to the actual data being stored, a nullable column with a large percentage of nulls can consume several times the amount of space as you have actual data to store. In cases such as this, SQL Server has a storage optimization for nullable columns that have a large percentage of NULLs. By adding the SPARSE property, a NULL will not consume any storage space. There are a set of restrictions for columns with the SPARSE property as follows:

- The column must be nullable, which should be obvious since it is very hard to store a NULL in a column that does not allow nulls.
- Cannot have the ROWGUIDCOL or IDENTITY properties assigned
- Cannot be a GEOMETRY or GEOGRAPHY data type
- Cannot have a default assigned
- Cannot be part of a clustered index or a primary key

When a column is designated as SPARSE, the maximum size of any row is reduced to 8018 byes, because the storage engine needs 42 bytes to store the structural information about the data in a row. You will only want to designate a column as SPARSE when you would achieve at least 30% - 40% space savings, because non-null values in a SPARSE column will consume more space than normal. In the Books Online article on sparse columns, there is a table that you can use to estimate the percentage of rows that need to be NULL in order to achieve a 40% space saving based on the data type of the column.

If you are removing the SPARSE property from a column, you need to ensure that enough free space exists in the row for a second copy of the data in the column that you are changing. The extra space is required, because SQL Server will add a new column to the table, copy the data from the old column, and then remove the old column. So, while the copy operation is occurring, you will have two copies of the column being changed counting against your row size limit. If during the ALTER operation, the row size is exceeded, the ALTER will fail.

While 1024 columns per table may seem like a lot, and it is for most well-designed applications, certain applications need more than 1024 columns in a table, for example a table storing survey responses or medical histories. If you have SPARSE columns, the number of columns allowed in a table is increased to 30,000 with a maximum of 1023 columns being non-sparse.

In order to exceed 1024 columns, you will need to define a column set encompassing all of the SPARSE columns in the table. A column set is an XML document with a schema that matches the set of columns designated as SPARSE. When a column set is defined, SQL Server will store non-sparse columns normally plus an XML column with the name of the column set that contains the collection of sparse columns. Referencing the columns within a column set is the same as referencing non-sparse column and SQL Server will implicitly perform the XML conversions.

A column set is defined using a special syntax that is very similar to a column definition as follows:

```
CustomerAddress XML COLUMN_SET FOR ALL_SPARSE_COLUMNS
```

A column set is required to be defined with an XML data type, the keyword COLUMN_SET, and specify the property FOR ALL_SPARSE_COLUMNS. As you can imagine from the structure as well as the property name, it might be possible in future versions of SQL Server to have multiple column sets per table, just like you can have multiple XML columns per table. However, in SQL Server 2012, you can only have a single column set per table.

Different countries can have different formats for addresses, although in a connected world where packages are shipped across borders, address formats have become largely standardized. Customer addresses can contain multiple parts such as a street address, suite number, etc. To more accurately capture address information for Champion Valley Pens, we need to modify the Customers.Address table to allow for multiple address parts.

Since only a small percentage of addresses will have multiple parts, we will take advantage of sparse column storage and specify a column set for the sparse columns.

```
CREATE TABLE Customers.Address
(AddressID         INT            IDENTITY(1,1),
 AddressTypeID     INT            NOT NULL,
 AddressLine1      VARCHAR(75)    NOT NULL,
 AddressLine2      VARCHAR(75)    SPARSE NULL,
 AddressLine3      VARCHAR(75)    SPARSE NULL,
 City              VARCHAR(100)   NOT NULL,
 StateProvinceID   INT            NOT NULL,
 PostalCode        CHAR(10)       NOT NULL,
 CustomerAddress XML COLUMN_SET FOR ALL_SPARSE_COLUMNS,
 CONSTRAINT pk_address PRIMARY KEY (AddressID))
GO
```

Computed Columns

You can store calculations within a table as computed columns. A computed column does not consume any space or require any additional overhead in the table. The definition of the calculation is stored with the table definition, but the actual result of the calculation is not stored. When you retrieve data from the table, SQL Server will evaluate the calculation and return the result as part of the result set, just as if it were an actual column of stored data in the table.

You can choose to avoid the calculation when the data is read by storing the computed value with the rest of the data in the table. To store the value; you need to specify the PERSISTED option for the computed column. In cases when the data is frequently read or the calculation is used for searches, it is more beneficial to consume storage by persisting the computed column.

Champion Valley Pens has to charge sales tax for customers residing in the state of Texas as well as shipping charges. After adding these two columns, it would be beneficial to specify an order total that includes the price of the products, sales tax, and shipping amount so that business users have the correct business calculation. We'll also persist the calculation since searches will be performed on the order total. The addition of these three columns would change the definition of the Orders.OrderHeader table to the following:

```
CREATE TABLE Orders.OrderHeader
(OrderID         INT       IDENTITY(1,1),
 CustomerID      INT       NOT NULL,
 OrderDate       DATE      NOT NULL CONSTRAINT df_CurrentDate DEFAULT (GETDATE()),
 OrderTime       TIME      NOT NULL CONSTRAINT df_CurrentTime DEFAULT (GETDATE()),
 OrderSubTotal   MONEY     NOT NULL CONSTRAINT ck_OrderSubTotalGreaterThanZero
                                               CHECK (OrderSubTotal > 0),
 SalesTax        MONEY     NOT NULL CONSTRAINT df_SalesTax DEFAULT (0),
                           CONSTRAINT ck_SalesTaxNotNegative CHECK (SalesTax >=0),
 ShippingAmount MONEY      NOT NULL CONSTRAINT ck_ShippingAmountNotNegative
                                               CHECK (ShippingAmount >= 0),
 OrderTotal      AS OrderSubTotal + SalesTax + ShippingAmount PERSISTED,
 CONSTRAINT pk_orderheader PRIMARY KEY (OrderID))
```

Exercise 4: Building the Champion Valley Pens Database

In the following exercise, you will build out several of the tables we've defined within this chapter within the ChampionValleyPens database. Scripts to create all of the database objects can be found in the Chapter 5 folder of the companion scripts to this book. If you do not have the companion scripts, please refer to the Book Organization section at the font of the book for how to download the scripts. To conserve space, we will not repeat the table definitions previously defined in this chapter.

> **Note:** Most of the objects listed in this exercise can only be found in the companion scripts as well as the full definition for all of the tables to be created. If you choose to skip this exercise, a backup is included with each chapter so you can start each chapter with an updated version.

1. Open a new query window and create the 28 tables in the Lookups schema.
2. Create the Products.Product, Products.SKU, and Products.Inventory tables. The Products.Product table will use a typed XML column for the Description with the XML schema collection created earlier in this chapter.
3. Create the Customers.Customer, Customers.Address, and Customers.Contact tables.
4. Create the HumanResources.Employee, HumanResources.EmployeeAddress, HumanResources.EmployeeDocument, and HumanResources.EmployeeContact tables.
5. Create the Orders.OrderHeader, Orders.OrderDetail, Orders.Shipment, and Orders.ShipmentXRefOrderDetail tables.
6. Create the foreign keys by running the ChampionValleyPensForeignKeys.sql script found in the companion scripts for the book.
7. Right click the Database Diagrams node underneath the ChampionValleyPens database and select New Database Diagram (you may be prompted to install supporting objects if this is your first diagram).
8. When the Add Table dialog displays, select all of the tables, click Add, and then click Close. You should have a database structure that looks like the following diagram. (Note: The diagram will look UGLY when you initially generate it.)
9. Save and close the database diagram.

> **Note:** Database Diagrams can provide a visual image of the database that you have designed. Pictures of your database become increasingly important as the number of tables increases and can provide very compact documentation for anyone trying to write queries or develop applications. The Database Diagrams in SSMS are not a substitute for specialized data modelling tools. You also have to be extremely careful with a database diagram; it is not just a pretty picture. You can make changes within the database diagram and upon saving changes; the underlying database structure will be modified.

The image below shows the completed ChampionValleyPens database. Most of the model should be reasonably self-explanatory as the basic elements of a business with customers, employees, and products. However, the SKU table might look a bit strange to some, make perfect sense to others, and some "purists" will say that this design is stupid.

One of the primary purposes of a database is to make data consistent so that it can be easily and reliably stored and retrieved, which takes us to a more detailed discussion of "code" tables or "lookup" tables. Every database will have one or more of this type of table, which contains standardized lists of values used throughout the organization such as colors, dimensions, countries, job titles, etc. These values are encoded in one or more tables to provide standardization in the values that can be supplied and usually wind up in applications as radio button and drop down lists.

Champion Valley Pens sells a small group of products, but almost every one of these products can have dozens, hundreds, or even thousands of small customizations. For example, while Acrylic Acetate is a product designating a specific chemical formula and manufacturing process, an unlimited number of colors and color combinations can be added. So, we have created a SKU table to capture each of these permutations, because a customer doesn't buy generic acrylic acetate, they purchase the red, black, and white swirled Acrylic Acetate, which is a physical item in a specific shelf location. You'll see the description in the product table, because it is a generic description for acrylic acetate that applies to every color permutation in the SKU table. The colors available are encoded in a lookup table called Lookups.Color. A sparse, ColorID column is added to the SKU table and enforced with a foreign key.

Chapter 5: Designing Tables   69

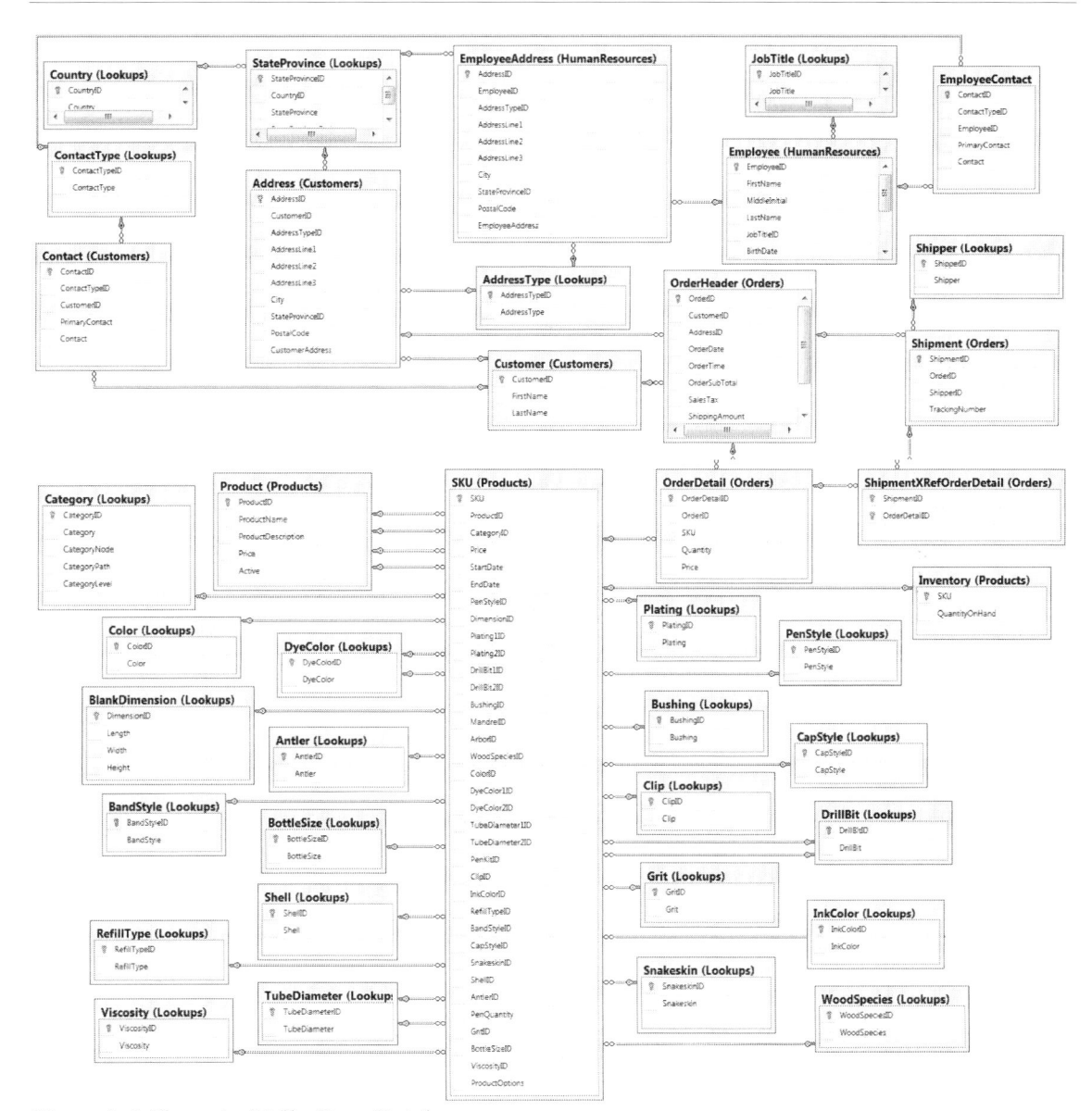

Figure 5-6 ChampionValleyPens Database

There are four basic designs for encoding lookup tables in a database:

- Each independent list of values has its own lookup table.
    - The lookup value is added directly to the child table. (This is the design that we've used.)
    - The lookup value is associated to the child table through an intermediate cross reference table.
- A single lookup table contains all of the standardized values.
    - The ID of each code is added directly to the corresponding child table.
    - The ID value is associated to the child table through an intermediate cross reference table.

Many of the "purists" want to see a design where you put each independent list in its own lookup table and then use an intermediate table to cross reference the child to the SKU. In our database, this would mean we would have Lookups.Color, Products.SKU, and Products.SKUXRefColor tables. The Products.SKUXRefColor table would have an ID along with the SKU and ColorID. They would push for this design to keep things "flexible" while arguing that it will perform better since all of the tables have few columns. While you could design like this, it won't perform any better than the design you see above while also needlessly overcomplicating the database design. We already have 28 lookup tables. We don't need an additional 28 cross reference tables when we can just add the ID from the lookup directly to the child table.

You could have combined all 28 of the lookup tables into a single "code" table. But, this poses a significant challenge in enforcing consistency within the database. Regardless of whether you created a foreign key to a column in the child table or used a cross reference table, the foreign key could not enforce a subset of values in the lookup table as valid for a given child value. For example, it would be impossible to enforce that values from 1 – 140 are valid for the ColorID column without introducing code into the database, thereby making the foreign key worthless for enforcing data consistency.

The way the SKU table is designed, as well as any lookup structure I design into a database, you preserve the ability to create foreign keys to enforce validity and consistency in the data while utilizing the minimum number of tables possible.

The application developers who are reading this book might be saying that I missed a design option. After all, the SKU table contains a handful of mandatory values along with a large number of optional values. Furthermore, a given set of optional columns is only valid for a small set of rows in the SKU table. The answer from the application development community would be to remove all of these columns and just use an XML column. An XML column would work, but you cannot create a foreign key to an XML column or even more specifically to a specific attribute within an XML schema.

If you look closely at the SKU table, we've actually defined an XML column in the table – ProductOptions. All of the optional columns, which have foreign keys defined, are sparse columns. ProductOptions is a column set for all of the sparse columns. This column set provides the best of both worlds. You get individual columns that you can enforce referential integrity on while being able to query just like any other column. However, you can also query and manipulate the ProductOptions column set which is exposed as an XML document. Going one step further, if you run a query that selects all columns from the table, SELECT *; all of the sparse columns will appear as an XML document under the ProductOptions column as shown below.

```
SELECT * FROM Products.SKU
SKU      ProductID    CategoryID   Price    StartDate    EndDate     ProductOptions
AA-1-1 1              39           2.49     2001-01-01   NULL
                                                <DimensionID>1</DimensionID><ColorID>1</ColorID>
```

Special Tables

SQL Server has two types of tables with special functions. Temporary tables have existed in the product since the first version of Microsoft SQL Server. FileTable is a feature new to SQL Server 2012.

Temporary Tables

Temporary tables (temp table) have all of the features available to regular tables, but are always stored in the tempdb database. There are two types of temp tables – global and local. A local temp table is automatically destroyed once the connection which created the temp table is terminated. A global temp table will be automatically destroyed once the last connection using the temp table has been closed. A local temp table is prefixed with # and a global temp table with ## For example:

```
CREATE TABLE #OrderHeader
(OrderID        INT         NOT NULL IDENTITY (1, 1),
CustomerID      INT         NOT NULL,
OrderDate       DATE        NOT NULL CONSTRAINT df_CurrentDate DEFAULT (GETDATE()),
OrderTime       TIME        NOT NULL CONSTRAINT df_CurrentTime DEFAULT (GETDATE()),
OrderAmount     MONEY       NOT NULL CONSTRAINT ck_OrderAmountGreaterThanZero
                                             CHECK (OrderAmount > 0),
CONSTRAINT pk_orderheader PRIMARY KEY (OrderID))
CREATE TABLE ##OrderHeader
(OrderID        INT         NOT NULL IDENTITY (1, 1),
CustomerID      INT         NOT NULL,
OrderDate       DATE        NOT NULL CONSTRAINT df_CurrentDate DEFAULT (GETDATE()),
OrderTime       TIME        NOT NULL CONSTRAINT df_CurrentTime DEFAULT (GETDATE()),
OrderAmount     MONEY       NOT NULL CONSTRAINT ck_OrderAmountGreaterThanZero
                                             CHECK (OrderAmount > 0),
CONSTRAINT pk_orderheader PRIMARY KEY (OrderID))
```

The difference between a global and local temp table is visibility. A local temp table is only accessible within the connection that created the temp table. A global temp table is accessible to everyone with a connection to the instance. Since names are unique within the scope with which they are available, it is possible for every connection to create their own, local copy of the #OrderHeader table, while only a single copy of the ##OrderHeader table can exist at any time on the instance.

While temp tables have special properties, the definitions are stored in the database catalog within tempdb just as any other table would be stored. So, how could you have a copy of a local temp table created within each connection when the properties of sys.tables require the table names to be unique within each schema? When you create a local temp table, SQL Server appends a connection specific suffix to the name. You don't need to know the suffix applied as SQL Server will transparently translate the name for you. In this way, your code can use a specific table name without needing to dynamically generate a unique name while at the same time, the SQL Server development team didn't need to create large numbers of exceptions to handle objects in tempdb.

The reason the special naming of a temp table is important is due to the fact that this special naming method was not applied to any other object in tempdb. Remember that constraints use the namespace of <schema>.<constraint>, so if you create a named constraint on a temp table, it has to be unique across ALL connections. The actual name of the temp table is modified by SQL Server, but the name of every other object you create in tempdb is left unmodified.

Complicating this issue is SQL Server's behaviour with respect to where code is executed *from*, not where the objects are actually created. If your current database context is the ChampionValleyPens database and you attempt to execute the following code, the collation sequence that would be applied is not the default collation sequence of tempdb, where the table is actually created, but the default collation sequence of the database where the code was executed *from*. So, the column would use the default collation sequence of the ChampionValleyPens database.

```
CREATE TABLE #temp
(Column1    VARCHAR(20) COLLATE DATABASE_DEFAULT)
```

If you weren't already confused enough, Microsoft has thrown yet another curve ball in SQL Server 2012. If you were to attempt to create the #OrderHeader table from the context of the ChampionValleyPens database, you would receive the following error message:

```
Msg 12827, Level 16, State 1, Line 1
User-named PRIMARY KEY constraint 'pk_orderheader' is not allowed on temp table
'#OrderHeader' because it is being created in a contained database. Please consult
the Books Online topic Understanding Contained Databases for more information on
contained databases.
Msg 1750, Level 16, State 0, Line 1
Could not create constraint. See previous errors.
```

However, the same code executed from the context of the tempdb database would create the table without any errors. If another person attempted to create the #OrderHeader table while your copy is still active, an error message would occur due to a duplicate constraint name. The fact that the table will create when run from the context of tempdb is behaviour which has always existed even though another connection running the same code would produce an error. The reason that you now receive this ***very badly worded error message*** when run *from* the ChampionValleyPens database is because ChampionValleyPens is set to partial containment.

You can't set the containment property on a system database, but SQL Server is using the database properties of where you execute the code from to determine what is or is not allowed. Tempdb is not a contained database and you aren't attempting to create the table in a contained database. In fact, the code has nothing to do with the containment feature at all. Someone on the SQL Server development team decided to add this check and the error message to SQL Server 2012 under the false assumption that if you were to have code in a stored procedure in a contained database and then moved the database to another instance where someone had already created the #OrderHeader table, the code would suddenly fail. Well, that's no different than what would have happened in previous versions or if the containment property were set to NONE. So, all Microsoft has managed to do is create even more confusion.

The only thing to remember, regardless of the containment level, is that constraints have a namespace of <schema>.<constraint>, therefore if you are explicitly naming constraints, you can only create one per schema even though you appear to be able to create the same temp table many times as long as it is in a separate connection. You can avoid ever having to think about or even deal with this design flaw by never specifying constraint names for temporary tables.

FileTables

SQL Server 2008 introduced a new storage method called FILESTREAM as discussed previously in this chapter. One of the downsides to FILESTREAM is the need either modify existing applications or create new applications to stream files through SQL Server in order to store the files using FILESTREAM. Built on top of FILESTREAM technology, a FileTable makes the process of managing files seamless to an application. With a FileTable, SQL Server manages all of the access to files, but applications interact with files the same way as they currently do, by reading and writing data to a folder on the file system. SQL Server seamlessly and transparently stores and manages these files by intercepting and processing the call to the Windows API.

You can see this by performing the following steps:

1. Create a FileTable pointed at a directory on the file system.
2. Open Windows Explorer or any other application and drop a file in the directory
3. Read the contents of the FileTable in SQL Server and see that an entry is created for each file dropped in the folder concurrent with the write to the file system.
4. Read and write the contents of the file directly to the directory without ever having to go through SQL Server.

What normally occurs when you read a file from the file system is the application makes a call to the Windows API to request a file. The Windows API performs all of the operations necessary to retrieve the file and present it to the application where it is displayed. A similar process happens in reverse when you are writing a file where the application sends the data to the Windows API, the Windows API performs all of the operations to write the file, and then returns a success/fail message to the application.

When you read/write to a folder that is managed through the FileTable feature, SQL Server intercepts the Windows API call, performs the processing just as an application directly using FILESTREAM would, and returns the response to the application as if it were the same Windows API that all applications are coded to use. What that means is that no changes are needed for any application to utilize SQL Server 2012 to store and manage files.

Still think I'm crazy when I say that it might not be very far into the future when the Windows file system will be stored and managed through SQL Server?

FileTable has a fixed structure of 15 columns that store the location and attributes of the files in the folder designated for the FileTable. To create a FileTable, you specify a name for the table along with the parent folder and a collation sequence to be applied to the file name property. Because the Windows file system is case insensitive, the collation sequence specified must also be case insensitive. If you attempt to specify a case sensitive collation sequence, the CREATE TABLE statement will fail.

Pre-requisites

Prior to creating a FileTable, you must set the FILESTREAM directory name for the database which specifies the root of the file namespace to be used. The namespace specified is appended to the default UNC path used to read and write files which are controlled by SQL Server. The UNC path to access the directory storing files is \\<machine name>\mssqlserver\<FILESTREAM directory name>\<file table name>. While a UNC path is defined for accessing files stored with the FileTable feature, this path is not a share on the machine.

You can utilize FileTable in two basic application modes – behaving with basic FILESTREAM capabilities or with the ability of applications to directly interact with files. The non_transacted_access property of a database controls the operating mode and has three settings – OFF, READONLY, and FULL. The settings have the following behaviour:

- OFF – Applications must first connect to the SQL Server instance and obtain a transaction before reading or writing files. You cannot browse or connect to the UNC path to view files or file properties.
- READONLY – Application can browse to and read files using the UNC path.
- FULL – Application can browse to and read/write files using the UNC path.

Restrictions

FileTable also removes the nested folders limitation of FILESTREAM by allowing you to nest folders inside other folders, exactly like you would on any file system. However, FileTable does place a very low limit on nesting. You can only nest 15 levels and if the 15th level is a folder, the folder cannot contain any files.

There are two methods for accessing files in Windows – direct file I/O or memory mapping. The most common method of reading files is by using direct I/O. In the direct I/O method, a Windows API call is made to obtain a handle to the file and then the file is read/written by streaming the bytes to/from the file. Memory mapping is a secondary method where a portion of virtual memory is allocated in a one-to-one correspondence to the file allowing applications to access the file as if it were physical memory. Memory mapping allows for better, but is limited to the memory that is available for the processing architecture (32 bit or 64 bit). Since many applications can be running and accessing files along with the limitations in the memory available, the most common method of file access is by using direct I/O. The most common applications using memory mapping on a Windows platform are Notepad and Paint.

FileTable is incompatible with applications that use memory mapping. Therefore any applications which utilize memory mapping to read/write files cannot be used with the FileTable feature.

Exercise 5: Create a FileTable for the Employee Documents

In the following exercise, we will replace the HumanResources.EmployeeDocuments table with a FileTable. Employees of Champion Valley Pens will then be able to store and process documents such as tax forms and resumes without needing specialized applications while still being able to maintain all of the documents within SQL Server.

1. Open a new query window and execute the following code to set the directory name:

    ```
    ALTER DATABASE ChampionValleyPensDocs SET FILESTREAM
    (DIRECTORY_NAME = 'ChampionValleyPensDocs')
    ```

2. Execute the following code to set the non_transacted_access level:

    ```
    ALTER DATABASE ChampionValleyPensDocs SET FILESTREAM(non_transacted_access = FULL)
    ```

3. Execute the following code to drop the existing HumanResources.EmployeeDocument table from the ChampionValleyPensDocs database:

    ```
    DROP TABLE HumanResources.EmployeeDocument
    ```

4. Execute the following code to recreate HumanResources.EmployeeDocument as a FileTable:

    ```
    CREATE TABLE HumanResources.EmployeeDocument AS FILETABLE
    FILESTREAM_ON EmployeeDocuments
    WITH (FILETABLE_DIRECTORY = N'EmployeeDocs',
          FILETABLE_COLLATE_FILENAME = SQL_Latin1_General_CP1_CI_AS)
    ```

5. Execute the following code to create an auxiliary table which can be used to attach additional information to the employee documents.

    ```
    CREATE TABLE HumanResources.EmployeeDocumentProperties
    (DocumentPropertyID     INT                  IDENTITY(1,1),
    EmployeeID              INT                  NOT NULL,
    DocumentTypeID          INT                  NOT NULL,
    StreamID                UNIQUEIDENTIFIER     NULL,
    CONSTRAINT pk_EmployeeDocumentProperties PRIMARY KEY (DocumentPropertyID))
    GO

    ALTER TABLE HumanResources.EmployeeDocumentProperties
        ADD CONSTRAINT fk_EmployeeDocumentToEmployeeDocumentPropertiesOnStreamID
            FOREIGN KEY (StreamID)
        REFERENCES HumanResources.EmployeeDocument (stream_id)
    GO

    ALTER TABLE HumanResources.EmployeeDocumentProperties
        ADD CONSTRAINT fk_DocumentTypeToEmployeeDocumentPropertiesOnDocumentTypeID
            FOREIGN KEY (DocumentTypeID)
        REFERENCES Lookups.DocumentType (DocumentTypeID)
    GO
    ```

6. Open Windows Explorer and go to \\<machine name>\mssqlserver\ChampionValleyPensDocs to view the EmployeeDocs folder that was created. Substitute <machine name> with the actual name of your computer. This is the UNC path you can use to directly add files to the FileTable.

7. Run the scripts in the companion files to create the Products.ProductDocument, Products,ProductImage, Products.ProductDocumentProperties, and Products.ProductImageProperties tables.

Summary

Something very interesting has just happened at this point. You just designed a database based on *__putting stuff where it belongs__*. You spent your time defining the information that needed to be stored. You then expanded on the basic information in order to minimize the administrative overhead when the company wanted to simply add another one of a given set of data. You defined some basic business rules that govern the type and size of data that can be stored in each column. You added an element that allowed you to uniquely identify every piece of data. You added items that tied all of the information together while also enforcing some rules that didn't allow rows to exist in one table unless there was a corresponding entry in another table. What did you wind up with? You just designed what is called a 3rd normal form database. We didn't have to explain the different normal forms, talk about set theory, or even get into anything technical. We spent our time breaking down the information so that it could be stored in a flexible manner. More importantly, we didn't get bogged down in a bunch of rules, formulas, and technobabble.

The process that we went through could be duplicated by anyone and wind up at the same place. It should come as no surprise databases have existed in one form or another for millennia. You also shouldn't be surprised that relational databases reside at the heart of just about anything that needs to store and manipulate data. The demise of the relational database is just a bunch of hot air, because the structure of a relational database simply mimics the way human beings think about and organize the vast amounts of information that we consume and recall. Millennia from now, businesses will still have Cobol programs and data will still be stored in relational databases.

Chapter 6
Data Storage Structures

In chapter 5, we created the tables and constraints that Champion Valley Pens will need. Along the way, we had a brief discussion of storage space based on data types. The storage structures SQL Server uses to manage databases and all of the objects within a database are quite a bit more complicated, but knowledge of the internal storage will be helpful in understanding several features which will be discussed throughout this book. In this chapter, we will cover some of the details of the storage structures that underpin a database as well as how space is allocated to data storage.

Database Allocation

As you learned in Chapter 4, "Creating Databases" a database consists of at least 1 data file and 1 transaction log file and data files are associated to a filegroup. In chapter 5, "Designing Tables", you learned that objects which contain data can be placed on a specific filegroup in order to control the placement of data on one or more physical files. This structure doesn't explain the limits imposed on the size of a row, nor does it explain how SQL Server manages I/O in a reliable way since it isn't possible to read/write all of a file every time a data request is made.

Data is served up in a series of 8K pages. Within each data file, pages are numbered starting at 0 and increment sequentially to the maximum size of the data file. When you expand a data file, the pages are added to the end of the file. When you shrink a data file, pages are removed from the end of the file, starting with the highest number page. Therefore, each data file will always have a contiguous sequence of page numbers that start at 0. Since data rows are required to fit entirely on a page, the 8K size of a page dictates the maximum size of a row.

Eight pages are grouped into extents, which forms the minimum I/O structure within SQL Server. While many will talk about reading/writing a page of data for simplicity, including later in this book, keep in mind that whenever SQL Server performs either a logical or physical I/O operation, an entire extent is always operated on.

Extents can be either mixed or uniform. Each object which contains data, table or index, is allocated a minimum of 1 page when it is created. So, even a table without any data will still consume 8K of storage space. In order to optimize the storage space, when an object is created, SQL Server allocates a single page within an extent along with a page for up to 7 other objects. An extent which contains one or more pages for more than one object is called a mixed extent.

As data is added to an object and space is consumed, SQL Server continues allocating space, one page at a time to the object. Once the object needs 8 pages of storage, SQL Server will allocate a full extent, move the pages within the mixed extent(s) to this new extent, and from that point forward, no other object will share space on the extent. Additionally, at that point, SQL Server stops allocating space one page at a time and instead allocates space one uniform extent, 64K, at time to the object.

> **Note:** When I refer to objects in this chapter, I mean either a table or an index, because tables and indexes are the only objects within a SQL Server database that consume space. All other SQL Server objects such as functions, views, and stored procedures, exist as data within one of the system tables, also known as the system catalog, that every database has.

Page Chains

Each data page consists of a 96 byte page header, followed by the actual rows of data, and at the bottom of the page is a block of row offsets as shown in Figure 6-1 below.

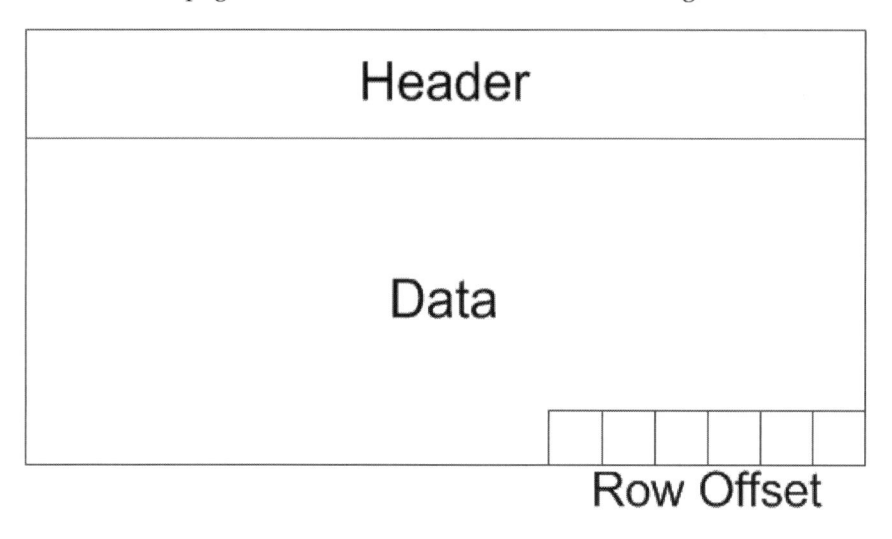

Figure 6-1 Basic Page Structure

Pages have a standard numbering scheme of <Database ID>:<File ID>:<Page ID>. All three elements allow SQL Server to uniquely identify every page either on disk or in memory. However, the last two elements are generally used when referring to pages. For example: 1:217 refers to page 217 within the first file of a given database. From this point forward, all page numbers will be assumed to reference the current database context unless explicitly noted otherwise.

With some of the tables I've worked with reaching several trillion rows, you would think that SQL Server would be consuming a very large amount of space just keeping track of all of the pages that belong to each object. That assumption is very far from reality. While objects can consist of hundreds of thousands or millions of 8K pages, SQL Server only needs to maintain a pointer to the very first page of the object in order to find any piece of data in a table. The reason that only a single page pointer is needed is due to the internal structuring of pages associated to an object.

Pages for each object are chained together in what is known as a doubly linked list. In a doubly linked list, each page contains a pointer to both the next and previous page within the chain. Since a doubly linked list never has any gaps, by knowing the first page in the chain, you can follow the internal links from one page to another until you reach the last page allocated to the object as shown in Figure 6-2 below.

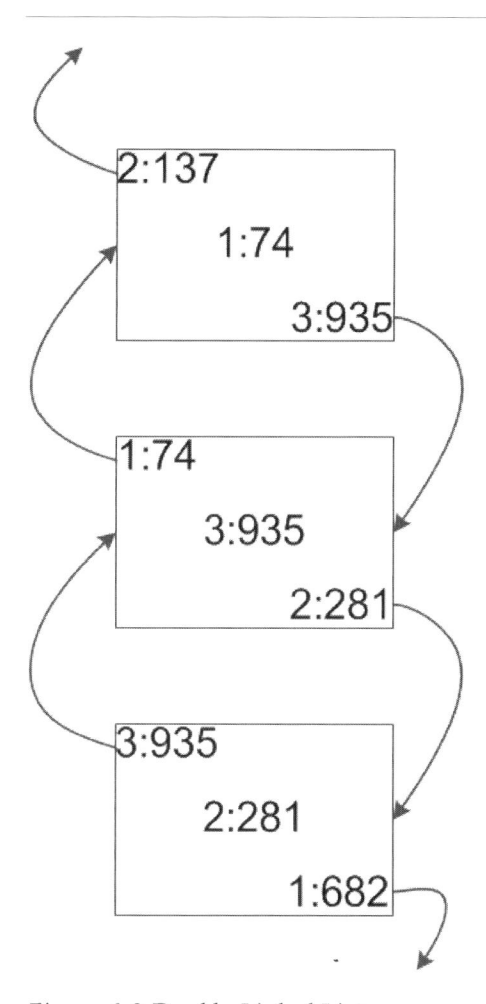

Figure 6-2 Doubly Linked List

The problem with a doubly linked list is that the first page in the chain doesn't have a previous page while the last page in a chain doesn't have a next page. Database files start numbering at 1, data pages start numbering at 0, and both are always positive numbers. SQL Server uses a page number convention of 0:0 to indicate either the first or last page in the chain. The first page in the chain will have a previous page entry of 0:0 and the last page in the chain will have a next page entry of 0:0. With this convention, SQL Server only needs to keep track of the first page of the object. The database engine will start reading the first page in the chain, designated with a previous page value of 0:0, and then simply needs to follow the next page value from one page to the next until it reaches a page where the next page value is 0:0 indicating that no additional pages exist for the object.

You can inspect any page within a database, given that you have sufficient security clearance, using the DBCC PAGE command. The output below shows the page header of page 1:217 in the ChampionValleyPens database which corresponds to the Lookups.Shipper table. You'll note that m_prevPage and m_nextPage are both set to 0:0 which tells you that this table only requires a single page to store all of its data.

```
PAGE HEADER:
Page @0x00000000392AC000
m_pageId = (1:217)                m_headerVersion = 1              m_type = 1
m_typeFlagBits = 0x0              m_level = 0                      m_flagBits = 0x8000
m_objId (AllocUnitId.idObj) = 117    m_indexId (AllocUnitId.idInd) = 256
Metadata: AllocUnitId = 72057594045595648
Metadata: PartitionId = 72057594040745984                          Metadata: IndexId = 1
Metadata: ObjectId = 1397580017   m_prevPage = (0:0)               m_nextPage = (0:0)
pminlen = 8                       m_slotCnt = 2                    m_freeCnt = 8055
m_freeData = 133                  m_reservedCnt = 0                m_lsn = (52:420:5)
m_xactReserved = 0                m_xdesId = (0:1213)
m_ghostRecCnt = 1
m_tornBits = 0                    DB Frag ID = 1
```

> **Note:** We will discuss DBCC PAGE in more detail in Chapter 14, "Partitioning Tables and Indexes" where we will again discuss doubly linked lists and page chains.

Page Structure

The present structure of a page was set down when SQL Server switched to 8K pages in SQL Server 2000. Each page has 8192 bytes of storage space and along with a page header of 96 bytes leaving a total available of 8096 bytes. However, you can only have a maximum row size of 8060 bytes. Of the remaining 36 bytes of storage space, 34 bytes was reserved for use by future features. Some of this space has been allocated in versions since SQL Server 2000 and a small portion still remains reserved and unused as of SQL Server 2012, however, the exact usage of that space is not relevant to any development or administration activities and is left to a purely academic discussion that I'll leave to others to write about.

This still leaves 2 bytes unaccounted for. The remaining two bytes is consumed by the row offset table at the end of the page. Each row stored on the page will consume 2 bytes of storage for the row offset, which indicates the byte position on the page where each row starts. So, for a single row that consumes all 8060 bytes, there will be a single 2byte row offset entry for the 1 row. However, if the row size is small enough for multiple rows to fit on a single page, each row will consume 2 bytes of storage on the page. Below is an example of a row offset for page 1:217 whose header was previously shown.

```
OFFSET TABLE:
Row - Offset
1 (0x1)  - 115 (0x73)
0 (0x0)  - 96  (0x60)
```

> **Why Should I Care?** I'm continually amazed by the amount of stuff, which I refer to as "SQL Server trivia", which gets thrown around as well as by the number of people this seems to impress. Trivia is simply an endless parade of factoids that people seem to spend a lot of time memorizing, but which have no actual use for anything that you are doing. Being able to spout KB article numbers, parse every bit value on a SQL Server page, and rattle off SQL Server trace flags are nothing more than interesting factoids, not a single one of which is of any real use in your job. Microsoft documents and search engines can find any trace flag or KB article that would be of use in your job and you can't change the way data is stored internally within SQL Server.
>
> So, just why am I spending an entire chapter walking you through some of the internal storage structures? SQL Server runs on a computer, which is based on binary math, and is bound by a set of rules that are defined by Microsoft. Nothing happens by accident within SQL Server and there is a reason every feature in the product behaves as it does, in every possible scenario, as well as a reason behind every limitation placed on every feature in the product. What I won't do is waste a lot of your time with endless pages of trivia, but will instead deal with just enough of the internal architecture so that you can understand how things behave as they do and be better prepared to apply various features to your applications.
>
> Understanding a doubly linked list and being able to actually read it from a page header won't do a single thing for any project you will ever work on. However, it provides background information which will explain how partitioning works and why it behaves as it does.
>
> Understanding the maximum of 8060 bytes of data space along with the 2 byte offset for each row will help you better design tables to maximize the available space. One of the worst things you can do, from a storage efficiency perspective; is create a table with a row size between 4030 bytes and about 6400 bytes. If you have a row size of exactly 4030 bytes, you will waste exactly 50% of every page, because there isn't enough space on a page to store 2 rows. You only have 8060 bytes of storage. Each row will consume 4030 bytes + a 2 byte row offset. The first row offset can essentially be considered free since it was already accounted for when the SQL Server team set the maximum row size to 8060 bytes. So, after storing the first row, you have 4030 bytes remaining. The second row would consume 4032 bytes and since that won't fit on a page, the row will be written to a new page, leaving every page allocated to the table ½ full. That same applies for any row size between 4030 bytes and 8060 bytes. However, as the row size gets closer to the maximum size allowed, you have less and less space wasted on a page. This doesn't mean you should immediately go out and re-design your tables, because you first "put stuff where it belongs". What it does mean is that you might want to more carefully consider the data types you are using and possibly even the columns defined for the table if you happen to have a table design that puts you at a row size where you will wind up wasting a large amount of space per page.

Slots

Each page is sub-divided into one or more slots, each of which contains a row. One slot is allocated on a page for each row which will fit. Rows are written to a page in any order, regardless of the order imposed on a table by a clustered index. The row offset table is the only element on the page that is maintained in clustered index order. You will learn about clustered indexes in Chapter 12, "Designing Indexes".

Row Structure

Within a page, as you can imagine, each row has a defined structure which depends upon whether variable length columns exist. For each row stored on a page, there is a small amount of space consumed, which impacts the number of rows that can be stored on a page.

Fixed Length Rows

Fixed length rows are constructed entirely with columns whose data types are fixed length such as INT, CHAR, DECIMAL, and UNIQUEIDENTIFIER. A fixed length row requires at least 7 bytes of storage space per row. The row overhead required is used as follows:

- 2 bytes of the row status
- 2 bytes to store the length of the fixed width portion of the row
- 2 bytes for the number of columns
- 1 bit per column for the NULL bitmap, rounded up to a whole byte

Row structure with only fixed length columns

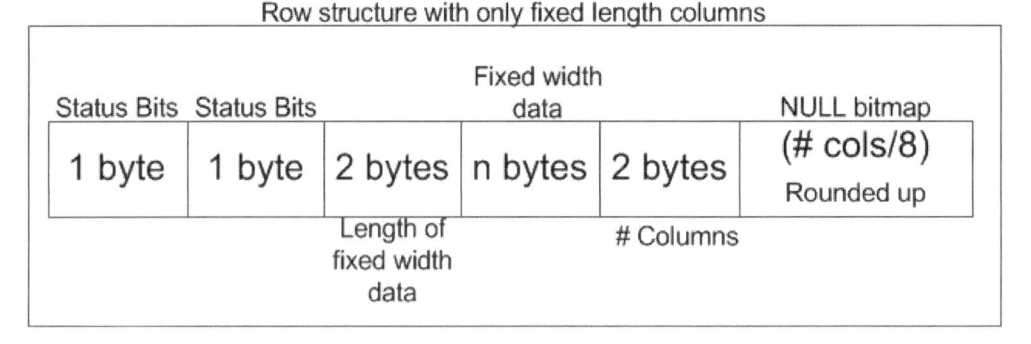

Status Bits	Status Bits	Length of fixed width data	Fixed width data	# Columns	NULL bitmap (# cols/8) Rounded up
1 byte	1 byte	2 bytes	n bytes	2 bytes	

Figure 6-3 Structure of a Fixed Length Row

The NULL bitmap makes the row overhead vary depending upon the number of columns. Each column defined in the table gets a bit in the NULL bitmap. Since storage is allocated 1 byte at a time in a row, you always allocate the NULL bitmap in increments of 1 byte. Therefore, for every 8 columns defined or fraction thereof, you will consume 1 byte of storage in the NULL bitmap e.g. a row with 7 columns will require 1 byte for the NULL bitmap, a row with 24 columns will require 3 bytes, and a row with 25 columns will require 4 bytes.

The NULL bitmap became necessary when SQL Server began allowing an empty string to be stored in a column. When an actual value is not specified for a fixed length column, SQL Server has to store something on the page in order to consume the fixed number of bytes the column is allocated for. The storage engine team decided to store the value of 0 in the column when a value was not supplied. Storing the value of 0 when a value wasn't specified creates a problem. On disk, it becomes impossible to distinguish an actual value of 0 from a NULL for numeric data or the difference between an empty string and a NULL for character data, hence the NULL bitmap. When SQL Server reads a bit value of 0 from disk, it uses the NULL bitmap to determine if the column is actually NULL.

While each row is allowed to consume 8060 bytes of space, you can now see that you can't actually store 8060 bytes of your own data in a row, because you have a minimum of 7 bytes of row overhead. So, the earlier comment about a row size of 8060 bytes was accurate enough for what you knew at the time, but with this additional information you know that you have to factor in the additional row overhead to come up with a maximum length of 8053 bytes of data storage. For a table with only fixed length columns, this is 6 bytes + the NULL bitmap lowers the value to 4026 bytes for a row size where you will only consume ½ of each page.

Variable Length Rows

Rows that have variable length columns such as VARCHAR, VARBINARY, and XML require additional overhead bytes in the row as shown in Figure 6-4. The first part of the row will contain the same structure as a fixed length row and then will add on 2 bytes to store the number of variable length columns, 2 bytes for every variable length column, and then n bytes for the variable length data. While you may have defined columns in a table in a particular order, SQL Server does not store them the way you have defined. The fixed length columns are separated from the variable length columns and placed in different sections of the row storage on disk in the order that the columns were defined in the table. If you think about it for a second, this arrangement makes a lot of sense. If fixed and variable length data were mingled together, a change that causes the length of the variable data to increase/decrease would also require relocating the fixed data, just to maintain a column order structure. By placing the variable data at the end of the row, the position of all of the fixed length columns remains static while allowing the variable length data to expand and shrink as needed.

Row structure with fixed and variable length columns

Fixed length structure	# Variable Columns 2 bytes	Var column Offset 2 bytes * # var cols	variable width data n bytes

Figure 6-4 Structure of a Variable Length Row

The column offset array indicates the position in the row where the column ends. The offset indicates the end of the column, so that you do not have to also store the number of bytes contained in the column. When a variable length column does not contain any data, the column does not consume any space on disk. You can see this by reading the column offset array. While each variable length column consumes 2 bytes of storage in the offset array, for any column that does not contain any data, the offset value will be the same as the offset value of the previous column in the table. The only exception is when the last variable length column contains a NULL, SQL Server does not store anything in the row or in the offset array.

Going back to the example we've been discussing about the size of a row where you can wind up leaving up to ½ of a page empty since no other row would fit on the page, you can see how to modify the basic premise based on whether you have variable length columns, even if those columns do not contain any data.

Large Objects

While the fixed and variable length row structures described above explain the limitations on the size of a row, it isn't the entire picture. If a row has to fit entirely on a page and the maximum size of a row is 8060 bytes, then how can you possibly store 2GB of data in a column with a data type of VARCHAR (MAX)/NVARCHAR (MAX), VARBINARY (MAX), or XML?

Restricted Length Data

In SQL Server 2005, an extension to the storage algorithm for variable length columns, the row overflow page, was introduced allowing a single row to span multiple pages. The fixed length data portion of a row + all of the overhead bytes are still bound by the 8060 byte limit, but variable length columns can expand to additional pages if the data will not fit on a single page. Row overflow pages apply to variable length columns which are limited in size, those less than 8000 bytes in length. Through the use of row overflow pages, you can define a table with variable length columns capable of storing many times the amount of data as SQL Server 2000 and prior. For example a table with 4 VARCHAR (8000) columns, fully populated with data would cause an error in SQL Server 2000, but can be stored on a regular page + 4 overflow pages in SQL Server 2005 and above.

As long as the row length is less than 8060 bytes, the row will be stored on a single page. However, once the row size exceeds 8060 bytes, SQL Server will allocate one or more overflow pages and move one or more variable length columns to the overflow page(s). A regular variable length column cannot span pages, so the column will exist either on the page with the rest of the row or the row overflow page.

> **Note:** Row overflow pages exist for variable length columns. Fixed length columns still cannot exceed 8060 bytes. Additionally, the fixed columns and all of the overhead bytes have to fit within 8060 bytes.

When a column is moved to a row overflow page, SQL Server leaves a 24 byte pointer in the row to indicate the column's location on the row overflow page. While a table can have 1024 columns and you might have thought, for a minute, that you could now create extremely wide tables with huge amounts of data per row by taking advantage of row overflow pages, the 24 byte pointer in the row quickly reduces the number of possible overflow columns.

The storage engine has a couple of optimizations for dealing with row overflow data. The first rule is that the length must exceed 24 bytes before it can even be written to a row overflow page. Since each overflow column requires 24 bytes of storage in the row for the overflow pointer, it would be pointless for SQL Server to attempt to move a column containing less data than the pointer would consume. Additionally, SQL Server will not even check if the column could be stored with the rest of the row until the size decreases by a minimum of 1000 bytes. The 1000 byte minimum was added to prevent SQL Server from constantly having to check if the column could be moved along with the deallocation of row overflow pages.

Unrestricted Length Data

While the row overflow page covers the case of variable length columns overflowing the 8060 bytes available in a row, it cannot account for the four data types which allow up to 2GB of data in a single column. For these four data types, SQL Server stores the data on a stack of pages organized in a B-tree. B-tree is shorthand for balanced tree and is a structure that looks very similar to the trees in nature you are used to. A B-tree consists of a root node, one or more intermediate levels, and a leaf level. The reason it is a balanced tree is that at any level you can draw a line vertically through the structure and there will be an equal number of nodes to the left and right of the node you are starting from. A portion of a B-tree is showing in Figure 6-5 below.

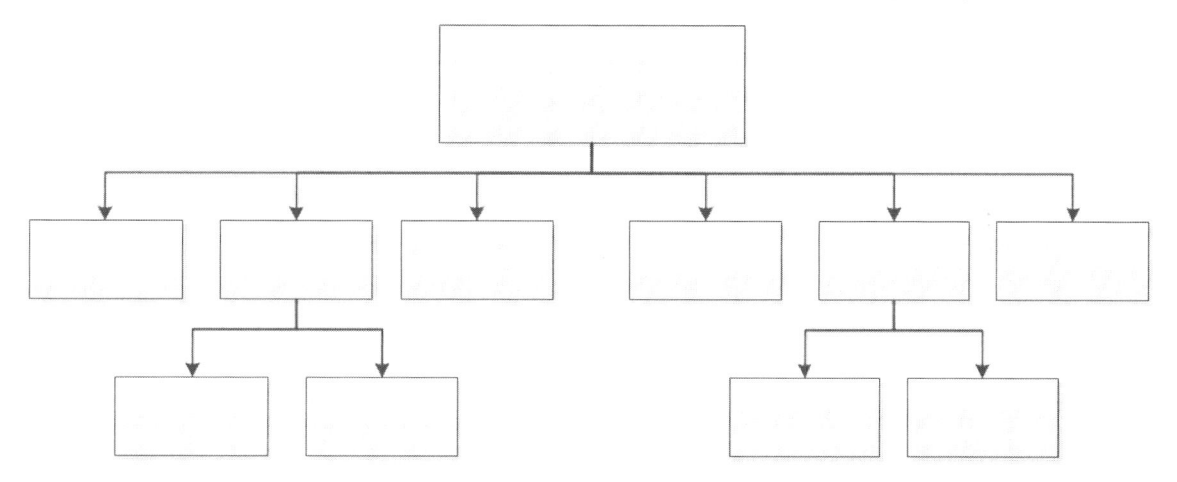

Figure 6-5 B-tree

SQL Server stores a 16 byte pointer to the root page of each object's B-tree. Depending upon the volume of data stored, the B-tree can vary from a single data page to several thousand pages. It is the lowest level in the B-tree which contains the data. The upper levels only contain pointers to the various blocks of data.

> **Note:** Indexes are also stored in a B-tree structure. We will discuss B-tree in more detail in Chapter 12 "Designing Indexes". While we could cover B-trees in detail in this section, going over the way B-trees are built will make a lot more sense when using actual data values instead of page pointers.

MAX Length Data Types

VARCHAR(MAX), NVARCHAR(MAX), and VARBINARY(MAX) can use either row overflow pages or a B-tree to store data. If the length of the data in the column is 8000 bytes or less, SQL Server will treat the column as if it were a restricted length column and utilize row overflow pages as needed. If the length is greater than 8000 bytes, a 16 byte pointer will be placed in the row, and the data will be stored in a B-tree structure.

Sparse Columns

In chapter 5, we described the use of sparse columns and column sets to allow you to define up to 30,000 columns in a table while not consuming space when the column is NULL. However, as we noted, you should only specify a column as SPARSE if you expect to achieve at least a 40% space savings.

When you store data in a SPARSE column, you will consume more storage space than normal due to the additional overhead required by the storage engine. The additional overhead is necessary, because when we say that no space is consumed by a SPARSE column that contains a NULL, not only is there no space consumed in the fixed or variable length data areas, space isn't even allocated for column offsets. The column also isn't counted in the number of fixed or variable length columns. So, from a very real sense, the column does not even exist to the storage engine if the column is NULL. This is different from a non-sparse column, which will have a column offset entry for either fixed/variable length data types as well as consume actual space if the data type is fixed length. Because the column does not exist to the storage engine, when you store a value in a SPARSE column, SQL Server needs to not only store the data, but also identify the column in the table.

When you store a value in a SPARSE column, the storage engine will create what is known as a sparse vector. Only one sparse vector exists per row and contains all of the overhead bytes as well as the data for all sparse columns which contain values. The sparse vector is placed at the very end of the row, after the NULL bitmap and is structured as follows:

- 2 byte header
- 2 bytes for number of populated sparse columns
- 2 bytes for each populated sparse column
- 2 bytes for end position of each populated sparse column

Row structure with at least one populated sparse column

Fixed length data	Variable length data	Header	# Pop Columns	Column ID	Column Offset	Data
		2 bytes	2 bytes	2 bytes * # cols	2 bytes * # cols	n bytes

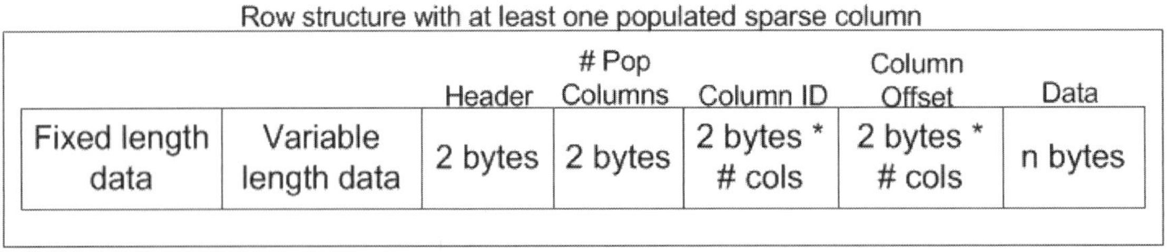

Figure 6-6 Structure of a Sparse Column Vector

Compression

The row structure we've been talking about up to this point is referred to as FixedVar due to the fixed length and variable length sections of the row structure. SQL Server 2008 introduced a new row structure called column descriptor to handle the storage for the new compression feature.

The Enterprise Edition of SQL Server 2008 and higher has the ability to compress rows, pages or both and can be applied to tables as well as indexes. The two compression methods utilize different algorithms, but the end goal is to be able to store more rows on every page as well as require fewer pages to store data for each table.

Storing the same amount of data on fewer pages means that SQL Server has to access fewer pages possibly giving you a performance boost. Compression follows the same reasoning as to why many people shop at these massive one-stop retailers such as WalMart, by going to a store that has an item in almost every category you need, you only need to stop at one place instead of having to go into many different stores to finish your shopping. However, just like going to a WalMart at the busiest time of the week, applying compression to a table on an instance that doesn't have sufficient CPU capacity to perform the compress/decompress operations as data is accessed can actually cause a decrease in performance. The storage engine takes on the task of compressing/decompressing data as needed, so you do not need any special considerations for your applications to work with compressed objects.

Compression in SQL Server follows the same basic principles for compressing files and folders:

- Remove white space
- Replace commonly occurring patterns with small tokens

> **Note:** Compression cannot be enabled on a table with sparse columns.

Compressed Row Structure

When a row is compressed, the structure is changed from the FixedVar format to the column descriptor format. Within this structure, data is broken into short and long data regions. The short data region is composed of all of the columns that require 8 bytes or less of storage. The long data region is for all of the columns that require more than 8 bytes of storage.

The header contains a series of status bits. The next section contains up to 2 bytes for the number of short data columns followed by 4 bits for the length of each column. Any column with data in the long data area is set to a value of 10. By using the values of 0 – 9 to indicate the length of each column in the short data area, SQL Server is able to parse each column's value without needing to store position or offset information. The next section, short data, contains the values for every column that is less than 8 bytes. The long data section contains all of the values that were greater than 8 bytes in length along with a 2 byte offset for each long data column. The final section is only used if the row has a forwarding pointer, back pointer, or is row versioning is in effect for the row. We will discuss forwarding and back pointers in Chapter 12 "Designing Indexes" and row versioning in Chapter 8 "Managing Concurrency".

The combination of all of these bit values as well as splitting the columns on an 8 byte length boundary allows SQL Server to remove the maximum amount of space while minimizing the space needed to track column position.

The structure of a compressed row is shown in Figure 6-7.

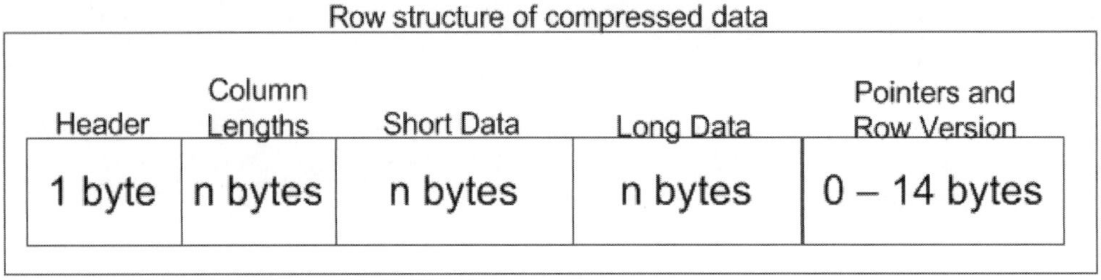

Row structure of compressed data

Header	Column Lengths	Short Data	Long Data	Pointers and Row Version
1 byte	n bytes	n bytes	n bytes	0 – 14 bytes

Figure 6-7 Structure of a compressed row

Row Compression

Row compression implements a basic white space removal algorithm. When you enable row compression, each row is compressed to the smallest possible size by removing extraneous white space. For example, an INT data type with a value of 7 in it will have 3 bytes removed since it only takes 1 byte to store the value on disk. Since variable length data types already have all of the white space removed, row compression will not have any effect on variable length data.

> **Note:** Row compression only applies to data stored in row, so any data on row overflow of LOB pages will not be compressed.

Page Compression

Page compression applies two additional algorithms that rely on replacing repeating values on a page with compact, substitute values called tokens. The first tokenize process replaces portions of string values with a shorter representation plus a difference value for example *deer, dear, deed, deem, beer*, and *bear*. You could use *dee* as a base value represented by a 1 byte base value + "r" and *deed* or *deem* would simply need that same 1 byte value along with a "d" or "m" to compress the value from 4 bytes to 2 bytes. Once the first tokenize pass is made, a second pass is applied that finds duplicate values along with the number of occurrences of that value. SQL Server will store the repeating value, whether it was already tokenized or not in a page dictionary represented by a replacement token which is then substituted for every occurrence of the value. Once page compression is complete, row compression is applied to eliminate an unnecessary white space in each row.

While row compression occurs at the time a row is written to a page, page compression is only applied to full pages. The reason for applying page compression to full pages only should be obvious; page compression is not only expensive to compute, but it also becomes more efficient as the volume of data increases. Additionally, SQL Server will not always compress a page. The storage engine will only compress a page if it determines that the reclaimed space will hold 5 additional rows or 25% more rows on a page, whichever is greater.

> **Note:** The actual tokenizing process as well as the internal storage of the tokens is only relevant if you are writing a compression algorithm.

Compression Considerations

- Since row compression only removes extraneous white space, variable length columns are not affected.
- Row compression has the greatest effect when a large percentage of fixed width data only consumes a small fraction of the available bytes.
- Compression is not valid for row overflow or LOB pages.
- Page compression has the greatest effect when data has a large number of repeating values.
- The storage engine performs all of the compression/decompression operations, so a system that does not have enough CPU capacity can have performance decline.

Storage Metadata

The metadata view, sys.indexes, stores a single row for each table. Each table can be split across many partitions, which we will discuss in detail in chapter 14. For now, we will assume that each table only has a single partition. The same metadata structure for tables also applies to indexes, which we will cover in Chapter 12. This structure is shown in Figure 6-8 below.

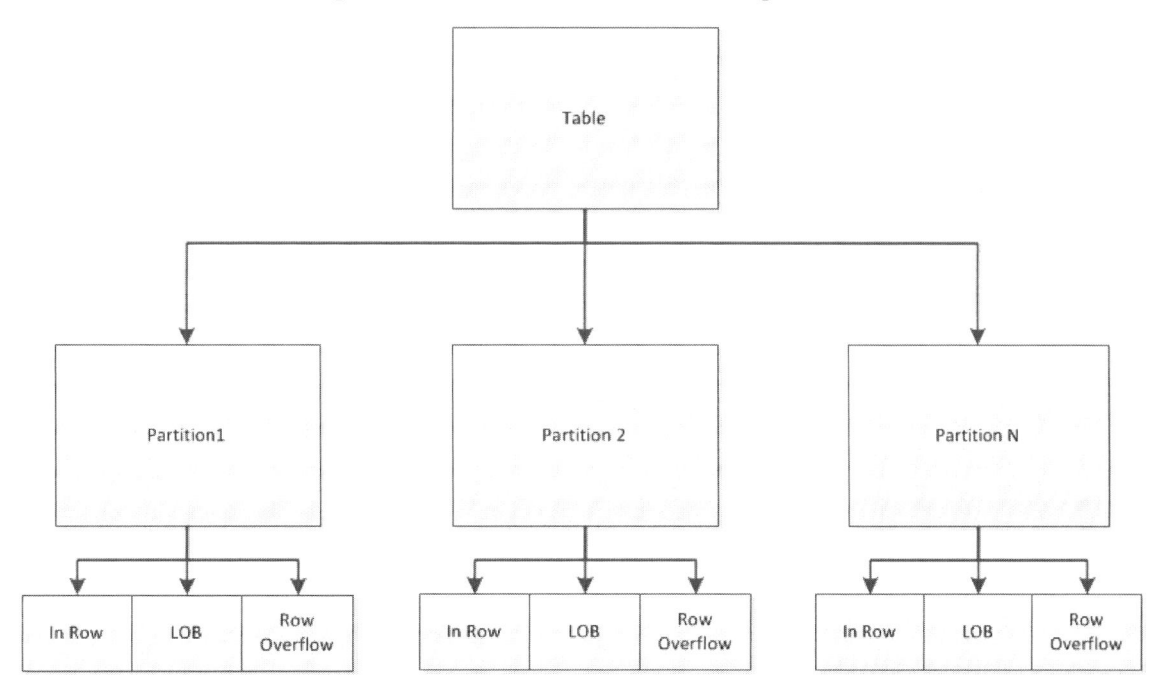

Figure 6-8 Table Structure

Each table can have up to 3 types of IAM pages allocated to it – in row data, row overflow, and LOB. Each type of data page assigned to a table is tracked in a separate IAM page. An entry is made in the IAM page for each extent containing one of the corresponding page types assigned to the table. The IAM is very densely packed, allocating a single bit for each extent. So there will be an IAM page for each data page type allocated for each 517,632 pages allocated to a table for each type of data. For example, in a table which does not have any row overflow or LOB pages, SQL Server will allocate an IAM page for in row data every 517,632 pages within each partition.

Earlier in this chapter, we discussed page chains and how everything is maintained in a doubly linked list. But, pages are only maintained in a doubly linked list when an order to the pages is enforced. There are only two cases when a doubly linked list is maintained – when a clustered index is present on the table and when you are looking at a non-clustered index, both of which will be discussed in Chapter 12. When a table does not have a clustered index, pages are simply maintained in a pile, called a heap. For a heap, the IAM pages are the only way which SQL Server can determine which pages belong to a given object.

Summary

Rows are stored in slots on pages which are arranged in a doubly linked list. A doubly linked list allows you to start at any page and traverse both forward and backward through the data set to find data. Data is stored randomly on a page, while the row offset table in the page footer is used to maintain a sort order on the data if necessary. Within each slot, rows are stored which contain structural information about the layout of the row, reducing the amount of space available on a page for your data. While fixed length data cannot span pages, variable length data can be stored on a series of row overflow of LOB pages to accommodate up to 2GB of data for some data types. In order to conserve space, you can apply both row and page compression at the expense of additional processor overhead for the storage engine to perform the compress/decompress operations.

Chapter 7
Data Manipulation

> **Setup:** Please run the Chapter 7 Setup script in the companion files prior to starting the exercises in this chapter to ensure that your databases are at the correct starting point. Every exercise in this book assumes that you have created the c:\ChampionValleyPress\Data and c:\ChampionValleyPress\Log folders, contained databases are enabled, and this is the location of all of the data, log, and filestream files which will be used for this book. If you have chosen a different path, you will need to adjust the paths listed accordingly. Every setup script also assumes that you have enabled FILESTREAM access for the instance. When executing commands, it is assumed that you will change context to the appropriate database since understanding the contents of each database in this book is the same skill you will need for working with your databases. All scripts also assume you are using a default instance.

In chapter 5 you learned how to construct a database and in chapter 6 you learned how the internal storage structures dictate the space required to store data as well as how the internal structure could affect your database design. While understanding how to design a database and how data is stored is important, a database is quite useless without any data. So, in this chapter, you will learn how to manipulate data in a SQL Server database.

Retrieving Data

The goal of writing this series was to provide complete coverage of SQL Server 2012 features for those just starting out with SQL Server as well as for those who have been working with SQL Server for years or decades. This chapter presents the first "educational issue" in addressing the needs of those just starting with SQL and SQL Server. You can't learn how to retrieve data if you don't have any data in your tables to help understand the queries. You also can't manipulate data in a table, unless you can retrieve data. Chapter 9 "Data Retrieval" and Chapter 10 "Advanced Data Retrieval" will cover all of the options available for retrieving data. However, basic data retrieval will be covered in this section in order to understand the subsequent sections for manipulating data.

The T-SQL language is split into two major groups: Data Definition Language (DDL) and Data Manipulation Language (DML). DDL is the section of the language, consisting of hundreds of commands, responsible for creating, modifying, and removing objects within SQL Server. DML is the section of the language which contains six commands responsible for manipulating data. Three of the commands READTEXT, WRITETEXT, and UPDATETEXT have been deprecated.

Within DML, there is exactly one command (SELECT), also referred to as a statement, which is used to retrieve data. While most programming languages have hundreds or thousands of specialized commands to return information, T-SQL has only one. At the same time, it is possible to construct a single SELECT statement to perform any data retrieval, from any database structure that you will ever design or work with. While there is only a single statement to retrieve data, there are infinite number of ways to construct a SELECT statement ranging from an extremely simple single line to a SELECT statement that would require many pages to print out.

The most basic SELECT statement that you can create is to return a statically defined constant.

```
SELECT 'a character constant'
```

It might seem that being able to do something as simple as returning a statically defined constant would be worthless, you'll see in subsequent chapters how you can use this feature of a SELECT statement to manipulate data and even build highly automated administrative routines.

A SELECT statement is constructed of one or more clauses with the SELECT clause being the only required clause. The SELECT statement can contain constants, columns, and calculations. If you want to return data from a table, you need to tell SQL Server which table to retrieve data from. This is done by using the FROM clause as follows:

```
SELECT *
FROM Customers.Customer
```

The FROM clause should always fully qualify the object you are retrieving data from, which at a minimum is <schema name>.<object name>. As was noted in Chapter 5, object names have 4 parts. Unless you are running a query that spans databases, you only need to specify the last two parts of the name. The * in the SELECT clause is a shorthand for "all columns".

> Note: SELECT * will be used in several points throughout this book in order to save space. You will also see SELECT * used in many demos for simplicity. When you write code for your applications, you should **_NEVER_** use SELECT *. When you use SELECT *, it becomes impossible to gauge the impact of database changes on your code if a column needs to be changed or modified, because your code doesn't contain the column name being modified. Additionally, if you subsequently add columns to a table, SELECT * will retrieve all of the new columns and if your application was not coded to handle additional columns you can introduce applications errors which could have been easily avoided.

The proper way to construct the query above is as follows:

```
SELECT CustomerID, FirstName, LastName
FROM Customers.Customer
```

With the basic SELECT and FROM clause, you now have the basic background for retrieving data to be able to work with the remaining DML statements within this chapter. Chapters 9 and 10 will cover the remainder of the clauses available to a SELECT statement as well as how to construct more complex SELECT statements.

Adding Data

Data is added to a table by using an INSERT statement. An INSERT statement has two formats, depending upon whether you are adding values directly or inserting data into a table based on retrieving data from another table.

The first clause of an INSERT statement is always the same and defines the table to insert data into as well as the column list as follows:

```
INSERT INTO <schema>.<table>
(<column1>,<column2>,…>)
```

The second clause of an INSERT statement will vary. If you are inserting explicit values, you will use a VALUES clause. If you are inserting data based on retrieving data from another table, you will use a SELECT statement. Examples of the two formats are as follows:

```
INSERT INTO <schema>.<table>
(<column1>,<column2>,…>)
VALUES (<value1>,<value2>,…)

INSERT INTO <schema>.<table>
(<column1>,<column2>,…>)
SELECT column1, column2, …
FROM …
```

> **Note:** The SELECT statement that you specify can be any valid SELECT statement and is not limited to a single table. If you can write a SELECT statement, the output of the SELECT statement can be used as the source for the INSERT.

The column list as well as the VALUES/SELECT clause are related by position i.e. the first column in the column list will receive the data from the first item in the VALUES/SELECT list.

> **Note:** If you are specifying a value for every column in a table and supplying the values in the same order as the columns in a table, the column list is optional. However, as was mentioned with respect to using SELECT * an INSERT without a column list is very poor programming practice.

The value supplied to the column must be compatible with the data type and any constraints defined. You must supply a value in the VALUES/SELECT clause for every column that is specified in the column list. You also have to specify a value for every column defined as NOT NULL. For columns that are defined as NULL, you can either explicitly specify NULL in the VALUES/SELECT clause or you can omit the column from the INSERT statement.

Prior to SQL Server 2008, an INSERT statement was only capable of adding a single row of data at a time when you used a VALUES clause. So, if you had to insert 1000 rows of data, you would have had to create and execute 1000 separate INSERT statements. In SQL Server 2008 and later, you can now specify multiple inserts in a single VALUES clause by separating each set with a comma as follows:

```
INSERT INTO <schema>.<table>
(<column1>,<column2>,…>)
VALUES (<value1>,<value2>,…), (<value1>,<value2>,…), …
```

Identities

Columns defined with an IDENTITY property are self-managing. When you insert rows into a table, any column designated with an IDENTITY property will automatically be assigned the next value in the range. The value for each row inserted will increase by the increment amount specified. Since identity columns are automatically assigned values, these columns are not included in the column list for an INSERT statement.

If you do include an identity column and attempt to assign a value, you will receive an error message. If you want to explicitly assign a value to an identity column, you must first execute the SET IDENTITY_INSERT command for the table as follows:

```
SET IDENTITY_INSERT <schema>.<table> ON
```

Once you are done inserting data, you need to turn this feature off by executing:

```
SET IDENTITY_INSERT <schema>.<table> OFF
```

IDENTITY_INSERT can only be enabled for a single table in each connection. You will receive an error message if you attempt to enable IDENTITY_INSERT on more than one table at a time.

When you specify a value which is higher than the current identity value, the newly inserted value is used as the current identity value. If you specify a value which is less than the current identity value, the current identity value is not reset. You can see this behaviour by executing the following code:

```
CREATE TABLE #test
(TestID     INT          IDENTITY(1,1),
Test        VARCHAR(75) NOT NULL)

SELECT * FROM #test
INSERT INTO #test
(Test)
VALUES ('initial')

SELECT * FROM #test

SET IDENTITY_INSERT #test ON
INSERT INTO #test
(TestID, Test)
VALUES(10,'Identity insert 1')
SET IDENTITY_INSERT #test OFF

SELECT * FROM #test
INSERT INTO #test
(Test)
VALUES('normal insert 2')

SELECT * FROM #test
SET IDENTITY_INSERT #test ON
INSERT INTO #test
(TestID, Test)
VALUES(5,'Identity insert 2')
SET IDENTITY_INSERT #test OFF

SELECT * FROM #test
INSERT INTO #test
(Test)
VALUES('normal insert 3')

SELECT * FROM #test
```

The current identity value is a property of the table. No matter how many connections are inserting data into the table, each row will be assigned a different value. Under normal operations, an identity column will start at the seed value and increase by the increment until you reach the maximum value for the defined data type without ever repeating a value, even if the SQL Server is restarted. The durability of an identity value is possible, because SQL Server physically stores the current value of the identity for each table. Each time an identity value is incremented due to the insert of a new row, the current value will be physically persisted to the database.

If you want to permanently reset the seed value, you can use the DBCC CHECKIDENT command as shown in the code below:

```
CREATE TABLE #test
(TestID     INT         IDENTITY(1,1),
Test        VARCHAR(75) NOT NULL)

INSERT INTO #test
(Test)
VALUES('First row')

SELECT * FROM #test
DBCC CHECKIDENT ("#Test", RESEED, 3)

INSERT INTO #test
(Test)
VALUES('Second row')

SELECT * FROM #test
DBCC CHECKIDENT ("#Test", RESEED, 5)

INSERT INTO #test
(Test)
VALUES('Third row')

SELECT * FROM #test
```

> NOTE: If you have a primary key or unique constraint on the identity column and you reset an identity value to less than the maximum value currently assigned in the column, subsequent insert operations can fail due to a duplicate value being generated.

Exercise 1: Inserting Data

In the following exercise, you will load data into the Lookups.Shipper, Lookups.Country, and Lookups.StateProvince tables.

1. Open a new query window and execute the following code:
    ```
    INSERT INTO Lookups.Shipper
    (Shipper)
    VALUES('US Postal Service')
    ```
2. Execute the following code to review the results and inspect the identity value assigned:
    ```
    SELECT * FROM Lookups.Shipper
    ```
3. Add the following values to the Lookups.Shipper table: UPS, FedEx, DHL, Royal Mail, and Canada Post.

4. Execute the following code to insert United States, Canada, and United Kingdom into the Lookups.Country table. Retrieve the contents of Lookups.Country to obtain the identity values for each country.

    ```
    INSERT INTO Lookups.Country
    (Country)
    VALUES('United States'),('Canada'),('United Kingdom')
    ```

5. Execute the following code to insert China and specify the CountryID:

    ```
    SET IDENTITY_INSERT Lookups.Country ON
    INSERT INTO Lookups.Country
    (CountryID, Country)
    VALUES(5,'China')
    SET IDENTITY_INSERT Lookups.Country OFF
    ```

6. Execute the following code to add Wisconsin, Tennessee, Illinois, California, Texas, Maryland, Pennsylvania, Iowa, and Ohio into the Lookups.StateProvince table.

    ```
    INSERT INTO Lookups.StateProvince
    (CountryID, StateProvince, StateProvinceCode)
    VALUES(10,'Wisconsin','WI'), (10,'Tennessee','TN'), (10,'Illinois','IL'),
    (10,'California','CA'), (1,'Texas','TX'), (10,'Maryland','MD'),
    (10,'Pennsylvania','PA'), (10,'Iowa','IA'), (10,'Ohio','OH')
    ```

> **Foreign Keys:** In my database, United States is assigned a CountryID of 1, Canada = 2, and United Kingdom = 3. Since these are the only values in the Lookups.Country table, attempting to use an invalid CountryID in the Lookups.StateProvince table will produce an error message and the INSERT will fail. Even though Texas is assigned the correct value for the CountryID, since an error was produced by one of the other rows specified, none of the data has been inserted. We will cover errors and transaction handling chapter 8, "Transaction Management".

7. Correct the statement above by specifying the correct CountryID, insert the data, and retrieve the contents of the Lookups.StateProvince table to inspect the results.

> **Identity Assignment:** When an INSERT is executes against a table with an identity column, SQL Server will acquire the current identity value and then increment the value stored. Even though no data was inserted in step 6 due to the error, SQL Server still acquired an identity value and incremented the value by 1. So, the failed INSERT statement had the effect of "burning" a value in the range. The subsequent insert assigned values contiguously. Thus the importance of retrieving the identity value of the corresponding row when specifying values for foreign keys since identities will always increment, but are not guaranteed to produce a contiguous range of values.

8. Insert the remainder of the states/provinces for the United States, Canada, and United Kingdom. A good reference for states/provinces around the world can be found at
    http://code.google.com/apis/adwords/docs/appendix/provincecodes.html

> Note: A single quote is used to designate text values, so in order to specify values with embedded single quotes such as the province of Hawke's Bay in New Zealand you need to include an escape character. Unfortunately T-SQL uses a single quote as the escape character, so the values clause would look like the following: VALUES (154,'Hawke''s Bay','HKB')

Hierarchies

Hierarchies are used to store the position within a structure that a particular object is located. Hierarchy data is stored in a binary format, but normally manipulated in a human-readable format known as canonical form. Canonical format encodes the positions of each element from the root node to each node in the hierarchy which allows you to easily navigate through each layer to the root element. Canonical format also provides an easy way to determine which other elements reside at the same level as well as levels above and below. This should explain how to store and read hierarchy data about as clear as mud, so let's look at an example.

In order to easily group similar products together, Champion Valley Pens assigns products to a category and categories can be nested inside of other categories. A small piece of this product category hierarchy is shown below:

```
Products
    Turning Kits
        Pen Kits
                Fountain Pens
                Rollerball Pens
        Accessories
                Clips
                Caps
                Nibs
                Bands
    Turning Blanks
        Natural
            Wood
                    Hardwood
                    Burl
                            Stabilized
                            Unstabilized
                    Other
        Man Made
                Plastic
    Adhesives
    Finishing
    Project Displays
        Boxes
        Pouches
        Cases
```

The root node, *Products*, in canonical form is /. Since *Turning Kits* is the first descendant of *Products*, it is represented as /1/. *Pen Kits*, as the first descendant of *Turning Kits* would be represented as /1/1/. *Accessories* as the second descendant of *Turning Kits* would be represented as /1/2.

The entire structure shown above, with canonical representations would be as follows:

```
Products                                    /
   Turning Kits                             /1/
      Pen Kits                              /1/1/
            Fountain Pens                   /1/1/1/
            Rollerball Pens                 /1/1/2/
      Accessories                           /1/2/
            Clips                           /1/2/1/
            Caps                            /1/2/2/
            Nibs                            /1/2/3/
            Bands                           /1/2/4/
   Turning Blanks                           /2/
      Natural                               /2/1/
         Wood                               /2/1/1/
            Hardwood                        /2/1/1/1/
            Burl                            /2/1/1/2/
                  Stabilized                /2/1/1/2/1/
                  Unstabilized              /2/1/1/2/2/
         Other                              /2/1/2/
      Man Made                              /2/2/
         Plastic                            /2/2/1/
   Adhesives                                /3/
   Finishing                                /4/
   Project Displays                         /5/
      Boxes                                 /5/1/
      Pouches                               /5/2/
      Cases                                 /5/3/
```

By looking at the canonical representation, we can quickly determine that *Natural* and *Man Made* are direct subcategories of *Turning Blanks* since the second element for both is 2/ and no further element exists. We can likewise select any element within the hierarchy and determine which category it is a subcategory of as well as what other categories are at the same level.

Don't get caught up in the apparent sequential, whole number nature of the canonical representation above. In the real world, once you start modifying hierarchies and moving elements around, you won't have such a neat structure to work with. As we noted in chapter 5, trees don't have to be numbered without gaps. When you modify the structure by doing something like moving the *Burl* category out 1 level so that it is between *Wood* and *Other*, SQL Server will change the reference to a decimal value such that it fits between 1 and 2. So, you would wind up with something like /2/1/1.4/ for *Burl*, /2/1/1.4/1/ for *Stabilized*, and /2/1/1.4/2/ for *Unstabilized*.

Variables

Within the DDL subset of T-SQL commands is a programming language that allows you to create code modules which can be executed. We will cover the entire programming language in chapters 18 – 20, however in order to load data into the hierarchies contained in our HumanResources.Employee and Lookups.Category tables, we need to cover one element within the programming set.

Like almost every programming language ever created, T-SQL allows you to create variables to store data. Variable definitions consist of two parts – variable name and a data type. A variable name follows a restricted set of rules for identifiers. The variable name must start with an @ symbol, has a maximum length of 128 characters, and is not allowed to contain a space. There are two types of variables, local and global. Local variables are designated by a single @ symbol while global variables are designed by a double @ symbol.

Global variables are created and managed by SQL Server and can be scoped at either the entire instance or a per connection basis. You can retrieve values from global variables, but you cannot create or assign values. Global variables scoped to the instance will return the same value to every connection while global variables scoped to a connection will return a value unique to each connection. The @@version global variable is scoped to the instance and will return the version of SQL Server that you are connected to. The @@SPID global variable is scoped to a connection and will return the process ID of the connection.

Local variables can be created and assigned values. To create a variable, you use the DECLARE statement as follows:

```
DECLARE @var    INT
```

You can declare as many variables as you need. You can use a separate DECLARE statement for each variable or you can combine multiple variables into a single DECLARE statement as follows:

```
DECLARE @var1    INT,
        @var2    VARCHAR(20),
        @var3    HIERARCHYID
```

There are three ways to assign a value to a variable: in the DECLARE clause, with a SET statement, or with a SELECT statement. The SELECT statement is the only method which will allow you to assign values to multiple variables in a single statement. Examples of the three methods are as follows:

```
DECLARE @var1    INT = 10,
        @var2    VARCHAR(20) = 'Test',
        @var3    HIERARCHYID,
        @var4    INT,
        @var5    DATE

SET @var3 = CAST('/' AS hierarchyid)

SELECT @var4 = 3, @var5 = '1/1/2012'
```

The statement to retrieve a value from a variable should be obvious from the preceding section since we said that T-SQL has exactly 1 command to retrieve data. So, to return the values of all five variables above, we would use the following statement:

```
SELECT @var1, @var2, @var3, @var4, @var5
```

Local variables are scoped to the block of code that is being executed. Once the block of code completes, SQL Server automatically destroys all local variables which were created.

Local variables can be declared with any data type and the data type cannot be changed once declared. In addition to all of the data types available, you can also declare a variable of type table. While most other variables are scalars, they can contain a single value, a variable declared as a table will function just like a table except that it will be automatically destroyed once the code that created it finishes. The declaration of a variable as type table must have its own DECLARE statement.

An example of a table variable is as follows:

```
DECLARE @Category TABLE
    (CategoryID     INT             IDENTITY(1,1),
    Category        VARCHAR(75)     NOT NULL,
    CategoryNode    HIERARCHYID     NOT NULL)
```

Hierarchy Functions

Prior to SQL Server 2005, all data types were built using C libraries which were integrated into the core storage engine. SQL Server 2005 introduced Common Language Runtime, CLR, capabilities which allowed .NET code to run inside the SQL Server engine. While the CLR enabled capabilities for functions, stored procedures, and triggers, the most visible result of the inclusion of CLR capabilities is the explosion of data types. Every new data type introduced from SQL Server 2005 on has been built in C# relying on the .NET framework and the CLR integration.

The reason this is important is that variables are no longer simple scalar values or even the more complex table structures, but can now behave as full programming objects depending upon the data type. A variable declared as an INT data type will store a scalar value and will only accept SET and SELECT operators acting upon the variable. However, a variable declared as GEOMETRY, GEOGRAPHY, HIERARCHYID, or XML will take on the characteristics of a programmable object complete with APIs to call methods and access properties. We'll discuss XML data in Chapter 12 and GEOMETERY/GEOGRAPHY in chapter 13, but we'll need to cover HIERARCHYID in detail if we are going to load products or employees.

The HIERARCHYID data type supports 10 methods, 8 of which are supported within T-SQL. You've already used two of the functions – GetLevel and ToString in the computed columns defined in the Lookups.Category table. The table below describes all of the hierarchy functions available in T-SQL.

Function	Description
GetAncestor	The nth level ancestor of the specified value
GetDescendant	A child of the specified node. Allows two parameters: child1 and child2 which are used to specify the return of a node between the two specified nodes.
GetLevel	The depth in the hierarchy of the specified node.
GetRoot	Returns the root element of the hierarchy. Function is always called with the following syntax hierarchyid::GetRoot()
IsDescendantOf	Returns true or false if the node is a descendent of the specified parent node.
Parse	Converts canonical representation of a node to the internal representation of a HIERARCHYID
GetReparentedValue	Returns a node in the hierarchy that is the new node along with the value of the old node for use when modifying the hierarchy.
ToString	Converts the internal representation of a HIERARCHYID to a canonical representation

> **Note:** Normally T-SQL keywords are case insensitive, so SELECT, select, and SeLeCt are all interpreted by the query engine as the same keyword. The hierarchy functions are exceptions to this and require a case sensitive match on the function name. While GetRoot will return the root element of the hierarchy, getroot will return an error. The case sensitivity stems from the fact that HIERARCHYID is implemented as a .NET library written in C#.NET.

There are a variety of ways to insert values into a HIERARCHYID column:

- Convert the canonical form to an internal hierarchy representation
- Convert a binary value to an internal hierarchy representation
- Use variables and hierarchy functions to generate hierarchy values

I've found that the easiest way is to simply convert the canonical form to an internal hierarchy representation by using the Parse() function as follows:

```
SELECT hierarchyid::Parse('/1/1/1/')
```

The code above will generate the internal HIERARCHYID value for the Fountain Pens category shown above.

- The process that I use to load values into a HIERARCHYID data type is as follows:
- Open Excel with a blank workbook and enter each hierarchy node in a separate row
- Indent each level of the hierarchy so you can visually see the structural relationship
- Select a column to the right that is visible to all of the nodes you've listed
- Enter / for the root node
- Label all of the direct descendants of the root as /1/, /2/, /3/, etc.
- Starting with /1/, label each descendants and repeat until all nodes have been labeled
- Copy both columns back into a query window or some other application and use the Parse() function to generate the necessary values

You can see the results of this process in the product category list above. The code to load the category structure above would look as follows:

```
INSERT INTO Lookups.Category
(Category, CategoryNode)
VALUES ('Products', hierarchyid::Parse('/')),
('Turning Kits', hierarchyid::Parse('/1/')),
('Pen Kits', hierarchyid::Parse('/1/1/')),
('Fountain Pens', hierarchyid::Parse('/1/1/1/')),
('Rollerball Pens', hierarchyid::Parse('/1/1/2/')),
('Accessories', hierarchyid::Parse('/1/2/')),
('Turning Blanks', hierarchyid::Parse('/2/')),
('Natural', hierarchyid::Parse('/2/1/')),
('Wood', hierarchyid::Parse('/2/1/1/')),
('Hardwood', hierarchyid::Parse('/2/1/1/1/')),
('Burl', hierarchyid::Parse('/2/1/1/2/')),
('Stabilized', hierarchyid::Parse('/2/1/1/2/1/')),
('Unstabilized', hierarchyid::Parse('/2/1/1/2/2/'))
```

An alternative method is to utilize the hierarchy functions along with variable assignments is shown below:

```
--Insert Root Node
INSERT Lookups.Category (Category,CategoryNode)
VALUES ('Products',hierarchyid::GetRoot());
GO

--Insert first descendant
DECLARE @Category HIERARCHYID;
SELECT @Category = hierarchyid::GetRoot() FROM Lookups.Category;
INSERT Lookups.Category (Category,CategoryNode)
VALUES ('Turning Kits',@Category.GetDescendant(NULL,NULL));
GO

--Insert second descendant
DECLARE @Category HIERARCHYID;
DECLARE @FirstDescendant HIERARCHYID;
SELECT @Category = hierarchyid::GetRoot() FROM Lookups.Category;
SELECT @FirstDescendant = @Category.GetDescendant(NULL,NULL);
INSERT Lookups.Category (Category,CategoryNode)
VALUES ('Turning Blanks',@Category.GetDescendant(@FirstDescendant,NULL));
GO

 --Insert first descendant of Turning Kits
DECLARE @Category HIERARCHYID;
SELECT @Category = CategoryNode FROM Lookups.Category WHERE Category = 'Turning Kits';
INSERT Lookups.Category (Category,CategoryNode)
VALUES ('Pen Kits',@Category.GetDescendant(NULL, NULL));
GO
```

Exercise 2: Inserting Data Into a Hierarchy

In the following exercise, you will load data into Lookups.Category table.

1. Open a new query window and execute the following code to load the first group of categories:

    ```
    INSERT INTO Lookups.Category
    (Category,CategoryNode)
    VALUES ('Products',hierarchyid::Parse('/')), ('Turning
    Kits',hierarchyid::Parse('/1/')),
    ('Pen Kits',hierarchyid::Parse('/1/1/')),
    ('Fountain',hierarchyid::Parse('/1/1/1/')),
    ('Ballpoint',hierarchyid::Parse('/1/1/2/')),
    ('Rollerball',hierarchyid::Parse('/1/1/3/')),
    ('Accessories',hierarchyid::Parse('/1/2/')),
    ('Clips',hierarchyid::Parse('/1/2/1/')),
    ('Caps',hierarchyid::Parse('/1/2/2/')), ('Nibs',hierarchyid::Parse('/1/2/3/')),
    ('Bands',hierarchyid::Parse('/1/2/4/')), ('Refills',hierarchyid::Parse('/1/2/5/')),
    ('Pencil Kits',hierarchyid::Parse('/1/3/')), ('Wine
    Bottles',hierarchyid::Parse('/1/4/')),
    ('Stoppers',hierarchyid::Parse('/1/4/1/')),
    ('Corkscrews',hierarchyid::Parse('/1/4/2/')),
    ('Letter Openers',hierarchyid::Parse('/1/5/')),
    ('Flashlights',hierarchyid::Parse('/1/6/')),
    ('Shaving',hierarchyid::Parse('/1/7/')), ('Key Chains',hierarchyid::Parse('/1/8/')),
    ('Grinders',hierarchyid::Parse('/1/9/')), ('Perfume',hierarchyid::Parse('/1/10/')),
    ('Game Call',hierarchyid::Parse('/1/11/')), ('Other',hierarchyid::Parse('/1/12/'))
    ```

2. Retrieve the contents of the Category table and inspect the node, path, and level assigned

3. Open a new query window and execute the following code to load the second group of categories:

```
INSERT INTO Lookups.Category
(Category,CategoryNode)
VALUES ('Turning Blanks',hierarchyid::Parse('/2/')),
('Natural',hierarchyid::Parse('/2/1/')),
('Wood',hierarchyid::Parse('/2/1/1/')),
('Hardwood',hierarchyid::Parse('/2/1/1/1/')),
('Burl',hierarchyid::Parse('/2/1/1/2/')),
('Stabilized',hierarchyid::Parse('/2/1/1/2/1/')),
('Unstabilized',hierarchyid::Parse('/2/1/1/2/2/')),
('Other',hierarchyid::Parse('/2/1/2/')),
('Corn Cob',hierarchyid::Parse('/2/1/2/1/')),
('Horn',hierarchyid::Parse('/2/1/2/2/')),
('Snakeskin',hierarchyid::Parse('/2/1/2/3/')),
('Shell',hierarchyid::Parse('/2/1/2/4/')),
('Man Made',hierarchyid::Parse('/2/2/')), ('Plastic',hierarchyid::Parse('/2/2/1/')),
('Acrylic Acetate',hierarchyid::Parse('/2/2/1/1/')),
('Crushed Velvet',hierarchyid::Parse('/2/2/1/2/')),
('Diamondwood',hierarchyid::Parse('/2/2/1/3/')),('Acrylester',hierarchyid::Parse('/2/2/1/4/')),
('AquaPearl',hierarchyid::Parse('/2/2/1/5/')), ('Mica Pearl',hierarchyid::Parse('/2/2/1/6/')),
('Inlay',hierarchyid::Parse('/2/2/2/')), ('Other',hierarchyid::Parse('/2/2/3/'))
```

4. Finally execute the following code to add the remaining set of categories:

```
INSERT INTO Lookups.Category
(Category,CategoryNode)
VALUES ('Tooling',hierarchyid::Parse('/3/')),
('Bushing',hierarchyid::Parse('/3/1/')),
('Drill Bit',hierarchyid::Parse('/3/2/')), ('Arbor',hierarchyid::Parse('/3/3/')),
('Mandrel',hierarchyid::Parse('/3/4/')), ('Adhesives',hierarchyid::Parse('/4/')),
('Finishing',hierarchyid::Parse('/5/')), ('Project Displays',hierarchyid::Parse('/6/')),
('Boxes',hierarchyid::Parse('/6/1/')), ('Pouches',hierarchyid::Parse('/6/2/')),
('Cases',hierarchyid::Parse('/6/3/')), ('Displays',hierarchyid::Parse('/6/4/'))
```

Default Constraints

Default constraints are used to set a value for a column when a value is not supplied with the INSERT statement. For example, the Active column in the Products.Product table will assign the value of Y if you do not specify a value since it is assumed that a newly added product would be active in the company's product catalog.

Exercise 3: Inserting Data with a Default

In the following exercise, you will insert a row into the Products.Product table.

1. Open a new query window and execute the following code to insert a new product:

```
INSERT INTO Products.Product
(ProductName, ProductDescription, Price)
VALUES ('Acrylic Acetate Pen Blank','<ProductDescription
xmlns="urn:ChampionValleyPens-com:product:ProductDescription">
  <MetaDescription>Acrylic acetate features stunning colors and finishes to a very
high polish.  Our acrylic acetate is specially formulated for turning
pens.</MetaDescription>
  <MetaKeywords>wood turning, wood working, turning, acrylic acetate, pen, pen
turning, pen blank, acrylic acetate pen, acrylic acetate pen blank, acrylic
pen</MetaKeywords>
  <MetaTitle>Champion Valley Pens. Stunning acrylic acetate pen blanks</MetaTitle>
<Description>Acrylic acetate is a very spectacular material for your small turning
projects such as pens, bottle stoppers, letter openers, etc.  Our acrylic acetate is
specially formulated for turning and comes in a variety of rich, shimmering,
translucent colors. It looks spectacular in pens and related items. This form of
Acrylic Acetate is specially formulated to be extremely easy to work: drills, turns,
sands, polishes like a dream.</Description>
</ProductDescription>',2.49)
```

2. Execute the following code to review the results:

```
SELECT * FROM Products.Product
```

You should have noticed three things about the exercise above:

- The Active column was not specified in the column list
- The INSERT did not fail even though the Active column is NOT NULL
- A value of Y was populated in the column

If you would have included the Active column in the column list for the INSERT statement, SQL Server would have required you to specify a value in the VALUES clause. The value supplied in the VALUES clause would have populated the Active column, not the DEFAULT that was defined.

When you submit a query to SQL Server, before the query is executed, the SQL Server Query Processor will parse the query to ensure that it is syntactically correct. During the parse process, SQL Server will detect that the number of values supplied does not match the number of columns specified in the INSERT statement and reject the query. The parser will not run a query against the database catalog to determine if a default constraint exists for all NOT NULL columns which were omitted from the INSERT clause.

Mass Loading Data

The process of writing data to SQL Server is referred to as a transaction. While we will cover transactions in detail in chapter 8, there are a few things we need to cover first in order to understand the different ways you can insert data into tables.

Every time you perform a write operation, your action is wrapped in a transaction. In general, a transaction covers everything you submit to SQL Server in a single action. For example, the single row insert to the products table above is one transaction and the multi-row insert into the categories table is also a transaction. As you may have guessed, transactions are written to the transaction log. A transaction log record consists of some header information along with the data that was affected by the transaction.

Data is stored in pages in a database's data files on disk, but your transactions will never directly interact with a data file. When you submit a request to SQL Server, regardless of whether you are reading or writing data, SQL Server first looks to see if the data page(s) which correspond to your request are in a memory area known as the data cache. If the pages are not in the data cache, the Storage Engine will retrieve the requested pages from disk and load them into the data cache to be operated upon.

Pages in the data cache which are pristine (they contain exactly the same information as exists on disk) are referred to as clean pages. Pages which have been modified from their state on disk are referred to as dirty pages.

Once any necessary pages are loaded to the data cache, the changes you submitted will be written to the copy of the page in the data cache. At the same time, the transaction is sent to a component of the Storage Engine called the Log Writer. The Log Writer assigns the header information, packages the changes you made into a log record, and writes the log record to the transaction log. If a change was made to a clean page, a bit will be flipped on the page to designate it as a dirty page. Once the Log Writer has successfully written your transaction to the transaction log, then and only then will the transaction be complete and a response returned to the application that submitted the transaction.

The transaction log does not exist in memory, so all writes must be written directly to disk by the Log Writer. Since SQL Server is a multi-user environment, as the number of users submitting transactions increases, the disk contention for the transaction log will increase. It does not matter whether you are working with Microsoft SQL Server, Sybase SQL Server, Oracle, or DB2, every transaction is written directly to disk prior to the transaction completing. This is done to ensure data integrity and persistence across restarts of the database engine. This means that the maximum rate at which you can write to any of these four DBMS engines is bound by the maximum throughput of the disk(s) underneath the transaction log. While each vendor is constantly submitting new Transaction Processing Council (TPC) benchmarks to "one up" the competition in terms of throughput, every drop of performance from the raw transaction handling code was squeezed out of these engines years ago, leaving the TPCC benchmark nothing more than an escalating, creative exercise in configuring ever more powerful hardware.

A background process called a checkpoint runs periodically and flushes dirty pages to disk. In general, this checkpoint process runs every 5 minutes, although you can change the frequency. When the database is check pointed, any page in the data cache that is marked as dirty is written out to the appropriate location on disk, overwriting the page that was stored on disk. Once the page has been successfully written to disk, the dirty bit is flipped in the data cache such that the page is now a clean page.

What this means at a practical level is that your application is going to dictate whether you even care about what is going on with write activity to the transaction log. The vast majority of applications have extremely low write requirements, usually on the order of 1 write every few minutes or even every few days. Unless you are making changes to a few dozen or more rows per second, you really aren't going to care about the write performance to the transaction log simply because your users will never be able to detect the time required to perform any write operation. However, as you scale up the number of writes per second, isolating the transaction log to the disk(s) with the highest write throughput can have a dramatic effect on the performance of your transactions.

> **More Information:** For a detailed discussion of the structure of a transaction log record and the behavior of the transaction log and associated engine components, please refer to Chapter 6, "Managing Transaction Logs" in "SQL Server 2012: Database Administration".

From time to time, you will need to load large amounts of data into one or more tables in your database. You could package the thousands, millions, or billions of row you are loading into a series of insert statements. However, this would be extremely expensive both in terms of writes to the transaction log as well as processing in the Log Writer. SQL Server has two specialized methods for loading large amounts of data, Bulk Copy Program (BCP) and BULK INSERT, which minimize the transaction logging overhead.

BCP and BULK INSERT are two of the operations in a class of operations known as minimally logged. When a minimally logged operation is performed, instead of logging all of the information to the transaction log, the only information that is logged is page allocation and deallocation. The data that you submit will never be written to the transaction log. However, to ensure data integrity and consistency even through a restart, instead of pushing the writes to the data files off to the checkpoint process, any data pages affected by a minimally logged operation are required to be flushed to disk before the operation can complete.

Recovery Models

> **More Information:** More a detailed discussion of recovery models, please refer to Chapter 6, "Managing Transaction Logs" and Chapter 22, Data Recovery in "SQL Server 2012: Database Administration".

To control the behavior of transactions, each database has a recovery model property that can be set to one of three values – FULL, BULK_LOGGED, or SIMPLE.

When the database is set to FULL recovery model, it does not matter whether you are running a minimally logged operation or not. Every row will be fully logged, meaning that every row of data affected will be written to the transaction log.

When the database is in BULK_LOGGED or SIMPLE recovery model, minimal logging can occur, however there are restrictions. If the table is empty or does not have any indexes (a primary key is an index as you'll learn in Chapter 12) minimal logging will occur. If the table already has data, you will get full logging occurring. This is why you will find processes which bulk load incremental data dropping and then recreating indexes.

BCP

BCP is a command line utility that has been in the SQL Server product, largely unchanged, since before Microsoft had a SQL Server database engine. While several updates have been made through the versions to add support for new data types and a handful of new options, the majority of the features from its Sybase roots are still the same and behave the same way.

As the name implies, BCP is a very narrowly built utility designed to bulk copy data with exactly 2 functions:

- Take data from a file and put it into a table
- Take data from a table or query and put it into a file

The general syntax for BCP is:

```
bcp databasename.schema.table [in | out]filename -options
```

BCP is a command line executable, so it follows the standard DOS convention for specifying command line parameters to an application. Immediately following the BCP command, which is shorthand for bcp.exe, you specify the table or view that you want to export data from or load data into. The table or view can use either a two part or three part naming convention. If you use a two part name, you will need to specify the –d parameter to specify the database, so it's a bit simpler to just use a three part name. Following the object you want to operate on, you specify the keyword of either in or out. In is used when you want to import data from a file into a table/view. Out is used when you want to export data from a table/view to a file. Following the direction, you specify the fully qualified file name that is either the source or the target of the operation. The file name is followed by one or more parameters.

The most common parameters, command line switches, which you will use with BCP are as follows:

Parameter	Purpose
-c	The data in the file is in a character format. The default field terminator is a tab.
-d	Database name
-E	Used when importing data into a table with an identity column. Specifies to use the identity value present in the file. If this parameter is left off, BCP will ignore the field in the file corresponding to the identity column and SQL Server will assign new values.
-n	The data in the file is in SQL Server's native storage mode.
-P	Password. Used in conjunction with the –U parameter.
-S	Name of the instance. If –S is not specified, BCP will attempt to connect to the default instance on the machine that BCP is running from. If a default instance does not exist, an error will be returned.
-T	Uses the Windows credentials of the account which BCP is running under to connect to the instance.
-U	User name

Parameter	Purpose
-?	Help. Dumps the DOS style help information to the screen showing the basic syntax and parameters available to the BCP command.

If you wanted to export the Customers.Customer table from the ChampionValleyPens database from the SQLPROD01 instance to the Customer.txt file in the c:\ChampionValleyPress folder in a character format using a trusted connection, you would use the following command line:

```
bcp ChampionValleyPens.Customers.Customer out c:\ChampionValleyPress\Customer.txt
    -SSQLPROD01 -c -T
```

If you wanted to perform the reverse operation and load the data from this file into the Customers.Customer table, you would use the following command line:

```
bcp ChampionValleyPens.Customers.Customer in c:\ChampionValleyPress\Customer.txt
    -SSQLPROD01 -c -T
```

> **Note:** bcp, the object name, direction, and file name are not case sensitive, unless you are using a collation sequence that is case sensitive. However, all parameters are case sensitive. -c specifies character mode while -C specifies the code page to use.

Notice that you utilize a space to separate each parameter, but do not use a space between a parameter and its value. Additionally, if you have an object name or a path which contains a space, it must be enclosed in double quotes otherwise; BCP will consider this embedded space as a separator and return an error message of invalid syntax.

> **Note:** If you are exporting data to a file and the file already exists, BCP will overwrite the file. BCP does not append rows to an existing file.

A little known, little used, but extremely powerful extension to BCP is the ability to use a SELECT statement as the source. SQL Server will execute the SELECT statement and the result set will be transferred to BCP to format the results and load them to the specified file. By using the query capabilities, you can export a portion of a table or even the combination of multiple tables to a file. Using the query option of BCP to perform the same export as above would result in the following command:

```
bcp "SELECT * FROM ChampionValleyPens.Customers.Customer" queryout
                    c:\ChampionValleyPress\Customer.txt -SSQLPROD01 -c -T
```

Exercise 4: Bulk Loading Customer Addresses

In the following exercise, you will load the Customers.Address table.

1. In the companion files, extract the contents of the Chapter7\Data\Customer.zip file to the C:\ChampionValleyPress folder.
2. Open a command prompt by clicking the Start button | Run, typing cmd in the field labelled Open and clicking OK.

3. Execute the following command from the command prompt using the –E parameter to preserve the identity values already set in the file:

   ```
   bcp ChampionValleyPens.Customers.Address in c:\ChampionValleyPress\Address.txt
                                                                            -c -T -E
   ```

4. It should take approximately 20 – 40 seconds to load the almost 1 million addresses and at the end, your screen should look something like the following:

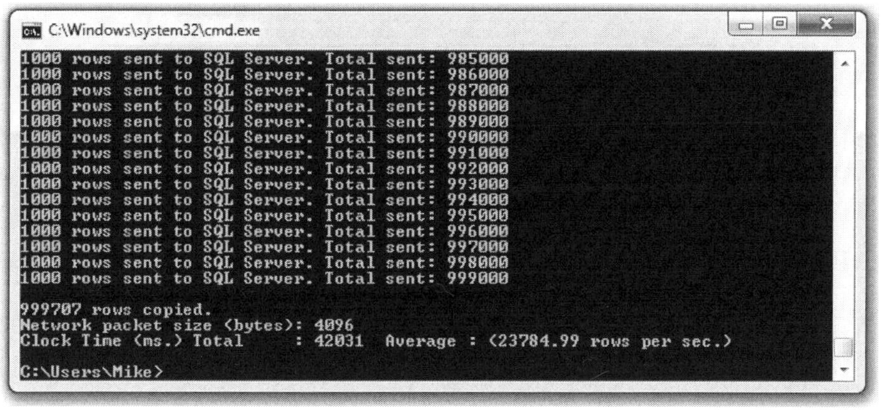

Figure 7-1: Loading the Customers.Address table

The exercise above worked and data was loaded to the Customers.Address table. For those paying attention, a big red flag should have gone off indicating something we just did was very wrong. If you'll recall, there is a foreign key between the Customers.Customer and Customers.Address table which is supposed to ensure you can't insert an address for a customer that doesn't exist. Unfortunately, you now have almost a million customer addresses in your database that do not correspond to a customer. To verify this, query the Customers.Customer table to verify that it is currently empty.

So, how is it possible to have data in the Customers.Address table without a corresponding customer? BCP is optimized for high performance loading of data into a table. When you create a foreign key, every insert has to check the parent table to see if the value you are inserting into the column exists. The query to check the parent table slows down the insert operation, so by default, a BCP operation bypasses the checking of a foreign key as well as a check constraint. If you need to enforce foreign keys or check constraints during a BCP, then you need to specify the –h parameter along with the CHECK_CONSTRAINTS property as follows:

   ```
   -h"CHECK_CONSTRAINTS"
   ```

BULK INSERT

The BULK INSERT command operates almost exactly the same as BCP, except it does not have the capability to export data from a table. Since BULK INSERT runs as a T-SQL command and does not need to authenticate to an instance, the list of options are limited to properties of the data file being imported as well as optional insert behaviors.

Exercise 5: Bulk Loading Customers, Contacts, Products, and SKUs

In the following exercise, you will load the Customers.Customer, Customers.Contact, Products.Product, Product.SKU, and Products.Inventory tables.

1. Open a new query window and execute the following command:

   ```
   BULK INSERT Customers.Customer FROM 'c:\ChampionValleyPress\Customer.txt' WITH
   (KEEPIDENTITY)
   ```

2. Retrieve the contents of the Customers.Customer table to verify that 999,706 customers were loaded.

3. Execute the following command to load the Customers.Contact table:

   ```
   BULK INSERT Customers.Contact FROM 'c:\ChampionValleyPress\Contact.txt' WITH
   (KEEPIDENTITY)
   ```

4. In the companion files, extract the contents of the Chapter7\Data\Products.zip file to the C:\ChampionValleyPress folder.

5. Execute the following commands to load the remainder of the Products.Product table along with the Products.SKU and Products.Inventory tables:

   ```
   BULK INSERT Products.Product FROM 'c:\ChampionValleyPress\Products.txt'
       WITH (KEEPIDENTITY, DATAFILETYPE = 'native')
   BULK INSERT Products.SKU FROM 'c:\ChampionValleyPress\SKU.txt'
       WITH (KEEPIDENTITY, DATAFILETYPE = 'native')
   BULK INSERT Products.Inventory FROM 'c:\ChampionValleyPress\Inventory.txt'
       WITH (KEEPIDENTITY)
   ```

Loading FileTable Data

Loading data into a FileTable is the easiest operation that you can do in SQL Server, because it doesn't even require that you connect to the SQL Server or execute any T-SQL. Loading data into FileTable is simply a matter of writing the file to the appropriate Windows share that is exposed for each FileTable that is defined.

Exercise 6: Bulk Loading Customers and Customer Contacts

In the following exercise, you will load the Customers.Customer and Customers.Contact tables.

1. In the companion files, extract the contents of the Chapter7\Data\EmployeeDocs.zip file to the C:\ChampionValleyPress folder.

2. Open Windows Explorer and go to \\<machine name>\mssqlserver\ChampionValleyPensDocs to view the EmployeeDocs folder that was created. You will need to substitute <machine name> with the actual name of your computer.

3. Using Windows Explorer, copy the contents of the c:\ChampionValleyPress\Resumes folder to EmployeeDocs.

4. Using Windows Explorer, copy the contents of the c:\ChampionValleyPress\W4s folder to EmployeeDocs.

5. Execute the following query to verify that you have 86 employee documents in your HumanResources.EmployeeDocument table:

```
SELECT * FROM HumanResources.EmployeeDocument
```

SELECT INTO

SELECT INTO is a minimally logged variation of a SELECT statement which will generate a new table as well as load data with minimal logging. Just like the SELECT statement we have covered previously, the SELECT clause defines the columns to be retrieved and the FROM defines the table to retrieve the data from. The INTO clause specifies the name of the new table.

The new table will be created based on the data type, identity, and nullability properties defined for the corresponding column(s) in the SELECT list. Default, check, foreign key, and primary key constraints are not automatically generated. An example of a SELECT INTO statement is:

```
SELECT EmployeeID, FirstName, MiddleInitial, LastName
INTO #Employee
FROM HumanResources.Employee
```

Modifying Data

In a perfect world, data would be written to a table and never be changed. Unfortunately, we don't live in a perfect world, so we need a way to modify data once it has been inserted. Data is modified using an UPDATE statement that has two main components: UPDATE and SET. The UPDATE clause specifies the table that contains the data to be modified while the SET clause specifies the columns and value that should be assigned as follows. (*This is an example. Do **NOT** run this query against your database. The reason why will be explained in the next 2 paragraphs.*)

```
UPDATE Products.Product
SET Price = 4.99
UPDATE Products.Product
SET Price = Price + 2
```

The first update statement will assign the value of $4.99 to all products while the second update will increase the price of all products by $2.00.

This is the simplest form of an UPDATE, but potentially has a small problem. An UPDATE statement of the form above will modify every row in the products table. While you might want to increase the price of every product by $2.00, it is highly unlikely that you would set the price of every product to $4.99.

To get around this problem, you can specify an optional clause that we showed, but didn't discuss, in the section on loading hierarchy data. A WHERE clause, which we will cover in detail in Chapter 8; will allow you to restrict the rows that are affected by the UPDATE. If you only wanted to change the price of the crushed velvet pen blanks to $4.99, you could run the following statement:

```
UPDATE Products.Product
SET Price = 4.99
WHERE ProductName = 'Crushed Velvet Pen Blank'
```

If a column has a default constraint defined and you wanted to reset the value in the column to the default value, instead of specifying a value, you can use the DEFAULT keyword in the SET clause as follows:

```
UPDATE Products.Product
SET Active = DEFAULT
WHERE ProductName = 'Crushed Velvet Pen Blank'
```

Exercise 7: Modifying Data

In the following exercise, you will modify products and the product category hierarchy.

1. Open a new query window and execute the following code to deactivate the crushed velvet, dymondwood, acrylester, and mica pearl pen blanks.

    ```
    UPDATE Products.Product
    SET Active = 'N'
    WHERE ProductID = 3
    UPDATE Products.Product
    SET Active = 'N'
    WHERE ProductID = 4
    UPDATE Products.Product
    SET Active = 'N'
    WHERE ProductID = 5
    UPDATE Products.Product
    SET Active = 'N'
    WHERE ProductID = 7
    ```

2. If you look in the product category table, you will find three different categories with the name of *Other*, which is very user unfriendly. Execute the following code to make these categories more explicit:

    ```
    UPDATE Lookups.Category
    SET Category = 'Misc. Natural Blanks'
    WHERE CategoryID = 32
    UPDATE Lookups.Category
    SET Category = 'Misc. Man-Made Blanks'
    WHERE CategoryID = 46
    ```

3. Execute the following code to create a *Miscellaneous* category underneath *Turning Kits*.

    ```
    INSERT INTO Lookups.Category
    (Category, CategoryNode)
    VALUES('Miscellaneous',hierarchyid::Parse('/1/11.5/'))
    ```

4. Execute the following code to move the *Wine Bottles* category underneath the *Miscellaneous* category and rename it to *Wine and Spirits*.

    ```
    DECLARE @Category hierarchyid,
            @OldParent hierarchyid,
            @NewParent hierarchyid

    SELECT @Category = CategoryNode
    FROM Lookups.Category
    WHERE Category = 'Wine Bottles';
    SELECT @OldParent = CategoryNode
    FROM Lookups.Category
    WHERE Category = 'Turning Kits';
    SELECT @NewParent = CategoryNode
    FROM Lookups.Category
    WHERE Category = 'Miscellaneous';
    ```

```
UPDATE Lookups.Category
SET CategoryNode = @Category.GetReparentedValue(@OldParent, @NewParent),
    Category = 'Wine and Spirits'
WHERE CategoryNode = @Category;
```

5. Repeat step 4 to move the *Letter Openers, Flashlights, Shaving, Key Chains, Grinders, Perfume,* and *Game Call* categories underneath the *Miscellaneous* category (don't rename these categories).

6. Execute the following code to create a new category called *Games* underneath the *Miscellaneous* category and after the *Game Calls* and then modify the Products.SKU table to move the chess kits and dart kits to the new category:

```
INSERT INTO Lookups.Category
(Category,CategoryNode)
VALUES('Games',hierarchyid::Parse('/1/11.5/12/'))
UPDATE Products.SKU
SET CategoryID = 60
WHERE ProductID = 93
UPDATE Products.SKU
SET CategoryID = 60
WHERE ProductID = 97
```

7. Execute the following code to create a new category called *Custom* as a top level category underneath *Products* and after the *Project Displays* category and then modify the Products.SKU table to move the custom plating and custom finish to the new category:

```
INSERT INTO Lookups.Category
(Category,CategoryNode)
VALUES('Custom',hierarchyid::Parse('/7/'))
UPDATE Products.SKU
SET CategoryID = 61
WHERE ProductID = 131
UPDATE Products.SKU
SET CategoryID = 61
WHERE ProductID = 132
```

8. Review the contents of the Lookups.Category table.

You should have noticed that the second value for each of the categories that you moved is now set to 11.5. However, the *stoppers* and *corkscrews* categories, which were previously underneath the *Wine and Spirits* category are now orphaned since a path of /1/4/ no longer exists. When you move a parent within a hierarchy, the children are not automatically moved as well. It is up to you to perform the maintenance and modify all child levels if you want to move an entire sub-tree within a hierarchy.

Exercise 8: Fix the Orphaned Categories

In the following exercise, you will fix the orphaned categories created in the previous exercise and move the entire sub-tree underneath *Miscellaneous*.

1. Execute the following query to set the *Wine and Spirits* category back to its original value.

```
UPDATE Lookups.Category
SET CategoryNode = hierarchyid::Parse('/1/4/')
WHERE CategoryID = 14
```

2. Execute the following code to move the entire *Wine and Spirits* sub-tree:

```
DECLARE @node hierarchyid,
        @newparent hierarchyid
SELECT @node = CategoryNode
FROM Lookups.Category
WHERE Category = 'Wine and Spirits';
SELECT @newparent = CategoryNode
FROM Lookups.Category
WHERE Category = 'Miscellaneous';

SELECT @newparent = @newparent.GetDescendant(MAX(CategoryNode), NULL)
FROM Lookups.Category
WHERE CategoryNode.GetAncestor(1)=@newparent;

UPDATE Lookups.Category
SET CategoryNode = CategoryNode.GetReparentedValue(@node, @newparent)
WHERE CategoryNode.IsDescendantOf(@node) = 1;
```

At this point, we need to stop and re-examine the HIERARCHYID data type and hierarchies in general. In chapter 5, you learned about trees, how to number a tree, and all of the neat properties that are revealed just by manipulating the numbers assigned as you moved around the tree. At the beginning of this chapter, we looked at the canonical representation and how you assign values to a HIERARCHYID data type. Once the data was inserted, we had a clean hierarchy, without holes, that was very easy to follow. We then messed up the neat little sequence of values when we started to re-organize the product categories, just like would happen in the real world.

This "mess" was created on purpose, along with the orphaned data, to show you that just because the data type is named HIERARCHYID, doesn't mean that it automatically has logic to enforce an actual hierarchy. It was also meant to demonstrate a maintenance issue with any tree.

There are two methods to maintaining a tree when you add, remove, or re-arrange nodes in the tree. If you want mathematical purity in your trees, then every time you add, remove, or re-arrange nodes in a tree, you have to re-number all of the nodes so that our values are sequential, without gaps. This would be a minor inconvenience with something like our 61 product categories, simply because modifying the category structure doesn't happen very often and there are a relatively small number of nodes in the tree. Would you really want to re-number the nodes in an organization tree or bill of materials that could contain tens of thousands of nodes? In cases where you don't want to re-number the nodes, you are left with the second maintenance method, assign a value to the node which lies between the nodes to the left or right. It is this second method that we demonstrated in these exercises when we assigned a value of /1/11.5/ to *Miscellaneous* so that it would lie between /1/11/ of the *Game Calls* category and /1/12/ of the *Other* category. The downside to using intermediate values is that all of the nice math rules which could be applied to the node numbers are destroyed, but that's why we have computers to calculate those kinds of values for us.

If you really wanted to close the large gap between /1/3/ and /1/11.5, you could re-assign the value of /1/4/ to the *Miscellaneous* category and then re-parent the entire sub-tree using a variation of the code in step 2 above as shown by the following SELECT statement:

```
DECLARE @node hierarchyid,
        @newparent hierarchyid

SELECT @node = CategoryNode
FROM Lookups.Category
WHERE Category = 'Miscellaneous';

SELECT @newparent = hierarchyid::Parse('/1/4/')

SELECT CategoryID, Category, CategoryNode.GetReparentedValue(@node, @newparent),
CategoryNode.GetReparentedValue(@node, @newparent).ToString()
FROM Lookups.Category
WHERE CategoryNode.IsDescendantOf(@node) = 1;
```

While we could have just modified the categories by directly assigning values to the CategoryNode using the Parse() function of the canonical representation, we relied instead on four of the hierarchy methods: GetReparentedValue, GetDescendant, GetAncestor, and IsDescendantOf.

```
SELECT @newparent = CategoryNode
FROM Lookups.Category
WHERE Category = 'Miscellaneous';

SELECT @newparent = @newparent.GetDescendant(MAX(CategoryNode), NULL)
FROM Lookups.Category
WHERE CategoryNode.GetAncestor(1)=@newparent;
```

In the code above, the first select statement retrieves the CategoryNode for the *Miscellaneous* category and assigns it to the @newparent variable. We want to ensure that we aren't assigning a duplicate CategoryNode when we move a value, so, we have to get the next number available in the hierarchy where the node is being moved. This requires that we retrieve all of the nodes directly underneath the *Miscellaneous* node, which is accomplished with the WHERE clause. We then use the GetDescendant function to retrieve the next available value. The MAX function returns the largest child currently existing underneath *Miscellaneous* and since the second parameter is null, a value that is greater than the maximum child currently assigned which is a descendant of *Miscellaneous* is returned and then assigned to the @newparent variable.

```
UPDATE Lookups.Category
SET CategoryNode = CategoryNode.GetReparentedValue(@node, @newparent)
WHERE CategoryNode.IsDescendantOf(@node) = 1;
```

The mistake most people make when working with the HIERARCHYID data type is to attempt to manipulate the actual binary value assigned. To understand GetReparentedValue, and everything else about HIERARCHYID, you need to work with the human readable canonical form. @node is assigned the node for the existing parent value while @newparent is assigned the node for the parent at the new location. In our update statement in the exercise above, @node was /1/4/ and @new parent was /1/11.5/. All GetReparentedValue is doing is to locate the value of /1/4/ and replace it with /1/11.5/ and preserving any values to the right, in essence nothing more than a simple string search and replace. It then translates the canonical result to a binary value and assigned it to the CategoryNode column.

The reason that the entire sub-tree, including the *Wine and Spirits* category is moved is due to the IsDescendant function. IsDescendant returns a value of 1 for all children, regardless of level, of the *Wine and Spirits* category. By default, a node is always considered a descendent of itself.

If you can't depend upon an application to properly manage the relationships in a HIERARCHYID column and wanted to enforce a tree structure, you can create a foreign key constraint that references within the same table. This would require the HIERARCHYID column to be the primary key of the table, so it would not work for either the category or employee hierarchies that we have defined. However, if we had used an alternate definition for the category table, the constraint to enforce the tree would look as follows:

```
CREATE TABLE Lookups.Category
(CategoryNode       HIERARCHYID    NOT NULL,
 Category           VARCHAR(75)    NOT NULL,
 CategoryPath       AS CategoryNode.ToString(),
 CategoryLevel      AS CategoryNode.GetLevel(),
 ParentNode AS CategoryNode.GetAncestor(1) PERSISTED
      REFERENCES Lookups.Category(CategoryNode),
 CONSTRAINT pk_Category PRIMARY KEY (CategoryNode))
```

Assign a Value While Updating

One of the interesting features of an UPDATE statement, proprietary to T-SQL, is the ability to modify data while at the same time assigning a value to a variable and then reusing the variable value. You could use this when you want to quickly number a set of data using a custom sequence.

```
CREATE TABLE #Temp
(ID         INT    NOT NULL,
 Sequence   INT    NULL)

INSERT INTO #Temp
(ID)
VALUES(1),(2),(3),(4),(5),(6)

SELECT * FROM #Temp

DECLARE @var   INT
SET @var = 10

UPDATE #Temp
SET @var = Sequence = @var + 1

SELECT * FROM #Temp
```

The SET clause is evaluated from right to left. The code first increments the variable @var by 1, then assigns the result to the first row in the #Temp table, then assigns the value to the variable @var. The second row is likewise incremented by 1, etc. This causes the Sequence column to be sequentially numbered from 11 to 16.

Removing Data

The DELETE statement is used to remove rows from a table and only has one required value, the name of the table to delete data from. However, if you were to use the simplest form of a DELETE statement, just like the simplest form of an UPDATE statement, you would affect every row in the table.

> **Best Practice:** It is very unlikely that you would delete every row in a table, especially within code that is part of an application. So, if you ever see a DELETE statement without a WHERE clause, you should always require an explanation of why it is necessary to empty the entire table. As a general rule, a DELETE statement should always have a WHERE clause.

The following two DELETE statements are equivalent to each other. While the FROM clause is optional for a DELETE statement, it does improve the readability of your code.

```
DELETE Customers.Customer
DELETE FROM Customers.Customer
```

While it would appear that the first statement would remove the entire table, remember from chapter 5, the command to remove an entire table is DROP TABLE.

Exercise 9: Delete Rows

In the following exercise, you will delete the *Other* category underneath Turning Kits since it is no longer needed.

1. Execute the following query to remove the *Other* category.

   ```
   DELETE FROM Lookups.Category
   WHERE CategoryID = 24
   ```

2. Observe that an error message was generated, because there are still rows in the Products.SKU table that reference the *Other* category and the foreign key constraint will prevent these rows from being orphaned

3. Execute the following code to add 2 new categories to move the remaining SKUs associated to the *Other* category:

   ```
   INSERT INTO Lookups.Category
   (Category, CategoryNode)
   VALUES('Equipment', hierarchyid::Parse('/1/4/'))
   INSERT INTO Lookups.Category
   (Category, CategoryNode)
   VALUES('Replacements', hierarchyid::Parse('/1/5/'))
   ```

4. Execute the following code to move the remaining SKUs to their new categories:

   ```
   UPDATE Products.SKU
   SET CategoryID = 62
   WHERE ProductID = 114
   UPDATE Products.SKU
   SET CategoryID = 62
   WHERE ProductID = 112
   UPDATE Products.SKU
   SET CategoryID = 59
   WHERE ProductID = 113
   UPDATE Products.SKU
   SET CategoryID = 63
   WHERE CategoryID = 24
   ```

5. Now, execute the following query to remove the *Other* category:

   ```
   DELETE FROM Lookups.Category
   WHERE CategoryID = 24
   ```

In chapter 5, we briefly discussed the CASCADE option for a foreign key and explained that you should never enable this option. It's rare that I'll put something in such absolute terms, after all, there are always multiple ways of doing things. The CASCADE option is one of the very few items that fall into the **_NEVER_** category. It's there for those who want to be lazy and not have to either think or understand their database structure, none of which are justifications for using an option which can be extremely damaging to your data.

If we had enabled the CASCADE option on the foreign keys, step 1 in the exercise above would have succeeded. Not only would it have removed the 1 row for the Other category from the category table, it would have cascaded and removed over 150 rows from the Products.SKU table, which in turn would have cascaded to the Products.Inventory table where it would have also removed over 150 rows. It would have them cascaded to the Orders.OrderDetail table and removed every row corresponding to a SKU that was assigned to the Other category which had been deleted and then proceeded to cascade to the Orders.Shipment table, removing any rows for those SKUs as well. While you might have thought you were only deleting a single row from the category table that you no longer needed, you could have wound up affecting thousands or millions of rows, damaging customer orders, shipments, and the ability to sell products.

Consider one step worse. We could have setup the Lookups.Category table with a foreign key which enforced a tree structure as shown previously in this chapter. Then someone could have accidentally deleted the Products category, causing every category, SKU, inventory, order detail, and shipment related to an order detail to be deleted leaving you with almost complete data loss for your orders.

If instead you had defined the foreign keys, as we have, without the CASCADE option, someone would have had to deliberately code the deletion of every child row before the parent could be removed, which can't be done on accident. Does anyone still think it is a good idea to cascade foreign keys?

Mass Removal of Data

On very rare occasions, you will need to remove all rows from a table. While this can be accomplished with a DELETE statement that does not have a WHERE clause, a high performance, minimally logged option TRUNCATE TABLE exists as shown below:

```
TRUNCATE TABLE Customers.Customer
```

When you delete rows from a table, every row that is deleted is written to the transaction log. However, when you execute TRUNCATE TABLE, SQL Server will de-allocate entire pages and the only thing logged to the transaction log is the page de-allocation.

Since TRUNCATE TABLE is designed as a high performance method to remove all rows from a table, it requires that the table being truncated is not being referenced by a foreign key constraint. Even if the child table is empty, TRUNCATE TABLE will fail, because SQL Server does not check foreign key constraints to ensure data is not being orphaned. The only exception to this rule is when you have a self-referencing table – the foreign key points back to another column in the same table.

Data Modification Tables

There are times when you are modifying data that you will want to access the state of the data during the modification process. For example, you may want to archive the previous version of a row before it was modified or deleted or you might want to maintain an aggregate value as data is added, modified, or removed from a table.

SQL Server makes two special tables available to you that are automatically materialized within the scope of the change being made. These tables are named *inserted* and *deleted* and do not belong to any schema. While they appear and behave as tables, what SQL Server is really doing behind the scenes is materializing the portion of the transaction log corresponding to the transaction that you are currently executing. The *inserted* and *deleted* tables are scoped to a connection and cannot be accessed across connections, the same way that a local temp table is scoped to a connection.

The *inserted* table contains the image of the row after the modification has been made while the *deleted* table contains the image of the row before the modification. In the case of an INSERT, the *deleted* table will be empty while for a DELETE, the *inserted* table will be empty. When an UPDATE is executed, both tables will be populated.

The structure of both the *inserted* and *deleted* tables is always the same as the table being modified in terms of the column names, data types, and nullability.

You access the *inserted* and *deleted* tables by using the OUTPUT clause as follows:

```
UPDATE Lookups.Category
SET CategoryNode = CategoryNode.GetReparentedValue(@node, @newparent)
OUTPUT $action, 'deleted - Before Image', deleted.*, 'inserted - After Image',
inserted.*
WHERE CategoryNode.IsDescendantOf(@node) = 1;
```

The $action is one of several special functions that are available within T-SQL. $action is only valid within an OUTPUT clause and returns one of three values: INSERT, UPDATE, or DELETE.

This UPDATE statement will return the entire contents of both the *inserted* and *deleted* tables as a result set. If you want to dump the contents of *inserted*, *deleted*, or both to a table or table variable, you would use the INTO clause as follows:

```
UPDATE Lookups.Category
SET CategoryNode = CategoryNode.GetReparentedValue(@node, @newparent)
OUTPUT 'Before Image', deleted.*, 'After Image', inserted.*
INTO <table or table variable>
WHERE CategoryNode.IsDescendantOf(@node) = 1;
```

The target table or variable must have the correct structure to accept the data being sent by the OUTPUT clause. Additionally, the target table cannot be either the parent or child in a foreign key relationship nor can the table have CHECK constraints or triggers. Additionally, since the *inserted* table is never populated during a delete, it cannot be referenced in the OUTPUT clause of a DELETE statement just as the *deleted* table cannot be referenced in the OUTPUT clause of an INSERT statement.

Multiple Modifications

Applications, particularly state-less web application, frequently want to just "throw data over the wall" and have SQL Server figure out what to do with it. If the row doesn't already exist, insert the row. If the row already exists, update the row with the values sent in. This particular capability is referred to as an UPSERT and does not exist in SQL Server. A variation of UPSERT, MERGE, will take the contents of one table, compare it to the contents of another table, and perform INSERT, UPDATE, and DELETE operations.

> Note: While some have referred to MERGE as the equivalent of an UPSERT that is not accurate. You cannot pass values to a MERGE statement from an application like you can with an INSERT, UPDATE, or DELETE. You have to first load all of the data being considered to a table and then execute the MERGE statement against this already existing data. Additionally, MERGE allows you to perform more actions than a simple UPSERT statement would.

The MERGE statement is a relatively complex DML statement consisting of at least 3 main clauses and can have up to 8 main clauses + 5 additional clauses, performing INSERTs, UPDATEs, and DELETEs in a single statement. The INSERT, UPDATE, and DELETE portions of the MERGE statement are slightly modified versions of what we have covered so far in this chapter and do not specify a table name for their actions. The general syntax for a MERGE statement is as follows:

```
[ WITH <common_table_expression> [, ...n] ]
MERGE
    [ TOP ( expression ) [ PERCENT ] ]
    [ INTO ] <target_table > [ WITH ( <merge_hint> ) ] [ [ AS ] table_alias ]
    USING <table_source>
    ON <merge_search_condition>
    [ WHEN MATCHED [ AND <clause_search_condition> ]
        THEN <merge_matched> ] [ ...n ]
    [ WHEN NOT MATCHED [ BY TARGET ] [ AND <clause_search_condition> ]
        THEN <merge_not_matched> ]
    [ WHEN NOT MATCHED BY SOURCE [ AND <clause_search_condition> ]
        THEN <merge_matched> ] [ ...n ]
    [ <output_clause> ]
    [ OPTION ( <query_hint> [ ,... n ] ) ] ;
```

The syntax shown above is the way all command syntax is formatted in Books Online. Using a specialized set of rules, brackets, braces, angle brackets, bold, italics, upper/lower case, etc. are used to convey what is valid syntax for the given command. The exact details of all of the operators can be found behind a link at the top of every Books Online article. The basic rules for this syntax are that items in brackets, [ ], are optional clauses or syntax elements.

The TOP expression will be covered in Chapter 9 and the WITH expression in Chapter 10. The OUTPUT clause, we have already discussed previously in this chapter. Thus far in this chapter we have been using extremely simple search conditions, WHERE <column> = <value>, and will cover all of the options for search conditions in Chapter 9. This leaves the core elements of the MERGE statement.

The first piece of a MERGE statement is to specify the table that will be modified, *target*, USING data in another table, *source*. The *source* can either be a table or a SELECT statement. The ON clause is used to specify the column(s) used in each table to match. Following the ON clause, you can specify up to 5 additional clauses defining the actions to be performed.

When you execute a MERGE statement, SQL Server lines the two tables up based on the column(s) that you specified. It will check every value in the *source* and *target*. When a match between the two is found, the action defined in the WHEN MATCHED clause will be executed if it is defined. For values in the *target* that are not found in the *source*, the WHEN NOT MATCHED BY TARGET clause will be executed if it is defined. For values in the *source* that are not found in the *target*, the WHEN NOT MATCHED BY SOURCE clause will be executed if it is defined.

You can have a maximum of 2 WHEN MATCHED clauses. If two clauses are defined, you are required to specify additional search criteria on the first WHEN MATCHED clause defined. This feature exists to allow you to perform varying actions on a match such as with a banking application when debits are added to one general ledger account while credits are added to a different general ledger account.

The 2nd WHEN MATCHED clause can have additional search criteria. The 2nd WHEN MATCHED clause will only be considered if the row doesn't match the search criteria of the first WHEN MATCHED clause.

> **Caution:** If additional search criteria exist on the 2nd WHERE MATCHED clause that do not correspond to the row being considered, no action will be performed on that row. It might sound rather strange that you can find a match and then perform no action on either of the WHEN MATCHED columns. Remember that the match is made on the column(s) defined in the ON clause, not the ON clause + additional search criteria. The additional search criteria is used strictly to control the subset of rows that are affected by the WHERE MATCHED action.

If two WHEN MATCHED clauses are specified, then one of the clauses must specify an UPDATE action while the other specifies a DELETE action. You cannot perform an INSERT in the WHERE MATCHED clause.

Additionally, you have to ensure that you aren't affecting a row in the *target* table more than once. If you match more than one row of the *source* to the *target* table, you will get an error and the entire command will abort. The *source* is scanned and checked, one row at a time. If you had a single row in the *source* that matched more than one row in the *target*, then you could either update the target multiple times or update and delete the same row. It doesn't matter how many rows in the target table are affected by a given action, only that the rows in the *source* match once and only once.

> **Best Practice:** It you are using an entire table as the *source*, the easiest way to ensure you don't have any problems is to create a primary key on the *source* table that corresponds to the column(s) specified in the ON clause. If you don't have a primary key, or are using a SELECT statement as the *source*, it is your responsibility to make sure the rows in the *source* are unique with respect to the column(s) defined in the ON clause.

There can only be one WHEN NOT MATCHED BY TARGET clause which specifies the INSERT into the *target* table. A value is inserted only when the *source* row doesn't exist in the *target* and any optional search criteria are satisfied. If the *source* row does not match and the row does not match the additional search criteria, no action is performed.

The WHEN NOT MATCHED BY SOURCE specifies the UPDATE and/or DELETE action to be performed when a value in the *target* table does not exist in the *source*. The WHEN NOT MATCHED BY SOURCE clause follows all of the same rules as the WHEN MATCHED clause. Additionally, you can only reference the columns in the *target* in the UPDATE/DELETE statement, because when a match to the *source* is not found, no *source* column definition is available to the UPDATE/DELETE and error 207, invalid column name, will be returned.

Foreign Keys

MERGE allows you to make multiple modifications to a single table with one pass. Coupled with the OUTPUT clause, the MERGE statement can be also used as the source for any other DML statement. In fact, every DML statement gives you the capability of using the inserted, deleted, or both as a source for another DML statement. The MERGE statement also allows you to specify columns from the source or target table.

The simplest version is to just specify OUTPUT along with a list of columns to return a result set to an application which called the DML command. Since the OUTPUT clause returns a result set, you can use it as the source for any other DML command. For example:

```
INSERT INTO <table>
(<Column List>)
FROM (MERGE...
      OUTPUT <columns>) a
```

You can also add the INTO clause to direct the OUTPUT columns into a table or table variable. The nested example above is equivalent to using OUTPUT...INTO.

If the target table for the nested DML or the INTO clause is participating on either side of a forcign key, you will receive an error message. OUTPUT...INTO and nested DML with the OUTPUT clause is incompatible with foreign keys. You can have a target table for MERGE which is either the parent or child of a foreign key; you cannot direct output to that table.

You can work around this using two methods:

1. You can wrap the MERGE statement into a dynamic SQL call.
2. You can direct the output to a temp table or table variable and then use the temp table/table variable in a subsequent statement to perform the extra DML operation.

Terminators

T-SQL has two blocks of code execution, statement and batch, with a statement being a subset of a batch. You've actually executed both types thus far in this book. A statement is a single command that can be executed such as a SELECT, CREATE, INSERT, UPDATE, etc. A batch is one or more statements that are executed together.

All statements and batches have terminators which designate where one statement/batch ends and another one begins. Up to this point, we have largely ignored both statement and batch terminators, because they have been optional up until this point. When you execute multiple commands, SSMS automatically adds the batch terminator, GO; before the batch is submitted to SQL Server. The parser in SQL Server figures out where each command in a batch ends and automatically adds the statement terminator, semi-colon (;).

While a batch terminator is still optional, certain statements require a terminator either on the statement itself or on the prior statement in the batch. MERGE is one of the statements which require a terminator.

> **Best Practice:** Using statement terminators is a good structural practice in your code and it also means you don't have to remember which statements require a terminator. So, from this point forward, we will always show all code with statement terminators.

Exercise 10: Reconcile Inventory on Hand with Shipments

Champion Valley Pens owns a manufacturing facility that produces every product that is sold. Products are packaged on the manufacturing line and delivered to the warehouse when they undergo a receiving process before being loaded on to shelves for subsequent picking and shipping to a customer. The website maintains an inventory on hand value that is debited each time a product is ordered in order to provide stocking status messages to customers. In the following exercise, you will create the statements which will increase the inventory on hand as products are received at the warehouse. You will also create the statements required to update the inventory on hand when the warehouse does a physical inventory.

1. Execute the following to create the Products.ShipmentHeader and Products. ShipmentDetail tables:

```sql
CREATE TABLE Products.ShipmentHeader
(ShipmentID        INT          IDENTITY(1,1),
ReceiveDate        DATE         NOT NULL,
AddedToInventory   CHAR(1) NOT NULL,
CONSTRAINT pk_ShipmentHeader PRIMARY KEY (ShipmentID));
GO
CREATE TABLE Products.ShipmentDetail
(ShipmentDetailID  INT          IDENTITY(1,1),
ShipmentID         INT          NOT NULL,
SKU                CHAR(30)     NOT NULL,
Quantity           INT          NOT NULL,
CONSTRAINT pk_ShipmentDetail PRIMARY KEY (ShipmentDetailID));
GO
ALTER TABLE Products.ShipmentDetail
    ADD CONSTRAINT fk_ShipmentHeaderToShipmentDetailOnShipmentID FOREIGN KEY
(ShipmentID)
    REFERENCES Products.ShipmentHeader (ShipmentID);
GO
ALTER TABLE Products.ShipmentDetail
    ADD CONSTRAINT fk_SKUToShipmentDetailOnSKU FOREIGN KEY (SKU)
    REFERENCES Products.SKU (SKU);
GO
```

2. Execute the following to create a new shipment:

   ```
   INSERT INTO Products.ShipmentHeader
   (ReceiveDate, AddedToInventory)
   VALUES ('3/5/2012', 'N');
   INSERT INTO Products.ShipmentDetail
   (ShipmentID, SKU, Quantity)
   VALUES (1,'DRILLBIT-9mm',20000),(1,'AA-1-1',2000),(1,'EW-1-1',1000);
   ```

3. Execute the following to review the inventory information for the newly arrived products:

   ```
   SELECT * FROM Products.Inventory WHERE SKU = 'DRILLBIT-9mm';
   SELECT * FROM Products.Inventory WHERE SKU = 'AA-1-1';
   SELECT * FROM Products.Inventory WHERE SKU = 'EW-1-1';
   SELECT * FROM Products.ShipmentHeader;
   SELECT * FROM Products.ShipmentDetail;
   ```

4. Execute the following code to MERGE the shipment into the inventory table:

   ```
   MERGE INTO Products.Inventory AS Target
   USING (SELECT SKU, Quantity FROM Products.ShipmentDetail WHERE ShipmentID = 1)
         AS Source
   ON Target.SKU = Source.SKU
   WHEN MATCHED THEN
       UPDATE SET QuantityOnHand = QuantityOnHand + Source.Quantity
   WHEN NOT MATCHED BY TARGET THEN
       INSERT (SKU, QuantityOnHand) VALUES (SKU, Quantity)
   OUTPUT $action, inserted.*, deleted.*;
   UPDATE Products.ShipmentHeader
   SET AddedToInventory = 'Y'
   WHERE AddedToInventory = 'N';
   ```

5. Review the results.

6. Execute the following to create the Products.PhysicalInventoryHeader and the Products.PhysicalInventoryDetail:

   ```
   CREATE TABLE Products.PhysicalInventoryHeader
   (InventoryID           INT           IDENTITY(1,1),
    InventoryDate         DATE          NOT NULL,
    ReconcileToInventory  CHAR(1)       NOT NULL,
    CONSTRAINT pk_PhysicalInventoryHeader PRIMARY KEY (InventoryID));
   GO
   CREATE TABLE Products.PhysicalInventoryDetail
   (InventoryDetailID  INT          IDENTITY(1,1),
    InventoryID        INT          NOT NULL,
    SKU                CHAR(30)     NOT NULL,
    Quantity           INT          NOT NULL,
    CONSTRAINT pk_PhysicalInventoryDetail PRIMARY KEY (InventoryDetailID));
   GO
   ALTER TABLE Products.PhysicalInventoryDetail
       ADD CONSTRAINT fk_PhysicalInventoryHeaderToPhysicalInventoryDetailOnInventoryID
           FOREIGN KEY (InventoryID)
       REFERENCES Products.PhysicalInventoryHeader (InventoryID);
   GO
   ALTER TABLE Products.PhysicalInventoryDetail
       ADD CONSTRAINT fk_SKUToPhysicalInventoryDetailOnSKU FOREIGN KEY (SKU)
       REFERENCES Products.SKU (SKU);
   GO
   ```

7. Execute the following to create a new physical inventory:

   ```
   INSERT INTO Products.PhysicalInventoryHeader
   (InventoryDate, ReconcileToInventory)
   VALUES ('3/10/2012','N');
   INSERT INTO Products.PhysicalInventoryDetail
   (InventoryID, SKU, Quantity)
   VALUES (1,'DRILLBIT-9mm',19964),(1,'AA-1-1',14800),(1,'EW-1-1',32850),(1,'EW-1-2',0);
   ```

8. MERGE the physical inventory to the inventory table:

   ```
   MERGE INTO Products.Inventory AS Target
   USING (SELECT SKU, Quantity FROM Products.PhysicalInventoryDetail WHERE InventoryID = 1)
        AS Source
   ON Target.SKU = Source.SKU
   WHEN MATCHED AND Source.Quantity = 0 THEN
       DELETE
   WHEN MATCHED THEN
       UPDATE SET QuantityOnHand = Source.Quantity
   WHEN NOT MATCHED BY TARGET THEN
       INSERT (SKU, QuantityOnHand) VALUES (SKU, Quantity)
   OUTPUT $action, inserted.*, deleted.*;
   ```

9. Review the results

Tracking Changes

In many applications, requirements exist to audit changes to data. Data auditing requirements can range from simple, knowing what data changed; to the complex, knowing the current and prior values for each change along with when and who made the change. Prior to SQL Server 2008, if you wanted to audit data changes, you had to design your own infrastructure and code to log changes as they occurred.

SQL Server 2012 provides two features to accomplish the simple form of data auditing – *change tracking* and *change data capture*. Both change tracking and change data capture are enabled on a table by table basis. Change tracking will log the primary key of each row that is changed, the type of change that was made, and which columns were changed, but does not log the actual values that were changed in the row. Change data capture logs each change that occurred along with the actual data that was changed. Neither auditing method will track the user making the change.

Change Tracking

Change tracking provides the simplest auditing possible, logging that a change has been made to a row within a table. Change tracking is first enabled at the database level by changing the CHANGE_TRACKING database property. In addition to enabling change tracking for the database, you can optionally specify retention and automatic clean up. For example if you set CHANGE_RETENTION to 5 days and AUTO_CLEANUP to ON, then SQL Server will automatically remove any change tracking information older than 5 days.

Once enabled on the database, you enable change tracking on a table by table basis by enabling the CHANGE_TRACKING property for each table. When change tracking is enabled for a table,

SQL Server will automatically create a change table to log the changes made.

Changes can be tracked at the table or column level. TRACK_COLUMNS_CHANGED is turned off by default, because it requires additional storage space. However, when enabled SQL Server will log information that designates each column in a table that was changed by an UPDATE statement.

Change tracking is always a synchronous process that logs the primary key, a version number for the creation of a row, version number for the last change to a row, the type of change made, and optionally the column(s) changed during an UPDATE.

Any INSERT, UPDATE, or DELETE statement can be modified using a WITH clause that specifies a CHANGE_TRACKING_CONTEXT. CHANGE_TRACKING_CONTEXT accepts a single, VARBINARY(128) value. The change tracking context allows additional information to be stored in the change tracking tables that can be used later. For example, an application can pass information designating the name of the application and user making the change which will then be stored with the rest of the automatically generated change tracking data.

Exercise 11: Tracking Employee Changes

In the following exercise, you will enable change tracking, make multiple modifications to the employee table, and observe the corresponding change tracking information that is stored.

1. Execute the following code to enable change tracking on the database:

    ```
    USE master;
    GO
    ALTER DATABASE ChampionValleyPens
    SET CONTAINMENT = NONE WITH NO_WAIT;
    GO
    ALTER DATABASE ChampionValleyPens
    SET CHANGE_TRACKING = ON
    (CHANGE_RETENTION = 7 DAYS, AUTO_CLEANUP = ON);
    GO
    ```

2. Execute the following code to enable change tracking on the Employee table.

    ```
    USE ChampionValleyPens;
    GO
    ALTER TABLE HumanResources.Employee
    ENABLE CHANGE_TRACKING
    WITH (TRACK_COLUMNS_UPDATED = ON);
    GO
    ```

3. Execute the following code to return the change tracking version and insert a new row:

    ```
    SELECT CHANGE_TRACKING_CURRENT_VERSION();
    GO
    INSERT INTO HumanResources.Employee
    (FirstName, MiddleInitial, LastName, JobTitleID, BirthDate, SSN, Gender, OrganizationNode)
    VALUES('Lorraine','A','Peters',3,'6/14/1968','053-82-4617','F',hierarchyid::Parse('/7/3/3/'));
    GO
    SELECT CHANGE_TRACKING_CURRENT_VERSION();
    GO
    ```

4. Execute the following code to view the change tracking information:

   ```
   SELECT a.EmployeeID, a.SYS_CHANGE_VERSION, a.SYS_CHANGE_CREATION_VERSION,
   a.SYS_CHANGE_OPERATION, a.SYS_CHANGE_COLUMNS, a.SYS_CHANGE_CONTEXT
   FROM CHANGETABLE(CHANGES HumanResources.Employee, NULL) AS a;

   SELECT a.EmployeeID, a.SYS_CHANGE_VERSION, a.SYS_CHANGE_CREATION_VERSION,
   a.SYS_CHANGE_OPERATION, a.SYS_CHANGE_COLUMNS, a.SYS_CHANGE_CONTEXT
   FROM CHANGETABLE(CHANGES HumanResources.Employee, 0) AS a;
   GO
   ```

   > **Note:** A value of NULL in the 3rd parameter means to retrieve all tracked versions while a value of 0 means to retrieve all versions since version 0.

5. Execute the following code to modify a row and view the new version number:

   ```
   UPDATE HumanResources.Employee
   SET LastName = 'Chester'
   WHERE SSN = '053-82-4617';
   GO
   SELECT CHANGE_TRACKING_CURRENT_VERSION();
   GO
   ```

6. Execute the following code to view the change tracking information:

   ```
   SELECT a.EmployeeID, a.SYS_CHANGE_VERSION, a.SYS_CHANGE_CREATION_VERSION,
   a.SYS_CHANGE_OPERATION, a.SYS_CHANGE_COLUMNS, a.SYS_CHANGE_CONTEXT,
   CHANGE_TRACKING_IS_COLUMN_IN_MASK
       (COLUMNPROPERTY(OBJECT_ID('HumanResources.Employee'),
               'LastName', 'ColumnId'),a.SYS_CHANGE_COLUMNS)
   FROM CHANGETABLE(CHANGES HumanResources.Employee, 1) AS a;
   GO
   ```

7. Execute the following code to clean up the employee table and disable change tracking.

   ```
   ALTER TABLE HumanResources.Employee
   DISABLE CHANGE_TRACKING;
   GO
   DELETE FROM HumanResources.Employee
   WHERE SSN = '053-82-4617';
   GO
   USE master;
   GO
   ALTER DATABASE ChampionValleyPens
   SET CHANGE_TRACKING = OFF;
   GO
   ```

Before we turned change tracking on, we had to turn containment off for the database. One of the requirements of a contained database is that it does not utilize features which either depend upon services outside of the database or utilize features that might not be available if the database is transferred to another instance. Due to these requirements, change tracking and change data capture cannot be enabled for a database that is set to PARTIAL containment.

When you enable change tracking, SQL Server requires exclusive access to the database. If any other connections are present, the ALTER DATABASE command will fail, return an error, and abort. Prior to turning on change tracking, you must ensure that all connections to the database are terminated.

When you enabled change tracking for a table, SQL Server automatically creates a table to hold the change tracking information for the table. Each table you enable will have a corresponding change tracking table. However, if you were to go looking for any of these change tracking tables in the Object Explorer or system catalog, you would not find any of them. Prior to SQL Server 2005, you could view and even manipulate internal, system tables. SQL Server 2005 introduced a new table property, hidden, that is used for all internal tables. Change tracking tables, while they consume space, are hidden tables that are only exposed through a set of change tracking functions.

Change Tracking Functions

Change tracking data is exposed through a set of four functions shown in the table below:

Function	Purpose
CHANGETABLE()	Returns the change tracking information for the specified table
CHANGE_TRACKING_CURRENT_VERSION()	Returns the change version of the last change that was made
CHANGE_TRACKING_MIN_VALID_VERSION()	Returns the minimum version number that can be used for the specified table
CHANGE_TRACKING_IS_COLUMN_IN_MASK()	Returns a 1 if the specified column was changed based on the CHANGE_COLUMNS returned from the CHANGETABLE() function.

CHANGETABLE accepts one of two parameters – CHANGES and VERSION. When you use the CHANGES parameter, the name of the table and a version is specified. The version specified designates the point at which to start returning changes. A NULL will return all changes for the specified table, while a version number will return all changes after that version. When you use the VERSION parameter, you specify the name of the table and the primary key value(s). VERSION will then return the change tracking information corresponding to the last change made to the designated row(s).

CHANGETABLE returns a different result set based on the parameter specified. When you specify the CHANGES parameter, the result set will contain the following columns:

Column	Purpose
SYS_CHANGE_VERSION	Version number of the row
SYS_CHANGE_CREATION_VERSION	Version number when the row was created
SYS_CHANGE_OPERATION	Single character for the type of change made – *I*nsert, *U*pdate, or *D*elete
SYS_CHANGE_COLUMNS	Stores column(s) changed in a binary encoding Use with CHANGE_TRACKING_IS_COLUMN_IN_MASK().
SYS_CHANGE_CONTEXT	Optional context information specified by the application performing the change
<primary key>	One column for each column in the primary key of the table

When you specify the VERSION parameter, only the SYS_CHANGE_VERSION, SYS_CHANGE_CONTEXT, and primary key columns are returned.

Change Data Capture

The main purpose of change tracking is to provide information to applications that synchronize changes periodically. The application can store the current change version, disconnect, perform processing, and at a later time connect up and retrieve any rows that have changed since the last synchronization. If the application doesn't care about the state of a row between synch cycles, only that it has the most recent set of data, change tracking will serve the application's needs. Change Data Capture, CDC, logs each change that was made to a table and instead of just noting the operation performed, stores the actual values in the row. So, CDC gives applications the ability to retrieve an entire change history for a row. Logging the change history for a row is especially useful for ETL applications which load incremental changes to a data warehouse or are responsible for maintaining a set of master data across an enterprise.

Change tracking is an internal, synchronous process that occurs while changes are being made. CDC operates in an asynchronous mode, using components from the replication engine (sp_replcmds), to read the contents of the transaction log and capture the changes.

> **Note:** If transactional replication is also configured for the database, CDC will use the Log Reader Agent to capture changes instead of making a separate call to sp_replcmds. This allows the Log Reader Agent to make a single scan of the transaction log and satisfy the needs of both CDC and replication.

You enable CDC by executing the sys.sp_cdc_enable_db stored procedure.

> **Note:** Since change data capture relies on SQL Server Agent, the service needs to be running. You should also set the service to start automatically so that if the server restarts, SQL Server will be automatically started by Windows.

CDC consumes more storage and processing capacity than change tracking due to the additional information stored; but has minimal impact on applications since all changes are logged asynchronously by reading the transaction log. However, in situations where you have a very high volume of changes occurring, change data capture can have an impact on application performance since all changes have to be written to the transaction log while the Log Reader agent is continuously reading the log. Access to the transaction log is a single threaded, sequential operation, so the writes from your application have to compete with the reads from the Log Reader agent. The architecture of the Log Reader agent minimizes contention, even in high volume situations, but it can have a noticeable impact.

Once enabled, you execute the sys.sp_cdc_enable_table stored procedure to enable change data capture for a table. The procedure will create a table to track changes that contains a column for each column in the table being tracked along with several additional columns to track the change operation. In addition to enabling CDC for the table, you can specify that only certain columns in the table are tracked using the @captured_column_list parameter. Columns are specified in a comma separated list with the default being to capture all columns for the table. If you specify columns, you must always include the column(s) for the primary key or for the unique index which can be defined separately for CDC.

One of the biggest differences between change tracking and CDC is that CDC stores the actual data. With data being stored in the tracking tables, CDC has a security property that you can choose to set. If you specify a role name when you enable CDC for a table, only users who are a member of the specified role will have access to the data in the tracking tables. This prevents the possibility of exposing data to someone through CDC when they might not be able to access the data normally.

In addition to specifying the schema name and table name to enable CDC on, you also specify a capture instance. When enabled, SQL Server will create several objects to support CDC and the capture instance is used within the names of the objects created. Each table can have up to 2 capture instances defined. The capture instance is used by the CDC functions to specify the set of change data to retrieve.

Each record in the transaction log is uniquely identified by a number known as the Log Sequence Number, LSN. The LSN starts at 1 for each database and increments forever, never reusing a value or generating values less than 1.

One of the data points that CDC logs is the LSN of the change. Changes are then retrieved based on the LSN. You can specify a single LSN or a range of LSNs. Since multiple changes to the same row can occur across a range of LSNs, CDC has a feature which controls the way data is returned in the event of multiple changes. By setting the @supports_net_changes parameter to 1, a single row is returned for the change set reflecting the sum of all of the changes within the specified LSN range. If you set @supports_net_changes to 1 and the table does not have a primary key, then you must specify the name of the index to be used to uniquely identify each row in the table. By default, @supports_net_changes is set to 0, which means in the event of multiple changes to the same row across a specified LSN range, a separate row for each change will be returned.

CDC logs change information such as the start/end LSN, a sequence number, the operation performed, and an update mask column along with the data in the row. While the change related information is relatively small, storing the row data can consume a considerable amount of space. So, CDC allows you to specify a filegroup to store the change data in order to manage the space consumption.

> **Best Practices:** Instead of mixing the change data on the filegroup(s) where your data resides, it is recommended that you designate one or more dedicated filegroups to store the change data. This allows you to manage the space consumed by the change data separately. Additionally, if you decide to disable CDC, you can easily reclaim the disk space used by dropping the corresponding filegroup(s)

Exercise 12: Tracking Employee Changes

In the following exercise, you will enable change data capture, make multiple modifications to the employee table, and observe the corresponding change data capture information that is stored.

1. Execute the following code to add a new file and filegroup to the ChampionValleyPens database:

    ```
    ALTER DATABASE ChampionValleyPens
        ADD FILEGROUP CDC;
    GO
    ALTER DATABASE ChampionValleyPens
        ADD FILE (NAME = CDC, FILENAME =
    'C:\ChampionValleyPress\Data\ChampionValleyPens_CDC.ndf')
        TO FILEGROUP CDC;
    GO
    ```

2. Launch SQL Server Configuration Manager, Select SQL Server Services, and start SQL Server Agent.

3. Execute the following code to enable CDC for the database and the HumanResources.Employee table:

    ```
    USE ChampionValleyPens;
    GO
    EXEC sys.sp_cdc_enable_db;
    GO
    EXEC sys.sp_cdc_enable_table
        @source_schema = N'HumanResources',
        @source_name   = N'Employee',
        @role_name     = NULL,
        @filegroup_name = N'CDC',
        @capture_instance = N'HumanResources_Employee',
        @supports_net_changes = 1;
    GO
    ```

4. Expand the System Tables node underneath ChampionValleyPens | Tables to review the tables that are created for managing CDC.

5. Insert Lorraine Peters into the Employee table, just like we did in the change tracking exercise.

    ```
    INSERT INTO HumanResources.Employee
    (FirstName, MiddleInitial, LastName, JobTitleID, BirthDate, SSN, Gender,
    OrganizationNode)
    VALUES('Lorraine','A','Peters',3,'6/14/1968','053-82-
    4617','F',hierarchyid::Parse('/7/3/3/'));
    GO
    SELECT *
    FROM HumanResources.Employee
    WHERE SSN = '053-82-4617';
    GO
    ```

6. Execute the following code to review the CDC information:

    ```
    DECLARE @from_lsn binary(10),
            @to_lsn binary(10);

    SET @from_lsn = sys.fn_cdc_get_min_lsn('HumanResources_Employee');
    SET @to_lsn   = sys.fn_cdc_get_max_lsn();

    SELECT *
    FROM cdc.fn_cdc_get_all_changes_HumanResources_Employee (@from_lsn, @to_lsn,
    N'all');
    SELECT *
    FROM cdc.fn_cdc_get_net_changes_HumanResources_Employee(@from_lsn, @to_lsn, N'all');
    SELECT sys.fn_cdc_map_lsn_to_time(@to_lsn);
    GO
    ```

7. Execute the following code to modify Lorraine's last name:
   ```
   UPDATE HumanResources.Employee
   SET LastName = 'Chester'
   WHERE SSN = '053-82-4617';
   GO
   ```

8. Execute the code in step 6 to review the CDC information. Note that the first function returns both the insert and the update as separate rows while the second function only returns the end result of all changes in the LSN range.

9. Disable CDC on the table and the database, remove Lorraine from the Employee table, and drop the CDC filegroup and file.
   ```
   EXEC sys.sp_cdc_disable_table
       @source_schema = N'HumanResources',
       @source_name   = N'Employee',
       @capture_instance = N'HumanResources_Employee';
   GO
   EXEC sys.sp_cdc_disable_db;
   GO
   DELETE FROM HumanResources.Employee
   WHERE SSN = '053-82-4617';
   GO
   ALTER DATABASE ChampionValleyPens
       REMOVE FILE CDC;
   GO
   ALTER DATABASE ChampionValleyPens
       REMOVE FILEGROUP CDC;
   GO
   ```

10. Launch SQL Server Configuration Manager, Select SQL Server Services, and stop SQL Server Agent.

Change Data Capture Functions

Function	Purpose
cdc.fn_cdc_get_all_changes_<capture_instance>	Returns all changes which have occurred to a capture instance between the specified LSN values
sys.fn_cdc_has_column_changed	Returns true or false if a specified column in the designated change instance has been modified.
cdc.fn_cdc_get_net_changes_<capture_instance>	Consolidates all changes to a given row between the specified LSN values so that only a single row per unique key is returned.
sys.fn_cdc_increment_lsn	Returns the next LSN available in the CDC data based on the specified LSN
sys.fn_cdc_decrement_lsn	Returns the prior LSN available in the CDC data based on the specified LSN
sys.fn_cdc_map_lsn_to_time	Converts an LSN to the time the change occurred.
sys.fn_cdc_get_max_lsn	Returns the maximum LSN in the change table for the specified change instance.
sys.fn_cdc_map_time_to_lsn	Converts a time to an LSN available in the change data.

Function	Purpose
sys.fn_cdc_get_min_lsn	Returns the minimum LSN in the change table for the specified change instance.

The sys.fn_cdc_map_time_to_lsn and sys.fn_cdc_map_lsn_to_time functions are based on a system table maintained for all CDC operations. When each change is logged, the time for each LSN is recorded in the cdc.lsn_time_mapping table. This provides a time based tracking mechanism based on the system clock for every change logged by CDC. The function to return an LSN based on a time can be utilized by applications for those cases where time based incremental changes need to be extracted, e.g. a daily ETL routine that needs to extract all changes since the last daily processing run. In addition to specifying the time to map for the sys.fn_cdc_map_time_to_lsn, the function takes an additional parameter that specifies the LSN to return. You can return the smallest LSN possible that is either > or >= to the specified time or you can return the largest LSN possible that is < = <= to the specified time. In this way, you can get an absolute set of boundary LSNs to feed to either the cdc.fn_cdc_get_all_changes_<capture instance> or the cdc.fn_cdc_get_net_changes_<capture instance> functions.

CDC Capture and Cleanup

When you configure the first table within a database for CDC, a pair of jobs is created to capture and cleanup changes and values are loaded to the msdb.dbo.cdc_jobs table with hard-coded parameters. The parameters in the cdc_jobs table control the behavior of both the capture and cleanup jobs.

> **Note:** If the database has a transactional publication created, the capture job will not be created.

The first job runs the collection of changes on a continuous basis by executing scans of the transaction log. The default behavior of the capture job is to continuously log changes with a maximum of 500 changes at a time being logged. While the job is set to run "continuously", it simply means the job is always running. Having SQL Server endlessly executing a block of code is a huge waste of resources, so CDC uses a basic "batching" methodology. The polling interval parameter is set to 5 seconds by default, which means that CDC will wake up every 5 seconds, look for any changes, log any changes it finds, and then go back to sleep. The impact of reading the transaction log and logging changes is controlled by the maxtrans and maxscans parameters. The maxtrans parameter is set to 500 by default, which means that CDC will process a maximum of 500 transactions in a single scan. The maxscans parameter is set to 10 by default, which means that CDC will perform a maximum of 10 read operations of the transaction log before sleeping for 5 seconds. Using the default parameters, CDC can capture and log 5000 transactions each time it runs before going to sleep for 5 seconds.

If the tables you have enabled for CDC are receiving more than 5000 transactions every 5 seconds on a sustained basis, you will need to modify the parameters of the capture job by running the sys.sp_cdc_change_job stored procedure. Only change these parameters if the change volume is consistently above 5000 every 5 seconds otherwise you can run into resource contention on the transaction log when writing changes. If your change volume occasionally exceeds this threshold, CDC will periodically fall behind and then take a few seconds to catch up which shouldn't pose any issues with applications using the CDC data.

While change retention and automatic clean up are visible and configurable when you enable change tracking, the automatic clean up and retention are almost completely hidden with CDC.

The second CDC job is responsible for automatically cleaning up the CDC logging tables based on a hard coded interval. By default, the job runs once per day at 2AM. When the job starts, it accesses the msdb.dbo.cdc_jobs table and retrieves the value in the retention column for the database. By default, the retention is set to 3 days (4320 minutes).

Once the retention interval is retrieved, the procedure will subtract the retention interval from the current system time to determine the minimum allowed time, known as the low watermark. This time is then mapped to the largest LSN in the cdc.lsn_time_mapping table that is <= the low watermark as follows:

```
SELECT @lsn = sys.fn_cdc_map_time_to_lsn ('largest less than or equal',
@extraction_time);
```

Once the appropriate LSN for the new low watermark is computed, the cleanup routine first removes any entries in the cdc.lsn_time_mapping table that are <= to this LSN. The entries are first removed from cdc.lsn_time_mapping, because this table is used by all CDC functions which return data to determine the minimum allowed change set. By removing the entries from cdc.lsn_time_mapping first, any applications retrieving changes can continue to function even as the remainder of the CDC tables are cleaned up, as the cleanup process can take a considerable amount of time for database where a large number of changes are occurring.

Once the low watermark is set in the cdc.lsn_time_mapping table, the cleanup routine then removes all entries in the remaining CDC tables for all capture instances with LSNs less than the low watermark. The maximum number of rows removed in a single operation is governed by the threshold parameter in cdc_jobs which by default is 5000.

You can change the retention interval or the threshold by executing the sys.sp_cdc_change_job stored procedure. You can change the schedule on which the cleanup job runs by modifying the schedule of the cleanup job.

You can have a maximum of two capture instances configured for each table, but the cleanup job removes entries for all capture instances on the same retention interval. If you need to clean up the CDC data on different intervals for each capture instance or you need the retention interval to vary on a table by table basis, you cannot use the built in cleanup job. In this case, you will need to disable the default cleanup job and build your own cleanup routine based on the sys.sp_cdc_cleanup_change_table stored procedure.

Summary

In this chapter, we covered the basics of retrieving data and variables. You learned how to add, modify, and remove data from tables. We covered how to load and manipulate hierarchy data. You learned how the MERGE statement allows you to synchronize the contents of two tables. Finally, you learned how to deploy change tracking and CDC.

Chapter 8
Managing Concurrency

> **Setup:** Please run the Chapter 8 Setup script in the companion files prior to starting the exercises in this chapter to ensure that your databases are at the correct starting point. Every exercise in this book assumes that you have created the c:\ChampionValleyPress\Data and c:\ChampionValleyPress\Log folders, contained databases are enabled, and this is the location of all of the data, log, and filestream files which will be used for this book. If you have chosen a different path, you will need to adjust the paths listed accordingly. Every setup script also assumes that you have enabled FILESTREAM access for the instance. When executing commands, it is assumed that you will change context to the appropriate database since understanding the contents of each database in this book is the same skill you will need for working with your databases. All scripts also assume you are using a default instance.

If Microsoft SQL Server were simply a local database accessed by a single person or process at a time, we could continue on with our current understanding of how to access and manipulate data. SQL Server is designed to allow tens of thousands of users to simultaneously access data in a controlled manner.

As a multi-user system, a mechanism has to be in place to govern access to the data to ensure conflicting access doesn't happen. Conflicts can occur when two users attempt to change the same row of data at the same time or when one user is attempting to read data while another is changing it.

In this chapter, you will learn how you can manage concurrent access to data while still ensuring data consistency by manipulating the behavior of SQL Server's basic unit of work.

Concurrency Models

Databases can handle concurrency using two different models – pessimistic and optimistic.

A pessimistic concurrency model, the default model for SQL Server assumes that data access patterns will have users attempting to read the same block of data as is being changed by other users. In a pessimistic model, the database engine will lock resources to prevent users from reading data that is in the process of being changed or changing data that is in the process of being read. Put another way – readers block writers and writers block readers.

An optimistic concurrency model assumes that it is unlikely that users reading data will be attempting to access rows that are undergoing changes. In an optimistic concurrency model, when a user attempts to read data that is being changed, the database engine will create a copy of the row as it existed prior to the change starting and return data based on that prior image. Put another way – readers don't block writers and writers don't block readers. However, in an optimistic concurrency model, writers will still block other writers.

Transactions

The basic unit of work in SQL Server, as well as any DBMS, is a transaction. Regardless of whether you are reading or writing data or manipulating objects, everything that you submit to SQL Server is contained within a transaction. Transactions are used to maintain consistency in data while also controlling concurrent access in a multi-user environment.

Types of Transactions

Transactions can be either implicit or explicit, but every batch that is submitted will be wrapped inside at least one transaction.

Explicit transactions occur when you include the BEGIN TRANSACTION command within your batch. Shorthand is available for transaction of TRAN, which we will use from this point forward. Each BEGIN TRAN command starts a new transaction and you can have as many transactions in a batch as you have commands and transactions can be nested within each other. A transaction is terminated by either a COMMIT TRAN or ROLLBACK TRAN.

The COMMIT TRAN permanently saves any changes made within the transaction. Once committed, the change cannot be undone. A COMMIT TRAN command is paired with the closest BEGIN TRAN within the batch. It takes one COMMIT TRAN for every BEGIN TRAN to commit every transaction opened within a batch.

A ROLLBACK TRAN will undo any changes performed to the outermost BEGIN TRAN statement. If the transactions are nested, even if all inner transactions have been committed, a ROLLBACK TRAN will undo all of the changes of the inner, committed transactions. Consider the following examples:

```
CREATE TABLE #Test
(ID     INT     NOT NULL)

BEGIN TRAN
INSERT INTO #Test
VALUES(1)
COMMIT TRAN

BEGIN TRAN
INSERT INTO #Test
VALUES(2)
ROLLBACK TRAN

SELECT * FROM #Test
```

In this example, we have two explicit transactions within the batch. The first transaction inserts a value of 1 and then commits the transaction. The second one inserts the value of 2 and rolls back the transaction. The end result is that the table contains a single row with a value of 1, because the first transaction was committed and the second transaction was rolled back.

```
CREATE TABLE #Test
(ID INT NOT NULL)

BEGIN TRAN
    BEGIN TRAN
    INSERT INTO #Test
    VALUES(1)
    COMMIT TRAN

INSERT INTO #Test
VALUES(2)

ROLLBACK TRAN
SELECT * FROM #Test
```

In this example, the same changes are made, however; note that the insert of the value of 1 is nested inside the outer transaction. In this case, the end result will be an empty table. Even though the value of 1 was committed in the inner transaction, the rollback undoes every change to the BEGIN TRAN that it is paired with. As of the writing of this book, SQL Server Books Online (BOL) will tell you: "A transaction cannot be rolled back after a COMMIT TRANSACTION statement is executed." This is a bug in BOL. Any nested transactions, regardless of whether committed or not, can be rolled back if contained within another transaction that has a ROLLBACK TRAN statement executed for it.

If you explicitly start a transaction and do not terminate the transaction with either a COMMIT TRAN or ROLLBACK TRAN, the transaction will be held open for as long as the connection is active to the instance. Depending upon the locking behavior you have specified, this can cause locks to remain open for a very long duration possibly causing severe contention in your database.

An implicit transaction is one that SQL Server automatically starts for each batch submitted if you do not specify an explicit transaction. Implicit transactions are always committed when the batch finishes execution. Up to this point, every command you have executed has been within an implicit transaction.

Even when you explicitly specify a transaction, every batch is also implicitly wrapped in a transaction. Consider the following example, which is a slight variation of the nested transactions issue.

```
CREATE TABLE #Test
(ID INT NOT NULL)

BEGIN TRAN
    BEGIN TRAN
    INSERT INTO #Test
    VALUES(1)
    ROLLBACK TRAN

INSERT INTO #Test
VALUES(2)

COMMIT TRAN
SELECT * FROM #Test
```

In this example, all we have done is swapped the COMMIT TRAN and ROLLBACK TRAN commands. The end result of this code is both an error message and the value 2 being saved to the #Test table. The batch explicitly starts two transactions, inserts a value of 1 and then issues a ROLLBACK TRAN. This rolled back and closed both of the BEGIN TRAN statements, undoing the insert of the value 1. We then insert the value of 2 and explicitly commit the value. This will first produce an error message that the COMMIT TRAN doesn't have a corresponding BEGIN TRAN, because the ROLLBACK TRAN closed both of the BEGIN TRAN statements. However, the value of 2 will still be saved to the table, because the entire batch is wrapped inside an implicit transaction that commits the value of 2 to the table.

ACID properties

SQL Server is no different than most other database management systems in obeying a variety of ANSI standards. One of the core standards are the ACID properties of database transactions. ACID stands for Atomicity, Consistency, Isolation, and Durability.

Atomicity refers to the behavior that a database transaction is not allowed to partially commit. The transaction either commits completely or rollback completely. To understand atomicity, consider the transfer for funds from your checking account to your savings account. Funds are first debited from your checking account and then credited to your savings account. If the debit of the checking account were allowed to commit while the credit to the savings account failed, you would be losing money (and be very unhappy). On the other hand, if the debit from the checking account failed, but your savings account was still credited, you would be happy, but your bank wouldn't be. Atomicity of a transaction ensures that both the debit from the checking account as well as the credit to the savings account have to either both commit or both rollback.

Consistency means that at the end of the transaction, the database has to be in a logical state. Consistency is also at play in our banking scenario since it wouldn't be logical for money to either magically appear or disappear.

The isolation behavior ensures that transactions aren't stepping on each other. Isolation ensures that one transaction cannot see intermediate results of another transaction. In our banking example, another process shouldn't be able to access the checking account balance while the transfer transaction is occurring. If it were allowed to access the balance and the transfer was ultimately aborted, the process would be retrieving a checking account balance that never existed since an abort means that the transfer never occurred. If that process were a bill payment process, it could wind up rejecting a bill payment due to insufficient funds, when there actually were funds available since the transfer aborted. You would be left wondering why you were charged a late fee for a payment which was never sent since you had sufficient funds at every point in time. SQL Server isolates transactions by locking the rows that are being changed so that another process cannot read them. It will also lock rows that are being read so that another process cannot change the data until the read is complete.

This is not the same thing as application processes or users stepping on each other. Two users can still change the same row. The first change will block the second change until it completes and then the second change will execute. If the second change commits, then it will have the effect of overwriting the first change. This situation is something which needs to be handled at the application tier as SQL Server is not responsible for making assumptions as to which transaction should be committed.

Database management systems, like SQL Server, are built to service large numbers of requests concurrently. When a DBMS locks data to guarantee isolation, the concurrency goes down as processes get serialized when attempting to access data. You can manipulate the amount of transaction isolation SQL Server enforces to suit the needs of your applications and users.

Durability ensures that all committed changes persist within the database, even in the event of a system failure. If a transaction has started, but is interrupted by a system failure, the transaction is guaranteed to be rolled back. Additionally, if system failure occurs following a commit of a transaction, that transaction is guaranteed to exist when the system is brought back online. SQL Server, and most DBMSes, uses the transaction log to ensure durability. Every transaction is written to the transaction log prior to the commit, which can then be used in the event of a system restart to reconcile changes to the data files. The transaction log writes are always written to disk, so unless you suffer a major disk failure, something outside the control of SQL Server, durability of transactions are always guaranteed.

Locking

Locking is used to maintain transaction isolation and control concurrent access to data. SQL Server uses two locking systems. Locks are acquired when you read and write data. Latches are used to control access to internal data structures as well as for portions of the index structure which we will discuss in chapter 12. The reason for having two different locking systems is latches allow lightweight, optimized control of internal resources where it isn't necessary to incur all of the overhead of a full lock.

> **More Info:** There is an even lighter weight type of lock used for access to internal resources which are normally expected to be idle. A spin lock is really nothing more than the code within SQL Server going into a retry loop when certain resources can't be locked. Instead of ceding control of the processor to another request, the process basically spins around a loop of attempting to lock a resource until that resource is released by another process, hence the term SPINLOCK. Spin locks are used to prevent SQL Server from context switching in those cases where the context switch would be more expensive that just spinning around in a loop trying to lock a resource. Spin locks are never acquired on user data and you have no control over them.

Lock Types

When locking data, SQL Server uses five locking types. Shared (S) and Exclusive (X) locks are the most common. Bulk update, schema modification, and schema stability locks are used for DDL changes and a few other special operations. Shared and exclusive locks can also have special behavior, sometimes referred to as separate lock types, of Intent (I) and Update (U).

A shared lock is taken out during a read operation while an exclusive lock is taken out during a write operation. As the name implies, you can have multiple shared locks on the same data concurrently. Shared locks are automatically acquired when you begin reading data and are normally held until you finish reading the data at which time they are automatically released. As long as a shared lock exists, any process attempting to change the data being read will be blocked.

An exclusive lock is automatically acquired when data is being changed. As the name implies, you can only have a single exclusive lock active on a piece of data at any time. Any process that needs either a shared or exclusive lock will be blocked and have to wait until the existing exclusive lock is released.

When you update data, SQL Server first has to find the row(s) being modified and then change the data. Sometimes referred to as an update lock, it is really just a behavior of shared and exclusive locking where the lock starts out as a shared lock on each row being modified. Once all of the rows to be modified have a shared lock acquired, SQL Server will convert the shared locks into exclusive locks prior to changing the data. Of course, if another connection has a shared lock on any row within the set, the conversion to an exclusive lock will be blocked until the exclusive lock can be acquired.

Locking occurs in the order in which requests are executed. The first request into the processing queue will acquire the necessary locks and all other processes will line up behind it. As long as no competing lock exists on a piece of data required by a request, you won't experience any blocking. When competing lock requests exist, the requests will stack up in a queue on a first in, first out basis.

> **Note:** Blocking is normal in a multi-user system and in a healthy system blocking will periodically come and go at a relatively rapid rate. As the volume of changes increases, you can expect to see more blocking, however, this is not necessarily a problem. You only have a concurrency problem that needs to be addressed when requests get blocked for an unacceptably long time.

When you execute a query, SQL Server first has to compile the query into a useable internal format. Part of that process is converting all of your object names into internal modifiers. The compilation process would be nearly impossible and could produce unexpected errors if you were allowed to modify objects during the compilation process. Schema stability locks are acquired on all of the objects affected by a query compilation event which will block any structure changes.

Likewise, you wouldn't want anyone attempting to read, write, or modify an object while you were changing the structure. Schema modification locks are acquired on objects that are being changed so that competing operations cannot interfere with the change.

> **Best Practice:** It should be obvious that while schema stability and schema modification locks prevent unexpected errors while object structures are being changed, you should make every effort to modify objects either when no one is using the object or during a time when it is least likely to impact a query.

BCP and BULK INSERT have a TABLOCK hint that can be specified which will cause a bulk update lock to be acquired. You can also set the *table lock on bulk load* property on the table and every BULK INSERT or BCP will automatically request a bulk update lock. A bulk update lock will lock the entire table during the bulk operation and prevent any other resources from accessing the table. If the table has indexes or another process has locks already acquired on the table, the bulk update lock will not be granted. While non-bulk operations will be prevented from accessing the table while a bulk update lock is acquired, other bulk operations can still load data to the table. This allows parallel bulk load operations to occur.

You cannot block yourself. Blocking only occurs across connections. Within the same connection, you acquire locks, but those locks don't block any other requests within the same connection.

Lock Structures

Information about each lock is maintained in a set of internal memory structures by a component called the *lock manager*. Lock information is maintained in memory, because the information does not have to be persisted through an instance restart. The memory allocated to the lock manager is an instance-wide resource which is shared by all connections.

Data can be locked at a row, page, and table level. When a lock is acquired, SQL Server determines the level of locking based on internal statistics which are maintained about the distribution of data in a table with respect to the query that you are running.

Each lock is identified by the resource that is being locked – row, page, table, etc. In addition to the resource being locked, state information about the lock is also maintained in a structure called a *lock block*. Each lock block consumes 128 bytes.

Since locks can exist independent of a process needing the lock, every lock must have an owner. SQL Server tracks information about the lock owner and a lock block in a 64 byte structure called a *lock owner block*.

Locks can be acquired on the same resource by multiple requests. You can also have multiple lock types on a single resource. This means you can have many lock blocks associated to a single resource and each lock block can have many lock owner blocks. To minimize the work required to check locks on a resource SQL Server maintains relationships between resources, lock blocks, and lock owners.

Each resource that has a lock granted or requested is hashed, assigned a slot number, and stored in a lock hash table, consuming 16 bytes. The lock block then references this slot number using a 15 byte reference. All lock blocks referencing the same hash slot are chained together. The lock blocks are also chained to any lock owner blocks.

> **Note:** On a 32 bit system, lock blocks consume 64 bytes and lock owner blocks consume 32 bytes. Since it is unlikely that you will be running SQL Server 2012 in a production environment on a 32 bit system, we will only consider 64 bit systems for all discussions in this book.

All of the lock blocks and lock owner blocks are created prior to use and allocated as needed to a transaction.

Static Allocation

If the number of locks is statically configured for the instance, when the instance starts, all of the lock blocks and lock owner blocks are created. For example, if you used *sp_configure* to set the locks to 5000, then 5000 lock blocks and 5000 lock owner blocks would be allocated. However, the amount of memory allocated statically for locks cannot exceed 25% of the committed buffer pool size, regardless of the number of locks that you configure for the system.

Dynamic Allocation

If you leave the locks value at the default of 0, which means to dynamically allocate as needed, SQL Server will create 2500 lock blocks and 5000 lock owner blocks on start up. If all of the existing locks are allocated to transactions, the lock manager will create additional lock blocks along with twice the number of lock owner blocks. In a dynamically configured instance, the number of lock owner blocks will always be twice the number of lock blocks. In the case of dynamic allocation, the lock manager is limited to 60% of the committed target size for the buffer manager.

Lock Escalation

If you were to acquire a single, shared lock on the HumanResources.Employee table, it would consume 16 bytes in the lock hash table, 128 bytes for the lock block, and 64 bytes for the lock owner block for a total memory consumption of 208 bytes for the single lock request. As you can see, acquiring large numbers of locks can consume significant amounts of memory. Additionally, since the amount of memory allocated to locks is limited, you could run out of locks available if every process were forced to only use row locks.

When the optimizer determines how to satisfy a query, the lock granularity is determined based on internal statistics the engine manages related to the distribution of the data you are querying. While usually accurate, this is only an "educated guess". The engine will only know how many locks are needed by actually acquiring the lock necessary to complete the request. If the engine determines that you are accessing far more data than originally estimated, the lock can be escalated. The lock escalation occurs in order to minimize the resources required by any transaction and to make a best effort to see that you do not run out of locks.

Lock escalation occurs from a row lock to a table lock or a page lock to a table lock. It is a common misunderstanding that SQL Server will escalate from a row to a page and then to a table. Lock escalation is done to reduce the resources consumed by locks while balancing concurrent access to the table. When a lock is escalated, the same type of lock is acquired on the less granular resource first and then the more granular locks are released.

> **Note:** You can also escalate locks to a partition. Partitioning will be covered in Chapter 14, "Partitioning Tables and Indexes".

Lock escalation occurs automatically as a request acquires locks as part of a read or a write operation. Lock escalation occurs on a statement by statement basis and not across multiple statements in a single batch. Lock escalation occurs based on two thresholds:

- When the number of locks held by a single statement exceeds 5000 on a single object, then the lock manager attempts to escalate the lock.
- When the amount of memory exceeds:
    - Static allocation – 40% of the memory reserved for lock resources
    - Dynamic allocation – 40% of the enabled memory

> **Note:** If you have a partitioned table and have enabled escalation to a partition LOCK_ESCALATION = AUTO, then locks can be escalated from a row/page to a partition and partition locks will not be later escalated to a table lock. We will discuss table partitioning in Chapter 14.

Just because you have passed a threshold, does not mean your locks will be escalated. A lock has to be first requested and granted on the larger resource (partition or table), before the less granular locks can be released. If a competing lock is already acquired on the larger resource, the escalation request fails. For example, if Request 1 has acquired exclusive locks on 5000 rows while at the same time Request 2 has shared or exclusive locks on a different set of rows, Request 1 cannot escalate to an exclusive lock on the table. If the escalation request fails, the lock manager will continue allocating the granular locks (row/page) and will only re-attempt to escalate every additional 1250 locks granted to the same object.

The reason that SQL Server escalates directly from a row/page lock to a table lock is to minimize the resources needed. If an escalation occurred from a row to a page and then a page to a table, you could wind up acquiring 5000 row locks, escalate those to hundreds or even thousands of page locks, continue acquiring page locks and again exceed the 5000 threshold, and have to escalate to a table lock. This wastes valuable time and lock manager resources, so SQL Server is configured to escalate locks aggressively in order to minimize the impact of the lock infrastructure.

Intent Locks

When locks are acquired, SQL Server keeps track of the type of lock and the resource that is locked such as the table, page, and/or row. When a new lock request occurs, a check is made against the lock information to determine if a competing lock is already acquired on the resource. Due to the granularity of a lock, this poses a potential issue. If one request already has an exclusive lock on a row and another request wants an exclusive lock on the page that the row is on, how would SQL Server know that the exclusive page lock should be blocked until the exclusive row lock has been released?

When attempting to acquire a page lock, SQL Server could retrieve the IDs for all of the rows on the page and compare those to the locks already granted to determine if any of the rows on the page has a competing lock. While this might sound like a reasonable idea, what about needing to acquire a lock on several hundred or thousand pages? Consider what would have to happen if the request wanted to take out a table level lock. Having to retrieve the IDs of all of the more granular level resources to determine if a lock can be granted would quickly become prohibitive.

To get around this problem, SQL Server uses an Intent (I) lock to indicate that a lock has been acquired on a more granular resource. SQL Server can then simply do an exact match on the resource that the lock is being requested for to determine if any competing locks already exist. For example, if a request had an exclusive lock on row 42 of page 98 in the Customers.Customer table, SQL Server would log the X lock on row 42, an IX lock on page 98, and an IX lock on the Customers.Customer table. If a resource were requesting a lock on either page 98 or the Customers.Customer table, with very little effort, SQL Server could determine that the request had to be blocked, because any lock on either page 98 or the Customers.Customer table would be incompatible with the exclusive lock on row 42.

The following table describes the locks that you can encounter.

Lock	Description
Shared (S)	Acquired for reads and blocks writes
Exclusive (X)	Acquired for writes and blocks reads and writes
Update (U)	Acquired for updates – works like an S lock during the read phase and an X lock during the write phase
Schema Stability (Sch-S)	Acquired during query compilation – prevents structure changes
Schema Modification (Sch-M)	Acquired during structure changes – blocks all other operations
Bulk Update (BU)	Acquired during a bulk load with the TABLOCK hint, blocks other processes but allows multiple bulk loads
Intent Shared (IS)	Acquired at a page or table level, indicates that an S lock exists at a row or page level
Intent Exclusive (IX)	Acquired at a page or table level, indicates that an X lock exists at a row or page level
Intent Update (IU)	Acquired at a page or table level, indicates that a U lock exists at a row or page level
Shared with intent exclusive (SIX)	Process has an S lock as well as an IX lock
Shared with intent update (SIU)	Process has an S lock as well as an IU lock
Update with intent exclusive (UIX)	Process has a U lock as well as an IX lock

Lock Timeout

By default, a request with a competing lock request will be blocked until the competing lock has been released. If the competing lock is never released, the request will be blocked forever. To modify the default behavior, you can utilize the lock timeout setting.

When you execute the SET LOCK_TIMEOUT statement, a request will only wait for the specified number of milliseconds for a competing lock to be released. If the request is still blocked after the timeout period has expired, an error will be thrown and the statement will be aborted. The following code would set a 5 second timeout period.

```
SET LOCK_TIMEOUT 5000
```

Transaction Behaviors

Transactions can exhibit several behaviors which may or may not be desirable in your environment. The behaviors that you can have are: dirty reads, nonrepeatable reads, phantoms, and lost updates. Of these behaviors, only lost updates are undesirable in all cases. The remainder of the behaviors will depend upon your application requirements as to whether they are undesirable or not. You can control whether or not to allow a behavior by controlling the isolation level of your transactions, which we will discuss in the next section.

Dirty Reads

A dirty read occurs when a process is allowed to read data while another process is modifying the same data. If the change is subsequently rolled back, data could have been read in an inconsistent state. Dirty reads are neither good nor bad; it is up to you whether allowing dirty reads is acceptable. Consider a retail business with an e-commerce site which displays the inventory on hand to customers placing orders. When customers are browsing products, you really don't care whether the inventory being displayed is an exact value or an approximation. You would rather have an inventory on hand display that is slightly higher or lower than the actual value rather than wait for an exclusive lock to be cleared on the inventory from another customer ordering the item and your application then debiting the quantity on hand. However, you probably don't want to allow dirty reads to occur for an internal application which is used by a buyer to replenish inventory. You could have had a customer start to place an order for several thousand of an extremely expensive item only to realize that it is the wrong item and cancel the order. If the buyer were to be allowed to see the quantity on hand before the order transaction completes, you could end up with a glut of very expensive inventory on the shelf.

The process that is making the change doesn't have any control over whether dirty reads are allowed or not. You make the decision to allow dirty reads for any process that is reading data.

Lost Updates

A lost update occurs when two processes modify the same data to a different value. The first change is overwritten by the second change, thereby "losing" an update. For example, you could have 500 Cocobolo pen blanks in stock. You had a shipment of 3000 pen blanks come into the warehouse and for some reason another shipment of 1000 pen blanks were delivered to the corporate office. A receiving clerk who is filling in for the receptionist decides that he's going to add the new inventory so that it is available to customers for ordering and then take the shipment to the warehouse when he returns there in the afternoon. The warehouse manager and receiving clerk both open the inventory management application at the same time and pull a value of 500 for the current inventory. The warehouse manager updates the value to 3500 and saves the new inventory. The receiving clerk then updates the value to the 1500 that he thinks should be there, which results in the shipment of 3000 pen blanks being lost.

Lost updates are undesirable in any application and there isn't anything you can implement in SQL Server to prevent a lost update. The prevention of lost updates has to be handled by your applications, which is yet another reason why users shouldn't be connecting directly to tables in a database and directly manipulating data with either T-SQL or applications like Access. You can build logic into your application to detect if a value has changed since it was read prior to allowing an update using a variety of methods. Two of those methods we covered in chapter 7 – change tracking and change data capture. Another method would be to simply add a DATETIME column to hold the last time the row was modified and then check this value against the value when you retrieved the row to determine if another change has occurred since you read the data.

Nonrepeatable Reads

When a process reads the same data more than once inside a single transaction, you produce a behavior called a nonrepeatable read. A nonrepeatable read occurs when another process changes data between the read operations within the transaction.

For example, a buyer is reviewing the inventory on hand for 7MM Slimline pens as part of placing orders for raw materials and notes that there are 355 currently in stock. While the buyer's transaction is still open, the nightly process runs which updates the inventory on hand with the 10,000 7MM Slimline pens which arrived at the warehouse this afternoon. The buyer then re-reads the inventory for 7MM Slimline pens and sees that the value is now 10,355. This is a nonrepeatable read since the value for the inventory on hand changed from 355 to 10,355 during the transaction.

Phantom Reads

Up to this point, we have only dealt with simple transactions where you only executed a single statement. A transaction can consist of multiple statements and be open for an extended period of time, although it is not recommended to create long running transactions since you will introduce severe blocking problems in your database. A phantom occurs when the number of rows you previously read changes within the same transaction.

As an example of a phantom, you could be preparing a list of customers in Texas for a special promotional offer. You start a transaction and retrieve the list of customers in Texas and then perform some additional processing to prepare the list. Meanwhile a new customer in Texas has created an account, which wasn't part of your original query. After performing all of the other processing required, you recheck the list of customers in Texas and now have a new entry appear that wasn't there before. The new customer would be considered a phantom, because running the same query twice in the same transaction produced a different set of rows.

Transaction Isolation Levels

SQL Server 2012 has five isolation levels to allow you to customize transaction behavior. Isolation levels control the scope and duration with which locks are held and can affect both read and write operations, although read operations are more affected since it is possible to read data while it is being changed but not possible for a change to occur while another process is changing a row.

In addition to the five isolation levels, SQL Server also provides a database property which is applied to all transactions in the database which can further modify locking behavior. While we will briefly cover snapshot isolation level and the read committed snapshot property in this section, a more detailed discussion will be held until the section on the version store.

Read Uncommitted

Read uncommitted allows you to read data that has not been committed. As such, read uncommitted allows all of the transaction behaviors to occur – lost updates, dirty reads, phantoms, and nonrepeatable reads. Under read uncommitted SQL Server does not attempt to acquire shared locks, so no blocking occurs.

Read uncommitted can also have a side effect of either reading data twice or not at all. As we discussed in Chapter 6, pages are allocated to tables an extent at a time. The page numbers in each extent do not have to be in order. The storage engine will maintain a doubly linked list of page pointers that allows you to transit from one page to another in a table. This has the effect of having two possible transit paths through a table. You can either follow the page pointers, a logical order scan, or you can scan the pages in page order, an allocation order scan.

Under read uncommitted, SQL Server will determine which scan method uses the least resources. However, if an allocation order scan is selected, you can read a row more than once or even miss rows.

For example, you begin scanning the Orders table and read part way through the table. While your process is reading data, someone comes in and changes the OrderDate on one of the orders you already read that causes it to move to a higher page number which you haven't already scanned. Your process then moves through the higher number page to read the row whose OrderDate was changed, causing your result set to have more orders than actually existed. Likewise, if a row was moved from a higher number page, before it was read, to a lower number page, after it was read, you can miss data in your result set.

You would use read uncommitted in those cases where exact results are not necessary such as doing sales trend analysis or retrieving the current quantity on hand for an e-commerce application.

Read Committed

The default option in SQL Server 2012, the read committed isolation level prevents dirty reads. When a read operation encounters an exclusive lock, the operation is blocked until the exclusive lock has been released. Additionally, the request will take out shared locks on all rows, pages, and tables that are being read, which will block exclusive locks from being acquired.

> **Note:** For simplicity, we will only reference exclusive locks. If an exclusive lock will be blocked or cause blocking, so will a bulk insert or schema modification lock. Exclusive locks are always held for the duration of the transaction in case a ROLLBACK is issued. So, when we talk about the duration of locks being held in a transaction, we are always referring to shared locks.

Under read committed isolation, shared locks are held only for as long as it takes to read the data. Once the data has been read, the lock can be released, even if the process still needs to read other data. For example, if you acquire shared locks on a set of rows, as soon as each row is read the shared lock on that row is released even though the request hasn't read all of the rows required yet.

While dirty reads are not allowed, you can still have lost updates, phantoms, and nonrepeatable reads.

Repeatable Read

Repeatable read prevents nonrepeatable reads from occurring by holding shared locks for the duration of a transaction. Once a COMMIT or ROLLBACK is issued, all shared locks are released. Since the shared locks are held, subsequent read operations in the same transaction are guaranteed to read the same values. However, you will be holding shared locks for a much longer time than with read committed, which can lead to concurrency issues.

Even though locks are held for the duration of the transaction, repeatable read will still allow phantoms.

Serializable

Serializable is the most restrictive isolation level and prevents all of the transaction behaviors mentioned. As the name implies, *serializable* serializes access to a set of data, holding all locks until the completion of the transaction. Multiple read operations in the transaction will always return the same data set.

A phantom is a new row which was introduced to a result set. The interesting side effect is that in order to accomplish the prevention of phantoms, read serializable has to be able to lock data that actually doesn't exist in the table yet. For example, if we are reading the list of customers in Texas, in order to prevent a phantom, SQL Server has to lock all data which would produce a customer in Texas. To enforce this lock, SQL Server uses one of two different methods. If an index exists on the column(s) in the query criteria, SQL Server will acquire a key range lock on the index to prevent the introduction of a row that would produce a phantom. If an index does not exist on the column(s) in the query criteria or you are reading the entire table, SQL Server will acquire a table level lock.

Snapshot

Snapshot isolation was introduced to allow read and write operations to not conflict with each other while also preventing dirty reads, nonrepeatable reads, and phantoms. Like any isolation level, an exclusive lock will always block another exclusive lock, because allowing more than one request to change the same data at the same time would produce inconsistent results.

Since snapshot isolation level ensures that exclusive locks can't block read operations or that shared locks can't block write operations. If SQL Server were to accomplish this by simply ignoring locking, as happens with read uncommitted, read operations would be able to view data that had not been committed yet, which is not allowed by the snapshot isolation level. So, to accomplish the requirements of snapshot isolation level, SQL Server uses the only other alternative – copies. When a request running under snapshot isolation needs to read rows that are being modified, SQL Server makes a copy of the row as it existed before the modifying transaction started, a row version, and writes it to a version store in the tempdb database. The request then uses this prior version to satisfy the read quest. Likewise, when a process needs to modify rows that are being read, SQL Server creates a row version for any read operation such that it is always reading data as it existed prior to the data modification, thereby preventing phantoms and non-repeatable reads.

Key Locks

In addition to the key range locks discussed above which are acquired under READ SERIALIZABLE isolation level, SQL Server can also acquire key locks on individual keys under read committed, repeatable read, and snapshot. Instead of locking actual rows of data by default, it is more efficient to locate index keys for the rows concerned and lock the index keys instead. If the table has a clustered index, you will see key locks acquired on the lead level of the index, which are also the actual data rows. If the table does not have a clustered index, you will see key locks acquired on the lead level of a non-clustered index along with row locks on the actual rows of data.

View Lock Information

You can view lock information by querying sys.dm_tran_locks. This management view lists all of the locks currently held within the entire instance, so you will want to be careful when querying this view on an instance with a lot of activity. Usually, you are going to be looking for lock information for a particular database and object such as a table or index.

The first set of columns in the view show the resource being locked such as the database, object, and type of lock. The second group of columns contains information about the session requesting the lock such as the session ID, status of the lock request, and how many times the lock request has been made.

The information contained in sys.dm_tran_locks is used by the Lock Manager to determine whether a lock can be granted. The process used to make the determination was described earlier in the lock granularity section.

In addition to all of the shared, exclusive, update, and intent locks acquired on keys and data, you will also see locks acquired at a database level. Every session that is using a database will have a shared lock on the database recorded in sys.dm_tran_locks. When you execute a command which requires exclusive access to the database such as DROP DATABASE, RESTORE, and ALTER DATABASE, the process will be blocked if any entry exists for the database.

> **Best Practice:** It is very common for your DBA to be attempting to make changes to a database only to be stopped because the database is in use. I've watched DBAs then go off to do a search to try to find a script that will tell them who is using a database. Many even fall back on executing sp_who or sp_who2, which is a leftover from the very early days of SQL Server; and scanning through pages of results trying to find that one connection to the database they need to manage. The proper way to figure this out is the same way that SQL Server determines if the database is in use. You simply query sys.dm_tran_locks for the database you are interested in.

Exercise 1: Reading data using Repeatable Read

In order to get consistent results, please make sure all other connections to the ChampionValleyPens database have been closed.

1. Open a new query window and execute the following code:

    ```
    USE ChampionValleyPens;
    SET TRANSACTION ISOLATION LEVEL REPEATABLE READ;
    BEGIN TRANSACTION;
    SELECT * FROM Products.SKU
    WHERE SKU LIKE 'CUSTOM-FINISH%';
    SELECT resource_type, resource_description,  request_mode, request_type,
    request_status
    FROM sys.dm_tran_locks
    WHERE resource_database_id = DB_ID(DB_NAME());
    COMMIT TRANSACTION;
    ```

You should have returned 1 row of data from the table along with four locks granted. The first row will be the shared database lock you acquired due to the USE <database> command. The other three rows are due to the read of the single row. Because the Products.SKU table has a clustered index on the SKU column, you see a shared lock granted with a resource type of KEY instead of a row lock (resource type = RID). The remaining two locks are intent locks. You placed an IS lock on the page which contained the SKU for the custom finish as well as the Products.SKU table. You are able to view the lock information, because locks are held until the end of the transaction for the repeatable read isolation level.

Exercise 2: Reading data using Read Serializable

1. Execute the following code:

    ```
    USE ChampionValleyPens;
    SET TRANSACTION ISOLATION LEVEL SERIALIZABLE;

    BEGIN TRANSACTION;
    SELECT * FROM Products.SKU
    WHERE SKU LIKE 'CUSTOM-FINISH%';
    SELECT resource_type, resource_description,  request_mode, request_type,
    request_status
    FROM sys.dm_tran_locks
    WHERE resource_database_id = DB_ID(DB_NAME());
    COMMIT TRANSACTION;
    ```

The only difference in this query is that we changed from REPEATABLE READ to SERIALIZABLE for the isolation level. You see the same shared lock on the database as well as the intent shared lock on both the page and table. New inside of this result is the RangeS-S lock. The range lock is a key range lock that locks the keys that span the row being returned. In the Products.SKU table, this locks the range of keys from CRYSTALPOLISH-8OZ through CUSTOM-PLATING-AG. The range locks ensure that a new row can't be added to the result set if the SELECT runs again within the transaction. By locking the keys on either side of the key being returned, you will not be able to introduce a row with a SKU between the value of CRYSTALPOLISH-8OZ or CUSTOM-FINISH e.g. CRYSTALPOLISH-16OZ. You also will not be able to introduce a value between CUSTOM-FINISH and CUSTOM-PLATING-AG e.g. CUSTOM-PLATING. Even though neither of these values would be returned by the SELECT statement, the key range lock will still prevent insertion of these values until the serializable transaction has been committed.

Exercise 3: Modifying a row

1. Execute the following code to modify the Products.SKU table

   ```
   USE ChampionValleyPens;
   SET TRANSACTION ISOLATION LEVEL READ COMMITTED;
   BEGIN TRANSACTION;
   UPDATE Products.SKU
   SET Price = Price * 1.1
   WHERE SKU LIKE 'CUSTOM-FINISH%';
   SELECT resource_type, resource_description,  request_mode, request_type,
   request_status
   FROM sys.dm_tran_locks
   WHERE resource_database_id = DB_ID(DB_NAME());
   ROLLBACK TRANSACTION;
   ```

While you can't view locks in READ COMMITTED isolation level by the method we've been using to show the contents of sys.dm_tran_locks because shared locks are released as soon as the data is read, you can view the locks for any DML statement. Exclusive locks are always held until the transaction is committed or rolled back. Just like the SELECT in REPEATABLE READ isolation, we are locking the key for the row that is being modified as well as the page the row is on and the object that the row is in. Since this is a modification, you are seeing exclusive locks acquired on the row along with intent exclusive locks on the page and table. The reason that you don't see a shared/intent shared lock for the UPDATE statement is because by the time you read the lock information, the shared lock has been escalated to an exclusive/intent exclusive lock.

Through this small number of exercises, in addition to retrieving lock information and seeing the locks that are acquired, you should have learned several other items:

- Locks are constantly being acquired and released on any instance that has activity.
- Locks are being acquired and released very rapidly.
- A single query can acquire a very large number of locks, spanning multiple objects.
- You should always target your request for lock information to as short of a list of objects as possible.
- Locking is normal and desired, however holding locks for a long time will create problems.
- By the time you retrieve lock information, the actual set of locks acquired has probably changed.
- If the lock information is still the same 5 seconds later, you very likely have one or more applications that need to be re-written.

Deadlocks

Locks are granted on a first come, first served basis and under most circumstances, any blocking that occurs simply introduces small delays in processing a request. However, you can have a situation created where it becomes impossible to grant locks between a pair of requests, because each request is blocking the other. This situation is called a deadlock and SQL Server has a mechanism to resolve deadlocks when they occur.

Consider the following example:

- Request 1 acquires an exclusive lock on EmployeeID 1 in order to make a change.
- Request 2 acquires an exclusive lock on EmployeeID 2 in order to make a change.
- With the transaction still open, request 1 then requests a shared lock on EmployeeID 1.
- With the transaction still open, request 2 then requests a shared lock on EmployeeID 2.

The shared lock from request 1 is blocked, because request 2 has an exclusive lock on the row. The shared lock from request 2 is also blocked, because request 1 has an exclusive lock on the row. Neither transaction can complete, because request 1 and request 2 are blocking each other in such a way that prevents the locks from being resolved.

Without a means to deal with this deadlock scenario, request 1 and request 2 would remain blocked forever. So, SQL Server implements a deadlock resolution and terminates one of the requests, rolling back all changes the request had made. The request that is terminated is referred to as the deadlock victim.

By default, the deadlock victim is chosen based on the request that is least expensive to rollback. For example, if request 1 has changed 100 rows of data and request 2 has only changed 1 page of data, request 2 will be chosen as the deadlock victim because it is cheaper to rollback the change to the single page than it is to rollback changes to 100 individual rows.

You can influence the selection of the deadlock victim by setting the DEADLOCK_PRIORITY of a request. The deadlock priority accepts a value from -10 to 10. You can also specify the value as LOW, NORMAL, or HIGH. LOW corresponds to a value of -5, NORMAL to a value of 0, and HIGH to a value of 10. 0 is the default value for a session if the deadlock priority is not explicitly set.

When two sessions are deadlocked, the session with the lowest value for the deadlock priority will be chosen as the deadlock victim. If both sessions have the same deadlock priority, then the deadlock victim will be chosen based on the least expensive to rollback.

In most cases, the cause of the deadlock is simply bad timing. If an application receives a 1205 error, the first thing that should be done is for the request to simply be re-submitted to SQL Server. It is very likely that the re-submission will succeed the second time, so there isn't any reason to alarm a user of your application by displaying an error message. If the re-submission also fails, then you likely have a much bigger problem on your hands and many users are probably being impacted by repeated deadlocks.

There are several ways to fix an application so that it does not produce deadlocks:

- Always access tables in the same order, which would prevent deadlocks from occurring across tables.
    - Keep your transactions as short as possible.
- Change your transactions to use snapshot isolation, which ensures that readers and writers do not block each other.
- If you can't modify the application to use snapshot isolation level, then you could turn on the READ_COMMITTED_SNAPSHOT property of the database to force all requests running under the read committed isolation level to behave as if they were running under the snapshot isolation level.

Accessing tables in the same order for all transactions will not fix an issue where a deadlock occurs internally in a table, which we will demonstrate in Exercise 4 below. If your transactions are running under serializable or repeatable read, the only way to prevent deadlocks from occurring is to ensure that tables are always accessed in the same order and you do not attempt to read data that the transaction is not modifying.

Deadlock detection is not an immediate process. Approximately every 5 seconds, a system thread called the lock monitor will run and scan the lock blocks looking for cycles which indicate a deadlock has occurred. A deadlock victim will then be chosen based on the rules defined above. Once a deadlock occurs, the scan interval is reduced, and the lock monitor goes back to sleep. If subsequent deadlocks are detected, the scan interval will continue to be reduced to a minimum value of 100 milliseconds. If a deadlock is not detected on the next scan, the scan interval will be increased up to a maximum of 5 seconds. So, the lock monitor will run scans at a frequently ranging from 100 milliseconds to 5 seconds and as the number of deadlocks increases, a deadlock victim is chosen more rapidly.

Exercise 4: Producing a Deadlock

In the following exercise, you will produce a cycle deadlock on the HumanResources.Employee table. To ensure that the following exercise is not impacted by any other transaction in the ChampionValleyPens database, as well as to avoid confusion, commit any open transactions and close all query windows.

1. Open two new query windows, which will be referred to as request 1 and request 2 for the remainder of this exercise.

2. In request 1, execute the following code:
    ```
    USE ChampionValleyPens;
    SET TRANSACTION ISOLATION LEVEL READ COMMITTED;
    BEGIN TRANSACTION;
    UPDATE HumanResources.Employee
    SET MiddleInitial = 'D'
    WHERE EmployeeID = 1;
    ```

3. In request 2, execute the following code:

   ```
   USE ChampionValleyPens;
   BEGIN TRANSACTION;
   SET TRANSACTION ISOLATION LEVEL READ COMMITTED;
   UPDATE HumanResources.Employee
   SET MiddleInitial = 'J'
   WHERE EmployeeID = 2;
   ```

4. In request 2, execute the following code which should produce blocking:

   ```
   SELECT *
   FROM HumanResources.Employee
   WHERE EmployeeID = 1;
   ```

5. In request 1, execute the following code to close the cycle and produce a deadlock:

   ```
   SELECT *
   FROM HumanResources.Employee
   WHERE EmployeeID = 2;
   ```

Step 4 should have caused request 2 to become blocked waiting for the exclusive lock on EmployeeID 1 to be released. As soon as you executed the SELECT in step 5, you would have closed the loop by attempting to acquire a shared lock on the row that request 2 had exclusively locked. This would have produced the following error message for one of the requests in 5 seconds or less from the time you executed the SELECT on request 1:

```
Msg 1205, Level 13, State 51, Line 1
Transaction (Process ID 57) was deadlocked on lock resources with another process
and has been chosen as the deadlock victim. Rerun the transaction.
```

Row Versioning

Earlier in this chapter, we introduced the two possible concurrency models and have discussed pessimistic concurrency extensively. Now that we understand how locking prevents access to rows, optimistic concurrency should make more sense.

Prior to SQL Server 2005, the challenge in being able to utilize optimistic concurrency was that we had to allow transactions to read data which had not yet been committed. What if you only wanted to read committed data, but did not want writes and reads to block each other? A read cannot access data that is in the process of being changed; otherwise you would get inconsistent results. A read caused a write operation to be blocked to ensure that the write operation couldn't change data as it is being read. This catch-22 was solved by literally mimicking the way data was handled prior to computers.

Before we had computers, information would be printed out on a variety of materials such as stone, feathers, animal hides, and various forms of paper. The information, in physical form, would be distributed to the person requesting the data. If the data needed to change after it was printed, a new copy of the information would be created. The old version still existed and the requester could read it without stopping someone else from changing the information. Since the requester couldn't read the new information as it was being changed as the physical copy wasn't yet complete, none of the changing data was accessible.

This process of making copies of data was added in SQL Server 2005 and everyone in the SQL Server world hailed this as a novel new feature. Oracle had been beating the SQL Server world over the head for years since this method of data copying had existed in their DBMS as the default isolation level since the earliest versions. Yet, as I said in chapter 1, there isn't a single feature found in a DBMS that didn't already exist in some kind of physical form millennia before computers were even invented.

The process that started out with stone tablets is now manifested in SQL Server with a feature called row versioning. When a process is making changes, a copy of the prior committed version is made so that any transactions reading data can use the copy without seeing any changes which had not yet been committed. Since these transactions are reading a copy of the row, locks aren't acquired which would block modifications from occurring.

> **Note:** Row versioning applies when UPDATE and DELETE operations are performed. It has no effect on INSERT operations since a prior version of a row does not exist when you are inserting data.

Isolation Levels

Row versioning is an internal process that is invoked when a transaction runs under one of two isolation levels – read committed or snapshot.

Under the default isolation level of read committed, transactions will run under snapshot isolation if the database owner has set the READ_COMMITTED_SNAPSHOT property of the database on. Once this option is turned on, any transaction running under read committed isolation will no longer cause blocking between readers and writers. Read operations will access prior versions of a row. However, the duration of this effect is the same as any read committed transaction. The prior versions of a row only apply on a statement by statement basis, not at the transaction level. Therefore, your transaction could read one version of a row and at a later time read a different version of the row since any read committed transaction will always access the most recent version of a row. This is why the READ_COMMITTED_SNAPSHOT property is referred to as statement level snapshot isolation.

Row versioning also occurs when you explicitly change the isolation level to SNAPSHOT. Before snapshot transactions are allowed in the database, the database owner must first enable the ALLOW_SNAPSHOT_ISOLATION database option as shown below:

```
ALTER DATABASE ChampionValleyPens
    SET ALLOW_SNAPSHOT_ISOLATION ON;
```

If snapshot isolation has not been enabled for a database, changing your connection's isolation level will not result in an error. However, if you attempt to execute any read or write operation under snapshot isolation you will receive the following error message:

```
Msg 3952, Level 16, State 1, Line 1
Snapshot isolation transaction failed accessing database 'ChampionValleyPens'
because snapshot isolation is not allowed in this database. Use ALTER DATABASE to
allow snapshot isolation.
```

Version Store

Row versions are stored in a special table called the version store in the tempdb database. Once snapshot capabilities are enabled for the database, any update or delete operation will generate row versions in tempdb for all rows affected by the data modification, regardless of whether anyone is currently reading the rows being modified. Row versions are generated, because SQL Server doesn't know when a read operation will start, so it has to ensure that the prior version of the row is accessible at any time.

Since the generation of row versions can have a significant impact on the size and activity in tempdb, along with transaction performance in the source database, snapshot behaviors are not enabled by default. A DBA is required to explicitly enable snapshot capabilities because of the possibility of performance degradation along with additional capacity planning for tempdb.

The version store is global to the instance, so each row version stored in tempdb contains a column corresponding to the database where the row originated. The other piece of information identifying the row is a transaction sequence number, XSN.

An XSN is a sequential number that starts at 1 and increments by 1. Each database has its own XSN sequence, with each starting at 1. Any transaction that modifies data or read data in a snapshot mode will be assigned an XSN. Each time the database is restarted, the XSN is reset back to 1.

Beyond the additional space required in tempdb, row versioning requires 14 bytes of storage per row. The storage required is broken down into two sections. The first section is 8 bytes in length and tracks the file, page, and row location in the version store for the most recent version created. The remaining 6 bytes stores the XSN.

When you enable snapshot capabilities, SQL Server does not go through every existing row in a database and add 14 bytes as this would be prohibitive and not make any sense. The only time a read operation cares about a row version is if the row had been modified. If the row was never modified, there isn't any need to carry 14 bytes of additional storage for the row.

Any new rows added to a table after snapshot capabilities have been enabled will include a 14 byte row version consisting of all zeros since new rows aren't visible to any snapshot transaction until the row has been committed. Any update of a row will add a 14 byte row version and write the row to the version store. Any delete operation will write a row to the version store and leave a ghost record in the row with a pointer to the row version. The ghost record will be cleaned up via a background process just like any other ghost record.

> **Note:** If you remove snapshot capabilities from the database, the same process will occur to remove the extra 14 bytes for the row version. Each time you modify a row that contains version information; the extra 14 bytes will be removed.

If you recall from chapter 6 where we discussed page layouts, each row allows a maximum of 8060 bytes. You might be wondering what happens when you create a row that is 8060 bytes in length, enable snapshot capabilities, and then update the row. The row is already 8060 bytes in length, so you might assume that the update would fail because the additional 14 bytes of space is not available.

On a page with 8192 available bytes, you have 96 bytes for the header, 8060 bytes for the row, and

2 bytes per row for the offset, leaving 34 bytes unaccounted for. These 34 bytes are designated for "future use". Row versioning is one of the "future use" capabilities. It would create a very bad user experience if someone were to enable row versioning and updates suddenly started failing, which is why an 8K page will always have a small amount of space reserved so that future capabilities will succeed when enabled.

You will need to account for the additional 14 bytes of storage space per row in most cases. There are two exceptions if you have a table with very large rows. If you can only fit 1 or 2 rows per page, then you won't see any added effect on space consumption, because the 14 or 28 bytes of additional storage needed is less than the 34 bytes of reserved space. Anything beyond 2 rows per page will produce page splitting and/or variable length data being moved to row overflow pages if the page size will be exceeded.

Each row stores the most recent XSN, but a single row can be modified multiple times with different read operations needing different versions of the row. Each version is written to the version store and a linked list is maintained between each of the row versions. Each read needing to access a row version will first read the XSN from the row. The XSN from the row is then located in the version store.

If multiple versions exist, the chain of row versions will be scanned to find the version which is valid for the read operation, which is based on the XSN of the read request. The version chain is traversed to find the maximum XSN which is less than the XSN of the read operation.

Version Store management

Management of the version store is automatic via a background thread. Once per minute a cleanup thread scavenges the version store to remove versions which are no longer valid. Under normal circumstances, the automated cleanup routine should keep your version store to a stable size.

Beyond the cleanup process, the only other management you need to do for the version store is to manage the space allocated to tempdb. Keep in mind that tempdb affects the entire SQL Server instance. If you run out of space in tempdb, the entire instance can become unusable, making the management of space in tempdb one of the most critical tasks of an administrator.

The following are a set of performance counters under the SQLServer:Transactions object that you can use to monitor the version store:

- Free Space in tempdb (KB) – The amount of free space in tempdb.
- Longest Transaction Running Time – The number of seconds for the longest running snapshot transaction.
- Version Cleanup Rate (KB/s) – The rate at which version store space is being cleaned up
- Version Generation Rate (KB/s) – The rate at which version store space is being consumed
- Version Store Size (KB) – The total size of the version store

Having transactions with a long running time means versions are being kept in the version store longer than necessary. Keeping snapshot transactions short allows the versions to be cleaned up more quickly and also reduces the possibility of long version chains due to multiple changes to the same row.

Exercise 5: Transactions Running Under Read Committed Snapshot

In the following exercise, you will observe the behavior of the generation of row versions and the impact on row size when the read committed snapshot property is enabled for a database.

1. Open a new query window and execute the following code to create a new database along with a table that has a fixed length row which is the maximum size allowed. You'll recall from chapter 6 that a row with all fixed length columns will consume 7 bytes of space for the row header, which results in a maximum size of 8053 bytes for the row.

    ```
    CREATE DATABASE Test;
    GO
    USE Test;
    GO

    CREATE TABLE dbo.Fixed
    (ID    INT         NOT NULL,
     Val1  CHAR(49)    NOT NULL,
     Val2  CHAR(8000)  NOT NULL,
     CONSTRAINT pk_Fixed PRIMARY KEY (ID));
    ```

2. Execute the following query to review the allocation information for the table:

    ```
    SELECT OBJECT_NAME(OBJECT_ID) name, partition_id, partition_number, rows,
        allocation_unit_id, type_desc, total_pages
    FROM sys.partitions p INNER JOIN sys.allocation_units a ON p.partition_id =
    a.container_id
    WHERE OBJECT_ID = OBJECT_ID('dbo.Fixed');
    ```

3. Execute the following code to insert a row into the table, verify that only 1 page is allocated to the table, and that the row size is 8060 bytes. You'll recall from chapter 6 that the previous and next page will both be set to 0:0 when only a single page exists for the table.

    > **Note:** The 2nd parameter of DBCC PAGE is the file number and the 3rd parameter is the page number. The sys_fn_PhysLocFormatter function will return the file number and page number for the row you inserted. Mine happens to be 1:274. File Number = 1 and Page Number = 274. Yours might be different. You'll need to modify the parameters to match your database.

    ```
    INSERT INTO dbo.Fixed
    VALUES (1,'a','a');
    GO

    SELECT sys.fn_PhysLocFormatter(%%physloc%%), *
    FROM dbo.Fixed;
    GO
    DBCC TRACEON(3604);
    DBCC PAGE('Test',1,274,1);
    ```

4. Review the m_prevPage, m_nextPage, and Record Size information in the page output.

5. Scroll down to the bottom of the output where the last row of the output should be as follows:

    ```
    0000000000001F68:    20202020 20202020 20202020 20202020 20030000
    ```

6. Execute the following code to turn on the read committed snapshot database property and verify that the row is still the same size.

    ```
    USE master;
    GO
    ALTER DATABASE test
    SET READ_COMMITTED_SNAPSHOT ON;
    GO
    USE test;
    GO

    SELECT sys.fn_PhysLocFormatter(%%physloc%%), *
    FROM dbo.Fixed;
    GO
    DBCC TRACEON(3604);
    DBCC PAGE('Test',1,274,1);
    ```

7. Now update the row and review the contents of the version store.

    ```
    UPDATE dbo.Fixed
    SET Val1 = 'b';
    GO

    SELECT * FROM sys.dm_tran_version_store;
    ```

8. Review the contents of the page to see that a 14 byte row version has been added to the end of the row.

    ```
    DBCC TRACEON(3604);
    DBCC PAGE('Test',1,274,1);
    GO

    0000000000001F7C:    51030000 01000000 d1020000 0000
    ```

9. If you wait approximately 1 minute from the time you run the UPDATE statement and then re-query sys.dm_tran_version_store, you will see that the row version has been removed by the cleanup process.

10. Execute the following code to remove the test database:

    ```
    USE master;
    GO
    DROP DATABASE test;
    ```

As you saw in the previous exercise, row versioning information is only added to existing rows when they are modified. Since we created a maximum sized row, the only way for the update operation to succeed was for SQL Server to consume 14 bytes of the page storage that was designated for "future use".

Finally, since we used the read committed snapshot property of a database, row versions are valid on a statement by statement basis. Once the statement completes, the row version can be removed from the version store if another process wasn't running a SELECT statement while the UPDATE was happening. In the following exercise, we'll see that row versions can stay around a lot longer under snapshot isolation if your transactions are not committed quickly.

Exercise 6: Transactions Running Under Snapshot Isolation

In the following exercise, you will enable snapshot transactions on the database and observe the effect on transactions.

1. Close all other query windows in order to avoid confusion and conflicts.
2. Open a new query window, which we will refer to as Q1 for this exercise, and turn on snapshot isolation by executing the following query:

    ```
    USE master;
    GO
    ALTER DATABASE ChampionValleyPens
    SET ALLOW_SNAPSHOT_ISOLATION ON;
    ```

3. Open a second query window, which we will refer to as Q2 for this exercise.
4. In Q1, execute the following code, ensuring that you do not commit or rollback the transaction:

    ```
    USE ChampionValleyPens;
    GO

    BEGIN TRAN;
    UPDATE HumanResources.Employee
    SET MiddleInitial = 'Z'
    WHERE EmployeeID = 1;

    SELECT *
    FROM sys.dm_tran_version_store;

    SELECT *
    FROM sys.dm_tran_active_snapshot_database_transactions;
    ```

5. Unless you've run other snapshot tests in the database, there should be only 1 row in the version store. Note the value in the transaction_sequence_num column for the single row in sys.dm_active_snapshot_database_transactions. Mine is 15.

6. In Q2, execute the following code, ensuring that you do not commit or rollback the transaction:

    ```
    USE ChampionValleyPens;
    GO
    SET TRANSACTION ISOLATION LEVEL SNAPSHOT;
    BEGIN TRAN;
    SELECT *
    FROM HumanResources.Employee
    WHERE EmployeeID = 1;

    SELECT *
    FROM sys.dm_tran_version_store;

    SELECT *
    FROM sys.dm_tran_active_snapshot_database_transactions;
    ```

7. The version store should only have a single row since only 1 update is active. You should now have 2 rows in sys.dm_tran_active_snapshot_database_transactions since 2 transactions are active. Notice that the second row has a value for first_transaction_sequence_number that points back to the transaction_sequence_num for the update transaction. You should also notice that you are seeing Steven D Silas, which is the previous version of the row since the update has not been committed. The value for the max_version_chained should be set to 1 since there is only 1 version currently active for the row.

8. Go back to Q1, commit the transaction, and observe the snapshot metadata.
   ```
   COMMIT TRAN;
   SELECT *
   FROM sys.dm_tran_version_store;

   SELECT *
   FROM sys.dm_tran_active_snapshot_database_transactions;
   ```
9. You should only be seeing a single transaction still active for the SELECT in Q2.
10. In Q1, modify the row again and observe the snapshot metadata:
    ```
    BEGIN TRAN;
    UPDATE HumanResources.Employee
    SET MiddleInitial = 'Y'
    WHERE EmployeeID = 1;

    SELECT *
    FROM sys.dm_tran_version_store;

    SELECT *
    FROM sys.dm_tran_active_snapshot_database_transactions;
    ```
11. Observe that the version store now has 2 rows in it since the read operation in Q2 is still running and still needs the first version.
12. Execute the following in Q2:
    ```
    BEGIN TRAN;
    SELECT *
    FROM HumanResources.Employee
    WHERE EmployeeID = 1;

    SELECT *
    FROM sys.dm_tran_version_store;

    SELECT *
    FROM sys.dm_tran_active_snapshot_database_transactions;
    ```
13. Note that the max_version_chain_traversed is now set to 2 meaning this transaction had to traverse 2 versions in the version store in order to find the version applicable to the transaction.
14. Go back to Q1, commit the previous update, and update the row again:
    ```
    COMMIT TRAN;
    BEGIN TRAN;
    UPDATE HumanResources.Employee
    SET MiddleInitial = 'D'
    WHERE EmployeeID = 1;

    SELECT *
    FROM sys.dm_tran_version_store;

    SELECT *
    FROM sys.dm_tran_active_snapshot_database_transactions;
    ```

15. Go to Q2 and execute another read of the row and observe that the max_version_chain_traveresed has again increased.

    ```
    BEGIN TRAN;
    SELECT *
    FROM HumanResources.Employee
    WHERE EmployeeID = 1;

    SELECT *
    FROM sys.dm_tran_version_store;

    SELECT *
    FROM sys.dm_tran_active_snapshot_database_transactions;
    ```
16. Commit all of the transactions in Q1 and Q2.

Transactions will remain in the version store for as long as a snapshot transaction needs the versions.

- If an UPDATE or DELETE is executed and committed before a SELECT operation needs to read the row, the version can be cleaned up during the next cleanup cycle since any SELECT statements run after the commit read from the actual data in the table.
- If a SELECT operation reads a row before the UPDATE or DELETE is executed, the row version will stay for as long as a SELECT operation needs the row version.

You may have noticed that in Q2, I used nested transactions, which caused us to read a middle initial of D every time we ran a SELECT. This was because the outer transaction was "holding our place" within the version chain and no matter how many levels we nest transactions; we would only see the row version valid for the outer transaction.

If you were to use separate query windows and hence separate transactions for a read operation following each UPDATE, each separate transaction would show a different state of the row. The max version chain traversed would still increase for every subsequent update operation as follows:

In Q1, execute the first update leaving the transaction open:

```
BEGIN TRAN;
UPDATE HumanResources.Employee
SET MiddleInitial = 'Z'
WHERE EmployeeID = 1;
```

In Q2, execute a read operation, keeping the transaction open:

```
SET TRANSACTION ISOLATION LEVEL SNAPSHOT;
BEGIN TRAN;
SELECT *
FROM HumanResources.Employee
WHERE EmployeeID = 1;

SELECT *
FROM sys.dm_tran_version_store;

SELECT *
FROM sys.dm_tran_active_snapshot_database_transactions;
```

In Q1, commit the update, and update the row again:

```
COMMIT TRAN;
BEGIN TRAN;
UPDATE HumanResources.Employee
SET MiddleInitial = 'Y'
WHERE EmployeeID = 1;
```

In Q2, run the same SELECT statement, still keeping the transaction open:

```
SELECT *
FROM HumanResources.Employee
WHERE EmployeeID = 1;

SELECT *
FROM sys.dm_tran_version_store;

SELECT *
FROM sys.dm_tran_active_snapshot_database_transactions;
```

You should see the max version chain traversed increase to 2 in Q2. Run the same SELECT in Q3 and observe that you are now a middle initial of Z and the max version chained for Q3 is 1.

```
SET TRANSACTION ISOLATION LEVEL SNAPSHOT;
BEGIN TRAN;
SELECT *
FROM HumanResources.Employee
WHERE EmployeeID = 1;

SELECT *
FROM sys.dm_tran_version_store;

SELECT *
FROM sys.dm_tran_active_snapshot_database_transactions;
```

In Q1, commit the transaction, and update the row a 3rd time:

```
COMMIT TRAN;
BEGIN TRAN;
UPDATE HumanResources.Employee
SET MiddleInitial = 'D'
WHERE EmployeeID = 1;
```

Going back to Q2 and re-running the SELECT, without committing the transaction, you will now see a max version chained of 3. Q3 will show a max version chained of 2. Executing the same SELECT in Q4 will show a max version chained of 1. Remember to commit any open transactions you have.

You should have also see versions stacking up in the version store. The longer you keep transactions open, the longer versions will stay in the version store. You can also get escalating performance degradation due to an increase version chain traversal. This was on a simple test environment. Your production environment will be producing row versions at a much higher rate, so you need to be very aware of how your transactions behave and how long they are open.

> **Caution:** You might be thinking that creating nested transactions for SELECT statements or holding transactions open for a long time doesn't apply to you. You are forgetting the default behavior of the code frameworks that most applications are built on. These frameworks will automatically issue a BEGIN TRAN before every command that you execute. If you then explicitly execute a BEGIN TRAN, you might think you only have a single transaction when in fact you have a nested transaction. You might commit your transaction, but the framework might still be holding its transaction open, causing row versions to continue to be held as well as producing other, undesirable, locking side effects.

Snapshot Conflicts

While snapshot isolation allows you to read the prior version of a row, there are two possibilities of conflicts which will throw an error and rollback a transaction.

Only rows in a table are versioned, not DDL changes. As long as a DDL operation does not produce a case where it would be impossible for an active snapshot transaction to avoid including the change, the DDL operation is allowed. For example, you can create a new table inside a snapshot transaction.

However consider the following scenario:

- Connection 1 starts a snapshot transaction and reads from TableA
- Connection 2 inserts a new row into TableA and commits it
- Connection 1 then attempts to create an index on TableA inside the snapshot transaction

The creation of the index would generate an error and not be allowed, because the snapshot transaction in connection 1 shouldn't see the newly inserted row. But, the creation of the index can't skip the new row that was inserted, so it would be forced to include a row that should not be visible to the snapshot transaction. The following scenario will also produce a snapshot conflict:

- Connection 1 starts a snapshot transaction and reads from TableA
- Connection 2 alters TableA and adds/removes/modifies a column
- Connection 1 attempts to read from TableA a second time

The second read on connection 1 would fail, because the table definition changed since the snapshot transaction started. This would force the snapshot transaction to read data that is in a state that shouldn't exist to the snapshot transaction.

The other way to produce a snapshot conflict is to introduce a lost update issue. A lost update can be produced by the following scenario:

- Connection 1 starts a snapshot transaction and reads row 1 from TableA
- Connection 2 starts a transaction and updates row 1 in TableA
- Connection 1 then attempts to update row 1 in TableA and is blocked by the exclusive lock in connection 2
- Connection 2 commits successfully

Connection 1 will receive error number 3960 because if the update in connection 1 were allowed to commit, the update from connection 2 would be wiped out and produce a lost update issue. Since lost updates are not allowed under snapshot isolation, the only possible result is an error and rollback of the conflicting transaction.

Summary

Transaction handling and the locking semantics associated with various isolation levels allow multiple users to concurrently access data while avoiding unintended side effects. Isolation levels control the duration with which locks are held in order to arbitrate access to data between read and write operations. Two write operations attempting to modify the same data or overlapping blocks of data will always block each other.

You can use the new snapshot capabilities to ensure that read operations are always looking at committed data, but do not block write operations. However, snapshot transactions incur a performance penalty due to having to maintain versions of rows in tempdb.

Chapter 9
Data Retrieval

> **Setup:** Please run the Chapter 9 Setup script in the companion files prior to starting the exercises in this chapter to ensure that your databases are at the correct starting point. Every exercise in this book assumes that you have created the c:\ChampionValleyPress\Data and c:\ChampionValleyPress\Log folders, contained databases are enabled, and this is the location of all of the data, log, and filestream files which will be used for this book. If you have chosen a different path, you will need to adjust the paths listed accordingly. Every setup script also assumes that you have enabled FILESTREAM access for the instance. When executing commands, it is assumed that you will change context to the appropriate database since understanding the contents of each database in this book is the same skill you will need for working with your databases. All scripts also assume you are using a default instance.

Through the previous 8 chapters, you learned how to install SQL Server, build a database, populate your database with data, and manage multi-user access. We've had a brief introduction to retrieving data and kept the data retrieval very simple. In this chapter and Chapter 10, we'll cover everything you need to know about retrieving data from your databases.

> **Note:** In almost all cases where we reference a table in this chapter, you can also use a view or a table expression. We'll cover table expressions in Chapter 10.

General Select Statement

At this point, you've been introduced to 6 commands to manipulate data, over a dozen to manipulate objects, and the T-SQL language has hundreds more commands that we have yet to cover. You have about 2 dozen data types to use in designing any database you can conceive of. Yet with the infinite ways to design tables and databases and the infinite ways that you might need to retrieve data, ANSI SQL as well as any variants such as SQL Server's T-SQL dialect has exactly one command to retrieve data.

The SELECT statement will probably be the most powerful and flexible command that you will ever encounter in a development language. The general syntax for a SELECT statement is as follows:

```
SELECT statement ::=
    [WITH <common_table_expression> [,...n]]
    <query_expression>
    [ ORDER BY { order_by_expression | column_position [ ASC | DESC ] }   [ ,...n ]
]
    [ COMPUTE    { { AVG | COUNT | MAX | MIN | SUM } ( expression ) } [ ,...n ]
  [ BY expression [ ,...n ] ]    ]
    [ <FOR Clause>]
    [ OPTION ( <query_hint> [ ,...n ] ) ];
```

```
<query expression> ::=
    { <query specification> | ( <query expression> ) }
    [ { UNION [ ALL ] | EXCEPT | INTERSECT }
        <query specification> | ( <query expression> ) [...n ] ]

<query specification> ::=
SELECT [ ALL | DISTINCT ]
    [TOP expression [PERCENT] [ WITH TIES ] ]
    < select_list >
    [ INTO new_table ]
    [ FROM { <table_source> } [ ,...n ] ]
    [ WHERE <search_condition> ]
    [ GROUP BY [ ALL ] group_by_expression [ ,...n ]
    [ WITH { CUBE | ROLLUP } ]      ]
    [ HAVING < search_condition > ]
```

The syntax specifications for every T-SQL command can be found in Books Online, BOL, and follow a compact set of conventions. Square brackets denote optional elements while curly braces denote sets of possible choices. Square brackets around a ,...n mean that you can have any number of that element in the statement. Angle brackets designate where you need to substitute an object or expression. Square brackets with two values separated by a pipe symbol designate two options, one of which has to be specified.

The general syntax above is an abbreviated version of the full syntax possible, but it is sufficient for our purposes at this point as it describes most of what we will be covering in this chapter. If you look carefully at the general syntax, you will note that virtually everything in a SELECT statement is optional. In fact, the only clause of a SELECT statement which is required is the SELECT clause. That means the most basic SELECT statement that you can run is:

```
SELECT 0;
```

> **Note:** This chapter will contain a significant amount of code. It would be helpful for you to execute the queries as we go along, inspect the results, and compare what you expected with the discussions in this chapter. I will be refraining from pasting extensive result sets into the chapter following the queries, due to the large number of pages it would consume. So, in lieu of me consuming 40 – 50 pages in this chapter just to display result sets, I am expecting that you will be executing these queries and reviewing them on your screen. Result sets may also be truncated in order to show the effect of the query referenced, so they won't necessarily exactly match the size of a result set or even the exact order if you run the corresponding query. However, the values in the result set will always match your database unless you have modified the data from the starting state defined at the beginning of the chapter.

Obviously, this returns a single row in the result set with a value of 0. If you want to specify character, date, time, or date/time data, you need to use single quotes. Most of your application development languages use double quotes for character/date/time constants, but T-SQL always uses single quotes. For example:

```
SELECT 1, 'character constant', '7/27/2008';
```

As noted previously, keywords in T-SQL are case insensitive, so the following are all valid:

```
SELECT 'Keywords are case insensitive';
select 'Keywords are case insensitive';
SeLeCt 'Keywords are case insensitive';
```

You might be asking, what is the point in writing a SELECT statement to return statically defined values? By themselves, SELECT statements like the ones shown above are completely worthless for an application. However, you will find the ability to include constants in the SELECT clause extremely useful and something that you will do repeatedly in your career. For example, how would you concatenate a first and last name or an address and format it so that it is valid without being able to add in a space where needed? This feature of a SELECT statement is one of the most useful capabilities for DBAs as well. You've already be introduced to the metadata information that SQL Server stores about every object. DBAs can use the metadata coupled with constants to build SELECT statements that return T-SQL commands which can then be executed in less time than someone could pointy, clicky in the SSMS GUI.

The SELECT clause is used to specify the information that you want to return. The information could be columns, constants, or calculations. Since we are interested in running queries that actually have business value, we need to utilize a second clause in our SELECT statements.

FROM Clause

The FROM clause is used to specify the table(s) that you want to query. You can specify up to 256 tables in the FROM clause, although if you have to go anywhere near that number of tables, you really need to re-evaluate your database design.

To retrieve all of the data from the HumanResources.Employee table, you would execute the following query:

```
SELECT *
FROM HumanResources.Employee;
```

This query should return all 44 rows in the table and all columns. The * is a shorthand notations for "all columns". However, just as we explained earlier that you should always explicitly specify the schema name with any object you are referencing, you should always explicitly specify the columns you are retrieving.

While you might use a * to get a "quick and dirty" idea of the data in a table, you should never have SELECT * in any application that ever queries a production database. SELECT * will always retrieve every column in a table and it will return every column present at the time the query is executed. If the structure of the database has changed since your application was developed, SELECT * will never tell you that there is a problem in your code that needs to be fixed, because an explicit list of columns is not present in the SELECT statement. Additionally, if the SELECT doesn't return a column that your code is looking for or returns columns your code is not expecting, your application can suddenly fail and display very alarming error messages to your users. On top of all of that, SELECT * returns the columns in the order of the CREATE TABLE statement. If your application is referencing columns in the result set by ordinal position and the table is modified such that columns are now in a different order, your application will either get data type mismatch errors or using the wrong column for display or calculations. For all of these reasons, it is very strongly recommended that you never use SELECT * in an application.

The way you should have specified the query above is:

```
SELECT EmployeeID, FirstName, MiddleInitial, LastName, JobTitleID, BirthDate, SSN,
Gender,
OrganizationNode
FROM HumanResources.Employee;
```

At this point, someone is going to say something like "but, my tables have dozens or hundreds of columns with really long names and it takes a lot of time and effort to type all of the column names". The answer to every permutation of "it takes too long to type out all of the names" is that you need to understand how to use the tools at your disposal.

If you don't have SSMS open, launch SSMS and connect to your instance. In the Object Explorer, expand the Database node, then the ChampionValleyPens database, then the table node underneath it, and finally the HumanResources.Employee node. Your Object Explorer should look like the following:

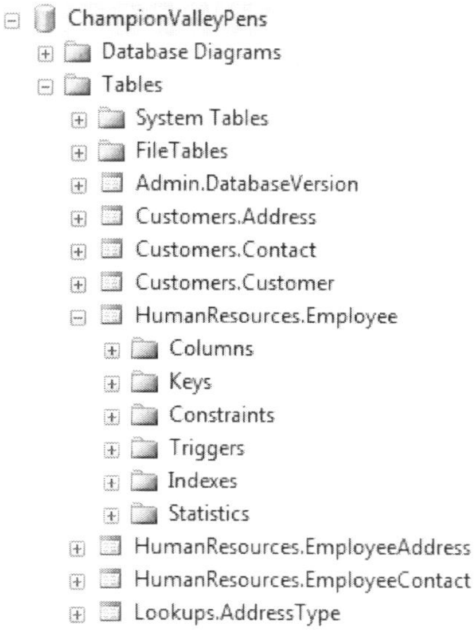

- ChampionValleyPens
  - Database Diagrams
  - Tables
    - System Tables
    - FileTables
    - Admin.DatabaseVersion
    - Customers.Address
    - Customers.Contact
    - Customers.Customer
    - HumanResources.Employee
      - Columns
      - Keys
      - Constraints
      - Triggers
      - Indexes
      - Statistics
    - HumanResources.EmployeeAddress
    - HumanResources.EmployeeContact
    - Lookups.AddressType

Figure 9-1 Object Explorer showing HumanResources.Employee

Now, open a new query window and type in the following:

```
SELECT
FROM
```

Click HumanResources.Employee in the Object Explorer and drag and drop it after the FROM. Click the Columns folder underneath HumanResources.Employee and drag and drop the entire columns folder after the SELECT.

Your query should now look like the following (assuming you put a space after both SELECT and FROM):

```
SELECT EmployeeID, FirstName, MiddleInitial, LastName, JobTitleID, BirthDate, SSN,
    Gender, OrganizationNode
FROM HumanResources.Employee;
```

At this point the argument of "it takes too long…" should no longer exist. Therefore, there isn't a valid reason for not explicitly specifying every object that you are going to query.

You may have square brackets around both the schema name and object name. This is a behavior of the scripting engine in SSMS. It does not evaluate the names of the objects, so it does not know if you have violated the naming conventions and the object needs to be delimited by square brackets. Therefore, it takes the safest route and always includes brackets around object names. I don't design databases that would ever need to delimit names with brackets, because I don't want to have to type brackets all over my code, so I automatically remove brackets.

The query window in SSMS is also enabled with Intellisense should you choose to use it. If you start typing your queries with the FROM clause, Intellisense will pop-up a selection list that enables rapid selection of object names relevant to the clause you are typing in.

> **Note:** I disable Intellisense when I'm doing development. In order for it to work properly, you have to type your queries starting with a FROM clause, which is something I rarely do. It can also get in your way when you have object names that closely resemble the names of objects that ship with SQL Server. Finally, if you are working with very large databases containing thousands or tens of thousands of objects, Intellisense will perform extremely poorly. In general, I find Intellisense gets in my way a lot more than it helps. You might have different experiences or opinions. Whether you utilize Intellisense or not it is your choice and you can enable/disable it under the Query menu.

As mentioned in Chapter 5, every object in a database can be referenced through its associated namespace. For a column, the full namespace is instance.database.schema.table.column. If the instance is not specified, the instance the query is being run on is assumed. If the database is not specified, the database context of your connection is assumed.

Queries can be run across instances by using the linked server feature. Although you can run queries across instances, it is strongly discouraged due to the performance issues you will encounter. In all of the systems I've worked on, I have never found a case where linked server queries produced a benefit that outweighed the significant performance impact. If you are running queries across instances, you will need to specify both the instance and database portion of the namespace.

Likewise, you can run queries across databases. If you are querying an object in a database different from the current execution context, you will need to specify the database name portion of the namespace.

The schema name is also optional, although I would very strongly discourage omitting the schema name. When you omit the schema name, SQL Server attempts to resolve the object name by first looking for the object in a schema that matches your login and if not found, then attempts to find the object in the dbo schema. For example, if I'm logged in as LAB\mhotek and was running a query to retrieve data from Table1, SQL Server would first look for [LAB\mhotek].Table1 and if the table wasn't found, would then look for dbo.Table1. If dbo.Table1 didn't exist, you would receive an error message. You'll notice from the structure of the sample databases that I don't design databases with any objects in the dbo schema or in a schema corresponding to a login. Therefore, the schema is required in all of the databases I design.

The following query is the completely explicit specification of the query above:

```
SELECT HumanResources.Employee.EmployeeID, HumanResources.Employee.FirstName,
HumanResources.Employee.MiddleInitial, HumanResources.Employee.LastName,
HumanResources.Employee.JobTitleID, HumanResources.Employee.BirthDate,
HumanResources.Employee.SSN, HumanResources.Employee.Gender,
HumanResources.Employee.OrganizationNode
FROM HumanResources.Employee;
```

While syntactically correct and completely explicit, you aren't required to specify the full namespace for each column in the SELECT clause. As long as the column can be uniquely resolved to a single table in the FROM clause, you only need to specify the column name.

> **Note:** As you're going through school, you learn a lot of different things. Every once in a while, you learn something profound, and it will almost never be found in a textbook. Long after you have forgotten much of what you learned, these profound nuggets will stay with you. One of my nuggets came from Mr. Harshbarger who taught me Calculus in 11th and 12th grade. "The best mathematician is a lazy mathematician, not lazy enough that they don't do their work, but lazy enough to find the easiest way." While I'm not doing pure mathematics anymore, I apply this extensively when writing queries. I'll only include something if it is necessary and try to write code as compactly as possible. Some might say that my code is a bit hard to read, but I've found that anyone who spent more than a couple of minutes reading my code quickly forgets all of the shortcuts that I use and can understand all of the code constructs without any problems.

Aliasing

In Chapter 5, we discussed naming conventions and one of the items mentioned was to avoid convoluted abbreviations, because it made reading a database structure almost impossible for anyone, even the person who originally designed the database. Inevitably, you'll run across a database filled with objects that have convoluted abbreviations or even worse, randomly generated names. Usually, these will be found in some of the major systems running an organization such as an ERP or CRM application. Fortunately, we have a way around all of the user unfriendly names that a lot of 3rd party applications use.

T-SQL allows you to rename a column in the result set through the use of an alias. In fact, there are three ways to express an alias.

Alias Method 1

The first method specifies the alias followed by an = and then the column from the table to be aliased:

```
SELECT Address = AddressLine1, City, StateProvinceID, PostalCode
FROM HumanResources.EmployeeAddress;
```

Alias Method 2

The second method specifies the column to be aliased, followed by the keyword AS, and then the alias as follows:

```
SELECT AddressLine1 AS Address, City, StateProvinceID, PostalCode
FROM HumanResources.EmployeeAddress;
```

Alias Method 3

The third method is the most compact way to alias because it simply uses a space between the column and the alias.

```
SELECT AddressLine1 Address, City, StateProvinceID, PostalCode
FROM HumanResources.EmployeeAddress;
```

All three methods are exactly equivalent and there is no performance difference between the methods. Some people will argue that method 2 is the way you should alias everything in your code, because it is explicit and avoids the following potential coding error:

```
SELECT AddressLine1 City, StateProvinceID, PostalCode
FROM HumanResources.EmployeeAddress;
```

Can you spot the error? Instead of returning 4 columns in the result set, a comma was omitted and the AddressLine1 column was aliased as City. While, the comma was omitted, creating an error, this type of error should never make it into your application. If an error such as the one above gets into your application, it means you have violated development best practices and deployed your code without ever testing it. A simple test of the query above would show that you had an error.

I use method 3 in my code simply because it is the most compact form of a query I can write and it fits with the "lazy" part as well in that I have less to type.

> **Note:** You have a NUMERIC and DECIMAL data type that are exactly equivalent and in Chapter 5, I said that it doesn't matter which you use as long as you are consistent. Aliasing is the same way. It doesn't matter which method you use to alias, just be consistent so that everyone knows what to expect when reading code.

In addition to aliasing columns, you can also alias tables in your query as follows:

```
SELECT AddressLine1, City, StateProvinceID, PostalCode
FROM HumanResources.EmployeeAddress a;
```

Once aliased, the table alias can be used anywhere in the query that you would specify the schema.table. For example:

```
SELECT a.AddressLine1, a.City, a.StateProvinceID, a.PostalCode
FROM HumanResources.EmployeeAddress a;
```

Exercise 1: Retrieving Data

Up to this point in the book, all of the exercises allowed you to pretty much blindly follow along while various features were demonstrated with all of the necessary code included in the exercise. While you might not install SQL Server, design a database, or even manipulate data very frequently, your entire career involving databases will require you to write SELECT statements. So, the exercises in this chapter and the next will introduce a new format where you are given one or more problems to solve. The solutions along with explanations are included at the end of the chapter.

1. Write a query to retrieve all of the employees.
2. Write a query to retrieve all of the employee addresses, omitting the EmployeeAddress column set.
3. Write a query to produce the following output from the Products.Product table

```
Name       Description    Price
---------  -------------  --------
...Rows removed for brevity
(119 row(s) affected)
```

Query Results

Under the Query menu, there is a "Results To" submenu second from the bottom. This allows you to change the way a result set is displayed in SSMS. The output shown was generated using the Results to Text option, which is how you'll see result sets displayed in this book, because it includes a message of how many rows were returned at the bottom of the result set.

You can retrieve data using any display method for the results; however, Results to Grid can require significant resources if your result sets are large. In order to for SSMS to display the results in a grid, the results need to be loaded into a data set in memory, a grid control needs to be loaded with any associated .NET assemblies required for its display, and then the data set mapped to the grid control. In extreme situations, displaying results in a grid can consume all of the available resources on your machine, which is another reason to always test your queries to ensure that you are returning results sets that are a manageable size.

Data Manipulation

Along with just returning the data in a column, you can manipulate data in your SELECT statements using a variety of functions and operators.

Determinism

All functions can be classified under one of two definitions – deterministic and nondeterministic. A deterministic function always returns the same result when called with a specific input value.

Nondeterministic functions can return a varying result each time they are called even when supplying the same input value.

The SQRT function computes the square root of a number. No matter when you ask for SQRT(4), you will always get back a value of 2. The GETDATE function returns the current date and time from the machine that the instance is running on and doesn't accept any parameters, so each time the GETDATE function is called, you will get a different answer. SQRT is deterministic while GETDATE is nondeterministic.

Whether a function is deterministic or not only matters if you are using it to store data. Recall from chapter 5 that you can create a computed column in a table. A computed column can contain any valid function, but if you want to persist the calculation, all functions must be deterministic. If you think about it, the determinism requirement for persisted computed columns makes sense. The results of the calculation are physically stored on disk. If you were allowed to persist a computed column with a nondeterministic function, SQL Server would never be able to store the value, because the result of the calculation would be constantly changing.

Built-in Functions

There are four types of functions available: rowset, aggregate, ranking, and scalar.

Row set functions provide a means to access external resources and expose them to a query as if they were another table in your database such as retrieving the contents of a comma delimited text file. The rowset functions available are OPENDATASOURCE, OPENQUERY, OPENROWSET, and OPENXML. Rowset functions are nondeterministic and can be used anywhere a table is specified in a SELECT statement.

Aggregate functions, which we will discuss and provide many examples for in this chapter and Chapter 10, return a single value as the result of a calculation across a set of values e.g. average (AVG), COUNT, minimum (MIN), maximum (MAX), and SUM. All aggregate functions are deterministic.

Ranking functions are always non-deterministic and will be covered in Chapter 10.

Scalar functions accept 0 or 1 inputs and return a single value. Scalar functions can be either deterministic or nondeterministic e.g. SQRT and GETDATE. You will be introduced to a variety of scalar functions throughout this book.

Data Type Conversion

You can convert data from one data type to another using either the CAST or CONVERT functions.

The syntax for CAST and CONVERT are:

```
CAST(<column> AS <data type>)
CONVERT(<data type>,<column>)

SELECT CAST(AddressID AS VARCHAR(30)) AddressID, EmployeeID, AddressTypeID,
AddressLine1,
AddressLine2, AddressLine3, City, StateProvinceID, PostalCode
FROM HumanResources.EmployeeAddress;

SELECT CONVERT(VARCHAR(30),AddressID) AddressID, EmployeeID, AddressTypeID,
AddressLine1,
AddressLine2, AddressLine3, City, StateProvinceID, PostalCode
FROM HumanResources.EmployeeAddress;
```

Instead of specifying VARCHAR(30), you could simply use the shortcut of VARCHAR, because the default length of a VARCHAR data type is 30 characters. But, just like any default behavior, Microsoft reserves the right to change the behavior at any time. So, you should always specify the number of characters when you use CHAR and VARCHAR to ensure that the results are always the same.

```
SELECT CAST(AddressID AS VARCHAR) AddressID, EmployeeID, AddressTypeID,
AddressLine1,
AddressLine2, AddressLine3, City, StateProvinceID, PostalCode
FROM HumanResources.EmployeeAddress;
```

The only difference between CAST and CONVERT is when working with dates and times. For dates and times, CONVERT has a 3rd parameter that allows you to specify the display format.

```
--Month/Day/2 digit year
SELECT EmployeeID, FirstName, MiddleInitial, LastName, JobTitleID,
CONVERT(VARCHAR(30),BirthDate,1), SSN, Gender, OrganizationNode
FROM HumanResources.Employee;

--Month/Day/4 digit year
SELECT EmployeeID, FirstName, MiddleInitial, LastName, JobTitleID,
CONVERT(VARCHAR(30),BirthDate,101), SSN, Gender, OrganizationNode
FROM HumanResources.Employee;

--Day/Month/4 digit year
SELECT EmployeeID, FirstName, MiddleInitial, LastName, JobTitleID,
CONVERT(VARCHAR(30),BirthDate,103), SSN, Gender, OrganizationNode
FROM HumanResources.Employee;
```

If you attempt to convert a value to an invalid data type such as attempting to convert a character value to an integer, SQL Server will return an error. To get around this issue, SQL Server 2012 has a new function TRY_CONVERT

The syntax is the same as the CONVERT function

```
TRY_CONVERT(<data type>,<column>,style)
```

If you attempt an invalid conversion, TRY_CONVERT will return a NULL instead of an error. A valid conversion will return the same results as the CONVERT function. However, there are some data type conversions which are not valid such as attempting to convert an integer to XML or HIERARCHYID which will still cause TRY_CONVERT to return an error message.

If you need to type cast string values to date/time and numeric data which is sensitive to a locale, SQL Server 2012 includes a PARSE and corresponding TRY_PARSE function which accepts a culture. In the US, we use a decimal place to represent fractions of a dollar amount whereas in Europe, a comma is used to represent fractions of a Euro. If you use the CONVERT function, the language settings of your machine will be used to determine how to convert the data.

```
SELECT CAST('€89,52' AS money) Euros;
```

On my machine, this produces the following invalid result:

```
Euros
--------------------
8952.00
```

But, using a culture specification in the PARSE function, the value is correctly converted:

```
SELECT PARSE('€89,52' AS money USING 'es-ES') Euros;
Euros
--------------------
89.52
```

Books Online lists all of the valid culture specifications. TRY_PARSE works in the same manner as TRY_CONVERT. If the parse succeeds, the value is returned otherwise a NULL is returned unless the data type conversion is invalid.

It is interesting to note that attempting to use en-GB which is Great Britain yields an error. Since Great Britain didn't change currencies to the Euro, the en-GB culture apparently doesn't understand what a Euro is even though using the CAST function on my US locale based machine produces the correct result as long as I replace the comma with a decimal point. But, using the en_US culture with the PARSE function produces the same error as attempting to use en-GB.

```
SELECT CAST('€89.52' AS money) Euros;

Euros
--------------------
89.52
```

All of these options will leave many with a simple question, "which one should I use"? Since there really isn't any noticeable performance difference between any of the 5 conversion functions, my recommendations are as follows:

- If your code has to be backwards compatible, you need to use CAST or CONVERT
- Only use CONVERT if you need to utilize the 3rd parameter for formatting a date otherwise use CAST
    - This causes date format manipulations to stand out in your code
- If your code does not have to be backwards compatible, use TRY_CONVERT or TRY_PARSE depending upon whether you need to utilize the culture sensitive conversion

Using TRY_CONVERT/TRY_PARSE if your code doesn't have to be backwards compatible, allows you to easily test for a NULL in the return, and make any desired corrections without having to use any error handling routines.

Variables

A complete discussion of T-SQL programming and in particular variables will be done in the next book, "SQL Server 2012 Database Development", but a brief overview will be helpful since I'll be using them to demonstrate functionality in the next 5 chapters.

T-SQL has two types of variables: local and global. A global variable is visible to any connection and you can only have a single instance of a global variable at any time. A global variable is designated by two @ symbols, e.g. @@VERSION, @@MyGlobalVariable. A local variable is visible to the connection which created it and each connection can have its own copy of the variable active at any time. A local variable is designated by a single @ symbol, e.g. @LocalVariable.

There are two types of global variables: system defined and user defined. System variables are always global variables and you cannot assign a value to a system variable. User defined global variables have the same properties as a local variable, except for the visibility across connections.

You create a variable by using the DECLARE keyword along with specifying a data type. Variables are always strongly typed, meaning that you have to specify the data type for the variable at the time the variable is declared. The data type can be any valid data type for the instance except for TEXT, NTEXT, and IMAGE. You don't specify nullability for a variable and every variable starts out assigned NULL.

You can assign a value to a variable either by using the SET command or a SELECT statement. The SET command will allow you to assign a static value to a single variable. The SELECT statement will allow you to assign values to multiple variables as well as assigning a value from a column or expression in the SELECT statement to a variable. You retrieve a value from a variable by using a SELECT statement.

```
DECLARE @Var1    INT,
        @Var2    DATE,
        @Var3    CHAR(1);

SET @Var1 = 1;
SELECT @Var2 = '2012-05-17', @Var3 = 'A';

SELECT @Var1, @Var2, @Var3;
```

The variables we will be using are all scalars meaning the variable holds a single value. Keep this in mind if you are assigning a value to a variable from a column or an expression while querying a table which can return more than 1 value. You won't receive an error; the variable will simply hold the last value that was assigned to it.

```
DECLARE @EmployeeID INT;

SELECT @EmployeeID = EmployeeID
FROM HumanResources.Employee;

SELECT @EmployeeID;
```

A "unique" feature of a variable is that character data will be silently truncated if you attempt to assign a value which is longer than the data type allows. This is not the same behavior as you get with a table. If you attempt to store a character value that exceeds the size of the data type definition, the transaction will fail and rollback with a truncation error.

```
DECLARE @Var      CHAR(3);

SET @Var = 'A very long string'

SELECT @Var
```

Variables of any other data type will throw an error is you attempt to assign a value which is outside their range.

```
DECLARE @DateTime    DATETIME,
        @TinyInt     TINYINT;

SET @DateTime = '1752-12-31';
SET @TinyInt = 1000000;

Msg 242, Level 16, State 3, Line 4
The conversion of a varchar data type to a datetime data type resulted in an out-of-range value.
Msg 220, Level 16, State 2, Line 5
Arithmetic overflow error for data type tinyint, value = 1000000.
```

Handling NULLs

You concatenate character data using the + symbol. If you are concatenating data of any other type than character, you must first explicitly convert it using CAST or CONVERT before concatenating it.

```
SELECT EmployeeID, AddressLine1 + ' ' + AddressLine2 + ' ' + AddressLine3,
City, StateProvinceID, PostalCode
FROM HumanResources.EmployeeAddress;

EmployeeID   Address   City            StateProvinceID    PostalCode
----------   -------   --------        ---------------    ---------------
1                      NULL   Irving              6                        75038
2                      NULL   Mansfield           6                        76063
3                      NULL   Dallas              6                        75212
...
(44 row(s) affected)
```

The results of the query might look a little strange since every Employee has an address, because the AddressLine1 column is defined as NOT NULL. The problem is when concatenating AddressLine1 with AddressLine2 and AddressLine3 which are both NULL. Since NULL does not equal another NULL, if you calculate or concatenate any value with a NULL, you will get NULL as a result.

To get around this issue, SQL Server provides two functions ISNULL and COALESCE to substitute a value for a NULL. This does not change the fact that NULL is the nonexistence of a value. It just means you are deciding that in a particular case, you want to replace NULL with something.

The following queries produce the same result by substituting an empty string where a NULL exists.

```
SELECT EmployeeID, AddressLine1 + ' ' + ISNULL(AddressLine2,'') + ' ' +
ISNULL(AddressLine3,'') Address, City, StateProvinceID, PostalCode
FROM HumanResources.EmployeeAddress;

SELECT EmployeeID, AddressLine1 + ' ' + COALESCE(AddressLine2,'') + ' ' +
COALESCE(AddressLine3,'') Address, City, StateProvinceID, PostalCode
FROM HumanResources.EmployeeAddress;

EmployeeID   Address              City         StateProvinceID  PostalCode
-----------  -------------------  -----------  ---------------  ----------
1            3817 Charla Lane     Irving       6                75038
2            326 Waldeck Street   Mansfield    6                76063
3            1228 Whitetail Lane  Dallas       6                75212
...
(44 row(s) affected)
```

While the example above produced the same result using either ISNULL or COALESCE, there are some differences between the two functions.

In some cases, COALESCE will perform slightly better than ISNULL while in other cases ISNULL performs slightly better. By slightly better I mean on the order of 0.5 to 1.5 seconds over a million rows. While you can measure a performance difference, it is so small that for all practical purposes the two functions perform the same. Even over a million row result set, you can chew up the entire difference in performance just in IP packet retries when sending the results across the network.

If you are using SELECT INTO to generate a table with results from a SELECT statement, then COALESCE will produce a NULL column whereas ISNULL will produce a NOT NULL column.

ISNULL only supports a single argument while COALESCE supports multiple arguments. COALESCE will return the first argument in the list that is NOT NULL. If all of the values in the list are NULL, then COALESCE will return NULL.

The most important difference is the data type handling. ISNULL returns the result using the data type of the first argument. COALESCE uses data type precedence as well as a best fit when dealing with values of the same data type.

```
DECLARE @Var1   INT,
        @Var2   DATETIME,
        @var3   DATETIME;

SET @Var3 = '2012-05-17'

SELECT COALESCE(@Var2, 2);
SELECT COALESCE(@Var1, @Var3);
```

> **Note:** Data type precedence can be found in Books Online.

DATETIME has a higher precedence than INT. In the first SELECT statement, we have a DATETIME which is NULL that is replaced by the integer value of 2. Instead of returning 2, COALESCE converts the 2 to a DATETIME because of the higher data type precedence and instead returns the DATETIME value of 1900-01-03. Just as the second SELECT also returns a

DATETIME value.

Now, consider the same example using ISNULL.

```
DECLARE @Var1    INT,
        @Var2    DATETIME,
        @Var3    DATETIME;

SET @Var3 = '2012-05-17'

SELECT ISNULL(@Var2, 2);
SELECT ISNULL(@Var1, @Var3);
```

The first SELECT will still return a DATETIME value of 1900-01-03, because the first argument is a DATETIME. However, the second SELECT will fail since a DATETIME cannot be converted to an INT and ISNULL sets the data type of the return value based on the first argument.

An additional side effect of the data type precedence behavior between ISNULL and COALESCE is the possibility of truncating character values.

```
DECLARE @Var1    CHAR(3);
SELECT ISNULL(@Var1,'Not Specified'), COALESCE(@Var1,'Not Specified')
```

Date and Time Data

Date and time data have a large number of functions that return the date/time from the SQL Server instance, parse out portions of a date/time value, or perform temporal calculations.

There are 6 functions to return the current system date/time. All of the functions return a date and time from the computer the SQL Server instance is running on. Three functions are high precision with an accuracy of 100 nanoseconds and three are lower precision with an accuracy of 3 milliseconds.

```
SELECT SYSDATETIME(), SYSDATETIMEOFFSET(), SYSUTCDATETIME()

SYSDATETIME                  SYSDATETIMEOFFSET                      SYSUTCDATETIME
--------------------------   ------------------------------------   --------------------------
2012-05-17 14:09:23.8298772  2012-05-17 14:09:23.8298772 -05:00     2012-05-17 19:09:23.8298772


SELECT CURRENT_TIMESTAMP, GETDATE(), GETUTCDATE()

CURRENT_TIMESTAMP         GETDATE                   GETUTCDATE
-----------------------   -----------------------   -----------------------
2012-05-17 14:09:23.827   2012-05-17 14:09:23.827   2012-05-17 19:09:23.827
```

You'll notice that the UTC date functions return a UTC time. Since the machine my SQL Server is running on has its clock set to US Central time, I'm at a -5 time zone offset from Greenwich Mean Time (GMT) as shown in the SYSDATETIMEOFFSET function, which also adds 5 hours to the two functions returning UTC times. The SYSDATETIMEOFFSET returns the value using a DATETIMEOFFSET data type. All of the other functions return the data using a DATETIME2 data type.

SQL Server doesn't have functions to just return the system date or the system time individually. However, you can obtain either of these portions by just converting the return value to a DATE or TIME data type.

```
SELECT CAST(GETDATE() AS DATE) DateOnly, CAST(GETDATE() AS TIME) TimeOnly

DateOnly            TimeOnly
----------          ----------------
2012-05-17          14:23:06.3770000
```

The ISDATE() function returns a 1 or 0 based on whether the input value is a valid date or time value. The input value is required to be a character string or a variable of a CHAR/VARCHAR/NCHAR/NVARCHAR data type.

```
SELECT ISDATE('14:23:06.3770000') TimeOnly, ISDATE('2012-05-17') DateOnly,
ISDATE('2012-05-17 14:23:06.3770000') DateAndTime,
ISDATE('2012-05-17 14:09:23.8298772 -05:00') DateTimeOffset,
ISDATE('1752-12-31 00:00:00.000') PriorToDateTime, ISDATE('abc') Invalid

TimeOnly   DateOnly DateAndTime DateTimeOffset PriorToDateTime Invalid
---------- -------- ----------- -------------- --------------- ---------
0          1        0           0              0               0
```

If you look closely, you might be wondering why ISDATE() returned a 0 (invalid) for the TimeOnly, DateAndTime, DateTimeOffset, and PriorToDateTime since these are all valid dates/times in SQL Server 2012. After all, we just used the values from above that either the system generated or we type cast to a DATE or TIME data type. The TimeOnly and DateAndTime values are invalid, because ISDATE() cannot handle the high precision times from SQL Server 2012 which are actually DATETIME2 data types.

```
SELECT ISDATE('14:23:06.377') TimeOnly, ISDATE('2012-05-17') DateOnly,
ISDATE('2012-05-17 14:23:06.377') DateAndTime

TimeOnly      DateOnly      DateAndTime
-----------   -----------   -----------
1             1             1
```

The DateTimeOffset and PriorToDateTime are invalid for the ISDATE function, because it can only test for valid DATE, TIME, SMALLDATETIME, and DATETIME values. ISDATE() cannot handle time zone offsets or dates prior to January 1, 1753.

The DATETIMEOFFSET data type has two specialized functions.

TODATETIMEOFFSET() function takes an existing DATETIME, SMALLDATETIME, or DATETIME2 value and adds a time zone offset returning a DATETIMEOFFSET value. The time zone offset is based on the time zone setting on the machine that SQL Server is running on.

SWITCHOFFSET operates on a DATETIMEOFFSET value and moves the time zone offset to a new offset value while preserving the UTC representation of the value. In the following example, the UTC time is 2012-05-18 04:59:59.7134500. In US Central Time (-05:00), it is only just slightly before midnight on May 17 while US Eastern Time (-04:00) is it almost 1AM on May 18. The actual UTC time didn't change. The value is simply represented with the new time zone offset specified.

```
SELECT SWITCHOFFSET(CAST('2012-05-17 23:59:59.71345 -5:00' AS DATETIMEOFFSET),'-04:00')

----------------------------------
2012-05-18 00:59:59.7134500 -04:00
```

There are 3 specialized and 2 general purpose functions to return a portion of a date/time value.

DAY(), MONTH(), and YEAR() return an integer value representing the portion of a date as you would expect. DATENAME() and DATEPART() are general purpose functions that allow you to slice out various portions of a date/time value. Books Online lists the 14 date parts which are valid for DATEPART() and DATENAME()

> **Note:** Remember our discussion in Chapter 5 on date formats. Be very careful you are consistent with the storage and calculations of dates. In the US, we use mm/dd/yyyy while in most of the rest of the world it is dd/mm/yyyy making a value like 02/06/2012 ambiguous. If you're passing dates around as string values, SQL Server will parse the value differently based on your DATEFORMAT setting.

```
SELECT DAY(GETDATE()) DayPortion, DATEPART(dd,GETDATE()) DayPortion,
YEAR(GETDATE()) YearPortion, DATEPART(yy,GETDATE()) YearPortion,
DATEPART(dy,GETDATE()) DayOfYear

DayPortion  DayPortion  YearPortion  YearPortion  DayOfYear
----------- ----------- ------------ ------------ -----------
17          17          2012         2012         138

SELECT DATENAME(mm,GETDATE()) Month, DATENAME(weekday,GETDATE()) DayOfWeek

Month                            DayOfWeek
-------------------------------- --------------------------------
May                              Thursday
```

SQL Server 2012 introduce 6 new functions to assemble a DATE, TIME, DATETIME2, DATETIME, or DATETIMEOFFSET from constituent parts e.g. DATEFROMPARTS(2012,5,17). I'm still not sure where I would apply any of these functions since I've never encountered an application which sent me dates or times broken down into pieces.

If all of the functions noted above weren't enough, you can also perform calculations on dates such as the number of days/weeks/months between two dates or take a given date and add a number of days/weeks/months to it.

The DATEDIFF function allows you to specify one of the 14 valid date parts along with two dates to calculate against.

```
SELECT DATEDIFF(dd,'2012-01-01',GETDATE()) DaysBetween,
DATEDIFF(hh,'2012-01-01',GETDATE()) HoursThisYear

DaysBetween HoursThisYear
----------- -------------
137         3303
```

DATEADD allows you to modify a given date by a number of date parts. For example:

```
SELECT DATEADD(wk,1,GETDATE()) SameDayNextWeek, DATEADD(wk,-1,GETDATE())
SameDayPriorWeek, DATEADD(mm, DATEDIFF(mm, '2012-01-01', GETDATE()) + 1, '2012-01-
01') FirstDayOfNextMonth

SameDayNextWeek              SameDayPriorWeek             FirstDayOfNextMonth
---------------------------- ---------------------------- -----------------------
2012-05-24 15:58:06.383      2012-05-10 15:58:06.383      2012-06-01 00:00:00.000
```

If I didn't mention it already and as you've seen with a few examples, you can nest functions to pretty much an unlimited length. There is an actual nesting limit, but you'll reach the point of your code being impossible to figure out long before you hit a nesting level. The first parameter for DATEADD() is the date part to use. The second parameter is the number of units to move the value by with positive being forward in time and negative being backward in time.

So, let's focus on this convoluted piece of code I have for calculating the first day of next month from any date within a month. I used January 1, 2012 as the anchor date to compute against, but I could have used January 1 of any year. I could have even specified a value of 0, which SQL Server interprets as January 1, 1900. The DATEDIFF function simply calculates the number of months between the date I'm interested in (GETDATE() in this case) and the anchor date. I then add 1 to that number since I wanted the next month. If I wanted 5 months from now, I would have added 5 to the result of DATEDIFF. I then take that result and use it as the second parameter of the DATEADD function to compute a given number of months from my anchor date. If I had wanted to compute the 2nd day of a month, I could have specified something like January 2, 2012.

You could have used DATEPART to slice off the month and year of your date, added 1 to the month, and concatenated it all back together as a string and converted that result back to a date value, but you'll find that to be much slower than the example above nesting DATEDIFF inside DATEADD. This also turns out to be faster than using any of the new date/time assembly functions.

New in SQL Server 2012 is the EOMONTH function which computes the last day of any month and optionally allows you to specify an offset.

```
SELECT EOMONTH(GETDATE()) EndOfThisMonth, EOMONTH(GETDATE(),1) EndOfNextMonth,
    EOMONTH(GETDATE(),-1) EndOfPreviousMonth
```

If your code needs to be backwards compatible to a version of SQL Server that doesn't have a DATE or TIME data type, you can easily strip the date or the time portion off a DATETIME value by taking advantage of the way that dates and times are stored internally as was discussed in Chapter 5 "Designing Tables". Below is a calculation to strip the time off a DATETIME value that will work for all versions of SQL Server going back to at least SQL Server 6.5.

```
SELECT CONVERT(DATETIME, FLOOR(CONVERT(FLOAT, GETDATE())))
```

Many people have this notion that T-SQL is of limited use and that lots of problems simply can't be solved using a SELECT statement. They're then amazed when someone produces a calculation which not only runs quickly, but provides lots of flexibility. It is simply a matter of understanding what each function can do for you as well as being able to understand basic mathematics and you can solve a wide range of interesting problems while amazing your co-workers.

For example, we noted that dates are simply stored as the number of days after a specified anchor date for the data type. That means the date is actually a number to SQL Server, not what you are really seeing. Translating that, it means that if you store the actual anchor date for the data type, SQL Server stores 0, not the date you specified.

So, I'll leave our discussion of date functions with a SELECT statement for you to mull over and consider just what "impossible" means when computing dates and times.

```
SELECT DATEADD(mm, DATEDIFF(mm, 0, '2012-05-17') + 1, 0),
DATEADD(mm, DATEDIFF(mm, 1, '2012-05-17') + 1, 1),
DATEADD(mm, DATEDIFF(mm, 2, '2012-05-17') + 1, 2),
DATEADD(mm, DATEDIFF(mm, 18, '2012-05-17') + 1, 18),
DATEADD(mm, DATEDIFF(mm, 31, '2012-05-17') + 1, 31),
CAST(CAST(GETDATE() AS INT) AS DATETIME);
```

Exercise 2: Manipulating Data

1. Write a query to prepare a customer mailing. Make sure that you include all of the parts of the customer addresses. You results should look like the following: Note: We will enhance this query later to retrieve the actual customer name along with the actual state/province.

   ```
   CustomerID  Address               City         StateProvinceID  PostalCode
   ----------- --------------------- ------------ ---------------- ----------
   1           1167 Goldcliff Circle Washington   1075             20032
   2           2875 Godfrey Street   Portland     1100             97205
   (999707 row(s) affected)
   ```

2. The average transit time for an order is 5 days from the date the order was placed by the customer. Compute the estimated arrival date for each order.

   ```
   OrderID     OrderDate    EstimatedArrival
   ----------- ----------   ----------------
   1           2001-01-01   2001-01-06
   2           2001-01-01   2001-01-06
   3           2001-01-01   2001-01-06
   (8088 row(s) affected)
   ```

3. Compute the same day of the week, 3 weeks from the current date along with the number of days between the current date and 3 weeks later. Remove the time portion and return the date in the format of mm/dd/yyyy. The example output is based on the current date being May 21, 2012.

   ```
   ------------------------------ ----------
   06/11/2012                     21
   (1 row(s) affected)
   ```

Calculations

The functions covered above are only a small fraction of what is available within SQL Server. You have:

Function Category	Examples
Logical	CHOOSE() and IIF()
Math	ABS(), SIN(), PI(), ROUND() and CEILING()
Metadata	DB_NAME() and SCHEMA_NAME()
System	CHECKSUM(), ISNUMERIC(), and HOST_NAME()
String	REPLACE(), SUBSTRING(), UPPER(), and RTRIM()

You can also perform aggregations such as COUNT(), SUM(), MIN() along with any of the standard mathematical operators +, -, /, *, % (MODULO or the remainder of division).

To return the number of rows in the HumanResource.Employee table, you would execute the following:

```
SELECT COUNT(*), COUNT(1), COUNT('a')
FROM HumanResources.Employee;
```

The standard way is to use COUNT(*), but you can place any static value as the argument without affecting the computation. The * is simply a placeholder.

You can specify a column name from the table instead of a * or static value, but the results will depend upon the presence of NULLs.

```
SELECT COUNT(*) Count, COUNT(EmployeeID) EmployeeIDs, COUNT(AddressLine2)
AddressLine2
FROM HumanResources.EmployeeAddress;

Count        EmployeeIDs  AddressLine2
-----------  -----------  ------------
44           44           0
Warning: Null value is eliminated by an aggregate or other SET operation.
(1 row(s) affected)
```

When you specify a column name as the argument for COUNT(), SQL Server will return the number of rows that have a non-NULL value. It doesn't care if the values are repeated in the column only that a value exists.

LEN is used to return the number of characters while DATALENGTH returns the number of bytes.

```
DECLARE @Char      CHAR(10),
        @Varchar   VARCHAR(10),
        @Nchar     NCHAR(10),
        @Nvarchar  NVARCHAR(10);

SELECT @Char = REPLICATE('a',5), @Varchar = REPLICATE('a',5),
    @Nchar = REPLICATE('a',5), @Nvarchar = REPLICATE('a',5);

SELECT @Char, @Varchar, @Nchar, @Nvarchar;

SELECT LEN(@Char) LenChar, DATALENGTH(@Char) DataLenChar,
LEN(@Varchar) LenVarchar, DATALENGTH(@Varchar) DataLenVarchar,
LEN(@Nchar) LenNvar, DATALENGTH(@Nchar) DataLenNchar,
LEN(@Nvarchar) LenNvarchar, DATALENGTH(@Nvarchar) DataLenNvarchar;

----------  ----------  ----------  ----------
aaaaa       aaaaa       aaaaa       aaaaa
(1 row(s) affected)

-----  --------  -------  ------  -------  ------  ------  -------
5      10        5        5       5        20      5       10
(1 row(s) affected)
```

The REPLICATE() function is used to simply seed the variables with a string of 5 a's as shown in the first result set. Notice the difference in the results between the LEN and DATALENGTH functions for each of the four character data types. Since LEN is counting the number of characters, it ignores any spaces, regardless of whether the data is fixed length or Unicode. DATALENGTH is counting bytes, so it computes the number of bytes SQL Server stores. Remember that a fixed length data type always stores the same number of bytes regardless of the length of the actual data.

When performing mathematical operations, the operator precedence you learned in your first few years in school still applies. For example, 1 + 5 * 6 produces 31, not 36, because multiplication is evaluated from left to right first before addition. Consider the following calculation:

```
SELECT 1 + 2 * 3 * 2 + 1 / 7 * 5;
```

Not only does this look like a mess, it produces a result that many will find unintelligible because of the way SQL Server handles data types with computations. The way this is evaluated in mathematics is to multiply 2 * 3 * 2, divide 1/7 and multiple the result by 5, then add one to the result of 2 * 3 * 2 which is then added to the result of 1/7 * 5. 1/7 * 5 is approximately 0.71. So, you would think that SQL Server would return a result of 13.71. SQL Server in fact returns a result of 13.

Notice that every value we specified was an integer. That means SQL Server has to return the result as an integer. Since 1/7 produces 0 with a remainder of 1, the 1 is simply thrown away leaving a result of 1/7 = 0, because an integer cannot accept any decimal places. This is where data type precedence intersects with math operator precedence to produce some seemingly strange results. In pure mathematics, you would have rounded this off to 14, based on a concept called the least significant digit to determine how to handle calculations of numbers with different precisions. SQL Server is designed to store data and therefore has to enforce a data type on any piece of data you manipulate. When mathematics collides with data types, data types win out.

You can force the issue by doing the following:

```
SELECT 1 + 2 * 3 * 2 + 1 / 7. * 5;
```

This produces a result of 13.714285. What is different between the two? I added a decimal point after the 7 to force SQL Server to treat this value as a decimal. Since decimal takes precedence over integer, SQL Server no longer has to drop the decimal portion since the data type of the result has been transformed to a decimal.

You will see all kinds of examples that force an integer into a decimal value in order to preserve the fractions, but I consider this just as bad as the calculation we are using. It is obtuse and very easy to miss. Just like you were taught how to clarify your calculations using parenthesis, I would write the calculation above as follows:

```
SELECT 1 + (2 * (3 * 2)) + ((1 / 7.0) * 5);
```

Now you don't have to squint to figure out that I'm forcing the calculation to a decimal, because the 7.0 makes that very clear. You also don't have to remember the precedence of math operators, because the parenthesis makes it very clear how I want the calculation performed.

This section was just a small taste of the dozens of functions and infinite permutations that you can apply to manipulate data. Books Online has a complete function reference along with simple examples showing how to use each function. Pay particular attention to the data type(s) of the argument(s) and the data type is the output in order to understand how you can nest functions within each other. A function which returns a data type of float cannot be used as an argument for a function when the argument requires an integer value.

CASE

A CASE expression is used to return a value based on a selection list that you specify. Each CASE expression starts with the CASE keyword and is terminated by the END keyword. You must have at least WHEN comparison and can optionally specify an ELSE which will be assigned if a match is not found to any of the WHEN criteria. If no match is found and you have not specified an ELSE, the CASE expression returns NULL. There are two forms or a CASE statement: simple and searched.

An example of a simple CASE statement is:

```
SELECT EmployeeID, Contact, CASE ContactTypeID
                WHEN 1 THEN 'Cell Phone'
                WHEN 2 THEN 'Home Phone'
                WHEN 3 THEN 'Work Phone'
                WHEN 4 THEN 'E-Mail'
                ELSE 'UNKOWN' END ContactType
FROM HumanResources.EmployeeContact;
```

In a simple CASE statement, you specify a column, calculation, or variable to test for a value and then provide a list of values to compare to followed by an optional ELSE and closed with the END keyword. SQL Server will compare the contents to the list and return the first value that exactly matches.

A simple CASE expression only allows equality in the matches. A searched CASE provides more flexibility by allowing you to specify complex and compound comparisons. For example:

```
SELECT EmployeeID, Contact, CASE WHEN ContactTypeID = 4 THEN 'E-Mail'
                WHEN ContactTypeID < 4 THEN 'Cell Phone'
                WHEN ContactTypeID > 2 THEN 'Home Phone'
                WHEN ContactTypeID = 3 AND EmployeeID = 22 THEN 'Work Phone'
                ELSE 'UNKOWN' END ContactType
FROM HumanResources.EmployeeContact;
```

While the searched CASE expression shows that you can use a variety of comparison operators as well as compound criteria, it also demonstrates that CASE will return the first matching value it finds. Since the values in the ContactTypeID column range from 1 to 4, the last two WHEN comparisons will never be evaluated since a value of 4 will produce E-Mail while any other value in the column will produce Cell Phone.

The value you are comparing can be a single column or it can be a complex calculation involving multiple columns. I've shown a comparison to a single, static value simply to make the example easy to understand. However, the value you are testing for can also be a complex calculation involving multiple columns, or even another CASE statement. The searched CASE expression offers virtually unlimited flexibility and can be nested up to 10 levels deep. You need to ensure that you adequately test your queries for not only common, known values, but also for all of the boundary points possible.

Sorting Data

The only way to guarantee results sorted in a particular order is to include an ORDER BY clause, which is almost always the last clause of any SELECT statement. Without an ORDER BY clause, SQL Server simply returns the results as it finds the rows. While it might appear that your results are sorted in some manner, it is an accident.

```
SELECT FirstName, MiddleInitial, LastName, BirthDate, SSN, Gender, OrganizationNode
FROM HumanResources.Employee
ORDER BY LastName;
```

The default sort order is ascending, but you can use the DESC keyword to sort in descending order.

```
SELECT FirstName, MiddleInitial, LastName, BirthDate, SSN, Gender, OrganizationNode
FROM HumanResources.Employee
ORDER BY LastName DESC;
```

You can sort data based on multiple columns. The data will be sorted by the first column and then within that by the second column, etc. The DESC or ASC keyword is specified for each column you want to sort the results by.

```
SELECT FirstName, MiddleInitial, LastName, BirthDate, SSN, Gender, OrganizationNode
FROM HumanResources.Employee
ORDER BY LastName DESC, FirstName;
```

The sort is not required to be on a column in the SELECT clause. You can sort on any column in any table in the FROM clause or by any valid calculation

```
SELECT FirstName, MiddleInitial, LastName, BirthDate, SSN, Gender, OrganizationNode
FROM HumanResources.Employee
ORDER BY EmployeeID;

SELECT FirstName, MiddleInitial, LastName, BirthDate, SSN, Gender, OrganizationNode
FROM HumanResources.Employee
ORDER BY LastName + ',' + FirstName DESC;

SELECT AddressID, EmployeeID, AddressLine1, City, StateProvinceID, PostalCode
FROM HumanResources.EmployeeAddress
ORDER BY CASE PostalCode
    WHEN '75051' THEN 1    WHEN '75760' THEN 2    WHEN '76001' THEN 3
    WHEN '75038' THEN 4    WHEN '75039' THEN 5    WHEN '76053' THEN 6
    WHEN '75244' THEN 7    ELSE 8 END;
```

You can have ties when sorting a result set. If the ORDER BY clause does not include enough columns to break ties and determine a unique, repeatable order of the rows in the result set, ties will be returned in the order that SQL Server found them in the table.

```
SELECT AddressID, EmployeeID, AddressLine1, City, StateProvinceID, PostalCode
FROM HumanResources.EmployeeAddress
ORDER BY City;
```

If you want to ensure a stable, repeatable result set, always include enough columns in the ORDER BY clause to uniquely identify any row in the result set.

This is usually done by including the column(s) in the primary key.

```
SELECT AddressID, EmployeeID, AddressLine1, City, StateProvinceID, PostalCode
FROM HumanResources.EmployeeAddress
ORDER BY City, AddressID;
```

You can specify a sort either based on names or position in the SELECT list.

```
SELECT AddressID, EmployeeID, AddressLine1, City, StateProvinceID, PostalCode
FROM HumanResources.EmployeeAddress
ORDER BY City;

SELECT AddressID, EmployeeID, AddressLine1, City, StateProvinceID, PostalCode
FROM HumanResources.EmployeeAddress
ORDER BY 4;
```

While specifying based on position can give you quick shorthand when you are building queries and investigating data, it is extremely bad coding practice to specify based on position. You included an ORDER BY clause because you wanted the data sorted in a given order. If you specify an ORDER BY clause based on position, all someone needs to do is rearrange the order of columns in the SELECT statement to blow up your sort order. An application won't receive an error, because the same columns are being returned, but the results will no longer be in an expected order. If you specified the ORDER BY clause based on names, then it doesn't matter how someone arranges the SELECT clause and it makes your code clear to whoever comes behind you to maintain the code.

> **Note:** Sorting results can be a very expensive operation, so if you really don't need the results sorted, don't include an ORDER BY clause. Additionally, keep in mind that you have 1 database server while you might have hundreds or thousands of applications retrieving data. Those applications can sort results just as easily as specifying an ORDER BY clause. However, you spread the overhead of sorting to those hundreds or thousands of applications instead of having a single SQL Server have to perform hundreds or thousands of sorts. I almost never use an ORDER BY clause in my code, instead relying on the applications to sort the data as they need it.

Exercise 3: Computing and Sorting Data

1. Return the number of customers.

2. Compute the maximum length of a customer's address along with the maximum number of bytes consumed by just the data in a customer's postal code.

3. Return the orders sorted by order date within each customer starting with the most recent orders.

4. Using the OrderSubTotal, SalesTax, and ShippingAmount columns, compute the order total. Return a result set that has the OrderID and order total.

5. Return a result set with a subjective description for the size of a customer's order using the following criteria: orders less than $40 are small, orders between $40 and $100 are medium, and orders larger than $100 are large.

Returning a Subset of Rows

Up to this point, we've written queries which return all of the rows in a table. For most applications, returning an entire table is not very useful and in many cases completely impossible. You might be able to store several trillion rows in a SQL Server table, but you certainly don't want to return all of them to an application. So, the SELECT statement obviously has mechanisms to allow you to return only a subset of rows.

TOP

The TOP operator allows you to return a number or percentage of rows. For example:

```
SELECT TOP 100 OrderID, CustomerID, OrderDate, OrderTime, OrderTotal
FROM Orders.OrderHeader;

SELECT TOP 10 PERCENT OrderID, CustomerID, OrderDate, OrderTime, OrderTotal
FROM Orders.OrderHeader;
```

When you specify TOP n, the first n rows that SQL Server finds in the table are returned. If you specify TOP n PERCENT, then SQL Server determines the number of rows in the table, computes the percentage of those rows rounded up to the next whole number, and returns the first n rows it finds in the table based on the calculation.

You can use TOP in conjunction with an ORDER BY clause to return the first n rows within an ordered list. However, as was noted in the section above, if the ORDER BY clause does not include enough columns to uniquely identify each row, SQL Server will still return the first n rows it encounters after applying the ORDER BY clause. So, repeated queries could produce different result sets even if the data has not changed.

```
SELECT TOP 5 OrderID, CustomerID, OrderDate, OrderTime, OrderTotal
FROM Orders.OrderHeader
ORDER BY OrderDate;
```

You can eliminate the variability in the result set by either ensuring the ORDER BY clause has enough columns to uniquely identify each row or you use the WITH TIES option. The WITH TIES option first sorts the result set and retrieves the first n rows required by the TOP operator. SQL Server then appends any additional rows to the result set which have the same value and the last row based on the ORDER BY clause.

```
SELECT TOP 5 WITH TIES OrderID, CustomerID, OrderDate, OrderTime, OrderTotal
FROM Orders.OrderHeader
ORDER BY OrderDate;
```

The Orders.OrderHeader table has 11 rows with an OrderDate of January 1, 2001. If you just specified TOP 5, SQL Server would return the first 5 rows with an order date of January 1, 2001 and the list could vary each time you ran the query. By specifying WITH TIES, SQL Server retrieves the first 5 rows for January 1, 2001 that it encounters. It then looks at the value for the OrderDate column in the last row retrieved, determines that the value was January 1, 2001, and appends any other rows in the table with an order date of January 1, 2001.

TABLESAMPLE

SQL Server 2012 added a TABLESAMPLE operator to allow you to return a subset of rows. TABLESAMPLE is specified in the FROM clause and has the following generic syntax:

```
<tablesample_clause> ::=
    TABLESAMPLE [SYSTEM] ( sample_number [ PERCENT | ROWS ] )
        [ REPEATABLE ( repeat_seed )
```

The keyword SYSTEM specifies the sampling method that is used to retrieve the set of rows. Currently SQL Server only supports a single sampling method, although you can imagine that additional sampling methods might be added in the future. The sampling method is based on data pages in the table. SQL Server randomly selects data pages and returns all of the rows on the selected page, which means the overall number of rows you will get back will be variable. Each time you execute the query, you should return a different result set, unless you specified 100 PERCENT. If you want SQL Server to return the same sample set repeatedly, you can use the REPEATABLE clause with a seed value.

```sql
SELECT CustomerID, FirstName, LastName
FROM Customers.Customer TABLESAMPLE SYSTEM (1 PERCENT) ;

SELECT CustomerID, FirstName, LastName
FROM Customers.Customer TABLESAMPLE SYSTEM (1 PERCENT) REPEATABLE (1);
```

WHERE

While the TOP operator can be used to limit the number of rows returned from a SELECT statement, it is very limited. The most common and flexible way to limiting rows is with a WHERE clause, which is specified in your SELECT statement immediately following the FROM clause.

```sql
SELECT OrderID, CustomerID, OrderDate, OrderTime, OrderTotal
FROM Orders.OrderHeader
WHERE OrderDate = '2001-01-01';
```

Comparison Operators

You can use all of the math operators to make comparisons e.g. =, <, >, <=, >=, <>.

```sql
SELECT OrderID, CustomerID, OrderDate, OrderTime, OrderTotal
FROM Orders.OrderHeader
WHERE OrderTotal > 200;

SELECT OrderID, CustomerID, OrderDate, OrderTime, OrderTotal
FROM Orders.OrderHeader
WHERE OrderTotal <= 20;
```

Inequality can be expressed using either <> or the older syntax of !=

```sql
SELECT OrderID, CustomerID, OrderDate, OrderTime, OrderTotal
FROM Orders.OrderHeader
WHERE ShippingAmount <> 5;
```

Comparison operators don't just apply to numbers. They can be used with any data type.

```
SELECT FirstName, LastName
FROM HumanResources.Employee
WHERE FirstName > 'H';
```

In the above example, SQL Server will return anything that starts with the letter H or higher in the alphabet. To every computer system, letters are simply display encodings for numbers. Each letter in an alphabet is assigned a number which is also known as the letter's ANSI character code. So, the H is converted to its ANSI equivalent code and then retrieves every character with a higher ANSI character code.

Likewise, you can use comparison operators on dates and times as well. You need to be careful with a datetime data type since you can inadvertently leave values when using an equality operator since the date could have a time component stored. In terms of dates and times, the less than operator means dates/times prior to the date/time specified while the greater than operator means dates/times after the date/time specified.

```
SELECT OrderID, CustomerID, OrderDate, OrderTime, OrderTotal
FROM Orders.OrderHeader
WHERE OrderDate < '2001-06-01';
```

You can specify compound criteria using AND and OR. AND means both criteria must be true for a row to be returned. OR means either of the criteria can be true for a row to be returned.

```
SELECT OrderID, CustomerID, OrderDate, OrderTime, OrderTotal
FROM Orders.OrderHeader
WHERE OrderTotal > 100 AND OrderTotal < 200;

SELECT OrderID, CustomerID, OrderDate, OrderTime, OrderTotal
FROM Orders.OrderHeader
WHERE OrderTotal > 100 OR OrderTotal < 200;

SELECT OrderID, CustomerID, OrderDate, OrderTime, OrderTotal
FROM Orders.OrderHeader
WHERE OrderTotal >= 100 AND OrderTotal <= 200;
```

When you have criteria that includes two specified endpoints, you can change the >=…<= to a BETWEEN operator.

```
SELECT OrderID, CustomerID, OrderDate, OrderTime, OrderTotal
FROM Orders.OrderHeader
WHERE OrderTotal BETWEEN 100 AND 200;
```

Parenthesis can be used to group criteria together, much like you group expressions in math

```
SELECT OrderID, CustomerID, OrderDate, OrderTime, OrderTotal
FROM Orders.OrderHeader
WHERE (OrderTotal >= 100 AND OrderTotal <= 200)
    OR OrderTotal < 20;
```

> **Note:** While the parenthesis are not technically necessary in the query above since AND takes precedence over OR, the parenthesis makes the code's intent clear to anyone.

The criteria in a WHERE clause is not required to evaluate to a true value. While this looks a bit strange, it is an extremely useful technique. The following query will return 0 rows, because 1 can never equal 2. However, it does retrieve the columns in the table for those cases where you know the table name, but not all of the columns in the table. This technique can also be used in conjunction with a SELECT INTO statement to quickly generate an empty table.

```
SELECT * INTO SomeOtherTable FROM Products.Product WHERE 1 = 2;
```

If you are trying to return rows based on a criteria where the row can match any one of a list of values, you can use the IN operator to specify the list.

```
SELECT SKU, ProductID, CategoryID, Price, StartDate, EndDate
FROM Products.SKU
WHERE CategoryID IN (4,5,6);
```

You can embed a SELECT statement as criteria in a WHERE clause which returns a single column of data although you have to be careful with the comparison operator. If the SELECT statement returns a single value, you can use any of the comparison operators. A SELECT statement which returns multiple rows can only be used with the IN operator.

```
SELECT a.FirstName, a.LastName
FROM HumanResources.Employee a
WHERE a.EmployeeID IN (SELECT b.EmployeeID
                       FROM HumanResources.EmployeeAddress b
                       WHERE b.StateProvinceID = (SELECT c.StateProvinceID
                                                  FROM Lookups.StateProvince c
                                                  WHERE c.StateProvince = 'Texas'));
```

Wildcards

Equality and inequality operators work well for numbers and dates/times, but character data needs a little more flexibility. You might want to return rows with a column that starts with one or more characters or where a value contains a specified string. The LIKE operator allows you to do wildcard searches. TSQL has two wildcard operators: % means any number of characters and _ means a single character.

```
SELECT FirstName, LastName
FROM HumanResources.Employee
WHERE FirstName LIKE 'M%';

SELECT FirstName, LastName
FROM HumanResources.Employee
WHERE FirstName LIKE 'M_r%';
```

The first example says to return employees with a first name that begins with M and has any number of characters following the M. The second example says to return employees that start with the letter M, have any character as the second letter of their name, followed by an r, and then any number of characters.

You can place the wildcard anywhere.

```
SELECT FirstName, LastName
FROM HumanResources.Employee
WHERE FirstName LIKE '%ar%';
```

Some people will tell you that you should never write the query above, which is referred to as a full wildcard search based on the beginning of the string being a wildcard character. While this example is extremely inefficient, sometimes you really don't know what characters are at the beginning of the data, therefore you don't have any option other than to use a full wildcard search. When the first character is defined, SQL Server can use an index, if one exists, to quickly find the matches to the pattern you are searching for. When you execute a full wildcard search, SQL Server doesn't have any ability to use an index and instead must read and evaluate every row in the table to find a match.

In addition to wildcard characters, you can also specify string patterns using square brackets as follows: [<list of characters>], [<char>-<char>], [^<char>].

The following example shows how to return valid US Social Security Numbers.

```
CREATE TABLE #Test
(SSN     CHAR(11)    NOT NULL);

INSERT INTO #Test
VALUES('000-00-0000'),('001-00-1000'),('001-01-0000'), ('457-55-5462'),('666-45-1234');

SELECT * FROM #Test
WHERE REPLACE(SSN,'-','') LIKE '[0-9][0-9][0-9][0-9][0-9][0-9][0-9][0-9][0-9]'
    AND SSN NOT LIKE '000%' AND REPLACE(SSN,'-','') NOT LIKE '____00%'
    AND REPLACE(SSN,'-','') NOT LIKE '_____0000' AND SSN NOT LIKE '666%'
    AND REPLACE(SSN,'-','') NOT IN ('987654320','987654321','987654322','987654323',
                                    '987654324','987654325','987654326','987654327',
                                    '987654328','987654329', '078-05-1120');
```

The basic SSN is 9 digits in three groups with each group separated by a -. The - is optional and used as a formatting device. The REPLACE function removes any - before making the comparisons.

```
CREATE TABLE #Test
(Value   CHAR(20)    NOT NULL);

INSERT INTO #Test
VALUES('Resist'),('Resisting'),('Resistor'),('Resisted');

SELECT * FROM #Test
WHERE Value LIKE 'Resist[^oe]%';
```

The example above shows how to exclude one or more characters from a result set by using the ^ (NOT) operator. The example will return anything that begins with 'Resist' and exclude anything where the seventh character is 'o' or 'e'.

At this point someone will be thinking "these wildcards are great, but what if I want to find one of the wildcard characters in my data". SQL Server has three methods to search for a wildcard character as a literal string value.

We've already covered one method in Chapter 6 when we inserted Provinces into the Lookups.StateProvince table, but we'll cover all three methods here.

```
CREATE TABLE #Test
(Value    CHAR(10)    NOT NULL);

INSERT INTO #Test
VALUES ('Te[st'),('Te]st'),('Te%st'),('Te_st'),('Te''st');

SELECT * FROM #Test
WHERE Value LIKE 'Te[[]st';

SELECT * FROM #Test
WHERE Value LIKE 'Te#%st' ESCAPE '#';

SELECT * FROM #Test
WHERE Value LIKE 'Te#'st' ESCAPE '#';

SELECT * FROM #Test
WHERE Value LIKE 'Te[']st';
```

Remember that square brackets tell SQL Server to look for the character(s) specified between the square brackets. So, if you are looking for [,], %, or _ you can simply enclose the characters in square brackets for SQL Server to interpret them as literals as shown in the first SELECT statement. You can also use the ESCAPE keyword to define what is known as an "escape" character for the SELECT statement. You specify the escape character immediately preceding the wildcard character you are trying to find as shown in the second SELECT statement.

I've included the single quote in this discussion even though it isn't one of the wildcard characters, because you might think that you could use either the square brackets or ESCAPE operator to search for a single quote within a character string. Attempting to run either of the last two SELECT statement to find a single quote will produce the following error message:

```
Msg 102, Level 15, State 1, Line 2
Incorrect syntax near 'st'.
Msg 105, Level 15, State 1, Line 2
Unclosed quotation mark after the character string ';'.
```

Remember that single quote is the terminator for character strings. So, as soon as you specify a single quote SQL Server interprets that as either the start or end of a string, in our example the end of the string, and since the remainder of the command is invalid SQL, produces an error. If you are looking for a single quote or need to store a single quote, you need to use a special case of an escape character, which is also a single quote as shown below:

```
SELECT * FROM #Test
WHERE Value LIKE 'Te''st';
```

That is not a double quote in the middle of the string; it is two single quotes side by side. The first single quote escapes the second single quote such that SQL Server treats the second single quote as a literal character.

NULLs

There are times when you want to find all of the rows where a NULL exists. So, taking what you already know about writing queries, you might try the following SELECT statement:

```
SELECT AddressID, EmployeeID, AddressLine1, AddressLine2, City, StateProvinceID,
PostalCode
FROM HumanResources.EmployeeAddress
WHERE AddressLine2 = NULL;
```

This is NOT the way to find a NULL. Remember NULL means the non-existence of a value. If a value doesn't exist, it certainly can't be equal to anything. To find NULLs, you have to use the special IS NULL operator as follows:

```
SELECT AddressID, EmployeeID, AddressLine1, AddressLine2, City, StateProvinceID,
PostalCode
FROM HumanResources.EmployeeAddress
WHERE AddressLine2 = NULL;
```

Likewise to find rows that are not NULL, use the IS NOT NULL operator.

```
SELECT SKU, ProductID, CategoryID, Price, StartDate, EndDate
FROM Products.SKU
WHERE PenStyleID IS NOT NULL;
```

You could have used the ISNULL() and COALESCE functions to translate a NULL to some specified value and then looked for that value in the results as shown below, but this is extremely inefficient.

SQL Server has to first compute the result of the ISNULL function for each row before comparing the results to determine if the row should be returned. Remember our discussion in Chapter 6 on how NULLs are actually stored on a data page. By simply looking for rows when a column IS NULL, SQL Server has to just look for a 0 in the column along with the NULL bitmask to determine if a row should be returned. In order to find rows where a column IS NOT NULL, SQL Server simply has to return all rows where the column does not have a 0 stored in it or the ones where a 0 is stored but the NULL bitmask is turned off for that column.

Operator Precedence

Just as math and data types have a precedence order, the precedence on operators is as follows:

1. () Parenthesis

2. * Multiply, / Divide, % Modulo (remainder of division)

3. +, -

4. =, <, >, <=, >=, <>, !=

5. NOT

6. AND

7. BETWEEN, IN, LIKE, OR

Basic Performance Tuning

This is also where we need to have a basic discussion on performance. I've lost count of the number of times I've been called by customers to deal with poor performance in their applications. The common misconception is that I'd have some "magic bullet" tweak of a setting in SQL Server, Windows, or the hardware that would suddenly make an application perform better. Lacking that, many of them seem to think that you can just "throw more hardware" at the problem. The real source of their performance problems was really in either design or knowledge.

While processors have gotten faster, servers have become more powerful, memory sizes have increased dramatically, and "disk space is cheap", the core principles of application design that we used "in the dark ages" of computing where you were lucky to have 8K of RAM still apply. Unfortunately, lost in this soup of development tools claiming to let you build applications very quickly with off the shelf software components that "shield" you from the "complexities" of databases are the three basic concepts of good application development:

1. If you don't need it, don't retrieve it.
2. Retrieve only what a user needs at the time, not everything they think they might want.
3. Make a single pass through the data or code.

Performance Tuning Rule 1

One of my all-time favorites for violating rule #1 is a legal application that I had to deal with several years ago. This company had a major performance issue with an application that was central to managing all of their legal cases. The application ran extremely quickly during testing and development, but now that it was in production, it was taking several minutes for a single screen to display to a user. After asking several standard questions about the environment and application I determined that I couldn't simply give them a piece of code or some simple advice to fix something simple that had been overlooked…until I got out to their office the following week and found out that the answers I had gotten weren't completely accurate.

The application in question pulled up full contact information about a client along with any legal matters the firm was dealing with. For each of these legal matters, all of the details of the legal matter were returned to the application and displayed on a single screen. This by itself might sound reasonable until you understand that "all of the details" meant pulling back 290+ columns of data, many of which had lengthy legal notes in them, and sticking all of the details in a grid control in the middle of the screen. The contact information for the client fit neatly in a small number of columns, but to get to any of the case details, you might have to scroll 150+ pages to the right in the grid, that was for a single case. If the client had hundreds of legal matters, they would all be pulled back into the grid with all 290+ columns of data.

This was compounded by a second grid which displayed the detailed billing history for the client. It turns out that most of the time, people using the application only needed the contact information for the client, only two people in the office cared about the detailed billing information, and no one was going to scroll several hundred times to the right to find data they needed.

The queries to retrieve this information ran in less than 3 seconds, but it took more than 2 minutes for the application to render a screen. I fixed the short term performance issue by pulling both grids off the main screen and stuck them behind two tabs which would only be filled when a user activated the tab. The application was suddenly displaying screens in less than 3 seconds. The application ran quickly in development and testing, because they were only testing against a database with 1 client who had 1 legal matter, no billing information, and the data was dummied up such that almost all of the columns were NULL. I left them to re-design the rest of the application so that screens only pulled data that a user needed.

Don't write your queries to pull every column from a table if your application only needs one or two columns. It is a waste of time, resources, and does nothing except slow your application down.

Performance Tuning Rule 2

My all-time favorite for only retrieving data that a user needs at the time comes from a recruiting application I was called in to fix performance issues with almost 15 years. This was in the SQL Server 6.5 days when we didn't have FileTable and Full-Text indexing which allowed us to just index and search documents. The application was hooked up to a scanner with OCR capabilities that would extract the contents of a resume, split it into 255 character chunks and store it in however many rows were required to capture the resume. I know, arcane and difficult, but the way things were stored wasn't much of a problem and wasn't the cause of performance issues.

A recruiter would input a keyword and run a search. The application would display the number of resume that matched the search. If the number was too large to deal with, they would add another search term and re-run the query, which would then be displayed as the number of resumes now matching. They would repeat this process of narrowing down the results until they had a set that was reasonable enough to go through. At that point, they would click the button to show the resumes and they would immediately appear on the screen.

There was only one problem. They had several thousand people needing to run searches and each person would usually run 15 – 20 staffing searches per day. When the system was only capable of serving up an average of 10 – 15 searches a minute on the largest, fastest hardware currently available, there was a bit of a problem.

It turns out that each person ran 6 – 8 searches on average before ever looking at the list of resumes. Unfortunately, the application pulled the entire contents of every resume each time a search was performed so that the results would appear immediately when the user wanted them.

What does that look like as a real world example? Suppose you are going to take a 2 day road trip with your family. You take the entire contents of your house and move it out to the driveway next to your car. You look at the large pile and decide that you really can't haul everything. You haul everything back into the house and put it back where it was. You then haul everything in the house back out into the driveway, except what is in the kitchen because you decided that you didn't need that. You look at the pile and decide it is still too much, so you haul it all back inside. You repeat this process over and over until the pile in the driveway is small enough to deal with before you start picking through and deciding what items are going to be packed into the car. Sounds completely crazy right? So, why would we do the same thing in an application and expect something different?

I introduced their developers to COUNT(*) and had them spend about 10 minutes making a tiny change in the application. Now when a search was performed and the result was simply going to display a number of resumes on the screen, they returned the results of COUNT(*) instead of the entire result set. The users could then refine their searches and once they got the results to a manageable list, clicking the button would then send a query off to collect only the resumes they really needed.

We terminated the load test when we passed 30,000 queries per minute, because that was more than their projected query load for an entire day.

Don't retrieve any data that you aren't actually going to use at the time the result is displayed to the user. You can always go back and get additional information when the user asks for it and if the user never asks for the additional information you didn't waste any time retrieving something they never used.

Performance Tuning Rule 3

One example, out of an unfortunately large number I've encountered, for making a single pass through the data to get what you need comes from a customer in the travel industry. Customers would go out to a website and search for vehicle, flight, or hotel for a destination. What they would get back is a page of up to 20 results sorted according to the order specified.

> This sounds reasonably straight forward, run a query to return the TOP 20 hotels for a destination ORDER BY some criteria. What happened to my SQL Server was an entirely different matter.
>
> The application was developed using nHibernate as the middle tier broker for managing access to the database. The developers went click, click, click to generate an object model and then used the object model without any modifications. They happily coded away, oblivious to what was actually being executed to retrieve the data they were after. After testing the application by running a couple dozen concurrent queries on a data set with a few hundred rows, they released the code to production.
>
> The customer was planning on rolling this out on a regional basis using localized language content. The marketing department had already started to blast advertisements out, complete with dates, as to when the new platform was going to be available in various markets. We were given the rollout schedule so we could manage our workload with respect to an increase in load on our database servers. The DBAs had never been involved in the design or testing of this application and the first time we saw the effect is when it went live in the first market. Instead of a couple dozen concurrent queries running against a few hundred rows, we had tens of thousands of customer attempting to run searches against millions of rows of data.
>
> We immediately saw our database server utilization suddenly jump by almost 20% when the first market went online. At about 30% utilization, it wouldn't have been a problem if this was the last market to come online. Instead it was the first market of almost 30 markets that was going to be put on this platform. When I looked at the query traffic coming through I was appalled. Taking the web stats on the number of page views and plotting that against the number of queries, we determined that each page served was averaging over 5,000 database queries. Even if you haven't ever worked in the IT industry, you'll quickly realize that asking for a single web page shouldn't kick off 5,000 queries to a database unless someone did something VERY wrong in the code.
>
> We spent the next week arguing with the developers about the application, with management only caring about moving forward with the rest of the rollout as promised by the marketing campaign. Instead of running a simple query, what the code did was to retrieve a list of hotel IDs from the database that matched the search criteria and load those into a data set. The code then looped across the data set and ran a query for each hotel ID to pull the rest of the data. Since the data was spread across multiple tables and just about everything had multiple attributes such as images, descriptions, amenities, the code ran an individual query for each hotel ID, then within each hotel ID pulled a list of the IDs for each of the child tables, and looped across each of those lists running a query for each ID. The code then reassembled the results of the thousands of single row queries into a useable web page to display to the user.
>
> This shows a fundamental implementation issue with any development framework, code generator, or object model. The tools that generate them are designed to be platform agnostic, so they are capable of generating code that will run against an RDBMS like SQL Server or against a bunch of spreadsheets and text files. That produces code which uses the least common denominator in functionality. In this case, the default nHibernate was using SQL Server to retrieve data as if it were just a bunch of text files sitting on a file system. This wasn't a problem with nHibernate, it was a problem with the developers understanding and implementation of the tool.
>
> Even after pulling the data and demonstrating what the code was doing based on the queries being executed, we spent another week arguing with the developers with them saying their application wasn't built the way we said it was with all of the looping going on. No matter what we presented, even going as far as to capture the query activity off a single page execution, we didn't get anywhere. We finally had to tell management that the rollout had to be stopped or we were going to melt down our database servers. We also sent them an infrastructure proposal based on the statistics we had gathered on how many additional database servers we were going to have to deploy to handle the load from this application. Things didn't start turning around until they brought in an outside expert of nHibernate and we sat on a conference call where he showed the developers the exact lines of code in their application where the nested loop for the queries was defined.

> SQL Server is designed to return result sets, which means it has the capability of joining multiple tables together and presenting a multi-row result set which an application can easily consume and display to the user. Don't make your application run multiple queries to return something that can be done is a single SELECT statement.
>
> **Performance Tuning Realities**
>
> Over the years, I've covered numerous performance issues to get an application running "good enough" by increasing the hardware and performing a lot of various tricks and tweaks, because organizations almost never want to deal with the actual root cause of performance problems, inefficient code. Throwing more hardware at the problem, tweaking settings, and manipulating SQL Server behaviors only covers up a performance issue. At some point in time, the performance problem will come back.
>
> People constantly marvel at how those "old-time" developers managed to write the applications they did with so few resources. We did it by paying attention to every byte that went into an application along with ensuring that we always executed the minimum amount of code necessary to accomplish a task. This might have resulted in some rather difficult to read code, but the fact is the code worked, ran fast, and used very little resources. The accounting application I wrote for a multi-million dollar company that ran in 8K of memory wouldn't be possible in today's development environment of frameworks and pre-built modules and my accounting application would still run circles around anything built today while only using 8K of RAM. While I wouldn't return of those days of having to count every character used in a program, the basic principles are still the same if you want an application to perform well.
>
> The real and permanent solution to almost every performance issue I've encountered was to either re-write code so that it was more efficient, re-design a database, or both. If you take the time to write code that is as efficient as possible, you can spend your time building new applications and new features, not re-writing/replacing poorly performing applications.

Exercise 4: Limiting Result Sets

1. Return a result set with a subjective description for the size of a customer's order using the following criteria: orders less than $40 are small, orders between $40 and $100 are medium, orders larger than $100 are large.
2. Return the first and last name of the first 100 customers in the state of Texas.
3. Retrieve the provinces that contain a single quote.
4. Return all of the provinces that start with M or N.

Multi-table queries

In chapter 5, we discussed how to design a database for transaction processing. In that design, we split out logical groups of data into separate tables and also ensured that we weren't repeating information within a table. This process causes your data to be spread out across several tables and while the query below will work to allow you to retrieve data from one table based on data in another table, it is extremely convoluted, cumbersome, and requires that you have significant understanding of the data in all of the tables combined. The query below only works as long as you have a single row in the Lookups.StateProvince table with a value of Texas. As soon as someone adds a second row either by accident or on purpose, the query fails.

```
SELECT TOP 100 a.FirstName, a.LastName
FROM Customers.Customer a
WHERE a.CustomerID IN (SELECT b.CustomerID
                       FROM Customers.Address b
                       WHERE b.StateProvinceID = (SELECT c.StateProvinceID
                                                  FROM Lookups.StateProvince c
                                                  WHERE c.StateProvince = 'Texas'));
```

As you can imagine, the SQL language wasn't designed to be that brittle and error prone and we've alluded to the fact that you can place multiple tables in a FROM clause. You can combine up to 256 tables in a FROM clause using 5 different join operators.

You will always see me alias tables when more than one table exists in a query. Additionally, when I alias a table, I will always explicitly apply the corresponding table alias to every column in a query. Not only does this make the code explicit, it avoids a possible error in your code that can be very hard to detect. The only time you are required to qualify a column name is when the same column name occurs in more than one table in the query. However, SQL also has another feature which can trip you up. Any column in an outer query can be referenced in an inner query. Consider the following query and please do not run this query unless you are prepared to wait a very long time.

```
SELECT TOP 100 FirstName, LastName
FROM Customers.Customer
WHERE CustomerID IN (SELECT CustomerID
                     FROM Customers.Address
                     WHERE StateProvinceID IN (SELECT AddressID
                                               FROM Lookups.StateProvince
                                               WHERE StateProvince = 'Texas'));
```

You might think you are still returning customers in the state of Texas, but you will in fact return an empty result set even though there are 76,519 customers in Texas. But, you will receive an empty result set based on a fortunate accident in the data instead of something **much** worse.

The AddressID column does not exist in the Lookups.StateProvince table, but it is perfectly valid to include AddressID in the SELECT clause since it belongs to the Customers.Address table in the outer query. The code also will not return an error since both the AddressID and StateProvinceID are integers.

What this query will actually do is the following:

- Since there is 1 row in the Lookups.StateProvince table that matches the criteria of Texas, retrieve the first AddressID from the Customers.Address table.
- Take this AddressID and match it to the StateProvinceID to return a list of CustomerIDs in the Customers.Address table.
- Use that list of CustomerIDs to retrieve the first 100 rows.

The reason this was a fortunate accident in the data is because AddressIDs start at 1001 and SQL Server would read the first value in the table, which happens to be an AddressID of 1001. This would then be compared to the StateProvinceID column to find the list of CustomerIDs with a StateProvinceID = 1001. That result would have been returned to the Customers.Customer table to retrieve the customer names. Since none of the customers resides in Kayseri, Turkey (StateProvinceID = 1001), you received an empty result set. If Champion Valley Pens actually had customers in Kayseri, Turkey, this query would have returned those customers instead of the intended list of customers in Texas.

INNER JOIN

An INNER JOIN tells SQL Server to take the two tables and match the rows on the columns specified in the ON clause. Any place the values match, return a row. Anywhere the values do not match, drop the row from the result set. This feature makes an INNER JOIN another way to limit your result sets. The query above can be written as a simple INNER JOIN as follows:

```
SELECT TOP 100 a.FirstName, a.LastName
FROM Customers.Customer a INNER JOIN Customers.Address b ON a.CustomerID = b.CustomerID
    INNER JOIN Lookups.StateProvince c ON b.StateProvinceID = c.StateProvinceID
WHERE c.StateProvince = 'Texas';
```

Not only is this query a lot easier to write and understand, it is doesn't have the brittle nature of the queries nested in the WHERE clause. It no longer matters how many times Texas occurs in the Lookups.StateProvince table. SQL Server will simply match the values and return rows where a match occurs. The query above tells SQL Server to first look in the Lookups.StateProvince table to find all of the StateProvinceIDs which correspond to a value of Texas. Then take that list of StateProvinceIDs and find every CustomerID that matches the list. Based on the list of CustomerIDs found, return the FirstName and LastName for the first 100 rows.

You'll notice that we used the primary key column along with the foreign key to create the join criteria in the ON clause. SQL doesn't care if the columns that you use in the ON clause are primary key/foreign key pairs, although this is the most common way you'll join tables together since it is how you split the data apart to start with. It doesn't even care if the data types match as long as the data can be implicitly converted to make a comparison.

For example, you could join an INT column to a DECIMAL column with 0 decimal places or a CHAR to a VARCHAR, but you can't join an INT to a CHAR because a CHAR can't be implicitly converted to an INT.

```
SELECT a.ShipmentID, a.ReceiveDate, b.OrderID
FROM Products.ShipmentHeader a INNER JOIN Orders.OrderHeader b ON a.ReceiveDate =
b.OrderDate;
```

The query above doesn't use either the primary key or foreign key, yet returns a valid result set which is a list of the orders placed on the same day as a shipment arrived at the warehouse.

The ON clause is not limited to a single set of columns in a join. You can specify multiple criteria using the same operators as you used to specify multiple criteria in a WHERE clause. Interestingly, you can use both the NOT and OR operators in addition to the AND operator.

```
SELECT a.ShipmentID, a.ReceiveDate, b.OrderDate
FROM Products.ShipmentHeader a INNER JOIN Orders.OrderHeader b
    ON NOT a.ReceiveDate = b.OrderDate;

SELECT a.ShipmentID, a.ReceiveDate, b.OrderDate
FROM Products.ShipmentHeader a INNER JOIN Orders.OrderHeader b
    ON NOT a.ReceiveDate = b.OrderDate AND a.ReceiveDate = b.OrderDate;

SELECT a.ShipmentID, a.ReceiveDate, b.OrderDate
FROM Products.ShipmentHeader a INNER JOIN Orders.OrderHeader b
    ON NOT a.ReceiveDate = b.OrderDate OR a.ReceiveDate = b.OrderDate;
```

I would strongly discourage you to avoid using the NOT operator in a join. Not only is it terrible for performance, it will cause a lot of confusion for anyone else reading your code. If you are forced to use an OR operator, you really need to go back and fix the table design. The OR operator tells you that two tables can be joined together multiple ways and that case will clearly violate all database design rules.

You can mix selection criteria and join criteria as shown below:

```
SELECT TOP 100 a.FirstName, a.LastName
FROM Customers.Customer a INNER JOIN Customers.Address b ON a.CustomerID =
b.CustomerID
    INNER JOIN Lookups.StateProvince c ON b.StateProvinceID = c.StateProvinceID
        AND c.StateProvince = 'Texas';
```

There are cases where placing selection criteria in the join can be an advantage, but you should leave all of your selection criteria to the WHERE clause where it belongs.

The default for a join is INNER JOIN, but just like any default, it can change at any time. As I've said several times already, don't depend on the default behavior; always explicitly specify INNER JOIN if that is what you really want. It not only makes the intention of your code clear, it also makes your code independent of any behavior changes.

In addition to NOT and OR being valid in the ON clause, you don't always have to use an equality operator. You can use any valid comparison operator.

The query below returns all of the products which were discounted from the default pricing.

```
SELECT a.OrderDetailID, a.SKU, a.Price, b.Price
FROM Orders.OrderDetail a INNER JOIN Products.SKU b ON a.SKU = b.SKU AND a.Price <>
b.Price;
```

A table can appear in the FROM clause as many times as you choose. Joining a table to itself is referred to as a self-join. The following query returns all of the accessories that are available for the Gatsby pen kit.

```
SELECT DISTINCT b.SKU
FROM Products.SKU a INNER JOIN Products.SKU b ON a.ProductID = b.PenKitID
WHERE a.SKU LIKE 'TK-GATSBY%';
```

OUTER JOIN

When you model data and create tables, certain columns in a table can be optional. The optional columns are defined as NULLable. Additionally, data in dependent tables can also be completely optional. For a company that ships products to customers, it might seem a little strange to have a customer without an address or an order, but if you consider marketing capabilities this is possible. A person might want to be added to a mailing list to be informed about upcoming sales even though they aren't ready to make a purchase yet. That means you could have a row in the customer table that has contact information, but no orders or addresses.

What if you wanted to retrieve a list of all customers and include any orders that the customers had placed. If you use an INNER JOIN, you would only retrieve the customers who had placed an order and would eliminate any customers who had not yet placed an order. You can preserve all rows in a given table and include data from one or more other tables if the data exists by using an OUTER JOIN.

There are three types of OUTER JOIN: LEFT OUTER JOIN, RIGHT OUTER JOIN, and FULL OUTER JOIN. The keyword OUTER is optional, but as I've said many times before the shorthand notation isn't worth the confusion that your code would cause for most developers.

```
SELECT a.CustomerID, a.FirstName, a.LastName, b.OrderID, b.OrderTotal
FROM Customers.Customer a LEFT OUTER JOIN Orders.OrderHeader b ON a.CustomerID =
b.CustomerID
WHERE a.CustomerID IN (10,35,41,611,720,800)
ORDER BY a.CustomerID DESC;
```

Every LEFT OUTER JOIN can be expressed as a RIGHT OUTER JOIN by simply changing the order of the tables as follows:

```
SELECT a.CustomerID, a.FirstName, a.LastName, b.OrderID, b.OrderTotal
FROM Orders.OrderHeader b RIGHT OUTER JOIN Customers.Customer a ON a.CustomerID =
b.CustomerID
WHERE a.CustomerID IN (10,35,41,611,720,800)
ORDER BY a.CustomerID DESC;
```

When you specify LEFT OUTER JOIN, SQL Server preserves all of the rows in the table on left hand side of the outer join operator which match the selection criteria and appends data from the table on the right hand side of the outer join operator if a match exists based on the ON clause. For a RIGHT OUTER JOIN, it is simply the opposite effect.

If a matching row does not exist, SQL Server fills the corresponding columns with a NULL. Using this behavior is the first way that most developers learn to find rows in one table that do not have a match in the other table. You could write the following query to return just the customers who have not yet placed an order.

```sql
SELECT a.CustomerID, a.FirstName, a.LastName, b.OrderID, b.OrderTotal
FROM Customers.Customer a LEFT OUTER JOIN Orders.OrderHeader b ON a.CustomerID = b.CustomerID
WHERE a.CustomerID IN (10,35,41,611,720,800)
    AND b.OrderID IS NULL
ORDER BY a.CustomerID DESC;
```

```
CustomerID   FirstName         LastName      OrderID      OrderTotal
-----------  -----------       --------      --------     -----------
720          Adria             Crowe         NULL         NULL
611          Allen             Smith         NULL         NULL
(2 row(s) affected)
```

You could also specify a FULL OUTER JOIN which would preserve all of the rows from both sides of the outer join operator and append NULLs where rows did not exist on either side.

Joins are logically processed from left to right, so simply rearranging the join order in a FROM clause can produce different results.

Taking the same query as above and adding in the order details will produce a logic error.

```sql
SELECT a.CustomerID, a.FirstName, a.LastName, b.OrderID, b.OrderTotal
FROM Customers.Customer a LEFT OUTER JOIN Orders.OrderHeader b ON a.CustomerID = b.CustomerID
    INNER JOIN Orders.OrderDetail c ON b.OrderID = c.OrderID
WHERE a.CustomerID IN (10,35,41,611,720,800)
    AND b.OrderID IS NULL
ORDER BY a.CustomerID DESC;
```

This will result in no rows returned even though customers 611 and 720 haven't placed any orders. The issue here is with the INNER JOIN that follows the LEFT OUTER JOIN. SQL Server first evaluates the outer join which produces NULLs for the OrderID for both of these customers. It then does an INNER JOIN of that result to the OrderDetail table. Since a NULL doesn't equal anything else, the two rows with a NULL for an OrderID are eliminated from the result set. So, in general, if you follow an OUTER JOIN with an INNER JOIN where the join is based on the optional table in the OUTER JOIN, you will nullify the results of the OUTER JOIN.

You can fix this problem three ways:

- Use parenthesis to make the order of operations clear

```sql
SELECT a.CustomerID, a.FirstName, a.LastName, b.OrderID, b.OrderTotal
FROM Customers.Customer a LEFT OUTER JOIN (Orders.OrderHeader b
    INNER JOIN Orders.OrderDetail c ON b.OrderID = c.OrderID) ON a.CustomerID = b.CustomerID
WHERE a.CustomerID IN (10,35,41,611,720,800)
    AND b.OrderID IS NULL
ORDER BY a.CustomerID DESC;
```

- Change the INNER JOIN to a LEFT OUTER JOIN

```
SELECT a.CustomerID, a.FirstName, a.LastName, b.OrderID, b.OrderTotal
FROM Customers.Customer a LEFT OUTER JOIN Orders.OrderHeader b ON a.CustomerID =
b.CustomerID
    LEFT OUTER JOIN Orders.OrderDetail c ON b.OrderID = c.OrderID
WHERE a.CustomerID IN (10,35,41,611,720,800)
    AND b.OrderID IS NULL
ORDER BY a.CustomerID DESC;
```

- Rearrange the joins in the FROM clause

```
SELECT a.CustomerID, a.FirstName, a.LastName, b.OrderID, b.OrderTotal
FROM Orders.OrderHeader b INNER JOIN Orders.OrderDetail c ON b.OrderID = c.OrderID
    RIGHT OUTER JOIN Customers.Customer a ON b.CustomerID = a.CustomerID
WHERE a.CustomerID IN (10,35,41,611,720,800)
    AND b.OrderID IS NULL
ORDER BY a.CustomerID DESC;
```

CROSS JOIN

A CROSS JOIN is used to produce all combination of rows between two tables, in other words a cross product. This is a highly unusual join to use in an application and should raise a huge, red flag when you find one. A cross product is extremely bad for performance and can produce incredibly large result sets. For example, if you cross join two tables with 1000 rows each, you will produce a result set of 1,000,000 rows.

If you are encountering CROSS JOINs between tables in your database, you most likely have a database that needs to be redesigned to be useable for a business. Sometimes, a CROSS JOIN is either necessary or useful for what you need to accomplish. However, in all cases where a CROSS JOIN is present, you should include a comment so that anyone looking at the code knows you used a CROSS JOIN for a very specific purpose.

One of the useful applications of a CROSS JOIN is in generating sample data. CROSS JOINs were used extensively to generate the sample data in the Champion Valley Pens database. I started by defining the data in the Products.Product table and populated all of the lookup tables with valid values. Once those were done, I used CROSS JOINs to derive all of the rows in the Products.SKU table. For example, the following query generates a piece of the data set for Gatsby pens:

```
SELECT 'TK-GATSBY-' + CASE WHEN c.PenStyle = 'BallPoint' THEN 'BP'
                           WHEN c.PenStyle = 'Rollerball' THEN 'RB'
                           ELSE 'FP' END + '-' + b.Plating SKU,
    a.ProductID, CASE WHEN c.PenStyle = 'BallPoint' THEN 5
                      WHEN c.PenStyle = 'Rollerball' THEN 6
                      ELSE 4 END CategoryID, a.Price, '2001-07-01' StartDate
FROM Products.Product a CROSS JOIN Lookups.Plating b
    CROSS JOIN Lookups.PenStyle c
WHERE a.ProductName LIKE 'Gatsby%'
```

If you compare the results from above to the contents of the Products.SKU table, you'll realize that instead of using the fully spelled out plating, I used an abbreviation. I also modified the price based on the style of pen and the plating (Rose Gold is more expensive than Silver). A second pass was made to produce the SKUs that have dual platings. I also populated the drill bits, bushing, mandrel, arbor, plating1, plating2, and pen style although those have been left out of the query simply for brevity. You will get greater insight into the data when we start working with the business documents in Chapter 14, "Full Text Indexing".

Subqueries

You can nest one SELECT within another SELECT. The nested query is referred to as a subquery and can be either correlated or non-correlated. A non-correlated subquery is also referred to as self-contained, because it does not depend on the outer query. You saw an example of a non-correlated subquery when we return customers in the state of Texas before we introduced joins.

When a subquery returns a single value, scalar, it can be used anywhere a single value is allowed such as the SELECT or WHERE clauses. A subquery which returns a list of values can be used in a WHERE clause with the IN operator. A subquery which returned an entire table can be used anywhere a table is allowed. The special case of a subquery returning an entire table is referred to as a derived table and will be covered at the end of this chapter.

```
SELECT TOP 100 a.FirstName, a.LastName
FROM Customers.Customer a
WHERE a.CustomerID IN (SELECT b.CustomerID
                      FROM Customers.Address b
                      WHERE b.StateProvinceID = (SELECT c.StateProvinceID
                                                FROM Lookups.StateProvince c
                                                WHERE c.StateProvince = 'Texas'));
```

Non-Correlated Subqueries

If the non-correlated subquery from the Lookups.StateProvince table returns more than one row, you will get an error unless you change the = operator to an IN operator. Since we know that we should have multiple customers in the state of Texas, an IN operator was specified with the CustomerIDs.

You have to be careful with the results of a subquery. If the subquery does not return any rows, it is converted to a NULL. This has the effect of returning an empty result set from the outer query. If the subquery returns an actual NULL from the table, the same thing occurs as if the subquery produced no rows. If the subquery returns a list of values and one of those values is NULL, the results will depend upon the operator used with the set. Consider the following queries:

```
SELECT a.ProductID, a.ProductName
FROM Products.Product a
WHERE a.ProductID IN (SELECT b.PenKitID FROM Products.SKU b);

SELECT a.ProductID, a.ProductName
FROM Products.Product a
WHERE a.ProductID NOT IN (SELECT b.PenKitID FROM Products.SKU b);
```

Only a small portion of rows in the Products.SKU table have a value in the PenKitID column. This column started off being used for accessories which were specific to a single pen kit and the definition was later expanded to cover all turning kits. Parts on kits are not interchangeable, for example a center band on a Gatsby pen will not fit on an Astronaut pen. So, the parts which are not interchangeable are designated to specific pen kits by assigning the ProductID from the Products.Product table corresponding to a given turning kit to the PenKitID column in the Products.SKU table.

So, the first query says to retrieve a list of all of the products that have accessories specific to the product. The second query is intended to retrieve the opposite of that, namely the list of products which do not have accessories associated to them. Running the queries, you'll find that the first query returns list of turning kits while the second query returns an empty result set. You would expect a list of turning kits from the first query, since turning kits are going to have accessories associated to them. However, there are a large number of products that aren't turning kits, so why did the second query return an empty result set.

To understand this, let's first break down the results of the subquery. The subquery will return a list of values such as 46, 92, NULL, 42,... SQL Server will find each of these values in the Products.Product table and return the corresponding row. Since a NULL isn't possible in the ProductID column, SQL Server obviously doesn't find a match and throws that value away. Even if the ProductID column contained a NULL, that row would still not be returned since a NULL can't equal another NULL.

What happens when we negate this subquery with the NOT operator? We still get the same result from the subquery, but this time SQL Server has to eliminate any row in the Products.Product table which is in the list. This works fine until the NULL is encountered. To SQL Server, the NULL is unknown or non-existent. Since the NULL can't possibly equal another value, it also can't be used to determine a non-match. What results when you combine NOT IN with a list that contains a single NULL is the entire list is wiped out and SQL Server returns an empty result set.

We'll see how to fix this problem in just a little bit.

When you use a subquery in the SELECT statement, it behaves much like an outer join with one restriction. Each time the subquery is invoked, it must return a single value. If you think about this, it does make a lot of sense. You generally place columns in the SELECT clause and return 1 or more rows from a SELECT statement. The format of that result set looks very much like a table.

You can't embed columns within columns or a table within a single column, so it wouldn't make any sense to attempt to return multiple values from a subquery in the SELECT statement or multiple rows.

```
SELECT a.CustomerID, a.FirstName, a.LastName, (SELECT b.OrderID FROM
Orders.OrderHeader b)
FROM Customers.Customer a
WHERE a.CustomerID IN (10,35,41,611,720,800)
ORDER BY a.CustomerID DESC;
```

The query above would return an error since the subquery returns more than one order for each customer. You can fix this error by ensuring that only a single row is returned from the subquery.

```
SELECT a.CustomerID, a.FirstName, a.LastName,
    (SELECT TOP 1 b.OrderID FROM Orders.OrderHeader b)
FROM Customers.Customer a
WHERE a.CustomerID IN (10,35,41,611,720,800)
ORDER BY a.CustomerID DESC;
```

When I said that subquery in the SELECT statement behaves much like an OUTER JOIN, you might have thought this query was going to return the first OrderID for each customer in the list if an order exists. This is not what this query produces. The query above is a bit nonsensical from a business perspective. Since it is a non-correlated subquery, it does not rely on any values from the outer query, so it just returns an OrderID of 1 for every row returned in the outer query. Since

OrderID = 1 doesn't correspond to any of the CustomerIDs, it doesn't make any sense.

Correlated Subqueries

A correlated subquery uses values from the outer query. This makes the subquery dependent upon the outer query. Logically, it is as if the subquery is executed once for each row in the outer query.

To fix our customer orders example above, we would need to use a correlated subquery. The following subquery will return the first order placed by each customer in the list. Note that since customers 611 and 720 have not placed any orders, a NULL is returned, just like an OUTER JOIN would have.

```
SELECT a.CustomerID, a.FirstName, a.LastName,
    (SELECT TOP 1 b.OrderID
     FROM Orders.OrderHeader b
     WHERE a.CustomerID = b.CustomerID
     ORDER BY b.OrderID)
FROM Customers.Customer a
WHERE a.CustomerID IN (10,35,41,611,720,800)
ORDER BY a.CustomerID DESC;
```

If you only care that something occurs at least once, but not how many times it occurred, you can use the EXISTS operator. For example, if you wanted to return the list of customers who placed an order, you can get this list using an INNER JOIN as follows:

```
SELECT a.FirstName, a.LastName
FROM Customers.Customer a INNER JOIN Orders.OrderHeader b ON a.CustomerID = b.CustomerID;
```

But, this will return many duplicates since a customer can place more than one order and an INNER JOIN simply matches the values no matter how many times the value occurs. You can fix this by switching to a subquery with an EXISTS clause as follows:

```
SELECT a.FirstName, a.LastName
FROM Customers.Customer a
WHERE EXISTS (SELECT * FROM Orders.OrderHeader b
              WHERE a.CustomerID = b.CustomerID);
```

The EXISTS will also perform better than an INNER JOIN, because SQL Server doesn't have to scan to the end of the results to check for matches. As soon as it encounters the first match, it is done checking.

We can also fix the issue where the subquery after the NOT IN operator returned a NULL in the set thereby wiping out the entire set by using a correlated subquery as follows:

```
SELECT a.ProductID, a.ProductName
FROM Products.Product a
WHERE NOT EXISTS (SELECT * FROM Products.SKU b
                  WHERE a.ProductID = b.PenKitID);
```

The EXISTS operator always returns a TRUE or a FALSE from any comparison. When a NULL is encountered, EXISTS returns FALSE. A value of NOT FALSE is also FALSE, so EXISTS and NOT EXISTS effectively drop any NULLs returned by the subquery.

You could use SELECT *, SELECT 1, SELECT 'some constant', or SELECT <column> for the subquery. It really doesn't matter what is in the SELECT list for an existence check, only that a row exists/does not exist based on the WHERE clause.

SQL Server has an additional performance optimization when you use the EXISTS operator with columns which match a foreign key. The foreign key enforces that a row in a child table cannot have a value that does not exist in a parent table. So, if you asked for the orders which have a valid customer, SQL Server wouldn't even have to check the parent table. You would simply return any rows matching the criteria for the outer table, because there is a foreign key defined between the Customers.Customer and Orders.OrderHeader table that does not allow an invalid CustomerID to be written to the Orders.OrderHeader table. SQL Server simply determines that a foreign key exists and automatically knows that every CustomerID in the Orders.OrderHeader table has to exist in the Customers.Customer table.

```
SELECT a.*
FROM Orders.OrderHeader a
WHERE EXISTS (SELECT * FROM Customers.Customer b
              WHERE a.CustomerID = b.CustomerID);
```

There is a catch to this optimization. Foreign keys can be disabled and you can BCP/BULK INSERT data into a table. If you run a BCP/BULK INSERT with default settings or you disable a foreign key, the foreign key constraint is not checked. This can allow values to exist in the child table which do not exist in the parent. You can actually see this where the Customers.Address table has an address with a CustomerID that does not exist in the Customers.Customer table due to the bulk load operation we performed in Chapter 5.

Internally, when a foreign key is disabled, SQL Server changes the trusted flag on the foreign key. Likewise, if you BCP/BULK INSERT without having the operation check constraints, any foreign keys that reference the table being bulk loaded are also set to not trusted.

You can see this by executing the following query against the ChampionValleyPens database:

```
SELECT * FROM sys.foreign_keys
WHERE is_not_trusted = 1;
```

When you execute an EXISTS query and a foreign key covers the columns in your correlated subquery and the foreign key has is_not_trusted = 0, then SQL Server will ignore the table in the subquery and only query the outer table. You can see this by looking at the execution plan of the query above. Note, the OrderHeader table is the only one that appears in the query plan. We will cover query plans in detail in the next book, "SQL Server 2012 Database Development".

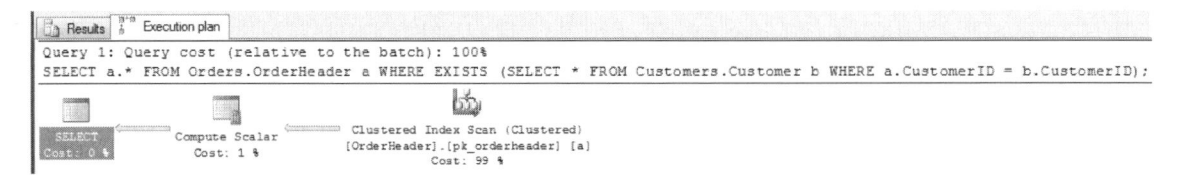

Figure 9-2 Foreign Key Optimization

However, if is_not_trusted is set to 1, SQL Server has to actually query the data since the foreign key was not checked for every row that is in the table.

You can make the foreign key trusted by executing an ALTER TABLE statement as follows:

```
ALTER TABLE Customers.Address
WITH CHECK
CHECK CONSTRAINT fk_StateProvinceToAddressOnStateProvinceID;
```

The CHECK CONSTRAINT clause enables the foreign key while the WITH CHECK clause tells SQL Server to scan the table and check that none of the rows violate the constraint.

Unique Results

As you've seen from the examples above, you can easily return result sets with repeating values since SQL Server will match all occurrences of a value without regard to whether the rows duplicate in a result set. If you want to eliminate duplicate values in any result set, you can use the DISTINCT operator in the SELECT clause. The DISTINCT applies to all columns in the SELECT list, not to a subset of columns.

The following query returns one row for each customer that has placed more than one order.

```
SELECT a.CustomerID, a.FirstName, a.LastName
FROM Customers.Customer a INNER JOIN Orders.OrderHeader b ON a.CustomerID = b.CustomerID
    INNER JOIN Orders.OrderHeader c ON b.CustomerID = c.CustomerID AND b.OrderID <> c.OrderID
ORDER BY a.CustomerID;
```

If you want to eliminate the duplicates, all you need to do is add the DISTINCT operator as follows:

```
SELECT DISTINCT a.CustomerID, a.FirstName, a.LastName
FROM Customers.Customer a INNER JOIN Orders.OrderHeader b ON a.CustomerID = b.CustomerID
    INNER JOIN Orders.OrderHeader c ON b.CustomerID = c.CustomerID AND b.OrderID <> c.OrderID
ORDER BY a.CustomerID;
```

However, if you were to include a column from the OrderHeader table which was unique for each row, no rows would be eliminated, because the DISTINCT applies to all columns in the SELECT list.

```
SELECT DISTINCT a.CustomerID, a.FirstName, a.LastName, b.OrderID
FROM Customers.Customer a INNER JOIN Orders.OrderHeader b ON a.CustomerID = b.CustomerID
    INNER JOIN Orders.OrderHeader c ON b.CustomerID = c.CustomerID AND b.OrderID <> c.OrderID
ORDER BY a.CustomerID;
```

Recall that COUNT(*) will return the number of rows based on the selection criteria of the query and COUNT(<column>) will return the number of non-NULL values in a column based on the selection criteria for the query. So, how do you find the number of unique values in a column based on selection criteria? For example, what if you wanted to know how many unique job titles exist within the company?

Since you know that DISTINCT removes duplicates, you might try the following query:

```
SELECT DISTINCT COUNT(JobTitleID)
FROM HumanResources.Employee;
```

You would get an incorrect answer. The COUNT(JobTitleID) will remove any NULLs, but it will count every occurrence of a non-NULL value in the JobTitleID column. Once the count has been computed, the DISTINCT operator is applied to the result. Since there is only one value, you are in fact returning the number of rows with a non-NULL JobTitleID. What you want to do is get a distinct list of JobTitleIDs first and then count the number of values in the set as follows:

```
SELECT COUNT(DISTINCT JobTitleID)
FROM HumanResources.Employee;
```

When we discussed the ORDER BY clause, we said that you can put any column or expression in the ORDER BY clause that is valid for the table(s) in the query, even if you do not include that column/expression in the SELECT clause. However, if your query has a DISTINCT, the ORDER BY clause is limited to the columns specified in the SELECT list. This is because a given row in the result set can correspond to multiple rows in the table and sort order between the elements would be ambiguous.

```
SELECT b.OrderID, a.CustomerID, a.FirstName, a.LastName
FROM Customers.Customer a INNER JOIN Orders.OrderHeader b ON a.CustomerID =
b.CustomerID
WHERE a.CustomerID IN (10,35,41,611,720,800);
```

```
OrderID        CustomerID     FirstName      LastName
-----------    -----------    ------------   --------
223            41                            Gabriel        Parrish
264            41                            Gabriel        Parrish
283            10                            Donna          Fierro
287            41                            Gabriel        Parrish
```

If you were to sort this query by the OrderID column, but not include the OrderID in the SELECT clause, SQL Server wouldn't care, because each row in the table would correspond to a row in the result set. (Although, a result set like that would probably confuse your users who wouldn't be able to understand how a result is sorted.) However, if we apply a DISTINCT to this query while leaving the OrderID out of the SELECT clause, SQL Server no longer has a way to determine how the results should be sorted. Should Fierro appear before or after Parrish if you are sorting by OrderID when the value of Parrish corresponds to OrderIDs 223, 264, and 287?

Exercise 5: Joining Tables and Returning Unique Results

1. Return the first name and last name of customers in the state of Illinois sorted by last name, first name using 2 different methods.

2. Find the customer address that does not match a customer.

3. Find the employee that does not have a phone number.

4. Retrieve the unique list of products which have been ordered. Hint: The Products.Product table contains a master grouping of a set of products, while the Products.SKU table contains the unique products that the company sells.

5. Return the number of different products which have been ordered.

6. Return the number of customers who have not placed an order with a CustomerID less than the maximum CustomerID in the Orders.OrderHeader table.

7. Retrieve the number of different pen kits which have accessories using 2 different methods. Hint: The PenKitID column will be non-NULL.

Aggregation – GROUP BY Clause

Earlier in the chapter, we introduced a variety of aggregation function such as SUM(), COUNT(), MIN(), MAX(), and AVG(). Computing these aggregates for an entire table or a filtered result set has some use, but of even greater use is the ability to compute aggregates based on groupings of data. The GROUP BY clause allows you to define groupings of data for an aggregate to be computed across. The query below computes the amount of money spent and number of orders placed by each customer within each calendar year.

```
SELECT a.CustomerID, a.FirstName, a.LastName, YEAR(b.OrderDate),
    SUM(b.OrderTotal) TotalRevenue, COUNT(b.OrderID) NumberOfOrders
FROM Customers.Customer a INNER JOIN Orders.OrderHeader b ON a.CustomerID = b.CustomerID
GROUP BY a.CustomerID, a.FirstName, a.LastName, YEAR(b.OrderDate);
```

```
CustomerID  FirstName  LastName   OrderYear   TotalRevenue   NumberOfOrders
----------  ---------  ---------  ----------  -------------  --------------
413         Martha     Toledo     2001        147.22         6
1021        Lucille    Peterson   2001        36.18          1
1472        Karen      Mora       2001        51.29          2
1923        Lakeisha   Borchardt  2001        240.2733       4
2531        Anthony    Bradley    2001        16.58          1
2982        Edward     Lilly      2001        64.60          1
159         Kenneth    Greer      2001        157.50         5
```

Looking at the result set, you might initially think that you have magically sorted the results by CustomerID. However, the 7th row in the result set demonstrates that you would be wrong. SQL Server does some internal manipulation of the data in order to compute the aggregate and in many cases; it might appear that the data comes out sorted. But, as we've already noted earlier, the only way to guarantee a specific sort order is to include an ORDER BY clause. The same rules noted for a DISTINCT with an ORDER BY clause also apply to GROUP BY.

A GROUP BY will aggregate multiple rows together, so the ORDER BY clause is restricted to columns and/or expressions used in the SELECT list.

```
SELECT a.CustomerID, a.FirstName, a.LastName, YEAR(b.OrderDate) OrderYear,
    SUM(b.OrderTotal) TotalRevenue, COUNT(b.OrderID) NumberOfOrders
FROM Customers.Customer a INNER JOIN Orders.OrderHeader b ON a.CustomerID = b.CustomerID
GROUP BY a.CustomerID, a.FirstName, a.LastName, YEAR(b.OrderDate)
ORDER BY TotalRevenue DESC;
```

The GROUP BY clause is required to contain every non-aggregate column in the SELECT clause. The following query would be invalid:

```
SELECT a.CustomerID, a.FirstName, a.LastName, YEAR(b.OrderDate) OrderYear,
    SUM(b.OrderTotal) TotalRevenue, COUNT(b.OrderID) NumberOfOrders
FROM Customers.Customer a INNER JOIN Orders.OrderHeader b ON a.CustomerID =
b.CustomerID
GROUP BY a.CustomerID, YEAR(b.OrderDate);
```

As I've said before, SQL Server doesn't do anything that is particularly unique or magical. The way data is processed is really no different than how things were done efficiently long before computers were invented. Computers simply allow us to operate on much larger sets of data in a much shorter time period than was possible before.

Take a moment to think through how you would create this type of calculation if all you had was a paper ledger book listing the orders as they occurred. There are two basic methods and each involves you taking out one or more blank pieces of paper to perform the calculation.

The first method would have you start at the top of the list and write down the first CustomerID and next to that the amount of the order with a 1 to designate this is the first order for the Customer. You would repeat this for every subsequent CustomerID in the ledger. When you encountered a CustomerID you had already written down on your scratch paper, you would increment the orders and revenue. You would repeat this process until you had gone through the entire ledger. (Yes, you would also account for one row per customer for each year they placed an order, but the process doesn't change, just the volume of data.)

The second method would be to re-write the ledger to your scratch paper and sort the contents of the ledger by CustomerID and order year. Once the list was sorted, it is a simple matter of starting with the first row and accumulating the order total and number of orders until the combination of customer and order year changes at which point you would start back from 0 for the next group of data.

SQL Server logically uses the second method with the "scratch paper" being the tempdb database. The data is first going to be sorted and then the engine scans down through the sorted list creating each aggregate. The aggregated data is then combined with anything else requested in the query and the results returned to you. This is why it may appear that the results of a GROUP BY are in a sorted order, but as we've demonstrated above, this is how SQL Server logically processes, not how it actually processes the query.

This may also lead you to ask why SQL Server can't just perform the aggregate based on the CustomerID and order year since the FirstName and LastName are simply additional data attached to a CustomerID and don't contribute to any kind of tie-breaking in the groups created. You may know that the CustomerID is simply a representation of a customer name, but SQL Server can't assume that.

So, if you want to return the customer name, you have to include the FirstName and LastName in the GROUP BY and incur the overhead of these columns in the grouping operation. Or do you......? Consider the following query:

```
SELECT a.CustomerID, MIN(a.FirstName) FirstName, MIN(a.LastName) LastName,
    YEAR(b.OrderDate) OrderYear, SUM(b.OrderTotal) TotalRevenue,
    COUNT(b.OrderID) NumberOfOrders
FROM Customers.Customer a INNER JOIN Orders.OrderHeader b ON a.CustomerID =
b.CustomerID
GROUP BY a.CustomerID, YEAR(b.OrderDate);
```

Since the CustomerID is really equivalent to the FirstName and LastName, I really don't have to create the overhead of grouping those columns. If I put FirstName and LastName inside an aggregate, those columns simply become computations and are no longer considered in the grouping. It doesn't change the result set, but it does reduce the overhead of the query in the tempdb database.

OUTER JOINS

The behavior of COUNT(*) exposes a logic issue when used with OUTER JOINs. Recall from our discussion that when you specify COUNT(*) SQL Server doesn't care whether a value exists in a particular column or not, only that a row exists. So, if you are using a COUNT(*) with an OUTER JOIN, you could get invalid results as follows:

```
SELECT a.CustomerID, a.FirstName, a.LastName, COUNT(*) CustomerOrders
FROM Orders.OrderHeader b RIGHT OUTER JOIN Customers.Customer a ON a.CustomerID =
b.CustomerID
WHERE a.CustomerID IN (10,35,41,611,720,800)
GROUP BY a.CustomerID, a.FirstName, a.LastName;
```

The query above will tell you that customers 611 and 720 have placed 1 order even though we already know neither of these customers has placed an order. COUNT(*) doesn't care if a NULL is present from the OrderHeader table, just that a row exists. You fix this by replacing the * with a column name so that NULLs are eliminated by the aggregate.

```
SELECT a.CustomerID, a.FirstName, a.LastName, COUNT(b.OrderID) CustomerOrders
FROM Orders.OrderHeader b RIGHT OUTER JOIN Customers.Customer a ON a.CustomerID =
b.CustomerID
WHERE a.CustomerID IN (10,35,41,611,720,800)
GROUP BY a.CustomerID, a.FirstName, a.LastName;
```

NULLs

Normally, a NULL does not equal another NULL. However, when grouping data, you aren't limiting a result set, so all values present need to be accounted for. So, with respect to a GROUP BY, the convention is to put all NULLs into a single group for aggregation.

```
SELECT PenKitID, COUNT(*)
FROM Products.SKU
GROUP BY PenKitID
ORDER BY PenKitID;
```

For the purpose of sorting, the NULL grouping will appear as the lowest value.

An interesting effect is when you combine a GROUP BY with COUNT(<column>) as follows:

```
SELECT PenKitID, COUNT(PenKitID)
FROM Products.SKU
GROUP BY PenKitID
ORDER BY PenKitID;
```

The GROUP BY aggregates all of the NULLs into a single group, but the COUNT (PenKitID) will only count non-NULL values. So, what you get as a result is the following:

```
PenKitID
-----------  -----------
NULL         0
28           1063
29           1063
```

Multi-Level Aggregates

The GROUP BY clause has two additional operators, ROLLUP and CUBE, which allow a GROUP BY clause to generate multiple levels of aggregates. In addition to the aggregation by groups from the GROUP BY, ROLLUP will add in an aggregation of groups along with a grand total for the result set.

ROLLUP

We previously used a GROUP BY to compute the revenue and number of orders for each customer within each year. Since the ChampionValleyPens database currently has data spanning January 1, 2001 through January 31, 2002, most of the customers have only placed orders in a single year. However, a few customers have orders in both years. A straight GROUP BY query would return a separate row for each year for the customers placing orders in more than one year. We can apply the ROLLUP function to include an additional layer of aggregation such that customers who have orders in both years will have one row for each year as well as a row that is an overall aggregate of their orders spanning all years. The ROLLUP function will also include a grand total row for the entire result set.

```
SELECT a.CustomerID, YEAR(b.OrderDate) OrderYear,
    SUM(b.OrderTotal) TotalRevenue, COUNT(b.OrderID) NumberOfOrders
FROM Customers.Customer a INNER JOIN Orders.OrderHeader b ON a.CustomerID = b.CustomerID
WHERE a.CustomerID IN (4,5)
GROUP BY ROLLUP(a.CustomerID, YEAR(b.OrderDate));

CustomerID    OrderYear     TotalRevenue            NumberOfOrders
-----------   -----------   --------------------    --------------
4             2001          218.81                  6
4             NULL          218.81                  6
5             2001          133.30                  7
5             2002          73.91                   1
5             NULL          207.21                  8
NULL          NULL          426.02                  14
(6 row(s) affected)
```

Note the row where CustomerID = 5 and the OrderYear is NULL. This represents the subtotal of all orders for CustomerID 5 spanning both years. The row where both CustomerID and OrderYear are NULL represents the grand total.

So, how do you know whether a NULL was actually in the results and when the NULL was generated by the ROLLUP function? SQL Server includes an addition function GROUPING to tell you whether the NULL you are seeing in the result set is an actual NULL or the NULL was generated as part of the ROLLUP function.

```
SELECT a.CustomerID, YEAR(b.OrderDate) OrderYear,
    SUM(b.OrderTotal) TotalRevenue, COUNT(b.OrderID) NumberOfOrders,
    GROUPING(a.CustomerID) CustomerRollup, GROUPING(YEAR(b.OrderDate)) YearRollup
FROM Customers.Customer a INNER JOIN Orders.OrderHeader b ON a.CustomerID =
b.CustomerID
WHERE a.CustomerID IN (4,5)
GROUP BY ROLLUP(a.CustomerID, YEAR(b.OrderDate));
```

```
CustomerID  OrderYear   TotalRevenue  NumberOfOrders  CustomerRollup  YearRollup
----------  ---------   ------------  --------------  --------------  ----------
4           2001        218.81        6               0               0
4           NULL        218.81        6               0               1
5           2001        133.30        7               0               0
5           2002        73.91         1               0               0
5           NULL        207.21        8               0               1
NULL        NULL        426.02        14              1               1
(6 row(s) affected)
```

The GROUPING function will return a 0 when the value comes from the actual data and a 1 when the NULL is produced by the ROLLUP function. Notice that you have to test each column in the GROUP BY clause separately and the case where all of the GROUPING tests evaluate to 1 is the grand total row.

Another function that helps you distinguish whether a row was generated by the ROLLUP function is GROUPING_ID(). Unlike the GROUPING function, GROUPING_ID can accept the entire list of columns/expressions in the GROUP BY clause and will produce a number corresponding to each group of results.

```
SELECT a.CustomerID, YEAR(b.OrderDate) OrderYear,
    SUM(b.OrderTotal) TotalRevenue, COUNT(b.OrderID) NumberOfOrders,
    GROUPING_ID(a.CustomerID,YEAR(b.OrderDate)) GroupID
FROM Customers.Customer a INNER JOIN Orders.OrderHeader b ON a.CustomerID =
b.CustomerID
WHERE a.CustomerID IN (4,5)
GROUP BY ROLLUP(a.CustomerID, YEAR(b.OrderDate));
```

```
CustomerID  OrderYear   TotalRevenue  NumberOfOrders  GroupID
----------  ---------   ------------  --------------  -------
4           2001        218.81        6               0
4           NULL        218.81        6               1
5           2001        133.30        7               0
5           2002        73.91         1               0
5           NULL        207.21        8               1
NULL        NULL        426.02        14              3
(6 row(s) affected)
```

GroupID = 0 is actual data in the table. GroupID =1 is the subtotals created by the ROLLUP function. GroupID = 3 is the grand total line.

CUBE

The CUBE function behaves similarly to the ROLLUP function in that it produces additional aggregation levels. Instead of just subtotals and a grand total, the CUBE function computes all possible combinations of the values in the GROUP BY clause. So, you will get rows grouped by CustomerID and OrderYear, rows grouped by CustomerID, rows grouped by OrderYear, and a grand total. You can use the GROUPING and GROUPING_ID functions to distinguish the rows generated by the data and the rows generated by the CUBE function.

```
SELECT a.CustomerID, YEAR(b.OrderDate) OrderYear,
    SUM(b.OrderTotal) TotalRevenue, COUNT(b.OrderID) NumberOfOrders,
    GROUPING(a.CustomerID) CustomerRollup, GROUPING(YEAR(b.OrderDate)) YearRollup
FROM Customers.Customer a INNER JOIN Orders.OrderHeader b ON a.CustomerID = b.CustomerID
WHERE a.CustomerID IN (4,5)
GROUP BY CUBE(a.CustomerID, YEAR(b.OrderDate));

SELECT a.CustomerID, YEAR(b.OrderDate) OrderYear,
    SUM(b.OrderTotal) TotalRevenue, COUNT(b.OrderID) NumberOfOrders,
    GROUPING_ID(a.CustomerID,YEAR(b.OrderDate)) GroupID
FROM Customers.Customer a INNER JOIN Orders.OrderHeader b ON a.CustomerID = b.CustomerID
WHERE a.CustomerID IN (4,5)
GROUP BY CUBE(a.CustomerID, YEAR(b.OrderDate));
```

Multiple Groupings

In addition to the CUBE and ROLLUP capabilities, in SQL Server 2008, Microsoft added the ability to compute aggregates across multiple groupings in a single SELECT statement. The GROUP BY clause was extended with the GROUPING SETS function. Take the following base query:

```
SELECT a.CustomerID, b.City, c.StateProvince, YEAR(d.OrderDate), OrderTotal
FROM Customers.Customer a INNER JOIN Customers.Address b ON a.CustomerID = b.CustomerID
    INNER JOIN Lookups.StateProvince c ON b.StateProvinceID = c.StateProvinceID
    INNER JOIN Orders.OrderHeader d ON a.CustomerID = d.CustomerID;
```

An application might want to compute the total revenue and number of orders for the combination of customer and order year. The same application might also want the total revenue and number of orders broken down by city, state/province, and order year along as well as by state/province and order year, plus add a grand total.

This would be four different aggregate groupings all from the same basic query. You could accomplish this by using the CUBE function and then eliminating all of the permutations that you don't want or you can use the GROUPING SETS function as follows:

```
SELECT a.CustomerID, b.City, c.StateProvince, YEAR(d.OrderDate) OrderYear,
    SUM(OrderTotal) TotalRevenue, COUNT(*) NumOrders
FROM Customers.Customer a INNER JOIN Customers.Address b ON a.CustomerID =
b.CustomerID
    INNER JOIN Lookups.StateProvince c ON b.StateProvinceID = c.StateProvinceID
    INNER JOIN Orders.OrderHeader d ON a.CustomerID = d.CustomerID
GROUP BY GROUPING SETS ((a.CustomerID,YEAR(d.OrderDate)),
                       (b.City,c.StateProvince,YEAR(d.OrderDate)),
                       (c.StateProvince,YEAR(d.OrderDate)),());
```

```
CustomerID  City         StateProvince  OrderYear  TotalRevenue  NumOrders
----------  -----------  -------------  ---------  ------------  ---------
NULL        Albertville  Alabama        2001       545.77        16
NULL        NULL         Wisconsin      2002       794.11        16
NULL        NULL         NULL           NULL       368044.0022   8088
1021        NULL         NULL           2001       36.18         1
```

The rows where the CustomerID and OrderYear have values and City and State are NULL correspond to the first grouping. The rows where the City, StateProvince, and OrderYear have values and CustomerID is NULL correspond to the second grouping. The rows where the StateProvince and OrderYear have values and the CustomerID and City are NULL correspond to the third grouping. The single row where all four of the columns are NULL corresponds to the fourth grouping specified by () which is also known as a grand total.

You can use the GROUPING_ID function as follows to provide a column which allows you to separate each of the aggregation levels:

```
SELECT a.CustomerID, b.City, c.StateProvince, YEAR(d.OrderDate) OrderYear,
    SUM(OrderTotal) TotalRevenue, COUNT(*) NumOrders,
    GROUPING_ID(a.CustomerID, b.City, c.StateProvince, YEAR(d.OrderDate)) GroupID
FROM Customers.Customer a INNER JOIN Customers.Address b ON a.CustomerID =
b.CustomerID
    INNER JOIN Lookups.StateProvince c ON b.StateProvinceID = c.StateProvinceID
    INNER JOIN Orders.OrderHeader d ON a.CustomerID = d.CustomerID
GROUP BY GROUPING SETS ((a.CustomerID,YEAR(d.OrderDate)),
                       (b.City,c.StateProvince,YEAR(d.OrderDate)),
                       (c.StateProvince,YEAR(d.OrderDate)),())
ORDER BY GroupID;
```

When we explained the CUBE and ROLLUP functions, you might have been wondering why anyone would want to subject themselves to having to break apart a result set instead of just running separate queries for the different grouping levels. GROUPING SETS probably just made your eyes cross and your head hurt.

Including multiple aggregations or multiple levels of aggregation in a single query can provide you with a performance improvement since you are making a single pass through the data. However, you now pushed a bunch of complicated logic upstream to your applications which have to now decompose a result set to figure out how to display the data properly. If you're trying to do something like this in a report, you'll definitely fry your brain getting it to break the result set and display anything properly

There are a lot of things you can do in SQL Server, but just because you can do something doesn't mean you should. If you are simply exploring data and trying to get an idea of what various computations produce, CUBE, ROLLUP, and GROUPING SETS can return all of the combinations very quickly. However, if you are building applications around multiple permutations of aggregates, there is a much better and simpler way of providing all of these permutations. The entire purpose of SQL Server Analysis Services is to compute aggregates across all permutations of a set of input columns in a way that allows users to very easily explore and analyze their data. I haven't found a case yet where CUBE, ROLLUP, and GROUPING SETS provided any benefit over using Analysis Services, so you won't find these functions in my code.

> **Note:** We'll cover Analysis Services in detail in the third book in our SQL Server 2012 series, "SQL Server 2012 Business Intelligence".

Filtering Aggregates – HAVING clause

Just as you can filter data in a WHERE clause, you can provide additional filtering when computing aggregates by using the HAVING clause. HAVING is only valid when you have a GROUP BY clause in the query.

The WHERE and HAVING clauses confuse many when they are new to writing queries. Both are used to filter data, but they are evaluated at different times. SQL Server applies the WHERE clause as well as the FROM clause to filter out the set of data available for aggregation. Once the data is filtered, the GROUP BY clause is applied to compute any aggregates. After the aggregates are computed, the HAVING clause can be applied to the data set to provide an additional level of filtering.

For example, if you wanted to look at customers with revenue greater than $100, you might think to write the following query:

```
SELECT a.CustomerID, MIN(a.FirstName) FirstName, MIN(a.LastName) LastName,
    YEAR(b.OrderDate) OrderYear, SUM(b.OrderTotal) TotalRevenue, COUNT(*)
NumberOfOrders
FROM Customers.Customer a INNER JOIN Orders.OrderHeader b ON a.CustomerID =
b.CustomerID
WHERE b.OrderTotal > 100
GROUP BY a.CustomerID, YEAR(b.OrderDate);
```

If you look at the results, CustomerID 6 is showing total revenue of $115.35 for a single order in 2002. But, if you look at the Orders.OrderHeader table, CustomerID 6 placed 7 orders in 2001 and 1 order in 2002. So, why does the query above only return a single order for this customer? It turns out that all 7 orders placed in 2001 were less than $100 while a single order in 2002 was more than $100 ($115.35). What the query does is first eliminate all orders from the table with a total less than $100 and then apply the GROUP BY to compute aggregates on what is left.

The correct query is as follows:

```
SELECT a.CustomerID, MIN(a.FirstName) FirstName, MIN(a.LastName) LastName,
    YEAR(b.OrderDate) OrderYear,  SUM(b.OrderTotal) TotalRevenue, COUNT(*)
NumberOfOrders
FROM Customers.Customer a INNER JOIN Orders.OrderHeader b ON a.CustomerID =
b.CustomerID
GROUP BY a.CustomerID, YEAR(b.OrderDate)
HAVING SUM(b.OrderTotal) > 100;
```

You'll now find that Todd Sawyers is included twice in the result set. The 6 orders he placed in 2001 totaled to more than $100 while the single order placed in 2002 also totaled to more than $100.

```
CustomerID  FirstName   LastName   OrderYear     TotalRevenue    NumberOfOrders
----------  ----------  ---------  ------------  -------------   ---------------
1           Lorraine    Peters     2001          477.02          10
...
6                       Todd       Sawyers       2002            115.35          1
6                       Todd       Sawyers       2001            202.14          7
```

You might be wondering why I specified the calculation in the HAVING clause instead of the alias for the calculation that was used in the SELECT clause. If I had specified the alias for the calculation, SQL Server would have returned an error message that the column TotalRevenue was not found. The section below on processing order explains why you can't reference an alias from the SELECT clause in the HAVING clause.

Even though the calculation is specified twice, SQL Server doesn't actually perform the computation twice. When the query is physically processed, the calculation is made once. The results of the calculation are then filtered by the criteria in the HAVING clause.

Derived Tables

For the last trick in this chapter, let's return to the aggregation query we've been using for the last several pages.

```
SELECT a.CustomerID, a.FirstName, a.LastName, YEAR(b.OrderDate) OrderYear,
    SUM(b.OrderTotal) TotalRevenue, COUNT(*) NumberOfOrders
FROM Customers.Customer a INNER JOIN Orders.OrderHeader b ON a.CustomerID =
b.CustomerID
GROUP BY a.CustomerID, a.FirstName, a.LastName, YEAR(b.OrderDate);
```

Ideally, I would like to compute the aggregates by having SQL Server build groups just on the CustomerID and OrderYear, but I also want the FirstName and LastName of the customer included in the result set. That forces me to either include those two columns in the GROUP BY clause or use a "trick" to turn them into aggregates.

I can accomplish my goals by taking advantage of something that is available, but essentially hidden within the syntax of a SELECT statement. When we defined a table, we specified a set of columns with data types and nullability and then gave the definition a name. If you'll recall when we executed a SELECT INTO statement, the resulting table had the column names, data types, and nullability of the corresponding columns in the SELECT clause. Since the definition of the columns was picked up from the SELECT list, it really means that every result set produced is a table definition. The only thing lacking is an actual name for the definition in order for the result set to actually become a table.

Using this, it would stand to reason that you can actually embed an entire SELECT statement into a FROM clause as long as you can make it look like an actual table. The FROM clause needs a name to reference, so by providing an alias for the SELECT statement, we've met all of the requirements of a table, which is then valid to embed inside a FROM clause.

```
SELECT a.CustomerID, a.FirstName, a.LastName, d.OrderYear, d.TotalRevenue,
    d.NumberOfOrders
FROM Customers.Customer a INNER JOIN
    (SELECT b.CustomerID, YEAR(c.OrderDate) OrderYear,
        SUM(c.OrderTotal) TotalRevenue, COUNT(*) NumberOfOrders
    FROM Customers.Customer b INNER JOIN Orders.OrderHeader c ON b.CustomerID =
c.CustomerID
    GROUP BY b.CustomerID, YEAR(c.OrderDate)) d ON a.CustomerID = d.CustomerID;
```

This technique is called a derived table. I took our SELECT...GROUP BY, wrapped it in parenthesis and aliased it as d. The SELECT..GROUP BY defines the structure of the table and the letter d provides the name for SQL Server to reference the structure. The derived table is computed first and the results are then joined back to the customer table to pick up the customer name. Just like you have to provide a name for every column in a table, every column/expression has to have a name in the SELECT list of the derived table.

We could have simply used a SELECT INTO to dump the contents of the GROUP BY query into a temp table and then joined this temp table back to the customers table. However, this incurs physical writes to disk and can have a significant performance impact. The derived table on the other hand is a memory only structure which in most cases will outperform a temp table.

> **Note:** One of the biggest performance drains for applications is the extensive use of temp tables to stash intermediate results. This usually happens, because a developer really doesn't understand how to do set oriented processing. The developer will retrieve a piece of data and perform an operation, stashing the result in a temp table. They will then retrieve the contents of the temp table to perform the next step in the operation, only to stash the data back into the same or a different temp table. This process could be repeated dozens of times before a final result is returned to an application. At each step, the developer is incurring physical disk I/O. Each read of a different temp table also consumes additional memory, because it is a different table and set of data pages. I've lost track of the number of times all I had to do to fix a performance issue in an application was to get rid of the temp tables and replace them with derived tables. It's happened so frequently, that it is the first thing I look to eliminate when I have to work with anyone's code.

Exercise 6: Aggregating Data

1. Retrieve the top 10 products in terms of quantity sold. Hint: a sellable product is a SKU.

2. Retrieve the quantity sold and total sales amount for each product. Sort the list from highest to lowest sales.

3. Retrieve the products which have total sales greater than $500. Sort the list from highest to lowest sales.

4. Retrieve the quantity sold and total sales for each product broken down by year and include a grand total in the results.

Processing Order

The ANSI standard defines a logical processing order for clauses in a SELECT statement. Although SQL Server is free to optimize this process and frequently does.

The logical order in which clauses are processed is:

- FROM
- ON
- JOIN
- WHERE
- GROUP BY
- HAVING
- SELECT
    - OVER
    - DISTINCT
    - TOP
- ORDER BY

If you think about the processing order based on what you now know about retrieving data, the order makes a lot of sense, although there is some inefficiency. It would be very difficult to retrieve data if you didn't first know where to get the data. However, retrieving the entire contents of a table into memory and then filtering the results is very inefficient, so SQL Server applies some optimization to avoid retrieving data which doesn't match the filter criteria in the WHERE clause.

Once you retrieve the base set of data, you can then produce groupings and aggregate as necessary. Since the HAVING clause operates on grouped data, the evaluation of HAVING must follow the GROUP BY clause.

The SELECT is almost the last clause evaluated, however it makes very little sense to retrieve all of the columns in a table and carry those columns around in memory for each of the subsequent operations only to return a small fraction of the columns to an application. So, just like the processing of a FROM clause, some optimization is applied to only retrieve columns into memory which is necessary for processing the query.

The final step in the process is to sort the results before returning the set to an application. This also makes sense since the number of rows in the result set is now fixed; SQL Server has all of the data that it needs to sort. However, additional optimizations occur within SQL Server on the ORDER BY clause. If you have a clustered index or primary key which is clustered, which corresponds to the ORDER BY clause, SQL Server does not need to perform the sort operation since the data is already properly ordered coming out of the table. However, you should always include the ORDER BY clause if you need the results sorted; the query processor will determine if work actually needs to be performed to meet your sorting requirements.

Of special note is the place where the SELECT clause is logically processed. In your SELECT clause you can alias columns; however, those aliases will not be valid for any clause logically processed prior to the SELECT clause. The following query is invalid, because the Orders.OrderHeader table does not contain a GrandTotal column and the alias in the SELECT statement is not valid for the WHERE clause since a WHERE clause is logically processed before a SELECT clause:

```
SELECT OrderID, OrderDate, OrderTotal AS GrandTotal
FROM Orders.OrderHeader
WHERE GrandTotal > 100
```

However, since the ORDER BY clause is logically processed after the SELECT clause, the following statement is valid:

```
SELECT OrderID, OrderDate, OrderTotal AS GrandTotal
FROM Orders.OrderHeader
WHERE OrderTotal > 100
ORDER BY GrandTotal;
```

Each element within each clause has the same execution precedence and in fact all elements in a clause are executed as if they are processed at the same time. Just because you specified one element before another doesn't mean SQL Server will process that way. The following query will return a syntax error, because even though you specified the GrandTotal alias first in the SELECT clause, SQL Server evaluates all elements of the SELECT clause as if they were processed at the same time.

So, GrandTotal doesn't have any validity in the OrderSubTotal computation.

```
SELECT OrderID, OrderDate, OrderTotal AS GrandTotal,
    GrandTotal - SalesTax - ShippingAmount AS OrderSubTotal
FROM Orders.OrderHeader
WHERE OrderTotal > 100
```

Exercise 1: Solutions

1. You should have returned 44 rows of data. You might have written SELECT * and while technically correct, you shouldn't be using SELECT * in any application that you write.

    ```
    SELECT EmployeeID, FirstName, MiddleInitial, LastName, JobTitleID, BirthDate, SSN,
        Gender, OrganizationNode
    FROM HumanResources.Employee;
    ```

2. You should have returned 44 rows of data. Removing the column set is simply a matter of not specifying the EmployeeAddress "column" in the SELECT list.

    ```
    SELECT AddressID, EmployeeID, AddressTypeID, AddressLine1, AddressLine2,
        AddressLine3, City, StateProvinceID, PostalCode
    FROM HumanResources.EmployeeAddress;
    ```

3. You should have returned 119 rows of data. The ProductName and ProductDescription need to be aliased to produce this output.

```
SELECT ProductName Name, ProductDescription Description, Price
FROM Products.Product
```

Exercise 2: Solutions

1. You should have returned 999707 rows of data, which will consume a significant amount of resources on your machine and take quite a while to render the result set. Don't worry, I did this on purpose as both an example in how to deal with NULLs and the effect pulling large result sets has on an application. We will fix this problem in subsequent queries and won't dump massive result sets again.

```
SELECT CustomerID, AddressLine1 + ' ' + ISNULL(AddressLine2,'') + ' ' +
ISNULL(AddressLine3,'')
Address, City, StateProvinceID, PostalCode
FROM Customers.Address;
```

2. You should have returned 8088 rows of data. You would have needed to add 5 days to the OrderDate column and aliased the calculation to produce the required output.

```
SELECT OrderID, OrderDate, DATEADD(dd,5,OrderDate) EstimatedArrival
FROM Orders.OrderHeader;
```

3. You should have returned 1 row of data. The trick on the first column is that formatting date/time data is a display function and only has an effect when the output data type is a character string. You first needed to convert the 3 week result to a DATE to strip off the time portion and then format this by converting the result to a character string.

```
SELECT CONVERT(VARCHAR(30),CAST(DATEADD(wk,3,GETDATE()) AS DATE),101),
DATEDIFF(dd,GETDATE(),DATEADD(wk,3,GETDATE()));
```

Exercise 3: Solutions

1. You should have returned a single row with a value of 999,706.

```
SELECT COUNT(*)
FROM Customers.Customer;
```

2. You should have returned 1 row with the maximum length of 29 and maximum bytes of 5. You needed to remember that there are 3 address lines in a customer address and you have to translate the NULLs in order to get a valid result. Since the PostalCode is stored in a CHAR(10) column, you had to remove the trailing spaces from the data before computing the data length.

```
SELECT MAX(LEN(AddressLine1+ ISNULL(AddressLine2,'')+ ISNULL(AddressLine3,'')))
MaxLength,
MAX(DATALENGTH(RTRIM(PostalCode))) MaxBytes
FROM Customers.Address;
```

3. You should have returned 8088 rows of data. You needed to sort first by the CustomerID column and then in descending order by the OrderDate column.

```
SELECT OrderID, CustomerID, AddressID, OrderDate, OrderTime, OrderSubTotal,
SalesTax,
ShippingAmount, OrderTotal
FROM Orders.OrderHeader
ORDER BY CustomerID, OrderDate DESC;
```

4. You should have returned 8088 rows of data. If you had included the OrderTotal computed column in your query, you could have verified if you calculation was correct. An even easier comparison to the computed column would have been if you had subtracted your calculation from the OrderTotal computed column. If your calculation was correct, it should have produced a result of 0. You could have further simplified inspecting the results by sorting by this comparison calculation and then looking at the first and last rows in the result set to verify both were 0.

```sql
SELECT OrderID, OrderSubTotal + SalesTax + ShippingAmount OrderTotal
FROM Orders.OrderHeader;
```

5. You needed to use a searched CASE for the correct result. You could have had 3 WHEN expressions, however, since the first two covered every other possibility for the business rules provided, all you needed was 2 WHEN expressions along with an ELSE.

```sql
SELECT OrderID, OrderTotal, CASE WHEN OrderTotal < 40 THEN 'Small'
                                 WHEN OrderTotal >= 40 AND OrderTotal <= 100 THEN 'Medium'
                                 ELSE 'Large' END
FROM Orders.OrderHeader;
```

Exercise 4: Solutions

1. Your result set should be identical to part 5 in exercise 3. The only difference in the query is using the BETWEEN operator to simplify the code.

```sql
SELECT OrderID, OrderTotal, CASE WHEN OrderTotal < 40 THEN 'Small'
                                 WHEN OrderTotal BETWEEN 40 AND 100 THEN 'Medium'
                                 ELSE 'Large' END
FROM Orders.OrderHeader;
```

2. You should have returned 100 rows. You would have needed to retrieve the StateProvinceID for Texas from the Lookups.StateProvince table. You then used this to retrieve the set of customer IDs with addresses that were in Texas. You then used the set of customer IDs with an IN operator to retrieve customer names, limiting the results to the first 100 rows. For those who read ahead before doing this exercise, you could have solved this using a join, but we haven't covered joins yet by the time you do this exercise.

```sql
SELECT TOP 100 a.FirstName, a.LastName
FROM Customers.Customer a
WHERE a.CustomerID IN (SELECT b.CustomerID
                       FROM Customers.Address b
                       WHERE b.StateProvinceID = (SELECT c.StateProvinceID
                                                  FROM Lookups.StateProvince c
                                                  WHERE c.StateProvince = 'Texas'));
```

3. You should have returned 32 rows. The key to this query is that in order to find a single quote, you had to escape the quote with another single quote while performing a full wildcard search.

```sql
SELECT StateProvinceID, CountryID, StateProvince, StateProvinceCode
FROM Lookups.StateProvince
WHERE StateProvince LIKE '%''%';
```

4. You should have returned 135 rows by using the LIKE operator in conjunction with square brackets to list the characters that you wanted.

   ```
   SELECT StateProvinceID, CountryID, StateProvince, StateProvinceCode
   FROM Lookups.StateProvince
   WHERE StateProvince LIKE '[MN]%';
   ```

Exercise 5: Solutions

1. You should have returned 48004 rows. No matter how you construct the query, you need to find the StateProvinceID that corresponds to Illinois. The StateProvinceID is linked to the customer through the Customers.Address table. You could have written this query as a series of nested, non-correlated subqueries or as an INNER JOIN.

   ```
   SELECT a.FirstName, a.LastName
   FROM Customers.Customer a
   WHERE CustomerID IN (SELECT b.CustomerID
                        FROM Customers.Address b
                        WHERE b.StateProvinceID = (SELECT c.StateProvinceID
                                                   FROM Lookups.StateProvince c
                                                   WHERE c.StateProvince = 'Illinois'))
   ORDER BY a.LastName, a.FirstName;

   SELECT a.FirstName, a.LastName
   FROM Customers.Customer a INNER JOIN Customers.Address b ON a.CustomerID = b.CustomerID
      INNER JOIN Lookups.StateProvince c ON b.StateProvinceID = c.StateProvinceID AND
   c.StateProvince = 'Illinois'
   ORDER BY a.LastName, a.FirstName;
   ```

2. You should have returned 1 row. If you outer join the Customers.Address to Customers.Customer and check the CustomerID, the customer that does not have an address will have a NULL in the CustomerID column.

   ```
   SELECT b.AddressID
   FROM Customers.Customer a RIGHT OUTER JOIN Customers.Address b ON a.CustomerID = b.CustomerID
   WHERE a.CustomerID IS NULL;
   ```

3. You should have returned 1 row. The trick to this solution is that you had to filter out the E-Mail contact type in order to work only with phone number rows.

   ```
   SELECT c.EmployeeID
   FROM HumanResources.EmployeeContact a
       INNER JOIN Lookups.ContactType b ON a.ContactTypeID = b.ContactTypeID
                                        AND b.ContactType <> 'E-Mail'
       RIGHT OUTER JOIN HumanResources.Employee c ON a.EmployeeID = c.EmployeeID
   WHERE a.EmployeeID IS NULL;
   ```

4. You should have returned 505 rows. This solution required a self-join of the Orders.OrderHeader table. In order to find products that were ordered more than once, you needed to find all of the cases where a SKU existed on more than one OrderID. You needed to add a DISTINCT to the SELECT clause in order to return a result set that did not have repeating values.

   ```
   SELECT DISTINCT a.SKU
   FROM Orders.OrderDetail a INNER JOIN Orders.OrderDetail b
      ON a.SKU = b.SKU AND a.OrderID <> b.OrderID;
   ```

5. You should have returned 637 rows. You needed to count up the distinct occurrences of a SKU in the Orders.OrderDetail.

    ```
    SELECT COUNT(DISTINCT SKU)
    FROM Orders.OrderDetail;
    ```

6. You should have returned 1134 rows. You could have written this query two ways. The first method would have been the same as exercise 2 where you outer joined the tables and then looked for the NULLs. A more efficient way is to use the NOT EXISTS operator as shown below. You also needed a non-correlated subquery to retrieve the maximum CustomerID in the Orders.OrderHeader table. Why did I include this requirement? There are almost 1 million customers in the database and at this point in the book, only a small fraction of the orders have been entered so that the queries you are running do not take very long. By limiting this query to a range of CustomerIDs which are possible to have an order generated, we avoid having you retrieve more than 90% of the customers which haven't been used in the database at this point.

    ```
    SELECT COUNT(*)
    FROM Customers.Customer a
    WHERE NOT EXISTS (SELECT *
                      FROM Orders.OrderHeader b
                      WHERE a.CustomerID = b.CustomerID)
          AND a.CustomerID < (SELECT MAX(CustomerID) FROM Orders.OrderHeader);
    ```

7. You should have returned 51 rows. I've included 3 ways to write this query even though the exercise only asked for 2. The EXISTS deals with the fact that multiple rows in the Products.SKU table do not have a PenKitID specified. The IN has a NULL in the set returned from the subquery, but ignores the NULL since it doesn't match to anything. The 3rd query simply ensures that NULLs are returned in the list to the IN operator.

    ```
    SELECT COUNT(*)
    FROM Products.Product a
    WHERE EXISTS (SELECT * FROM Products.SKU b
                  WHERE a.ProductID = b.PenKitID);

    SELECT COUNT(*)
    FROM Products.Product a
    WHERE a.ProductID IN (SELECT b.PenKitID
                          FROM Products.SKU b);

    SELECT COUNT(*)
    FROM Products.Product a
    WHERE a.ProductID IN (SELECT b.PenKitID
                          FROM Products.SKU b
                          WHERE b.PenKitID IS NOT NULL);
    ```

Exercise 6: Solutions

1. You should have returned 10 rows. You needed to compute a SUM(Quantity), sort the results in descending order, and then use the TOP operator to return the top 10 rows.

    ```
    SELECT TOP 10 SKU, SUM(Quantity) QuantitySold
    FROM Orders.OrderDetail
    GROUP BY SKU
    ORDER BY QuantitySold DESC;
    ```

2. You should have returned 637 rows. You needed to remember that the OrderDetail table contains the quantity sold and the price that the product was sold at. In order to get the total sales, these two values needed to be multiplied prior to computing a SUM.

   ```
   SELECT SKU, SUM(Quantity) QuantitySold, SUM(Quantity*Price) TotalSales
   FROM Orders.OrderDetail
   GROUP BY SKU
   ORDER BY TotalSales DESC;
   ```

3. You should have returned 172 rows. You needed to take the query from exercise 2 and add a HAVING clause to filter the aggregate.

   ```
   SELECT SKU, SUM(Quantity) QuantitySold, SUM(Quantity*Price) TotalSales
   FROM Orders.OrderDetail
   GROUP BY SKU
   HAVING SUM(Quantity * Price) > 500
   ORDER BY TotalSales DESC;
   ```

4. You should have returned 875 rows. This one should have been a bit tricky and it required you to carefully read the business requirement. Returning the quantity sold and total sales broken down by year should have been a simple case of modifying the query from exercise 2 to include the OrderHeader table so that you could compute the year the order was placed. Only returning the grand total was a bit harder. You needed to use the ROLLUP function, but this also produces subtotals which needed to be filtered out. So, you needed to add a HAVING clause with the GROUPING_ID function to remove the subtotal rows.

   ```
   SELECT a.SKU, YEAR(b.OrderDate) OrderYear, SUM(a.Quantity) QuantitySold,
       SUM(a.Quantity*a.Price) TotalSales,
     GROUPING_ID(a.SKU, YEAR(b.OrderDate)) GroupID
   FROM Orders.OrderDetail a INNER JOIN Orders.OrderHeader b ON a.OrderID = b.OrderID
   GROUP BY ROLLUP(a.SKU, YEAR(OrderDate))
   HAVING GROUPING_ID(a.SKU, YEAR(b.OrderDate)) <> 1;
   ```

Summary

SQL gives you exactly one statement, SELECT, to retrieve data from the infinite permutations or tables you can design coupled with the infinite permutations of the question you might want to ask. In this chapter, we discussed how to limit the list of columns returned as well as include a variety of calculations in the SELECT clause. You saw how to specify the table you wanted to query as well as join tables together in the FROM clause. You even saw how to embed an entire query into the FROM clause. The WHERE clause was used to limit rows from the result set and the HAVING clause was used to filter aggregations. The GROUP BY clause, with its many permutations was used to compute various levels of aggregation for your applications. Hopefully, you've gotten a taste for the power and flexibility that a SELECT statement allows and you are now ready to extend that in Chapter 10 with some more complicated and interesting problems.

Chapter 10
Advanced Data Retrieval

> **Setup:** Please run the Chapter 10 Setup script in the companion files prior to starting the exercises in this chapter to ensure that your databases are at the correct starting point. Every exercise in this book assumes that you have created the c:\ChampionValleyPress\Data and c:\ChampionValleyPress\Log folders, contained databases are enabled, and this is the location of all of the data, log, and filestream files which will be used for this book. If you have chosen a different path, you will need to adjust the paths listed accordingly. Every setup script also assumes that you have enabled FILESTREAM access for the instance. When executing commands, it is assumed that you will change context to the appropriate database since understanding the contents of each database in this book is the same skill you will need for working with your databases. All scripts also assume you are using a default instance.

In chapter 9, you were introduced to the SELECT statement and all of the clauses available to mold your queries to return the exact set of data that you need. If you stopped learning about a SELECT statement with what we've covered in chapter 9, you would be able to construct queries to satisfy virtually every question that could be asked about your data. This chapter will extend your knowledge with additional SELECT capabilities which you might find useful from time to time to improve performance, simplify code, or tackle some relatively challenging problems.

Set Operations

A set operation is defined as two input queries that are processed by an operator to produce a result set. SQL Server has three set operations: UNION, INTERSECT, and EXCEPT.

Without getting into the details of the mathematical definition of sets, an actual set consists of 0 or more values which can be in any order and do not contain duplicates. I've never needed, nor do I ever expect to need to apply a mathematical definition of a set. So, I use the term "set" very loosely to mean any set of values produced by a query regardless of whether duplicates exist.

Set operations make comparisons based on all columns present. In order to compare the results of two input queries, you have to have a pair of result sets with the following characteristics:

- Both queries produce the same number of columns
- The data types of columns, based on position in the result set, are compatible
- You can use any clause or operator available to a SELECT statement, except ORDER BY
- NULL = NULL

If you are making comparisons, none of these requirements should surprise you at this point. It wouldn't make any sense to attempt to compare a result set containing 2 columns with a result set containing 17 columns. Likewise, it would be impossible to make a comparison if the first column in one result set was a CHAR(30) while the first column in the second result set was an INT.

Additionally, you can't use an ORDER BY clause in either of the input queries, which also makes sense when you think about it. The two input queries are executed and the results are operated upon. Only once the results are operated upon does SQL Server return a result set to an application. The ORDER BY clause is used to sort data for presentation purposes, which means that it is only valid for sorting a final result set for presentation to an application, not for intermediate calculations.

The column names do not have to match between the two queries. The column names which are returned in the final result set come from the first query in the set operation.

The strangest characteristic of set operations is that NULLs are treated as equivalent to each other. Just like a GROUP BY clause, rows have to be preserved within the comparison, so SQL Server has to do something with NULL values. So, the convention chosen is to treat NULLs as equivalent to each other in the comparison.

UNION

The UNION operator allows you to combine multiple results into a single result set. T-SQL has two flavors of the UNION operator – UNION and UNION ALL. The UNION operator combines the two result sets and removes duplicates while the UNION ALL operator preserves duplicates.

```
SELECT LastName, FirstName
FROM HumanResources.Employee
WHERE EmployeeID = 24
UNION
SELECT LastName, FirstName
FROM HumanResources.Employee
WHERE EmployeeID = 24
UNION
SELECT LastName, FirstName
FROM HumanResources.Employee
WHERE EmployeeID = 24;

LastName    FirstName
----------  ---------
Hotek       Michael
```

Since the query above uses the UNION operator, instead of returning 3 rows in the result set with the same values, the duplicates are removed and only a single row is returned. Compare this with the query below where the duplicates are preserved and all 3 rows are returned.

```
SELECT LastName, FirstName
FROM HumanResources.Employee
WHERE EmployeeID = 24
UNION ALL
SELECT LastName, FirstName
FROM HumanResources.Employee
WHERE EmployeeID = 24
UNION ALL
SELECT LastName, FirstName
FROM HumanResources.Employee
WHERE EmployeeID = 24;

LastName    FirstName
----------  ---------
Hotek       Michael
Hotek       Michael
Hotek       Michael
```

While the queries above were rather artificial since it is highly unlikely you will ever return the same employee multiple times and UNION the result together, the example was chosen to simply show the difference between UNION and UNION ALL.

One of the more common tasks you will have from time to time that can be easily solved with the UNION operator is to de-dupe data. You may receive data files from a partner which have not been validated and contain duplicates or you may have had a primary key/unique constraint dropped off a table which allowed duplicates to be entered and you need to clean all of these duplicates out. Since the rows are duplicates, you can't simply delete one row over the other, because you have no way of specifying a WHERE clause to tell the rows apart. So, you can use the UNION operator to deal with the duplicates. You can simply write a SELECT statement to return the duplicate rows and UNION the SELECT statement with itself as shown below to produce a unique result set.

```
SELECT column1, column2
FROM Table1
UNION
SELECT column1, column2
FROM Table1;
```

> **Note:** Using UNION to de-dupe a set of data is just one method. You could also use a GROUP BY where the grouping effectively removes the duplicates. You could also utilize the method with ranking functions shown a little later in this chapter.

INTERSECT

The INTERSECT operator returns the distinct rows from the first query that also exist in the second query as shown in the diagram below. The INTERSECT operator is also transitive, meaning that it does not matter which query is placed first, you will always return the unique set of rows that exist in both queries.

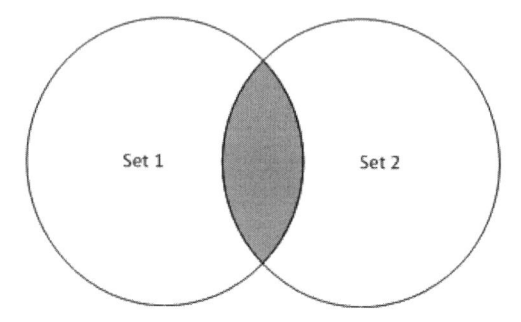

Figure 10-1 Venn Diagram of the INTERSECT operator

For example, if you wanted to return the unique list of customers that have placed an order, you could INNER JOIN the Customers.Customer and Orders.OrderHeader tables. The INNER JOIN would include the customer as many times as an order was placed, so to get a unique list of customers, you would have to apply the DISTINCT operator.

Alternatively, you could use the INTERSECT operator to return a distinct list as shown below.

```
SELECT CustomerID
FROM Customers.Customer
INTERSECT
SELECT CustomerID
FROM Orders.OrderHeader;
```

If you inspect the results, it might appear that you are returning the results in a sorted order, but this is simply an accident. If you want the results to be sorted, you need to include an ORDER BY clause at the end of the operation. Remember, you can't sort the queries inside the set operation, but you can sort the results.

```
SELECT CustomerID
FROM Customers.Customer
INTERSECT
SELECT CustomerID
FROM Orders.OrderHeader
ORDER BY CustomerID;
```

EXCEPT

You can think of the EXCEPT operator as subtracting the second result set from the first and returning the distinct rows that remain from the first query. Put another way, the EXCEPT operator compares the first and second queries and returns the distinct rows in the first query that do not exist in the second query. The EXCEPT operator is intransitive, meaning you cannot interchange the order of the queries and obtain the same result. So, the order of the queries does matter for EXCEPT.

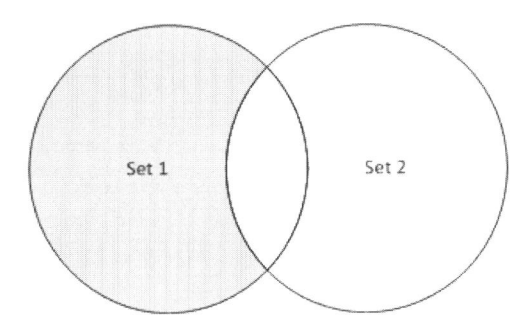

Figure 10-2 Venn Diagram of the EXCEPT Operator

In the previous chapter, we showed a technique using an OUTER JOIN to find a list of the customers that have not placed an order. You can solve the same problem by using the EXCEPT operator as follows:

```
SELECT CustomerID
FROM Customers.Customer
WHERE CustomerID < (SELECT MAX(CustomerID) FROM Orders.OrderHeader)
EXCEPT
SELECT CustomerID
FROM Orders.OrderHeader;
```

As I explained in the last chapter, the non-correlated subquery is simply used to reduce the list of customers considered since only a small fraction of the 1 million customers have data loaded for them at this point in the book.

> **Why Should You Care?**
> You might be wondering why the EXCEPT and INTERSECT operators were even added since you could accomplish the same result by using outer and inner joins. These operators were added for performance and I wouldn't underestimate the usefulness.
>
> At one of my customers, we had a routine that loaded a data warehouse from a large set of files that arrived every day. Files could be sent multiple times and processed multiple times based on a set of business rules. Once loaded, a variety of processes were kicked off to compute data for various business functions. One of these processes computed a set of aggregates and had a rule that the aggregate was computed once and only once. So, we needed a way to filter out any of the detail data corresponding to aggregate rows which had already been computed. The process was written using the OUTER JOIN…WHERE …NULL technique. This worked ok in a test environment, but when it was run in a production environment where we had millions of rows in one table and billions of rows in another table; the performance was a challenge, to put it mildly.
>
> This single query to filter out rows that had already been processed took between 1.5 and 3 hours and caused unacceptable delays in data availability to the business. The query was rewritten to use an EXCEPT operator and the query time dropped to less than 1.5 minutes, a better than 99% performance improvement.
>
> While EXCEPT and INTERSECT appear to behave like the equivalent join operation, these are specialized and highly optimized operators which can perform a tremendous amount of work in a very short time.

Data Modification

In Chapter 7, we kept the discussion of data modification reasonably simple. Now that we've covered a SELECT statement, we can complete the discussion of data modification. In addition to performing data modification based on static data, you can leverage all of the capabilities of a SELECT statement with an INSERT and the capabilities of a FROM clause with UPDATE and DELETE statements.

Instead of specifying a VALUES clause with an INSERT statement, you can use a SELECT statement to insert rows into a table as follows:

```
INSERT INTO TableA
(Column1, Column2, Column3)
SELECT Column1, Column2, Column3
FROM TableB;
```

You can also perform join operations with an UPDATE or DELETE statement. For example, you can update the values in inventory based on the physical inventory taken this month as follows:

```
UPDATE a
SET a.QuantityOnHand = b.Quantity
FROM Products.Inventory a INNER JOIN Products.PhysicalInventoryDetail b ON a.SKU = b.SKU
    INNER JOIN Products.PhysicalInventoryHeader c ON b.InventoryID = c.InventoryID
WHERE YEAR(c.InventoryDate) = YEAR(GETDATE())
    AND MONTH(c.InventoryDate) = MONTH(GETDATE());
```

You could delete customers who have not placed an order with the following query:

```
DELETE a
FROM Customers.Customer a INNER JOIN
    (SELECT CustomerID
    FROM Customers.Customer
    EXCEPT
    SELECT CustomerID
    FROM Orders.OrderHeader) b ON a.CustomerID = b.CustomerID;
```

Table Expressions

Table expressions are named SELECT statements that you can either store in your database or are evaluated at execution time. Regardless of whether they are stored or only available at run-time, a table expression is a SELECT statement. The table expressions that are available only at run-time are derived tables, row/table constructors, common table expressions (CTEs), and the PIVOT/UNPIVOT operators.

We've already covered derived tables at the end of chapter 9, which should give you a basic understanding of how table expressions work. The SELECT statement defined in the table expression is executed. The results are stored in memory and referenced within DML statements. By themselves, table expressions don't confer any specific performance benefits, but they do make your code more modular and understandable. Although due to the results being stored in memory, table expressions have a significant performance advantage over temp tables.

Row/Table Constructors

As you saw in Chapter 7, "Data Manipulation", you can use a VALUES clause with an INSERT statement to specify static values. The INSERT statement was enhanced to allow you to specify multiple rows in the VALUES clause.

Additionally, the VALUES clause itself was enhanced to allow you to construct a row or even an entire table of static values. This enhancement is called a row or table constructor and can be used anywhere a table expression is allowed such as in the FROM clause of a SELECT statement as follows:

```
SELECT OrderID, Product, OrderDate
FROM (VALUES(1,'Product4','2012-05-29'),(2,'Product2','2012-04-22'),
      (3,'Product3','2012-02-28')) Orders(OrderID, Product, OrderDate);
```

If you recall the way we constructed a derived table in Chapter 9, a table constructor is very similar. Instead of retrieving data from a table, the table constructor is created from one or more hard coded values. You specify a VALUES clause the same way as you would if you were creating an INSERT statement. The VALUES clause is then wrapped in parenthesis and aliased, in our case the alias is Orders. Following the table constructor alias, you alias each of the columns of data specified in the VALUES clause. The SELECT clause then references the column aliases.

Common Table Expressions (CTEs)

CTEs are very similar to derived tables where you can define a SELECT statement that is then embedded into another statement. Like a derived table, the result set of a CTE is stored in memory and automatically discarded once the statement completes.

There are two important differences between a derived table and a CTE. CTEs can reference any previously defined CTEs within the same statement. If you need to reference the results of a derived table more than once or reference the results of one derived table from within another derived table, you have to repeat the derived table definition and nest it in the statement. CTEs also have a special construct which allows for recursion.

The generic syntax for a CTE is as follows:

```
WITH <cte_name> (<column list>)
AS
(<select statement>)
SELECT <columns>
FROM <cte_name>…;
```

The column list is optional. If you do not specify the column list, then the column names will come from the SELECT statement in the definition of the CTE, which means that every column has to either be named or aliased in the SELECT clause. Additionally, the WITH keyword is used for multiple purposes in T-SQL, so if you are specifying a CTE, the preceding command in a batch must be terminated with a semicolon (;). This is the main reason why I have been recommending that all of your statements are terminated with a semicolon so that you don't have to remember which commands require a semicolon, which ones don't, and where the semicolon is required in a batch for various command.

Regular CTEs

To illustrate the use of a CTE and the difference with a derived table, let's take a look at how to solve a problem that stumps most people. Suppose you have a table that has some sequence of events – orders placed, purchase orders issued, sequence numbers allocated, driver's license numbers assigned, etc. You suspect that gaps in the sequence of values might exist such as days when no orders were placed, purchase order numbers that have never been issued, driver's license numbers not assigned. The general question is – find me all of the places in the sequence where data does not exist.

The query below uses a derived table to find the days where ChampionValleyPens did not have any orders.

```
SELECT StartGap, EndGap, DATEDIFF(dd,StartGap,EndGap) + 1 AS NumberMissingDays
FROM
    (SELECT t1.OrderDate AS StartGap, MIN(t2.OrderDate) AS EndGap
       FROM
       (SELECT DATEADD(dd, 1, OrderDate) AS OrderDate FROM Orders.OrderHeader tbl1
          WHERE NOT EXISTS(SELECT * FROM Orders.OrderHeader tbl2
                    WHERE DATEDIFF(dd, tbl1.OrderDate, tbl2.OrderDate) = 1)
         AND OrderDate <> (SELECT MAX(OrderDate) FROM Orders.OrderHeader)) t1
       INNER JOIN
       (SELECT DATEADD(dd, -1, OrderDate) AS OrderDate FROM Orders.OrderHeader tbl1
          WHERE NOT EXISTS(SELECT * FROM Orders.OrderHeader tbl2
                    WHERE DATEDIFF(dd, tbl2.OrderDate, tbl1.OrderDate) = 1)
         AND OrderDate <> (SELECT MIN(OrderDate) FROM Orders.OrderHeader)) t2
        ON t1.OrderDate <= t2.OrderDate
        GROUP BY t1.OrderDate) a
ORDER BY StartGap;
```

> **Note:** You could solve this problem by first generating a table containing all possible order dates and then finding the dates in the generated table which do not exist in the Orders.OrderHeader table, but I try to not embed the generation of auxiliary tables in my code when possible. Instead, I simply work with the data as presented so that I'm not constantly generating different auxiliary tables with various definitions.

Yes, this query looks pretty complicated, so let's take a look at what is going on. Let's first look at the derived table t1.

```
(SELECT DATEADD(dd, 1, OrderDate) AS OrderDate FROM Orders.OrderHeader tbl1
        WHERE NOT EXISTS(SELECT * FROM Orders.OrderHeader tbl2
                    WHERE DATEDIFF(dd, tbl1.OrderDate, tbl2.OrderDate) = 1)
        AND OrderDate <> (SELECT MAX(OrderDate) FROM Orders.OrderHeader)) t1
```

The query, t1 finds all of the order dates before a gap by filtering out all of the cases where dates are adjacent to each other, DATEDIFF = 1. It also excludes the case for the last row in the table to ensure that you are only considering date inclusive to the contents of the Orders.OrderHeader table. Since the query finds the points BEFORE a gap occurs, you need to add 1 to the value to find the actual order date where the gap actually starts.

The query, t2 performs a similar operation in finding the dates where the gaps end. You subtract 1day to find the actual order date at the end of the gap.

The two derived tables are then joined together where the OrderDate from the first derived table is less than or equal to the OrderDate from the second derived table to return the start and end of each gap as well as how large the gap is. You could also write this using a CTE as follows:

```
WITH StartGap_CTE (OrderDate)
AS
(SELECT DATEADD(dd, 1, OrderDate) AS OrderDate FROM Orders.OrderHeader tbl1
        WHERE NOT EXISTS(SELECT * FROM Orders.OrderHeader tbl2
                    WHERE DATEDIFF(dd, tbl1.OrderDate, tbl2.OrderDate) = 1)
        AND OrderDate <> (SELECT MAX(OrderDate) FROM Orders.OrderHeader)),
EndGap_CTE (OrderDate)
AS
(SELECT DATEADD(dd, -1, OrderDate) AS OrderDate FROM Orders.OrderHeader tbl1
        WHERE NOT EXISTS(SELECT * FROM Orders.OrderHeader tbl2
                    WHERE DATEDIFF(dd, tbl2.OrderDate, tbl1.OrderDate) = 1)
        AND OrderDate <> (SELECT MIN(OrderDate) FROM Orders.OrderHeader)),
Gaps_CTE (StartGap, EndGap)
AS
(SELECT t1.OrderDate AS StartGap, MIN(t2.OrderDate) AS EndGap
    FROM  StartGap_CTE t1 INNER JOIN EndGap_CTE t2
      ON t1.OrderDate <= t2.OrderDate
      GROUP BY t1.OrderDate)
SELECT StartGap, EndGap, DATEDIFF(dd,StartGap,EndGap) + 1 AS NumberMissingDays
FROM Gaps_CTE a
ORDER BY StartGap;
```

While you don't save any code and it looks a little strange at first for a SELECT statement, you should be able to clearly understand where each section of the query is located and how each section builds on each other to produce the final result. This is just one way of solving the general "sequence gaps" problem. Finding sequence gaps through this method can also be quite time consuming and resource intensive. For example, when you run this query, you can expect the results to return in about 1 minute, depending upon your hardware.

Another solution, which is a lot less code and hence a lot easier to understand is to first create a list of OrderDate pairs in the table. You do this by essentially joining the Orders.OrderHeader table to itself with an offset via a correlated subquery to return pairs of adjacent values and then finding the ones where the difference is more than 1.

```
WITH Pairs_CTE (StartDate, EndDate)
AS
(SELECT DISTINCT OrderDate AS StartDate,
    (SELECT MIN(OrderDate) FROM Orders.OrderHeader AS b
      WHERE b.OrderDate > a.OrderDate) AS EndDate
 FROM Orders.OrderHeader AS a)
SELECT DATEADD(dd, 1,StartDate) AS StartGap, DATEADD(dd,-1,EndDate) AS EndGap,
 DATEDIFF(dd,StartDate,EndDate) - 1 AS NumberMissingDays
FROM Pairs_CTE
WHERE DATEDIFF(dd,StartDate,EndDate) > 1;
```

The CTE embeds a correlated subquery into the SELECT clause. The purpose of the correlated subquery in the SELECT clause is to take each OrderDate in the Orders.OrderHeader table and produce a list of all other order dates in the Orders.OrderHeader table which are greater than the date. The MIN then throws away all of the rows generated leaving just a single value. The DISTINCT eliminates all of the duplicate values generated to produce a result set like the sample below:

```
StartDate   EndDate
----------  ----------
2001-02-19  2001-02-20
2001-12-09  2001-12-10
2002-01-19  2002-01-20
2001-04-30  2001-05-01
2001-06-10  2001-06-11
```

The outer query then computes the gaps by only returning the rows where the difference between the two dates is more than 1. While this query produces the same results as the two prior queries, it executes in approximately 2 – 3 seconds. Additionally, as the volume of data increases, the performance of this query will hardly be affected.

Let's look at another common problem – running calculations such as running totals, running averages, etc. The following query is a solution using derived tables to compute a running total over our sales.

```
SELECT a.OrderDate, a.DailyTotal, SUM(b.DailyTotal) RunningTotal
FROM (SELECT OrderDate, SUM(OrderTotal) DailyTotal
        FROM Orders.OrderHeader
        GROUP BY OrderDate) a
INNER JOIN (SELECT OrderDate, SUM(OrderTotal) DailyTotal
        FROM Orders.OrderHeader
        GROUP BY OrderDate) b
ON a.OrderDate >= b.OrderDate
GROUP BY a.OrderDate, a.DailyTotal
ORDER BY a.OrderDate;
```

In order to compute a running total, what we want to do is return a total sales amount of each day. The running total for the current day then becomes the running total from the previous day + the current day's total. Put another way, the running total for the current day is the sum of all of the sales for every date prior to the current day. The first thing you should notice is that the same derived table is repeated. The first derived table is used for the current day's total. The second derived table is used to compute the running total by summing up all daily totals for all order dates prior to the current date. Yes, we could have dispensed with the second derived table and just joined to the Orders.OrderHeader table, but that wouldn't make for nearly as interesting of an example.

If we had solved this problem using a CTE, we could have simply self-joined the CTE to produce the results making for more compact code.

```
WITH DailyTotal_CTE (OrderDate, DailyTotal)
AS
(SELECT OrderDate, SUM(OrderTotal) DailyTotal
      FROM Orders.OrderHeader
      GROUP BY OrderDate)
SELECT a.OrderDate, a.DailyTotal, SUM(b.DailyTotal) RunningTotal
FROM  DailyTotal_CTE a INNER JOIN DailyTotal_CTE b
ON a.OrderDate >= b.OrderDate
GROUP BY a.OrderDate, a.DailyTotal
ORDER BY a.OrderDate;
```

Recursive CTEs

CTEs have a unique capability, recursion, within all of the table expressions.

The CTE is formed with the following basic structure:

```
WITH <cte_name> (<column list>)
AS (<anchor SELECT>
UNION ALL
<recursive SELECT>)
```

The recursive SELECT will have a join to the CTE in order to specify how the recursion occurs. The result of the anchor query is stored in the result set and then that anchor element is fed to the recursive portion which iteratively executes the recursive SELECT until an empty result occurs. All of the recursive rows generated are appended to the result set, which forms the final set of rows in the CTE. An outer query is then executed to return the values desired from the CTE. This should explain a recursive CTE about as clear as mud. So, let's take a look at an example to understand what is going on.

```
WITH Category_CTE(CategoryID, CategoryNode, Category, RecursionLevel)
AS (SELECT a.CategoryID, a.CategoryNode, a.Category, 0
    FROM Lookups.Category a
    WHERE CategoryID = 1
    UNION ALL
    SELECT b.CategoryID, b.CategoryNode, b.Category, RecursionLevel + 1
    FROM Lookups.Category b
       INNER JOIN Category_CTE c ON b.CategoryNode.GetAncestor(1) = c.CategoryNode)
SELECT d.RecursionLevel, d.CategoryID,
REPLICATE('   ',d.RecursionLevel -1) + d.Category Category,
d.CategoryNode.ToString() AS CategoryNode, e.Category ParentCategory
FROM Category_CTE d INNER JOIN Lookups.Category e
   ON d.CategoryNode.GetAncestor(1) = e.CategoryNode
ORDER BY d.CategoryNode.ToString(), RecursionLevel
OPTION (MAXRECURSION 25);
```

The anchor query is executed and returns the CategoryID, CategoryNode, and Category for CategoryID of 1, which is Products. This row is placed in the Category_CTE which is then joined to the recursive member. The join says to return the row(s) whose direct ancestor is Products. This returns Turning Kits, Turning Blanks, Tooling, Adhesives, Finishing, Project Displays, and Custom and assigns each of these rows a RecursionLevel = 1. Since the results are not blank, the recursive query is run again, this time looking for all of the rows whose direct ancestor are the categories at a RecursionLevel = 1 and assigns these a recursion level of 2. Since that result produced rows, the process is repeated looking for all of the rows whose direct ancestor is one of the rows at a RecursionLevel = 2 and so on until no rows are returned. All of these results are appended to the row where CategoryID = 1 to produce the contents of the Category_CTE. We then execute the outer query to return the results of the Category_CTE. The REPLICATE() function was used to simply indent values to make them appear in a format like we are used to seeing for hierarchies. Sorting by the text representation of the category hierarchy produces a nicely formatted list of values.

One thing with recursive CTEs that creates problems for many people, including myself, is the desire to create a single, general purpose query that will just display the entire hierarchy. You might think that you could do this by just removing the WHERE clause from the anchor query. While this might appear to work on initial inspection of your result set, what you've produced instead is a lot of duplication within the result set as a result of the recursion. At this point, I'd encourage you to execute the query below and verify that instead of returning 62 rows, you instead returned 235 rows with a small piece of the result shown below:

```
RecursionLevel   CategoryID   Category       CategoryNode   ParentCategory
--------------   ----------   --------       ------------   --------------
0                2            Turning Kits   /1/            Products
1                2            Turning Kits   /1/            Products
0                3            Pen Kits       /1/1/          Turning Kits
1                3            Pen Kits       /1/1/          Turning Kits
2                3            Pen Kits       /1/1/          Turning Kits
0                4            Fountain       /1/1/1/        Pen Kits
1                4            Fountain       /1/1/1/        Pen Kits
2                4            Fountain       /1/1/1/        Pen Kits
3                4            Fountain       /1/1/1/        Pen Kits
```

Why did you get 235 rows instead of 62? The anchor query returned 63 rows. Those 63 rows are handed to the recursive query which then does the level 1 recursion, etc. until an empty result set occurs. You can see from the above query that one occurrence of each of the duplicate rows came from the anchor query – RecursionLevel = 0. The Products category (CategoryID = 1) is then recursed to return all of the rows in RecursionLevel 1. The Turning Kits category (CategoryID = 2) is then recursed to return all of the rows in RecursionLevel 2. Finally, the Pen Kits category (CategoryID = 3) is recursed to produce all of the rows in RecursionLevel 3. So, Turning Kits at RecursionLevel 1, Pen Kits at RecursionLevel 2, and Fountain at Recursion Level 3 come from recursing Products. Pen Kits at Recursion Level 1 and Fountain at Recursion Level 2 come from recursing Turning Kits. Fountain at Recursion Level 1 comes from recursing Pen Kits. What you actually did is completely recurse every category, individually, and then combine the results of all of the recursion operations.

You might think that you can "fix" this result set by simply restricting the outer query to where the RecursionLevel = 0. But, all you've really done is return the contents of the Lookups.Category table minus the root node and not actually built a recursion.

When you remove the WHERE clause from or even when you include multiple rows in the anchor query, you are basically telling SQL Server to fully recurse each of the rows in the anchor query and then combine the result together. This can produce duplicates with no ability to differentiate one recursive hierarchy in the result set from another.

PIVOT

When data is pivoted, you are turning data values into columns while applying an aggregate. Groupings are calculated and the aggregate applied to the grouping to produce the body of the pivot table. A SELECT statement is defined that encompasses the columns used for grouping, the column that calculations are spread across, and the column used for the aggregate. In our query below, the FOR clause defines the column which is used to spread the data with the IN clause defining the data values you want to spread the aggregate across. What SQL Server does is computes SUM(c.Quantity * c.Price) grouping by product name and month name. It then rotates the month name to the columns and spreads the appropriate aggregate based on the intersection of the product name and month name.

You should notice that the query does not have a GROUP BY clause. Any column which is not specified in either the aggregate or the spreading column (FOR clause) forms the set of columns for the implicit GROUP BY. So, you need to ensure that you do not include additional columns in the SELECT statement which you don't want the grouping to be defined on.

```
SELECT f.ProductName, f.January, f.February, f.March
FROM (SELECT a.ProductName, DATENAME(mm,OrderDate) OrderMonth, c.Quantity * c.Price
SalesAmount
      FROM Products.Product a INNER JOIN Products.SKU b ON a.ProductID = b.ProductID
         INNER JOIN Orders.OrderDetail c ON b.SKU = c.SKU
         INNER JOIN Orders.OrderHeader d ON c.OrderID = d.OrderID
      WHERE YEAR(d.OrderDate) = 2001) e
   PIVOT
      (SUM(SalesAmount)
      FOR OrderMonth
      IN (January,February,March)) f
ORDER BY f.ProductName;
```

You could produce the same result by leveraging a CASE statement as shown below. Pivoting data using a CASE expression is also backwards compatible to versions prior to SQL Server 2005.

```
SELECT a.ProductName, SUM(CASE WHEN DATENAME(mm,OrderDate) = 'January'
                        THEN c.Quantity * c.Price END) January,
                     SUM(CASE WHEN DATENAME(mm,OrderDate) = 'February'
                        THEN c.Quantity * c.Price END) February,
                     SUM(CASE WHEN DATENAME(mm,OrderDate) = 'March'
                        THEN c.Quantity * c.Price END) March
FROM Products.Product a INNER JOIN Products.SKU b ON a.ProductID = b.ProductID
      INNER JOIN Orders.OrderDetail c ON b.SKU = c.SKU
      INNER JOIN Orders.OrderHeader d ON c.OrderID = d.OrderID
WHERE YEAR(d.OrderDate) = 2001
GROUP BY a.ProductName
ORDER BY a.ProductName;
```

What if you wanted to pivot multiple columns e.g. pivoting both a sales amount and a quantity sold? The PIVOT operator will only accept a single aggregate function along with a single spreading column. But, there isn't a restriction on the number of PIVOT operators you can include in a single SELECT statement. Ok, for those who want to be completely accurate, you can only include 256 PIVOT operators in a single SELECT statement, but you have an almost impossible task of figuring out what the query is doing if you had 256 PIVOTs in a single statement.

You solve the double pivot problem using the query below where I've used a CTE to simplify the code so that the double pivot is easier to see.

```
WITH ProductTotals_CTE (ProductName, OrderMonth, QuantitySold, SalesAmount)
AS
(SELECT a.ProductName, DATENAME(mm,OrderDate) OrderMonth, SUM(c.Quantity)
QuantitySold, SUM(c.Quantity * c.Price) SalesAmount
FROM Products.Product a INNER JOIN Products.SKU b ON a.ProductID = b.ProductID
        INNER JOIN Orders.OrderDetail c ON b.SKU = c.SKU
        INNER JOIN Orders.OrderHeader d ON c.OrderID = d.OrderID
WHERE YEAR(d.OrderDate) = 2001
GROUP BY a.ProductName, DATENAME(mm,OrderDate))

SELECT f.ProductName, f.JanuaryQty, g.JanuaryAmount, f.FebruaryQty,
g.FebruaryAmount, f.MarchQty, g.MarchAmount
FROM (SELECT ProductName, OrderMonth + 'Qty' PivotKey, QuantitySold
      FROM ProductTotals_CTE) e
    PIVOT
        (SUM(QuantitySold)
        FOR PivotKey
        IN (JanuaryQty, FebruaryQty, MarchQty)) f
INNER JOIN
    (SELECT ProductName, OrderMonth + 'Amount' PivotKey, SalesAmount
      FROM ProductTotals_CTE) e
    PIVOT
        (SUM(SalesAmount)
        FOR PivotKey
        IN (JanuaryAmount, FebruaryAmount, MarchAmount)) g ON f.ProductName =
g.ProductName
ORDER BY f.ProductName;
```

From a performance perspective, the CASE representation and a single PIVOT are about equivalent. However, if you need to double pivot, triple pivot, etc., the CASE expression will outperform the PIVOT by 50% or more in most cases. The explanation for the performance difference is rather straightforward. Each PIVOT operator has to perform a grouping and an aggregation before the results are joined together, which in a double pivot case means two passes through the data to compute the aggregate. The CASE expression only requires a single pass through the data, so you would expect the CASE expression to complete in approximately ½ the time as a double pivot. The triple pivot would make three passes through the data while the equivalent CASE expression still only requires a single pass.

UNPIVOT

The UNPIVOT operator rotates one or more columns into rows. While the PIVOT operator can aggregate values as it rotates rows to columns, the UNPIVOT cannot split aggregates back out to their constituent values. It should be obvious that SQL Server has no idea if a value of 10 should be split into a single row or multiple rows or how 10 should be distributed across multiple rows, although many people ask the question of how to split the aggregate back out.

The general syntax of UNPIVOT is as follows:

```
SELECT …
FROM <source table>
UNPIVOT (<target quantity column name>
    FOR <target values column name> (<source columns>)) <alias>;
```

Since our database doesn't have any data that is in a format to use for UNPIVOT, let's take our double pivot example and generate a temp table to work with:

```
SELECT a.ProductName, SUM(CASE WHEN DATENAME(mm,OrderDate) = 'January'
                   THEN c.Quantity END) JanQty,
               SUM(CASE WHEN DATENAME(mm,OrderDate) = 'January'
                   THEN c.Quantity * c.Price END) JanAmount,
               SUM(CASE WHEN DATENAME(mm,OrderDate) = 'February'
                   THEN c.Quantity END) FebQty,
               SUM(CASE WHEN DATENAME(mm,OrderDate) = 'February'
                   THEN c.Quantity * c.Price END) FebAmount,
               SUM(CASE WHEN DATENAME(mm,OrderDate) = 'March'
                   THEN c.Quantity END) MarchQty,
               SUM(CASE WHEN DATENAME(mm,OrderDate) = 'March'
                   THEN c.Quantity * c.Price END) MarchAmount
INTO #ProductSales
FROM Products.Product a INNER JOIN Products.SKU b ON a.ProductID = b.ProductID
       INNER JOIN Orders.OrderDetail c ON b.SKU = c.SKU
       INNER JOIN Orders.OrderHeader d ON c.OrderID = d.OrderID
WHERE YEAR(d.OrderDate) = 2001
GROUP BY a.ProductName
ORDER BY a.ProductName;
```

This produces a result set that looks like the following:

```
ProductName         JanQty  JanAmount  FebQty  FebAmount  MarchQty  MarchAmount
-------------       ------  ---------  ------  ---------  --------  -----------
Flat Top American   NULL    NULL       NULL    NULL       NULL      NULL
Pen Disassembly     31      774.69     28      699.72     31        774.69
Cigar Pen           475     1895.25    549     2190.51    593       2366.07
Pen Press           31      929.69     28      839.72     31        929.69
```

What we want to do is turn the sales amount columns into rows with the following query:

```
SELECT ProductName, SalesAmount, Month
FROM #ProductSales a
UNPIVOT(SalesAmount FOR Month IN (JanAmount, FebAmount, MarchAmount)) b;
```

The ProductName column is returned directly from the table. The SalesAmount is the name of the column where we will put the values from the JanAmount, FebAmount, and MarchAmount columns. The Month is the column name where we will store a value that corresponds to the column names in the original table. This produces a result that looks like the following:

```
ProductName         SalesAmount   Month
-----------------   -----------   -------
Pen Disassembly     774.69        JanAmount
Pen Disassembly     699.72        FebAmount
Pen Disassembly     774.69        MarchAmount
Cigar Pen           1895.25       JanAmount
Cigar Pen           2190.51       FebAmount
Cigar Pen           2366.07       MarchAmount
Pen Press           929.69        JanAmount
Pen Press           839.72        FebAmount
Pen Press           929.69        MarchAmount
```

You'll notice that the NULLs are removed from the result set, so in the case of the Flat Top American pen kit, it will not even appear in the result. Therefore, in some cases, the UNPIVOTed result cannot be turned back into the original data set by a PIVOT operation. The "Month" column doesn't actually contain a month. This was done on purpose to show you where the data values for the column specified in the FOR clause come from.

The values in the Month column also lead us to the second example from this same temp table. Just like PIVOT, you can put multiple UNPIVOT operators in a single statement. However, it is not as straightforward as the multiple PIVOT. If you look back at the multiple PIVOT example, we used a join on the product name between the two PIVOT expressions to associate the aggregates to the correct product name. It isn't that straight forward with an UNPIVOT, because we are turning columns into rows and an UNPIVOT will rotate one set of values. To do a double UNPIVOT, you need to rotate multiple columns as a set and produce a multi-column result.

```
SELECT ProductName, REPLACE(Month,'Amount','') Month, SalesAmount, SalesQty
FROM #ProductSales a
UNPIVOT(SalesAmount FOR Month IN (JanAmount, FebAmount, MarchAmount)) b
UNPIVOT(SalesQty FOR Qty IN (JanQty, FebQty, MarchQty)) c
WHERE REPLACE(Month,'Amount','') = REPLACE(Qty,'Qty','');
```

To understand what is going on, take a look at each of the UNPIVOT separately. The first UNPIVOT returns the results shown above. The second UNPIVOT will return a similar result set with the quantities instead of sales amounts and the Qty column names as data values in the rows. The <target quantity column name> has to be unique within the query. Likewise, the <target values column name> also has to be unique, because the aliases for the UNPIVOT table expression cannot be used to reference columns. The WHERE clause is how everything gets put together properly. We've constructed the column names such that we can parse something out of each pair of column names that is distinct within the result set. Once the UNPIVOT occurs, the columns names are just data values in the table, so we can manipulate the data anyway we need to. So, with the two UNPIVOT operators we end up with two table expressions that we then join back together by parsing the common string out of the Month and Qty columns of the UNPIVOT table expression.

Set Operators

SQL Server 2005 introduced an APPLY set operator which can be used in the FROM clause. The APPLY operator is available in two different types, CROSS APPLY and OUTER APPLY. The APPLY operator executes against two table expressions. You can use any combination of tables, table expressions, or derived tables on either side of the APPLY operator.

The CROSS APPLY operator functions very much like a CROSS JOIN where each row on the left side is combined with every row on the right side. The following queries produce the same results. The CTE has been removed so that you can clearly see the queries involved.

```
SELECT b.ProductName, a.CustomerID, a.QuantitySold
FROM ProductSales_CTE a CROSS JOIN Products.Product b
ORDER BY b.ProductID;

SELECT b.ProductName, a.CustomerID, a.QuantitySold
FROM ProductSales_CTE a CROSS APPLY Products.Product b
ORDER BY b.ProductID;
```

Since you can specify table expressions with the APPLY operator, you can vary the results returned for each row in the left hand table expression which is not possible with a CROSS JOIN. You vary the results on the right side of the APPLY by applying the same technique you learned with correlated subqueries where the right hand table expression references one or more rows in the left hand table expression. If a row on the left side does not have a corresponding row on the right side, the row is dropped from the result set when using CROSS APPLY. If you want to preserve all rows on the left hand side, you can use OUTER APPLY.

The following example returns the top 5 customers for each product based on the quantity purchased. The CTE is used simply to produce the base level aggregate. Notice that the ProductID from the left hand table is referenced in the WHERE clause for the derived table on the right hand side. This causes the right hand query to be evaluated against each ProductID on the left hand side.

```
WITH ProductSales_CTE (ProductID, CustomerID, QuantitySold)
AS
(SELECT d.ProductID, b.CustomerID, SUM(a.Quantity) QuantitySold
FROM Orders.OrderDetail a INNER JOIN Orders.OrderHeader b ON a.OrderID = b.OrderID
    INNER JOIN Products.SKU c ON a.SKU = c.SKU
    INNER JOIN Products.Product d ON c.ProductID = d.ProductID
    GROUP BY d.ProductID, b.CustomerID)
SELECT a.ProductName, c.CustomerID, c.QuantitySold
FROM Products.Product a CROSS APPLY
    (SELECT TOP(5) CustomerID, QuantitySold
    FROM ProductSales_CTE b
    WHERE a.ProductID = b.ProductID
    ORDER BY QuantitySold DESC) c
ORDER BY a.ProductID;
```

Because not all products have sales, you can modify the query above to replace CROSS APPLY with OUTER APPLY to preserve all products while still including the top 5 customers for products which have sales.

```
WITH ProductSales_CTE (ProductID, CustomerID, QuantitySold)
AS
(SELECT d.ProductID, b.CustomerID, SUM(a.Quantity) QuantitySold
FROM Orders.OrderDetail a INNER JOIN Orders.OrderHeader b ON a.OrderID = b.OrderID
    INNER JOIN Products.SKU c ON a.SKU = c.SKU
    INNER JOIN Products.Product d ON c.ProductID = d.ProductID
    GROUP BY d.ProductID, b.CustomerID)
SELECT a.ProductName, c.CustomerID, c.QuantitySold
FROM Products.Product a OUTER APPLY
    (SELECT TOP(5) CustomerID, QuantitySold
    FROM ProductSales_CTE b
    WHERE a.ProductID = b.ProductID
    ORDER BY QuantitySold DESC) c
ORDER BY a.ProductID;
```

CROSS APPLY and OUTER APPLY operate on a set. Thus far, we've shown how to combine CROSS APPLY and OUTER APPLY to a table and a SELECT statement. But, you can use the APPLY operator with any set expression. One of the more interesting examples is when used with a row constructor.

A row constructor is not restricted to static values as we covered previously in this chapter, but instead can reference columns in a table within the FROM clause in addition to statically defined values.

Remember from our double unpivot example that you needed to create this weird looking join which relied on precisely controlling the names of the columns in order to be able to match up pairs of values.

```
SELECT ProductName, REPLACE(Month,'Amount','') Month, SalesAmount, SalesQty
FROM #ProductSales a
UNPIVOT(SalesAmount FOR Month IN (JanAmount, FebAmount, MarchAmount)) b
UNPIVOT(SalesQty FOR Qty IN (JanQty, FebQty, MarchQty)) c
WHERE REPLACE(Month,'Amount','') = REPLACE(Qty,'Qty','');
```

What would happen if the columns were instead named as follows: JanuaryAmount, FebruaryAmount, MarchAmount, JanQty, FebQty, MarQty? You would have to create a CTE to first alias the column names into some artificial naming construct in order to parse the column names apart to produce a match on the pairs. While the double unpivot is complicated enough, picture how quickly this escalates when you have to do a triple, quadruple, etc. unpivot. We can utilize a row constructor to simplify this multiple unpivot example as follows:

```
SELECT a.ProductName, b.Month, b.SalesAmount, b.SalesQty
FROM #ProductSales a CROSS APPLY
    (VALUES ('January', JanAmount, JanQty), ('February', FebAmount, FebQty),
    ('March', MarchAmount, MarchQty)) b (Month, SalesAmount, SalesQty);
```

The results produced are not exactly equivalent to an UNPIVOT. The UNPIVOT will eliminate any rows where either the SalesAmount or SalesQty is null while the CROSS APPLY will preserve all rows. If you want to make the query equivalent to an UNPIVOT, you can apply a WHERE clause to filter out the NULLs.

```
SELECT a.ProductName, b.Month, b.SalesAmount, b.SalesQty
FROM #ProductSales a CROSS APPLY
    (VALUES ('January', JanAmount, JanQty), ('February', FebAmount, FebQty),
    ('March', MarchAmount, MarchQty)) b (Month, SalesAmount, SalesQty)
WHERE SalesAmount IS NOT NULL AND SalesQty IS NOT NULL;
```

However, there is a slight problem with both this query and the implementation of UNPIVOT. Anywhere a NULL exists in either the quantity or amount will be eliminated when the data is UNPIVOTed. What if you had a quantity for January, but the amount was NULL? While this would surely violate a business rule in having product sold with a nonexistent sales amount, the fact is that a set of related columns in a multiple unpivot can contain a mix of NULL and not NULL values. You get around this problem by changing the AND to an OR in the query above.

```
SELECT a.ProductName, b.Month, b.SalesAmount, b.SalesQty
FROM #ProductSales a CROSS APPLY
    (VALUES ('January', JanAmount, JanQty), ('February', FebAmount, FebQty),
    ('March', MarchAmount, MarchQty)) b (Month, SalesAmount, SalesQty)
WHERE SalesAmount IS NOT NULL OR SalesQty IS NOT NULL;
```

The UNPIVOT operator does not have the same capability. In order to preserve the row where you have a mixture of NULL and not NULL values, you would have to first translate the NULLs to an actual value, UNPIVOT, change the value back to NULL, and then filter out the rows where all values in a row are NULL.

Exercise 1: Set Operations and Table Expressions

1. Display Stephen Silas' org chart. Hint: You need to build a recursive CTE on the HumanResources.Employee table.

2. Compute the total sales by master product for customers in Illinois, Texas, California, and Maryland. Display the results in the following format sorted by product name. Hint: Master product = Products.Product table.

   ```
   Product         Illinois       Texas        California     Maryland
   -------------   -----------    --------     -------------  -----------
   Product1        $Amount        $Amount      $Amount        $Amount
   ```

3. Extend the result from item 2 to include both the total sales and quantity sold using the most efficient method possible.

4. One of the first applications of a double unpivot was when I needed to process baseball statistics for the Texas Rangers. Each game's lineup was stored as a pivoted set, 1 row per game/team combination with 20 columns to list each of the 10 players and their positions. I needed to unpivot the data so that I could compute stats for each player. The schema below is simplified in that it simply embeds the player's name instead of having an ID with the player name stored elsewhere. Given the following schema and data to populate it, produce a result set with the following columns: GameID, TeamID, PlayerID, and Position.

   ```
   CREATE TABLE #GameLineup
   (GameID              INT        NOT NULL,
   TeamID               INT        NOT NULL,
   Player1ID            CHAR(20)   NOT NULL,
   Player1Position      CHAR(2)    NOT NULL,
   Player2ID            CHAR(20)   NOT NULL,
   Player2Position      CHAR(2)    NOT NULL,
   Player3ID            CHAR(20)   NOT NULL,
   Player3Position      CHAR(2)    NOT NULL,
   Player4ID            CHAR(20)   NOT NULL,
   Player4Position      CHAR(2)    NOT NULL,
   Player5ID            CHAR(20)   NOT NULL,
   Player5Position      CHAR(2)    NOT NULL,
   Player6ID            CHAR(20)   NOT NULL,
   Player6Position      CHAR(2)    NOT NULL,
   Player7ID            CHAR(20)   NOT NULL,
   Player7Position      CHAR(2)    NOT NULL,
   Player8ID            CHAR(20)   NOT NULL,
   Player8Position      CHAR(2)    NOT NULL,
   Player9ID            CHAR(20)   NOT NULL,
   Player9Position      CHAR(2)    NOT NULL,
   Player10ID           CHAR(20)   NULL,
   Player10Position     CHAR(2)    NULL)

   INSERT INTO #GameLineup
   VALUES (1,1,'Rod Carew','2B','Cal Ripken Jr.','SS','Ted Williams','LF',
   'Babe Ruth','DH','Hank Aaron','RF','Joe DiMaggio','CF', 'Lou Gehrig','1B',
   'George Brett','3B','Yogi Berra','C', 'Nolan Ryan','P'),
   (1,2,'Pete Rose','3B', 'Rickey Henderson','RF', 'Ryne Sandberg','DH',
   'Willie Mays','CF', 'Johnny Bench','C', 'Willie McCovey','1B',
   'Ernie Banks','SS','Jackie Robinson','2B', 'Willie Stargell','LF',
   'Steve Carleton','P');
   ```

5. Retrieve the 2 most recent orders for each customer.

Window Functions

A SELECT statement retrieves a set of data that is subsequently operated on to produce a result. If you just take the SELECT, FROM, and WHERE clauses, the result of these three clauses defines a subset of data that you are going to either return to an application or perform further operations against before returning a final result. The GROUP BY clause operates against this entire subset retrieved to compute aggregates. You might optionally apply a HAVING clause against the computed aggregates. However, the GROUP BY doesn't have a role in defining a subset of data, only operating across the entire subset that is presented to GROUP BY. The HAVING clause operates against the aggregated data, therefore by extension, also operates against the entire subset and does not define the initial subset of data being operated against.

So, when a database platform is finished evaluating the SELECT, FROM, and WHERE clauses, the subset of data defined can be thought of as a window into the overall set of data available in your database. You can then apply functions and operators to this window of data to do analysis or perform a variety of aggregates.

This section will focus on the application of a class of functions to this window of data, also known as window functions. All of the window functions are going to operate against the subset of data exposed by the SELECT, FROM, and WHERE clauses with the SELECT clause being a special case in that it encompasses all possible columns and expressions which are valid against the FROM and WHERE clauses. So, the definition of a window function is a function that is applied over the subset of data exposed by the FROM and WHERE clauses.

With the exception of the FROM and WHERE clauses, any other clause valid for a SELECT statement do not play a role in defining the window of data you will operate against. This might seem like splitting hairs, but it is an important concept to understand the result set that will be returned. Many of the window functions are going to be familiar from our discussion of a GROUP BY clause e.g. SUM(), MIN(), MAX(), AVG(), etc. But just using a SUM in your query does not mean you are applying a function in a window mode. Window functions are a special class of behaviors for the set of functions discussed below.

You could write a SELECT statement using window function behavior that is exactly equivalent to a SELECT statement which computes an aggregate with a GROUP BY clause. However, writing the SELECT statement with a GROUP BY clause to produce the same behavior as a window function, while doable, can be extremely complicated and the performance would be terrible. Window functions are implemented in SQL Server through an extension to a small group of functions with the OVER operator.

Without getting into an even longer explanation of the exact differences in behavior with windows functions and the broader group of functions, let's get into how to apply window functions and hopefully you'll understand what the big deal really is.

Aggregate Functions

The following table lists the aggregate functions compatible with the OVER clause. All of the aggregate functions ignore any NULLs in the result set, except COUNT(*). You can also specify

DISTINCT with any of the aggregate functions to only include unique values in the set being aggregated e.g. SUM(DISTINCT...), MIN(DISTINCT...), and COUNT(DISTINCT...).

As I said in the intro to this section, the subset of data defined for a window function comes from the FROM and WHERE clauses. While the functions listed below have the capability to apply a DISTINCT, DISTINCT is not compatible with the OVER operator. The reason that DISTINCT is not compatible with the OVER operator is because a window function has to be applied to the entire window of data and the DISTINCT operator filters duplicate values from the set of data.

Function	Definition
AVG	Returns an average of the set of values
CHECKSUM_AGG	Computes a checksum over a group of values.
COUNT	Returns a count of the number of rows in a set. Returns an INT data type.
COUNT_BIG	Functions the same as the COUNT() function, except returns a BIGINT data type. Use this function when the count of the number of rows is expected to exceed the capacity of an INT.
GROUPING	Used to distinguish if a NULL value returned by ROLLUP, CUBE, or GROUPING SETS is an actual NULL in the source data.
MAX	Returns the maximum value of a set.
MIN	Returns the minimum value of a set.
SUM	Returns the sum of the values in a set.
STDEV	Returns the standard deviation of all values in a sample set. Mathematically known as the sampled standard deviation.
STDEVP	Returns the standard deviation of a population. Mathematically known as the population standard deviation.
VAR	Returns the variance of all values in a sample set. Mathematically known as the sample variance.
VARP	Returns the variance of a population. Mathematically known as the population variance.

You can compute the total of all orders by using the following query:

```
SELECT SUM(OrderTotal)
FROM Orders.OrderHeader;

--------------------
368044.0022
(1 row(s) affected)
```

You can accomplish the same thing using the window function extension to SUM as follows:

```
SELECT SUM(OrderTotal) OVER ()
FROM Orders.OrderHeader;


---------------------
368044.0022
368044.0022
...
368044.0022
(8088 row(s) affected)
```

Each version of the query produced the answer of $368,044.00, but the result sets are very different between the two queries. So, why is there a difference? The first query uses the regular version of the SUM function and tells SQL Server to retrieve all of the rows from the Orders.OrderHeader table, sum up the OrderTotal for all rows, and return the result. The second query tells SQL Server to retrieve all rows from the Orders.OrderHeader table and for each row in the subset, apply the SUM function to the OrderTotal column for every row in the subset.

At first read, the explanation might seem to be the same between the two queries, but look at the difference very carefully. When you specify OVER without any parameters, OVER(), you are saying that the computation window for the SUM function is the entire window of data. So, for every row in the subset, compute the total of all orders in the subset. Adding in the OrderID column makes the behavior more apparent.

```
OrderID
-----------   ---------------------
1             368044.0022
2             368044.0022
3             368044.0022
4             368044.0022
...
8101          368044.0022
(8088 row(s) affected)
```

If you wanted the two queries to produce the same result, not just the same calculation, you would have needed to do the following:

```
SELECT DISTINCT SUM(OrderTotal) OVER ()
FROM Orders.OrderHeader;
```

While the window function with a DISTINCT produces the same result, it is a horribly inefficient query. The GROUP BY computes the total once while the window function computes the total 8088 times and then throws away 8087 of the computations to produce a single row. So, when you have simple aggregation, you are usually better off writing a GROUP BY query instead of using the windowing extension to the function.

Let's take a look at the next feature of the OVER clause which applies a sort to the result set before applying the computation, which also limits the window of data available to each row during the calculation.

Recall the query we wrote to compute a running total shown below:

```
WITH DailyTotal_CTE (OrderDate, DailyTotal)
AS
(SELECT OrderDate, SUM(OrderTotal) DailyTotal
      FROM Orders.OrderHeader
      GROUP BY OrderDate)
SELECT a.OrderDate, a.DailyTotal, SUM(b.DailyTotal) RunningTotal
FROM  DailyTotal_CTE a INNER JOIN DailyTotal_CTE b
ON a.OrderDate >= b.OrderDate
GROUP BY a.OrderDate, a.DailyTotal
ORDER BY a.OrderDate;
```

The CTE was used to first compute a daily total since we only want to calculate a running total from one day to the next across the entire Orders.OrderHeader table. This query required you to join the CTE to itself with this weird looking inequality join. What this query forces SQL Server to do is to compute the contents of the CTE twice, store both results in memory, join the two result sets together, and compute the aggregate for each row in the set.

The same result can be accomplished with a window function as follows:

```
WITH DailyTotal_CTE (OrderDate, DailyTotal)
AS
    (SELECT OrderDate, SUM(OrderTotal) DailyTotal
     FROM Orders.OrderHeader
     GROUP BY OrderDate)
SELECT OrderDate, DailyTotal, SUM(DailyTotal) OVER(ORDER BY OrderDate) RunningTotal
FROM  DailyTotal_CTE
ORDER BY OrderDate;
```

The CTE still exists, because we want to operate on daily totals. However, you'll notice a dramatic difference in the outer SELECT statement. What this query does is tells SQL Server to compute the CTE and store the results in memory. Then take a single calculation pass across the results of the CTE and compute the SUM of the DailyTotal for each row in the set. The OVER(ORDER BY OrderDate) tells SQL Server that the data should be sorted by OrderDate and the window of the data available to the SUM function changes for each row as it moves down the result set. The window of the data available to the SUM function at each row is the current row + all rows prior to the current based on the ORDER BY specification. So, the January 1, 2001 row only has the data for January 1 visible through the window for the SUM function while January 2, 2001 has both January 2 and January 1 visible through the window for the SUM function.

The OVER(ORDER BY…) will produce a simple running total that doesn't require a GROUP BY in the outer query nor does it require the CTE to be joined to itself or the use of an inequality join. Additionally, if you look at the performance, the window function will perform the same amount of work with an almost 90% reduction is resources.

Another difficult problem is trying to compute when someone has met or exceeded a quota. You want to return all prior values up to the point where the quota is met or exceeded. This requires you to compute a running total and at each step compare to see if the running total is greater than or equal to the quota.

Now that we have a simpler and more efficient way to compute a running total, you might think to solve the problem using the query below:

```
WITH DailyTotal_CTE (OrderDate, DailyTotal)
AS
    (SELECT OrderDate, SUM(OrderTotal) DailyTotal
     FROM Orders.OrderHeader
     GROUP BY OrderDate)
SELECT OrderDate, DailyTotal, SUM(DailyTotal) OVER(ORDER BY OrderDate) RunningTotal
FROM   DailyTotal_CTE
WHERE SUM(DailyTotal) OVER(ORDER BY OrderDate) <= 50000
ORDER BY OrderDate;
```

From our discussion of order of operations, you know that you couldn't reference the column alias RunningTotal in the WHERE clause, because the alias doesn't exist until the SELECT clause is evaluated. So, you might have attempted to put the actual window function into the WHERE clause and received an error message. Recall our discussion from above. The window of data that the function is applied across is defined by the FROM and WHERE clauses. So, how could you embed a window function into a WHERE clause to compute the subset of data that could be available to the window function? This is cyclical logic and makes it impossible for SQL Server to ever resolve the query. The OVER operator is only valid in the SELECT and ORDER BY clauses.

The proper way to solve this problem is to compute the running total in a CTE and then return the rows that meet the criteria as shown below:

```
WITH DailyTotal_CTE (OrderDate, DailyTotal)
AS
    (SELECT OrderDate, SUM(OrderTotal) DailyTotal
     FROM Orders.OrderHeader
     GROUP BY OrderDate),
Totals_CTE (OrderDate, DailyTotal, RunningTotal)
AS
    (SELECT OrderDate, DailyTotal, SUM(DailyTotal) OVER(ORDER BY OrderDate) RunningTotal
     FROM   DailyTotal_CTE)
SELECT OrderDate, DailyTotal, RunningTotal
FROM Totals_CTE
WHERE RunningTotal <= 50000
ORDER BY OrderDate;
```

If instead of computing just a running total or a running average, you wanted to compute a moving aggregate. Computing a moving aggregate is also known as computing over a sliding window such as calculating a moving 3 month average of sales. The trick to computing a moving 3 month average is to be able to restrict the computation to the current month plus the two prior months.

The query below shows how you would compute a moving average, in this case a moving 3 day average without using a window function.

```
WITH DailyTotal_CTE (OrderDate, DailyTotal)
AS
    (SELECT OrderDate, SUM(OrderTotal) DailyTotal
     FROM Orders.OrderHeader
     GROUP BY OrderDate)
SELECT a.OrderDate, a.DailyTotal, AVG(b.DailyTotal) Moving3DayAverage
FROM  DailyTotal_CTE a INNER JOIN DailyTotal_CTE b ON
    b.OrderDate > DATEADD(dd,-3,a.OrderDate)
    AND b.OrderDate <= a.OrderDate
GROUP BY a.OrderDate, a.DailyTotal
ORDER BY a.OrderDate;
```

By now, you should be familiar with the CTE we are using to compute a single sales amount for each OrderDate. As a running aggregate, you should also expect that we need to join the CTE to itself. The way the CTE is joined is where you get the moving average. You want the OrderDate from the second copy of the CTE to be greater than 3 days ago in the first copy while also being less than or equal to the OrderDate in the first copy. This defines a 3 day range that you shouldn't have any problem extending to a moving 3 months, 6 months, 1 year, etc.

```
WITH DailyTotal_CTE (OrderDate, DailyTotal)
AS
    (SELECT OrderDate, SUM(OrderTotal) DailyTotal
     FROM Orders.OrderHeader
     GROUP BY OrderDate)
SELECT OrderDate, DailyTotal,
    AVG(DailyTotal) OVER(ORDER BY OrderDate
                 ROWS BETWEEN 2 PRECEDING AND CURRENT ROW) Moving3DayAverage
FROM  DailyTotal_CTE
ORDER BY OrderDate;
```

New in SQL Server 2012, you can specify a ROWS clause to define a window extent that allows you to easily compute sliding aggregates. What the ROWS clause says is to compute the average of the DailyTotal based on the current row in the set plus the 2 rows before the current row. The ORDER BY is required in order to make the calculations repeatable.

The ROWS window extent can be defined with the PRECEDING or FOLLOWING keywords and you specify both an upper and lower bound for the extent. The lower bound for the extent can be specified as the current row, an integer number of rows, or the beginning of the window. The upper bound can be specified as the current row, an integer number of rows, or the end of the window. The current row is specified with the CURRENT ROW keyword. The beginning of the window is specified by UNBOUNDED PRECEDING. The end of the window is specified as UNBOUNDED FOLLOWING.

Window Extent	Meaning
BETWEEN UNBOUNDED PRECEDING AND CURRENT ROW	Compute from the beginning of the window up to and including the current row.
BETWEEN 4 PRECEDING AND CURRENT ROW	Compute from the current row to 4 rows prior to the current row.
BETWEEN 3 PRECEDING AND UNBOUNDED FOLLOWING	Compute from 3 rows prior to the current row through the end of the window.

Window Extent	Meaning
BETWEEN CURRENT ROW AND CURRENT ROW	Compute using only the current row.
BETWEEN CURRENT ROW AND 5 FOLLOWING	Compute from the current row through 5 rows following the current row.

As if the capabilities already mentioned weren't enough, OVER has one final trick up its sleeve. So far, we've been aggregating across the entire window of data and saw how the visibility of the aggregate could be limited by the addition of the ORDER BY and ROWS clauses. You can also scope the calculations to subsets of data within the window. For example, what if we wanted to compute a running total for each year? We know that we can use the ORDER BY clause within the OVER operator to produce a running total. But how do we get it to reset the calculation for each year? The ROWS clause isn't going to help, because it just restricts the calculation to a number of rows and won't accomplish an actual reset of the running total at each yearly inflection point.

To accomplish resetting the calculation, we need to be able to break the window into distinct segments of data based on the order year. The PARTITION BY clause is used to break the window into segments such that the aggregate is applied within each partition. This allows a running total to be computed where the calculation resets each time the year changes as follows:

```
WITH MonthlyTotal_CTE (OrderYear, OrderMonth, MonthlyTotal)
AS
    (SELECT YEAR(OrderDate), MONTH(OrderDate), SUM(OrderTotal) MonthlyTotal
    FROM Orders.OrderHeader
    GROUP BY YEAR(OrderDate), MONTH(OrderDate))
SELECT OrderYear, OrderMonth, MonthlyTotal,
    SUM(MonthlyTotal) OVER(PARTITION BY OrderYear ORDER BY OrderMonth) SalesToDate
FROM  MonthlyTotal_CTE
ORDER BY OrderYear, OrderMonth;

OrderYear    OrderMonth    MonthlyTotal             SalesToDate
---------    ----------    --------------------     --------------------
2001         1             18417.1881               18417.1881
2001         2             22386.943                 40804.1311
2001         3             24544.0024                65348.1335
...
2001         11            52678.9974               255447.6778
2001         12            76610.3186               332057.9964
2002         1             35986.9958                35986.9958
```

Notice that we got the same running total as shown before, because the ORDER BY clause exposed an increasing window of data for each subsequent row in the window we are calculating over. However, you should also notice that the calculation resets based on the PARTITION BY clause so that the running total starts over with each year.

You might be wondering why I keep showing these examples based on a CTE that computes an aggregate and then proceed to compute an additional aggregate using a window function instead of just using the base table. Recall that the SELECT is applied across the entire window of data exposed by the FROM and WHERE clauses. We have more than 1 order in a day, so we could compute a running total directly from the Orders.OrderHeader table. But, instead of getting 1 row for each of the days or one row for each month, we would get all 8088 rows.

```
SELECT YEAR(OrderDate) OrderYear, MONTH(OrderDate) OrderMonth, OrderTotal,
    SUM(OrderTotal) OVER(PARTITION BY YEAR(OrderDate) ORDER BY MONTH(OrderDate))
SalesToDate
FROM Orders.OrderHeader
ORDER BY OrderYear, OrderMonth;

OrderYear    OrderMonth       OrderTotal              SalesToDate
-----------  -----------      --------------------    --------------------
2001         1                16.39                   18417.1881
2001         1                16.39                   18417.1881
2001         1                29.80                   18417.1881
...
2001         1                85.35                   18417.1881
2001         2                17.45                   40804.1311
2001         2                29.90                   40804.1311
2001         2                141.33                  40804.1311
...
(8088 row(s) affected)
```

In the first few examples, the CTE was used to pre-aggregate the data at a day or month level to make the result set clear and manageable. But, notice that even though the result above looks a bit unwieldy, the running total still computes properly at a month level. Each row in the window defined by the FROM clause has the SUM applied to the portion of the window defined by the OVER clause. While you could easily devise a way of modifying this query to return 1 row for each OrderYear, OrderMonth pair with the running total by removing the OrderTotal column and applying a DISTINCT, if you wanted to compute a moving 3 month average you would have a problem.

The ROWS clause deals with rows within the window. Each month has a varying number of rows. So, it would be impossible to specify a value for the number of rows preceding. If you had said ROWS BETWEEN 2 PRECEDING AND CURRENT ROW, what you would be doing is computing a moving average over 3 orders, not 3 days or even 3 months. So, when calculating moving averages, you need to ensure that the window of data defined by the FROM and WHERE clause produces 1 row for each level you are going to compute a moving aggregate across e.g. 1 row per day for an n day moving average, 1 row per month for an n month moving average, etc.

There is an alternative solution to the running total problem which doesn't require us to create a CTE or derived table to pre-aggregate data. Instead of using ROWS, we can specify RANGE as follows:

```
SELECT DISTINCT YEAR(OrderDate), MONTH(OrderDate),
    SUM(OrderTotal) OVER(PARTITION BY YEAR(OrderDate)
                    ORDER BY YEAR(OrderDate), MONTH(OrderDate)
                    RANGE BETWEEN UNBOUNDED PRECEDING AND CURRENT ROW) SalesToDate
FROM Orders.OrderHeader
ORDER BY YEAR(OrderDate), MONTH(OrderDate);
```

The DISTINCT is used to eliminate duplicates giving us a result that has one row per order year and order month combination. The PARTITION BY clause segments the data by year and the ORDER BY clause causes the running total to be computed within each yearly segment. If we had specified ROWS BETWEEN UNBOUNDED PRECEDING AND CURRENT ROW, we would still get a running total, but the running total would have been computed moving from one order to the next and you would have had to then apply a MAX operator to pick out the maximum amount for each OrderYear, OrderMonth combination. The calculation would have occurred on an order by order basis, because the ROWS operator only cares about rows in the window, not actual data values. The RANGE operator works based on the actual data values, so it combines duplicates as can be seen in the comparison between the two methods below:

```
SELECT OrderID, YEAR(OrderDate), MONTH(OrderDate),
    SUM(OrderTotal) OVER(PARTITION BY YEAR(OrderDate)
                    ORDER BY YEAR(OrderDate), MONTH(OrderDate)
                    ROWS BETWEEN UNBOUNDED PRECEDING AND CURRENT ROW) SalesToDate
FROM Orders.OrderHeader
ORDER BY YEAR(OrderDate), MONTH(OrderDate);

OrderID          OrderYear          OrderMonth          SalesToDate
-----------      -----------        -----------         --------------------
1                2001               1                   16.39
2                2001               1                   32.78
3                2001               1                   62.58
4                2001               1                   92.48
....
521              2001               1                   18417.1881
522              2001               2                   18434.6381

SELECT OrderID, YEAR(OrderDate), MONTH(OrderDate),
    SUM(OrderTotal) OVER(PARTITION BY YEAR(OrderDate)
                    ORDER BY YEAR(OrderDate), MONTH(OrderDate)
                    RANGE BETWEEN UNBOUNDED PRECEDING AND CURRENT ROW) SalesToDate
FROM Orders.OrderHeader
ORDER BY YEAR(OrderDate), MONTH(OrderDate);

OrderID          OrderYear          OrderMonth          SalesToDate
-----------      -----------        -----------         --------------------
1                2001               1                   18417.1881
2                2001               1                   18417.1881
3                2001               1                   18417.1881
4                2001               1                   18417.1881
....
521              2001               1                   18417.1881
522              2001               2                   40804.1311
```

What RANGE is doing is based on the value in the current row, compute the SUM(OrderTotal) from the beginning of the window through all rows which have the same value for the OrderYear, OrderMonth combination.

You might be thinking that you can now solve the sliding aggregate problem using RANGE across the base table(s) instead of computing a CTE. While this would make sense, you would receive an error message. RANGE is only valid using UNBOUNDED and CURRENT ROW. You cannot specify a number of values preceding or following. So, while RANGE can be used to compute running totals, you must use ROWS to compute sliding aggregates.

There is also a performance difference between ROWS and RANGE. ROWS uses an in-memory structure to perform calculations. RANGE uses a worktable in tempdb to perform calculations. So, when you specify RANGE, you will incur physical disk I/O in the calculation. For small windows, the performance difference between ROWS and RANGE is virtually undetectable. As the number of rows in the window increases, ROWS will outperform RANGE to produce the same running total.

While window functions allow you to solve some problems that previously required very complicated SQL involving nested derived tables, multi-level CTEs, self-joins, and unequal joins, you might have missed one of the most useful capabilities of window functions. If you were stuck with a GROUP BY to compute an aggregate and then wanted to combine the aggregate with other data, you would have to compute the aggregate in one step and then join the result to the other tables. Window functions compute the aggregates in-line with the rest of the data being retrieved so you eliminate the additional step.

For example what if you wanted to compute a running total for both sales and quantity sold along with moving 3 and 6 month averages for sales and quantity sold and then wanted to compute the percentage of the total sales that each month contributed. If you didn't have window functions, you would have to rely on the other methods we've shown. The running totals would require a CTE self-joined to itself using an unequal join and since you wanted running totals for both quantity and sales, you would need a CTE for each one as shown at the beginning of this section. But, combining both results into a single result set is even more complicated. You would need a CTE that computed the daily totals. You would need a second CTE to compute the running total sales, a third CTE for the running total quantity, and an outer query that brought both running total CTEs into a single result set. It would require another set of CTEs for the moving 3 month average sales and quantity, another set for the moving 6 month sales and quantity, etc. To accomplish a single result set with all of these aggregates would require an extremely complicated query containing 10 – 12 CTEs before you even got to the complicated outer query to bring everything together. Just think what it would look like if you couldn't use CTEs. All of that is before you even get to the performance issues that would be involved with multiple passes through the same sets of data.

We can accomplish all of these requirements using window functions as shown below:

```
WITH DailyTotal_CTE (OrderYear, OrderMonth, MonthlyTotal, MonthlyQuantity)
AS
    (SELECT YEAR(a.OrderDate), MONTH(a.OrderDate), SUM(a.OrderTotal) MonthlyTotal,
        SUM(b.Quantity) MonthlyQuantity
    FROM Orders.OrderHeader a INNER JOIN Orders.OrderDetail b ON a.OrderID = b.OrderID
    GROUP BY YEAR(a.OrderDate), MONTH(a.OrderDate))
SELECT OrderYear, OrderMonth, MonthlyTotal, MonthlyQuantity,
    SUM(MonthlyTotal) OVER(PARTITION BY OrderYear ORDER BY OrderMonth) SalesToDate,
    AVG(MonthlyTotal) OVER(PARTITION BY OrderYear ORDER BY OrderMonth) AverageSalesToDate,
    SUM(MonthlyQuantity) OVER(PARTITION BY OrderYear ORDER BY OrderMonth) QuantityToDate,
    AVG(MonthlyQuantity) OVER(PARTITION BY OrderYear ORDER BY OrderMonth)
                                                            AverageQuantityToDate,
    AVG(MonthlyTotal) OVER(PARTITION BY OrderYear ORDER BY OrderMonth
                    ROWS BETWEEN 2 PRECEDING AND CURRENT ROW)
                                                        SalesMoving3MonthAverage,
    AVG(MonthlyQuantity) OVER(PARTITION BY OrderYear ORDER BY OrderMonth
                    ROWS BETWEEN 2 PRECEDING AND CURRENT ROW)
                                                        QuantityMoving3MonthAverage,
    AVG(MonthlyTotal) OVER(PARTITION BY OrderYear ORDER BY OrderMonth
                    ROWS BETWEEN 5 PRECEDING AND CURRENT ROW)
                                                        SalesMoving6MonthAverage,
    AVG(MonthlyQuantity) OVER(PARTITION BY OrderYear ORDER BY OrderMonth
                    ROWS BETWEEN 5 PRECEDING AND CURRENT ROW)
                                                        QuantityMoving6MonthAverage,
    (MonthlyTotal / SUM(MonthlyTotal) OVER()) * 100.0 PercentOfTotalSales,
    SUM(MonthlyTotal) OVER() TotalSales
FROM  DailyTotal_CTE
ORDER BY OrderYear, OrderMonth;
```

The CTE first computes the window of data which we are going to operate on. Then for each row in the window, we scope the aggregate differently for each result that we need to return. So, in a single pass through the data, we can calculate not only running totals but also moving averages. We can also directly combine base data with any of the windowed aggregates as shown by the computation of the PercentOfTotalSales. Hopefully you have grasped how window functions can dramatically transform the way you write aggregates while making the solution to some complicated problems very straightforward and easy to understand even for those with very little experience writing queries.

Ranking Functions

SQL Server has 4 functions used to rank data in a result set as follows:

Function	Purpose
ROW_NUMBER()	Number a data set from 1 and increment by 1
RANK()	Number a data set from 1, increment by 1, and assign the same number to duplicate values
DENSE_RANK()	Number a data set from 1, increment by 1, and assign the same number to duplicate values
NTILE(n)	Split a data set into n groups

All of the ranking functions require an OVER clause and the ORDER BY parameter to be specified, since it doesn't make any sense to rank data without having a sort order to determine the ranking. You can optionally specify PARTITION BY to perform ranking within groups of data. However, unlike aggregate function, you cannot use ROWS or RANGE with ranking functions.

The following query applies the ROW_NUMBER and NTILE(n) functions.

```
WITH Orders_CTE (StateProvince, SalesAmount)
AS
(SELECT c.StateProvince, SUM(a.OrderTotal)
FROM Orders.OrderHeader a INNER JOIN Customers.Address b ON a.AddressID = b.AddressID
    INNER JOIN Lookups.StateProvince c ON b.StateProvinceID = c.StateProvinceID
    INNER JOIN Orders.OrderDetail d ON a.OrderID = d.OrderID
GROUP BY c.StateProvince)
SELECT StateProvince, SalesAmount,
    ROW_NUMBER() OVER(ORDER BY SalesAmount DESC) RowNumber,
    NTILE(6) OVER(ORDER BY SalesAmount DESC) Tile
FROM Orders_CTE
ORDER BY SalesAmount DESC;

StateProvince    SalesAmount      RowNumber    Tile
--------------   -------------    ----------   -------
California       112254.0036      1            1
Texas            72430.0988       2            1
Illinois         65391.4482       3            1
New York         61797.00         4            1
...
Massachusetts    42160.1097       9            1
Georgia          37418.403        10           2
...
Maine            1507.51          51           6
(51 row(s) affected)
```

ROW_NUMBER()

We have sales for 51 states/provinces in the database, so as you should expect, the ROW_NUMBER() function starts at 1 and ends at 51. The rows will be numbered from highest sales to lowest sales based on the ORDER BY parameter in the OVER clause. The ROW_NUMBER() function is non-deterministic, because you can have ties in the ORDER BY. When more than one row has the same value based on the ORDER BY specification, the rows will be numbered as SQL Server found them in the table and the order can change with subsequent queries. If you want to ensure repeatable ordering, you need to include enough columns to uniquely identify each row.

One of the interesting applications of the ROW_NUMBER() function is in finding groups of sequential values. This is the opposite of the sequence gaps problem discussed earlier. To find gaps in a sequence, we need to find each of the gaps and then return the range of values between two gaps.

```
WITH OrderDates_CTE (OrderDate)
AS
(SELECT DISTINCT OrderDate
FROM Orders.OrderHeader),
Pairs_CTE (OrderDate, DateGroup)
AS
(SELECT DISTINCT OrderDate,
        DATEDIFF(dd,0,OrderDate) - ROW_NUMBER() OVER(ORDER BY OrderDate) AS
DateGroup
FROM OrderDates_CTE)
SELECT MIN(OrderDate) AS StartDate, MAX(OrderDate) AS EndDate
FROM Pairs_CTE
GROUP BY DateGroup;
```

We start the sequence gaps problem by first retrieving a unique set of order dates. The second CTE is where the key to computing the start and end of each sequence that uses a trick with DATEDIFF and ROW_NUMBER(). As we saw in Chapter 9, dates are really stored as numbers. In this case, since the order date is a DATE data type, a value of 0 really means January 1, 1 AD. So the DATEDIFF(dd,0,OrderDate) is just calculating the number of days from the anchor date of the DATE data type. The ROW_NUMBER() function sequentially numbers the set starting at 1 from the earliest date to the most recent date. So, if you look at the DATEDIFF() function, if you have a sequential set of dates, the DATEDIFF() should increase by 1 for each subsequent row in the sequential group as the dates increase, which is the same thing which is happening to the ROW_NUMBER(). Therefore, if you subtract the two values, all of the sequential dates will have the same value for the calculation.

Once we have the calculation assigned to all of the dates, it is a simple matter of retrieving the MIN() and MAX() for each grouping value. You could have solved this using the same techniques we covered in the section on CTEs when we discussed finding gaps in a sequence, but you'll find that the example above will significantly outperform any alternate approach that does not utilize ROW_NUMBER().

NTILE(n)

NTILE(n) splits the results into n groups of rows of approximately equal size. When the set is not evenly divisible by the number of tiles specified, the first n groups are assigned an additional row.

51 is not evenly divisible by 6, but what we get is 8 with a remainder of 3. This means NTILE will assign tiles from 1 – 6 with 9 rows in each of the first three tiles and 8 rows in the last three tiles.

One application of NTILE is to retrieve rows at a given percentile in the result set. If you split a result set into 100 tiles, each tile mathematically represents 1% of the overall set. So, you could use NTILE(100) to find thing like the top 10% of customers or the 5% most frequently ordered products. Without using NTILE() or the TOP operator, you could solve the general purpose percentile problem with the following CTE definition.

```
WITH Orders_CTE (CustomerID, TotalSales)
AS
(SELECT CustomerID, SUM(OrderTotal)
FROM Orders.OrderHeader
GROUP BY CustomerID),
CustomerRank_CTE (CustomerID, TotalSales, Percentile)
AS
(SELECT CustomerID, TotalSales,
FLOOR((ROW_NUMBER() OVER ( ORDER BY TotalSales ) * 1.0) /
    ((SELECT COUNT(*) FROM Orders_CTE)) * 100.0) Percentile
FROM Orders_CTE)
```

The percentile computation relies on an ordered numbering of the customers by sales amount, which is a perfect application of the ROW_NUMBER() function. The ROW_NUMBER is multiplied by 1.0 in order to change the data type so that the division doesn't wipe out the data since we want all of the fractions generated. You'll note that customer sales were numbered from lowest amount to highest amount. So, as you go from lowest sales amount to highest sales amount, the division by the total number of rows gives you an ever increasing value. Since most business users deal with actual percentage values instead of their decimal equivalents, I multiplied by 100.0 to move the decimal point 2 places. Since I only cared about assigning whole number percentiles, I used the FLOOR function to remove the decimal places.

> **Note:** You could still accomplish this general purpose percentile calculation in versions prior to ROW_NUMBER() or CTEs being introduced. The CTEs would be replaced with derived tables or a temp table. The ROW_NUMBER() function would be replaced by an alternative numbering method like an identity. So, while I mentioned that when you are inserting into a table using a SELECT statement, you should never have an ORDER BY clause on the SELECT, this is one exception to that rule. Using a SELECT INTO with an ORDER BY clause to generate a temp table with an identity populated mimics the ordered numbering of the ROW_NUMBER() function.

Applying the general purpose percentile query to a business problem, the following query retrieves all customers in the 50% percentile based on total sales.

```
WITH Orders_CTE (CustomerID, TotalSales)
AS
(SELECT CustomerID, SUM(OrderTotal)
FROM Orders.OrderHeader
GROUP BY CustomerID),
CustomerRank_CTE (CustomerID, TotalSales, Percentile)
AS
(SELECT CustomerID, TotalSales,
FLOOR((ROW_NUMBER() OVER ( ORDER BY TotalSales ) * 1.0) /
    ((SELECT COUNT(*) FROM Orders_CTE)) * 100.0) Percentile
FROM Orders_CTE)
SELECT a.CustomerID, a.TotalSales, a.Percentile
FROM CustomerRank_CTE a
WHERE a.Percentile = 50;
```

This leads us to solving a problem which has come up at several of my customers, median. SQL Server has functions to compute all kinds of things, so people have been surprised for years that median wasn't one of those functions. Many of them resorted to building an application that pulled the data out, computed a median, and returned the result. Others have simply given up and found other ways to either avoid or work around a problem. The trouble is that a median is extremely useful when you are dealing with variance in values, but you need to come up with an answer that eliminates the outliers and gives a single answer.

The problem of SQL Server not having a median function is an example of a problem that occurs all too frequently in the IT world. All of these graphical tools, code analyzers, debuggers, code generators, and frameworks have allowed applications to be rapidly created and deployed at a cost. When something goes wrong, if the debugger doesn't show exactly where the problem is, most people lack the troubleshooting skills to isolate the problem and figure out how the problem was created. A simpler way of saying the same thing is that many people in the IT industry don't know how to restate problems if the tool of their choice doesn't provide exactly what they are looking for out of the box. Tackling this problem is one of the main things that I teach in all of the classes I've taught over the years.

I grew up on a farm and almost my entire family either works in construction or is a farmer. That's about as far from computers and all of the mathematics we use as you can get. While most of my family doesn't understand what I do beyond the fact that I'm a computer geek, I've been able to explain it to them by restating the problem using everyday objects they are likely to encounter. When you have to explain all of this database stuff in terms of a car, farm, or a building, you learn how to break down and restate problems.

What does this have to do with median? Everything. No, SQL Server does not have a median function, because SQL Server doesn't need a median function. A median is computed by finding the middle value in a set of numbers. If the set of numbers is odd, you simply find the number at the exact middle of the set. If the set of numbers is even, you find the two middle values and average them. Put another way, the median is the value at the 50th percentile in a set of numbers. The query above pulled the customer sales at the 50th percentile and you shouldn't have any problem computing the average to find the median sales amount across all customers.

However, there is a much simpler way of solving this problem using NTILE. You could use

NTILE(100) to split a set of numbers into 100 separate groups with each representing approximately 1% of the set and then pull the ones with a tile numbered 50. This has a major flaw in that it requires the set to have at least 100 values and your result wouldn't be the mathematical median. However, 50% is also ½ and we can divide any size set in half. When you use NTILE(2), you split the set in half and the way the set is split makes it very easy to compute the median. If the number of values in each tile is the same, then the median is the average of the maximum value from the first tile and the minimum value from the second tile. If the number of values in each tile is not the same, then the median is the maximum value of the first tile as shown in the example below:

```
WITH AssemblyLines_CTE (AssemblyLine, Defects)
AS
(SELECT AssemblyLine, Defects
FROM (VALUES('A',100),('A',152),('A',150),('B',98),('B',100))
        AssemblyLines(AssemblyLine, Defects)),
AssemblyLineDefects_CTE (AssemblyLine, Defects, Tile)
AS
(SELECT AssemblyLine, Defects,
     NTILE(2) OVER(PARTITION BY AssemblyLine ORDER BY Defects) AS Tile
 FROM AssemblyLines_CTE),
AssemblyLineDefectTiles_CTE
AS
(SELECT AssemblyLine, Tile, COUNT(*) AS Num,
    CASE WHEN Tile = 1 THEN MAX(Defects) ELSE MIN(Defects) END AS Defects
 FROM AssemblyLineDefects_CTE
 GROUP BY AssemblyLine, Tile)
SELECT AssemblyLine,
     CASE WHEN MIN(Num) = MAX(Num) THEN AVG(1.0 * Defects)
          ELSE MIN(Defects) END As Median
FROM AssemblyLineDefectTiles_CTE
GROUP BY AssemblyLine;
```

AssemblyLines_CTE is just a row constructor which contains a small amount of sample data for testing. AssemblyLineDefects_CTE splits the set into 2 tiles for each assembly line in the data set. AssemblyLineDefectTiles_CTE returns the assembly line, a count of the number of values in each assembly line tile, the maximum value from tile 1, and the minimum value from tile 2. The tile number is included in the CTE in case you want to look at intermediate results, but isn't used in the outer query. The outer query simply performs the calculation we discussed earlier. In the case when the number of values is the same, compute an average otherwise return the minimum value between tile 1 and tile 2. So, from the sample data, assembly line A has 3 values. Tile 1 contains 100 and 150 and tile 2 contains 152. The outer query sees values of 150 and 152 and selects 150 as the minimum value in the set for assembly line A. Assembly line B has an even number of values in each tile, so 98 and 100 are averaged to produce a result of 99.

RANK() and DENSE_RANK()

The RANK() and DENSE_RANK() functions allow you to apply a ranking to a data set. You can also apply a PARTITION BY parameter to compute rankings within groups such as ranking customer sales within a state/province or employee salaries within a department.

> **Note:** If the column(s) supplied in the ORDER BY parameter uniquely sort the list without ties, RANK() and DENSE_RANK() will produce the same output as the ROW_NUMBER() function.

The difference between RANK() and DENSE_RANK() is how numbering is applied when ties exist in the data set. RANK() will assign the same number to rows where the sort order results in a tie and then skip n values in the sequence to cover the number of rows that had a tie. DENSE_RANK() will assign the same number to rows where the sort order results in a tie, but will not skip any values in the sequence. For example, if you had 3 football teams with the same record leading all other teams, RANK() and DENSE_RANK() would assign a value of 1 to all three teams.

RANK() would assign a value of 4 to the team with the next best record while DENSE_RANK() would assign a value of 2.

```
WITH Orders_CTE (StateProvince, QuantitySold)
AS
(SELECT c.StateProvince, SUM(d.Quantity)
FROM Orders.OrderHeader a INNER JOIN Customers.Address b ON a.AddressID = b.AddressID
    INNER JOIN Lookups.StateProvince c ON b.StateProvinceID = c.StateProvinceID
    INNER JOIN Orders.OrderDetail d ON a.OrderID = d.OrderID
GROUP BY c.StateProvince)
SELECT StateProvince, QuantitySold,
    RANK() OVER(ORDER BY QuantitySold DESC) QtyRank,
    DENSE_RANK() OVER(ORDER BY QuantitySold DESC) QtyDenseRank
FROM Orders_CTE
ORDER BY QuantitySold DESC;
```

You can see this in the query above by looking at the row for South Carolina. The quantity sold for Colorado and South Dakota is 1035 and both are assigned a RANK() and a DENSE_RANK() of 29. However, the next row in the list, South Carolina, is assigned a RANK() of 31 and a DENSE_RANK() of 30.

You can take advantage of the way that ROW_NUMBER() and RANK() work to remove duplicates in a set of data as shown in the following example:

```
WITH AssemblyLines_CTE (AssemblyLine)
AS
(SELECT AssemblyLine
FROM (VALUES('A'),('A'),('A'),('B'),('B'),('C')) AssemblyLines(AssemblyLine)),
AssemblyLineRankings_CTE (AssemblyLine, Rank, RowNumber)
AS
(SELECT AssemblyLine, ROW_NUMBER() OVER(ORDER BY AssemblyLine) AS RowNumber,
    RANK() OVER(ORDER BY AssemblyLine) AS Rank
 FROM AssemblyLines_CTE)
SELECT AssemblyLine
FROM AssemblyLineRankings_CTE
WHERE RowNumber = Rank;
```

Analytic Functions

The set of analytic functions are all new in SQL Server 2012. The definitions of the analytic functions available are listed in the table below.

Function	Definition
FIRST_VALUE	The first value in the set based on the specified sort order.
LAST_VALUE	The last value in the set based on the specified sort order.
LEAD	Returns data from a row at a specified offset forward in the data set from the current row.
LAG	Returns data from a row at a specified offset backwards in the data set from the current row.
PERCENTILE_CONT	Percentile computed based on a continuous distribution of values
PERCENTILE_DISC	Percentile based on exact values within a set.
CUME_DIST	Cumulative distribution of a value within a set computed as the number of rows less than or equal to the specified value divided by the number of rows in the set.
PERCENT_RANK	Relative ranking of a value within a set.

FIRST_VALUE() and LAST_VALUE()

As the name implies, FIRST_VALUE() and LAST_VALUE() return the value in the specified column from the first and last rows, respectively, in the data set. As a practical example, suppose you wanted to return the customer with the most and least sales. You could solve this problem by using the TOP operator as follows:

```
WITH Orders_CTE (CustomerID, TotalSales)
AS
(SELECT CustomerID, SUM(OrderTotal)
FROM Orders.OrderHeader
GROUP BY CustomerID),
HighestSales_CTE (CustomerID)
AS
(SELECT TOP 1 CustomerID
FROM Orders_CTE
ORDER BY TotalSales),
LowestSales_CTE (CustomerID)
AS
(SELECT TOP 1 CustomerID
FROM Orders_CTE
ORDER BY TotalSales DESC)
SELECT a.CustomerID, b.CustomerID
FROM LowestSales_CTE a CROSS JOIN HighestSales_CTE b;
```

To return the customer with the least sales, we need to sort the sales in ascending order and retrieve the TOP 1. To return the customer with the most sales, we need to sort the sales in descending order and retrieve the TOP 1. You then CROSS join the two results to produce a single result set. If you wanted the result as two rows with 1 column instead of 1 row with 2 columns, you could have used the UNION operator. However, you can't solve this problem directly with a UNION operator, because the ORDER BY within the CTE is critical to retrieving the correct result and you cannot apply an ORDER BY clause within a UNION operator.

The same problem can be solved as follows:

```
WITH Orders_CTE (CustomerID, TotalSales)
AS
(SELECT CustomerID, SUM(OrderTotal)
FROM Orders.OrderHeader
GROUP BY CustomerID)
SELECT DISTINCT LAST_VALUE(CustomerID) OVER (ORDER BY TotalSales
                    ROWS BETWEEN UNBOUNDED PRECEDING AND UNBOUNDED FOLLOWING)
HighestSales,
    FIRST_VALUE(CustomerID) OVER (ORDER BY TotalSales
                    ROWS UNBOUNDED PRECEDING)   LowestSales
FROM Orders_CTE;
```

The key to returning the correct result is the ROWS parameter. The set needs to be ordered and as you'll recall from the section on aggregates, when an ORDER BY clause is applied, it scopes the calculation to the current row + all previous rows by default. In our case, we need to sort the list and also have the function consider the entire data set. That is why the LAST_VALUE() function is specified as unbounded for both preceding and following in order to retrieve the same value for the highest sales for each row in the set. Since the lowest sales will be the first value in the set based on the sort order, all we needed to do is specify UNBOUNDED PRECEDING. The DISTINCT operator is used simply to eliminate all of the duplicates and return a single row. The solution using FIRST_VALUE() and LAST_VALUE() has a slight performance advantage over the solution using the TOP operator since we only have to compute the results of the CTE once using the analytic functions.

> **Note:** Instead of using the LAST_VALUE() function to retrieve the highest sales, you could have sorted the sales in descending order and used the FIRST_VALUE() function. But, doing so would have meant not being able to use the LAST_VALUE() function in the example above.

LEAD() and LAG()

LEAD() and LAG() allow you to include data in your results from rows before or prior to the current row scoped by the window defined with the OVER clause. LEAD() and LAG() have three parameters which can be specified in addition to the OVER clause.

The first parameter is the expression to retrieve. The expression has to evaluate to a scalar value for each row in the set and you cannot nest another analytic function in the expression. The most common parameter is simply a column from a table, CTE, or derived table. You can also perform calculations such as multiplying a column by 100 or multiplying 2 columns together.

The second parameter is the offset. The offset specifies how many rows forward or backward within the window to retrieve rows from. The LEAD() function accesses rows forward of the current row. The LAG() function accesses rows backward from the current row.

The third parameter is the default value to include in the result set when a row does not exist at the offset specified. For example, if you ran a query with the LAG() function, the first row in the set does not have a prior row. The default value is NULL.

Since LEAD() and LAG() access rows forward and backward in a set, the set is required to be sorted. So, the OVER clause is required to have an ORDER BY parameter and can optionally include the PARTITION BY parameter.

The following query shows the previous and next year's sales amount by product group along with the percentage increase in sales for the current year vs. the prior year. Can you explain why every product group shows a very large drop in sales between 2001 and 2002?

```
WITH ProductSales_CTE (ProductID, SalesYear, Sales)
AS
(SELECT b.ProductID, YEAR(c.OrderDate) SalesYear, SUM(a.Quantity * a.Price) Sales
FROM Orders.OrderDetail a INNER JOIN Products.SKU b ON a.SKU = b.SKU
    INNER JOIN Orders.OrderHeader c ON a.OrderID = c.OrderID
GROUP BY b.ProductID, YEAR(c.OrderDate))
SELECT ProductID, SalesYear, Sales CurrentSales,
    LEAD(Sales,1) OVER (PARTITION BY ProductID ORDER BY SalesYear) NextYearSales,
    LAG(Sales,1) OVER (PARTITION BY ProductID ORDER BY SalesYear) PriorYearSales,
    ((Sales - LAG(Sales,1) OVER (PARTITION BY ProductID ORDER BY SalesYear))
        / LAG(Sales,1) OVER (PARTITION BY ProductID ORDER BY SalesYear)) * 100.0
PercentIncrease
FROM ProductSales_CTE
ORDER BY ProductID;
```

> **Lies, Damn Lies, and Statistics:** The query above is correct and the values being computed are also correct. But, the results are useless for business use. This is a perfect example of the old adage, "Lies, damn lies, and statistics". Just because the query and the results are mathematically correct, doesn't mean they show a true picture. The query does demonstrate the use of the LEAD() and LAG() functions, however, it is comparing 12 months of sales in 2001 to 1 month of sales in 2002. When you are building business applications, you need to ensure that you aren't producing flawed results due to comparing data sets of significantly different scope.

PERCENTILE_CONT() and PERCENTILE_DISC()

The PERCENTILE_CONT() and PERCENTILE_DISC() functions allow you to compute a value at the percentile specified. PERCENTILE_CONT() returns a value based on a continuous distribution, so if a value does not exist in the set for the percentile specified, a value will be interpolated. PERCENTILE_DISC() returns a value based on the discrete values in the set, so if a value does not exist in the set for the percentile specified, the value that is closest to and less than the percentile will be returned.

The values in the set must be one of the numeric data types such as INT, DECIMAL, or FLOAT. The percentile is specified as a value between 0.0 and 1.0. The OVER clause can include PARTITION BY to compute percentiles within groups, but cannot include either an ORDER BY or ROWS/RANGE parameters. A separate WITHIN GROUP (ORDER BY <expression> ASC|DESC) is used to specify the sort order to be applied to the set.

Earlier in the chapter, we computed a median using NTILE(2). The query below shows an even easier way to compute a median.

```
WITH AssemblyLines_CTE (AssemblyLine, Defects)
AS
(SELECT AssemblyLine, Defects
FROM (VALUES('A',100),('A',152),('A',150),('B',98),('B',100))
AssemblyLines(AssemblyLine, Defects))
SELECT DISTINCT AssemblyLine, PERCENTILE_CONT(0.5) WITHIN GROUP (ORDER BY Defects)
                              OVER (PARTITION BY AssemblyLine) AS Median,
                              PERCENTILE_DISC(0.5) WITHIN GROUP (ORDER BY Defects)
                              OVER (PARTITION BY AssemblyLine) AS Medoid
FROM AssemblyLines_CTE;
```

Notice that both functions return the same result when an odd number of values exist in the set, but different results when an even number of values exists. In this example, the PERCENT_CONT(0.5) function defines the mathematical median for the set while PERCENT_DISC(0.5) defines a value known as the medoid.

CUME_DIST() and PERCENT_RANK()

CUME_DIST() computes the relative position within a set of values by dividing the number of values less than or equal to a given value by the total number of values. PERCENT_RANK() computes the rank of a value in a set as a percentage. Both function require the ORDER BY parameter to be specified in the OVER clause. You can optionally specify PARTITION BY to segment the set.

The following query applies CUME_DIST() and PERCENT_RANK() to the set of values we've been using to demonstrate median and medoid.

```
WITH AssemblyLines_CTE (AssemblyLine, Defects)
AS
(SELECT AssemblyLine, Defects
FROM (VALUES('A',100),('A',152),('A',150),('B',98),('B',100))
   AssemblyLines(AssemblyLine, Defects))
SELECT AssemblyLine, Defects, CUME_DIST()
                              OVER (PARTITION BY AssemblyLine ORDER BY Defects) AS
CumeDist,
                              PERCENT_RANK()
                              OVER (PARTITION BY AssemblyLine ORDER BY Defects) AS
PercentRank
FROM AssemblyLines_CTE;
```

AssemblyLine	Defects	CumeDist	PercentRank
A	100	0.333333333333333	0
A	150	0.666666666666667	0.5
A	152	1	1
B	98	0.5	0
B	100	1	1

Now that we've dealt with CUME_DIST(), we need to amend the definition of PERCENTILE_DISC() to how it is actually computed. PERCENTILE_DISC() returns the value corresponding to the smallest CUME_DIST() greater than or equal to the percentile specified.

Window Function Performance

One of the traps that many people fall into is to perform one or two tests and then assert the results achieved apply universally. As I was writing this section on window functions, I ran across another example of this fault with an article published on the performance of window functions. That article prompted including this section in the book at this point, instead of saving the performance discussions until Section 6 "Performance Tuning and Analysis".

While window functions are powerful and allow you to dramatically simplify complex query problems, the OVER clause is not a replacement to GROUP BY. The OVER clause is just another tool for you to use in solving problems. Sometimes a window function will dramatically outperform an equivalent query which utilizes GROUP BY. Sometimes, the GROUP BY solution will perform better. You can even find differences between two solutions using window functions.

For example, if you look at the two queries we wrote to compute a median. One uses NTILE() and the other uses PERCENTILE_CONT(). The NTILE() solution looks complicated and takes a bit of study to understand while the PERCENTILE_CONT() function is very simple to read. However, the complicated NTILE() function which appears to do much more work, runs in half the time that PERCENTILE_CONT does. However, if you think about it, the NTILE() solution should run faster. The computation for both solutions is entirely in memory and the way SQL Server executes both queries is almost exactly the same. However, the PERCENTILE_CONT() solution requires a DISTINCT operator to remove duplicates that accounts for 50% of the total execution time of the query.

In general, if you are creating a query where you are joining a table/derived table/CTE to itself and computing one segment of data against another segment, such as in a running total problem, the window function will usually provide better performance. However, if you are computing a simple aggregation such as sales by customer or sales by product, a solution using GROUP BY will generally perform better. However, these are very broad generalities and should be taken as a very basic guideline. Your data sets will differ and your results may differ. You always need to test your solution to ensure that it achieves adequate performance.

For all the functionality present, SQL Server is just another computer program that has rules defined by the developers who wrote the code. Understanding how each option for your queries works against the data in your tables is the first step to unravelling the unending performance question. The performance you achieve in your applications is determined more by the code you write than the hardware your code is running on. If you are running code on a machine that is 8 times slower than my machine, but I write code that takes 10 passes through the data while your code takes a single pass to produce the same result, your code will perform better than mine on a machine 8 times slower. The only absolute to performance is that your code will get slower with each additional pass it has to take through the data.

Window Functions Reloaded

Hopefully by the time you have reached this point, you have a better appreciation not only for the queries which are possible but also the powerful features exposed by the OVER clause. So, we need to take a second look at the background information at the beginning of this section which attempted to explain and define a window function now that we have looked at multiple examples.

When you compute an aggregate using a GROUP BY clause, SQL Server performs many similar actions as you saw with window functions. That should be fairly obvious, because the definition of a SUM does not change just because you add an OVER operator. However, the GROUP BY has significantly different behavior in that the overall result set is reduced by the GROUP BY. The aggregate is computed within each specified group, but SQL Server then removes multiple occurrences of the values in each group to return a single row for each group. The aggregate is also computed across the entire group without respect to the position in each group where a row resides.

The addition of the OVER operator makes the aggregate computation sensitive to the position each row occupies in the result. Adding an ORDER BY parameter to the OVER operator scopes the aggregate computation to only the current row in the set plus all prior rows in the set. This has the effect of causing the scope of the aggregate computation to progressively increase as SQL Server moves from one row to the next in the set. For the functions which support ROWS and RANGE, you can manipulate the scoping of the aggregate to consider an arbitrary subset. The PARTITION BY parameter segments the set into groups and applies the aggregate within each group subject to the scoping specified by the ORDER BY and/or ROWS/RANGE parameters. In all cases, all rows in the original set defined by the FROM and WHERE clauses are preserved when using the OVER operator.

Exercise 2: Window Functions

1. Compute the monthly sales by product category. Include a running 3 month and 6 month sales average for each category with each year along with the percentage contribution of each category to the total sales.

2. Compute the amount of increase or decrease between each customer's first order and most recent order.

3. Retrieve the top selling customer within each state/province.

XML

XML is one of those data exchange protocols which create very strong emotions within IT departments. Many developers prefer XML, base most of the messaging within an application on XML, and think that XML should be used everywhere. Many DBAs hate XML and equate it with all things evil, dictating that XML doesn't belong anywhere near a SQL Server database. The developers are partially correct and the DBAs mandating that XML "does not belong in my database" are out of touch with the realities of today's applications.

XML has its place, just as relational databases have their place. XML is an excellent protocol for exchanging data between systems where you might not control the application you are sending data to because the XML is self-describing, packaging the data definition along with the data. However, if you wrote the application to access a database under your control, XML is an extremely poor choice for data exchange because it requires much more effort to package and unpackage than just using native access modes.

I'll leave the debate on when to use XML to you. I'll tell the DBAs that XML is here to stay, so deal with it. XML is not a substitute for a well-defined database. Used appropriately, XML is a very powerful tool in your toolbox that can greatly simplify database designs in many cases. One of the places that I frequently use an XML column in my application databases is when developers need to store configuration information for the application. I don't care to spend a considerable amount of time modelling the configuration information to handle all of the various types of data involved and I certainly don't want to have to spend time redesigning when an application needs to add or remove a configuration parameter. So, I'll usually just add a table to the database which has an ID along with possibly a column for the application name or module name and then an XML column and let the developers do whatever they want to with the XML document containing all of their configuration parameters. You usually wind up with a small number of rows in the table and the developers can manipulate the configuration structure on the fly as the application is being written or modified.

Why store XML inside SQL Server instead of just throwing the documents in a folder on the operating system? There are a variety of reasons, but they all boil down to access and data management. The applications already have access to the database to read and modify data, so with all of the XML documents inside the database you don't have to manage security separately. Because all of the XML documents related to the application(s) that are managing the data in the database are stored inside the database, you never have to deal with backups being out of synch or versioning issues that can arise from separated storage. Storing the XML documents in SQL Server also has significant advantages over storage on a file system. SQL Server can natively query large volumes of XML documents in place while an application has to load documents from a file system one at a time to locate what it needs. The access to the XML data can also be improved significantly when we get to chapter 12 and explain how to index XML data.

In chapter 5, we briefly discussed XML data types and how XML schema collections can be used to validate XML documents stored in a column. In this section, we'll take a look at how to query XML documents using XQuery as well as how to render the results or a query as XML.

Formatting Results as XML

You return data formatted as XML by appending the FOR XML clause to your SELECT statement. The FOR XML clause has four options as explained in the table below:

Option	Description
AUTO	Generates a nested XML document based on the relationship between tables in your SELECT statement. This is the most common way of generating XML documents from result sets.
EXPLICT	Allows complete control over the shape of the XML document. You explicitly specify all of the formatting and nesting within the document.
PATH	Allows you to specify elements and attributes in the XPath expression as an alternative to the much more complicated EXPLICIT mode.
RAW	A single row in the output is generated for each row in the result set

The simplest way to output a result set to XML is by using the AUTO option as shown below:

```
SELECT RTRIM(a.SKU) SKU, b.ProductName, a.Price, a.DrillBit1ID, a.DrillBit2ID
FROM Products.SKU a INNER JOIN Products.Product b ON a.ProductID = b.ProductID
WHERE a.CategoryID IN (4,5,6)
FOR XML AUTO;
```

This returns an attribute centric XML document based on the table relationships. A small piece of the result document is shown below:

```
<b SKU="TK-30CAL-BP-AG" ProductName="30 Caliber">
  <a Price="9.9900" DrillBit1ID="2" />
</b>
<b SKU="TK-30CAL-BP-AU" ProductName="30 Caliber">
  <a Price="9.9900" DrillBit1ID="2" />
</b>
```

If you want the output as element centric XML, you can specify the ELEMENTS directive.

```
SELECT RTRIM(a.SKU) SKU, b.ProductName, a.Price, a.DrillBit1ID, a.DrillBit2ID
FROM Products.SKU a INNER JOIN Products.Product b ON a.ProductID = b.ProductID
WHERE a.CategoryID IN (4,5,6)
FOR XML AUTO, ELEMENTS;

<b>
  <SKU>TK-30CAL-BP-AG</SKU>
  <ProductName>30 Caliber</ProductName>
  <a>
    <Price>9.9900</Price>
    <DrillBit1ID>2</DrillBit1ID>
  </a>
</b>
```

If you look closely at the result document, you should see a potential problem. While we specified the DrillBit2ID column in the query, it does not appear in the resulting XML document for all rows. By default, if a column returns a NULL, the element is dropped from the XML document. To force all elements to be included for all rows, you need to specify the XSINIL directive.

```
SELECT RTRIM(a.SKU) SKU, b.ProductName, a.Price, a.DrillBit1ID, a.DrillBit2ID
FROM Products.SKU a INNER JOIN Products.Product b ON a.ProductID = b.ProductID
WHERE a.CategoryID IN (4,5,6)
FOR XML AUTO, ELEMENTS XSINIL;

<b xmlns:xsi="http://www.w3.org/2001/XMLSchema-instance">
  <SKU>TK-30CAL-BP-AG</SKU>
  <ProductName>30 Caliber</ProductName>
  <a>
    <Price>9.9900</Price>
    <DrillBit1ID>2</DrillBit1ID>
    <DrillBit2ID xsi:nil="true" />
  </a>
</b>
<b xmlns:xsi="http://www.w3.org/2001/XMLSchema-instance">
  <SKU>TK-30CAL-BP-AU</SKU>
  <ProductName>30 Caliber</ProductName>
  <a>
    <Price>9.9900</Price>
    <DrillBit1ID>2</DrillBit1ID>
    <DrillBit2ID xsi:nil="true" />
  </a>
</b>
```

If you've executed any of the queries above while having results to grid turned on, you would have received a single row with a hyperlink that opened the entire document in a separate window. However, the output data type is a simple text string that SSMS is coded to recognize as XML and translate the format for you. If you need to explicitly return the XML document as an XML data type and not a text string, you need to specify the TYPE directive.

```
SELECT RTRIM(a.SKU) SKU, b.ProductName, a.Price, a.DrillBit1ID, a.DrillBit2ID
FROM Products.SKU a INNER JOIN Products.Product b ON a.ProductID = b.ProductID
WHERE a.CategoryID IN (4,5,6)
FOR XML AUTO, ELEMENTS, TYPE;
```

You can include an inline XSD by specifying the XMLSCHEMA directive. This will generate a document where the XML schema is listed first followed by the remainder of the data.

```
SELECT RTRIM(a.SKU) SKU, b.ProductName, a.Price, a.DrillBit1ID, a.DrillBit2ID
FROM Products.SKU a INNER JOIN Products.Product b ON a.ProductID = b.ProductID
WHERE a.CategoryID IN (4,5,6)
FOR XML AUTO, XMLSCHEMA;
```

When you retrieve data that includes binary information such as a file stored within a FileTable, the auto option only returns a reference to the binary by default. If you want to include the binary data in the XML document, you need to specify the BINARY BASE64 directive. When specified the binary data is base64 encoded and included as an element in the XML document.

```
SELECT c.ProductName, a.file_stream ProductImage
FROM ChampionValleyPensDocs.Products.ProductImage a
    INNER JOIN ChampionValleyPensDocs.Products.ProductImageProperties b
        ON a.stream_id = b.StreamID
    INNER JOIN ChampionValleyPens.Products.Product c ON b.ProductID = c.ProductID
FOR XML AUTO, BINARY BASE64;
```

> **Note:** The ChampionValleyPens database does not have any product images at this point, so you will get a blank result set. This is for example purposes. If you are using the XML RAW option, you must include the BINARY BASE64 directive when retrieving binary data.

The RAW option can be used instead of AUTO to provide a little more customization of the XML document.

```
SELECT RTRIM(a.SKU) SKU, b.ProductName, a.Price, a.DrillBit1ID, a.DrillBit2ID
FROM Products.SKU a INNER JOIN Products.Product b ON a.ProductID = b.ProductID
WHERE a.CategoryID IN (4,5,6)
FOR XML RAW;

<row SKU="TK-30CAL-BP-AG" ProductName="30 Caliber" Price="9.9900" DrillBit1ID="2" />
<row SKU="TK-30CAL-BP-AU" ProductName="30 Caliber" Price="9.9900" DrillBit1ID="2" />
```

Just like the AUTO option, specifying the ELEMENTS directive produces element centric XML.

```
SELECT RTRIM(a.SKU) SKU, b.ProductName, a.Price, a.DrillBit1ID, a.DrillBit2ID
FROM Products.SKU a INNER JOIN Products.Product b ON a.ProductID = b.ProductID
WHERE a.CategoryID IN (4,5,6)
FOR XML RAW, ELEMENTS;

<row>
  <SKU>TK-30CAL-BP-AG</SKU>
  <ProductName>30 Caliber</ProductName>
  <Price>9.9900</Price>
  <DrillBit1ID>2</DrillBit1ID>
</row>
<row>
  <SKU>TK-30CAL-BP-AU</SKU>
  <ProductName>30 Caliber</ProductName>
  <Price>9.9900</Price>
  <DrillBit1ID>2</DrillBit1ID>
</row>
```

An inline XSD is included with the XMLSCHEMA directive as follows:

```
SELECT RTRIM(a.SKU) SKU, b.ProductName, a.Price, a.DrillBit1ID, a.DrillBit2ID
FROM Products.SKU a INNER JOIN Products.Product b ON a.ProductID = b.ProductID
WHERE a.CategoryID IN (4,5,6)
FOR XML RAW, ELEMENTS, XMLSCHEMA;

<xsd:schema targetNamespace="urn:schemas-microsoft-com:sql:SqlRowSet4"
xmlns:xsd="http://www.w3.org/2001/XMLSchema"
xmlns:sqltypes="http://schemas.microsoft.com/sqlserver/2004/sqltypes"
elementFormDefault="qualified">
  <xsd:import namespace="http://schemas.microsoft.com/sqlserver/2004/sqltypes"
schemaLocation="http://schemas.microsoft.com/sqlserver/2004/sqltypes/sqltypes.xsd"
/>
  <xsd:element name="row">
  ...
  </xsd:element>
</xsd:schema>
<row xmlns="urn:schemas-microsoft-com:sql:SqlRowSet4">
  <SKU>TK-30CAL-BP-AG</SKU>
  <ProductName>30 Caliber</ProductName>
  <Price>9.9900</Price>
  <DrillBit1ID>2</DrillBit1ID>
</row>
<row xmlns="urn:schemas-microsoft-com:sql:SqlRowSet4">
  <SKU>TK-30CAL-BP-AU</SKU>
  <ProductName>30 Caliber</ProductName>
  <Price>9.9900</Price>
  <DrillBit1ID>2</DrillBit1ID>
</row>
```

You can change the namespace by specifying your own namespace following the XMLSCHEMA directive.

```
SELECT RTRIM(a.SKU) SKU, b.ProductName, a.Price, a.DrillBit1ID, a.DrillBit2ID
FROM Products.SKU a INNER JOIN Products.Product b ON a.ProductID = b.ProductID
WHERE a.CategoryID IN (4,5,6)
FOR XML RAW, ELEMENTS, XMLSCHEMA ('urn:ChampionValleyPens.com');

<xsd:schema targetNamespace="urn:ChampionValleyPens.com"
xmlns:xsd="http://www.w3.org/2001/XMLSchema"
xmlns:sqltypes="http://schemas.microsoft.com/sqlserver/2004/sqltypes"
elementFormDefault="qualified">
  <xsd:import namespace="http://schemas.microsoft.com/sqlserver/2004/sqltypes"
schemaLocation="http://schemas.microsoft.com/sqlserver/2004/sqltypes/sqltypes.xsd"
/>
  <xsd:element name="row">
…
  </xsd:element>
</xsd:schema>
<row xmlns="urn:ChampionValleyPens.com">
  <SKU>TK-30CAL-BP-AG</SKU>
  <ProductName>30 Caliber</ProductName>
  <Price>9.9900</Price>
  <DrillBit1ID>2</DrillBit1ID>
</row>
<row xmlns="urn:ChampionValleyPens.com">
  <SKU>TK-30CAL-BP-AU</SKU>
  <ProductName>30 Caliber</ProductName>
  <Price>9.9900</Price>
  <DrillBit1ID>2</DrillBit1ID>
</row>
```

You can change the default element of "row" by specifying your own element name immediately following the RAW option. You can also specify a root node by using the ROOT directive.

```
SELECT RTRIM(a.SKU) SKU, b.ProductName, a.Price, a.DrillBit1ID, a.DrillBit2ID
FROM Products.SKU a INNER JOIN Products.Product b ON a.ProductID = b.ProductID
WHERE a.CategoryID IN (4,5,6)
FOR XML RAW ('Product'), ELEMENTS, XMLSCHEMA ('urn:ChampionValleyPens.com'),
ROOT('Products');

<Products>
  <xsd:schema targetNamespace="urn:ChampionValleyPens.com"
xmlns:xsd="http://www.w3.org/2001/XMLSchema"
xmlns:sqltypes="http://schemas.microsoft.com/sqlserver/2004/sqltypes"
elementFormDefault="qualified">
    <xsd:import namespace="http://schemas.microsoft.com/sqlserver/2004/sqltypes"
schemaLocation="http://schemas.microsoft.com/sqlserver/2004/sqltypes/sqltypes.xsd"
/>
    <xsd:element name="Product">
…
    </xsd:element>
  </xsd:schema>
  <Product xmlns="urn:ChampionValleyPens.com">
    <SKU>TK-30CAL-BP-AG</SKU>
    <ProductName>30 Caliber</ProductName>
    <Price>9.9900</Price>
    <DrillBit1ID>2</DrillBit1ID>
  </Product>
  <Product xmlns="urn:ChampionValleyPens.com">
    <SKU>TK-30CAL-BP-AU</SKU>
    <ProductName>30 Caliber</ProductName>
    <Price>9.9900</Price>
    <DrillBit1ID>2</DrillBit1ID>
  </Product>
```

If you want even more control over the shape of the XML document generated, you can work with the PATH and EXPLICIT modes. Details for PATH and EXPLICT can be found in Books Online.

> **Note:** Instead of hand writing the XSD for an XML schema collection, you can take advantage of the XMLSCHEMA directive of the FOR XML clause to generate the XSD from existing tables in your database. If you don't have tables matching the structure required for your XSD, you can always create the tables temporarily to generate the XSD and then make any necessary adjustments. It's a lot easier to make adjustments to an XSD that is generated than it is to hand code every piece of the XSD.

Querying XML Data

The simplest way to query XML is to return the entire XML document. When you return the entire XML document, all you need to do is add the column to the SELECT clause. The data returned will contain the entire XML document as a VARCHAR data type. When the results are returned to a grid in SSMS, the format of the data is recognized as XML and you are provided a hyperlink to open the XML document in a separate window.

```
SELECT ProductID, ProductName, ProductDescription, Price, Active
FROM Products.Product;
```

If you only want to return documents where a node in the document matches a criterion, you need to use the query method of the XQuery language. The query method has the following general syntax:

```
<column>.query('<prolog>';<body>)
```

The prolog usually contains the XML namespace you are querying to restrict the query to a valid set of documents based on the namespace URI (Uniform Resource Indicator). You can create XML documents without a namespace declaration and then just reference document nodes in the query, but if the XML document has a namespace, then you must specify the namespace in the query to retrieve information from the document. As I mentioned with XML schema collections, all XML is case sensitive, even with comparison operators. While you can specify compound criteria *OR* will return an error while *or* will return results, just like specifying the incorrect case for any node or attribute will also cause an error.

The query method allows you to retrieve fragments of an XML document as well as specify search criteria. To retrieve a fragment of a document, you specify the namespace along with the node you want to retrieve separated by a semicolon as follows:

```
SELECT ProductID, ProductName,
    ProductDescription.query('declare namespace
        CVP="urn:ChampionValleyPens-com:product:ProductDescription";
        CVP:ProductDescription/CVP:Description')
FROM Products.Product;
```

The CVP that you see in the query is just an alias for the URI. You can also use the WITH clause to define the namespace(s) to apply to the query. The query criteria are specified in square brackets and the path specification to the left defines the fragment of the XML document to retrieve. The following query will return all products and include the XML fragment defined by CVP:ProductDescription for only products that use a 7MM drill bit.

Remember, some kits can have more than 1 drill bit, so we specify compound criteria to retrieve any product where either of the possible drill bits are 7mm.

```
WITH XMLNAMESPACES ('urn:ChampionValleyPens-com:product:ProductDescription' AS CVP)
SELECT ProductID, ProductName,
    ProductDescription.query('CVP:ProductDescription[CVP:DrillBit1 = "7mm"
                                            or CVP:DrillBit2 = "7mm"]')
FROM Products.Product;
```

If you only want to return the rows where either drill bit is 7mm, you can use the exist() method in the WHERE clause as follows:

```
WITH XMLNAMESPACES ('urn:ChampionValleyPens-com:product:ProductDescription' AS CVP)
SELECT ProductID, ProductName
FROM Products.Product
WHERE ProductDescription.exist('CVP:ProductDescription[CVP:DrillBit1 = "7mm"
                                            or CVP:DrillBit2 = "7mm"]') = 1;
```

Discrete values can be returned from the XML document by using the value method as follows:

```
WITH XMLNAMESPACES ('urn:ChampionValleyPens-com:product:ProductDescription' AS CVP)
SELECT ProductID, ProductName,
ProductDescription.value('(/CVP:ProductDescription/CVP:DrillBit1)[1]','VARCHAR(30)')
DrillBit1,
ProductDescription.value('(/CVP:ProductDescription/CVP:DrillBit2)[1]','VARCHAR(30)')
DrillBit2
FROM Products.Product
WHERE ProductDescription.exist('CVP:ProductDescription/CVP:DrillBit1') = 1
    OR ProductDescription.exist('CVP:ProductDescription/CVP:DrillBit2') = 1;
```

We used the exist method in the WHERE clause to limit the results to only the products which have drill bits defined in the product description. We then pulled the two possible values for the drill bit. The path to locate the item we wish to extract is enclosed in parenthesis. The [1] is a required element to indicate that only a scalar value can be returned to the value method. The second parameter specifies the data type definition for the value being extracted. The value method can be used to extract data either from an element or an attribute. You specify an attribute to extract by utilizing the @ symbol as a prefix to the attribute name.

> **Note:** Books Online has an extensive XQuery language reference which will show you how to construct virtually any query you can imagine for your XML documents. The XQuery language reference can be found at http://msdn.microsoft.com/en-us/library/ms189075.aspx.

Exercise 1: Solutions

1. You should have returned 43 rows. Stephen Silas is EmployeeID = 1. You need to build a recursive CTE to solve this problem. The single row for Stephen Silas is your anchor query while the HumanResources.Employee table is your recursive query. The anchor query is joined to the recursive query where the anchor OrganizationNode is an ancestor of the recursive OrganizationNode. The rest of the query is simply returning results and applying some formatting.

   ```
   WITH Employee_CTE(EmployeeID, OrganizationNode, Category, RecursionLevel)
   AS (SELECT a.EmployeeID, a.OrganizationNode,
           a.FirstName + ' ' + a.MiddleInitial + ' ' + a.LastName, 0
      FROM HumanResources.Employee a
      WHERE EmployeeID = 1
      UNION ALL
      SELECT b.EmployeeID, b.OrganizationNode,
           b.FirstName + ' ' + b.MiddleInitial + ' ' + b.LastName, RecursionLevel + 1
      FROM HumanResources.Employee b
          INNER JOIN Employee_CTE c ON b.OrganizationNode.GetAncestor(1) =
   c.OrganizationNode)
   SELECT d.RecursionLevel, d.EmployeeID, REPLICATE('
   ',d.OrganizationNode.GetLevel() -1) + d.Category, d.OrganizationNode.ToString() AS
   OrganizationNode,
         e.FirstName + ' ' + e.MiddleInitial + ' ' + e.LastName Manager
   FROM Employee_CTE d INNER JOIN HumanResources.Employee e
       ON d.OrganizationNode.GetAncestor(1) = e.OrganizationNode
   ORDER BY d.OrganizationNode.ToString()
   OPTION (MAXRECURSION 25);
   ```

2. You should have returned 22 rows. The joins to the required tables should be familiar by now. In order to produce the correct output, you had to pivot on the StateProvince column and aggregate the SalesAmount.

   ```
   SELECT h.ProductName, h.Illinois, h.Texas, h.California, h.Maryland
   FROM (SELECT a.ProductName, f.StateProvince, c.Quantity * c.Price SalesAmount
       FROM Products.Product a INNER JOIN Products.SKU b ON a.ProductID = b.ProductID
          INNER JOIN Orders.OrderDetail c ON b.SKU = c.SKU
          INNER JOIN Orders.OrderHeader d ON c.OrderID = d.OrderID
          INNER JOIN Customers.Address e ON d. AddressID = e. AddressID
          INNER JOIN Lookups.StateProvince f ON e.StateProvinceID = f.StateProvinceID
       WHERE f.StateProvince IN ('Illinois','Texas','California','Maryland')) g
      PIVOT
         (SUM(SalesAmount)
         FOR StateProvince
         IN (Illinois,Texas,California,Maryland)) h
   ORDER BY h.ProductName;
   ```

3. You should have returned 22 rows. You could have produced the result set using either a double pivot or a set of CASE expressions. However, the CASE expressions will outperform the double pivot by approximately 50%. At this point, you should stop and take a look at how far you've come. Just about 90 pages ago, you were learning SELECT 1. Now you're looking at queries that contain CTEs, CASE expressions embedded inside aggregates, grouping, filtering, multiple joins, double unpivots, and sorting and everything that you are seeing should be understandable. At this point you shouldn't be surprised that a single command, SELECT, can be used to retrieve and manipulate data any way that you can conceive of.

```
SELECT a.ProductName, SUM(CASE WHEN f.StateProvince = 'Illinois'
                        THEN c.Quantity END) IllinoisQty,
                SUM(CASE WHEN f.StateProvince = 'Illinois'
                        THEN c.Quantity * c.Price END) IllinoisAmount,
                SUM(CASE WHEN f.StateProvince = 'Texas'
                        THEN c.Quantity END) TexasQty,
                SUM(CASE WHEN f.StateProvince = 'Texas'
                        THEN c.Quantity * c.Price END) TexasAmount,
                SUM(CASE WHEN f.StateProvince = 'California'
                        THEN c.Quantity END) CaliforniaQty,
                SUM(CASE WHEN f.StateProvince = 'California'
                        THEN c.Quantity * c.Price END) CaliforniaAmount,
                SUM(CASE WHEN f.StateProvince = 'Maryland'
                        THEN c.Quantity END) MarylandQty,
                SUM(CASE WHEN f.StateProvince = 'Maryland'
                        THEN c.Quantity * c.Price END) MarylandAmount
FROM Products.Product a INNER JOIN Products.SKU b ON a.ProductID = b.ProductID
        INNER JOIN Orders.OrderDetail c ON b.SKU = c.SKU
        INNER JOIN Orders.OrderHeader d ON c.OrderID = d.OrderID
        INNER JOIN Customers.Address e ON d.AddressID = e.AddressID
        INNER JOIN Lookups.StateProvince f ON e.StateProvinceID = f.StateProvinceID
WHERE f.StateProvince IN ('Illinois','Texas','California','Maryland')
GROUP BY a.ProductName
ORDER BY a.ProductName;
```

4. You should have returned 20 rows. You needed to build a double UNPIVOT operation to rotate the player and position columns into a single player and a single position column with the players correctly matched up to the positions they played. You could have also solved this problem using a CROSS APPLY in conjunction with a row constructor.

```
SELECT GameID, TeamID, PlayerID, PositionID
FROM #GameLineup
UNPIVOT
(PlayerID FOR Player IN (Player1ID, Player2ID, Player3ID, Player4ID, Player5ID, Player6ID,
 Player7ID, Player8ID, Player9ID, Player10ID)) Player
UNPIVOT
(PositionID FOR Position IN (Player1Position, Player2Position, Player3Position,
 Player4Position, Player5Position, Player6Position, Player7Position, Player8Position,
 Player9Position, Player10Position)) Position
WHERE REPLACE(Player,'ID','') = REPLACE(Position,'Position','')

SELECT a.GameID, a.TeamID, b.PlayerID, b.PositionID
FROM #GameLineup a CROSS APPLY
        (VALUES (Player1ID, Player1Position), (Player2ID, Player2Position),
                (Player3ID, Player3Position), (Player4ID, Player4Position),
                (Player5ID, Player5Position), (Player6ID, Player6Position),
                (Player7ID, Player7Position), (Player8ID, Player8Position),
                (Player9ID, Player9Position), (Player10ID, Player10Position))
                    b (PlayerID, PositionID)
```

5. You should have returned 3813 rows. You needed to use the CROSS APPLY operator to retrieve the top 2 orders for each customer from the Orders.OrderHeader table and join that with the Customers.Customer table.

```
SELECT a.CustomerID, c.OrderID, c.OrderDate, c.OrderTotal
FROM Customers.Customer a CROSS APPLY
    (SELECT TOP(2) b.OrderID, b.OrderDate, b.OrderTotal
     FROM Orders.OrderHeader b
     WHERE a.CustomerID = b.CustomerID
     ORDER BY b.OrderDate DESC) c
ORDER BY a.CustomerID
```

Exercise 2: Solutions

1. You should have returned 130 rows. You first needed to build a CTE which aggregates the sales by year, month, and category. The rolling 3 and 6 month averages are computed by partitioning by the category and year and ordering by the month. The category sales and total sales are included below so you can see how they are used to compute the percentage. To correctly compute the percentage, the monthly total has to be partitioned differently than the rolling averages.

```
WITH DailyTotal_CTE (OrderYear, OrderMonth, Category, MonthlyTotal)
AS
    (SELECT YEAR(a.OrderDate), MONTH(a.OrderDate), d.Category, SUM(a.OrderTotal) MonthlyTotal
     FROM Orders.OrderHeader a INNER JOIN Orders.OrderDetail b ON a.OrderID = b.OrderID
         INNER JOIN Products.SKU c ON b.SKU = c.SKU
         INNER JOIN Lookups.Category d ON c.CategoryID = d.CategoryID
     GROUP BY YEAR(a.OrderDate), MONTH(a.OrderDate), d.Category)
SELECT OrderYear, OrderMonth, Category, MonthlyTotal,
    AVG(MonthlyTotal) OVER(PARTITION BY Category, OrderYear ORDER BY Category, OrderMonth
                          ROWS BETWEEN 2 PRECEDING AND CURRENT ROW)
SalesMoving3MonthAverage,
    AVG(MonthlyTotal) OVER(PARTITION BY Category, OrderYear ORDER BY Category, OrderMonth
                          ROWS BETWEEN 5 PRECEDING AND CURRENT ROW)
SalesMoving6MonthAverage,
    SUM(MonthlyTotal) OVER(PARTITION BY Category) CategorySales,
    SUM(MonthlyTotal) OVER() TotalSales,
    (SUM(MonthlyTotal) OVER(PARTITION BY Category) /
                            SUM(MonthlyTotal) OVER()) * 100.0
PercentOfTotalSales
FROM  DailyTotal_CTE
ORDER BY Category, OrderYear, OrderMonth;
```

2. You should have returned 2307 rows. This requirement could have been solved using several methods. You could have used a MIN/MAX in conjunction with a GROUP BY to retrieve the first and last order dates for each customer and then joined that back to retrieve the sales. This solution uses the FIRST_VALUE() and LAST_VALUE() window functions with the data partitioned by CustomerID and sorted by OrderDate.

```
SELECT DISTINCT CustomerID,
    FIRST_VALUE(OrderTotal) OVER (PARTITION BY CustomerID ORDER BY OrderDate
                          ROWS UNBOUNDED PRECEDING) -
    LAST_VALUE(OrderTotal) OVER (PARTITION BY CustomerID ORDER BY OrderDate
                          ROWS BETWEEN UNBOUNDED PRECEDING AND UNBOUNDED FOLLOWING)
FROM Orders.OrderHeader
ORDER BY CustomerID;
```

3. You should have returned 51 rows. This requirement could have been solved using a MAX with a GROUP BY to retrieve the maximum sales per state/province and then join that back to retrieve the corresponding customer information. The chosen solution first computes the customer sales by state/province, computes a ranking within each state/province, and then retrieves the customer at the 100% percentile for each state/province.

```
WITH Sales_CTE (CustomerID, StateProvince, SalesAmount)
AS
(SELECT a.CustomerID, c.StateProvince, SUM(a.OrderTotal)
FROM Orders.OrderHeader a INNER JOIN Customers.Address b ON a.AddressID = b.AddressID
    INNER JOIN Lookups.StateProvince c ON b.StateProvinceID = c.StateProvinceID
GROUP BY a.CustomerID, c.StateProvince),
CustomerRankings_CTE (CustomerID, Ranking)
AS
(SELECT CustomerID, PERCENT_RANK()
                        OVER (PARTITION BY StateProvince ORDER BY SalesAmount) Ranking
FROM Sales_CTE)
SELECT a.CustomerID, a.StateProvince, a.SalesAmount
FROM Sales_CTE a INNER JOIN CustomerRankings_CTE b ON a.CustomerID = b.CustomerID
WHERE b.Ranking = 1
ORDER BY a.StateProvince, a.CustomerID
```

Summary

A SELECT statement may have seemed reasonably innocuous when we first introduced it, a single statement to retrieve and manipulate data from the infinite possibilities which exist for database designs to satisfy the infinite possibilities for business requirements. In this chapter, you learned how to extend the basic SELECT statement with set operations and table expressions which can provide significant performance improvements while also simplifying your code. The basic aggregates that you learned about can be extended with an OVER clause to create powerful scoping capabilities. Finally, you learned how to output data as XML as well as querying XML stored in your tables. At this point, you should be able to retrieve just about any data that SQL Server can store in a relational database and manipulate the results to meet just about every business need. The next chapter on the SQL Server spatial capabilities will turn the "just about any data" into being able to manipulate every type of data that can be stored in your relational databases.

Chapter 11
Spatial Queries

> **Setup:** Please run the Chapter 11 Setup script in the companion files prior to starting the exercises in this chapter to ensure that your databases are at the correct starting point. Every exercise in this book assumes that you have created the c:\ChampionValleyPress\Data and c:\ChampionValleyPress\Log folders, contained databases are enabled, and this is the location of all of the data, log, and filestream files which will be used for this book. If you have chosen a different path, you will need to adjust the paths listed accordingly. Every setup script also assumes that you have enabled FILESTREAM access for the instance. When executing commands, it is assumed that you will change context to the appropriate database since understanding the contents of each database in this book is the same skill you will need for working with your databases. All scripts also assume you are using a default instance.

In Chapters 9 and 10, you learned about how to construct SELECT statements to retrieve and manipulate data within your tables. The SELECT statements we've covered thus far have applied, mostly, to the simple data types most commonly used in tables. We also went through how to retrieve and manipulate data by invoking CLR assemblies to work with data stored in a HIERARCHYID.

We've explicitly bypassed GEOMETRY and GEOGRAPHY data types since they need special treatment to explain and work with. In this chapter, you learn how to define, load, and query spatial data.

> **Note:** This chapter assumes a basic understanding of geometry, since it would be impossible to include basic high school geometry in this chapter.

Overview of Spatial Data

Spatial data is used to describe the shape and location of objects in space. Some would restrict this definition to the location of objects on the world. While geographic location is the primary use of spatial data, restricting our discussion to the location of objects on a globe would eliminate some extremely interesting uses of the spatial capabilities in SQL Server.

Spatial data can be used to describe the shape of everyday objects such as the components of a pen. Spatial data can also be used to describe cities, roads, or buildings such as the Pentagon in Washington D.C.

Some of the applications of spatial data are:

1. Storing 3D drawings for use by a CAD system.
2. Finding all of the Starbucks within a 5 mile radius of your office.
3. Determine the best location of a store based on distance and ease of access for customers.
4. Determining the optimal path for an explorer to take for a landing on Mars.
5. Tracking sightings of minions in order to achieve the optimal chance of catching one.

6. Plot the location of particles and particle decay paths to understand how high energy particles interact in a particle accelerator.
7. Determine the highest concentration of customers to optimize the return on investment for billboard advertising
8. Compute the shortest distance from Africa to New York so Alex, Marty, Gloria, and Melman can get home to the zoo.

You might think that defining the shape of an object is very simple. The shape of this book, whether you are reading the paper version or the electronic version is very well defined. The paper version is defined by the length, width, and height of the pages and cover that the book is composed of. The shape of the electronic version is defined by the fixed shape of the screen you are reading it on. But, the shape of every object depends upon your perception. The Pentagon appears much differently when viewed from a helicopter hovering 500 feet off the ground than it does when viewed from the Moon. When you are hovering 500 feet off the ground, the Pentagon appears as a large building composed of a pentagon cut out of a larger pentagon. When viewed from the Moon, the Pentagon is nothing more than a tiny pinpoint on the surface of the Earth. The way you measure the object can also change its definition. You might think the roof of the Pentagon, excluding any antennae sticking up is a flat surface. But, if you were to precisely measure the Pentagon's roof from a satellite stationary over the center point, you would find a very slight difference in the distance around the perimeter due to the natural curvature of the Earth. Even that slight difference would vary based on the time of the day due to the way the Moon affects the shape of the Earth.

When we store and manipulate spatial data, we are concerned with the location of the object as well as the best way to display the object for our application. If you wanted to display a map of the entire globe showing the location of cities, it wouldn't make any sense to display every city in the world since you would have an unintelligible mess. You would instead select the largest cities and represent them as simple points on the map. However, if you were to build a map that just covers the United States, you would probably still represent cites as simple points, but the larger cities would be represented by slightly larger points than smaller cities. If you zoomed into a map of the state of Texas, you would have smaller cities represented as points, but cities like Houston, Dallas, San Antonio, and Austin would be represented by polygons.

The additional issue we have is with producing an exact description of an object. It may seem like a man-made object such as a pen can be very clearly defined. Taking a tape measure and measuring around the entire perimeter of the pen would produce a number telling you the distance around the pen. Now, put the pen under a microscope and you'll see that the surface really isn't that smooth, but is instead made up of lots of tiny peaks and valleys. Now take your microscopic tape measure and measure the perimeter of the pen taking into account all of the peaks and valleys. If you compared this to the first measurement, you would find that the length of the perimeter of the pen is suddenly larger. Zoom in even more and repeat the process and the length would increase again. The further in you zoom, the longer the distance gets. This is one of the great paradoxes of measuring objects or in explicitly defining the shape of an object. If you thought measuring the perimeter of a pen was hard, try giving a precise definition of the shape of the United States.

What we're really doing when we store spatial data is storing the object with the best approximation that suits our purposes. In SQL Server 2008, you could store points, lines, and polygons. SQL Server 2012 introduced circular strings, compound curves, and curved polygons.

Points

A point is a zero dimensional object that represents a single position in space. A point has no length or area and is represented by a single set of coordinates. You use a point to represent an object at an exact location such as a city, building, street address, or the tip of a pen.

Lines

Lines don't exist, per se, in spatial systems, instead we deal with LineStrings. A LineString is used to represent a one-dimensional object; the object has a length, but not an area. LineStrings are defined by at least two points and can have any number of points in the definition. A LineString can cross itself and the start and end points can be the same. A LineString where the start and end point are the same is known as a closed line string. If the LineString does not cross itself and is also a closed string, it is known as a ring. Even if the LineString crosses itself, it does not define an area in the enclosed region, but only represents the points along the perimeter of the region.

A LineString can be used to represent a road, an airplane route, the trajectory of a high energy particle, or the outline of a cartoon character plastered against the back of a truck.

Figure 11-1 Examples of line strings

Polygons

A polygon is a two dimensional object that is defined by at least 1 ring, the start and end points are the same. You can also have one or more interior rings defined. The external ring defines the boundary of the polygon and any internal rings define areas which are not part of the polygon. You can think of the internal rings as "cutting out" pieces of the polygons. A polygon has an area defined as the area inside the external ring minus the area of any internal rings. The length of a polygon is a measure of the length of all segments which make up the external ring.

You generally use polygons to represent larger spatial objects such as buildings, lakes, and large cities. You could also use polygons to represent a floor plan or objects placed inside a room.

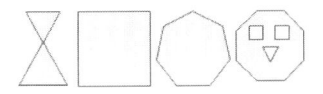

Figure 11-2 Examples of polygons

Circular Strings

Circular strings are new in SQL Server 2012. In prior versions, you could approximate a curve by using a series of very short LineStrings. However, you couldn't capture the true shape of an object with a curve. A CircularString is composed of zero or more circular arcs, which is a curved line represented by three points where the first and third points are not the same.

A circular string can be stored if it is empty or has an odd number of points, although it may not be valid. For example you could store the following in a circular string 0 0, 0 0, 1 1, 1 1, 0 0. This example has an off number of points and the first and third points are not the same, but it isn't a valid circular arc. This is instead a line that goes from 0,0 to 1,1. If the coordinates are collinear, the CircularString is treated as a LineString.

It might seem strange to have a CircularString seemingly morph from arcs to straight lines. However, a straight line is nothing more than an arc with zero curvature just as a point can also be defined as a LineString with zero length.

An example of a CircularString with straight line segments is a race track or a fish bowl which could be represented by the following series of points:

1 1, 3 -1, 1 -3, 1 -3, -1 -3, -3 -1, -1 1, -1 1, 1 1

Figure 11-3 CircularString with straight line segments

A CircularString does not have to define an actual circle. In other words, the first point of the first arc segment does not have to be the same as the last point of the final arc segment. However, it does have to define a continuous line or the last end point of each arc segment must be the first point in the next arc segment. A CircularString also cannot overlap itself within the same interval.

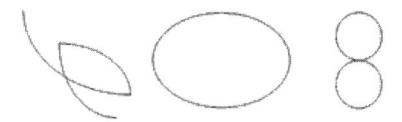

Figure 11-4 Examples of circular strings

Compound Curves

Compound curves were introduced in SQL Server 2012 and consist of zero or more circular strings and/or line strings. The strings must be continuous, i.e. the ending point of each string must be the same as the starting point of the next string except for the last string. The Z must be the same for all points in the compound curve, so you can't use a compound curve to represent a 3 dimensional object.

You should only use a compound curve if your object has a combination of circular strings and line strings; otherwise, it is much simpler to use CircularString or LineString.

Figure 11-5 Examples of compound curves

Curved Polygons

Curved polygons are new in SQL Server 2012. Just as a polygon is defined by a LineString that forms a ring, a curved polygon is defined by a CompoundCurve that forms a ring. A curved polygon can also have one or more internal rings which are LineString, CircularString, or CompoundCurve. An interior ring cannot cross the exterior ring and cannot also contain another interior ring. A ring cannot cross itself or another ring, but is allowed to touch another ring at a single tangent point.

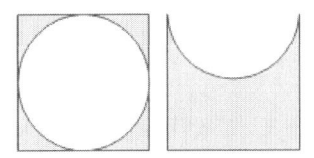

Figure 11-6 Examples of curved polygons

GeometryCollection

A geometry collection is the most general type available and contains any number of the other available shapes. In order to be valid, all objects must be accepted and valid. For example, it is possible to define a LineString using the points 1 1, 1 1 which is really a line of zero length or better known as a point. The definition will be accepted and can be displayed, but it is not valid according to the Open Geospatial Consortium (OGC) specifications. Therefore including this LineString definition in a geometry collection makes the collection invalid even though it is accepted and can be stored.

Boundaries

When working with spatial objects, you need to be aware of how the region in space is divided by the definition of the object. Every object has an interior, exterior, and boundary. The interior of an object is the collection of points that lies inside the space occupied by the object. The exterior of an object is the collection of points that are not inside the space occupied by the object. The boundary is the collection of points that lies on the edge of the object. In SQL Server, every point on the boundary is considered to be within the interior of the object.

Every object will have an interior and exterior, however, only certain objects will have a boundary.

Point and MultiPoint have an interior which is made up of each point and an exterior made up of all other points. However, Point and MultiPoint do not have a boundary. LineString, MultiLineString, CircularString, and CompoundCurve have an interior made up of all of the points on the line and an exterior of all points not on the line. The boundary of line strings which are not closed consists of the points at the beginning and end of the line string. Line strings which are closed do not have a boundary, which should make sense since the beginning and end of the line string is the same point and points do not have a boundary. Polygon, MultiPolygon, and CurvePolygon have an interior which consists of all points within the exterior ring minus any points in any interior rings and a boundary of the LineString defined by the exterior ring plus the LineString(s) defined by any interior rings.

The distinction between interior, exterior, and boundary is important when making comparisons between objects. An object intersects another object when they have at least one common point, but will only touch if any shared points lie solely on the boundary. When computing the area of a polygon, you only want to consider the interior space occupied by the object.

Defining Geometric Shapes

Geometric shapes are defined on an infinite plane using the same representation that you learned in your high school geometry class. The center point of the plane is a point at x=0 and y=0. SQL Server allows you to specify two additional values for points, line strings, and circular strings. These values are referred to as z and m. The z value is usually used to represent distance above the plane. The m value can be used to store a measurement of anything you want and is left open to interpretation by your application. You could store a time, temperature, unit conversion, sales amount, density, or any other value that makes sense for your application.

Even though you can store z and m values, SQL Server simply stores these values and ignores them in any calculation. For example, if you were to create a line that started at 0 0 0 and went to 0 1 10, SQL Server will tell you the length of this line is 1. However, if you were to actually measure the line taking into account the z axis, you would have a line that is much longer than 1.

The other thing to get used to is the way coordinates are represented in SQL Server. We are used to seeing coordinates listed with parenthesis wrapped around each comma separated set and each set separated by commas. So, the notation you probably learned in high school geometry would be (0,0,0),(0,1,10). SQL Server does not use the notation and in fact none of the tools you will encounter utilize this notation. Each coordinate is separated from another coordinate by a space and each set of coordinates are separated from other sets by a comma. The entire set of coordinates is then wrapped inside a single set of parenthesis. So, SQL Server would represent these same points as (0 0 0, 0 1 10).

Spatial objects, like the HIERARCHYID we've already worked with are implemented using the CLR integration within SQL Server. You can create spatial objects and perform a variety of operations on spatial object, but be aware that you are loading the .NET framework and making calls to external dlls. While the spatial capabilities are integrated into SQL Server, all of the heavy lifting is performed in the .NET assemblies loaded on the server hosting the SQL Server instance; which is responsible for unpacking the spatial objects and manipulating them one at a time in order to return results for your query. As such, you can experience a delay, sometimes a significant delay, when you execute spatial queries. This is due to the necessity of loading the .NET assemblies before computations can be performed. If your application relies heavily on spatial queries, you will want to execute a few basic spatial queries as soon as your instance starts up so that the .NET assemblies are already loaded before your users start executing queries.

All spatial objects are stored in a binary format and the most efficient way to write spatial objects is in the internal binary representation. However, a binary string is not very user friendly. The Open Geospatial Consortium, OGC, provides three formats for spatial objects. Well Known Text, WKT, is a human readable, plain text representation. Well Known Binary, WKB, is the industry standard binary format that SQL Server uses to store spatial objects. Geospatial Markup Language, GML, is a markup language which can also be used to represent the objects. Due to the simplicity and transportability of the format, you will almost always see objects represented using WKT while applications dedicated to exchanging and manipulating spatial data will always use WKB.

WKT, WKB, and GML can't be interpreted directly by SQL Server. You have to either cast the definition as a spatial data type or assign it to a variable/column defined as either GEOMETRY or GEOGRAPHY. Beyond that, defining a spatial object using WKT is very straightforward. You simply have to specify the type of spatial object and the coordinates. For example, the line represented as (0 0 0, 0 1 10) would be defined as follows:

```
DECLARE @var    GEOMETRY;
SET @var = 'LINESTRING(0 0 0,0 1 10)';
SELECT @var;
```

> **Note:** If you are executing any of this code, querying a spatial object causes an additional tab to be displayed in the results labeled Spatial Results which shows a visual image of the spatial object.

If you wanted the same coordinates stored as two points instead of a line, you would use the following:

```
DECLARE @var    GEOMETRY;
SET @var = 'MULTIPOINT(0 0 0,0 1 10)';
SELECT @var;
```

As mentioned earlier, spatial data types are implemented using the CLR in the same manner as a HIERARCHYID data type. Instead of being simple scalar values, spatial data types are implemented as objects with all of the features of a .NET object. The objects have a set of properties you can retrieve as well as a set of methods which can be called.

While you can define a spatial object using the syntax above, there is a lot going on in the background for you. First SQL Server implicitly derives the type of object from the variable definition and then invokes the default method for the object when a value is being assigned. The unambiguous way to define a spatial object is to explicitly specify the type of object along with the appropriate method for the object.

The type of object is specified by the name followed by a double colon e.g. geometry:: or geography::. Note, just like you saw with HIERARCHYID, the types, methods, and properties of spatial objects are case sensitive.

You follow the object type definition with the method you want to invoke. Spatial methods are broken down into 2 broad categories. The methods which are OGC compliant are all prefixed with ST. The methods which provide extended functionality which is not part of the standard do not have prefixes. For example, the STAsText method will return the WKT representation of the instance without any Z or M values while the ToString method also return the WKT representation with the Z or M values.

The group of OGC methods for creating an object are of the general form ST<type>From<Text | WKB>. For example: geometry::STPointFromText('POINT (0 0) ') creates a geometry object that is a point at 0,0 while geometry::STMPointFromText('MULTIPOINT(0 0 0,0 1 10)') creates a multi-point object with 0,0,0 and 0,1,10. If your data is in WKB format, then you simply change Text to WKB e.g. STPointFromText is for the WKT representation while STPointFromWKB is for the WKB representation.

Storing Complex Spatial Objects

One of the biggest challenges when manufacturing products is whether to use an "off the shelf" component from a supplier or to custom engineer the component. When you custom engineer the component, you get a component with the precise dimensions and material characteristics you need. However, custom engineering comes at a very steep price. Your engineering department or an outside engineering firm first needs to put together the detailed specifications which are then rendered by a drafting department. The drafting specifications are then taken to a manufacturer to build a prototype. The prototype needs to be evaluated and almost always results in changes being made, which then have to go back through the cycle of drafting and building a prototype. This process can occur many times before you have the prototype built exactly as you need it. The prototype then has to be turned into a mold so that a part can be manufactured to your precise specifications. All of these steps come at a significant cost of both time and money.

That screw you bought at the hardware store for a nickel had to first go through this process resulting in tens or hundreds of thousands of dollars of investment. It only costs you a nickel, because the company is producing billions of them per day. Because the company standardized the component and then mass produced it, the entire cost of the design, prototype, and mold is spread across the first few batches, making the component affordable. We see this play out every day. The first one or two products using a new material, process, or technology are extremely expensive. If the product is popular or the material/process/technology has enough promise, the volume starts to increase to the point where the price drops significantly as all of the upfront investment is paid back. NASA might have spent tens of millions of dollars on a toilet, but a toilet which can operate in zero gravity probably couldn't use much of anything you would find stocked by your local plumber.

Engineering firms all over the world deal with this constant struggle. If they can find an off the shelf component, they can save significant time and money. The challenge is finding that component. If you've ever been in an engineering firm for any length of time, you would have been introduced to the "library". A lot has been computerized, but many engineering libraries still contain hundreds or thousands of paper catalogs from parts suppliers.

> While the OGC has a spatial standard, the challenge in digitizing all of these parts catalogs so that engineering firms can use them directly with their CAD systems is that all of the objects they are dealing with are three dimensional. While you can specify a Z coordinate on some spatial types, if you look very carefully at the requirements, you will quickly realize that storing a 3D object is actually impossible. Curved polygons and compound curves either require the same Z for all points or do not allow a Z to be defined.
>
> So, how do you bridge this basic problem? The simple answer would be to get the SQL Server development team to remove the Z restrictions. That might be possible in the next few years, but we did have to wait more than 20 years for the backup compression feature despite hundreds of thousands of requests for it over the years. You solve the problem today by simply going around it with a technique generally referred to as layering or slicing. You simply take your 3D object and slice it into hundreds, thousands, or even millions of very thin, parallel slices. When you stack the slices on top of each other, it forms the 3D object. Your challenge is to determine how thinly to slice an object such that you don't lose any detail when it is reassembled. Then all you have to do is define the object as a sequence of rows, each containing the 2D definition of the particular slice. A program can then read the slices and reassemble the object according to the slice sequence.
>
> You can see this technique applied in the Champion Valley Pens database within the Manufacturing.Geometry table. The sequence of rows defines the shape of a pen nib used in the Cigar Pen kit.

Exercise 1: Defining spatial objects

Champion Valley Pens is designing a new conveyor belt. Powering this conveyor belt is a motor which drives a 4 gear assembly with a chain wrapped around the gears. The gears are setup as follows:

Gear Number	Radius	X center position	Y center position
1	4 inches	0	0
2	2.5 inches	10	4
3	2.5 inches	10	-4
4	1 inch	0	19

For the purposes of this exercise, we will approximate a gear as a circle just to keep the geometry definitions simple.

1. Define the geometry object representing each of the gears listed above.
2. Define a single geometry object that contains each of the gears above.

Spatial Calculations

Objects, such as objects in a .NET application, can have properties and methods. A property is nothing more than a value which is assigned either internally or externally that can be retrieved such as a salary, distance, weight, building number, name of the object, type of the object, or an airplane designation. Methods are blocks of code which are executed within the object when an application makes a request. All spatial objects are binary representations which are manipulated as .NET objects. So, spatial objects have properties you can retrieve as well as methods that you can execute. You aren't retrieving properties or executing methods on the object itself, rather on an instance of an object such as a specific point, line, or polygon. You retrieve a property by using Instance.Property and execute a method with Instance.Method(<optional parameter(s)>).

Retrieving Properties

The most fundamental property of a spatial object is the type of object stored in the instance. Thus far, we've used the WKT representation, so you might wonder why we would need a function to determine the type of object. While it is very clear from the WKT representation, if the object were in WKB format, you would have no idea what object type it is. Furthermore, when storing data in a table, you can have objects of different types stored in the same column and some of the properties you might retrieve or methods you might execute are only valid for certain types of objects. To retrieve the type of object, you would use the STGeometryType() method. Since you can store multiple objects in a single geometry instance, the STGeometryN() method will return the Nth object defined in the geometry. For example, the WKB representation of a multi-point object would look like the following code. We can test the object to prove that it is in fact a multi-point. Since it is a multi-point, each object must be a point, which we prove by retrieving and testing both of the points defined for the multi-point object shown below.

```
DECLARE @geom    GEOMETRY;
SET @geom =
geometry::STGeomFromWKB(0x010400000002000000010100000000000000000000000000000000000000010100000000000000000000F03F000000000000F03F,0);
SELECT @geom.STGeometryType(), @geom.STGeometryN(1).STGeometryType(),
       @geom.STGeometryN(2).STGeometryType(), @geom.STAsText();
------------ ---------- ------- -----------------------
MultiPoint   Point      Point   MULTIPOINT ((0 0), (1 1))
```

You might be wondering why Microsoft designated all of the OGC methods and properties with an ST prefix. Just as with the T-SQL extensions to the ANSI SQL standard, Microsoft has provided extensions to the OGC specification. You have to be careful when working with objects to ensure that you don't lose any information when applying the OGC methods and properties.

SQL Server allows you to specify Z and M values, but neither is recognized by the OGC standard. So, if you were to utilize an OGC method or property on an object which contained Z and M values, you would lose information.

```
DECLARE @geom1   GEOMETRY;

SET @geom1 = 'POINT(0 0 1 1)';
SELECT @geom1.STAsText(), @geom1.ToString();
------------------------ ----------------------
POINT (0 0)              POINT (0 0 1 1)
```

You can retrieve the X, Y, Z, and M values using the following functions:

```
DECLARE @geom   GEOMETRY;
SET @geom = 'POINT(0 1 3 5)';
SELECT @geom.STX, @geom.STY, @geom.Z, @geom.M, @geom.HasM, @geom.HasZ;
---- ---- ---- ---- ---- ----
0    1    3    5    1    1
```

HasM and HasZ are used to test whether an instance has Z or M values defined. The properties are returned as a Boolean value where 1 = true and 0 = false. STX, STY, Z, and M can only return a single value, so each of these are only valid when used with a POINT. Any other object will return a NULL for any of these properties. However, HasZ and HasM can be used with any object and will return 1 if any object in the instance being tested has a Z or M value.

The OGC specification defines a set of properties, which allow you to apply a special classification to a spatial object. Additionally, some objects are only valid if they meet one or more of these special classifications. An object is considered to be simple as long as each object in the instance does not intersect itself, except at the endpoints, while at the same time do not intersect each other at a point that is not in both of their boundaries. For example, a line string in the shape of a figure eight is not considered simple, but the same figure eight constructed of two circles is simple. An object is considered to be closed if the start and end point are the same. An object is a ring if it is both simple and closed. In order for a polygon to be valid, it must have at least 1 ring.

You can test geometry instances to determine if they meet a variety of conditions as well as extract portions of a geometry such as we saw with the STGeometryN() method.

The following table describes some additional properties which are commonly used:

Property	Purpose
STIsSimple	Tests whether the object meets the OGC specification for a simple type
STIsClosed	Returns 1 if the start and end points are the same
STIsEmpty	Returns 1 if the instance is empty, which is not the same as if the instance is NULL.
STIsRing	Valid for a LINESTRING. Returns 1 if the LINESTRING is closed and simple
STBoundary	Returns the boundary of the instance. Returns an empty instance if the instance tested is closed.
STDimension	Returns the number of dimensions in an object. Since SQL Server does not allow 3D objects, the only valid values are 0, 1, and 2.
STExteriorRing	Valid for polygons and returns the LINESTRING that defines the exterior ring
STNumInteriorRing	Returns the number of interior rings for a polygon
STInteriorRingN	Returns the LINESTRING that defines the Nth interior ring
STNumCurves	Returns the number of curves of any one dimensional object as long as the object is closed. Does not work on collections of objects like MultiLineString.
STCurveN	Returns the Nth curve in the instance
STNumGeometries	Returns the number of geometries
STNumPoints	Returns the number of points in the definition of any geometry instance
STPointN	Returns the Nth point in the instance

The STArea method returns the surface area occupied by the object. But, the area calculation is only valid for objects with a dimension of 2. So, if you were to define an object as a LINESTRING, even if the object is closed, the area would still compute to 0, because lines have a dimension of 0.

So, the only way to compute a non-zero area is if the object contains one or more polygons (POLYGON, CURVEPOLYGON, or MULTIPOLYGON). In the case of a polygon, the area is computed as the area occupied by the exterior ring minus the area occupied by any interior ring.

```
DECLARE @geom GEOMETRY;

SET @geom = 'LINESTRING(0 0,0 1, 1 1,1 0, 0 0)';
SELECT @geom.STIsSimple(), @geom.STIsClosed(), @geom.STIsRing(),
            @geom.STDimension(), @geom.STArea();

Simple  Closed  Ring   Dimension   Area
----    -----   -----  -----       -----
1       1       1      1           0
```

Centroids are used extensively in geospatial applications. If all spatial objects were simple geometric shapes such as circles, squares, and octagons, computing the center would be trivial. How do you compute the center point of an irregular shape such as the United States or even worse a Congressional district? We'll ignore Congressional district shapes since they defy all logic – human or mathematical. Keep in mind that you can also have holes cut out of the shape, which also need to be accounted for. A centroid is simply the geometric center of one or more polygons. The centroid is a point, but the point does not have to lie within the polygon.

```
DECLARE @geom GEOMETRY;
SET @geom = 'POLYGON((0 0, 13 0, 13 16, 0 16, 11 11, 11 4, 0 0))';
SELECT @geom, @geom.STCentroid().ToString();

Centroid
---------------
POINT (9.1656441717791513 8.3374233128834625)
```

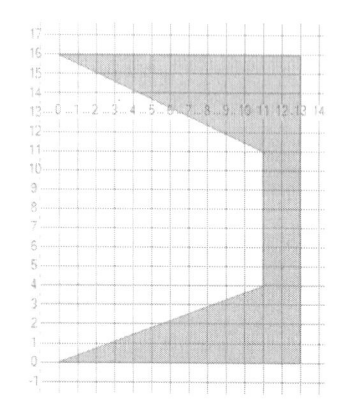

Figure 11-7 Centroid of an irregular shape

Delivery routes are one of the most basic spatial applications. The goal is to build the shortest route possible. If you are retracing part of your route or crossing back and forth over previous route segments, you do not have an optimal route. You can utilize the STIsSimple() method to quickly determine whether you have built an optimal route between a set of points. Recall that STIsSimple() requires that the object does not intersect itself along any segment.

Consider the following example:

```
DECLARE @geom   GEOMETRY;
SET @geom = 'LINESTRING(0 0, -1 7, 3 6, -2 3, 3 2, 0 0)';
SELECT @geom, @geom.STIsSimple(), @geom.STLength();

DECLARE @geom GEOMETRY;
SET @geom = 'LINESTRING(0 0, -2 3, -1 7, 3 6, 3 2, 0 0)';
SELECT @geom, @geom.STIsSimple(), @geom.STLength();
```

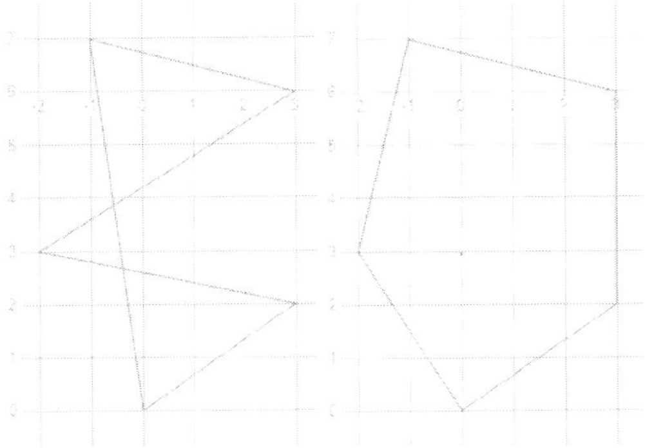

Figure 11-8 Shortest path between a set of points

The two line strings contain the same set of points. In the first instance, the line string intersects itself multiple times along the route. In the second instance, the order was changed to ensure that the segments did not cross. The STLength() is used to prove that the second instance is a shorter route with a length of 19.46 as compared to 25.73 for the first route.

The geometry data type is more forgiving than geography. As long as it meets the basic requirements of the shape, it is possible to store an object in a geometry data type which is not valid. For example, you could store a figure 8 or the outline of an hourglass in a geometry data type even though the shape would violate the intersection rules of a polygon. The STIsValid method will return 1 if the shape is valid and 0 if it is not. However, simply returning a 1 or 0 provides little useful information in correcting the object. Instead you should use the ISValidDetailed method which will provide a detailed explanation of why an object is not valid.

The following script creates a polygon which intersects itself. In order to be a valid polygon, the shape must form a closed ring and be simple, which means that the outer ring cannot intersect itself or any other ring. The shape below will create and can even be stored in a geometry data type, even though the shape is not valid.

```
DECLARE @geom   GEOMETRY;
SET @geom = 'POLYGON((0 0, 5 0, 0 5, 5 5, 0 0))';
SELECT @geom, @geom.STIsValid(), @geom.IsValidDetailed();
```

Modifying and Comparing Objects

In addition to the methods which return various properties about a spatial object, you can use another group of methods to create new objects.

STBuffer() is used to answer the most common question for spatial data – find me all of the objects within a specified distance from another object. STBuffer() accepts one parameter, the distance, and computes a new shape which is composed of the original shape plus all points within the distance specified of the original shape. Once the buffer is computed, you can simply use the STWithin() method to find any objects which fall inside the new shape.

```
DECLARE @geom1    GEOMETRY;
SET @geom1 = 'POINT(1 1)';
SELECT @geom1, @geom1.STBuffer(3), @geom1.STBuffer(3).ToString(),
       @geom1.STBuffer(3).STNumPoints();
```

While you might think that creating a buffer around a point would result in a circle, what you will actually get is a many sided polygon that is an approximation of a circle. In the example above, a 129 sided polygon was created. SQL Server 2012 added support for arcs and with it the BufferWithCurves() method. BufferWithCurves() acts the same as STBuffer(), but allows the use of curved segments when constructing a buffer around an object. Performing the same buffer computation yields a curved polygon with only 5 points instead of the 129 sided polygon returned by STBuffer(). A computation with 5 points will perform significantly better than a computation with 129 points.

```
DECLARE @geom1    GEOMETRY;
SET @geom1 = 'POINT(1 1)';
SELECT @geom1, @geom1.STBuffer(3), @geom1.STBuffer(3).ToString(),
       @geom1.STBuffer(3).STNumPoints(),@geom1.BufferWithCurves(3),
       @geom1.BufferWithCurves(3).ToString(),
@geom1.BufferWithCurves(3).STNumPoints();
```

If you want to further simplify a buffer calculation, you can use the BufferWithTolerance() method. BufferWithTolerance accepts three parameters. The distance parameter specifies the size of the buffer, the tolerance parameter specifies how much the result object is allowed to deviate from the specified distance, and the third parameter specifies whether the tolerance is relative or absolute.

> **Buffer Distances:** The distance parameter for any of the buffering methods can be positive or negative. You can use a negative distance to shrink the size of an object.

As we saw in the section above, it is possible to define and store objects which are not valid according to the OGC specifications. You can use the STIsValid() method to detect invalid objects. SQL Server ships with an extended method, MakeValid() which will create a new instance from the specified points which is valid to the OGC specifications. In the process, some of the points may shift slightly and the object may be broken into multiple objects. The following code generates a self-intersecting polygon which is invalid.

```
DECLARE @geom    GEOMETRY;
SET @geom = 'POLYGON((0 0, 5 0, 0 5, 5 5, 0 0))';
SELECT @geom, @geom.STIsValid(), @geom.IsValidDetailed();
```

The MakeValid() method breaks this object into a pair of triangles and defines a MULTIPOLYGON instance.

```
MULTIPOLYGON (((2.5000000000000089 2.5000000000000089, 5 5, 1.7763568394002505E-14
5, 2.5000000000000089 2.5000000000000089)), ((1.7763568394002505E-14
1.7763568394002505E-14,
5 1.7763568394002505E-14, 2.5000000000000089 2.5000000000000089,
1.7763568394002505E-14 1.7763568394002505E-14)))
```

If you look at the result of MakeValid(), it basically looks like a mess. You have all kinds of decimal places, including several points with values with 14 decimal places. All points in spatial objects are floating point decimals and just like a FLOAT or REAL data type, have inherent imprecision. The imprecision is the tradeoff in the data type to be able to store the full range of value required. Just because a point is represented with 14 decimal places doesn't mean it is more accurate. It just means that every point will have some minor variance that you simply have to accept. It is impossible to use a spatial object to precisely locate any given point. Instead you get an approximation of the location with a very tiny margin of error. This is why computations against objects that are extremely close can result in what would seem to be invalid results.

STUnion() will create a new object which is the simplest possible object that contains all of the points from the two objects being combined. If the objects are of different types, you will get a geometry collection. If the objects are of the same type, you will get an object of the same basic type. For example, the union of two polygons will either result in a polygon or a multi-polygon while the union of a line and a polygon will result in a geometry collection containing both objects.

```
DECLARE @geom1   GEOMETRY,
        @geom2   GEOMETRY;

SET @geom1 = 'POLYGON((0 0, 5 0, 2.5 3, 0 0))';
SET @geom2 = 'POLYGON((0 5, 5 5, 2.5 1, 0 5))';

SELECT @geom1.STUnion(@geom2);
```

The STUnion() method is basically equivalent to summing all of the numbers in a column. You take object 1 add object 2 to it, and return the result which contains all of the points of both objects. With a SUM, you can specify a column and SQL Server will aggregate all of the values for you. In order to do this with spatial objects, you have to loop through the rows and apply STUnion() one row at a time since spatial objects do not have aggregate functions. You can compare 2 instances or make computations between 2 instances, but you can't compute aggregates across more than 2 instances unless you do the looping yourself. For example, if you were storing a geometric shape representing each sales territory and you wanted to know the largest, smallest, and average area of sales regions. You cannot use the MIN(), MAX(), or AVG() aggregates to perform this calculation, you must instead loop across each row yourself and create the computation.

If instead of computing the union of two objects, you only wanted the points the objects have in common, you can use the STIntersection() method. If the intersecting points are all in a contiguous area, you will get a single geometry instance. Otherwise, you will get either a multi object instance or a geometry collection.

While STIntersection() returns the shape at the intersection of two geometries, you can simply test whether two objects intersect by using the STIntersects() method.

```
DECLARE @geom1   GEOMETRY,
        @geom2   GEOMETRY;

SET @geom1 = 'POLYGON((0 0, 5 0, 2.5 3, 0 0))';
SET @geom2 = 'POLYGON((0 5, 5 5, 2.5 1, 0 5))';

SELECT @geom1.STIntersection(@geom2);
```

The Filter() method is similar to STIntersects(), but can return false positives in some cases. While STIntersects() is computed for each row, Filter() uses a spatial index to determine if there is a match. We will discuss Filter() in Chapter 12, "Designing Indexes".

STDifference()will return all of the points from one instance which do not intersect with another instance.

```
DECLARE @geom1   GEOMETRY,
        @geom2   GEOMETRY;

SET @geom1 = 'POLYGON((0 0, 5 0, 2.5 3, 0 0))';
SET @geom2 = 'POLYGON((0 5, 5 5, 2.5 1, 0 5))';

SELECT @geom1.STDifference(@geom2);
SELECT @geom2.STDifference(@geom1);
SELECT @geom1.STDifference(@geom2).STUnion(@geom2.STDifference(@geom1));
```

STSymDifference() computes the set of points that are within each geometry instance, but not both. STSymDifference() would be equivalent to the union of differences between two geometries as was shown in the SELECT statement above.

```
DECLARE @geom1   GEOMETRY,
        @geom2   GEOMETRY;

SET @geom1 = 'POLYGON((0 0, 5 0, 2.5 3, 0 0))';
SET @geom2 = 'POLYGON((0 5, 5 5, 2.5 1, 0 5))';

SELECT @geom1.STDifference(@geom2).STUnion(@geom2.STDifference(@geom1));
SELECT @geom1.STSymDifference(@geom2);
```

STWithin() is used to test whether one geometry instance is completely inside another geometry instance. Remember that there is a difference between a point on a boundary and a point on the inside of an object. If you attempt to use STWithin against a point or a line, you will always receive a 0, false, answer. So, you need to understand that the instance you are testing against must be some form of a polygon which has an interior region. This is a subtle point which can trip you up when performing calculations. One of the more common calculations performed is to determine is some feature, represented by a point, is within a given target area. It would seem logical to use STWithin() to perform this calculation. However, STWithin() will exclude any points which are on the boundary of the target area. In order to get all of the points within a given target area, you would need to use STIntersects() which returns a value of true if any point is either on the boundary or within the target area.

STContains() is a complimentary function to STWithin() and both can be used interchangeably.

STTouches() is used to determine if two instance touch each other, but do not cross, intersect, or overlap. For two objects to touch, both objects must have at least 1 point on their boundaries in common, but cannot have any interior points in common.

STCrosses() returns a 1 if a geometry instance crosses another instance. STCrosses() will return 1 in the following cases:

- The reference instance is a polygon and the instance being compared intersects both the interior and exterior ring. This is only possible if the instance being compared is either a multipoint or some type of line string.

- Both of the instances are some type of line string and the intersection is zero dimensional. If the lines intersect each other along a section of the line, STCrosses() will return 0.

Two polygons cannot cross each other, but they can overlap. STOverlaps() returns a 1 if

- the instances being compared are of the same type
- they share at least 1 interior point
- the intersection created is of the same dimension as the objects being compared
- at least one interior point is not common between the two instances.

Tennessee and Arkansas touch each other at their boundaries in the middle of the Mississippi River. If you define the Hernando-Desoto bridge on I-40 as a narrow rectangle, it would overlap both of the polygons representing Tennessee and Arkansas. If you defined the bridge as a line, it would intersect Tennessee and Arkansas, but wouldn't overlap, touch, or cross.

An object that is convex does not contain any angles greater than 180° or in simpler terms does not bend backwards on itself or contain indentations. The convex hull or convex envelope is the smallest polygon that will fit around one or more objects. The easiest way to think of a convex hull is to stretch a rubber band around all of the spatial objects. The shape formed by the rubber band is the convex hull.

> **Why Should I Care?**
>
> Thus far, we've only discussed geometric objects. So, you might think that all of this spatial stuff doesn't apply to you or you're thinking that I just need to end this chapter since I already told you how to compute the shortest path between a series of points or how to find objects within a specified distance of a point. While we may have been talking exclusively about geometric objects so far, all of these objects have geographic applications.
>
> In 2012, the West Nile virus has caused significant illness and death across the US, with the hardest hit area being the state I live in, Texas. This has prompted several health emergency declarations and aerial spraying around the Dallas-Fort Worth metroplex among other areas in the state. However, officials do not want to indiscriminately spray an entire area and would instead prefer to concentrate their efforts on the worst spots.

> This can be accomplished by applying several spatial functions to determine the optimal areas to spray in an attempt to get rid of the mosquitos causing the West Nile outbreak. Researchers can capture mosquitos and test for the presence of West Nile, keeping track of the coordinates of each capture. You can then apply STBuffer() with a value of about 3000 meters as the average flight range of a mosquito. STUnion() can then be used to construct a polygon which represents the region where a positive occurrence of West Nile has been detected in order to determine the overall region affected.
>
> Since resources are not infinite, you want to target resources where they can have the greatest effect. This is where the use of STIntersects() and STIntersection() come in. When you use STBuffer() to compute a 3000 meter area around each positive occurrence of West Nile, you get a bunch of circles, some intersect each other while other don't intersect. When you do aerial spraying, you can simply drop pesticide on a bunch of circles 3000 meters in diameter from an airplane moving at 150+ miles per hour.
>
> You need to understand whether any of these buffer zones intersect each other and you also need to know if any other positive reports fit inside any other buffer zones. You can first apply STIntersects() to each buffer zone for all positive reports in order to compute the number of other reports that fall within each zone, in other words, compute the density of reports in each buffer zone. You can also use STIntersection() to compute the region where one or more buffer zones intersect each other and also apply the same STIntersects() method to this newly created target area. If you find more than one region with multiple reports that are within 3000 meters of each other, you can use STUnion to combine these areas and then repeat the density calculation.
>
> By iteratively applying STBuffer(), STUnion(), STIntersects(), and STIntersection(), you can quickly determine a series of target areas where the presence of West Nile has been reported. The density calculations can further rank these areas so that officials can target areas with warning signs and aerial spraying starting with the highest risk and proceeding down to the list until all available resources have been expended. They can additionally apply STDifference() to compute target areas which have no West Nile reports and avoid wasting scarce resources in those areas.

If you need to make your applications compatible between SQL Server 2012 and earlier versions which do not support curves, the STCurveToLine() and CurveToLineWithTolerance() methods will convert a shape with curved segments into the closest approximation using a series of straight line segments.

The Reduce() method accepts a tolerance amount and applies the Douglas-Peucker algorithm to reduce the number of points while attempting to preserve the overall shape on the object. This is a basic iterative process which starts with a straight line between the start and end points of the object. If the original shape has any points which are further way than the specified tolerance, the point furthest from the line is added back in. The resulting line string formed by the three points is then compared to determine if any points from the original shape are still outside the tolerance, which would then add back in the furthest point. This process continues until a shape is created where all points on the original shape are within the tolerance of the new shape.

When you want to compute the shortest distance between two objects, you can use the STDistance() method. The shortest distance between two points is always a straight line, so STDistance() first creates a straight line between the two points which are closest to each other and then returns the length of the line created. You can compute the distance between any two spatial objects; however, it cannot be used to compute the distance between geometry and geography shapes.

You can test to see whether 2 geometry instances are equal to each other by using the STEquals() method. Two instances are equal when they both contain the same set of points, regardless of whether the objects are of the same spatial type. For example, a point defined as 0 0 would equal a line string defined as 0 0, 0 0. You have to use some caution with STEquals(). You'll recall that all points in a spatial definition are stored using floating point numbers. However, a number such as 1.1 cannot be expressed exactly as a floating point value. So, you might have two objects which seem to be equal to each other, but STEquals() returns a 0 due to the imprecision in storing the floating point value.

> **Why Should I Care?**
>
> In the IT world, we like to live in the ideal world of designing the best solution to fit the problem based on estimates of the transaction volume, data size, number of concurrent users, and many other factors. Many of these solutions are denied by the business resulting in much disappointment by IT professionals. The solutions are turned down, not because they wouldn't work, but because the cost of the solution far exceeded the benefit to the business.
>
> What does that have to do with storing and manipulating spatial data? Storing spatial object requires a significant amount of space in comparison to the basic text representation. We could store an X and a Y coordinate at decimal values in less space than it takes to store the same coordinates as a point in a geometry or geography data type. Performing calculations with spatial objects is also significantly more expensive than manipulating a pair of decimals. If all you are doing is storing objects so that an application can pull them out for display, you don't even need to use the spatial data types. Most applications won't understand SQL Server's internal storage format, so you have to translate the spatial object back to a representation, usually WKT, which the application can understand. If you have to translate the spatial object back to WKT before an application can display it, there really isn't any point in storing the data in any other format than WKT.
>
> The only time you need to store the data using SQL Server's spatial data types is when you are going to actually have SQL Server perform calculations on the data. While SQL Server doesn't allow you to store 3D objects and it doesn't understand slicing algorithms used to turn a 3D object into a series of 2D objects, the time and effort which goes into the slicing algorithm and storage of each slice in a geometry data type is extremely useful for many engineering applications.
>
> Why would an engineering firm go to the expense of loading millions or billions of parts into a massive SQL Server database which is running on multiple machines with the maximum amount of RAM and processors you to stick into a server? You need the massive storage because of the large amount of space all of these objects require. You need the massive processing capacity, because performing computations across tens of billions of rows of spatial parts data is extremely challenging. Many of the queries take hours or days to complete. The reason for spending several million dollars on a system to store parts was due to the return on investment provided. If all we were doing was displaying the parts, the entire project would have never gotten off the ground, let alone funded. Even if the project would have started, it would have never received the funding approval for the hardware required just to display objects.

> How was it used? While used to search for matches on millions of different parts used in making equipment, the simplest example would be for a part like a bolt. We aren't talking about the common bolt that you find at your local hardware store. We're talking about the kind of bolt that holds the blades on a wind turbine, connects the shaft to the screw on an aircraft carrier, attaches a 16 foot tall tire to a dump truck used in an open pit mine, seats an oil derrick to a platform on an off-shore oil rig, etc. These types of bolts are big, heavy, cost a lot of money, and are critical to equipment working properly. These kinds of parts are also commonly custom engineered for a given application or piece of equipment. If you can find one that is already being made, which will work for your application, you can save a tremendous amount of money on something as simple as a bolt.
>
> A bolt has 4 critical dimensions for an engineering application: the diameter of the head of the bolt, the diameter of the shank of the bolt, and the length of both the head and shank. Every piece of equipment has some basic tolerance in the design. You could make a bolt hole slightly larger or smaller to accommodate a bolt with a larger/smaller diameter than your initial design. You could increase/decrease the distance required for a bolt shank to accommodate a bolt that is slightly longer/shorter than you initial design. As long as the changes did not impact the piece of equipment and create a failure point, you might be able to find an off the shelf part which meets your needs instead of custom engineering it.
>
> You could use STExteriorRing() to compute the outside edge of the head and shank of the bolt. You could then generate a polygon composed of the exterior ring plus an interior ring of the same shape that represents the minimum allowable diameter of the head and shank of the bolt. The resulting polygon can then be combined using STBuffer() to produce a comparison shape representing the minimum and maximum allowable diameters of the head and shank of the bolt. From that point, all you have to do is find all of the parts in your database where STContains() of your comparison object returns true when you compute STExteriorRing() on a part. You return the reference list to the engineering team for them to make a determination on whether to source the part from a supplier or custom create the part.

The most general spatial method is STRelate(). All other methods which compare two spatial instances can be derived from STRelate(). STRelate() uses a Dimensionally Extended 9-Intersection Model (DE-9IM), which is just a fancy way of saying 3x3 matrix, to express a pattern to match when comparing two spatial instances. If you find that you need to perform a custom comparison which is not possible using any of the dozens of built-in methods, STRelate() will allow you to specify the precise comparison required.

Exercise 2: Computing a Convex Hull

Having a set of gears exposed on the new conveyor belt is a safety issue for Champion Valley Pens. They need to build a housing to cover the gears you designed in Exercise 1, but want to use the minimum amount of material necessary.

1. Given that a ¼" chain will run through the gears and we want a ½" clearance between the chain and the housing, define the shape of the housing with the fewest number of points necessary.

Defining Geographic Shapes

The shapes available for the geography data type are the same as we've already covered for the geometry data type. Unlike defining objects on a plane, defining objects for a geography data type is dependent upon how you will be using the data. You could represent the Golden Gate Bridge in San Francisco as a point, line, or a polygon. From the perspective of an airplane flying at 20,000 feet, the bridge would be nothing more than a point. Descend to 5,000 feet and the bridge would look like a thin line going across the bay. Get in a car and drive across the bridge and the bridge surface would turn into a long rectangle. If you've ever looked at a map online such as Bing Maps, Google Maps, or Yahoo Maps, you would have encountered this effect by using the zoom feature of the maps. What you are actually doing when going from one zoom level to another is looking at a different version of the same map where objects are represented according to an expected visual perspective.

In this section, we will focus on some of finer details of defining spatial objects which were avoided when we were just dealing with a flat plane.

Objects on a Globe

Beyond the challenges with choosing the best spatial object to represent a particular feature, you also have to deal with the basic challenges of locating anything on the surface of the Earth. Going back to your first encounter with a globe in school, you were left with the impression that the Earth is a nicely shaped sphere. If you've ever walked up to the edge of a cliff, looked at a mountain range, or simply viewed a valley with rolling hills, you would know that the idealized, perfect sphere does NOT accurately represent the Earth.

As you saw in the previous section, you can include a Z coordinate, which in a geometry data type would correlate to an elevation, spatial calculations never consider the Z axis. So, from the perspective of the geography data type, all of the mountains, hills, valleys, gorges, etc. do not exist. That leaves you with an idealized smooth surface, with no elevation when plotting objects on the globe.

Even on this idealized surface, you would still have problems accurately locating any given object. That is because even the idealized version of Earth is still not a perfect sphere. The Earth is in fact what is known as an oblate spheroid or to use ultra-technical terminology, the Earth is smashed. Thanks primarily to the Moon, Earth is smashed at the poles and bulges at the equator. Additionally, the bulge is not the same throughout the day as anyone who has been near one of the oceans can attest to the difference between high and low tide. While you might think of high and low tide as an elevation issue which is ignored by SQL Server, the tides are in fact caused by stretch and compression of the Earth's crust. If you were able to precisely mark a spot from a satellite, you would find that the actual location of the spot would move between two extremes in the course of each day as the Moon orbits the Earth and stretches and compresses the crust.

One of the things you have to deal with is the inherent imprecision of any spatial object beyond the fact that spatial coordinates are floating point numbers. For most applications, the imprecision can be ignored. We don't drive a vehicle from one location to another based on the precise reading of an odometer. The directions get us close enough and then our brains extrapolate the rest. Even with most engineering applications requiring very high precision such building a skyscraper or a house, the imprecision due to the shape of the Earth can be ignored. This is because the distortion of a measurement on the surface of the Earth is negligible over very short distances. However, over long distances, the distortion does become noticeable and would create problems if not corrected. For example, if you started building one end of a railroad from San Diego and the other end from New York with each team following what they thought was a nice straight line on a map, by the time they reach the middle of the US, the segments could be separated by a mile or more. One of the things that many inexperienced engineers have to be taught is that there is a level of precision which simply can't be met when you are building large scale projects.

With all of this imprecision, how can you possibly define the location of an object on the Earth? Over the centuries, a variety of methods have been developed by cartographers. The first element necessary to locate a specific point is a coordinate system. There are two accepted models for coordinate systems, vector and raster. Raster model specify a series of tiny cells over the entire surface of the Earth and describing an object is simply a matter of specifying the set of cells which cover the object. The vector model utilizes a set of angular coordinates to designate an object. Raster models are commonly used when you need a very precise description of objects which have a continuous range of values. Vector models are used when you simply need to specify discrete points on the globe to describe an object. Raster models are most commonly used for the high precision maps you find on services such as Bing Maps, Google Maps, and Yahoo Maps. Vector models are used for all spatial features in SQL Server and are commonly used to overlay discrete objects on a raster rendering of a map.

In order to designate a set of angular coordinates, we first need to understand where to measure the angles from. The reference point that most people will be familiar with is the little town of Greenwich, England which is used as the reference point for designating time zones. The line joining the north and south poles through the town of Greenwich is also known as the Prime Meridian. If you set your reference point as the Prime Meridian, you can now specify a set of angular coordinates, or more common known as longitude and latitude, and everyone will understand where each object is located on the globe.

Why Greenwich, England? There are historical reasons that Greenwich, England is known as the Prime Meridian, but the simplest explanation is "because I said so". More specifically, Sir George Airy selected the Royal Observatory in Greenwich to be the Prime Meridian in 1851 and it became a de facto standard due to popularity. Sir George could have just as easily designated any point on the Earth; everyone could have ignored him and come up with a different reference point. However, if everyone had chosen a different reference point, it would have been virtually impossible to make comparisons or to understand where anything was located. So, just like your arguments over naming conventions and coding standards, enough people agreed on Greenwich, making it a standard reference point.

We know from geometry that the shortest path between two points is a straight line. But, it is impossible to draw a straight line on the surface of the globe. When you measure lines on a globe, the resulting line is actually an arc following the curvature of the Earth. These arc segments are known as geodesics.

Using the Prime Meridian as the basis of your measurements is really nice when you have a globe to take measurements on. How do you represent objects on the Earth when you want to plot them on a piece of paper which doesn't have any curvature? Cartographers have come up with various methods, called projections, to render these two dimensional images. However, every one of these projected coordinate systems introduce significant distortion based on the projection method used. You are probably most familiar with the common map of the globe found in virtually all primary school textbooks which does a pretty good job of providing an accurate picture when you are working around the equator, but is extremely inaccurate at the poles.

> **Prime Meridian**
>
> At least one person reading this book will be prepared to send an e-mail saying that the description and definition above of the Prime Meridian is wrong. For most people, the description above is adequate for what you need to accomplish with spatial data inside SQL Server. For everyone else, this sidebar is for you. Of course, this sidebar probably won't be sufficient even for this group, because they either have a background in Geodesy or work with spatial data for a career, so nothing related to spatial measurements can be described in simple terms.
>
> The line which creates a circle around the globe running through Greenwich and the north and south poles forms what is known as a great circle. If you are using Sir George's reference system, then the arc of this great circle running from the North Pole, through Greenwich, and to the South Pole is the Prime Meridian and designated with a longitude of 0°. The other half of the arc segment is designated with a longitude of 180°.
>
> However, this is only one of an infinite number of possible Prime Meridians. If you were using one of the reference systems centered on Paris, France, then the Prime Meridian would be designated by the arc segment which starts at the North Pole, goes through Paris, France, and to the South Pole. I could define any arbitrary location, such as the weather vane on the peak of the barn at our family farm outside of Hillsboro, WI. I could name this location George, of the Warner Brothers' cartoon fame not to be confused with Sir George. The Prime Meridian in the George reference system would be designated by the arc segment which joins the North and South poles through the George point.
>
> It really doesn't matter what you choose as your Prime Meridian as long as you have a definition which allows your spatial locations to be translated to anyone else's spatial locations. For virtually the entire world, this means Greenwich is sitting on the Prime Meridian.

Spatial Reference Systems

We have the natural distortion due to the shape of the Earth, various ellipsoids that describe the shape of the Earth, geodetic representations, projected coordinate systems, and completely arbitrary reference points. How are we ever supposed to be able to specify the location of any object and have anyone else understand what we mean?

Fortunately, very few applications have to understand any of this. We simply load data that is provided to us and make comparisons. As long as the data we load and compare against uses the same definition, we never have to care. There are numerous, standard spatial reference systems available and SQL Server recognizes 391 one different spatial reference systems which can be reviewed by querying the sys.spatial_reference_systems view. The European Petroleum Survey Group, EPSG, maintains the list of spatial reference systems which are used throughout the world and assigns each reference system a spatial reference ID, SRID. As long as you are using data sets defined with the same SRID, all of your comparisons will be valid. If the SRIDs are different, SQL

Server will return an error, because calculations across SRIDs are not valid.

The most common SRID you will come across is 4326, The 4326 SRID is used by all retail GPS devices as well as the most common map rendering applications – Google, Bing, and Yahoo maps.

If you retrieve the well_known_text column from sys.spatial_reference_systems, you can get an idea of how a reference system is defined. The definition for SRID 4326 is shown below:

```
GEOGCS["WGS 84", DATUM["World Geodetic System 1984", ELLIPSOID["WGS 84", 6378137,
298.257223563]], PRIMEM["Greenwich", 0], UNIT["Degree", 0.0174532925199433]]
```

The first code tells us that this is a geographic coordinate system which will be based entirely on some reference ellipsoid. The next piece provides the name of the reference system, WGS 84. The Datum provides the name and parameters of the definition. The World Geodetic System 1984 is based on a reference ellipsoid with a semi-major axis of 6,378,137 meters, an inverse flattening ratio of 298.257223563, a prime meridian defined as Greenwich where the longitude is set to 0, with measurements in degrees, and a conversion factor to radians of π/180.

If you were to look at the definition of a projected coordinate system, it would begin with PROJCS and a name. Following the name of the reference system would be a full definition of a geographic coordinate system since all projected coordinate systems are based on a geographic coordinate system. Following the GOGCS definition would be a set of parameters that define the projection to a flat plane.

In addition to the spatial definition of the object as we've seen throughout this chapter, every piece of spatial data must also specify the SRID used. If you do not specify an SRID for geometry data, the default of 0 will be used. The default for geography data is 4326. You can even specify your own SRIDs or an SRID that SQL Server does not support. However, if you are using a geography data type, you are restricted to one of the 391 geographic coordinate systems defined in sys.spatial_reference_systems. If you review the coordinate systems supported by SQL Server, you will find that the list does not contain any projected coordinate systems. You can store spatial data using a projected coordinate system, but you have to store the data in a geometry data type and not a geography data type. The geography data type only allows geodetic data to be stored.

The other important piece of information in sys.spatial_reference_systems is the unit of measure. This value tells us what unit of measure is used for any distance or area calculations. For example, 4326 uses a meter as the unit of measure, so any distances are expressed in meters and areas in square meters.

> **Unit Of Measure:** People in the United States and United Kingdom all speak English. But, that doesn't mean they can understand each other. I remember a class I taught in London several years ago to 12 attendees. Six came from an area on the east coast and six from an area on the west coast. All 13 of us were speaking English. The 12 attendees seemed to have no trouble understanding me, but I had to really concentrate to understand any of them. On our way to lunch, one person asked me if I could understand the people in the other group, because he couldn't. It turns out that the six from the east coast had no idea what the 6 from the west coast were saying and vice versa.

> Just like the spoken language, the written language also has differences. Words will be spelled differently in US English than they are in UK English. The spatial reference systems are maintained by the EPSG, which means the definitions will be using the UK English spellings. In UK English, it is metre, while in US English it is meter. Regardless of the spelling, it is still the same metric measurement unit.

Left Hand Rule

When we defined the points for a spatial object, we didn't pay attention to the direction in which the points were specified. We could have started at any point and proceeded to specify the points in either a clockwise or counter clockwise manner. Regardless of the direction, we would have defined a valid geometry. For any geometry that was closed, SQL Server would have implicitly understood which points were in the interior and which were in the exterior of the object. SQL Server implicitly understood the set of interior points, regardless of the direction of definition, because a geometry data type is defined on an infinite, flat plane. Because we are defining real objects, none of the object definitions can be infinite in scope.

When we define objects on a globe, we aren't dealing with an infinite plane. We also aren't dealing with an object which has edges. Any line can encircle the Earth and end up back at its starting point. This poses a problem when defining shapes. If you were to define a line that circled the equator, you split the globe into two hemispheres, but which hemisphere does the line around the equator represent?

To resolve this ambiguity, all spatial applications obey what is known as the left-hand rule when defining objects in a geodetic coordinate system. Very simply, the left-hand rules states that if you were to walk the path in the order in which points were defined for an object, the interior is the set of points on the left-hand side. So, if you were to draw a line around the equator by specifying points going in an easterly direction, the interior would be the northern hemisphere. If you were to define the same line, but specified the points going in a westerly direction, the interior would be the southern hemisphere.

Geography Methods

Geography points are normally specified in angular units as latitude and longitude. You need to convert these angular measurements to a decimal using the following formula:

```
Degrees + (Minutes / 60) + (Seconds / 3600)
```

New York is located at 40°39'51"N 73°56'19"W (40.66416666666667, -73.93861111111111) and Boston is located at 42°21'29"N 71°03'49"W (42.35805555555556, -71.06361111111111). The longitude is negative, because New York and Boston are west of the prime meridian. If you were to attempt to define a line string with these two points as defined above, you would receive an error message. While we have always been taught to specify geographic coordinates with latitude first followed by longitude, you need to switch the order to longitude and then latitude when defining a geography instance.

Just as you can perform computations on geometry instances, many of the same methods can be applied to geography instances. Geography instances have a more limited set of methods which can be applied and Books Online is your best source of information for the set of valid geography instances. Even if a geography instance does not support a particular method, you can always convert the instance to a geometry data type and perform the calculation.

You do need to take care when converting a geometry instance to a geography instance and performing a calculation. Geography calculations are based on a flat plane where straight lines exist. Geography calculations are all based on angular measurements since you are making measurements on the surface of an ellipsoid. The difference in the calculation methods can give significantly different results, even over short distances. Consider the following example which calculates the distance between New York and Boston.

```
DECLARE @geog    GEOGRAPHY,
        @geom    GEOMETRY

SET @geog = geography::STGeomFromText
('LINESTRING(73.93861111111111 40.66416666666667, 71.06361111111111
42.35805555555556)', 4326);
SELECT @geog.STLength()
SET @geom = geometry::STGeomFromText
('LINESTRING(73.93861111111111 40.66416666666667, 71.06361111111111
42.35805555555556)', 4326);
SELECT @geom.STLength()
```

When computed as a geography instance, we get a distance of about 304 kilometers. When computed as a geometry instance, we get a distance of about 3.3 units, which is a nonsensical answer. The reason we get an invalid answer from the geometry data type is because geometry only understands a flat plane and we stored coordinates based on geodesic measurements. This doesn't mean that you can't obtain reasonably accurate calculations from a geometry type. It means that you have to store the data in the appropriate format. In order to obtain a reasonably accurate calculation of the distance from New York to Boston, you have to first convert the geodesic coordinates to a corresponding set in a projected coordinate system before storing the result in a geometry data type for calculations. SQL Server won't convert coordinates from one coordinate system to another and also doesn't have any functions to perform the conversion. You would need to purchase an application such as ArcGIS from ESRI in order to perform the conversion.

Loading Real Geographic Objects

There is a wide array of websites where you can obtain extensive databases of geographic information. For US based information, the two biggest sources are the National Transportation Atlas maintained by the Bureau of Transportation Statistics (http://www.bts.gov/publications/national_transportation_atlas_database) and TIGER/Line from the US Census Bureau (http://www.census.gov/geo/www/tiger). The National Transportation Atlas contains data sets for items such as bridges/train stations/border crossings, state and county boundaries, national parks, and the national highway system. The TIGER/Line data contains streets, railroads, rivers, landmarks, and full address ranges.

You can also purchase additional databases or even use a service to geocode your data. However, if you spend a little bit of time with these data sets, you'll find a couple of really interesting things. First, the data sets contain virtually all of the information you will ever need. Secondly, almost every commercial geocoding service is actually using the free data set provided by TIGER/Line to geocode your data. Some of these services add additional value to the TIGER/Line data, but many of them simply import the updates into their database and then make you pay hundreds or thousands of dollars to geocode your data using this freely available data set.

The first challenge you'll encounter is that all of the data presented by these two sources is available in SHAPEFILE format, which is the internal format used by ArcGIS from ESRI. But, not everyone has the budget to purchase this product, so how do you work around it? Fortunately, Morten Nielsen has published a free tool at (http://www.sharpgis.net/page/SQL-Server-2008-Spatial-Tools.aspx). With this tool, you can simply select a shape file, specify a table, hit a button, and import the data.

> **Note:** The Shape2SQL utility was written for SQL Server 2008 and won't run right out of the box against SQL Server 2012. It relies on SqlServerSpatial.dll, but this file is named SqlServerSpatial110.dll for SQL Server 2012. To get the utility to work, go to Windows\System32, make a copy of SqlServerSpatial110.dll, and change the name of the copy to SqlServerSpatial.dll. You can now use Shape2SQL to import shape files into SQL Server 2012.

If you look in the Spatial schema of the ChampionValleyPens database, you will find 4 tables. The County, States, and Roads tables were imported from the 2012 National Transportation Atlas. The Starbucks table was imported from a file I found on the GPSPassion.com website which contained the coordinates of about 7600 Starbucks locations. So, armed with the roads and Starbucks tables, we can now locate the Starbucks nearest to you. If you know your exact GPS location, all you have to do is query the Starbucks table. If you don't know your GPS location, then you can use the roads table to perform a search from an intersection nearest you. Keep in mind that the roads table only contains US, state, and county roads, not streets. If you want to perform searches based on street intersections, you will need to download and import the TIGER/Line data from the US Census Bureau.

I won't cover how to load data to any of these tables, because I'm assuming you can figure out how to download files from either of the sites above, unzip the files to a folder, launch Shape2SQL, select a .shp file, fill out the rest of the configuration information, and click the import button. I also won't cover the contents of the State and County tables, because the data should be pretty self-explanatory.

For example, you display a county map of the state of Texas, you would run the following query:

```
SELECT county, geog
FROM Spatial.County
WHERE state = 'Texas'
```

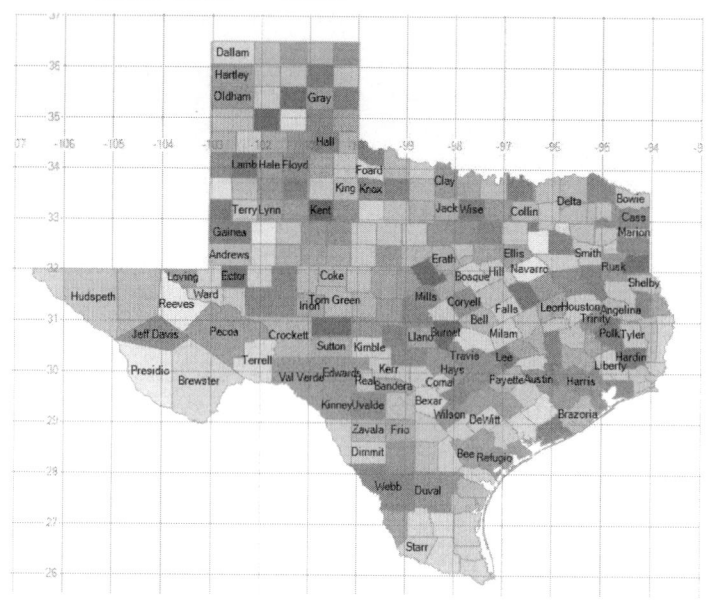

Figure 11-09 Map of Texas

The state and county tables are relatively simple and should be easily understood at this point in the book. You will want to be a little careful when querying the tables and displaying the results in the Spatial Results table in SSMS. Some of the shapes are quite large and might not even render in SSMS due to the amount of memory required.

The roads table is a bit more complicated and has many columns with unintelligible names. The roads are stored as LINESTRING objects and cover all of the US, state, and county roads in the United States. The CTFIPS column is the county FIPS code, which can be referenced from the county table. The STFIPS column is the state FIPS code, which can be referenced from the state table. For example, the state of Texas has a FIPS code of 48, so you can return the roads in the state of Texas with the following query:

```
SELECT *
FROM Spatial.Roads
WHERE STFIPS = 48;
```

This will return 13,483 rows. While Texas is a very large state, it doesn't have more than 13,000 different state, county, and federal roads. If you were to order the data by the LNAME column, you would see that many of the roads have multiple entries in the table. A single row does not represent a single road. For very short roads, which are reasonably straight, you'll find a single row in the table. For longer roads, you can find many rows each of which defines a small segment. For example, US Highway 30, which runs between the east and west coasts, passing through Dallas, has 884 segments.

You can see this by running the following query:

```
SELECT *
FROM Spatial.Roads
WHERE SIGNT1 = 'U' AND SIGNN1 = '30';
```

The SIGN1 column stores the recognized name of the road. SIGNT1 tells us whether it is a US (U), State (S), County (C), or Interstate (I) road. SIGNN1 tells us the main designation of the road. SIGNQ1 stores an optional identifier telling us whether it is an Alternate (A), Business (B), or Spur (S). If you want a detailed description of every column in the Spatial.Roads table, you can reference the documentation for the data set at
http://www.fgdl.org/metadata/metadata_archive/fgdl_html/nhpn.htm.

After reading this chapter, you might be in need of some caffeine, so we need to find a Starbucks. You could just pull out your "smart" phone, hit the maps icon, and type in Starbucks. But, if you're a real geek, you'll want to know what is going on to display the information. The mapping service that you are using has loaded up the nationwide business directory along with the mapping data sets from the National Transportation Atlas and the US Census Bureau's TIGER/Line. The phone takes your GPS location and does a search of the business directory which the mapping service has geocoded and finds Starbucks locations near you.

How it accomplishes this isn't rocket science, as long as you have the appropriate data sets. I didn't load the entire TIGER/Line data set due to space, so, you'll just have to be satisfied with a general approximation from the Roads table.

Six Flags Over Texas in Arlington, TX is near our home and right near the intersection of I-30 and State Highway 360. It also serves as a convenient location to find Starbucks locations near the house for those late nights spent writing books. The following query gives us an intersection point of I-30 and S-360 to work with:

```
WITH S360_CTE (geog)
AS
(SELECT geog
FROM Spatial.roads
WHERE stfips = 48 AND signt1 = 'S' AND signn1 = '360'),
I30_CTE (geog)
AS
(SELECT geog
FROM Spatial.roads
WHERE stfips = 48 AND signt1 = 'I' AND signn1 = '30')
SELECT TOP 1 i.geog.STIntersection(s.geog).STAsText()
FROM I30_CTE i CROSS JOIN S360_CTE s
WHERE i.geog.STIntersects(s.geog) = 1;
```

We first pull all of the segments for S360 and I30 that we're interested in. We then perform a CROSS JOIN so that we can compare each row in the first set to each row in the second set and pull out the rows where there is an intersection. We then just pull the first row and use the STIntersection method to return the point where the two lines intersect. This results in a point defined as POINT (-97.062972999999943 32.759602000000029).

We can then use this intersection point to find all Starbucks locations within 3 kilometers, which will be sufficient to find a nearby location.

```
DECLARE @Ref     GEOGRAPHY;

SET @Ref = geography::STPointFromText('POINT (-97.062972999999943
32.759602000000029)',4326);
SET @Ref = @Ref.STBuffer(3000);

SELECT @Ref, AddressLine1 + ' ' + City + ',' + State + ' ' + ZipCode Address,
Location
FROM Spatial.Starbucks
WHERE State = 'Texas'
    AND Location.STDistance(@Ref) <= 3000;
```

This resulted in a single row which was the Starbucks store at 2733 N. Collins Suite 117 in Arlington, Texas.

Exercise 1: Defining Spatial Objects

1. You need to create a set of 4 circular strings with the following coordinates:

   ```
   -4 0, 0 -4, 4 0, 0 4, -4 0
   18 0, 19 1, 20 0, 19 -1, 18 0
   7.5 4, 10 6.5, 12.5 -4, 10 1.5, 7.5 4
   7.5 -4, 10 -1.5, 12.5 4, 10 -6.5, 7.5 -4
   ```

2. In order to create a single geometry instance containing multiple objects, you need to use a GEOMETRYCOLLECTION and embed the definition of the 4 circular strings.

Exercise 2: Computing Spatial Objects

1. The key to computing the correct object is to create a geometry collection containing all four gears. You then need to apply the BufferWithCurves method with a parameter of .75 to account for the .25" of the chain along with the .5" for the clearance. You then compute the convex hull of the resultant object.

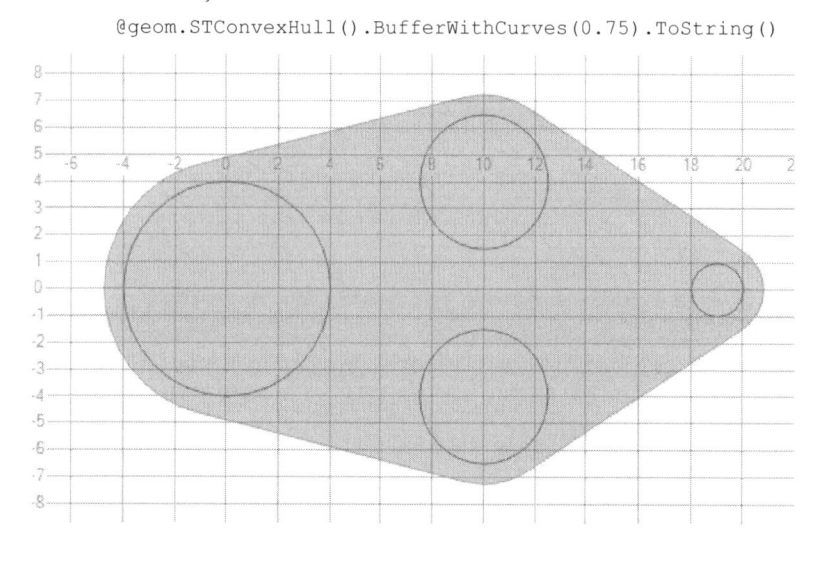

   ```
   @geom.STConvexHull().BufferWithCurves(0.75).ToString()
   ```

Figure 11-10 Create a gear assembly

> **Note:** I've applied a geometry collection including the 4 gears along with the convex hull so that you can see what the result would be if the part is manufactured using the spatial definition supplied in the exercise.

Summary

Prior to taking the time to really dig through the spatial capabilities, which also meant wading through reams of geospatial literature, how to work with and leverage spatial data was really a mystery. Even the examples you'll find online and in virtually every book are complicated, obtuse, and enough to scare most people away. Spatial really isn't that complicated once you understand some basic concepts.

For a few, you'll work with geometric shapes and a geometry data type to store and manipulate basic objects in a plane. For the vast majority, you'll be doing basic manipulation of geographic data. For those working with geographic data, all you really need to remember is that the Earth is neither flat nor a perfect sphere, every location is measured from an arbitrary location, and as long as all of your data uses the same spatial reference system, your analysis should be reasonably straight forward.

Storing spatial data is just one small step toward the overall goal of driving actionable and impactful information within your organization. Spatial data isn't just for niche applications where you're modeling products. Spatially enabled applications and reports can deliver insight into problems in ways that reams of tabular reports and spreadsheets can't. You can look at stacks of crime statistics and never understand the relationships, but as soon as you plot those same statistics on a map, you can suddenly see where resources need to be applied. As mapping technologies become easier to use, you'll start to see a major shift in analysis from simple reports to visual plots of data on maps being used to drive business decisions.

Chapter 12
Designing Indexes

> **Setup:** Please run the Chapter 12 Setup script in the companion files prior to starting the exercises in this chapter to ensure that your databases are at the correct starting point. Every exercise in this book assumes that you have created the c:\ChampionValleyPress\Data and c:\ChampionValleyPress\Log folders, contained databases are enabled, and this is the location of all of the data, log, and filestream files which will be used for this book. If you have chosen a different path, you will need to adjust the paths listed accordingly. Every setup script also assumes that you have enabled FILESTREAM access for the instance. When executing commands, it is assumed that you will change context to the appropriate database since understanding the contents of each database in this book is the same skill you will need for working with your databases. All scripts also assume you are using a default instance.

In Chapters 7 - 11, you learned how to store, manipulate, and retrieve data from a table. While the scenarios used resulted in code examples you would use in real world applications, the amount of data in the database was limited so that all of your queries would perform quickly. Real world systems have significantly more data and as the volume of data increases, the performance of your queries will decline. Indexes are used to improve the performance of queries and very few systems can function without indexes on your tables.

In this chapter, you will learn about most of the indexes that can be created in SQL Server 2012. We will reserve the creation of full-text indexes for the next chapter of the book.

Index Structure

Just like every feature in SQL Server, indexes existed for millennia before a computer existed, before relational database were "invented", and long before Microsoft SQL Server became a product. If you go back to the problem of our library from chapter 1, a method was devised to catalog and allow people to quickly find any volume among a massive collection of books. The title of each book was written on a card. Cards were alphabetized and placed in boxes. The ends of each box told you the first 1 - 3 letters for the first and last card in each box. All you had to do was start with the collection of boxes, find the box where the title of the book fell between the letters on the label on the outside of the box, open the box, and quickly flip through until you found the card that referenced the book. The card would then tell you where the book was located on the shelves.

The majority of the indexes that SQL Server uses work exactly like this card catalog. The only difference is that instead of having just a single index on the title of a book, you can create many indexes to allow rapid retrieval of information based on a variety of criteria such as subject, author, publication date, or even keywords within the book.

Indexes contain every value present in the column(s) that the index is defined for. As such, the index can be used to locate information as well as to tell you if information is not present. For example, we will use our card catalog example on an index of customers by City and

StateProvince. You create a card for each of the 1 million customers in the database with the City and StateProvince on each card and a reference to the ID of the customer it is associated to. You put these cards in alphabetical order. Now do a search for the customers who live in Dallas, TX. You would locate the drawer which contained Dallas and flip through the cards to locate the group for Dallas, TX. Since the cards are in alphabetical order, if you don't find a card for Dallas, TX where it should be in the drawer, you can say that you don't have any customers in Dallas, TX without having to look through the rest of the index.

B-Trees

Indexes are built and maintained in a doubly linked list that forms a B-tree (balanced tree). In a B-tree structure, the nodes are kept in balance such that the structure has as much data on the left side as exists on the right side. SQL Server doesn't implement a strict B-tree structure since doing so can incur a large amount of unnecessary I/O just to keep the tree balanced. Instead SQL Server implements what is referred to as a B+-tree where the left and right side don't strictly have to have the same number of values. However, the exact mechanics of a B+-tree are completely hidden within the storage engine so we'll simply base our discussion on a standard B-tree since it is much simpler to explain and still applies to how indexes are formed, used, and why indexes help you find data very quickly. An example of a B-tree is shown in Figure 12-1.

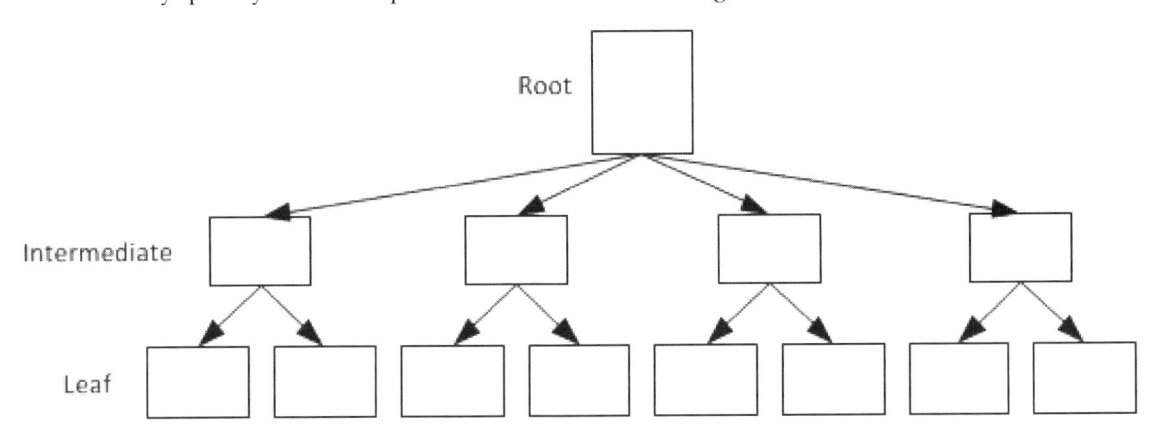

Figure 12-1 B-tree structure

A B-tree is constructed of a single 8K page of data at the root node, zero or more intermediate levels, and a leaf level. A B-tree is symmetrical. If you were to draw a vertical line through the B-tree structure, there would be just as much data on both the left and right side, at every level. Splitting the B-tree down the center of the root node will result in the same number of pages on the left and right. Splitting a B-tree down the center of any intermediate page also results in the same number of pages on each side.

The root node is constructed of the first entry on each page of the intermediate level just below the root. Each intermediate page is constructed from the first entry on every page below it. The lowest level intermediate page is constructed from the first entry on each leaf level page beneath it. Each page in the index, regardless of level has the entries sorted according to the definition of the index.

The detailed construction of an index is shown in Figure 12-2.

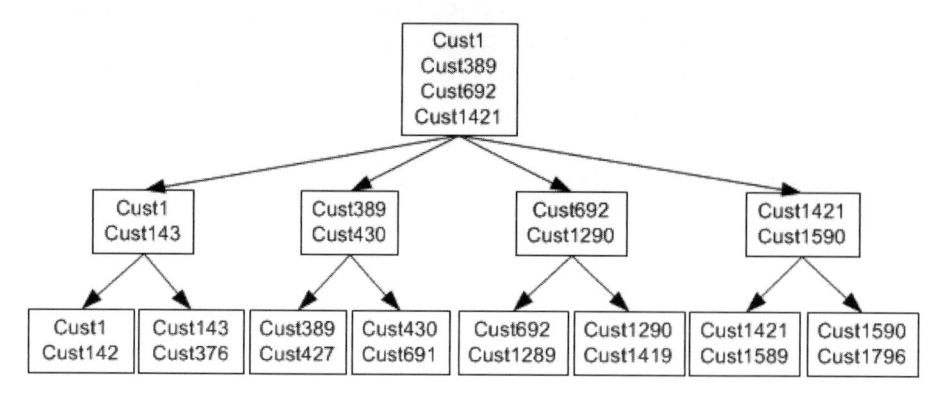

```
                          Cust1
                          Cust389
                          Cust692
                          Cust1421
         ┌───────────┬──────────┴──────┬────────────┐
      Cust1       Cust389          Cust692       Cust1421
     Cust143      Cust430          Cust1290      Cust1590
    ┌───┬──┐    ┌────┬───┐       ┌─────┬────┐   ┌─────┬────┐
 Cust1 Cust143 Cust389 Cust430 Cust692 Cust1290 Cust1421 Cust1590
 Cust142 Cust376 Cust427 Cust691 Cust1289 Cust1419 Cust1589 Cust1796
```

Figure 12-2 Constructing an index

> **A tree is a tree.** The biggest question you should be asking is "Why a B-tree?" The answer is really simple – Why not? A B-tree wasn't invented by a person. The B-tree was invented by nature. Just take a look outside and you'll find trees all over the place. The B-trees that we use are simply upside down trees. Ever wonder how trees stand up to high winds. Walk around a tree and take a really hard look at the simplicity and elegance of construction. Unless the tree has been damaged or something forced into growing at an odd angle, no matter what angle you look at the tree, you will see about as many branches on the left and right side. It's a very stable structure which distributes load evenly and disperses forces. It's also a structure that is extremely easy to build upon, allowing the tree to grow in every direction. Finding something in the tree is also extremely easy. You simply run up the trunk until you find a branch that holds the item you are looking for. You run along the branch, hopping to another branch at each successive intersection, until you reach the item you want. You don't have to comb through every branch of the tree, you only have to visit an extremely small number of branches to find an item, regardless of how large the tree actually is. Compare that to the structure above. If you started at the root node, how many pages would you have to read to find customer 502? Or, for that matter, any customer?

As we discussed in chapter 6, pages can store up to 8060 bytes of data. When SQL Server first builds an index, the process is very simple and straight forward. The index has to contain every value in the column(s) that define the index. For example, what if we were to define an index on the Customers.Customer.CustomerID column? From statistics maintained internally, SQL Server knows that there are 1 million customers. It also knows that each CustomerID is 4 bytes in size. Therefore, you can store 2015 customers on each page. That means SQL Server needs 497 pages at the leaf level to store all of the values. Since storage is allocated in extents, SQL Server initially allocates 63 extents to the index. All of the values in the CustomerID column are retrieved and sorted in numeric order since this is an integer column. SQL Server then chops the list into increments of 2015 values and writes each block of 2015 values to each data page, constructing a doubly linked list which maintains the pages in logical order. Since an index can't exist of just a leaf level, SQL Server allocates one more page as the root node of the index, and writes the first entry for each leaf level page to the root node. The index is now complete. In order to find any of the 1 million customers, you only have to read 2 pages of the index. You didn't need to allocate any intermediate level pages, because you didn't need more than 2015 pages on the leaf level. That means, you can have a little over 4 million customers in this index and still only need 2 levels. This is the power of a B-tree and why relational database scale so well when properly indexed.

> **Note:** All examples for clustered and nonclustered indexes within this chapter will be based on a single column index being created on an integer data type that does not allow nulls. This keeps the math simple and consistent when dealing with the storage structures so that you can learn the storage math behind these index structures. You will need to make adjustments to accommodate other data types and nullability for the indexes that you create.

Clustered Indexes

While SQL Server 2012 has several specialized indexes we will discuss later, the two most common types of indexes you will create are clustered and nonclustered indexes. Clustered and nonclustered indexes can have up to 16 columns or 900 bytes for the index key, whichever comes first.

Clustered and nonclustered indexes can also be defined as unique, which means that the index requires each index key to be unique. If you attempt to insert a duplicate value or modify an existing value to create a duplicate, the transaction will fail and be rolled back. This is how primary keys are actually enforced within SQL Server. By default, a primary key is created as a unique clustered index. You can override this behavior and create the primary key as a unique nonclustered index, but the primary key constraint always has to be enforced by a unique index.

A clustered index forces a physical sort order on the table. Since you can only sort a table in one physical order, you can only have a single clustered index on the table. When a clustered index is created on a table, the structure of an index changes slightly from what we've described previously.

Unique Clustered Indexes

SQL Server sorts the table based on the column(s) defined for the clustered index, also known as the clustering key. Instead of the leaf level of the index just containing the clustering key, the leaf level consists of the actual row of data. The non-leaf levels of the index are constructed as we've described previously in this chapter.

As an example, the Customers.Customer table has a primary key defined on the CustomerID column. Since we didn't override the behavior, a unique clustered index will exist on the Customers.Customer table with the clustering key being CustomerID. The leaf level of the index will consist of each row in the table. The non-leaf levels will consist of the first clustering key from each page in the level below. This arranges the entire table into a B-tree and not just the index on the CustomerID column.

The nice, simple storage example described earlier is a good place to start in understanding index structures. It's quite a bit messier in real life. Index pages are still 8K in size, just like all other types of pages. Index pages reserve 96 bytes for the header and then utilize the remainder of the page to store data. When dealing with a clustered index, we have a hybrid. The leaf level is the actual row of data, so the data storage on the leaf level obeys the storage rules you learned about in chapter 6. The non-leaf levels of the index only contain index entries, so 96 bytes is reserved in the header, and the remaining 8096 bytes are used for data.

Each index entry still obeys many of the same data storage rules as we discussed in chapter 6, which a few small exception. An index row only has a 1 byte overhead for the status bits unlike the 2 bytes for data rows. However, 2 bytes per row are still consumed for the row offset array. If you index a SPARSE column, a value is stored in the index as if the SPARSE property didn't exist for the column. A value in the page header called pminlen determines where the fixed length portion of each index key ends. If an index key does not contain any nullable columns, a null bitmap does not exist. Just like data rows with variable length columns, the overhead bytes only exist in the index key if variable length columns are part of the index definition.

If any of the columns in the index are nullable, you will have an additional 2 bytes of overhead per row to store the number of columns along with the storage overhead for a null bitmap which follows the same rules as were defined in chapter 6. If any of the columns in the index are variable length, you will have 2 bytes of overhead for the number of variable length columns, 2 bytes * number of variable length columns for the variable column offset array, and the number of bytes consumed by the data in the variable length columns.

What this all means for our clustered index is that each entry on a non-leaf level page will consume 13 bytes. The first 4 bytes is the lowest CustomerID from each page on the level below. Each of these entries has a pointer to the page where the clustering key came from in the form of FileID:PageID which consumes 6 bytes of storage. The final 3 bytes are 1 byte for the status bits and 2 bytes for the row offset entry for the row. A null bitmap does not exist since this is a not null column and there isn't any overhead for variable length columns since the index is defined on an INT data type.

You can inspect basic information about an index by using the sys.dm_db_index_physical_stats function which accepts 5 parameters, all of which can accept a NULL, as defined below:

- Database ID – If you do not specify a database ID, then you will retrieve index information from all databases. You can retrieve the ID of the database by querying sys.databases. You can also use the DB_ID() function to compute the ID of a specified database. Keep in mind that if you specify an invalid name to the DB_ID() function, the result is NULL, which is interpreted as not specifying a database.

- Object ID – If you do not specify an object ID, then you will retrieve index information for all objects. You can retrieve the object ID for a table by querying sys.tables. You can also use the OBJECT_ID() function, but keep in mind that OBJECT_ID() will return NULL, if you specify an invalid object name or have your database context set incorrectly.

- Index ID – This is the ID of the index you want information about, leaving this null returns information on all indexes for the specified object.

- Partition Number – This is the partition number of the index you want information for, leaving this null will return index information for all partitions.

- Mode – There are 3 modes: LIMITED, SAMPLED, and DETAILED. You can also specify DEFAULT or NULL, both of which mean LIMITED. LIMITED is the fastest and least detailed mode and will scan the first non-leaf level of the index and return basic information. SAMPLED returns more detailed physical information by reading 1% of the leaf level pages + all pages on the first non-leaf level of the index. DETAILED returns complete information about the index by scanning all pages of the index.

You can execute the following query to return information about the Customers.Customer table to verify the index information presented thus far in this chapter:

```
SELECT * FROM sys.dm_db_index_physical_stats
    (DB_ID('ChampionValleyPens'), OBJECT_ID('Customers.Customer'), null, null,
'DETAILED')
```

You can see from the results that the row size varies from 21 bytes to 41 bytes with an average of 29 bytes on index level 0, which is the leaf level. The leaf level consists of 999,706 rows stored on 3837 pages. The next level of the index, level 1 is the first non-leaf level which has a min, max, and average row size of 11 bytes (the 2 byte row offset is not included in the calculation). There are 13 pages with 3837 rows in level 1 corresponding to the number of pages in the leaf level. The root level, level 2, has a single page with 13 rows on it, each row being 11bytes in size.

Creating an Index

You create an index by using the CREATE INDEX statement as follows:

```
CREATE [ UNIQUE ] [ CLUSTERED | NONCLUSTERED ] INDEX index_name
    ON <object> ( column [ ASC | DESC ] [ ,...n ] )
    [ WITH ( <relational_index_option> [ ,...n ] ) ]
    [ ON { partition_scheme_name ( column_name ) | filegroup_name | default }]
    [ FILESTREAM_ON { filestream_filegroup_name | partition_scheme_name | "NULL" }
][ ; ]

<relational_index_option> ::=
{PAD_INDEX = { ON | OFF }
  | FILLFACTOR = fillfactor
  | SORT_IN_TEMPDB = { ON | OFF }
  | IGNORE_DUP_KEY = { ON | OFF }
  | STATISTICS_NORECOMPUTE = { ON | OFF }
  | DROP_EXISTING = { ON | OFF }
  | ONLINE = { ON | OFF }
  | ALLOW_ROW_LOCKS = { ON | OFF }
  | ALLOW_PAGE_LOCKS = { ON | OFF }
  | MAXDOP = max_degree_of_parallelism}
  | DATA_COMPRESSION = { NONE | ROW | PAGE}
    [ ON PARTITIONS ( { <partition_number_expression> | <range> } [ , ...n ] ) ]}
```

Indexes actually have two ON clauses with different purposes. The first ON clause specifies the table that you want the index created on while the second specifies the filegroup where you want the index stored. A second ON clause exists, because an index stores data, just like a table.

The simplest form of a CREATE INDEX statement specifies the type of index to create and the table and column to create the index on. For example, the statement that would create a clustered index equivalent to the primary key definition of the Customers.Customer table is:

```
CREATE UNIQUE CLUSTERED INDEX pk_Customer ON Customers.Customer (CustomerID);
```

While the primary key defined on the Customers.Customer table is physically implemented using a unique clustered index, a primary key is still slightly different. A unique clustered index will allow a null, whereas a primary key does not allow nulls.

The FILESTREAM option is only used with clustered indexes and allows you to specify a different filegroup for the FILESTREAM data than where the clustered index resides. Because the leaf level of the clustered index is the row of data, the ON clause for the clustered index will determine where the entire table is stored on disk.

The ASC and DESC options specify how the index is sorted. The default, ASC, is to sort the index in ascending order. You could also sort the data in descending order. The sort order can be specified for each column the index is created on. You would sort an index in descending order if the majority of your queries which will use the index need to return the data in a descending order such as returning orders with the newest order at the top of the list.

Page Splits

If all SQL Server did was build an index one time, it would quickly become useless as new rows are added, data is changed, and rows are deleted. So, with each data modification to the underlying table, SQL Server maintains all indexes created on a table so that the current set of data is always covered by the index.

The maintenance of an index poses an issue with storing the data. The data in an index is always maintained in order, so you can't simply add all new data to pages appended to the end of the index. SQL Server must find space on the appropriate page to store each index entry, even if the page is full.

We saw in chapter 6, that rows on a page aren't stored in physical order, but instead the order is maintained by the offset array at the end of the page. But, each page in an index must contain an ordered subset of the index. If you insert a new row of data, SQL Server will locate the page in the index which corresponds to the index key and if there is space on the page, it will simply append the row to the page and update the row offset array so that the rows are in the correct order. If the new index key will not fit on the page, SQL Server performs an operation called a page split.

When a page split occurs, SQL Server allocates a new page to the index, takes ½ of the data from the full page and writes it to the newly allocated page, inserts the new value into the appropriate page of the index, and then updates the pointers to maintain the list of index pages in the proper order. What would happen if a page split at the leaf level overflowed the storage at an intermediate level? SQL Server would do a page split at the leaf level as well as a page split at the intermediate level. More specifically, any time SQL Server can't find space on a page for a row which is required to be written to the page due to an ordering restriction, a page split could occur. This doesn't matter if it is a data page or an index page.

Page splits can also occur when you update variable length data and increase the storage space required. If the new value doesn't fit on the page, a page split can occur.

The cost of maintaining an index, both in writing the entries as well as possible page splits, is why you don't simply create an index on every possible combination of columns in a table. Indexes improve read operations, but slow down write operations.

Fill Factor

Picture what would happen if a new row is added to the table when all pages are full, which causes a page split at the table level, that then causes a page split at the leaf level of each index defined on the table, causing a page split at each intermediate level of each index, causing a page split of the root level of each index, and then a new root page to be allocated. All of this activity would be occurring behind the scenes of an INSERT statement. You may have only inserted a single row of data into the table, but it could have caused dozens of page splits and movement of hundreds of rows in the table.

To control the rate at which page splits occur, you can specify an option at the time you create the index called a fill factor. The fill factor tells SQL Server how full you want each leaf level index page when the index is initially created. A 100% fill factor means that SQL Server will place as many rows on each page as can fit within the 8096 bytes available. A 90% fill factor tells SQL Server that it only has 7286 bytes to write data, because you want to reserve 10% of the space on each page to accommodate new rows being added or updates to existing variable length data.

The fill factor is applied when the index is created. Any subsequent changes to the table will add rows to the index in the appropriate location until the page becomes full and then normal page splitting will occur.

> **Fill Factors** – One of the most frequently asked questions are what fill factor should I use? The answer is "it depends". There isn't a formula that you can use and the appropriate fill factor could change from one table to another or even one index to another on the same table. If you are working with a table that you only load once or you add data to very infrequently, but has a very high occurrence of reads, you would probably want to use a 100% fill factor because the data is either static or almost static and a 100% fill factor gives you the smallest possible number of pages in the index. If you have a table where you expect the number of rows to double every month, you might want to use a 50% or 60% fill factor so that you can avoid page splitting for as long as possible. However, if the rows being added always result in data being added to the end of the table, such as with an index on an identity column, you could safely specify a 100% fill factor, even if the table doubled in size every day, because you would have new pages allocated to the index, existing leaf level pages would never be split, and you would infrequently get page splits at the intermediate and root levels.

PAD_INDEX

The PAD_INDEX option is used in conjunction with FILLFACTOR. The PAD_INDEX option tells SQL Server to apply the FILLFACTOR to intermediate levels of the index to allow for new rows so that it takes a larger number of changes before a page split can occur. If the FILLFACTOR is not specified or is set to 100%, then the PAD_INDEX option is ignored.

SQL Server will always reserve enough space on an intermediate level page to accommodate 1 additional entry. If the FILLFACTOR is too small, then the storage engine will override the FILLFACTOR and ensure that space for at least 1 row exists on the page.

Compression

When the DATA_COMPRESSION option is specified, the index is compressed according to the option specified – NONE, ROW, or PAGE. However, it is impossible for the clustered index to have a different compression setting than the table.

Index Options Affecting Creation

There are a set of 5 options that affect storage engine behavior when an index is being created:

- SORT_IN_TEMPDB – One of the steps of creating an index is to sort the data. If you specify ON for the SORT_IN_TEMPDB option, SQL Server can utilize tempdb to store intermediate results of the sort operation. Otherwise, the intermediate results are stored in the same database as where the index is being created.

- DROP_EXISTING – Every once in a while, you will want to change the definition of an index. You could first drop the index and then recreate it, which can incur an incredible amount of overhead in some cases which we will discuss in the next section. When you specify the DROP_EXISTING option, SQL Server will replace the existing index with the new definition. While you can change columns, sort orders, and storage options, you can't change the type of the index between clustered and nonclustered when using the DROP_EXISTING option.

- ONLINE – Normally when an index is created, SQL Server will hold an exclusive table lock until the entire index is built. If you want to allow access to the table while an index is being built, you can specify that the index be created ONLINE which will cause SQL Server to leverage the row versioning capabilities we discussed in chapter 8.

- MAXDOP – The MAXDOP option allows you to override the max degree of parallelism during the creation of the index so that index creation can take advantage of more processors than are normally allowed for all other actions.

- DATA_COMPRESSION – You can compress indexes using the same options as were discussed from compressing data in tables in chapter 5. The clustered index always has the same compression setting as the table. If you create a clustered index on a heap, the clustered index will inherit the compression settings specified for the heap unless the compression option is explicitly specified during the creation of the clustered index.

Index Options Affecting Queries

As you saw in chapter 8, "Managing Concurrency", SQL Server will acquire locks at a row, page or table level in a way to reduce the resources required to manage the locking infrastructure. You can override this behavior on each index. If you do not want to allow row locks when a given index is used, you can set the ALLOW_ROW_LOCKS option to OFF. Likewise, you can disable page locking by setting ALLOW_PAGE_LOCKS to OFF.

Duplicate Keys

The last option we will cover in this section is one of those options I wish would be removed from the product. IGNORE_DUP_KEY, when enabled on a unique index, causes the storage engine to throw away a row of data if it would introduce a duplicate entry. Instead of receiving an error message, the engine just silently throws the data away. There is probably someone reading this who would argue that this is a very useful "feature", after all, they have it implemented all over the place on their systems so that they don't get key violation errors. At best, this is incredibly lazy and sloppy design. At worst, you are throwing away valid data which the business needs and violating the fundamental job of a DBA, protect the data.

Where I frequently see the IGNORE_DUP_KEY used is on data warehouses. They have a primary key defined on the tables. I then find a second index created, on the same columns as the primary key, with the IGNORE_DUP_KEY option enabled. They do this, so that their code can just blindly load the same data over and over and over again and SQL Server will just "throw away duplicates". There's only one problem with this, beyond the fact you are doubling the storage space and maintenance overhead of the primary key. You are throwing away the entire row when there is a duplicate key; you are not throwing away duplicate data.

I'm usually called in to "fix" a data warehouse, because the business no longer trusts the information that is coming out. By enabling the IGNORE_DUP_KEY option, the data warehouse has effectively implemented a rule that says "load the data once and ignore any subsequent changes". What happens when John Smith places an order for 10 gold plated cigar pens at a price of $3.20 each? The order gets loaded with an OrderID of 27 and an OrderDetailID of 163. The data warehouse picks up this data in a text file that is dropped on a daily basis and loads the data into the warehouse. The following morning, someone realizes that John Smith should have gotten a discount on their order and adjusts the price to $2.85. That evening, the order entry system dumps OrderID 27 with OrderDetailID 163 again since the order had a change. The data warehouse has IGNORE_DUP_KEY turned on and since OrderID 27 and OrderDetailID 163 already exist, the data is thrown away. The data warehouse now says that John Smith paid $3.20 for each of the pen kits while the order entry system says that he paid $2.85. Even worse, the following day, John Smith calls and says that he wants to change his order from cigar pen kits to executive pen kits. In the order entry system, OrderDetailID 163 is deleted and OrderDetailID 241 is added to the order. The data is dumped to a text file again that evening. If the data warehouse wasn't coded for incremental changes, which rarely happens when someone turns the IGNORE_DUP_KEY option on, the warehouse will now load OrderDetailID 241. The data warehouse now says that John Smith ordered 10 cigar pens at $3.20 each along with 10 executive pen kits.

It takes very little effort to detect if you are creating a duplicate key, BEFORE you process the transaction. It also takes very little effort to simply trap the duplicate key violation and make corrections. If you are doing either of these, then you can choose how to handle the issue. You may still throw the data away, but at least you are making a conscious decision to do so and your code provides a trace that you are throwing the data away. Turning the IGNORE_DUP_KEY option on and having SQL Server silently throw away data is just asking for trouble, because you'll only find this after you have destroyed the credibility of your system.

> **Tales from the Trenches** - Someone might be saying that the scenario above won't happen for a variety of reasons, many of which boil down to either arrogance or a lack of understanding in how a system is going to be used. In 2008 I was called into a very large, national, retail chain to help with their systems. They had a data warehouse that the business was trying to use which was designed by some "very smart" people. Beyond the fact that it was almost never available due to constant failures, the business couldn't trust the data, much of which was very obviously wrong. It was so bad that a new initiative was going on to build a new data warehouse to replace the existing one. Each day, every store would drop a file containing the previous day's sales and in many cases up to 10 – 30 days of sales in the past. The data was loaded into the warehouse and then aggregated and pushed over to a data mart which was used to build cubes. The data warehouse had indexes added on top of every primary key to ignore duplicate keys and so did the data mart. The only problem was that while yesterday's sales might have been dumped via an automated process, there were times when the data wasn't actually finalized at that point. We would find multiple files for a given store which had different numbers of sales records and different amounts on some sales records for the same date. It turns out that the LAST file that came in would contain the accurate set of sales data. The data warehouse and data mart was coded to only accept the FIRST set. The IGNORE_DUP_KEY option that someone added a year or more before was forgotten about and SQL Server was silently throwing away millions of dollars in valid sales.

Non-Unique Clustered Indexes

You can also create your clustered index without requiring the index key to be unique. The clustered index is built in the same way and consumes the same amount of space as when you defined the index as unique. There is one small exception to the storage on a non-unique clustered index. The storage engine requires each clustering key to be unique for reasons we'll explain when we get to nonclustered indexes. So, each time a duplicate occurs, the storage engine adds a 4 byte identifier called an uniquifier to the key in order to make it unique.

The uniquifier is simply an integer value which starts at 1 and increments for each non-unique value. The first entry is not assigned a uniquifier. The second entry is assigned 1 for a uniquifier. The third entry gets assigned 2, etc. The following example shows how uniquifiers are assigned:

```
CREATE TABLE dbo.Customer
(CustomerID     INT     NOT NULL);

INSERT INTO dbo.Customer
VALUES(1),(1),(1),(2),(2);

CREATE CLUSTERED INDEX ic_Customer on dbo.Customer(CustomerID) WITH FILLFACTOR = 100;

SELECT * FROM sys.dm_db_index_physical_stats (DB_ID('ChampionValleyPens'),
OBJECT_ID('dbo.Customer'),null,null,'detailed');
```

From the results, you can see that the minimum record size is 11 bytes as you would expect for a clustered index on an integer column. However, the maximum record size is 19. 4 bytes of that is the uniquifier, but to find the other 4 bytes, we have to take a closer look at the data structure on the index page.

To look into the detailed data structures, we need to use DBCC PAGE and DBCC IND.

DBCC IND is an "undocumented" DBCC command. DBCC IND is undocumented by Microsoft, but widely documented by others and used extensively throughout the industry. DBCC IND has four parameters with the 3rd parameter being overloaded and the 4th parameter, the partition number being optional. The first parameter specifies the database name or ID and the second parameter specifies the object name or ID.

DBCC IND is quite brittle and inflexible when it comes to specifying the first two parameters. As you saw with the code for sys.dm_db_index_physical_stats, if you didn't know the ID of the database or the object, you could use the DB_ID() and OBJECT_ID() functions to retrieve the IDs which would then be used. DBCC IND will throw an error message if you attempt to embed DB_ID() or OBJECT_ID() into the parameters. The first parameter doesn't pose much of a problem, because you should know the name of the database if you are going to poke around in the page structures. The second parameter poses a bit of a problem. While DBCC IND accepts the object name, it doesn't accept a schema qualifier. So, if the table you want to inspect isn't in the dbo schema, you have to first retrieve the ID of the schema qualified object and then substitute the ID into DBCC IND.

The third parameter is used to specify either a nonclustered index ID or the display mode. If you specify an index ID, then information will be displayed about the index specified. If you specify one of the four display modes, then DBCC IND will display the corresponding level of information about all indexes associated to the table. The display mode is not relevant for our purposes and I've never used it, so we'll ignore the displays modes, mostly. The table we want to inspect has a clustered index. All clustered indexes have an index ID = 1, which also happens to correspond to one of the display modes. So, whether you are specifying a display mode of 1 or simply specifying the ID of the clustered index is open to your interpretation.

```
SELECT OBJECT_ID('dbo.Customer');
DBCC IND(ChampionValleyPens,1981250113,1);
```

The ID of the dbo.Customer table in my database is 1981250113, so we substitute this value into the second parameter of DBCC IND. Your object ID may be different, so you will need to substitute the appropriate value. This will output a result set showing you the pages which belong to the dbo.Customer table. NextPagePID and PrevPagePID show you the actual doubly linked list which would allow you to navigate from any page to any page by following the links. The IndexLevel column tells you the level of the index you are looking at when the PageType = 1. We have a relatively uninteresting table for this test, but you could replace dbo.Customer with Customers.Customer and see a more interesting example of DBCC IND. The second row is the one we want to look at. When the PageType = 1, PrevPageFID = 0 and PrevPagePID = 0, the entry on the PagePID column will be the first page of the index level. In my case, this is page 58101 with a FileID of 1.

We'll then use DBCC page to look at the actual data on page 5101 as follows:

```
DBCC TRACEON(3604);
DBCC PAGE(ChampionValleyPens,1,58101,3);
```

The first parameter specifies the name or ID of the database. The second parameter is the ID of the database file containing the page. The 3rd parameter is the page you want to inspect. The 4th parameter is the display level. In this case, we used a display level of 3. The DBCC TRACEON(3604) command tells SQL Server to output the results of subsequent DBCC commands to the console. If you don't enable trace flag 3604, DBCC PAGE will not return any results that you can inspect.

After running the command, you will see the information that the 96 byte page header contains. Below that will be the actual data rows as follows:

```
Slot 0 Offset 0x60 Length 11
Record Type = PRIMARY_RECORD         Record Attributes =  NULL_BITMAP        Record Size
= 11
Memory Dump @0x000000004191A060
0000000000000000:   10000800 01000000 020000                              ...........
Slot 0 Column 0 Offset 0x0 Length 4 Length (physical) 0
UNIQUIFIER = 0
Slot 0 Column 1 Offset 0x4 Length 4 Length (physical) 4
CustomerID = 1
Slot 0 Offset 0x0 Length 0 Length (physical) 0
KeyHashValue = (de42f79bc795)
. . .Slot 1 removed from listing
Slot 2 Offset 0x7e Length 19
Record Type = PRIMARY_RECORD         Record Attributes =  NULL_BITMAP
VARIABLE_COLUMNS   Record Size = 19
Memory Dump @0x000000004191A07E
0000000000000000:   30000800 01000000 02000001 00130002 000000
0.................
Slot 2 Column 0 Offset 0xf Length 4 Length (physical) 4
UNIQUIFIER = 2
Slot 2 Column 1 Offset 0x4 Length 4 Length (physical) 4
CustomerID = 1
Slot 2 Offset 0x0 Length 0 Length (physical) 0
KeyHashValue = (0207a0a08e23)

Slot 3 Offset 0x91 Length 11
Record Type = PRIMARY_RECORD         Record Attributes =  NULL_BITMAP        Record Size
= 11
Memory Dump @0x000000004191A091
0000000000000000:   10000800 02000000 020000                              ...........
Slot 3 Column 0 Offset 0x0 Length 4 Length (physical) 0
UNIQUIFIER = 0
Slot 3 Column 1 Offset 0x4 Length 4 Length (physical) 4
CustomerID = 2
Slot 3 Offset 0x0 Length 0 Length (physical) 0
KeyHashValue = (9d6bf8154a2a)

Slot 4 Offset 0x9c Length 19
Record Type = PRIMARY_RECORD         Record Attributes =  NULL_BITMAP
VARIABLE_COLUMNS   Record Size = 19
Memory Dump @0x000000004191A09C
0000000000000000:   30000800 02000000 02000001 00130001 000000
0.................
Slot 4 Column 0 Offset 0xf Length 4 Length (physical) 4
UNIQUIFIER = 1
Slot 4 Column 1 Offset 0x4 Length 4 Length (physical) 4
CustomerID = 2
Slot 4 Offset 0x0 Length 0 Length (physical) 0
KeyHashValue = (0971161ce8c0)
```

We inserted the value of 1 three times and the value of 2 twice. You can see that the first occurrence of the values 1 and 2 have the uniquifier set to 0, meaning a uniquifier doesn't exist. Both of these rows have a size of 11 bytes. The second occurrence of a value of 1, the first duplicate value, is assigned a uniquifier = 1 and the second occurrence gets a uniquifier = 2. The same thing happens with the value of two where the first duplicate is assigned a value of 1. The interesting part is in the Record Attributes for any rows with a uniquifier. SQL Server 2012 had a behavior change from prior versions of SQL Server and now turns on the VARIABLE_COLUMNS attribute of the row, even though no variable length columns exist. By turning this attribute on, these rows now consume an additional 4 bytes of overhead in the index row to account for a non-existent variable length structure.

The reason SQL Server is consuming an additional 4 bytes when a fixed length uniquifier is added to non-unique rows is not clear. I can only surmise this was done to accommodate either future enhancements or unique capabilities that only appear with extremely large tables. The uniquifier is a whole number and 4 bytes in length or more specifically, the uniquifier is an integer data type which only appears to utilize the positive half of the value range. So, you can only have approximately 2 billion duplicates of a single value before the storage engine becomes incapable of storing and representing the data. That might sound like a lot, but there are applications that need to store hundreds of trillions of rows in a single table and a mere 2 billion is just a drop in the bucket to these types of applications. So, my best guess is that when you exceed approximately 2 billion duplicates of a single value, SQL Server will begin utilizing a variable length uniquifier that is already being accounted for in the row structure.

> **Moving tables:** Every object which contains data, a table or an index, has an ON clause which allows you to specify the storage location for the table. If you want to move a table to a new storage location, all you have to do is recreate the clustered index specifying the new storage location and the entire table will move. This does require approximately 2.5 times the space of the table as a duplicate copy of the table is made on the new storage location before the old copy is removed.

Nonclustered Indexes

In addition to the 1 clustered index allowed per table, you can also create up to 1000 nonclustered indexes on a single table. Nonclustered indexes are built very similar to clustered indexes with the exception that a nonclustered index does not order the rows in a table. Instead a completely separate index structure is maintained consisting of just the column(s) defined for the index which then maintains pointers at the leaf level of the index back to the corresponding rows in the table.

Heaps

While you can only create a single clustered index on a table, you don't have to create a clustered index at all. When a clustered index is created, it rearranges the table into a B-tree sorted by the clustering key. If you don't create a clustered index, the table remains unsorted and new rows are simply tossed on the end of the table as the rows are generated. A table that does not have a clustered index, which also means there isn't any order to the rows in the table, is called a heap. Regardless of whether there are nonclustered indexes or not, any table that does not have a clustered index is a heap.

Heaps create several special issues in locating the data you are after. If a table did not have any indexes, the only way to locate a piece of information would be to read every row in the table and pull out all of the rows that meet the search criteria. If a table had a clustered index which matched the search criteria you wanted, you could start at the root of the clustered index and quickly navigate to the leaf level where the rest of the data you were after was stored. If the table was a heap with a nonclustered index, you could navigate the index to the leaf level and then you would be stuck since the leaf level of a nonclustered index is not the actual row of data. You would need a way to hop from the leaf level of the nonclustered index to the actual row of data. The structure used to navigate from the leaf level of a nonclustered index in a heap is a Row Identifier, RID.

Non-Unique Nonclustered Indexes

A RID is an 8 byte identifier that uniquely identifies every row of data stored by SQL Server. RIDs reference the physical sector and block on disk where a row resides. A RID isn't a concept unique to SQL Server; it is used at the core of the storage engine of every modern relational database. Oracle DBAs have to deal with RIDs directly every time they reorg a table and were the primary reason why early Oracle versions required the table to be offline during the reorg. SQL Server hides the RIDs through an abstraction layer, so you don't have to get into the details of the particular block on disk where a row is stored, but RIDs are important since they consume space within a nonclustered index created against a heap.

Therefore a nonclustered index created against a heap will consume 15 bytes of storage for each row in the example we've been using of a single column index on an integer column which does not allow nulls. The first 4 bytes is for the integer data type, the next 8 bytes is for the RID, 1 byte for row overhead, 2 bytes for the row offset array. If you were to use sys.dm_db_index_physical_stats to inspect an index such as this, you would find that in SQL Server 2012, the index in fact consumes 18 bytes. In SQL Server 7.0 through SQL Server 2008 R2, a nonclustered index on a not null integer column on a heap only consumed 15 bytes for the index; however, SQL Server 2012 introduced an additional 3 bytes of overhead to the leaf level of the index increasing the storage requirements to 18 bytes per row.

When you have a non-unique nonclustered index, the RID is carried through all levels of the nonclustered index to ensure that each index entry can be uniquely identified across all index levels. That means each row on the non-leaf levels of the index will consume 21 bytes per row – 4 bytes for the integer, 8 bytes for the RID, 6 bytes for the page pointer, 1 byte for overhead, and 2 bytes for the offset array.

Unique Nonclustered Indexes

You can also enforce uniqueness on one or more columns by creating a unique nonclustered index. As we discussed back in chapter 5 with unique constraints, a NULL is treated as an actual value in terms of uniqueness. The index is still constructed in the same manner as discussed previously. For the example we've been using, the nonclustered index still consumes 16 bytes on the leaf level.

The storage changes on the non-leaf levels for a unique nonclustered index. Since the values at the leaf level are required to be unique, the non-leaf levels do not require the RID to be carried into the non-leaf levels. This saves 8 bytes of storage per row on the non-leaf levels. While the leaf levels consume 16 bytes for data + 2 bytes per row for the offset table, non-leaf levels only consume 11 bytes per row + the 2 bytes for the offset table.

> **Note:** If you simply want to know the number of pages occupied by a table and/or a specific index, all you need to do is retrieve the dpages column from the sys.sysindexes table. The number of rows in a table or index can be retrieved from the rows column of sys.sysindexes.

Forwarding Pointers

Thus far, we have dealt with a RID only as far as it contributes 8 bytes of storage to the nonclustered index key when you have a heap. RIDs have a critical role on the performance of queries against a heap and will determine your overall indexing strategy, even though many have never heard of a RID.

Beyond the fact that a RID contributes 8 bytes of storage to each row in a nonclustered index, the RID is the physical reference pointer to the location of the row on disk. The RID specifies the file number, page number, and slot number that allows SQL Server to find a specific row of data. The RID has to be used to locate a row, because a heap is an unordered pile of data contained in a storage structure separate from the nonclustered indexes created against it.

What happens if the row needs to be moved because it no longer fits on the page where it was originally written? SQL Server has two options to handle a row moving storage locations:

- Update the RID in all levels of all nonclustered indexes where it exists.
- Leave the RID stable and drop a placeholder in the original location to point to the new row location.

Updating the RID to reflect the new storage location at all levels of all nonclustered indexes could be an extremely expensive operation. Under this scenario, moving a single row of data could lead to dozens and possibly hundreds of RID updates.

SQL Server uses the second option. When a row is moved to another page in a heap, an 8 byte pointer is written to the slot on the page where the row originally existed. This 8 byte pointer is called a forwarding pointer. This allows the RID within each nonclustered index to maintain the same value, but the row can still move to the new location. This optimizes the write operation; however, it slows down read operations. SQL Server uses the nonclustered index to navigate to the leaf level, retrieves the RID to find the location of the row, reads the location where the RID points only to be directed to an additional page to find the actual data. This doubles the number of reads required to find the row.

Rows will get moved when the amount of storage space increases such that the row will no longer fit on the page where it was originally written. This only happens on a heap during an update and only with the following two scenarios:

- The row has variable length columns which are updated to increase the storage space required.
- The table is altered to add one or more additional columns which are then populated with data.

Exercise 1: Creating and Viewing Forwarding Pointers

In this exercise, you will create a set of forwarding pointers to see the effect that forwarding pointers have on a read operations.

1. Execute the following code to setup the dbo.Customer table as a heap for the test.

   ```
   DROP TABLE dbo.Customer;

   CREATE TABLE dbo.Customer
   (CustomerID    INT     NOT NULL);

   INSERT INTO dbo.Customer
   SELECT TOP 10000 ROW_NUMBER() OVER(ORDER BY (SELECT NULL)) ID
   FROM sys.all_columns sc1
   CROSS JOIN sys.all_columns sc2
   CROSS JOIN sys.all_columns sc3;

   CREATE UNIQUE NONCLUSTERED INDEX iun_Customer ON dbo.Customer(CustomerID)
        WITH FILLFACTOR = 100;
   ```

2. Execute the following code to review the index structure and page contents. Remember to replace the second parameter of DBCC IND with the object ID from your system and the 3rd parameter of DBCC page with the first page of the table (PageType = 1).

   ```
   SELECT * FROM sys.dm_db_index_physical_stats (DB_ID('ChampionValleyPens'),

   OBJECT_ID('dbo.Customer'),null,null,'detailed');
   SELECT OBJECT_ID('dbo.Customer');
   DBCC IND(ChampionValleyPens,2045250341,-1);
   DBCC TRACEON(3604);
   DBCC PAGE(ChampionValleyPens,1,71748,3);
   ```

3. Note that the forwarded_record_count for sys.dm_db_index_physical_stats is 0 for the table, the avg_page_space_used_in_percent has each page almost completely full, and that the first page of the table contains 11 byte rows with the actual values for the CustomerID.

4. Run the following code and review the information on the messages tab of the results pane:

   ```
   SET STATISTICS IO ON;
   SELECT * FROM dbo.Customer;
   SET STATISTICS IO OFF;
   ```

5. Notice that to retrieve all 10,000 rows required SQL Server to perform 17 read operations which correspond to the 17 pages the table is currently occupying.

6. Now alter the table to add a 200 byte column to the table.
   ```
   ALTER TABLE dbo.Customer
        ADD CustomerNotes   CHAR(200)    NULL;
   ```
7. If you review the table and index structure again, you shouldn't see any changes. This is because adding a nullable column to a table is a metadata operation only. The row structure is only affected when this column is updated for each row.

8. Now, update the CustomerNotes column to populate it with data, forcing a large number of rows to be moved to other pages.
   ```
   UPDATE dbo.Customer
   SET CustomerNotes = 'Test';
   ```
9. Look at the table and index structure and notice that the table now requires 308 pages of storage, but more importantly, there are now 9903 forwarded records. SQL Server also now says that the table has 19903 rows even though we didn't insert any additional data. This shows that the original 10,000 slots are still allocated although 9903 of them now contain a forwarding pointer and not any actual data.
   ```
   SELECT * FROM sys.dm_db_index_physical_stats (DB_ID('ChampionValleyPens'),
   
   OBJECT_ID('dbo.Customer'),null,null,'detailed');
   ```
10. Now inspect the first page of the table again:
    ```
    DBCC PAGE(ChampionValleyPens,1,71748,3);
    ```
11. Notice that there are now a very large number of 9 byte rows with Record Type = FORWARDING_STUB.
    ```
    Slot 0 Offset 0x60 Length 9
    Record Type = FORWARDING_STUB      Record Attributes =           Record Size
    = 9
    Memory Dump @0x000000003E44A060
    0000000000000000:   04083801 00010030 00                         ..8....0.
    Forwarding to   =   file 1 page 79880 slot 48
    ```

12. If we look at the page and slot referenced by the forwarding stub, in my case 1:79880:48, you can see the actual row of data.

    ```
    Slot 48 Offset 0x265 Length 225
    Record Type = FORWARDED_RECORD        Record Attributes =   NULL_BITMAP
    VARIABLE_COLUMNS
    Record Size = 225
    Memory Dump @0x000000003E7EA265

    0000000000000000:   3200d000 01000000 54657374 20202020 20202020   2.Ð.....Test
    0000000000000014:   20202020 20202020 20202020 20202020 20202020
    0000000000000028:   20202020 20202020 20202020 20202020 20202020
    000000000000003C:   20202020 20202020 20202020 20202020 20202020
    0000000000000050:   20202020 20202020 20202020 20202020 20202020
    0000000000000064:   20202020 20202020 20202020 20202020 20202020
    0000000000000078:   20202020 20202020 20202020 20202020 20202020
    000000000000008C:   20202020 20202020 20202020 20202020 20202020
    00000000000000A0:   20202020 20202020 20202020 20202020 20202020
    00000000000000B4:   20202020 20202020 20202020 20202020 20202020
    00000000000000C8:   20202020 20202020 02000001 00e18000 04f2e200   .....á...òâ.
    00000000000000DC:   00010000 00                                    .....
    Forwarded from   =   file 1 page 58098 slot 0
    Slot 48 Column 1 Offset 0x4 Length 4 Length (physical) 4
    CustomerID = 1
    Slot 48 Column 2 Offset 0x8 Length 200 Length (physical) 200
    CustomerNotes = Test
    ```

13. Run the following code to see what it now takes to read the entire table:

    ```
    SET STATISTICS IO ON;
    SELECT * FROM dbo.Customer;
    SET STATISTICS IO OFF;
    ```

The table now has 308 pages, but it requires 10,211 read operations. That is one read operation for each of the 308 pages along with 1 read operation for each of the 9903 forwarding pointers. What is happening is that SQL Server is reading the slots, in order, on each page. Each time it encounters a forwarding stub; it follows the pointer to read the row, and then returns to the original page to continue reading the next slot. Even a small number of forwarding pointers in a table can lead to a very large increase in the number of read operations. In our case, SQL Server had to perform 33.15 times as many read operations that would have been required if forwarding pointers did not exist.

Nonclustered Indexes with a Clustered Index

Forwarding pointers only occur on a heap and can cause severe performance degradation, so you want to avoid forwarding pointers at all costs. One of the ways to avoid forwarding pointers is to ensure that tables only utilize fixed length data types. But, this is not very practical and would lead to some extremely convoluted database designs. The other way is to ensure that you don't have a heap. A heap is eliminated by creating a clustered index. You can't randomly choose your clustered index just to ensure that the table is not a heap and will never have forwarding pointers, because an improperly chosen clustered index can lead to performance issues as well.

In SQL Server 7.0, the SQL Server team made many fundamental changes to the product which has enabled the explosion in capabilities. One of the changes was with the interaction between clustered and nonclustered indexes. Prior to SQL Server 7.0, nonclustered indexes were always independent and included the RID to locate rows in the table. In SQL Server 7.0 and beyond, nonclustered indexes are now linked to clustered indexes when present. If a clustered index is present on the table, the nonclustered index will not contain a RID, but will instead contain the clustering key.

This means that the clustering key is added to every nonclustered index entry when a clustered index is present on the table. You might have created a nonclustered index on a 4 byte integer column, but if the clustered index is defined on a 30 byte character column, the actual index key stored for each entry in the nonclustered index will be 34 bytes in size + the storage overhead.

When you create a clustered index on an existing table, SQL Server requires an additional approximately 1.5 times the amount of space as the original table plus its indexes. The additional space is required, because the creation process of a clustered index creates a completely new set of structures. The first step is to place a schema lock on the table and all nonclustered indexes to prevent DDL changes. A new, writable clustered index is then created which sorts and makes a complete copy of the table since the leaf level of a clustered index is the table. A new copy of each nonclustered index is also made in order to replace the RIDs with a clustering key. Once the new clustered index is created and all nonclustered indexes are recreated, a metadata update is performed so that the new structures are available, and the heap along with its nonclustered indexes is dropped. That is a lot of work and consumes a considerable amount of space, but is the most efficient way of accomplishing the operation since the table needs to be ordered and the nonclustered indexes need to include a clustering key.

Uniqueness

When you navigate an index, you have to be able to uniquely locate each row at every level of an index. This is where the RID and uniquifier come in.

We saw that when you built a unique nonclustered index on a heap, each entry on the leaf level of the index contained a RID, but the RID did not exist for any other level of the index. The RID was removed from the storage at all non-leaf levels, because SQL Server did not need the RID to uniquely locate a row when navigating from one level to the next. When you found the entry you were after on the root page, SQL Server knew that this value could only have 1 occurrence on the page pointer at the next level down since the index was defined as unique. The same is true for every intermediate level until you hit the leaf level. The only reason the RID was included on the leaf level was to point you to the location of each row and avoid having to scan an entire page of data to find the row you were after. If the nonclustered index on a heap was not unique, the RID was carried across all levels of the nonclustered index so that each row could be uniquely located when navigating from one level to the next.

When we created a non-unique clustered index, an uniquifier was added to each duplicate entry. The uniquifier was carried into every level of the clustered index, increasing the storage required by 8 bytes for each non-unique value.

Designing an Index

At this point, we know:

- Indexes will improve read performance.
- Indexes make read performance stable even when the data volume increases dramatically.
- You can create a single clustered index on a table.
- You can create up to 1000 nonclustered indexes.
- Non-unique clustered indexes have an uniquifier added to duplicate values.
- Non-unique nonclustered indexes have a RID added to all levels of the index when a clustered index is not present.
- Forwarding pointers are bad.

After 19 pages, all we've provided is storage calculations and background information about indexes, but we haven't provided anything that directly helps you decide what types of indexes to create or what column(s) indexes should be created on.

Over the years I've heard, too many times to count, that performance tuning is an art form or that indexing is an art form. What they're really saying is "Hire me for ridiculous amounts of money and I'll do the indexing and performance tuning for you". Performance tuning is **not** an art form. Designing appropriate indexes is **not** an art form. Designing indexes to improve performance is simply the application of the knowledge we've provided in the first 19 pages of this chapter.

Indexes are used to improve the performance of read operations, which means SELECT, INSERT, UPDATE, and DELETE statements. You need to consider UPDATE and DELETE operations as well, because each of these requires a read to locate the row being modified or deleted. INSERT operations can be improved by proper indexing when you have a clustered index, because SQL Server needs to place each new row in the proper location in the table, which also requires a read operation.

Put more generally, if a read operation is required against a table to accomplish the work you are trying to perform, then one or more indexes created on the table can improve performance, unless the table has a very small number of pages allocated. The corollary is that if you will never read from a table or use a column to locate data in a table, you can rule those out for creating indexes. It might seem strange to store data in a table that you will never read from, after all, the entire point of putting data into a database is to be able to use it. There is a class of tables which fall into this category of "never" being read or at least they are almost never read and any read operations are usually performed "offline". This class of tables is used for audit or logging purposes. You will insert your audit or logging information into these tables, but will almost never read from them, so they should be optimized for pure write activity, which means no indexes at all.

That leaves every other type of table which we read and write data to. The key is in providing a balance. We need to create enough indexes to achieve satisfactory performance for the majority of queries without creating so many indexes that writing data becomes so slow as to be almost useless.

We have two clauses which filter rows in a table – WHERE and FROM. Some would argue that HAVING also filters data, but HAVING filters aggregates which have already been computed from a table so that a HAVING clause will never utilize an index. Based on that, you can hopefully understand why indexing is **not** an art form. You should also realize that the list of candidate columns for an index was just reduced significantly when you look at your most frequently executed queries.

The first and easiest place to start is with the FROM clause. In most cases, you will be joining tables based on foreign key relationships. Since a foreign key can't be created without a primary key on the parent table and a primary key is always enforced with an index, you've already taken care of ½ of the indexes you need to create for FROM clauses. You'll also want to create an index on the other side of the join. For example, we have a foreign key defined between Customers.Customer and Orders.OrderHeader on the CustomerID column. We also run queries that join Customers.Customer to Orders.OrderHeader in order to retrieve the customer's name with the join being on the CustomerID column. Customers.Customer is the parent in the relationship and already has a primary key on the CustomerID column. So, creating an index on the CustomerID column in Orders.OrderHeader means that the join operation between two very large tables can utilize an index instead of having to scan every row in the table looking for a match.

That takes us to the WHERE clause and the area where you will spend the majority of your time evaluating which indexes to create. Some of the indexes will be pretty obvious as you design the database, after all the database design is based on real world problems with real applications built against it. The rest will only become apparent after you deploy the database and people start using it. The initial set of indexes you will deploy with should cover the most common search criteria, regardless of whether that search criteria is found in the WHERE clause or within the ON predicate of a FROM clause.

The ChampionValleyPens database has several logical candidates for indexes:

- Customers in a specific city and/or state
- Orders that occurred on a specific date
- The date an order shipped
- Orders for a specific product
- Orders for a specific SKU

978 columns in the ChampionValleyPens database to search on and there are only 5 basic searches for data which would make sense to perform a large number of times. That isn't all that unusual for transactional systems once you are done with the indexing for the FROM clause.

Now that we know how to determine what makes sense to index, the next question is whether the indexes should be clustered or nonclustered.

Unless you are dealing with an audit/logging table, every table should have a clustered index so that you avoid forwarding pointers. If the queries you are running have large, expensive sort operations such as when you are processing nonlinear aggregates for a cube or using window functions, I would place the clustered index on the column(s) which have the most expensive sort operation. The clustered index sorts the data in the table, so if your ORDER BY clause matches the clustered index definition, SQL Server eliminates the entire sort operation since the clustered index has already sorted the data appropriately. If you don't have expensive sort operations that you want to avoid, then the next candidate is the primary key of the table, which is the default for all primary keys. In either case, you want to define your clustered index on stable columns which are set when data is inserted and rarely, if ever, updated to avoid the performance hit required to modify the clustering key in all nonclustered indexes. But, even a volatile clustering key can be used if the performance benefit to avoiding a sort operation outweighs the write degradation of updating the nonclustered indexes.

That leaves nonclustered indexes to be created on all other candidates. The child column in a foreign key relationship when you are frequently joining on that column would normally be a nonclustered index. By the same token, the indexes you create based on search criteria will also normally be nonclustered indexes.

The only other nonclustered index you might want to create is for those cases where you want to enforce uniqueness on one or more columns. Unique constraints are enforced by the creation of unique nonclustered indexes.

> **Unique Clustered Indexes:** Some people have said that every table should have a clustered index and all clustered indexes should be unique. They usually go on to say that unique clustered indexes are so obvious that a detailed investigation of non-unique clustered indexes isn't important. This group of people design transactional databases, but almost never touch a data warehouse, the backbone of analytics in every organization. A clustered index defines the logical order of the pages in a table and should be very carefully chosen. While you could and frequently do place a clustered index on some unique ID column, in many cases that choice can lead to some severe performance problems. First and foremost, a clustered index sorts the data. If you need to perform a very expensive ORDER BY operation many, many times, creating your clustered index on the column(s) corresponding to the ORDER BY clause will eliminate the entire sort operation since SQL Server knows the data coming out of the table is already sorted in that order. You create your clustered index on the column(s) which provide the best benefit to your application. If a candidate is not immediately obvious, then your primary key should be the clustered index. The one part I do agree with is that with the exception of a table used purely for audit purposes which is always inserted to and never read online, every table should have a clustered index so that you don't create forwarding ..

If we are going to go to the time and effort to create an index, it should be obvious that we want the indexes to be useful. You can only determine if an index is useful by understanding the data which will be stored in the database, which also means understanding the business process(es) the database and its associated application(s) are implementing. It might seem logical to create a nonclustered index on the StateProvinceID in the Customers.Address table so that you can search for customers in a given state/province. If all of your customers have addresses in the state of Texas, a nonclustered index on the StateProvinceID column is worthless.

You determine if an index is useful by computing the selectivity of the index. In the simplest terms, the selectivity of an index is the number of unique values divided by the total number of values. An index on the Customers.Address.StateProvinceID column would have 51 unique values out of a total of 999,707 rows of data, which isn't very selective. However, an index on both the City and StateProvinceID would have 18581 unique values out of a total of 999,707 rows, which is much more selective.

The last piece of the puzzle for designing indexes is that order matters. SQL Server uses the first column of an index definition to determine if an index should even be considered. If it finds a match on the first column of the index definition, it will then take into account the selectivity of the index against just reading all of the rows of data when deciding whether an index would be beneficial for a query. For example, if you were to define an index as City and then StateProvinceID, then any query with a filter only on the StateProvinceID would not even consider the index even though StateProvinceID is part of the index definition it is not the first column in the index.

Exercise 2: Creating Nonclustered Indexes

If you recall from chapter 5, we created all of the tables using the default option for a primary key, therefore every table in the ChampionValleyPens and ChampionValleyPensDocs databases have clustered indexes on the primary key column, so we don't need to create any more clustered indexes as the primary key is a sufficient choice for now. However, we will create several nonclustered indexes to satisfy several query scenarios.

1. Execute the following command to create a nonclustered index to find customers based on where they live.

    ```sql
    CREATE NONCLUSTERED INDEX in_City_StateProvince
        ON Customers.Address (City,StateProvinceID);
    ```

2. Execute the following command to create an index to find orders for a specific SKU.

    ```sql
    CREATE NONCLUSTERED INDEX in_SKU
        ON Orders.OrderDetail(SKU);
    ```

3. Execute the following command to create an index used to query for orders with a specific product.

    ```sql
    CREATE NONCLUSTERED INDEX in_ProductID
        ON Products.SKU(ProductID);
    ```

4. Execute the following query to ensure that the product name is unique.

    ```sql
    CREATE UNIQUE NONCLUSTERED INDEX iun_ProductName
        ON Products.Product(ProductName);
    ```

Computed Columns

In chapter 5, we saw how you can create computed columns to encapsulate business rules that allow data to be queried directly without having to understand how to recreate the computation in every system needing to apply a given set of rules. The downside of a computed column is that the computation is performed when the data is retrieved and can lead to slow query performance. If you were to include a computed column in a WHERE clause such as retrieving all of the orders with an OrderTotal greater than a given value, SQL Server would first have to compute the OrderTotal for every row in the table before it could apply the filter.

In those cases where a computed column is querying frequently or used for selection criteria in either a FROM or WHERE clause, it would be beneficial to pre-compute the column and store the results. However, if you were to push this out to an application, it would defeat the purpose of creating computed columns since you would have to define the business rules the same way in every application which writes to the table. As long as the computed column is deterministic, meaning it does not contain any non-deterministic functions in the computed column definition, you can create an index on the computed column.

When you index a computed column, SQL Server performs the computation at the time the data is written and stores the actual result in the index. When a query accesses the computed column, the value is no longer computed on the fly, but simply retrieved from the index.

Exercise 3: Indexing a Computed Column

Since we will want to query orders based on the OrderTotal, we should materialize the computed column in order to avoid having to compute all rows before the filter can be applied.

1. Execute the following command to index the OrderTotal computed column.

```
CREATE NONCLUSTERED INDEX in_OrderTotal
    ON Orders.OrderHeader(OrderTotal);
```

Filtered Indexes

One of the challenges facing developers and DBAs is how to manage ever increasing volumes of data. As you can easily deduce from the math laid out in this chapter, tables with millions or billions of rows of data can consume significant amounts of storage space for the indexes necessary to achieve acceptable performance. However, if you were to evaluate the query patterns against databases, you would find that as data ages, the frequency with which it is retrieved declines rapidly. In a typical transactional system, the newest set of data is accessed and manipulated very frequently within the first few days or weeks of when it was created. You will generally only access data older than a couple of weeks as part of aggregates used in monthly, quarterly, or yearly reports. It is rare to access data older than a month within a transactional system and even rarer to access data older than 3 months.

Prior to SQL Server 2008, we didn't have many choices for how indexes were created. When you created an index, it contained every value in the column(s) defining the index. As the table grew so did the index, even as the query activity focused on a smaller and smaller subset of the table. Take the example of the Orders.OrderHeader table. This table contains data going all the way back to January 1, 2001. While we have been using this data as an example set for this book, it is very unlikely that anyone at Champion Valley Pens would be querying data beyond a week or so since the purpose of the database is to accept orders and get them shipped within 1 – 2 days of an order being placed. The employees of Champion Valley Pens simply don't have any need to query data older than about a week to manage customer orders.

Since it isn't necessary to query data older than about 1 week, why would we want to build an index that includes every OrderDate in the Orders.OrderHeader table? Starting with SQL Server 2008, an additional clause was added for a nonclustered index that allows us to index just a portion of a table. By adding a WHERE clause to the index definition, SQL Server will only create an index on the subset of the table specified. A nonclustered index with a WHERE clause is referred to as a filtered index.

Filtered indexes have a small number of restrictions:

- Must be a nonclustered index
- Cannot be created on computed columns
- Columns cannot undergo implicit or explicit data type conversion
- Can only reference deterministic functions
- ANSI_NULLS, ANSI_PADDING, ANSI_WARNINGS, ARITHABORT, CONCAT_NULL_YIELDS_NULL, and QUOTED_IDENTIFIER must be set to ON
- NUMERIC_ROUNDABORT must be set to OFF

Clustered indexes cannot be filtered, because it wouldn't make any sense to sort part of a table and not the rest of the table. By the same token, it also wouldn't make sense to filter an index on a computed column since the purpose of an index on a computed column is to materialize the calculation, not just the calculation on a portion of the rows in a table.

The rest of the restrictions might seem a bit strange until you think very carefully about what an index is and how an index is constructed.

In order to build an index, you have to retrieve all of the values in order to build the B-tree. Since the B-tree is based on data values, you have to be able to unambiguously determine the data type as well as the values for the B-tree.

If you are either implicitly or explicitly converting data types, you are not only introducing ambiguity in the values, but also ambiguity in the data type. What would it mean to create an index on a decimal column with a WHERE clause of a float value converted to a decimal? Would the index contain the same values on a machine that used an Intel processor and another using an AMD processor? Should the data type of the index be the data type of the underlying column, the data type of the value in the WHERE clause, or the data type of the conversion of the value in the WHERE clause?

It would be impossible to build a filtered index which was defined using a nondeterministic function. As you'll recall nondeterministic functions can return a different value every time the function is executed. If the function returns a different value every time it is executed, it would be impossible to build an index which relies on a static definition of the values. Any value which was computed would change the next time the function was executed, invalidating the entire index. This restriction poses a bit of a challenge in designing filtered indexes which are time based. It would be nice to create an index on the Orders.OrderHeader table which only included orders from the last 2 weeks. But the definition of orders from the last 2 weeks changes with every clock cycle. So, in this case you are left with building a filtered index based on a static date value along with a process that creates a new index covering the last 2 weeks once a day and dropping the index that it replaces.

The requirements for the SET options follow the same logic. These options are required to be set appropriately in order to ensure that the rows matching the filter criteria are always the same and are unambiguous.

Exercise 4: Creating Filtered Indexes

Champion Valley Pens requires all orders to be shipped within 1 week of the order creation. So, it is very rare to ever query data older than 2 weeks in the Orders.OrderHeader or Orders.Shipment tables.

1. Execute the following code to create an index to allow searching for orders by OrderDate.

    ```
    CREATE NONCLUSTERED INDEX ifn_OrderDate
        ON Orders.OrderHeader(OrderDate)
        WHERE OrderDate >= '20020115';
    ```

2. Execute the following code to create an index to allow searching for shipments by ShipDate.

    ```
    CREATE NONCLUSTERED INDEX ifn_ShipDate
        ON Orders.Shipment(ShipDate)
        WHERE ShipDate >= '20020115';
    ```

Covering Indexes

One of the interesting things about an index, beyond the search properties of a B-tree, is that the leaf level of nonclustered indexes contain every possible value in the table for the column(s) in the index definition or in the case of filtered indexes every possible value which matches the filter criteria. In an interesting way, you can look at the leaf level of an index as a miniature table.

If you can construct indexes such that a query only needs to access the data within the index to satisfy the query, the query does not need to utilize the RID or clustering key to retrieve data from the table, the index already contains all of the information necessary to satisfy the query. An index that completely satisfies a query is referred to as a covering index. Covering indexes are always nonclustered indexes since a nonclustered index is the only type of index which allows you to read just the index to satisfy a query. The leaf level of a clustered index is the table, so reading to the leaf level of a clustered index is the same thing as reading the actual table.

Covering indexes can improve the performance of queries by avoiding additional read operations from the underlying table. Covering indexes also have the potential to increase concurrency. If read operations are covered by an index, a lock does not have to be acquired on the row(s) of the underlying table so that a write to the row, which does not affect the index columns, does not have to be blocked by your read operation.

Included columns

While covering indexes can be extremely beneficial, as the size of the index key increases, the number of index rows stored per page decreases. As the number of rows per page decreases, SQL Server needs to utilize a larger number of pages to store the index which can also lead to an increase in the number of levels in the index and therefore the number of reads required to locate a piece of information. While adding a single read operation to every query by adding an additional level to the index might not sound like much, the accumulation of the additional read operation can outweigh the benefit of having a covering index. Additionally, you are still 16 columns and 900 bytes in an index, which effectively rules out columns with large data types that would be useful within a covering index so that a query did not have to pull the data from the underlying table.

SQL Server 2005 introduced a new index feature, included columns, which can be used to balance the size of an index key while at the same time creating more covering indexes. When you create an index using the INCLUDE clause, SQL Server will build the index based on the column(s) defined on the ON clause. At the leaf level only, the column(s) specified in the INCLUDE clause will be added to the index. Included columns only appear on the leaf level of an index, not non-leaf levels. So, an index can still be built on a small index key while also covering a larger number of queries by adding additional columns of data at the leaf level. The column(s) specified in the INCLUDE clause do not count against the 16 column or 900 byte limits of an index.

Exercise 5: Covering Indexes and Included Columns

Every quarter, Champion Valley Pens sends catalogs to every customer who has placed an order in the last 2 years. The 2nd page contains a Letter from the President highlighting interesting products, wood turning techniques, or other information of interest. The Letter from the President is always personalized to each customer and can contain localized items of interest as well such as disaster fund drives, local legislation, and location events. The customer's address is printed on the last page of the catalog in the provided mailing address block.

1. Special offers can be targeted on a state by state basis, so customer addresses are always queried and grouped by state. Execute the following command to create a covering index to handle retrieval of customer addresses.

   ```
   CREATE NONCLUSTERED INDEX in_StateProvince_Include_Address_City_PostalCode
       ON Customers.Address (StateProvinceID)
       INCLUDE (AddressLine1, City, PostalCode);
   ```

   > **Multiple Indexes:** One of the interesting capabilities of the SQL Server optimizer is that it is not limited to using just a single index for a given query. The optimizer will figure out whether it is less expensive to traverse an index and then read additional data from the table or whether it is cheaper to simply query two indexes. For example, if you had indexes on the Customers.Address table that were StateProvinceID, AddressLine1 and StateProvinceID, City, and your query asked for all 3 columns for customers with addresses in the state of Florida, SQL Server may select one of the indexes, traverse the B-tree, and retrieve the 3rd piece of information from the table. However, it may decide that it is cheaper to traverse both indexes and return all 3 pieces of information from the 2 indexes without ever touching the table.

Hierarchies

Queries against hierarchy data will traverse the hierarchy in one of two directions, depending upon the type of query. Depth first queries traverse the hierarchy structure from top to bottom. Breadth first queries traverse a hierarchy horizontally.

When you create a depth first index, children are stored near their parent's record. All nodes of a sub-tree will be co-located together in the index. Depth first indexes are good for answering question of the form "give me all of the descendants of a specified node".

When you create a breadth first index, all rows at a particular level in the hierarchy are stored near each other. All of the siblings will be co-located together in the index. Depth first indexes are good for answering questions of the form "give me all of the nodes at the same level as a specified node".

Creating depth first and breadth first indexes on a hierarchy is not a complicated process. In fact, there isn't even a specialized index structure for hierarchies. You simply create a clustered or nonclustered index on the appropriate columns.

If you create an index on a HIERARCHYID column, you have created a depth first index. This should be obvious just from querying the Lookups.Category table. All of the values in the CategoryNode column for turning kits start with 0x5. All of the values for the CategoryNode column for Pen Kits start with 0x5A, Accessories start with 0x5B, etc. So, simply indexing the CategoryNode column will arrange the nodes in a top to bottom manner.

Creating a breadth first index requires a little more work. What you want to do is co-locate all nodes at the same level together in the index or put another way, you want to sort all of the nodes by level, and then build an index with that sort order. As you'll recall all indexes are maintained as a sorted list, so you just have to construct the index such that all siblings are sorted together. To accomplish this, you create a computed column using GetLevel(), and then create your index on the level and the hierarchy column.

For small hierarchies, less than 5 – 6 levels and less than 200 – 300 values, you probably won't get any benefit from indexing the hierarchy data. For larger hierarchies, one or both types of indexes can provide a significant boost in performance. If you find yourself frequently adding or deleting child nodes, a depth first index may actually speed up DML operations. If you find yourself frequently moving sub-trees between nodes at the same level, a breadth first index may help improve performance. As with all indexes, you'll need to balance the performance gain of the index with the need to maintain the index as you manipulate the hierarchy structure.

Exercise 6: Indexing Hierarchies

Even though the product category hierarchy for Champion Valley Pens is rather small, the business has plans to significantly expand the product line and introduce many new product categories. Since queries are run against the product hierarchy in both directions, you decide to create both depth first and breadth first indexes.

1. Execute the following command to create a depth first index. At the same time we'll also ensure that duplicates are not allowed in the CategoryNode column by making the index unique.

    ```
    CREATE UNIQUE NONCLUSTERED INDEX iun_CategoryNode
        ON Lookups.Category(CategoryNode);
    ```

2. Execute the following command to create a breath first index. Since the level is already a computed column, we do not have to add one in order to create the appropriate index.

    ```
    CREATE NONCLUSTERED INDEX in_CategoryLevel_CategoryNode
        ON Lookups.Category(CategoryLevel,CategoryNode);
    ```

XML Data

We briefly covered the pros and cons around XML in chapter 5 and when you should and shouldn't use XML. SQL Server offers many advantages as a storage repository for XML documents. As we saw in chapter 5, you can create XML schema collections to enforce consistency within your XML documents. We saw how to query XML documents in chapter 10.

Searching XML documents whether they are stored in a SQL Server database or on a file system can create significant overhead and run very slowly. In order to search XML documents, regardless of where they are stored, each document must be opened and loaded to a Document Object Model, DOM. The header is inspected to determine if it matches the namespace of the query. If it does match, then the parsed document within the DOM is searched for the data, attribute, or element requested in the query. Once done with a document, it is unloaded from the DOM and the next document is loaded. This is repeated for every document you are attempting to search.

By storing the XML documents inside a SQL Server database, you can take advantage of the indexing and search engine built into SQL Server. You can create four types of indexes on an XML column. Unlike clustered and nonclustered indexes which allow multiple columns in the definition, XML indexes can only cover a single XML column.

Primary Index

Before you can create any of the 3 types of secondary XML index, you must first create a primary XML index. The table must first have a clustered index on the primary key. When you create a primary XML index, each XML document in the column is shredded and stored within the primary XML index. The primary XML index stores all tags, paths, properties, and values for each XML document. When a query retrieves the entire XML document, SQL Server retrieves the document from the column, but queries that return portions of a document will be satisfied with the primary XML index.

When you create a primary XML index, SQL Server shreds the XML document and creates one index row for each node in the document. Each index row contains the following information:

- Clustering key
- Value of the node
- Element of attribute name
- Type of node
- Path to the root of the document

By including the clustering key, the primary XML index correlates each document in the index to the underlying row in the table it was derived from. The primary XML index will help queries which specify the exists() method in the WHERE clause. Instead of having to shred the XML document on the fly, exists() queries will sequentially traverse the primary XML index looking for matches in the Path column of the index.

Once the primary XML index is created, you can create three types of secondary XML indexes – PATH, VALUE, and PROPERTY. Like PRIMARY XML indexes, all secondary XML indexes also contain 1 index row for each node in the XML document. Because each XML index contains 1 index row for each node in the document, you will want to carefully weigh the benefit to queries with the overhead such an index can have both in terms of storage as well as modifications when XML documents are inserted and modified. The XML indexes might improve performance, but on XML columns which are extremely volatile and contain very large XML documents, you could see a significant impact to write activities. Remember that if you create all 4 types of XML indexes on such an XML column, every change to these very large XML documents will need to write every node 5 times – once to the table and once to each of the 4 XML indexes. Before building XML indexes, you should clearly understand the XML query patterns and how XML documents are being used. If all of your queries simply retrieve XML documents based on the primary key of the table, you don't even need an XML index since the XML document will be retrieved from the table when you ask for the entire document.

PATH Index

A PATH XML index is constructed of the path to the root of the XML document, the node value, and the clustering key, in that order. Unlike the sequential search performed for a PRIMARY XML index, PATH indexes allow direct seeks for the path specified.

If your queries generally involve path expressions, then a PATH index will have better performance than a PRIMARY INDEX because it allows SQL Server to directly seek to the path requested. This is especially helpful when using the exists() method with a path expression. In the following query, the path and value you want are known, so using a PATH secondary index would provide better performance over a PRIMARY XML index.

```
WITH XMLNAMESPACES ('urn:ChampionValleyPens-com:product:ProductDescription' AS CVP)
SELECT ProductID, ProductName
FROM Products.Product
WHERE ProductDescription.exist('//CVP:ProductDescription/CVP:DrillBit1[.= "7mm"]')=
1;
```

VALUE Index

If you know the value you are searching for, but the node can appear anywhere in the path of the XML document, you can construct a VALUE secondary index. VALUE secondary indexes are constructed of the node value, path to the root of the XML document, and the clustering key, in that order. This allows for direct seeks on a value within the index. For example consider the following example which is a permutation of the previous query:

```
WITH XMLNAMESPACES ('urn:ChampionValleyPens-com:product:ProductDescription' AS CVP)
SELECT ProductID, ProductName
FROM Products.Product
WHERE ProductDescription.exist('//CVP:DrillBit1[.= "7mm"]')= 1;
```

In this example, we are still searching for any products with a value of 7mm for the DrillBit1 node. However, we don't necessarily know where in the path the DrillBit1 node will appear. So a value index allows us to search first on the value specified and then filter out all results which do not have the correct node path.

PROPERTY Index

If you are retrieving specific values using the values() method from one or more nodes when you know the primary key of the document(s) you are searching, a PROPERTY XML index will provide the best performance. A PROPERTY XML index is constructed from the clustering key, path to the root of the XML document, and node value, in that order. This allows a query to directly seek to the primary key and then extract the appropriate value for the specified node(s). For example, the following query would benefit from a PROPERTY index.

```
WITH XMLNAMESPACES ('urn:ChampionValleyPens-com:product:ProductDescription' AS CVP)
SELECT ProductID, ProductName,
ProductDescription.value('(/CVP:ProductDescription/@DrillBit1)[1]','VARCHAR(30)')
DrillBit1,
ProductDescription.value('(/CVP:ProductDescription/@DrillBit2)[1]','VARCHAR(30)')
DrillBit2
FROM Products.Product
WHERE ProductID = 34;
```

There is a very important difference between the query above, which will not run against the element centric XML documents in the Products.Product table and the query below which will run successfully.

```
WITH XMLNAMESPACES ('urn:ChampionValleyPens-com:product:ProductDescription' AS CVP)
SELECT ProductID, ProductName,
ProductDescription.value('(/CVP:ProductDescription/CVP:DrillBit1)[1]','VARCHAR(30)')
DrillBit1,
ProductDescription.value('(/CVP:ProductDescription/CVP:DrillBit2)[1]','VARCHAR(30)')
DrillBit2
FROM Products.Product
WHERE ProductID = 34;
```

PROPERTY XML indexes are used when you want to extract one or more values from a node for an attribute centric XML document. If you have element centric XML documents, the PRIMARY XML index will be used instead to satisfy the value() query.

Exercise 7: Indexing Product Descriptions

The product descriptions for Champion Valley Pens are relatively small, element centric, nonvolatile documents. But, these documents are queried in a variety of ways. In the following exercise, we will create the 3 XML indexes which can improve performance of a variety of queries.

1. Execute the following command to create the PRIMARY XML index.

    ```
    CREATE PRIMARY XML INDEX ipxml_ProductDescription
        ON Products.Product (ProductDescription);
    ```

2. Execute the following command to create the PATH XML index.

    ```
    CREATE XML INDEX ixmlp_ProductDescription
        ON Products.Product (ProductDescription)
        USING XML INDEX ipxml_ProductDescription FOR PATH;
    ```

3. Execute the following command to create the VALUE XML index.

    ```
    CREATE XML INDEX ixmlv_ProductDescription
        ON Products.Product (ProductDescription)
        USING XML INDEX ipxml_ProductDescription FOR VALUE;
    ```

Selective XML Indexes

While XML indexes improve the performance of a variety of XML queries and provide a large advantage over storing XML documents on a file system, they consume a significant amount of space and can take a very long time to build on large tables or large XML documents. XML indexes also index the entire XML document while many of your queries are only interested in a small portion of the nodes. To provide a more optimal balance between indexing the XML documents and the storage required, Service Pack 1 of SQL Server 2012 introduced Selective XML Indexes.

Selective XML indexes were added, not as an enhancement to the CREATE XML INDEX command, but as a new command CREATE SELECTIVE XML INDEX which uses a slightly different storage structure, rules, and capabilities. I would go a small step further and say that I believe the older XML indexes which index the entire document will eventually disappear from the product. It is very rare for an application to simply query the entire contents of an XML document, but instead to look at a small number of nodes. Selective XML indexes allow you to pull just the nodes you care about into the index, but also provide more targeted indexing of the documents. The selective XML index is just the starting point which defines the overall set of nodes you want included in the index. You can then specify up to 249 secondary XML indexes, based on the selective XML index, which index a single path in the document.

In SP1, support for selective XML indexes is limited to the exist(), value(), nodes(), query(), and modify() methods. However, selective XML indexes cannot be used to retrieve results for the query() method or update documents with the modify() method. You cannot index complex nodes such as union, sequence, and list or binary types such as base64 and hex encodings. You also can't index processing instructions, comments, or use the id() function to retrieve a node identifier. Path expressions have to be explicit and cannot contain a wildcard character at the end of the path expression.

Selective XML Index Storage

XML documents aren't simple linear arrangements of a flat set of data, but can have multiple levels of nesting. For example, you could have an order document which contains the following fragment:

```
<Order>
    <LineItem>
        <SKU>AA-A1</SKU>
        <Quantity>10</Quantity>
        <UnitPrice>2.30</UnitPrice>
    </LineItem>
    <LineItem>
        <SKU>AA-A2</SKU>
        <Quantity>10</Quantity>
        <UnitPrice>2.30</UnitPrice>
    </LineItem>
</Order>
```

What SQL Server does internally is turn the XML document into a relational table. Each node specified in the selective XML index definition becomes a column in the relational table. The table being indexed is required to have a primary key and the primary key must be clustered. The clustering key is propagated to the relational table in the same way as the clustering key is added to a nonclustered index to allow navigation from the nonclustered index to the associated row in the table. However, XML documents pose an additional challenge due to the possible nested structures. If you were to index the SKU, Quantity, and UnitPrice using a selective XML index, SQL Server would create a relational table with 3 columns corresponding to the 3 paths you were selectively indexing along with a column for each column in the clustered index of the table. But, you can't just take the 2 line items and stuff them into a single row in the table. The resulting table has to have 2 rows to store each of the line items. That requires an additional identifier to be added to the table to uniquely identify each row within the index.

Even though you are creating a selective XML index, the nodes are rendered as an internal table. That internal table has to uniquely identify every row. The only way SQL Server enforces uniqueness is to create a unique index. Indexes can only have a maximum of 16 columns. So, how do you handle a case where you are creating a selective XML index on a table with a 16 column primary key? The answer is that you can't, because it would force SQL Server to try to create a 17 column unique index on the resulting relational table. This is why a table with a selective XML index is limited to a maximum of 15 columns in the primary key and the size of the primary key is also limited to 128 bytes. Additionally, you can't index XML columns with documents containing more than 128 nested nodes simply because the internal identifiers used would cause the unique index to exceed the 900 byte limit on an index.

The fact that each path specified in the selective XML index becomes a column in the index table, places restrictions on the number of nodes which can be indexed. An XML schema can defined with nodes as required (not null) or optional (null). A table can only have a maximum of 1024 not null columns; therefore you can only specify a maximum of 1024 required nodes in the index. You can exceed this limit in the same way you can exceed the limit for a table. Optional nodes are added as sparse columns. However, internally a selective XML index can use between 1 and 4 columns for every node path which is indexed, further reducing the maximum number of nodes. Basically, it all boils down to being able to index between 60 and 200 nodes in a single selective XML index dependent upon the size of data in the indexed paths.

Since a selective XML index turns a portion of an XML document into a relational table, some of the other limitations should be fairly obvious. You can't combine multiple XML columns in a single selective XML index simply because it would create a nonsensical primary key structure in the index. You can't create a selective XML index on a column that is not an XML data type, even if the actual contents of the column is XML, because SQL Server isn't going to understand how to shred plain text into a table structure.

Creating a Selective XML Index

You use the following general syntax to create a selective XML index:

```
CREATE SELECTIVE XML INDEX index_name
  ON <table_object> (<xml_column_name>)
  [WITH XMLNAMESPACES (<xmlnamespace_list>)]
  FOR (<promoted_node_path_list>)
  [WITH (<index_options>)]
```

Creating a selective XML index on the ProductDescription column of the Products.Product table would look like the following:

```
CREATE SELECTIVE XML INDEX ixmlsp_ProductDescription ON Products.Product
(ProductDescription)
WITH XMLNAMESPACES ('urn:ChampionValleyPens-com:product:ProductDescription' AS CVP)
FOR (pathDrillBit1 = '/CVP:ProductDescription/CVP:DrillBit1',
     pathDrillBit2 = '/CVP:ProductDescription/CVP:DrillBit2',
     pathBushing = '/CVP:ProductDescription/CVP:Bushing',
     pathMandrel = '/CVP:ProductDescription/CVP:Mandrel',
     pathArbor = '/CVP:ProductDescription/CVP:Arbor');
```

As with all indexes, you give it a name and specify the table and column which the index is for. The WITH clause allows you to specify an XML namespace which simplifies the path expressions. The FOR clause is used to specify one or more paths to index. The first part of the path specification is the alias for the path, which will also become the name of the column within the relational table built for the index. The second part is the path specification to index.

Typing XML

Once you get past all of the sizing and nesting requirements, you run into another issue which might not be obvious at first. The issue is found buried in Books Online underneath a section on optimizing selective XML indexes. While you can get a benefit from a selective XML index, this particular issue, if overlooked can cost you as much as 90% of the benefit you could be getting.

XML documents are used to exchange data between systems because you get a structured set of data as well as a data definition. However, the data and the definition come as 2 separate documents. The XML schema is an independent document and the XML data is also an independent document. You have to put the two together, through an XML parser, in order to get the full power of XML. Without the XML schema all you really have is a bunch of character data within a structure and the XML data document does not have a reference to the XML schema which was used to generate it.

When a selective XML index is created, SQL Server creates a table. We learned in Chapter 5 that the column definitions have data types and nullability as required properties. The structure of the XML document provides the column names for the selective XML index, but where does the data type and nullability come from? The answer is those pieces of information come from the XML schema, which isn't stored with the XML data.

What if you don't have an XML schema? An XML document without a schema is referred to as untyped XML. If you create a selective XML index over untyped XML, SQL Server has to do something in order to create the relational table and load the data into the index. So, it falls back to the least common denominator – nullable, variable length strings. If your data isn't actually strings, SQL Server has to perform data type translation when querying the selective XML index, which impacts the performance of the index.

There are three way to solve this problem. The first method is to embed the XML schema into each XML document. XML schemas are separated in order to improve performance and reduce network bandwidth requirements. You can imagine how much bandwidth you would waste if you were exchanging hundreds, thousands, or more XML documents which all had the same schema and you embedded the schema into every XML document. The second solution is the best one for a database environment, use an XML schema collection to type the XML column. As we saw in chapter 5, the XML schema collection is used as a constraint to only allow XML documents to be stored for which you already understand the structure. The XML schema collection provides the data type information needed by the selective XML index to build an optimal index. The third solution is to embed the data type translations into the definition of the selective XML index.

> **SQL Types:** As I've stated throughout the book, you should always type your XML. This provides some level of predictability and prevents you from using SQL Server as a big XML garbage can. I even showed you how to make SQL Server generate an XML schema which can be added to an XML schema collection. This method of schema generation slams head first into a massive oversight by the SQL Server team in the initial implementation of selective XML indexes. SQL Server will dump an XML schema using SQL Server types. The SQL Server types are perfectly valid and recognized throughout all of the XML features in the engine….except selective XML indexes. Selective XML indexes have absolutely no support whatsoever for SQL types. You may actually stumble across a SQL Server type which works, but in my testing, it would not accept varchar, char, int, or decimal. Selective XML indexes only recognize native XML types found in the W3 XML schema. So, you have to convert your XML schema collections to use the base XML types in order to build a selective XML index over a typed XML column. Within the index creation statement, you can explicitly type cast untyped XML to a SQL Server type which makes the inability to use SQL Server types in an XML schema collection even more bizarre.

Index Optimizations

If you have untyped XML, you can still optimize the selective XML index by using the DATATYPE and MAXLENGTH options. These two options embed the data type information into the selective XML index definition. When you include type specifications, you include the AS XQUERY keywords followed by the data type you want to type cast the data to. For character data, you can also specify a maximum length. Data types can be either native XML types or SQL types, however, I would strongly recommend sticking with the native XML data types until SQL Server fully supports the SQL types. Below is an example of embedding type and length optimizations into the index definition.

```
CREATE SELECTIVE XML INDEX ixmlsp_ProductDescription ON Products.Product
(ProductDescription)
WITH XMLNAMESPACES ('urn:ChampionValleyPens-com:product:ProductDescription' AS PD)
FOR (pathDrillBit1 = '/PD:ProductDescription/PD:DrillBit1' AS XQUERY 'xs:string',
     pathDrillBit2 = '/PD:ProductDescription/PD:DrillBit2' AS XQUERY 'xs:string'
MAXLENGTH(10),
     pathBushing = '/PD:ProductDescription/PD:Bushing' AS SQL VARCHAR(10),
     pathMandrel = '/PD:ProductDescription/PD:Mandrel',
     pathArbor = '/PD:ProductDescription/PD:Arbor');
```

You can specify data type and length information for typed XML, but it really is a waste of time since you can't override the data type in the index definition. So, all you are really doing is making the definition of the selective XML index more complicated by repeating the type information from the schema collection. Additionally, SQL Server will give you an error message if you attempt to type cast in the index when the column is bound to an XML schema collection.

If the data in an XML document fails the type cast, SQL Server writes a NULL into the index. However, if you cause data to be truncated due to a MAXLENGTH being too small to accommodate all of the data, the index creation will fail. You are allowed to specify a path more than once in the FOR clause, but you can't specify the path more than once with the same data type. In some cases, a path may contain more than one type of data which you want to discretely index. You can include the path for each data type in the FOR clause. This is why a type case failure writes a NULL into the index.

You can apply two additional optimizations to a selective XML index.

The node() specification is used to satisfy those queries where all you care about is whether a value exists or not. When you include the node() specification, SQL Server will store the column using a BIT data type where 1 designates a value exists and 0 designates a value does not exist. Paths for node specifications can be used to satisfy queries which utilize the exists() method.

The SINGLETON keyword specifies that the path exists only once for a parent. When you index a path which has repeating children, such as the order line item example discussed earlier, a row has to be created in the index for each of the child elements. When you specify the SINGLETON keyword, SQL Server knows that only a single occurrence of the element exists for the specified path.

Enabling Selective XML Indexes

You've upgraded to SQL Server 2012 SP1 and are now ready to utilize selective XML indexes. Unfortunately, selective XML indexes are not available by default. You have to first enable selective XML indexes before you can use them, although the indexes will create and throw a 9539 error message. You enable selective XML indexes by executing the sys.sp_db_selective_xml_index stored procedure.

Exercise 8: Selectively Indexing Product Descriptions

The product descriptions for Champion Valley Pens are relatively small, element centric, nonvolatile documents. These documents are queried in a variety of ways. But, the queries are limited to searching on the drill bits, bushing, mandrel, and arbor. In the following exercise, we will create the selective XML indexes which can improve performance of a variety of queries.

1. Execute the following command to enable selective XML indexes on the Champion Valley Pens database.

    ```
    EXECUTE sys.sp_db_selective_xml_index ChampionValleyPens, TRUE;
    ```

2. We typed the ProductDescription column using an XML schema collection, but the XML schema was defined using SQL Server types which are currently incompatible with selective XML indexes. Execute the script Products.ProductDescriptionNative.XML Schema Collection.sql in the chapter 12 companion files to create a new XML schema collection using native types.

3. Execute the following code to drop our existing XML indexes because we are going to replace them with selective XML indexes.

    ```
    DROP INDEX ixmlv_ProductDescription ON Products.Product;
    DROP INDEX ixmlp_ProductDescription ON Products.Product;
    DROP INDEX ipxml_ProductDescription ON Products.Product;
    ```

4. Execute the following code to change the XML schema collection binding on the ProductDescription column and then drop the old schema collection since it isn't used anymore.
```
ALTER TABLE Products.Product
    ALTER COLUMN ProductDescription XML (Products.ProductDescriptionNative);

DROP XML SCHEMA COLLECTION Products.ProductDescription;
```
5. Execute the following code to create the selective XML index. We are indexing the 5 nodes for both filtering by value as well as existence checking. If you specify a node more than once and use the SINGLETON optimization, it has to be specified for all occurrences of the node.
```
CREATE SELECTIVE XML INDEX ixmlsp_ProductDescription ON Products.Product
(ProductDescription)
WITH XMLNAMESPACES ('urn:ChampionValleyPens-com:product:ProductDescription' AS CVP)
FOR (pathDrillBit1 = '/CVP:ProductDescription/CVP:DrillBit1' AS XQUERY SINGLETON,
     pathDrillBit2 = '/CVP:ProductDescription/CVP:DrillBit2' AS XQUERY SINGLETON,
     pathBushing = '/CVP:ProductDescription/CVP:Bushing' AS XQUERY SINGLETON,
     pathMandrel = '/CVP:ProductDescription/CVP:Mandrel' AS XQUERY SINGLETON,
     pathArbor = '/CVP:ProductDescription/CVP:Arbor' AS XQUERY SINGLETON,
     pathDrillBit1Exists = '/CVP:ProductDescription/CVP:DrillBit1' AS XQUERY 'node()'
SINGLETON,
     pathDrillBit2Exists = '/CVP:ProductDescription/CVP:DrillBit2' AS XQUERY 'node()'
SINGLETON,
     pathBushingExists = '/CVP:ProductDescription/CVP:Bushing' AS XQUERY 'node()'
SINGLETON,
     pathMandrelExists = '/CVP:ProductDescription/CVP:Mandrel' AS XQUERY 'node()'
SINGLETON,
     pathArborExists = '/CVP:ProductDescription/CVP:Arbor' AS XQUERY 'node()'
SINGLETON);
```
6. Execute the following code to create secondary XML indexes for improved performance on each of the filtering columns.
```
CREATE XML INDEX ixmls_ProductDescription_DrillBit1 ON
Products.Product(ProductDescription)
USING XML INDEX ixmlsp_ProductDescription
FOR (pathDrillBit1);

CREATE XML INDEX ixmls_ProductDescription_DrillBit2 ON
Products.Product(ProductDescription)
USING XML INDEX ixmlsp_ProductDescription
FOR (pathDrillBit2);

CREATE XML INDEX ixmls_ProductDescription_Bushing ON
Products.Product(ProductDescription)
USING XML INDEX ixmlsp_ProductDescription
FOR (pathBushing);

CREATE XML INDEX ixmls_ProductDescription_Mandrel ON
Products.Product(ProductDescription)
USING XML INDEX ixmlsp_ProductDescription
FOR (pathMandrel);

CREATE XML INDEX ixmls_ProductDescription_Arbor ON
Products.Product(ProductDescription)
USING XML INDEX ixmlsp_ProductDescription
FOR (pathArbor);
```

Spatial Indexes

Since we've discussed indexing just about every type of data you can store in SQL Server, it should come as no surprise that you can also index spatial data. The way you index non-spatial data should be relatively logical, after all, we've been indexing numbers and words for millennia. Hopefully by the time you reached the end of chapter 11, querying spatial objects and making comparisons is no longer an obtuse subject. But, just what in the heck does it mean to index an object?

At the core of any index is the principle of location. We use clustered and nonclustered indexes to locate rows in a table and XML indexes to locate nodes or values within an XML document. You index spatial data by using the same core principle of location. In the case of a spatial object, you need to be able to locate each object in relation to every other object within a spatial reference frame. The method used, called tessellation, has been around for millennia.

Tessellation is simply the process of filling a 2 dimensional space with a repeating geometric object with no gaps or overlaps. If you think tessellation is some kind of new mathematical construct invented for indexing spatial data, you've missed the repeating point throughout this book. Tessellation is not new and has been around since before modern humans ever walked the earth. One of the earliest examples of tessellation, which I know about, comes from nature around 100 million years ago with bees. It isn't known when the familiar honeycomb was first used to build nests by the ancient ancestors of bees and wasps, because people weren't around to document it.

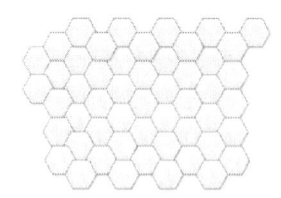

Figure 12-3 Honeycomb – a tessellation using hexagons

Tessellation was also used in ancient Moorish architecture and turned into an art which endures today in the works of M.C. Escher. SQL Server is quite a bit more boring than the wonderful Moorish designs or the impossible, tessellated drawings of Escher. SQL Server uses a simple grid.

The tessellation can be specified created in one of three allowed grid configurations: 4x4, 8x8, and 16x16. Each of the grid configurations have a standard alias where 4x4 = LOW, 8x8 = MEDIUM, and 16x16 = HIGH. Once you have a grid, it is a simple process of numbering each grid cell, overlaying your spatial object with the grid, and building a list of the cell numbers that contains a piece of your spatial object.

You might see a bit of an issue with these 3 grid configurations with respect to creating an index. Even a 16x16 grid isn't going to be very accurate. A 16x16 grid subdividing a square nanometer would be would be extremely accurate for indexing a football, but completely worthless if that same 16x16 grid subdivided a square mile. SQL Server solves this problem by utilizing 4 tessellation levels and allowing you to specify the cell density at each level. Even if you were to use the lowest density, 4x4 grids for all 4 levels, you would have 69,907 cells with which to locate your spatial object. A high density grid at each level would give you a whopping 4, 311,810,304 cells. Of course the time to compute the index increases as the density of the cells at each level increases. The figure below shows how a 4 level, tessellation using 4x4 grids works.

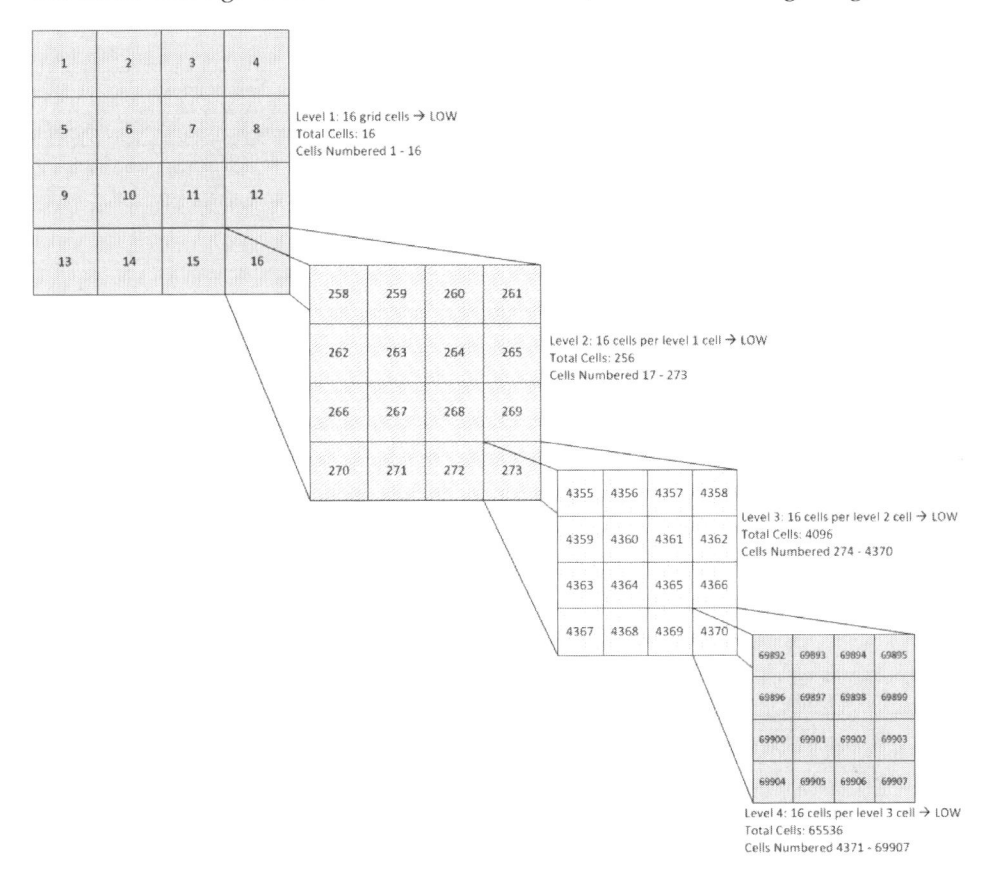

Figure 12-4 Tessellated 4x4 grid

The figure above might give the impression of the tessellation being 3 dimensional. Each of the levels is simply an explosion of the contents of one of the cells. Each cell, at every level except the final level contains a complete 4x4 grid inside it. So, each of the 16 cells in level 1 would be subdivided by 16 cells **per cell** at the second level bringing the number of level 2 cells to 256 and the total number of cells to 273. Each of the 256 cells in the second level would be subdivided into 16 cells **per cell** at the 3rd level making 4096 cells on level 3 and bringing the total number of cells to 4370. Each of the 4096 cells on the 3rd level would be subdivided into 16 cells **per cell** making 65536 cells on the 4th level and bringing the total number of cells to 69907. So even with a setting of LOW at all 4 levels, you can get a reasonable degree of accuracy in the index.

Since a spatial index can be applied to both geometry and geography data, SQL Server also has to deal with how to apply a tessellation to an ellipsoid used with all geographic data. As we saw in chapter 11, all lines on an ellipsoid are arcs and it would be impossible to apply a tessellation to an ellipsoid with cells of uniform size since the ellipsoid causes the grid to curve. Before applying a tessellation, SQL Server first converts the reference ellipsoid to a flat representation. The conversion is accomplished by first dividing the ellipsoid into hemispheres at the equator. Each hemisphere is then projected onto a quadrilateral pyramid. The two quadrilateral pyramids are smashed into a 2 dimensional plane and the two planes are then joined at the edge. A picture showing how this is accomplished would be nice, but it would exceed my artistic capabilities which stop at drawing stick figures. Instead I'll refer you to Books Online which has a decent graphical representation of this process.

The cell numbering scheme shown in Figure 12-4 is just a basic example. Another numbering approach uses a dotted notation for cells based on the level of the cell. Given a 4x4 grid, the lowest level cells would be numbered from 1 through 16. Within cell 1, the 16 cells for level 2 would be numbered 1.1 through 1.16. Within the 16 cells on level 3 within cell 1.1, the numbering scheme would be 1.1.1 through 1.1.16. Within the 16 cells on level 4 within cell 1.1.1, the numbering scheme would be 1.1.1.1 through 1.1.1.16. After studying hierarchies and indexes for the HIERARCHYID data type, it should be obvious why this type of numbering scheme can allow you to quickly locate objects based on proximity. This type of notation should also be familiar from IP address schemes. The actual numbering scheme used by SQL Server is a variation of the Hilbert space filling algorithm which would roughly approximate to the dotted numbering notation discussed above.

Tessellating Objects

After laying out the grid, SQL Server performs a tessellation process. The tessellation process maps the spatial object to the grid and records all of the cells that are touched by the object. For very small objects, the number of cells can be quite small whereas the number of cells for a large object can be quite extensive. While we want very accurate indexes, a perfectly accurate index could be extremely large and hence very slow. We build indexes to improve performance, so having a spatial index that can be as large as or possibly larger than the spatial object being indexed is counter-productive.

In order to limit the amount of space required for a spatial index, SQL Server applies three rules – covering, cells per object, and deepest cell.

Cells Per Object

The CELLS_PER_OBJECT is a configuration option you can specify for a spatial index, with a default of 16. You can specify a value between 1 and 8192. The CELLS_PER_OBJECT will limit the number of cells which are recorded for each spatial object in the index while still maintaining the best approximation of the object being indexed. CELLS_PER_OBJECT only applies to levels 2 through 4 of the tessellation. SQL Server will store as many level 1 cells as necessary to encompass the object, regardless of the limit you configure for the spatial index.

Covering

If the object completely covers a cell, the cell is considered to be covered. Covered cells are recorded for the index, but the cell is not further tessellated. The tessellation process within SQL Server is intelligent based on the object being indexed. Only the levels and cells necessary to compute the index will be created. If an object does not touch or cover a level 1 cell, none of the level 2 – 4 cells are even created for the untouched cells. You can think of the tessellation process as a sequential layering of successively smaller grid cells that stops either when the entire object is exactly mapped or you reach the 4th level of tessellation. Consider the following example:

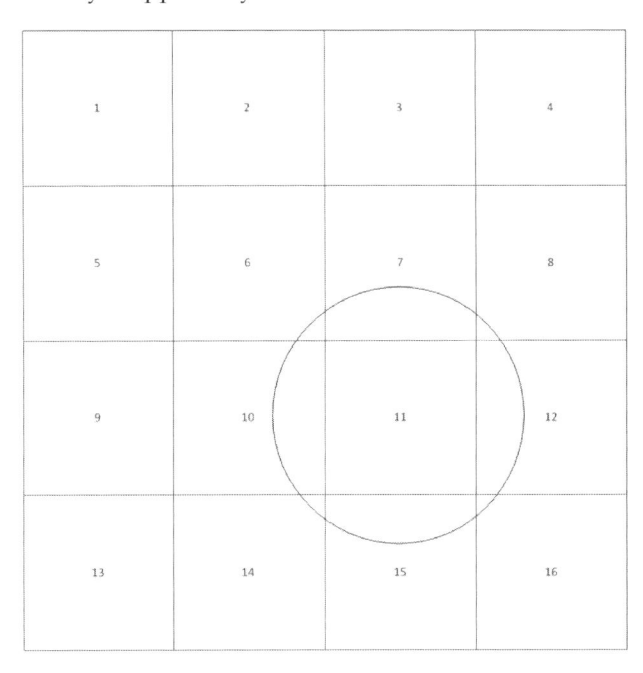

Figure 12-5 Covering Rule

Since the circle does not touch cells 1, 2, 3, 4, 5, 9, and 13, SQL Server does not compute the 2nd through 4th levels of the tessellation for those cells. Additionally, you can see that cell 11 is completely covered by the object. SQL Server will record cell 11 in the index, but will not further tessellate cell 11 since it would be pointless bloat in the index. If the object completely covers cell 11 at level 1, it will completely cover every cell at levels 2 – 4 tessellated within cell 11.

However, since cells 6, 7, 8, 10, 12, 14, 15, and 16 are only partially covered by the object, each of these cells will be tessellated to level 2 where the process will be applied again. Any cells on level 2 which are not touched by the object will be ignored and not tessellated any further. Any cells completely covered by the object will be recorded and not further tessellated. This process will continue through level 4 or until the CELLS_PER_OBJECT limit has been reached, whichever comes first.

The CELLS_PER_OBJECT also affects whether tessellation occurs. Even though cell 7 is partially covered on level 1 and a level 2 tessellation will be computed, if the number of cells recorded to the index when the level 2 tessellation of cell 7 is computed exceeds the CELLS_PER_OBJECT parameter, SQL Server will record cell 7 and not any of the level 2 tessellations of cell 7.

Deepest Cell

The deepest cell rule takes advantage of the hierarchical nature of the grid numbering system used within SQL Server. Under the deepest cell rule, only the deepest cells necessary to tessellate the object will be recorded. The 4th level cell at 1.4.12.7 is contained within the 3rd level cell at 1.4.12

which is contained within the 2nd level cell at 1.4 which is contained within the 1st level cell at 1. Therefore if an object is tessellated to the 4th level and is contained within cell 1.4.12.7, this is the only cell SQL Server will record within the index since recording any of the lower level cells is redundant under the numbering scheme used for spatial indexes.

Primary Key

Like we saw with an XML index, spatial indexes can only be created on tables that already have a clustered primary key. When the set of grid cells are computed by the tessellation process, the set of cells along with the clustering key are added to the spatial index. This allows you to search the spatial index while also having the ability to link back to the table to retrieve the spatial object.

Geometry Indexes

Spatial objects are indexed using tessellation. Tessellation is a process of repeating a geometric shape without overlaps or gaps such that it fills the entire area. Geometry objects are plotted against a 2 dimensional plane. So, how are you ever going to compute an index on a geometry data type whose objects are defined on an infinite plane? You certainly can't tessellate to infinity.

In order to get around this problem, one of the required options when you specify that you want the spatial index created for a geometry grid is a bounding box. A bounding box has 4 values – x_{min}, y_{min}, x_{max}, and y_{max}. SQL Server computes the tessellation for the spatial index within the bounding box specified. If an object lies outside of the bounding box, it will not be indexed. If an object lies partially outside the bounding box, only the portion within the bounding box will be indexed.

Supported Spatial Methods

Spatial indexes are also unique in the fact that an index won't improve the performance of every spatial query accessing a geometry or geography column. A small subset of spatial methods can utilize a two stage filter process. The spatial index allows a primary filter to be applied to reduce the set of rows for the method to operate on. Using just the spatial index can lead to false positives since the tessellation only produces a rough approximation of the space covered by the object. Once the set of rows to consider is reduced by the spatial index, a secondary filter is applied by executing the spatial method against each of the potential rows in order to obtain an exact match to the query.

> **Caution:** Spatial indexes behave unlike any other index. While you should always test your applications for improvements when creating indexes, testing is critical for spatial indexes. The same query using a spatial index can perform extremely well in one case and very poorly in another case. All other indexes improve performance slightly when you have very small data sets and really begin to shine when your data volumes get very large. Spatial indexes have the opposite performance curve. Spatial indexes are most useful against small, highly selective data sets. As the size of the data set increases, the performance when using a spatial index will generally decrease to the point where it would take less effort to simply compute the spatial method against every row in a table instead of using the index. A spatial index might be helpful for finding customers in the state of Texas, but would probably perform much worse than a table scan if you wanted all customers west of the Mississippi River.

Filter()

The filter method, available for both geometry and geography, is a specialized implementation of STIntersects(). When a spatial index exists, Filter() will use the index to produce a result set where one geometry instance possibly intersects another geometry instance. The approximation results by determining if any cells from the tessellation process are common between the two instances. However, it does not mean the two instances actually intersect.

If a spatial index does not exist, Filter() will simply scan all rows in the table and produce the same result set as STIntersects().

You will most commonly use Filter() with proximity searches when an index is present such as finding the nearest Starbucks, the closest hospital, or determining if a customer is within the delivery area of your pizza business. For example, you could use the following query to find the closest Starbucks within 3km of a specified location.

```
DECLARE @MyLocation    GEOGRAPHY;

SET @MyLocation = 'Your GPS coordinates';

WITH Starbucks_CTE (AddressLine1, City, Distance)
AS
(SELECT AddressLine1, City, Location.STDistance(@MyLocation)
FROM Spatial.Starbucks
WHERE Location.Filter(@MyLocation.STBuffer(3000)) = 1)
SELECT TOP 1 *
FROM Starbucks_CTE
ORDER BY Distance;
```

Geometry

Geometry data supports spatial index usage for STContains, STDistance, STEquals, STIntersects, STOverlaps, STTouches, and STWithin. For all of the supported methods, except STDistance, an index will only be used if the WHERE clause uses the spatial method in the following *precise* form: geom1.method(geom2) = 1. STDistance only supports < and <= if you want a spatial index to be used.

If you were to specify WHERE geom1.STDistance(geom2) <= 30 the spatial index would be used, but would not if you specified WHERE 30 >= geom1.STDistance(geom2) even though the two WHERE clauses produce the same result. Likewise WHERE geom1.STContains(geom2) = 1 would use a spatial index, but WHERE 1 = geom1.STContains(geom2) would not use a spatial index.

Geography

Geography data only supports STIntersects, STEquals, and STDistance with the same restrictions on the specification of the WHERE clause as a geometry data type.

Exercise 9: Creating Spatial Indexes

In order to customize the Champion Valley Pens catalog with local events, they need to be able to retrieve a list of customers within 100 miles of a wood turning event. The 100 mile radius only needs to be a rough approximation. The manufacturing department also needs to be able to compare parts in order to determine if substitutions can be made for new kits with previously designed parts. The majority of parts are 12 inches or less in length or width.

1. Execute the following command to create a geometry spatial index to improve search performance when the manufacturing department compares parts.

   ```
   ALTER TABLE Manufacturing.Geometry
       DROP CONSTRAINT pk_Geometry;
   GO
   ALTER TABLE Manufacturing.Geometry ADD CONSTRAINT
       pk_Geometry PRIMARY KEY CLUSTERED (SliceID);
   GO
   CREATE SPATIAL INDEX is_SliceShape ON Manufacturing.Geometry(SliceShape)
       USING GEOMETRY_GRID
       WITH (BOUNDING_BOX = ( xmin=0, ymin=0, xmax=12, ymax=12),
       GRIDS = (LOW, MEDIUM, MEDIUM, HIGH),
       CELLS_PER_OBJECT = 64);
   ```

   > **Clustered Primary Key:** We first had to drop and recreate the primary key, because it was initially created as nonclustered. In order to create a spatial index, the primary key is required to be clustered.

2. Execute the following command to create a geography spatial index to facilitate proximity queries for the catalog.

   ```
   CREATE SPATIAL INDEX is_Location ON Customers.Address(Location)
   USING GEOGRAPHY_GRID
   WITH (GRIDS = (LOW, LOW, LOW, MEDIUM),
       CELLS_PER_OBJECT = 4);
   ```

All of the customer locations are point objects and as such, shouldn't require more than 1 tessellation cell in the index. The radius only needs to be a rough approximation, so a value of LOW was specified for the first three levels and medium for the 4th level of the tessellation. The CELLS_PER_OBJECT was set to 4 just to get the index to compute through all 4 levels of the tessellation. A value of 2 would probably have been sufficient, but we could exceed that number if we had a point right on the boundary of 2 tessellation cells, so we chose 4 since it would be much harder to have a single point object lie on the boundary of more than one cell multiple times. We want the index to compute to all 4 levels so that the Earth's surface will be divided into about 265,000 cells. If we specified a value of 1 for the CELLS_PER_OBJECT, SQL Server would stop tessellating at the first level and each point object would be located within one of 16 cells dividing the surface of the Earth, which would be completely useless.

Indexes and the Optimizer

"There are three kinds of lies: lies, damned lies, and statistics."
-Mark Twain

With two exceptions, which we will get to shortly, we have covered the details about indexes in SQL Server. We've explained how indexes are created, the values stored in indexes, what types of indexes can be created, the rules behind the creation of indexes, and how indexes relate to each other. We've further explained how indexes are stored, why most indexes are constructed as B-trees (or B+ trees in SQL Server's case), and how SQL Server navigates indexes. We've even provided a set of rules for creating optimal indexes. To take a phrase from Sebastian, we've measured, counted, quantified, labelled, and categorized indexes, but we've still failed to answer the really important question.

The Vorlons say – "Who are you?" The Shadows say – "What do you want?" The equally "dangerous" question posed by Lorien – "Why are you here?" All of these boil down to THE question posed by children millions of times a day throughout the world, you know the question, the question which most people unfortunately seem to forget as they grow older and get more education.

I mentioned earlier that in the many years of my standard US education finishing out at the University of Illinois, I only learned 2 really important things. The first was something said to me by Mr Harshbarger after one of my Calculus classes in high school which I mentioned earlier in this book. The second:

"The uneducated accomplish the impossible every day, because they don't know any better."
-Unknown, a caption on a poster of Einstein in my physics advisor's office

It's the fundamental question that I constantly challenge everyone with who attends my classes, sessions, seminars. It's the fundamental question that I challenge everyone with that ever works with me. It's the fundamental question that I challenge everyone with who reads any of my books. WHY? How many times have you heard that? WHY? BUT, WHY? If you just want to memorize a bunch of stuff, that's why they write Books Online and what many of the other books on the market do – "Here's the information, memorize it, and go use it." You can create indexes. Why? Indexes improve performance. Why? SQL Server uses indexes to provide an optimal path to the data you want. Why? Because SQL Server can use the B-tree structure of an index to quickly locate your data. How? Oooooo!

It's great that we have indexes which SQL Server can use to improve the performance of queries, but WHY would it use an index and HOW does it determine whether an index should be used?

"The answers to the repeated use of HOW and WHY leads us to understand."
-Mike Hotek

SQL Server or more specifically, the Query Optimizer; doesn't just randomly select indexes to use to satisfy queries. SQL Server also doesn't just grab an index it finds where the first column of the index matches a WHERE or * JOIN condition. If you had two indexes, the first index on the LastName and City and the second index on the LastName and FirstName, and your query had a WHERE criteria of LastName and StateProvince, how is SQL Server going to know which index to use or whether to use an index at all? The Query Optimizer is tasked with finding the optimal path through the data which means minimizing the resources and number of operations required, which almost always leads to less time to execute the query. In this case, HOW can it determine the optimal path?

One valid way of determining the optimal path is to simply choose one at random, measure how long it takes to find the data, and store the knowledge gained. The next time the same query comes through, a different path could be chosen and the results for the resources consumed could be stored. You could repeat this until all possible paths have been investigated and from that point forward, the Query Optimizer would know which path was the most efficient and always select that path. While a perfectly valid methodology, it has several potential problems:

- The response time of queries could be wildly unpredictable
- It might take days, weeks, or even years to exhaust all of the possible paths
- It would take an infinite amount of time to investigate all of the paths for every possible filter criteria
- The data in the table could have changed thereby invalidating all of the knowledge gained
- The most efficient path might no longer exist due to changes in the structure of the table
- The most efficient path might no longer exist due to changes in the index structure

If logging the results of random choice doesn't work, SQL Server needs a more stable and predictable method for computing the most efficient query path. To meet the stable and predictable requirement, the information logged has to be the same size for every index so that it always takes the same amount of time to check each index to determine if it provides an optimal path. In order to compute an efficient query path, SQL Server needs to understand one basic metric –the percentage of each table a given query is going to need to access. The number of rows in a table or index along with the number of pages required to store the data is already stored and maintained in sys.sysindexes. This can give the divisor in the percentage calculation, but it can't provide a numerator. In order to provide a numerator, SQL Server needs to utilize a statistical sampling method; hence each index has an object behind it called distribution statistics.

Distribution Statistics

There are two methods to retrieve the values which are used to create statistics. The first and most obvious is to simply read all of the values from the table. The second method is to read a random sample of the data and use the random sample to interpolate the existence and quantity of a value. Reading all values produces the most accurate set of statistics, but is the slowest. Sampling the values produces less accurate statistics, but performs much better. When you create an index, SQL Server has to read all of the values in order to build the index, so statistics computed for an index are always built from all of the values.

So, if statistics for an index are always built by reading all values, why even discuss sampling data? While every index has a statistics object attached to it, you can also create standalone statistics on one or more columns which are not associated to an index. Regardless of whether the statistics are created for an index or as standalone, all of the definitions and rules are the same.

Density

When you compute distribution statistics, the primary concern is with distinct values. By capturing how many times a given value occurs, you can understand how much of a table you will need to read if your query was filtered by the value. For example, if you are building an index on the CustomerID column in the Customers.Customer table, you know that each value only occurs once since this is the primary key. That means any query specifying a CustomerID will select 1/999706 or approximately 0.00001% of the table. This value is also referred to as the density, which is computed as 1/(number of distinct values).

SQL Server tracks 2 types of density values for each statistics object. The value computed as 1/(number of distinct values) is actually named All_density by SQL Server within the statistics object. The density will be discussed in the next section.

You can create single column statistics or multicolumn statistics. When you create multicolumn statistics, SQL Server stores an All_density value for each prefix combination of columns. That is not the same as storing an All_density value for all combinations of columns defined for the statistics object. A prefix combination is obtained by successively adding the next column in the definition to create the computation. For example if you were to create a statistics object on the Customers.Customer table consisting of the CustomerID, FirstName, and LastName in that order, SQL Server would store 3 sets of All_density values – CustomerID, CustomerID + FirstName, and CustomerID + FirstName + LastName.

While density information can give you a basic idea for the selectivity, it is a single value computed for the entire table. When you are querying on any kind of unique index, the density information is all you really need, because SQL Server can easily see from a single density value that any query specifying a single value is highly selective, returning only a single row from the table. But, the majority of the indexes you will create to improve the performance of queries will not be unique.

While the density information provides a piece of the puzzle for a non-unique index, it can't be relied on by itself. For example, what if you stored the gender in the Customers.Customer table and were going to return a list of all of the female customers for some special promotion? The gender column is nullable, so it can store 3 values – Male, Female, and NULL. That means the density is 1/3 or 0.333333. So, would using an index defined on the gender column be useful? The answer is that you really don't know just from the density information. If there were only 82 female customers out of 999,706 total customers, the index would be extremely useful. But, if there were 998,462 female customers, the index would be useless and simply acquiring a table lock and reading every row would be more efficient. To solve this dilemma, SQL Server stores one more item in every statistics object, a histogram.

Histograms

Histograms are one of the core constructs in the field of statistics, both of which are credited to Karl Pearson right at the turn of the 20th century. At the most basic level, histograms provide an extremely compact way to represent the probability of the occurrence of a given value within a continuous range of values. The usual method is to plot the relative density of values on a graph whose area is normalized to 1. The graph is irrelevant to a computer, so SQL Server stores the values behind the graph, which is then called a histogram.

This is a really nice explanation of what a histogram is while also being utterly useless.

SQL Server computes histograms, because a histogram is extremely small even for very large sets of data. By being small, SQL Server has to perform very little work to read the histogram and determine if an efficient path has been found. While being very compact, a histogram also has to be able to represent the entire range of values in a set of data. A histogram also has to provide a positive hit for any value it is interrogated for. What the Query Optimizer is trying to answer with a histogram is how many rows in a table match a given value. A histogram plots a continuous range of values so that the Query Optimizer also receives a value for the number of rows which match a given value, even if the specified value never occurred in the data set or was not encountered when using a sampling method.

A continuous range, by definition, is infinite. SQL Server has to be able to store something in order to compute the probability of any given value and you can't store an infinite set of values. One of the core methods in statistics, which are the basis of histograms, is a methodology referred to as bucketing, binning, or discretization. Bucketing is simply defining a set of discrete values which are used to chop any data range into a set of buckets. When constructing a histogram, each of these buckets is plotted along the x axis, forming a series of blocks. On the y axis, you plot the number of values from the data set which belong to the specified bucket. Since the buckets are created without any gaps or overlaps, every value belongs to one and only one bucket. From there, you simply compute how many distinct values are within a given bucket as well as how many total values are in a given bucket to determine the probability for the occurrence of any specified value within the bucket.

The field of statistics has many equations to compute the size of each bucket, with no method superior to any other. When we refer to the size of a bucket, we mean the difference in the high and low value that the bucket cuts the data set into. You could simply divide the set of data into n equally sized buckets. You could divide the set of data into n buckets with each successive bucket being 50% larger than the previous bucket. You could make each successive bucket 50% smaller than the previous bucket. You could simply throw a random number generator and each successive bucket is a random amount larger or smaller than the previous bucket. It really doesn't matter how you compute your buckets only that your bucket size doesn't obscure important variations in the data. One equation for computing bucket sizes works best in some cases and not as well in others. What you are really after is finding a way to minimize the number of buckets you need to classify the data while still being able to accurately describe the relative distribution of all values in the data set you are considering. Figure 12-6 shows two examples of a histogram with the first using an equal buckets methodology and the other using a non-equal methodology.

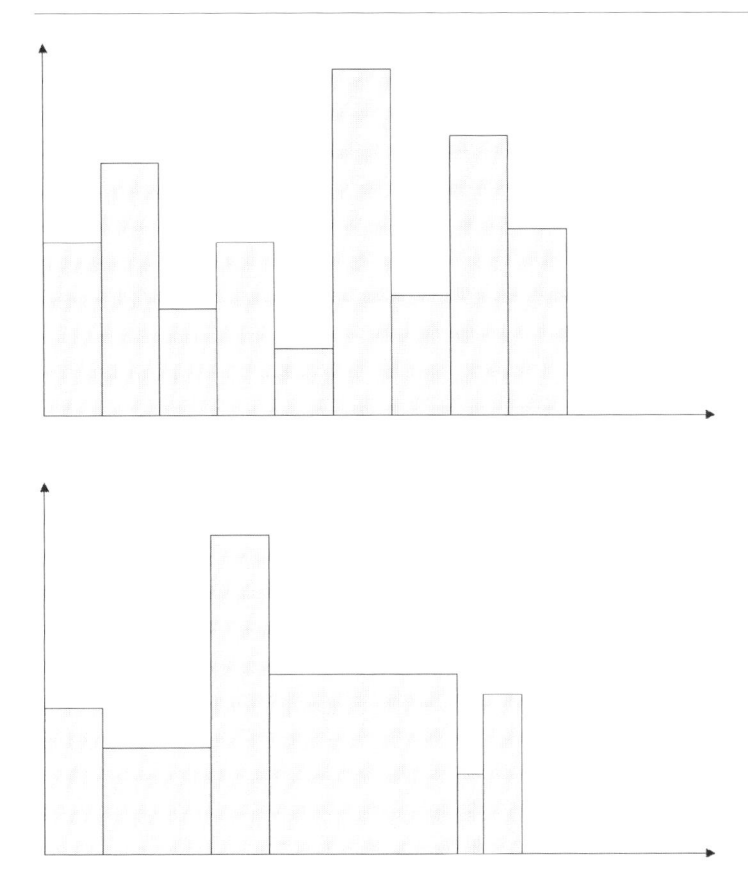

Figure 12-6: Histograms

The reason why the exact mechanics of computing the number buckets used for a histogram are not that important is because as long as the bucket methodology you choose doesn't obscure important features of the data, you can use any number. For example, if you had 1,000 unique integers, you could use 1 bucket with all 1000 values, 100 buckets with 10 values each, 500 buckets with 2 values each, 1000 buckets with 1 value each, or a variety of other bucket sizes. Every bucket size will produce the same understanding from the histogram, that of 1,000 unique values. However, if you had 999 unique integers along with 10,000 values of the number 500, you would have to be more careful. If you were to use a single bucket, you would have 10,999 values in a single bucket and the histogram would lead you to believe that each value represented 0.1% of the data set. That would lead you to believe that any value in the set occurs approximately 11 times, which is clearly false. If you were instead to use 3 buckets with the first bucket going from 0 to 499, the second bucket for 500, and the third bucket for 501 – 999, you would achieve an accurate representation of the data. The first and third buckets in this case could be subdivided into as many buckets as you wanted without losing information about the data set as long as a single bucket for the value 500 was maintained.

To compute a histogram, SQL Server uses a variation on the maxdiff methodology with a maximum of 200 buckets, also called steps, which works well enough to predict data distribution within a table.

Earlier in this chapter, we explained that SQL Server will only use an index if the first column of the index appears in the query. You might have found that statement to be a little strange and you should have been asking WHY? For every index, SQL Server builds a statistics object. Each statistics object contains a histogram which is used by the Optimizer to obtain a value which can be used to estimate the number of rows in a table which match a given query criteria. SQL Server builds a histogram based on the first column of the statistics object. The Optimizer can't consider an index if the first column is not specified in the query, because the histogram doesn't contain information on any other column in the statistics object.

Creating a Histogram

The generation of a histogram occurs in multiple stages. You first need to retrieve a set of values for the first column of the statistics object. During the creation of an index, the first stage is accomplished as part of building the index since all values need to be retrieved in order to create the B-tree structure. When creating a statistics object the first stage is a bit more complicated.

Sampling

One of the options for creating statistics is to specify a sampling value and method.

The biggest challenge when using a sampling setting is to sample just enough data to obtain accurate enough statistics. If you sample more data that you really need to in order to predict the distribution of the data, you have wasted resources. If you don't sample enough data to capture all of the patterns in the data, you can have statistics which predict accurately for some values are inaccurately for other values. Without accurate statistics, the Query Optimizer can choose a poorly performing method to satisfy a given query.

In order to build useful statistics when using a sampling methodology, you need to be able to build a subset that will represent the entire set of data such that accurate extrapolations can be made. To understand how to do this, let's take a page from the book of political polling. How do these pollsters make predictions on the outcome of a political race when they are only asking 500, 600, or 1000 people? Surely the opinions of 1000 people in Texas can't accurately predict the opinion of the 26 million Texas voters. When you are talking about a political race, each person polled usually only has 2 or 3 choices. If you were to poll 1,000 people on their choice for President of the United States and 500 said they were going to vote for Wakko Warner, 482 said they were going to vote for Escrow the crow, 16 said they were going to vote for Sue the T-Rex, and 2 were undecided, you might be able to predict that Wakko and Escrow were essentially tied and Sue was out of the race.

But, the accuracy of your prediction would depend on your sampling methodology. If I simply started on Collins Street in Arlington, TX, walked down the street knocking on every door to ask their opinion until I had asked 1000 people, I would have a set of statistics that would be accurate to predict how the people who live on Collins Street in Arlington, TX are going to vote. In order to be able to have statistics that can predict the result for the entire state of Texas, I need to do a much better job sampling. If instead I were to take the names of all 26 million Texas residents and toss them into a great big hat, it would have to be a 10 gallon hat like Yosemite Sam wore, and select out 1000 random names, I would be able to provide a much better prediction as long as those 1000 random people covered every property that I found useful in classifying them such as whether they are right handed, have hair or not, if they are a member of an extinct species, or wear baseball caps. If I had 10 classification categories and could put 100 random people spread across the state into each category, I would then have 100 opinions on 3 choices for each of my demographic categories. If the results on the polling for this random sample were 468 votes for Wakko, 481 votes for Escrow, and 51 votes for Sue, I would be able to make a much more accurate prediction.

When SQL Server samples the data in a table to produce statistics, it needs to randomly sample the data in an attempt to understand the general patterns. Just like in our political poll, if the number of data values is very small, it takes a very small sample to accurately make a prediction. If the number of data values is very large, it will require a larger sample size. After all, if you had 1000 choices and only asked 1000 people who they were voting for, it would be impossible to make any predictions since you can easily miss a pattern. This is why the default sampling method for SQL Server uses an algorithm where the sample size grows as the size of the table grows. For those who want a more complete treatment of sampling, I'll simply direct you to Amazon and the stack of books on statistics and polling methodologies.

When political or a wide variety of other polls are conducted, a very small sample is taken within dozens or even hundreds of different demographic classifications. This is done to be able to extrapolate results while using an extremely small sample size. SQL Server doesn't have demographics to categorize the data that is used to generate the statistics you define. Instead, SQL Server simply uses a much larger sample size to generate the statistics.

When you create a statistics object, you can use one of four options – FULLSCAN, sample by number of rows, sample by percentage of pages, or the default sample algorithm. FULLSCAN is the method used when creating statistics for an index, because a FULLSCAN builds the histogram based on reading every value. When you sample by percentage of pages, SQL Server selects every nth page starting at the beginning of the table and retrieves every value on the page. When you sample by number of rows, SQL Server retrieves the number of rows specified. Both percent of pages and number of rows are approximations and SQL Server may retrieve slightly more data than was specified. If you don't specify FULLSCAN or a SAMPLE value, SQL Server uses a default, unpublished algorithm. The default sampling algorithm uses a slowly growing function such that as the size of the table increases, the number of sample values also increases although the number of sample values does not increase as rapidly as the size of the table. In every case, SQL Server will always sample at least 8MB or 1024 pages of data, regardless of the sample setting.

The challenge SQL Server has in sampling data is that in order to produce the best random sample, it has to ignore or attempt to factor out structure that you have imposed on the database. When you create a clustered index on a table, you sort the data. If SQL Server just started at the beginning on the sorted table and read every n^{th} page, the sampling methodology wouldn't be any better than the example where we simply walked down Collins St. in Arlington, TX and used those results to try to extrapolate for the entire state of Texas. SQL Server explicitly ignores clustered indexes when using a sampling method to retrieve values such that your imposed sort order can't skew the results.

Buckets

Once SQL Server has completed the first stage, retrieving the values to build the histogram, the second stage sorts the data set and begins the process of assigning the data to buckets. To give you an idea of how the histogram is built, we'll use a very basic example with a very basic bucket assignment method.

Let's take the CustomerID column from the Customers.Customer table and use a full scan of the data. This results in 999,706 values. The values are sorted in ascending order starting at 1 and finishing at 1,000,000. The first 199 unique values are read with each unique value assigned to its own bucket. You now have 199 buckets with 1 value each in them, because the CustomerID column is a primary key and therefore does not allow duplicate values. The next value is read and since it does not belong to bucket number 199, a 200th bucket is created and assigned the value. You still have values to assign to buckets, but you have hit your limit for the number of buckets you are allowed. You take a look at the 200 existing buckets to see if you can combine 2 adjacent buckets together without losing information. You decide to combine buckets 62 and 63 into a single bucket, reducing the number of buckets back to 199. The next value is read, assigned to bucket 200, and the process is repeated. You continue the process of assigning the next value to the 200th bucket and then collapsing 2 adjacent buckets until all 999,706 values have been read.

Our collapse technique simply selected 2 adjacent buckets at random. Every time a new value from the sorted list was read and assigned to the 200th bucket, we randomly chose a bucket to be collapsed into its neighbour. The end result of all of our random collapses would be 199 total buckets with a varying amount of values inside each bucket. The number of values won't be exactly equal across all buckets, because in randomly selecting buckets, some buckets would simply be selected slightly more frequently than some other bucket. SQL Server builds buckets in much the same way as described above, but uses a more sophisticated variation of the maxdiff histogram.

Once all values have been read and assigned to buckets, the 3rd and final stage is initiated. In the final stage of processing the histogram, each of the buckets are inspected to determine if the histogram can be further collapsed without losing a significant amount of information. The final stage of further collapsing intervals will produce a histogram that has the smallest number of buckets possible as long as there wasn't any significant loss of information.

There are a couple of limitations on how few steps SQL Server will record in the histogram. If the table does not have any data, SQL Server does not bother to create a histogram since there aren't any values to assign to buckets. If the first column of the statistics object has 1 distinct value, you will get 1 step in the histogram. Likewise, 2 and 3 distinct values will result in a histogram with 2 and 3 steps respectively. For tables with 4 or more distinct values in the first column of the statistics object, the minimum number of steps in a histogram will be 3. Due to the way in which buckets are created, the actual number of steps in a histogram for tables with 4 or more values will be somewhere between 3 steps and the number of rows in the table – 3 with a maximum limit of 200 steps.

There are 5 values stored for each step in the histogram as shown in the table below:

Value	Description
RANGE_HI_KEY	The upper boundary of a histogram step.
RANGE_ROWS	The number of rows inside the histogram step.
EQ_ROWS	The number of rows which are exactly equal to RANGE_HI_KEY.
AVG_RANGE_ROWS	The average number of rows per distinct value inside the step.
DISTINCT_RANGE_ROWS	Number of distinct values in the step, not including RANGE_HI_KEY.

You can inspect the histogram by using the DBCC SHOW_STATISTICS command. DBCC SHOW_STATISTICS takes two parameters, the name of the table and the index. You can additionally specify a small number of options which control the type of data retrieved. The following command will retrieve the statistics information for the pk_Customer index in the Customers.Customer table.

```
DBCC SHOW_STATISTICS ("Customers.Customer","pk_Customer");
```

Take special note of the syntax. The table and index name need to be enclosed in double quotes, not the single quote which is standard T-SQL for character values. The first table in the results displays the statistics header. The second table displays the density vector for the statistics object. The third table displays the histogram, a portion of which is shown below:

RANGE_HI_KEY	RANGE_ROWS	EQ_ROWS	DISTINCT_RANGE_ROWS	AVG_RANGE_ROWS
1	0	1	0	1
2832	4219.379	1	2830	1.490947
16074	7067.978	1	7068	1.000046
19444	3532.263	1	3369	1.04846
25668	7067.978	1	6223	1.135783
31120	5300.12	1	5300	1
35533	3532.263	1	3532	1
43295	10603.69	1	7761	1.366279

What you'll almost always see SQL Server do is construct the first step and the last step in the histogram using the minimum and maximum value, respectively, in the data sampled. The minimum value is 1, so you see the first step with a bucket boundary of 1. Nothing exists in the set with a value lower than one and only one occurrence of the value 1 was found. So you see the bucket key set to 1 and there is exactly 1 row with a value of 1. The range rows and distinct range rows are both set to 0, because the first step only contains a value matching the key. If you look at the last step in the histogram, you will see a similar set of values for a RANGE_HI_KEY = 1000000. This is why a histogram with 3 or more distinct values will always have at least 3 steps in the histogram.

The key for the second step is 2832. That means this bucket contains the values between 2 and 2831. SQL Server counted 2830 unique values in the data set between those 2 values along with 1 row whose value was exactly equal to the RANGE_HI_KEY. The key for the third step is 16074, which means the bucket contains 7068 values between 2833 and 16073 with exactly 1 row being equal to 16074.

The strange numbers in the data are the values in the RANGE_ROWS and AVG_RANGE_ROWS. The values shown, which are the actual values computed by SQL Server for pk_Customer, actually don't make any sense for any step where decimals exist. The RANGE_ROWS column should actually exactly equal the DISTINCT_RANGE_ROWS in this case. The AVG_RANGE_ROWS should be exactly 1 for all steps in this particular histogram. The CustomerID column is an integer, it is unique, you can't store a fraction of a row in the table, and this histogram was built supporting an index which means to perform a FULLSCAN. For now, I'll leave you with a slight conundrum on the values SQL Server computed for these two columns, which will be cleared up when we get to the section on updating statistics.

Selectivity and Cardinality

The purpose for statistics objects to exist is to allow the Query Optimizer to compute cardinality. Cardinality is a single number that is obtained for each of the possible query paths. The Query Optimizer will choose the query path with the best cardinality since that path will result in the fewest resources.

In order to compute cardinality, you first need to compute selectivity. The selectivity is the fraction of rows in a table which match a query predicate, criteria contained in a WHERE clause or the ON predicate of a JOIN. This is where the histogram steps come in. SQL Server takes the value(s) in the predicate and locates the histogram step(s) which correspond to the values. If a value exactly matches a RANGE_HI_KEY, the value in EQ_ROWS determines the number of rows which match the value. If a value does not match a RANGE_HI_KEY, then the value in AVG_RANGE_ROWS is used. If a value falls outside of the last step of the histogram, SQL Server makes a guess on the value to use. If more than one value appears in the query predicate, values from the histogram for each predicate value are summed. The resulting value is divided by the number of rows in the table. To put this into an equation:

```
Selectivity = SUM(RANGE_HI_KEY or AVG_RANGE_ROWS or Guess) / Number of rows from stats header
```

The cardinality is an estimate of the number of rows which will be returned by the query predicate. Cardinality is the selectivity multiplied by the actual number of rows in the table as reported by sys.sysindexes.

The cardinality is used by the Query Optimizer to determine if an index would be useful in satisfying a query. Cardinality is also used to determine whether the query should initially request row, page, or table level locks. Cardinality is also used to determine the actual shape of a query plan, but the details of operators in query plans are outside the scope of this book and can be found in *Microsoft SQL Server 2012: Database Development*.

Creating Statistics

You can create statistics using the CREATE STATISTICS command as shown below:

```
CREATE STATISTICS statistics_name
ON { table_or_indexed_view_name } ( column [ ,...n ] )
    [ WHERE <filter_predicate> ]
    [ WITH  [ [ FULLSCAN | SAMPLE number { PERCENT | ROWS }] [ , ] ] [ NORECOMPUTE ]
] ;
```

The following code shows an example of creating a multi-column statistics object for the Products.SKU table:

```
CREATE STATISTICS st_ProductID_CategoryID ON Products.SKU (ProductID, CategoryID)
WITH FULLSCAN;
```

FULLSCAN was specified, because I wanted this example to be stable and allow for exact comparisons to the table itself so that you can see how each of the components of a statistics object is constructed.

You can query sys.stats or sys.indexes for basic definition level information on a statistics object. DBCC SHOW_STATISTICS will display the detailed information we want to use to inspect the stats object just created as follows:

```
DBCC SHOW_STATISTICS ("Products.SKU","st_ProductID_CategoryID");
```

Since we specified FULLSCAN, you would expect the header to tell us that the Rows and Rows Sampled are exactly equal and you can verify this information is accurate by running a COUNT(*) against the table. The second result set shows the density vectors for the ProductID by itself as well as ProductID + CategoryID. If you retrieve a distinct count of the ProductID column, you will find that there are 119 distinct values. 1/119 = 0.008403362 which is the All_density value for the first row. You'll also find that there are 155 distinct values for the two columns which results in 1/155 = 0.006451613. The average length for each should also come as no surprise since these are both integers.

The last result set is the histogram with 87 steps for the 119 distinct values in the first column of the statistics object. An initial inspection of the first few rows should make sense as each step in the histogram is simply each ProductID in ascending order.

RANGE_HI_KEY	RANGE_ROWS	EQ_ROWS	DISTINCT_RANGE_ROWS	AVG_RANGE_ROWS
1	0	4416	0	1
3	0	96	0	1
4	0	112	0	1
5	0	192	0	1
6	0	608	0	1
7	0	180	0	1
8	0	992	0	1

Skipping down a little bit in the results brings us to a couple of places where there is a skip in the numbers or more specifically, the step encompasses more than 1 value.

RANGE_HI_KEY	RANGE_ROWS	EQ_ROWS	DISTINCT_RANGE_ROWS	AVG_RANGE_ROWS
34	72	72	1	72
36	48	48	1	48
38	32	32	1	32
39	0	56	0	1
40	0	24	0	1
42	72	72	1	72
44	72	72	1	72

The step for a RANGE_HI_KEY = 36 has 48 rows which are exactly equal to 36 along with 48 rows for ProductID = 35. What SQL Server would have done to begin with is simply create 119 steps, one for each of the 119 unique values. Since 119 is less than the maximum number of steps, the second phase of histogram construction would have been complete. The third phase would have consolidated adjacent steps as long as significant information was not lost. The bucket for 35 happened to have exactly 48 rows and so did the bucket for 36, so SQL Server collapsed the two buckets together since the combined bucket would have preserved all of the information, since for each of these two values, exactly 48 rows exist. The same thing happened with 33 and 34, 37 and 38, 41 and 42, which you can easily verify counts by querying the table. 39 and 40 weren't collapsed, because the number of rows did not match either the 38 bucket or the 41 bucket.

In this example, FULLSCAN produced an exact set of statistics, so it is very easy to look at the values and understand how the histogram was constructed and how steps were collapsed. The Products.SKU table does not have enough pages to compare the histogram if a sampling method were used since it only has 490 pages which is less than the minimum of 1024 pages. If the Products.SKU table instead occupied 30,000 pages, but still only had 38,700 rows and 119 distinct values for the ProductID, you would end up with a slightly different histogram if the statistics object were created by sampling. SQL Server would first sample a random set of data and for the sake of this example; let's assume that it managed to obtain all 119 distinct values for ProductID. The initial histogram would have the same 119 steps as the one we just created. However, the collapse phase might have collapsed more buckets or collapsed them in a different way. If ProductID 36 had 29 values in the sample and ProductID 35 had 39 values, then the buckets most likely would not be collapsed since there is a large difference in the counts between the two buckets that could lead to significant overestimation or underestimation. However, if ProductID 36 had 29 values in the sample and ProductID 35 had 31 values in the sample, there is a strong possibility that the two buckets would be collapsed since very little difference exists between the two values.

Using a sampling method does not mean your statistics are flawed, just that the estimates will be less accurate than if you used a FULLSCAN. Sampling will produce estimates almost as accurate as FULLSCAN is you have a very low occurrence of duplicate values in a column. The estimates produced by sampling become less accurate as the occurrence of duplicates increases. The percentage of cases where sampling does not work well is very small, but still significant enough to impact applications. You still need to test your queries to determine if the sampling was sufficient and if not, then you need to override the default sampling with a larger sample set or a FULLSCAN.

Automatic Creation

In addition to manually creating statistics, SQL Server can also automatically create statistics. The auto creation of statistics is done to help the Query Optimizer make better decisions on the query plan to use. When you submit a query, SQL Server evaluates all of the query predicates – WHERE clause and ON predicates of a JOIN. If a query predicate does not have statistics, SQL Server will automatically create statistics.

The statistics objects created will contain all of the metrics as a manually created statistics object or statistics created in support of an index. But, the auto created statistics will always be for a single column and always using SQL Server default sampling methodology. The auto created stats will be named _WA_Sys_<unique sequential identifier>.

For example, if you were to execute the following query against the Products.SKU table, SQL Server would auto generate a statistics object for the CategoryID column since statistics do not already exist for the column, but would not create stats for the ProductID column since stats exist for this column as part of the creation of the in_ProductID index.

```
SELECT * FROM Products.SKU WHERE ProductID = 1 AND CategoryID = 39;
```

The auto creation of statistics is controlled by the AUTO_CREATE_STATISTICS configuration option. When set to ON, SQL Server will automatically create statistics for any column which does not already have a corresponding stats object. When set to OFF, SQL Server will not automatically created statistics. The default setting is ON and you should always leave this setting enabled.

You can use the sp_createstats stored procedure to create a statistics object for every column in a database. If a column already has a histogram built on it, sp_createstats will not build another statistics object. You shouldn't ever need to run the sp_createstats command and should simply rely on the auto creation of statistics when needed by the Query Optimizer.

> **Duplicate Stats:** One of the challenges of auto created statistics is that once created, SQL Server won't get rid of them, even if you explicitly create a statistics object or an index which duplicates or otherwise overrides the auto created statistics object. This is where the sys.stats view comes in. You should review your database every time you create/change an index of statistics object and remove any auto created stats which are no longer needed. This will reduce the overhead in managing statistics objects and accomplish one of the biggest challenges with every database ever created, keeping obsolete objects cleaned up.

Filtered Statistics

Every index has a supporting statistics object. Since you can filter an index, it would make sense to also be able to filter the statistics. After all, it wouldn't make any sense to poll residents of Japan for whether they were going to vote for Wakko, Escrow, or Sue for President of the United States. It also wouldn't make sense to build a statistics object with values which do not match the filter criteria of the index.

Correlated Columns

When SQL Server auto creates statistics, each column in a query predicate is treated independently. If the Query Optimizer is using multiple statistics objects and the query predicate for a single table has an AND operator, the selectivity of each stats object will be multiplied together to produce the total selectivity. For example, if the ProductID and CategoryID columns in the query above had a selectivity of 1/5 and 1/8 respectively, then the total selectivity for the query that had a predicate of ProductID AND CategoryID would be 1/40 or 0.025.

Take the additional example as shown below:

ModelID	Manufacturer	ModelNumber
17	Boeing	777
22	Airbus	A320
28	Embraer	ERJ-135
41	Boeing	787

SQL Server would treat the Manufacturer column independently of the ModelNumber column and a query that specified both a Manufacturer and a ModelNumber would produce a selectivity of ¼ * ¼ = 1/8 or 0.125. The real selectivity is ¼ or 0.25, because Boeing is always the manufacturer of a 777 or 787, Airbus is always the manufacturer of an A320, and Embraer is always the manufacturer of an ERJ-135.

There are many cases in which columns in a single table have a correlation which the auto stats generation will not detect. The ProductID and CategoryID are not independent columns. A given ProductID isn't assigned to any CategoryID and a given CategoryID can't contain any ProductID. In many cases, a single ProductID belongs to 1 and only 1 CategoryID while in a small number of cases a single ProductID can belong to as many as 3 categories.

When you have correlated columns in a table, the Query Optimizer can obtain a skewed result for the selectivity. You can avoid the potential skew three ways:

- Filtered statistics
- Multi-column statistics
- Multi-column index

The first way is to create filtered statistics for each one of the correlated options so that SQL Server can determine the correct selectivity. I hate this option, because while it solves the problem, you can wind up with a very large number of filtered statistics on a table that don't provide a compelling benefit for the amount of effort and continuous maintenance required.

Creating a multi-column statistics object gives you a much better option. SQL Server will build a histogram on the first column, but the density vector will provides an accurate computation for the selectivity of multiple columns. You end up with a single, multi-column statistics object which covers the entire range of values in the correlated column. The only drawback to this method would be the same drawback mentioned previously with sampling.

The best option would be to create an index on the correlated columns you are specifying in the query. A stats object by itself can help the Query Optimizer determine selectivity and improve a query plan, but without an index, SQL Server still has to scan the entire table to find the rows which match your query predicate. If an index were created on the correlated columns you are querying, you not only get accurate selectivity, but SQL Server can also utilize the index to quickly find the rows which match the criteria.

Exercise 10: Creating and Reviewing Statistics

Many product queries utilize both the ProductID and CategoryID column. The ProductID is always specified and in a smaller number of cases, the CategoryID is also specified. There aren't enough queries specifying the CategoryID to justify adding the CategoryID to the in_ProductID index, but since these two columns are correlated, you want to have accurate statistics.

1. Execute the following command to create statistics on the CategoryID column in Products.SKU.
   ```
   CREATE STATISTICS st_CategoryID ON Products.SKU (CategoryID)
   WITH FULLSCAN;
   ```
2. Execute the following command to create statistics on both the ProductID and CategoryID columns in the Products.SKU table.
   ```
   CREATE STATISTICS st_ProductID_CategoryID ON Products.SKU (ProductID, CategoryID)
   WITH FULLSCAN;
   ```
3. Execute the following command to view the density vectors applicable to a query specifying both ProductID and CategoryID.
   ```
   DBCC SHOW_STATISTICS ("Products.SKU","in_ProductID") WITH DENSITY_VECTOR;
   DBCC SHOW_STATISTICS ("Products.SKU","st_CategoryID") WITH DENSITY_VECTOR;
   DBCC SHOW_STATISTICS ("Products.SKU","st_ProductID_CategoryID") WITH DENSITY_VECTOR;
   ```

We've used the FULLSCAN option when creating the statistics object so that the density vector would be computed using all rows, just like the in_ProductID index was. You can see from the in_ProductID index that the ProductID has a density of 0.008403362. You can see from the st_CategoryID statistics object that CategoryID has a density of 0.02222222. If you hadn't explicitly created the st_CategoryID statistics object, SQL Server would have auto created it the first time a query ran which asked for both the ProductID and CategoryID. If these were the only two objects in the database, SQL Server would have computed the selectivity as:

```
0.008403362 * 0.02222222 = 0.000186741
```

If you look at the density vector for st_ProductID_CategoryID, you'll see that the actual selectivity for the ProductID and CategoryID column is 0.006451613. SQL Server can still use the in_ProductID index to quickly locate the necessary rows, but it can still make an accurate decision based on the selectivity of the st_ProductID_CategoryID statistics object.

String Statistics

Regardless of the data type, SQL Server will only use a maximum of 200 steps to build a histogram. Integers and decimal data types, while having a large range of potential values are still reasonably constrained and easily break down into manageable, contiguous ranges. Even date and time data will have a manageable number of ranges that can be easily divided into 200 or fewer steps.

Character data poses a much bigger challenge. The English language has hundreds of thousands or possibly millions of words, depending upon how you define a word. Inside a single column in a database, it is quite easy to have thousands of distinct character entries; the AddressLine1 column in Customers.Address has 923,925 unique entries. It is also very possible to have dramatically different statistics for each of the distinct character entries such that collapsing any range would lead to the loss of a significant amount of information.

Character data also has other challenges for the Query Optimizer. While we search for number, date, or time values based on either equality or some form of inequality, we aren't going to do a search for something like every OrderHeader where the 3rd digit of the OrderID is a 3. But, for character data, we are much more likely to search for a substring than for equality.

Prior to SQL Server 2005, when a character column was the first column of a statistics object, SQL Server made its best estimate on building a viable histogram that could be used for cardinality estimates. When it came to dealing with LIKE operators, you were left with a guess. SQL Server 2005 introduced an internal only structure in addition to the histogram called a Trie Tree that builds a statistical correlation of substrings across the rows sampled for the histogram. The algorithm is patented, so you could probably search the US Patent and Trademark Office site if you wanted deeper details into a Trie Tree. For our purposes, it simply means that the String Index column of the statistics header will be set to YES, the statistics object will be slightly larger due to the storage required of the Trie Tree, and the SQL Server Query Optimizer can make better cardinality estimates when you use the LIKE operator.

The Trie Tree does have certain limitations in order to control the amount of time required to compute and the amount of storage required. For strings that are 80 characters or less, SQL Server will build a Trie Tree on the entire string. For strings larger than 80 characters, SQL Server will build a Trie Tree on the first and last 40 characters of the string. The Products.SKU.pk_SKU index shows an example of a statistics object which includes a Trie Tree.

Updating Statistics

Just as indexes have to be maintained as rows are modified in the table, statistics have to be maintained in order to be useful. Statistics do not have to be updated continuously. Modifying a row in a table doesn't necessarily make the cardinality estimates obsolete. As the size of the table increases, the number of modifications necessary to invalidate cardinality estimates also increases.

Every time you modify a row in a table, the rowmodctr column in sys.sysindexes is incremented. If you make a modification to a column that has a statistics object, an internal counter called colmodctr is also incremented. SQL Server uses the colmodctrs value to determine when statistics need to be recomputed in order to ensure accurate cardinality estimates. Unfortunately, since the colmodctr value is not exposed, we are left using the rowmodctr value to make a basic guess when a stats object is out of date.

When you submit a query to SQL Server, the Query Optimizer identifies any statistics objects which match the query predicates which can be used to compute cardinality. Before inspecting the contents of the statistics object, a check is made against the colmodctr counter. If the value is beyond a specified threshold, the statistics object will be marked obsolete, and any query plans in the query cache will be invalidated. If you have left the AUTO_UPDATE_STATISTICS database property enabled, which is strongly recommended, SQL Server will automatically rebuild the statistics object and then use the rebuilt object to estimate cardinality.

The rules SQL Server uses to determine if statistics are out of date are as follows:

- If the table had 0 rows when statistics were last computed and the table sized has increased to more than 0 rows.
- If the number of rows in the table when the statistics were last computed was 500 or less and the colmodctr of the leading column of the statistics object has changed by more than 500.
- If the table had more than 500 rows when the statistics were last computed and the colmodctr of the leading column of the statistics object has changed by more than 500 + 20% of the number of rows in the table.
- For filtered statistics, the colmodctr is multiplied by the selectivity of the filter condition before the rules above are applied.
- If statistics are on a temp table, statistics are also recomputed when the table grows beyond 6 rows.

If you do not want to take the performance hit of automatically updating statistics while a query is running, you can enable the AUTO_UPDATE_STATISTICS_ASYNC database option. If this option is enabled, when the Query Optimizer encounters out of date statistics, the existing statistics object will be used and a rebuild of the statistics object will be initiated using a background thread.

You can retrieve detailed information about all of the statistics in a database with the following query:

```
SELECT OBJECT_SCHEMA_NAME(a.id), OBJECT_NAME(a.id), b.name,
    STATS_DATE(b.object_id, b.stats_id) StatisticsDate, a.*
FROM sys.sysindexes a INNER JOIN sys.stats b ON a.id = b.object_id AND a.indid = b.stats_id
WHERE OBJECT_SCHEMA_NAME(id) <> 'sys';
```

The STATS_DATE function returns the date and time that the statistics object was last modified.

You can disable the automatic update of statistics on a table, index, or statistics level with the sp_autostats stored procedure. When the auto update of statistics is disabled, SQL Server will invalidate any query plan for a statistics object that is out of date, but will not rebuild the statistics object. If you disable the update of statistics at a table level, SQL Server does not track any information that the statistics update on the table is disabled. Instead, the engine disables the auto update on every statistics object that exists on the table at the time you turned the auto update off. This does not prevent new statistics objects from being created on the table if AUTO_CREATE_STATISTICS is enabled and any newly created statistics will be automatically updated if you still have either AUTO_UPDATE_STATISTICS or AUTO_UPDATE_STATISTICS_ASYNC enabled. You can also disable the automatic update of a statistics object supporting an index at the time the index is created by specifying the STATISTICS_NORECOMPUTE option of the index.

If you disable auto update of statistics at a database level, you cannot enable the automatic update on a table, index, or statistics level. Auto update of statistics must be ON at a database level in order for the update of statistics to occur on any statistics object within the database.

> Disabling Auto Stats Update: As critical and good statistics are for optimal performance, it would seem that you should never disable auto update of statistics. Auto stats update is frequently disabled for tables that are used to stage data prior to populating one or more tables. In this type of scenario, your queries are always processing every row in the staging table. Since by design, you are going to scan the entire table, it doesn't make any sense for SQL Server to waste time updating statistics. You don't care about the cardinality estimate, because you aren't processing a subset of the rows in the staging table.

Most of the time, the auto update of statistics is sufficient to keep all statistics objects current enough to produce reliable cardinality estimates. If you've made substantial changes to a column in a filter predicate the statistics can be out of date, but SQL Server will never update them since changes to the filter predicate are not tracked. Additionally, you could have made mass changes to the table and do not want to incur a delay to recompute statistics automatically. For those cases where auto update of statistics will not occur or you do not want to incur the overhead while queries are executing, you can manually update statistics.

> Filtered Statistics: Filtered statistics are created when you either create a filtered index or when you add a WHERE clause to the CREATE STATISTICS command. SQL Server maintains statistics based on the columns defined for the statistics object, but doesn't maintain statistics on the filter. The stats will only contain values which match the filter criteria, but the column modification counters which determine whether the statistics are out of date will not be modified if a data modification action only affects the filter criteria and not any other column in the statistics.
>
> For example, if you were to define a statistics object on the Products.SKU table for the ProductID and CategoryID with a filter on the StartDate column, any change that affects the ProductID or Category columns will increment the column modification counters. But, an update that just affects the StartDate column will not cause the column modification counters to increment. If there is enough update activity of this pattern, the statistics object can become obsolete without SQL Server being aware or automatically updating the stats object. The only way to fix the statistics object in this case is to manually update the statistics.
>
> In the case of manually created statistics, you could avoid this situation by including the filter predicate as the last column in the definition of the statistics without affecting the actual stats definition. But, you wouldn't be able to affect the stats object underneath a filtered index the same way. While it might sound like an elegant way to avoid the problem of filtered stats becoming obsolete and not auto updating, you are much more likely to create filtered indexes than filtered statistics, so I wouldn't recommend doing this simply in order to avoid confusion for anyone having to manage the database. Every time you apply a "slick trick" to overcome a situation in a subset of cases, the solution will generally backfire in a production environment because everyone quickly forgets the "trick" you applied and wants to apply universal processes to manage databases in production.

Manual update of statistics can be accomplished by using either the UPDATE STATISTICS command or the sp_updatestats stored procedure. UPDATE STATSTICS is run either for all statistics on a specified table or for a specific statistics object. Sp_updatestats will rebuild all statistics for the entire database. Just because you told SQL Server to rebuild a statistics object, does not mean that the object will be rebuilt. When you manually update statistics, SQL Server will only update statistics for objects where necessary based on the value in sys.sysindexes.rowmodctr. For any statistics object which is updated, either manually or automatically, the rowmodctr and colmodctr values are reset to 0.

Prior to SQL Server 2012, if you manually updated statistics, any query plan which relied on the statistics being updated was immediately invalidated and removed from the query cache. SQL Server 2012 no longer invalidates the query plans in the query cache in all cases. If the statistics object was actually updated, the query plan will be invalidated. However, if SQL Server determines that the statistics object really doesn't need to be updated based on the rowmodctr value, the statistics object will not be updated and any associated query plan will not be invalidated. Prior to SQL Server 2012, the query plan would be invalidated even if SQL Server determined that it did not need to update the statistics object.

Now that we've covered how and when statistics are updated, we'll return to the histogram conundrum from earlier in the chapter. How did we manage to get decimal values in the RANGE_ROWS and AVG_RANGE_ROWS columns when it isn't possible to store a fraction of a row? How did we get a value for RANGE_ROWS on a primary key column which is greater than the number of values possible for the step? How did we get a value greater than 1 for the AVG_RANGE_ROWS column? The answer to all of these boils down to sampling.

RANGE_HI_KEY	RANGE_ROWS	EQ_ROWS	DISTINCT_RANGE_ROWS	AVG_RANGE_ROWS
1	0	1	0	1
2832	4219.379	1	2830	1.490947
16074	7067.978	1	7068	1.000046
19444	3532.263	1	3369	1.04846
25668	7067.978	1	6223	1.135783
31120	5300.12	1	5300	1
35533	3532.263	1	3532	1
43295	10603.69	1	7761	1.366279

We created the primary key when the table was created. That means the unique index which physically implements the primary key and the supporting statistics object were both created when the table was empty. We then loaded 999,706 rows into the Customers.Customer table. This set the rowmodctr value to 999,706 and the colmodctr to 999,706. The next time a query was run against the Customers.Customer table, the Query Optimizer determined the stats were out of date. Since AUTO_UPDATE_STATISTICS was enabled, the statistics object was automatically rebuilt. When the stats were automatically rebuilt, SQL Server used the default sampling rate. Since a sample was used, SQL Server created estimates for RANGE_ROWS and AVG_RANGE_ROWS and these values are not required to be whole number when a histogram is built using sampling.

Exercise 11: Updating Statistics

The following exercise will show you how to manually update statistics on a table as well inspect the histogram both before and after the statistics update.

1. Execute the following command to view the statistics object supporting the Customers.Customer primary key.

    ```
    DBCC SHOW_STATISTICS ("Customers.Customer","pk_Customer");
    ```

2. Manually update the statistics on Customers.Customer. Instead of sampling the data, use a FULLSCAN.

    ```
    UPDATE STATISTICS Customers.Customer WITH FULLSCAN;
    ```

3. View the statistics now that a complete rebuild has been done.

    ```
    DBCC SHOW_STATISTICS ("Customers.Customer","pk_Customer");
    ```

The histogram should now look like the following:

RANGE_HI_KEY	RANGE_ROWS	EQ_ROWS	DISTINCT_RANGE_ROWS	AVG_RANGE_ROWS
1	0	1	0	1
999999	999703	1	999703	1
1000000	0	1	0	1

This should be more in line with what you expected when we first looked at the histogram for pk_Customer. All of the decimal values are gone, because the histogram was built using the complete data set. Additionally, you can also see the effect of the collapse algorithm. The min and max values in the set will be the first and last step in the histogram. Since this is a unique column, all other values can be combined into a single step without losing any information on the data distribution.

Data Modifications

I've mentioned that indexes are maintained as data is modified and it should be obvious that in order for an index to be useful, it has to be maintained as data changes. We haven't delved into the details of how changes occur directly on a page, because it depends upon whether the change is being done to a page in a heap or a page in a B-tree, either a table with a clustered index or within an index, and we hadn't discussed B-trees until this chapter. In this section, when we discuss data changes, we are limiting the discussion to INSERT, UPDATE, and DELETE operations. MERGE, BCP, and BULK INSERT also change data in a table, but the effect of these three commands are already covered in the basic INSERT, UPDATE, and DELETE. Index maintenance operations for INSERT, BCP, and BULK INSERT will all be the same. We won't consider MERGE by itself, because MERGE is simply a way to package INSERT, UPDATE, and DELETE commands.

For every data modification made to a table, every index defined on the table will have a corresponding modification. When you are designing indexing strategies, you need to be aware of the rate of data modifications and the effect on applications. If you have a database which needs to have very low latency for a very high volume of transactions, you want to minimize the number of indexes, because the actual number of changes made in the database will be magnified by each index defined on the table.

Inserts

When data is inserted into a table, SQL Server must first figure out where to put the row and then add the row to the appropriate leaf level page of every index. If the table has a clustered index, the row is added to the appropriate data page based on the ordering of the clustered index. If the table is a heap, SQL Server scans the PFS pages associated to the table to locate the first page which has sufficient space available to accommodate the row.

If a page cannot be found with sufficient free space for the heap, a new extent will be allocated to the table and the row will be written to the first page allocated in the extent. SQL Server can simply plop data onto the first available page for a heap, because a heap does not define any kind of ordering.

If the table has a clustered index and the row will not fit on the required page, a page split will occur. SQL Server only performs page splits on INSERT operations and only on B-tree structures. A heap will never have a page split occur, but page splits can occur in the nonclustered, full-text, and XML indexes defined on a heap. Likewise, a table with a clustered index can have page splits occur.

Page Splits Revisited

Page splits begin at the leaf level first and then move up the levels of the index structure as needed. But, in order to find the appropriate leaf level page, SQL Server must transit from the root page through any intermediate level and then finally to the leaf level page. As it transits the index, it places a latch on each parent page. A latch can be considered as a type of lightweight lock which is applied to a page while it is being read from or written to in order to protect the integrity of the page. The latches acquired on parent pages are held for the duration of the transaction and prevent any other session from modifying the parent index pages.

When SQL Server reaches the appropriate leaf level page and determines that there isn't enough space for the new row, a new page is allocated to the index. The next page pointer on the existing page is updated to point to the newly allocated page. The previous page pointer on what used to be the next page in the chain is updated to point to the newly allocated page. The index page header is written with the appropriate values. SQL Server then takes the full page and splits it in half, where possible. Based on the row offset array in the page footer, the first half of the rows stay on the current page and the second half of the rows are moved to the newly allocated page. The new row is then written to whichever page the new row should belong based on the index keys and the row offset array is updated to reflect the correct logical ordering of the rows.

If SQL Server determines that the new row still can't fit on the newly allocated page, the page will be split again. This process can repeat several times. SQL Server will eventually do enough page splits to allow the row to fit on the page or it will simply place the row by itself on a newly allocated page.

Once the page splitting is complete at the leaf level, the parent page will be updated with the first entry for as many new pages as were introduced by the leaf level split. If there isn't enough room on the parent page, a page split will occur on the parent page using the same methodology as page splits occur on a leaf level page. Once all of the new entries have been written to the parent page, SQL Server will check to see if there is enough room for at least 2 more rows to be written to the parent page. If the page does not have enough room, a further split of the parent page will occur.

This process continues through all of the levels of the index until the root page is reached. If the root page does not have enough space for the new rows + 2 additional rows, the root page will be split. Splitting a root page is a little different than any other page in the index. When a root page is split, 2 new pages are allocated to the index. The first ½ of the rows on the root page based on the row offset array are written to one of the pages and the second ½ of the rows on the root page are written to the other new page. This introduces a new level in the index. Finally, the root page is updated to only contain the first key entry on each of the newly allocated pages.

When you query a table in SQL Server, your statement specifies a table name. The names in your query are converted into IDs and the Query Optimizer determines the optimal path to locate the data you asked for. The table(s) and/or index(es) used by the query are looked up in sys.sysindexes and the value in the FirstIAM column is retrieved. This values points at the first page for the object. The reason that root pages of an index are split by introducing 2 pages and writing ½ of the root page to each newly introduced page is to avoid having to do a metadata update on sys.sysindexes and potentially introducing locking contention.

Any page splits which occur are committed independently via a background system transaction. Even if the transaction which caused the page splits is rolled back, the page splits are still committed.

Deletes

When rows are deleted from a heap, the data is "removed" from the page. A delete from a heap occurs much in the same way as a when you delete a file from a file system. When deleting a file from the file system, you don't actually wipe out all of the bytes that constitute the file; you simply erase a small portion of the file header which tells the operating system that the file is valid along with the entry in the file allocation table that pointed to the file. When a row is deleted from a heap, nothing happens to the actual bytes which make up the row, but the 2 bytes corresponding to the slot in the row offset array is set to 0. A slot with a row offset of 0 tells SQL Server that the slot is no longer being used on the page. However, the space where the row was on the page is still consumed and SQL Server will never reclaim the space on the page. Reading the page, even with several display options for DBCC PAGE, will not show the deleted row. But, if you were to retrieve an actual binary dump of the page and reverse engineer the bytes, you would find the data. Since the slot in the row offset array is simply zeroed out, space is never reclaimed in a heap, just invalidated. You could delete every row on a page in a heap and the page would still be allocated to the table, consuming space, and the space would not be released.

When you delete a row from a B-tree, remember that the leaf level of a clustered index is the data row; SQL Server marks the row as a ghost record. The row offset array is not changed, but the status flag in the header of the row is changed. This status change marks the row as a ghost record so that it is not returned by any other process, but does not actually remove the row from the page or modify the row offset array. A background thread, called the ghost cleanup process, then runs against the page to remove the entry in the row offset table, allowing the space to be reused.

When a row is ghosted, the m_ghostRecCnt value in the page header is incremented. The PFS page which tracks the page where the row was deleted has a bit flipped that tells the engine at least 1 ghost record exists for the pages tracked by the PFS page. A status bit is also flipped for the database telling the process that at least 1 ghost record exists in the database.

The ghost cleanup is a single threaded process that runs a single occurrence for the entire instance. Every 10 seconds, the ghost cleanup starts, reads down the list of databases, in database ID order, and looks for the first database marked with ghost records existing. The process then removes the ghost entries on a maximum of 10 pages before shutting down and waiting 10 seconds for the next cycle. This allows the ghost cleanup process to minimize the impact on other processes. Once all ghost records have been cleaned up on a page, m_ghostRecCnt is set back to 0. Once all pages tracked by the PFS page are cleaned up, the bit on the PFS page is set back to false. Once all ghost records in a database are cleaned up, the database status flag is reset to false.

Once the ghost cleanup process has removed the entry for the slot in the row offset array, the space on the page can be reused. If the ghost cleanup removes all of the entries on a page in the row offset array, the entire page is deallocated from the table. If the deallocation would result in removing the last page attached to a table, the cleanup process leaves 1 slot allocated on the page with a null record since a table can't exist without at least one page allocated.

There is one exception to the ghost cleanup process. Ghost records are not created against heaps, unless a snapshot transaction was run against a heap during a delete operation. When a delete occurs within the pages accessed by a snapshot transaction, the deleted rows are ghosted. The ghost records will not be cleaned up on the page until all open snapshot transactions needing the page are closed.

You can force the cleanup of ghost records by executing either sp_clean_db_free_space or sp_clean_db_file_free_space. Sp_clean_db_free_space will clean up all ghost records within a database while sp_clean_db_file_free_space will clean up all records within a specified database file. You can also disable the ghost cleanup process by turning on trace flag 661.

> **Why Should I Care?**
> Normally, you wouldn't care. But, there are some very specific scenarios which are affected by the ghost cleanup process. The ghost cleanup process is responsible for cleaning up data pages to remove entries for ghosted records. This means write activity is occurring against the page. If the page is being changed, it will be locked, exclusively, which can cause blocking until the cleanup process completes and releases the exclusive lock. So, you could have a situation where you don't have any writes occurring against a database and suddenly have a bunch of your queries blocked, by the ghost cleanup process.

> On a database which is incurring very heavy delete activity, the ghost cleanup process can fall behind, sometimes so far behind that it is impossible for it to ever catch up. Space can't be reclaimed until the ghost cleanup process has scavenged the page. So, you might end up having to allocate additional pages to a table, because previously deleted rows are still ghosted. I've encountered cases where a process has emptied an entire table with a massive delete operation and then began inserting new rows into the table. At a certain point, all the rows would be deleted again and a new insert cycle would start. The developer thought the space was completely cleaned up and being reused by their process only to find the database growing uncontrollably because the ghost cleanup process fell further and further behind and space wasn't being reclaimed. They would have been much better off by dropping the table and re-creating it, which would have completely released the space.

Exercise 12: Deleting Rows

The following exercise will demonstrate how deletes occur both from a heap and a B-tree.

1. Execute the following command to create a copy of the Customers.Customer table.

    ```
    DROP TABLE dbo.Customer;
    SELECT *
    INTO dbo.Customer
    FROM Customers.Customer;
    ```

2. Retrieve the object ID of the dbo.Customer table and inspect the contents of the first page. Remember to change the object ID in DBCC IND to the object ID you retrieve from the first SELECT statement. Replace the page number in DBCC PAGE with the page number you retrieve from DBCC IND where the PageType = 1 and PrevPagePID = 0.

    ```
    SELECT OBJECT_ID('dbo.Customer');
    DBCC IND(ChampionValleyPens,425768574,1);
    DBCC TRACEON(3604);
    DBCC PAGE(ChampionValleyPens,1,81920,3);
    ```

3. Note that the m_ghostRecCnt = 0 in the header.

4. Scroll down and note that CustomerID = 1 is in slot 0 on the page.

5. Execute the following command to view the row offset array.

    ```
    DBCC PAGE(ChampionValleyPens,1,81920,2);
    ```

6. Scroll to the bottom of the results and note that slot 0 is at an offset of 96 on the page.

7. Execute the following code to delete CustomerID = 1 and view the contents of the page within the transaction to ensure that you are seeing the exact state of the page before the commit occurs.

    ```
    BEGIN TRANSACTION;
    DELETE FROM dbo.Customer WHERE CustomerID = 1;
    DBCC PAGE(ChampionValleyPens,1,81920,3);
    DBCC PAGE(ChampionValleyPens,1,81920,2);
    COMMIT TRANSACTION;
    ```

8. Note that m_ghostRecCnt = 0 as it should since this is a heap, slot 0 no longer exists on the page, and slot 0 still exists in the row offset array with an offset of 0.

9. Execute the following command to create a clustered index on dbo.Customer.

    ```
    CREATE UNIQUE CLUSTERED INDEX ic_Customer ON dbo.Customer(CustomerID);
    ```

10. Use DBCC IND to retrieve the new page number for the first page in the table PageType = 1 and PrevPagePID = 0.

11. Execute the following code to verify that CustomerID = 2 is in slot 0, at an offset of 96, and m_ghostRecCnt = 0. Make sure that you substitute the page number obtained from step 10.

    ```
    DBCC PAGE(ChampionValleyPens,1,82064,3);
    DBCC PAGE(ChampionValleyPens,1,82064,2);
    ```

12. Execute the following code to delete CustomerID = 2 and view the page contents and the row offset array.

    ```
    BEGIN TRANSACTION;
    DELETE FROM dbo.Customer WHERE CustomerID = 2;
    DBCC PAGE(ChampionValleyPens,1,82064,3);
    DBCC PAGE(ChampionValleyPens,1,82064,2);
    COMMIT TRANSACTION;
    ```

13. Note that m_ghostRecCnt = 1, the data still exists in slot 0 but with a Record Type = GHOST_DATA_RECORD, and slot 0 still exists at an offset of 96.

14. Wait a couple of minutes and run the following code.

    ```
    DBCC PAGE(ChampionValleyPens,1,82064,3);
    DBCC PAGE(ChampionValleyPens,1,82064,2);
    ```

15. You should see m_ghostRecCnt = 0, CustomerID = 2 no longer exists in slot 0 on the page, slot 0 is now at an offset of 129, and there are 258 rows on the page instead of 259 due to the ghost clean up thread removing the ghosted record.

Updates

Updates to a row can occur with two different methods. If you simply modify the contents of a row where it sits on a page, it is referred to as an update in place. You can also delete the existing version of the row from the page and insert the new version of the row back into the table. SQL Server 2012 does in place updates whenever possible, because only the bytes which have changed need to be modified on the page instead of moving the entire row.

There are several cases where SQL Server can't do an in place update with the most common three being:

- When the row has to move to a new page due to an update of the clustering key.
- An update of a nonclustered index key where the row has to move pages in the index.
- An update that increases the size of the row so that it no longer fits on the original page.

When SQL Server can't do an in place update, the update is internally changed into a DELETE of the existing version of the row followed by an INSERT of the new version of the row. If the row does not fit on the page, the INSERT portion of the update operation causes the page split following the same rules as described previously.

Changes to the clustering key will cause updates to all nonclustered indexes since all of the nonclustered indexes reference the clustering key. The only time nonclustered indexes are affected is when a row changes location in a heap, nonclustered index keys are modified, or the clustering key is changed. Since the nonclustered index points at the clustering key, if a clustered index exists, no changes are needed to the nonclustered index if you aren't changing the column(s) in the clustered index. If the entire table moves storage locations, the nonclustered indexes still don't need to be updated. But, if the table is a heap and the table moves to a new location, the entire nonclustered index has to be updated to reflect the new RID.

Unique Indexes

Unique indexes pose a particular challenge when making row modifications. A delete doesn't require any special handling beyond the normal maintenance that occurs for a DELETE. INSERT operations require SQL Server to check each unique index and reject any rows which would violate the unique index prior to any other changes occurring. Updates to a unique index key, however, can cause SQL Server to behave differently depending upon the actual values a key is being changed to.

What if you had a product table which looked like the table below with a unique index on the ProductName column and you wanted to perform an update that swapped the name of the products between the two rows? ProductID 2 would become a Cigar Pen and ProductID 1 would become a Slimline Pen.

ProductID	ProductName
1	Cigar Pen
2	Slimline Pen

Looking at this logically, there isn't an issue, because each of the product names still only occurs once in the table. But, how would SQL Server go about making the change? You can't change both rows simultaneously, so you would have to change first 1 row and then the other. If you changed ProductID 1 first to Slimline Pen, you would violate the unique index. If you changed ProductID 2 first, you would still violate the unique index. No matter which row was changed first, you would create a violation of the unique index even though the final result doesn't pose a problem. If SQL Server were to process this way, a SELECT statement running under the READ UNCOMMITTED isolation level could see a data violation. Reading uncommitted data is one thing, reading data which completely violates a uniqueness constraint would create a problem.

You can obviously perform the update mentioned above, so how does SQL Server get around this problem? The potential conflict is detected and the Query Optimizer re-writes the UPDATE using a technique referred to as expand/collapse. The UPDATE statement is first expanded into a series of DELETE/INSERT pairs. The resulting DELETE and INSERT statements are then ordered such that the DELETEs occur first followed by the INSERTs. In the collapse portion, the Query Optimizer collapses one or more DELETE/INSERT pairs back into an UPDATE as long as a violation of the unique index would not occur. The collapse portion is responsible for producing the set of statements equivalent to the original UPDATE which require the least amount of processing.

Take the following example UPDATE statement:

```
UPDATE Products.Product
SET ProductName = CASE WHEN ProductID = 1 THEN 'Slimline Pen'
                       WHEN ProductID = 2 THEN 'Cigar Pen' END;
```

SQL Server would first expand this UPDATE into the following:

```
DELETE FROM Products.Product WHERE ProductID = 1;
INSERT INTO Products.Product (ProductID, ProductName) VALUES (1,'Slimline Pen');
DELETE FROM Products.Product WHERE ProductID = 2;
INSERT INTO Products.Product (ProductID, ProductName) VALUES (2,'Cigar Pen');
```

The collapse portion would then produce the following:

```
DELETE FROM Products.Product WHERE ProductID = 1;
UPDATE Products.Product SET ProductName = 'Cigar Pen' WHERE ProductID = 2;
INSERT INTO Products.Product (ProductID, ProductName) VALUES (1,'Slimline Pen');
```

If ProductID 1 is first removed from the table before ProductID 2 is updated, the unique index is not violated. ProductID 1 can then be re-inserted into the table with the new value, again without any violation of the unique index. The expand/collapse shown above is just an example to illustrate what is going on when a temporary violation of a unique constraint occurs as part of an UPDATE. SQL Server could have decided to just delete both rows and insert them back with the new values or it could have decided to delete ProductID 2, update ProductID 1, and then re-insert ProductID 2. You can't dictate how SQL Server actually runs the UPDATE statement, unless you broke it apart into multiple steps yourself and ran each separately. You just need to be aware that this expand/collapse can be occurring as the result of an update to a unique key.

Under a very specific scenario with filtered unique indexes, all DML statements do not behave the same, even when they produce the same results. In one case an UPDATE will succeed while a MERGE will fail. This occurs when you have the following situation:

- You have a unique filtered index on the target table for the MERGE statement
- The filtering column is updated and has a transient key violation
- The key column is not updated

Consider the following example:

```
CREATE TABLE #Product
(ProductID    INT           NOT NULL,
ProductName VARCHAR(20) NOT NULL,
Active       CHAR(1)       NOT NULL,
CONSTRAINT pk_Product PRIMARY KEY (ProductID))

CREATE UNIQUE NONCLUSTERED INDEX iufn_ActiveProduct ON #Product (ProductName)
WHERE Active = 'Y';

INSERT INTO #Product
VALUES(1,'Cigar Pen', 'N'),(2,'Cigar Pen','Y');

SELECT * FROM #Product;

UPDATE #Product
SET Active = CASE WHEN ProductID = 1 THEN 'Y'
                  WHEN ProductID = 2 THEN 'N' END;

SELECT * FROM #Product;
DROP TABLE #Product;
```

The example above will successfully swap the Active designation between ProductID 1 and ProductID 2 even though a temporary violation of the unique constraint occurs.

Now, let's repeat the above scenario using a MERGE instead of a direct UPDATE.

```
CREATE TABLE #Product
(ProductID    INT           NOT NULL,
ProductName VARCHAR(20) NOT NULL,
Active       CHAR(1)       NOT NULL,
CONSTRAINT pk_Product PRIMARY KEY (ProductID))

CREATE UNIQUE NONCLUSTERED INDEX iufn_ActiveProduct ON #Product (ProductName)
WHERE Active = 'Y';

INSERT INTO #Product
VALUES(1,'Cigar Pen', 'N'),(2,'Cigar Pen','Y');

CREATE TABLE #Product2
(ProductID    INT           NOT NULL,
Active       CHAR(1)       NOT NULL,
CONSTRAINT pk_Product2 PRIMARY KEY (ProductID))

INSERT INTO #Product2
VALUES(1,'Y'),(2,'N');

SELECT * FROM #Product;
SELECT * FROM #Product2;

MERGE #Product AS target
USING #Product2 AS source
ON target.ProductID = source.ProductID
WHEN MATCHED THEN
    UPDATE SET Active = source.Active;

SELECT * FROM #Product;
SELECT * FROM #Product2;
```

The MERGE version of this same change will fail with a unique index violation. The MERGE applies the updates in primary key order. ProductID 1 is changed to Y, which results in two rows now having a value of Y and producing a duplicate within the unique index. The duplicate is not allowed by the storage engine, so the MERGE fails. As of this writing, the MERGE fails, because in this specific scenario with a filtered unique index, the Query Optimizer does not perform an expand/collapse of the UPDATE statement to take care of the transient key violation.

I first ran into this interesting little problem over 5 years ago as I was writing "SQL Server 2008 Step By Step", but wasn't allowed to include it in the book, because my publisher at the time said it was "beyond the scope of the book" and had to be left to some other author of SQL Server books for Microsoft Press. Since I no longer write for Microsoft Press, I can now include and discuss this interesting little gotcha. This issue exists in all versions, hotfixes, cumulative updates, and service packs from SQL Server 2008 Beta 1 through at least the updates available for SQL Server 2012 as of the writing of this book. This is a bug in SQL Server that has existed since filtered indexes were introduced in SQL Server 2008 that you will have to work around in your applications.

> **Microsoft Connect:** Microsoft has a website at Connect.Microsoft.com whose supposed purpose is to allow customers to submit bugs and feedback to improve Microsoft products. The specific bug related to MERGE and filtered unique indexes filed more than 5 years ago against SQL Server 2008, filed again against SQL Server 2008 R2, and yet again against SQL Server 2012 has been closed twice and still exists as of the writing of this book.

Multiple Changes

Now that we've covered changes to data pages as well as changes to index pages, we need to look at how SQL Server puts all of this together and the effect that it has on I/O. Any change has to modify the appropriate page(s) for the table, leaf level index pages along with possibly intermediate and root level index pages. We also have primary XML indexes pointing at a clustered index and secondary XML indexes pointing at the primary XML index. We can have filtered indexes in addition to spatial indexes and a single table can have all of these types of indexes present along with full-text indexes, which we will cover in the next chapter.

How is SQL Server supposed to maintain all of these structures? It could apply all of the changes to the table and then apply the same set of changes to each index. It could apply all of the changes to the table, all changes to the leaf level of each index, then apply all changes to the first intermediate level of all indexes, then the 2nd intermediate level, and progress through each index level to the root. It could process changes to the table and then each type of index in turn. The possible options are quite numerous and each has a corresponding impact on the amount of I/O required.

The Query Optimizer allows changes to be made via two different methods – table level and index level. The method chosen is based on which consumes the least resources.

When the table level change methodology is chosen, SQL Server applies the changes one row at a time. The first row to be changed is modified in the table and the change is then propagated to every index. Once complete, the process is repeated with the second row to be changed. This continues until all rows to be changed have been processed. Applying changes one row at a time causes a lot of random I/O in order to read and modify each of the index pages. Additionally, index pages could be accessed multiple times in order to apply all of the changes in the data modification operation. Table level changes are usually selected by the Query Optimizer when you are changing a small number of rows and the table and indexes are rather large.

When the index level change methodology is selected, SQL Server accumulates all of the changes and performs a sort operation for each index on the table. The changes are then applied to the table and each index in turn. Each index is only accessed once and each index page is only changed once when making changes via the index level methodology. However, the query plan will have a sort operation for each index in order to sort the changes for each index in index key order. SQL Server will normally select an index level change methodology when you are making a large number of changes in a single operation in order to minimize the random I/O to the index pages.

The Query Optimizer will select the change methodology based on statistics for the table. You need to be aware of the different methodologies, because if a table level change methodology is chosen for a very large data change due to poor statistics, you can incur a significant amount of unnecessary random I/O which will negatively impact performance as well as availability of data due to locks being held for an extended period of time.

Index Maintenance

Time and time again, I hear "performance tuning is an art form". That's the biggest load of BS that consultants have managed to feed businesses and many database professionals. It requires a special, artistic talent to take a blank canvas and turn it into painting. We're not talking about a painting that copies someone else's work or even incorporates elements designed by others, but a painting which is completely unique. It takes a special, artistic talent for a deaf Ludwig von Beethoven to create music which is still viewed as masterpieces today. The same can be said of a variety of other artistic endeavours which create something that is entirely unique.

There is absolutely nothing artistic about performance tuning a SQL Server. Microsoft built a piece of database software and programmed it to follow a large set of rules. Everything you do with SQL Server is bound by the rules coded by Microsoft engineers. Performance tuning might seem "magical" to someone without a lot of experience or knowledge of databases or SQL Server, but it is nothing more than applying a set of knowledge about the software rules available to come up with a solution which offers better performance. It is really nothing more than the application of a mathematical principle, millennia old to human beings, that the shortest path between two points is a straight line.

To put this into perspective, let's take an example which everyone encounters at least once per week. You need to go to the store to shop for groceries. Your grocery list consists of milk, bread, lettuce, tomatoes, peanut butter, and Vitamin L (otherwise known as licorice). You drive over to the store, fill your shopping cart, pay for everything, go back home, unpack, and put away your groceries. You don't even stop to think that there are multiple ways you could have done your shopping. Most of us would have gotten in a vehicle, driven to the store, mentally sorted the shopping list based on where we knew the products to be located in the store, took 1 pass through the store, went through the checkout, put our groceries in our vehicle, driven home, and put everything away. We could have also driven to the store, found the milk, checked out, put the milk in the car, drive back home, put the milk away, then driven back to the store to get the bread, checked out, put the bread in the car, driven back home, put the bread away, driven back to the store for lettuce, etc. Even though there are many different ways to accomplish our grocery shopping task, we know that the fastest and most efficient method is to do everything in a single pass without repeating steps or retracing our path. This isn't instinct and you wouldn't call grocery shopping using this method an art form. This method of grocery shopping is simply a learned behavior which resulted from years of learning from the time you were born. If we wouldn't call grocery shopping an art form, why do we allow consultants to feed us this line of BS that performance tuning is an art form?

How do you achieve optimal performance from a database? You figure out how to build a solution such that SQL Server has to read the fewest number of pages (shortest path between two points) without reading a page more than once (retracing our path). You still have to arrive at a valid answer, which means every query you execute will have a minimum amount of time required. You can't reduce the time beyond a certain point, because you have to do at least a certain amount of work to find your answer. If you went shopping and only returned with ½ of the list, your shopping trip was a failure. As the number of items on your shopping list increases, so does the minimum amount of time required to go shopping. As the number of locations in the store for the items on your shopping list increases, the minimum amount of time required to go shopping also increases.

SQL Server automatically maintains statistics in order to give the Query Optimizer the best information possible for finding the items on your data shopping list, also known as the queries you are running. In order to locate the data you are after in the most efficient way possible, you design indexes which fit all of the queries you are going to run. In order to reduce the number of pages in an index needing to be read to the minimum number possible, you set a 100% fill factor and pack the index pages completely full. That makes read operations as efficient as possible, but degrades the performance of write operations. So, you compromise to minimize the number of page splits such that you achieve a balance between reads and writes. As rows of data are deleted, SQL Server reclaims the space, keeping all of your indexes at an optimal density for the best balance of performance across read and write operations. And we all live happily ever after.

So says the happy hippy fairy tale. In the real world, people disagree, evil is lurking around the corner, and data maintenance in databases is messy. Once a page is split, SQL Server won't unsplit the page even if the reason for the page split no longer exists. Just because space freed up by the deletion of a row in a B-tree structure can be reused, doesn't mean you will be lucky enough to ever have a row which would belong on the page where the space was freed. You might have designed your database and loaded the initial set of data such that read and write performance was perfectly optimized. Just like any battle plan, that state would have been perfect right up to the first contact with the enemy, when your perfectly optimized system would have been destroyed. In the real world of data, your nice, svelte, high performance index structures get all kinds of lumps, warts, and flab. Pages split once and never have another row written to them. Rows are deleted, leaving behind holes. Just enough rows are written to a page so that nothing else will fit on the page even though a large amount of usable space still exists if you could only move the first row on the page to the previous page in the chain.

All of this flab in a B-tree structure is referred to as fragmentation. As soon as data modifications start against a database, the amount of fragmentation will almost always increase. The level of fragmentation is simply a measure of the percentage of the overall space within a B-tree is unused. An index which starts out with a 90% fill factor also starts out with 10% fragmentation. So, fragmentation in and of itself is not a problem. Excessive fragmentation is a problem as it leads to the requirement to read a much large number of pages than necessary in order to fulfil your data shopping list.

While SQL Server automatically maintains statistics, managing fragmentation is your responsibility. While data changes are under your control, you have no control over page splits and page splits contribute as much and often more to fragmentation than your data changes will. The storage engine is responsible for performing page splits and for writing every data change to a page. At the end of every write operation, the storage engine knows the exact number of bytes free on each page. Statistics are maintained, one way or another, on the number of pages, number of rows, min/max/average length of a row, and the amount of fragmentation in every index. Since a large portion of fragmentation is completely outside your control, why doesn't SQL Server have a way to automatically reduce fragmentation? That question is yet another one which you could put in the library of the great philosophical questions like which came first the chicken or the egg, the word or the thought behind the word, language or abstract thinking? Why did it take Microsoft 18 years to finally implement compression of backups when it was the single most asked for feature in the product when you add up all of the requests over those 18 years and the lack of the feature required Microsoft to spend hundreds of millions of dollars to 3rd parties who developed an entire product with the sole feature of compressing backups? But, I digress. The short, simple answer is that Microsoft will never include a feature to automatically control fragmentation simply because they don't want to. So, it is going to be up to you to write your own code to do something that Microsoft refuses to do. Well, you don't have to write your own, you can simply go online and find any one of the millions of permutations of a very simple routine to manage fragmentation and just plug it into your environment and go on with doing more important things. With the implementation of compressed backups, a feature to automatically manage fragmentation now is the most requested feature for the entire product, the lack of which has caused DBAs to spend tens of millions of hours writing their own and millions more searching for information about such routines. The lack of such a feature has led to the dumbest use of a highly compensated DBA's time and caused an uncountable number of performance issue. If Microsoft ever puts a feature into SQL Server to automatically manage fragmentation, I'll be posting a video of me eating this page.

So, you have to manage fragmentation yourself and you don't want to use a routine that someone else has written, where do you start. That is the subject of the remainder of this section. For those who are just going to use a routine written by someone else to maintain fragmentation, you can skip to the Disabling an Index section.

Fragmentation

You can have two types of fragmentation within an index structure, internal and external. Internal fragmentation occurs deliberately through the FILLFACTOR or PAD_INDEX options, via data modifications, or through data definitions. The FILLFACTOR and PAD_INDEX options contribute to fragmentation, but are desirable in order to minimize the amount of page splitting when data modifications occur. Fragmentation also occurs when pages are split via either an INSERT or UPDATE operation and when rows are deleted. You can also have fragmentation if you have data definitions which leave a large amount of free space on a page which does not have enough room to accommodate additional data. No matter how it occurs, internal fragmentation causes more I/O operations since the pages are not completely full.

External fragmentation occurs when pages are not stored in sequential order within the data files. That is, the pointer to the next page in the index is not the next physical page on disk within the data file. You'll normally get external fragmentation when page splits occur. External fragmentation affects the read ahead capabilities of the storage engine and is most noticeable when performing scans of an index.

Rebuilding Indexes

Since external fragmentation only impacts reads from physical disk, which you want to minimize wherever possible, I don't spend any time worrying about external fragmentation. I look at external fragmentation the same way I look at disk fragmentation within my file system, it is something that happens but I don't spend any time worrying about it. I've seen people stand in front of a room and jump up and down about defragging disk drives and external fragmentation within data files. It's all I can do to not laugh. In my entire IT career, you can count on a single hand the number of times I've defragged a hard drive. The system will spin away for hours moving file fragments around and when it is done, I still can't detect any improvement in performance. If you spend your time trying to get rid of external fragmentation, you are wasting your time, because a single query written slightly less than optimal will chew up more resources than you will ever gain from getting rid of external fragmentation. Additionally, internal fragmentation will cause more performance problems by bloating indexes than external fragmentation ever will.

Therefore, your focus should always be on internal fragmentation and the process of eliminating internal fragmentation will also reduce external fragmentation. Your goal is to maintain the amount of internal fragmentation such that you stay as close as possible to the optimal balance between read and write operations. This is a constant battle and is impossible to maintain on a continuous basis. Instead, you allow the amount of fragmentation to grow until it hits a threshold which you have determined is unacceptable for performance. Once it passes your threshold, you remove enough fragmentation to bring the system back to an acceptable performance level.

You can apply two different methods to your defrag process – index specific defragmentation and the sledgehammer approach. Unfortunately, almost everyone utilizes the one-size-fits-all approach, which I call the sledgehammer approach. You set one threshold for every single index in a database and defrag the index when it passes that threshold. While there technically isn't anything wrong with the sledgehammer approach, it does waste a lot of resources defragging indexes. I implement the sledgehammer defrag approach on databases which are very small simply because the amount of time to defrag every index is usually not much more than it takes to determine the fragmentation level in the first place. I also implement the sledgehammer defrag approach for organizations where they either don't have or don't want a DBA to manage their databases. In this case, all you are trying to do is keep the code as simple and straightforward as possible and the wasted resources are simply a cost of doing business without a DBA to manage the databases.

Applying index specific defragmentation takes much more effort and more complexity within your code. You need to determine the optimal fragmentation level for each index along with the fragmentation level which is unacceptable for each index. The index specific defragmentation method is the one I use the most often. Why do I use this approach? What happens if you say that you want every index to be defragged once it reaches 30% fragmentation? Most of the indexes in the database were created with a 90% fill factor, a small number were created with a 100% fill factor since you anticipated very rare changes, but you had about a dozen indexes which undergo extremely heavy modification so you created them with a 50% fill factor. The sledgehammer approach would say to defrag all of these heavily used indexes every single time you ran your defrag routine only to see every one of these indexes fragment beyond your 30% threshold almost immediately.

Not every index should be treated equally. There are some indexes which will be almost completely fragmented and there is nothing you can do to change it. What you are basically after is finding some kind of middle ground where you can maintain the database in a "good enough" state so that you can focus on more important things. The basic threshold that I use is one week. You want to determine your threshold levels based on how much fragmentation an index will acquire over a 1 week time period. I use a one week time interval, because I normally defrag indexes once per week. In terms of defragmentation, I determine my thresholds based on what is possible to even achieve. If I want to maintain 10% fragmentation in an index to account for data modifications and performance is noticeably impacted once the index reaches 30% fragmentation, but takes more than 1 week to reach 30%, I'll set my defrag interval at somewhere between 20% and 25% fragmentation. The index may or may not be defragmented every week, but it will usually be defragmented before it reaches the level where performance degrades.

Analysing Indexes

In order to defrag an index, you need to be able to determine the amount of fragmentation present in the index. In addition to reporting on the number of forwarded records, size of an index key, number of rows, and the number of pages used by an index, sys.dm_db_index_physical_stats also returns the amount of fragmentation present in the index.

There are two columns which are used to determine the level of fragmentation in an index, avg_fragmentation_in_percent and avg_page_space_used_in_percent.

The avg_fragmentation_in_percent returns the amount of external fragmentation present. The avg_fragmentation_in_percent is a measure of the percentage of pages which are not in the same physical order as logical order. The interesting thing about this piece of data is that almost every defrag routine you will encounter uses this number as the sole indicator of when to defrag an index. The amount of external fragmentation only matters when you are performing physical reads off disk. While you want to keep the external fragmentation low, since you can't completely avoid index scans or reads from disk in real world applications, the amount of external fragmentation will have very little impact in most databases designed for transaction processing.

The piece of data which very few people ever talk about is the avg_page_space_used_in_percent. This number tells you the amount of internal fragmentation present in an index. When this number is at 100%, you have completely filled every page and are at the smallest possible number of pages in the index. In reality, you want to keep this value near the fill factor you have established for the index.

Removing Fragmentation

You defragment an index with the DBCC DBREINDEX command, ALTER INDEX, or CREATE INDEX. DBCC DBREINDEX is left over from prior versions of SQL Server and while it can be used, you have better control and capabilities with ALTER INDEX or CREATE INDEX.

The nuclear option for defragging an index is to drop the index and recreate it using the CREATE INDEX statement. While this works for completely removing fragmentation, it has many downsides. Any code written as an automated routine will become very complex since you need to build a CREATE INDEX statement from the metadata stored within the database in order to recreate the index with the same definition as it originally had. While you are recreating the index, it is not available to SQL Server causing queries to degrade in performance. When the index is a primary key, you can't drop the index, but instead must issue an ALTER TABLE statement to drop the primary key constraint supported by the index. While the primary key is dropped, you can have duplicate keys written to the table. Additionally, you can't drop a primary key when it is being referenced by foreign keys. That means you have to drop all of the foreign keys before you can drop the primary key and referential integrity is not being enforced while the recreation of the index supporting the primary key is running. Also, remember that nonclustered indexes point to clustered index keys and if a clustered index does not exist, the nonclustered index contains a RID. If you drop a clustered index while nonclustered indexes still exist, SQL Server must re-write every nonclustered index entry to remove the clustering key and replace it with a RID. Then when you recreate the clustered index, the RID is removed from every nonclustered index key and replaced with the clustering key. You can use the CREATE INDEX…WITH DROP_EXISTSING clause to avoid many of these issues, but there are better options to rebuild an index using ALTER INDEX which avoid all of these problems. You should only use the DROP/CREATE method if you need to change the definition of an index or change the storage settings for the index.

ALTER INDEX has two options to remove fragmentation in an index, REBUILD and REORGANIZE. The REBUILD option will recreate the index with the existing definition. The REORGANIZE option compacts free space in the leaf level of an index along with reordering the pages in order to remove external fragmentation. The REORGANIZE option also allows you to separately compact LOB pages, pages which contain VARCHAR(max), NVARCHAR(max), VARBINARY(max), and XML data. LOB compaction is on by default and reorganizes LOB columns specified in the INCLUDE clause of a nonclustered index or LOB columns in a table when a clustered index is reorganized.

With either REBUILD or REORGANIZE, you can also change any properties set for the index such as the fill factor, data compression, and row/page locking, but you can't change the definition or storage location of the index. A REORGANIZE is always performed online, meaning the index is available for both read and write operations while the reorganization occurs. The REBUILD option allows you to specify that the rebuild should occur online. However, if an XML or spatial index exists on the table, the REBUILD must occur in offline mode. When an index build is in offline mode, the index is completely unavailable and SQL Server acquires a schema lock along with a shared lock on the table. The schema lock prevents all DDL changes while the rebuild is occurring and the shared lock prevents all write operations, but read operations are still allowed against the table. If you are rebuilding a clustered index offline, the entire table is unavailable until the rebuild completes.

> **Note:** Prior versions of SQL Server did not allow you to do an online index rebuild if the table has VARCHAR(MAX), NVARCHAR(MAX), or VARBINARY(MAX) columns. This limitation no longer exists in SQL Server 2012.

When an index is rebuilt, SQL Server keeps the existing index in place, builds a second copy of the index, modifies the metadata to point to the newly built copy, and then drops the original copy of the index.

When an index is reorganized, SQL Server performs two distinct phases in the process. The first phase of a REORGANIZE processes pages in logical index order in 8 page blocks. SQL Server inspects the contents of the 8 pages and if it determines that enough rows can be moved to completely empty at least one page in the 8 page segment, the rows are moved and empty page(s) deallocated. It then moves on to the next 8 page segment and repeats the process. Once all of the empty space is removed via this algorithm, a second pass is taken to remove external fragmentation. The external fragmentation algorithm applies a simple bubble sort algorithm to rearrange the pages such that the logical order matches the physical order on disk.

In the first phase, the REORGANIZE option operates on blocks of 8 pages and the second phase operates on 2 pages at a time. This requires page locks to be acquired on the pages being modified. If ALLOW_PAGE_LOCKS is set to OFF, the REORGANIZE will fail.

Since it is much harder to introduce fragmentation into intermediate levels of an index, a REORGANIZE is the most common defrag method. If you encounter significant fragmentation in the intermediate levels, the only way to remove the fragmentation is to rebuild the index.

Exercise 13: Internal Fragmentation

The following exercise takes a look at how internal fragmentation affects an index as well as how you can have significant internal fragmentation without any external fragmentation.

1. Execute the following code to create a test table, load with data, and create a nonclustered index with a 90% fill factor.

    ```
    CREATE TABLE dbo.Test
    (CustomerID INT NOT NULL);

    INSERT INTO dbo.Test
    SELECT CustomerID FROM Customers.Customer;

    CREATE NONCLUSTERED INDEX in_CustomerID ON dbo.Test (CustomerID) WITH FILLFACTOR = 90;
    ```

2. Execute the following code to inspect the index fragmentation and defined fill factor.

    ```
    SELECT * FROM sys.dm_db_index_physical_stats(DB_ID('ChampionValleyPens'),
                                    OBJECT_ID('dbo.Test'), NULL, NULL ,
    'DETAILED');
    SELECT * FROM sys.indexes WHERE object_id = OBJECT_ID('dbo.Test');
    ```

3. Note that the avg_fragmentation_in_percent is 0 for the nonclustered index while the leaf level, index_level = 0 has a value of approximately 90 for the avg_page_space_used_in_percent.

4. Now execute the following code to delete every 3rd row from the table. The % symbol is a modulo and the WHERE clause says to take the value in the CustomerID column, divide by 3, and delete any row where the remainder is 0.

    ```
    DELETE FROM dbo.Test WHERE CustomerID % 3 = 0;
    ```

5. Now execute the following code to look at the fragmentation information for the index.

    ```
    SELECT * FROM sys.dm_db_index_physical_stats(DB_ID('ChampionValleyPens'),
                            OBJECT_ID('dbo.Test'), NULL, NULL , 'DETAILED');
    ```

6. Notice that while the avg_fragmentation_in_percent is still 0, we now have an average of 40% unused space within the index. This basically means that we are consuming 30% more space than we need to and we have to read approximately 30% more pages to locate data than would be necessary. Note that there are 2469 pages on the leaf level of the nonclustered index.

7. Execute the following code to defrag the index.

    ```
    ALTER INDEX in_CustomerID ON dbo.Test REORGANIZE;
    ```

8. If you execute the following code to review the fragmentation now, you should see the avg_fragmentation_in_percent is still 0, the avg_page_space_used_in_percent is back to almost 90 and we've removed 815 pages from the leaf level of the nonclustered index or approximately 33% of the original pages.

    ```
    SELECT * FROM sys.dm_db_index_physical_stats(DB_ID('ChampionValleyPens'),
                            OBJECT_ID('dbo.Test'), NULL, NULL , 'DETAILED');
    ```

9. Execute the following code to drop the dbo.Test table and clean up the database.

    ```
    DROP TABLE dbo.Test;
    ```

Disabling an Index

The ALTER INDEX statement can also be used to disable an index. When an index is disabled, it is unavailable to the Query Optimizer and SQL Server no longer maintains the index when changes occur to the table. If you disable a clustered index, the entire table is unavailable since the leaf level of the clustered index is made up of the rows in the table.

The most common reason for disabling an index is to avoid the overhead of index maintenance when you are making mass changes such as importing a large volume of contacts for a marketing campaign from a 3rd party provider. You'll find that in many cases involving mass data loads that it takes less time to load the data into a table and then build indexes from scratch than it would take to load the data with the indexes already in place. As a general rule of thumb, if you are increasing the number of rows in a table by 20% or more using a bulk load routine such as BCP or BULK INSERT, it would take less time to drop and recreate the indexes than to perform all of the index maintenance during the load operation.

Of course, dropping and recreating indexes has all of the issues mentioned previously in this chapter. The way around having to drop the indexes is to simply disable the indexes. The metadata for the index is retained and all you need to know is the name of the index to re-enable it with the same definition. Since a disabled index is no longer maintained by SQL Server, you can't simply re-enable the index as it would not reflect the set of data present in the table. You re-enable an index by rebuilding it with an ALTER INDEX…REBUILD statement.

Designing Indexes Revisited

Now that we have a better understanding of how indexes are constructed, how statistics help the Query Optimizer determine an optimal path, how a B-tree structure allows us to scale to massive data volumes while keeping performance stable, and how fragmentation plays a role, we can take a look at some additional considerations when designing indexes.

When you have a table which handles large volumes of very small transactions, usually affecting only a single row, your main goal is to minimize the number of indexes since each additional index will decrease the performance of transactions. In many cases, a table which handles large volumes of very small transactions will also have large volumes of very small read operations and almost all the read operations will be accessing a single row based on the primary key. In almost all of these cases, you will want the table to have an integer based primary key which is also an identity and clustered. You will also want the index to have a very large fillfactor, generally 100%. By combining the identity based primary key with a 100% fill factor, you ensure that the pages are packed as tightly as possible with rows and that all new rows get appended to the table. Page splits should be very rare and would only occur on the upper levels of the index. Having the pages packed as full as possible minimizes the number or read operations required to locate a single row. You will also have a very small clustering key to be added to any nonclustered index, although you should have very few, if any created against tables which fit this activity pattern. A table with this type of activity pattern should also be defragmented frequently, with a REORGANIZE, if rows are being deleted to reclaim as much space as possible.

You begin to run into performance conflicts when the table needs to handle large volumes of very small transactions along with a lot of SELECT statements which retrieve multiple rows using criteria based on a wide range of columns. Here you need to make a trade off which will usually skew towards keeping the transactions at peak performance while slowing down read operations. In order to achieve peak performance on transactions, you may need to refrain from creating nonclustered indexes which would otherwise satisfy queries in order to avoid the index maintenance overhead. You make the trade off in favor of transactions to ensure that the data makes it into the database as quickly as possible. After all, if you optimized the table for read operations, you may have created a situation where transactions run slowly enough that it actually becomes impossible to write all of the data you need and if you can't capture the data then read operations become rather pointless.

The access pattern which almost always creates problems is when you are dealing with a table which frequently has a small number of large transactions while at the same time having to handle large volumes of SELECT statement retrieving large blocks of rows. This is the type of activity you see within databases which are the primary source for reporting and analytic applications. You perform large loads of data on a periodic basis which need to finish within tightly defined time periods and then run a large number of read operations, some of which can access very large sets of data. Since you are building a database primarily for reporting and analytic activities, you need to have a very high level of indexing to maintain adequate performance. However, the large number of indexes will significantly impact the periodic load operations. The reason this type of access pattern creates problems is many people design the system such that indexes are disabled, data is loaded, and indexes are then rebuilt. This usually works well for a short period of time before the system starts degrading and the load operations no longer complete on time. The problem is that the rebuild of the index is taking place on increasingly larger volumes of data to the point where you are loading a tiny fraction of the overall table size, but having to rebuild the entire table.

There isn't a simple solution to this problem. You can mitigate the situation by having the routine disable some, but not all of the indexes, load the data, and then rebuild the smaller number of indexes. The load degrades in performance, but hopefully degrades less than if the indexes which were left in place would take if rebuilt. This continues to the point where the load is occurring with all of the indexes in place due to the amount of time it would take to rebuild the index. Once you reach this state, the only way out of a performance issue is to redesign some or all of the system.

In the data load scenario, you also have an issue with clustered indexes. You can't disable the clustered index otherwise the load would fail due to the table being unavailable. You also can't drop the clustered index while leaving the nonclustered indexes in place because that would require rewriting all of the nonclustered indexes to replace the clustering key with a RID. For tables accepting periodic, mass data loads, you are almost always going to use the same clustered index design as I recommended for a large volume of small transactions – an integer type column which is an identity such that the clustered index really doesn't play a role in performance of the data load operation.

Sorting is one of the most expensive operations you can perform when reading data. However, if the data you are retrieving is already sorted as specified in a SELECT statement, SQL Server does not have to perform the sort operation. When you have applications which require large, expensive sort operations, you can utilize an index with the INCLUDE clause to build a covering index that not only satisfies the query, but also avoids the sort. Remember that ascending is the default sort order, but you can also specify the DESC keyword on any column in the index key. This could lead to indexes which have the same columns in the index key, might even have the columns in the same order, but specify different sort orders in order to satisfy different sort operations.

Complementary indexes

One of the least understood index design patterns is complementary indexes. Some mistakenly call these duplicate indexes, but there isn't anything duplicate about them. Complementary indexes always occur at least in pairs, but can occur in groups of 3, 4, 5, etc. indexes. A complementary index is simply an index with a definition which is similar to another index on a table, but complements the index by satisfying a slightly different set of queries. Duplicate indexes on the other hand are exactly what the name implies, exact duplicates of another index which should be dropped since a duplicate index serves no purpose other than to consume resources.

Consider the Customers.Customer table which has a LastName and FirstName column. You might search on the last name only, the first name only, or both first and last name. You might also sort the result set by the last name. You wouldn't want to perform these searches by having to read all 1 million rows in the table.

Designing a single index to meet all of these requirements is also impossible, so you might wind up with a set of complementary indexes which might look like the following:

```
CREATE NONCLUSTERED INDEX in_LastNameASC_Include_FirstName
    ON Customers.Customer (LastName) INCLUDE (FirstName);

CREATE NONCLUSTERED INDEX in_LastNameDESC_Include_FirstName
    ON Customers.Customer (LastName DESC) INCLUDE (FirstName);

CREATE NONCLUSTERED INDEX in_FirstName_Include_LastName
    ON Customers.Customer (FirstName) INCLUDE (LastName);

CREATE NONCLUSTERED INDEX in_LastNameFirstName
    ON Customers.Customer (LastName, FirstName);

CREATE NONCLUSTERED INDEX in_LastNameDESCFirstName
    ON Customers.Customer (LastName DESC, FirstName);
```

The first index would be optimal for a query that searched on the last name and also returned the first name and either didn't have an ORDER BY clause or sorted the results in ascending order by last name. The second index would be optimal for a query that searched on the last name, also returned the first name, and sorted the results by last name in descending order. The 3rd index would be optimal for a search on the first name which also returned the last name. The 4th and 5th indexes would be optimal for searches on both first name and last name with either an ascending or descending sort by last name. If you were just searching by the last name and didn't want to return the first name, then you could drop the INCLUDE clause off the first 2 indexes to achieve an optimal design for two different sort orders.

The indexes complement each other. Each index has a slightly different design even though the indexes only cover 2 columns in the table. Whether you create complementary indexes or not is a matter of balancing the maintenance required for write operations with the reduction in I/O for read operations. When you have a table which receives significantly more read activity, you will usually have more complementary indexes created. You are sacrificing performance of write operations in order to achieve a bigger reduction in resources from the much larger volume of read operations.

Monitor Index Usage

By now, you are probably trying to make sense of all of the design options and hoping for a simple cookbook that tells you how to design all of your indexes. Unfortunately, there isn't a simple cookbook and anyone attempting to present one is feeding you a line of BS. Your index strategy is dependent upon the mix of reads and writes from the application(s) accessing your databases. The indexing needs of a database may also change over time. Every index decision you make will be specific to your situation and all index designs will need to be re-evaluated periodically.

Missing Indexes

You could use a simple brute force method to determine the optimal indexing strategy. The brute force method is exactly what it sounds like. You first load a database with a representative sample of the data which will exist in production. You make sure the database also accurately represents the volume of data which will exist. You then create every permutation of index that is possible for every table in the database. Once that is done, all you need to do is run a representative sample of queries against the database and determine which indexes the Query Optimizer actually uses. You eliminate the indexes which are not used and run all the queries against the database again to see if the set of indexes selected has changed. You then evaluate all of the remaining indexes to achieve the optimal balance of index maintenance during write operations with the performance improvement for read operations.

The brute force method, while not very elegant, will give you a set of indexes which the Query Optimizer will use to improve read operations. But, the brute force method has some large drawbacks. Building a database with a representative sample of data as the production system will have is usually a rather difficult task for many developers. If you manage to build a sample set of data which has the proper volume without introducing skew in the data set, you will run into the biggest issue with the brute force method, time. Generating all possible permutations of indexes is a simple exercise in building a query which interrogates the table definitions and creates all of the index permutations. Creating all of those indexes is another matter. A single table could generate hundreds or even thousands of index definitions and you could wait weeks or months for all of the indexes to be created. Even if you managed to every permutation of index, you would still need to set of all of the possible queries which would be run against the database. From what you learned in chapters 9, 10, and 11, you should know that the set of possible queries might as well be considered to be infinite based on all of the different ways you could construct even rather simple queries. Using the brute force method, while effective, simply takes too long to achieve a result.

Fortunately, with SQL Server 2005 and above, you can narrow down your choices more quickly and easily than applying a brute force method. The potential choices are also much more accurate as they are based on statistical data from the Query Optimizer.

When you run a query against SQL Server, an index is not found to satisfy the query, but based on statistical information automatically computed against all columns SQL Server determines that an index might have been useful, you produce what is referred to as an index miss. In very simple terms, an index miss occurs when SQL Server can't find an index definition for a query but thinks one might have been useful. In SQL Server 2005 and above, when an index miss occurs, SQL Server logs detailed information about the event. You can use this information to determine where indexes might be useful to create. But using the metadata which SQL Server will build up over time, all you need to do is toss queries at the database and see what turns up in the missing index metadata.

The information is stored in a set of views which begin with sys.dm_db_missing_index. The two core views are sys.dm_db_missing_index_details and sys.dm_db_missing_index_group_stats. Sys.dm_db_missing_index_details view contains information about the table and columns involved in the index miss. Sys.dm_db_missing_index_group_stats contains the statistical information behind the index miss event such as how many times it occurred, the estimated cost, and the estimated impact. You can use this information to find cases where one or more queries could be helped with the creation of an index

The missing index Dynamic Management Views, DMVs, have some very large blind spots that you need to account for. Index misses on spatial or XML data will not result in an entry. Likewise, the missing index DMVs will not account for cases where a filtered index or a descending sort order would be appropriate. An index miss only occurs due to a read operation and does not factor in any cost for write operations. You are completely on your own for spatial indexes, XML indexes, and descending sort orders on index keys.

Using the missing index DMVs means that you have to have an index miss on a query in order for SQL Server to log any data. The data logged will point to an index possibly being useful, but it will not tell you whether applying a filter to the index will be useful. If an index exists to satisfy the query, even if a filtered index would be more efficient, SQL Server will not log any information to the missing index DMVs since the presence of an inefficient index still results in the Query Optimizer selecting the inefficient index. While the missing index DMVs might point you in the direction of a filtered index being needed, you will almost always be on your own when it comes to defining filtered indexes.

You can use the missing index views to quickly find candidates, but you always need to evaluate the indexes suggested to suit your applications. You can find the best candidates with the query below:

```
WITH Impact_CTE (IndexAdvantage, GroupHandle, UniqueCompiles, UserSeeks, UserScans,
    LastUserSeek, LastUserScan, AvgTotalUserCost, AvgUserImpact, SystemSeeks,
SystemScans,
    LastSystemSeek, LastSystemScan, AvgTotalSystemCost, AvgSystemImpact)
AS (SELECT user_seeks * avg_total_user_cost * (avg_user_impact * 0.01) AS
index_advantage, *
    FROM sys.dm_db_missing_index_group_stats)
SELECT *
FROM Impact_CTE i INNER JOIN sys.dm_db_missing_index_groups AS mig
        ON i.GroupHandle = mig.index_group_handle
    INNER JOIN sys.dm_db_missing_index_details AS mid ON mig.index_handle =
mid.index_handle;
```

The key to the query above is with the calculation for the column named index advantage. This calculation wasn't just made up and I don't know why you should only factor in 1% of the average user impact. I don't question the calculation since it was provided to me many years ago by one of the PMs at Microsoft who works on the Query Optimizer team. The basics of the calculation allow you to provide a statistical value to the possible advantage of a particular missing index in relation to all of the rest of the missing indexes. The first value in the calculation is the number of user seeks which is another way of saying how frequently a particular index miss occurs. Just because an index miss occurs doesn't mean you want to immediately create an index for it, because the query which produced the index miss might never happen again or happen only very infrequently. You want to focus on the most frequent queries that produce the largest amount of index misses. What I do know from using this query for many years on tens of thousands of databases is that when you see an index advantage which exceeds 20,000 you should very seriously consider creating the index and when it exceeds 50,000 the benefit of creating the index will far outweigh any possible index maintenance due to write operations.

The data in the missing index views is not persisted to disk, so when the instance is restarted the information on index misses is cleared. In order to obtain adequate information to make a decision, you need to ensure that the instance has been running for a long enough time period to yield adequate information. When you are using the missing index views on a development system to make initial estimates for indexes, you generally don't care how long the instance has been running since you are making evaluations on a reasonably controlled environment where you can limit the queries being run. When you look at the missing index information on a production system, you need to know how long the instance has been running and make adjustments accordingly. If the instance has been running for many years without a restart, even infrequently run queries can start reaching the 20,000 and 50,000 thresholds mentioned earlier which can lead to excessive creation of indexes. The 20,000 and 50,000 thresholds are good enough approximations for production instances which have been running for up to 6 – 9 months. Beyond that time frame, you may want to use slightly higher thresholds.

Exercise 14: Missing Indexes

The following exercise takes a look at how you can use the missing index DMVs to find potential index candidates.

1. Restart your SQL Server instance to ensure that the data underneath the missing index views has been cleared from any prior queries before doing this exercise.

2. Execute the following query:
   ```
   SELECT CustomerID, AddressLine1, City, StateProvinceID, PostalCode
   FROM Customers.Address
   WHERE City = 'Dallas';
   ```

3. Now run the following queries to inspect the statistics, index structures, and missing index details:
   ```
   DBCC SHOW_STATISTICS("Customers.Address","in_City_StateProvince");
   SELECT * FROM sys.dm_db_index_physical_stats(DB_ID('ChampionValleyPens'),

   OBJECT_ID('Customers.Address'),null,null,'DETAILED');


   WITH Impact_CTE (IndexAdvantage, GroupHandle, UniqueCompiles, UserSeeks, UserScans,
        LastUserSeek, LastUserScan, AvgTotalUserCost, AvgUserImpact, SystemSeeks,
        SystemScans, LastSystemSeek, LastSystemScan, AvgTotalSystemCost,
   AvgSystemImpact)
   AS (SELECT user_seeks * avg_total_user_cost * (avg_user_impact * 0.01) AS
   index_advantage,
             migs.* FROM sys.dm_db_missing_index_group_stats migs)
   SELECT *
   FROM Impact_CTE i INNER JOIN sys.dm_db_missing_index_groups AS mig
                                                   ON i.GroupHandle =
   mig.index_group_handle
        INNER JOIN sys.dm_db_missing_index_details AS mid ON mig.index_handle =
   mid.index_handle;
   ```

4. You should see an entry in the missing index DMVs indicating an index miss on the query that retrieved Dallas customer address information. You should also note that the table has 16,929 pages, the statistics on the City column sampled 100% of the rows in the table, and Dallas is a boundary point in the histogram.

5. Run the Dallas query again and check the missing index information.

6. You should see the value for UserSeeks increase by 1 to reflect the 2 times you've run this query and the IndexAdvantage should have also increased.

7. Now run the query below and then check the missing index information.
   ```
   SELECT CustomerID, AddressLine1, City, StateProvinceID, PostalCode
   FROM Customers.Address
   WHERE City = 'Davenport';
   ```

8. You should have seen that the UserSeeks remained the same.

9. Now take a look at the histogram for the City column again and note that Davenport is not a boundary point on the histogram and SQL Server would consider the statistics from the Dayton step which says there are 55 unique values within the step and an average of 59.96363 rows for each unique value.

10. Create the following index:
    ```
    CREATE NONCLUSTERED INDEX in_City ON Customers.Address (City);
    ```

11. Check the missing index information again and note that the row corresponding to the City column is gone..

12. Drop the in_City index on the Customers.Address table, because we really don't want it and it was used for simple demonstration purposes.
    ```
    DROP INDEX Customers.Address.in_City;
    ```

Some of those who have experience with SQL Server should have grasped the meaning behind all of the numbers mentioned in the exercise as well as where all of this leads. I am specifically trying not to take this chapter on a 200 or so page detour into query plans, performance analysis, and query tuning, because that is a subject for a large section of the next book and it will not fit within the page constraints I have for this book.

SQL Server can use more than 1 index to satisfy a query. This might sound strange, but consider a table with a clustered index. A query would have to be able to use more than 1 index per table otherwise it would become impossible to utilize any nonclustered index since gathering any data not in the nonclustered index requires reading from the clustered index whose leaf level is the table. Without getting into a lot of details, the two queries against the Customers.Address table used the clustered primary key along with the in_City_StateProvince index.

If SQL Server just scanned the table, it would have to read 16,929 pages. However, the in_City_StateProvince table is ordered by City, so SQL Server can determine from the statistics that there are 9043 entries from Dallas since it is a boundary point and that it would have to read about 32 pages to find all of the Dallas rows. 999707 rows / 3326 pages on the leaf level = 300 rows per page and 9043 rows / 300 rows per page comes out to 30 pages + 1 page for the root and 1 page for the intermediate level. It then has to perform 9,043 read operations to gather the additional data. This adds up to approximately 9,075 I/O operations, which is far less than the 16,929 pages which would have to be read if the table were simply scanned from start to finish. This is why the Query Optimizer chose to use the in_City_StateProvince index instead of scanning the table. However, it also understands average amount of space consumed by the CustomerID, AddressLine1, StateProvinceID, and PostalCode columns based on the statistics present for those columns and that if an index on just the City column that had an INCLUDE of the rest of the columns in the SELECT list were present, the number of I/O operations would be dramatically reduced. So, even though the Query Optimizer used the in_City_StateProvince index, it threw an index miss event or more specifically a missed index opportunity event.

SQL Server could make precise decisions for Dallas, because as a boundary point on an index with 100% sample rate, an exact number of rows could be determined for the value. Davenport is not a boundary value, so SQL Server has to rely on averages. The statistics tell the Query Optimizer that Davenport would yield approximately 60 rows of data which means that it would have to read approximately 3 pages from the index along with about 60 reads to gather the rest of the data for the query. Doing the same basic math considering the leaf level space consumed if an index existed on the City column which included the remainder of the columns in the SELECT statement, the Query Optimizer can quickly determine that the number of read operations would not substantially decrease from the estimated 63 reads currently required, so an index miss event does not occur in this case. The actual results are a bit different, because 822 rows were returned instead of the estimated 60, but the basic principle still applies.

Does anyone still think that a deep understanding of statistics is not important in building optimal database applications? Does anyone still think there is anything magical or "it's an art form" about determining when SQL Server might decide to utilize one index over another?

You should have also noted that the number of UserSeeks will increment each time an index opportunity is missed for a given potential index. This is how the IndexAdvantage metric segments the entries allowing you to focus on frequently occurring missed index opportunities.

The majority of the columns in the missing index query are devoted to metrics around each missed index opportunity. The last 4 columns provide the information about what the missed opportunity is. The included_columns column is simply a reflection of all of the columns from a table that are in the SELECT clause, but not the WHERE clause. The columns in the equality_columns column are simply the result of using = or IN within the WHERE clause. If we had used BETWEEN, LIKE, <, >, etc., values would have appeared in the inequality_columns column.

Each entry in the missing index DMVs is unique based on equality_columns, inequality_columns, included_columns, and statement. If you were to change the Dallas query slightly by removing the CustomerID column, you would get a second entry in the missing index DMVs. If you added in AddressLine2, you would get a 3rd entry. So, you can have a number of slightly different queries which produce missed index opportunities with slightly different definitions which might be satisfied by creating a single index. Steps 10 and 11 should have told you that SQL Server maintains this data both when missed index opportunities occur and when indexes are created.

SQL Server will remove any missing index entries which loosely correspond to the index that was created. It isn't going to remove a missing index entry for the StateProvince column when you create an index on the City column, but if you create an index on the City column, it will remove every entry where the City column is found in either equality_columns or inequality_columns regardless of whether the included_columns matches or not.

That takes us to the last column with a rather strange name compared to the data it contains. The column named statement contains the table corresponding to the missing index entry. The reason for the discrepancy is buried in the early beta releases of SQL Server 2005. In the initial beta releases, the statement column contained a complete CREATE INDEX statement matching the equality_columns, inequality_columns, and included_columns for the missing index entry. Microsoft quickly found out that a few customers, who didn't really understand how to use the missing index DMVs, had created a process that automatically created an index any time an entry appeared in the missing index DMV. This quickly lead to massive bloat of indexes on tables and in some cases brought write operations to a near halt. Of course, it was Microsoft's fault that SQL Server was slow and needed to be fixed, not the completely inappropriate way in which a feature was being used. So, they replaced the CREATE INDEX statement with the name of the table, but left the column name intact so they didn't have to refactor and retest a large block of code. This didn't prevent someone from doing something stupid with the missing index DMVs, but it did mean they had to deliberately create something stupid which Microsoft was not going to be responsible for.

The missing index data always needs to be evaluated based on your knowledge of the application. You also need to ensure you are minimizing the number of indexes on a table in order to maintain a proper balance between reads and writes. While the missing index data might contain a number of entries, a single index might be able to satisfy a wide range of queries which were producing a variety of missed index opportunities.

Evaluate Index Usage

Whether or not an index is used is highly dependent upon the statistics. If the statistics behind the in_City_StateProvince index were instead built with a 15% or 20% sample of the data, the Query Optimizer calculations may have said to just scan the table for both customers in Dallas and Davenport instead of using the in_City_StateProvince index which was still suboptimal for this particular query but still better than a table scan. While missing index information is maintained when an index miss occurs, a new index is created, and cleared when the instance is restarted, it is not maintained when statistics are updated or statistics become invalid. So, the choice of whether to use an index or scan a table is highly dependent upon the actual values used in the query, the volume of data in the table, and the accuracy of the statistics. Since the volume of data can change over time as can the accuracy of statistics, you need to periodically evaluate the indexes in your database to ensure that you still have optimal indexes. An index that is used heavily today might not be used at all tomorrow due to a shift in the data within the table.

Prior to SQL Server 2005, we found unused indexes the hard way. You dropped the index and waited to see if performance declined. If not, then you found an index which wasn't being used. Not only was this method invasive, it was also not very accurate, so many never attempted to clean out unused indexes and simply dealt with the bloated transaction logs and performance impact to write operations. SQL Server 2005 changed all of that through sys.dm_db_index_usage_stats and sys.dm_db_index_operational_stats.

Where sys.dm_db_index_physical_stats provides us information about the physical storage of each level of an index or heap, sys.dm_db_index_operational_stats provides details about the read and write activity occurring within each index. You can get details such as the number of inserts, updates, and deletes at both a leaf and non-leaf level. You can also get the number of each type of read operation such as whether the read was for a single row or a range of rows. In addition to the read and write activity, detailed information about locking and latching within each index is captured.

You use sys.dm_db_index_physical_stats to understand the relative amount of activity occurring with an index which helps determine whether the index is being used and is useful. Since indexes are used to improve read performance, all of your indexes should have much heavier read activity than write activity otherwise you are potentially spending more time maintaining the index than you are getting out of it for read performance. The statistics on the lock and latch waits tell you whether you have contention between reads and writes within the index which might be alleviated by increasing the fillfactor, defragging the index, or refactoring your code.

In addition to the detailed write related information in sys.dm_db_index_physical_stats, sys.dm_db_index_usage_stats provides additional breakdown of read and modification activity along with when the activity last occurred. This is useful in finding out if an index is even being used. Instead of dropping an index and waiting to see if there are any complaints, sys.dm_db_index_usage_stats will tell you the last time a read or update operation occurred against the index. You can then focus on indexes which haven't been accessed in a long time and determine if they can be dropped without affecting some operation that you might only perform once a week, month, or quarter.

Sys.dm_db_index_usage_stats will interact with index rebuilds. If you REORGANIZE an index all you are really doing is shuffling the entries around to compact space on the leaf level. When you REBUILD an index, you are re-computing the statistics in addition to any defragmentation. When you rebuild the statistics for an index, the Query Optimizer may decide that an index which was being used to satisfy one or more queries is no longer the optimal path. Since a re-computation of the statistics during an index rebuild can cause the index to no longer be used, SQL Server will remove the entry from sys.dm_db_index_usage_stats.

Columnstore Indexes

Now that we've gone into all of the details around indexes and index construction, let's take a small step back and look at indexes at a macro level and how they help our applications. An index's power comes not only from the B-tree structure which allows us to read a very small number of entries to find anything in a table, but also the fact that the index is always maintained in synch with the underlying data. Covering indexes take this a step further by allowing us to satisfy queries entirely from the contents of the index. For all of their power in improving the performance of queries, indexes as they are currently constructed, still have some significant inefficiencies. Additionally, tables can get so large that it doesn't matter how much indexing you do, queries are going to run painfully slow.

The inefficiencies within an index stem not from *how* they are built, but from *what* they contain. An index contains every value from the columns defined for the index which are present in the table. We can minimize the amount of data by applying a filter to the index, but the simple fact remains that the index still contains every value corresponding to the index definition. Consider the StateProvinceID column in the Customers.Address table. An index on the StateProvinceID column will contain 999,707 values since that is how many rows are in the table, but there are only 51 unique values in that column.

The question becomes, can we build a better index?

One of the most powerful things I ever learned in school didn't come from a course, a teacher/professor, or from any of my own research or discussions. Instead, it came from a simple poster hanging on the wall of my physics advisor's office at the University of Illinois Urbana-Champaign. It was a large poster of an elder Einstein staring straight forward with that stare which was blank and penetrating at the same time topped off with the unruly hair which only Einstein could have managed to pull off. The caption on the poster said – "The uneducated accomplish the impossible every day, because they don't know better." It took me a while to really understand that incredibly powerful statement and you can see it vividly in Einstein's life.

It doesn't mean that an education is worthless. It means we have to look beyond what we're taught and more importantly how we're taught, to break down the barriers that education throws into our minds, and think through problems free of the "can't", "don't", and "won't". Einstein made some of the most powerful and pivotal observations in physics precisely because he rejected the rote learning, memorization, and unbending rules present in the educational systems of his time and still seen today. Magic becomes science and impossible becomes possible, simply when we acquire enough knowledge to make it so. What does this have to do with indexes? Everything. Just as it has everything to do with everything I've ever studied, conceived of, written about, taught, and implemented in my career.

It was this principle which was at the core of a system I built back in 1994. It was an extremely elegant and advanced solution at the time, but something I see as quite obvious when you really think through it. That is because the solution really wasn't that novel. Sure, it was miles ahead of anything available at the time, but it still wasn't a novel solution. It was born out of needing to design a data warehouse where the fundamental question was "How in the heck are we going to do **THAT**!?"

The design problem was that we had to build a data warehouse which had an initial load of data between 7TB and 8TB. To some, a terabyte of data is still a lot to have to store, manage, query, and update. But, managing terabytes of data has become routine. So, you might be wondering why we were twisting our brains inside out trying to figure out how to deal with 7 – 8TB of data. The reason was that this wasn't something we were building in 2010, we were building this in 1994. For those who weren't in IT or who hadn't even been born yet, this was an era when we had just gotten shiny new 386s on our desks, RAM was still measured in megabytes, 10K RPM drives didn't exist let alone the solid state drives people are starting to take for granted and the big news was that we could put 4 whole processors in a server and the concept of multi-core processors was still years away. Word Perfect was our word processor and it shipped on 62 3.5" floppy disks, DVDs hadn't even been invented yet and downloading software was virtually unheard of. E-mail was just being deployed within companies, executives had secretaries who would print out their e-mail and put it in the physical inbox on their desk, and the "You've got mail" advertising campaigns were still years away. Windows 3.11 was just being deployed within the company where less than ½ of the staff even had a computer on their desks, there was barely a thing called HTML, the World Wide Web was in its infancy, and we certainly weren't designing websites or shopping online. A HUGE SQL Server database was considered to be 50GB. In this environment we were being tasked with building a data warehouse that would start out with 7 – 8TB of data and have more than 1,000 engineers pulling data and loading new data. Yes, back in 1994 I was designing data warehouses which were a hybrid between a transactional system, operational data store, data mart, and data warehouse so there was a section of the database accepting transactions. I could have simply followed all of the "can't", "don't", "won't" that we get taught growing up, but instead said that we could build it given the right resources.

There was absolutely no way of putting 7 – 8 TB in a single SQL Server database, you simply couldn't. The hardware and software did not support it. What we did was simply redefine the problem as well as redefining what a database was. What we did was physically split the database across a number of servers. The initial attempt split the database apart based on subject area. But, we quickly found that some subject areas wouldn't fit in a single database without becoming unusable. The second attempt applied the entire database structure across all of the servers and split individual tables at a row level. So, we wound up with a bunch of databases spanning the entire subject range of data, but with each database containing a sub-set of each table. This creates some issues with the tens of thousands of lookup tables in the database, so we dropped complete copies of the lookup tables and a few other master tables on every database server. We were left with a database structure which could handle the data we were going to throw at it.

This led to a second problem. We weren't designing a set of independent databases, but a set of data which had to be presented to the business as an integrated whole. We couldn't make users of the system connect to one database server to work with one piece of data, connect to another database server to work with another piece, and then leave it up to them to stitch everything together. To the business, it was one block of data. So, we had to make everything transparent. This was done by gating access to the data warehouse through an application tier I wrote in Powerbuilder. Nowadays, we hear about "self-service BI" and unlocking the data so that users can be creative with it, not burying the data behind an application where the application dictated what you got, how you got it, and what you did with it. Remember, this was designed in an era when secretaries printed out e-mails to executives, who wrote in them, and handed them back to secretaries to type their response. There was no self-service BI and you very rarely found someone on the business side who knew how to construct a basic report let alone doing data exploration against a data warehouse.

The Powerbuilder layer was left to solve the problem of stitching all of the pieces together so that it appeared as a single, integrated database. This was accomplished by building and maintaining a data catalog. Every request would be looked up against the catalog. The results from the catalog told the application where to find the data requested. The application would then spawn as many connections as necessary to retrieve the pieces from the various database servers, stitch everything back together, and then present it back to the person who requested it. We chose Powerbuilder, because it had a capability which was non-existent in every other development tool on the market – the Data Window. Before the "purists" start turning their noses up at someone using such an "antiquated" solution such as Powerbuilder, just consider that the "magical" ADO.NET component that millions of people write their applications around is nothing more than Microsoft's rendition of a Powerbuilder Data Windows…more than a decade after we had it in Powerbuilder. I believe that I mentioned earlier in this book that there are no new ideas in the database world, which also applies to the application development tools we use today.

The Powerbuilder application controlled all of the data going in as well as all of the retrieval and presentation. So, the application was responsible for maintaining the catalog server as data was written to the various databases. The application was also responsible for the algorithm which spread the data across the various database servers. I would create a much more general solution many years later, but you'll have to wait for the BI books in this series for that detailed discussion. This discussion of splitting a database apart to spread it across multiple servers and building a catalog in front of the pieces might be interesting, but what does it have to do with indexes?

Going back to the Customers.Address.StateProvinceID index example, we have 999,707 rows in an index where there are only 51 unique values. As the number of rows in the table increases, so does the number of rows in the index. It's a linear expansion relationship. A table with 1 billion rows would have 1 billion rows in the index. The number of reads to find any row increases by 1 at defined intervals. The number of reads required to determine if a value does not exist increases faster than finding values that do exist. But, if all of Champion Valley Pens' customers are in the

United States, the number of unique values does not change, even as the size of the table explodes. If I had simply built the catalog to hold every one of the searchable values from the set of databases which made up the data warehouse, the catalog would quickly exceed the capacity of a single machine. So, the algorithm which maintained the catalog had a de-duping mechanism in it. We only maintained unique values in the catalog along with a secondary set of tables which mapped each unique value to the location where it was stored. This kept the size of the catalog under control and also dramatically improved performance and scale.

I was proud of the novel approach of splitting our data warehouse across multiple servers and building a catalog layer in between to map the location of the pieces. That lasted for a very short time. Shortly after building this I was at the main Chicago Public Library looking for a couple of books. I walked up to not a small set, but to a very large section of drawers which made up the card catalog, organized slightly different than your normal catalog. I first had to look up my subject, which then pointed me to another section which contained the card catalog which would tell me where the 2 books I was looking for were located. I was looking at a catalog of a catalog pointing at books. My "novel" approach to the data scale problem was nothing more than repeating a solution that librarians had devised in multiple permutations centuries before I was born, centuries before the United States was even a country. There are no "new" ideas inside the database world. By the way, that entire architecture around splitting the data across numerous database servers and maintaining a mapping catalog…. Microsoft calls that the Parallel Data Warehouse; no, I didn't have a part in designing it.

Columnstore Indexes Defined

What does this all have to do with columnstore indexes? When you start getting very large amounts of data, all of the standard options no longer apply and all of the easy solutions have been exhausted. You have to build new capabilities, using a different approach. This is what happened as the genesis of columnstore indexes.

The SQL Server team built an entirely new set of capabilities into both the storage engine and the query processor which leave behind everything done with indexing up to this point. In building the first version of this technology, Microsoft targeted a very specific problem in data warehousing where you deal with very large volumes of data that you aggregate a variety of ways where the result set is generally very small. As with any initial feature implementation, you'll find a large number of restrictions on columnstore indexes. The specific goal behind columnstore indexes was to achieve up to a 90% improvement in certain types of queries. While I've seen improvements in the 10% - 30% range, I haven't gotten anywhere near the improvement you'll see in a lot of the demos that people are doing at various events. But the main reason behind that discrepancy can be found in the next book in this series where we will spend a considerable amount of time on performance analysis and tuning.

Columnstore Index Structure

At its core, columnstore indexes handle data much differently than other indexes we've discussed. All of the other indexes are used to filter data and locate rows in a manner which is much more efficient than simply scanning through all of the data. In order to locate the data you are after, you need to scan a series of rows in an index which can be made up of multiple columns in each index key. If you only care about the first column of the index, it would be much faster if you only had to scan the data corresponding to that column.

As its name implies, a columnstore index is built based on columns, not rows. So, a clustered or nonclustered index on two columns would be built on a row basis by loading all of the combinations of the two columns together as rows in the index. A columnstore index on the same two columns would instead pivot the data and write all of the values for each column separately into the columnstore index. The entire index is then compressed to reduce space. Because the types of data sets being targeted by columnstore indexes are generally very large volumes of data with a relatively small set of unique values, you can achieve much better compression rates than would be possible on a regular clustered or nonclustered index. However, compression is the only optimization currently occurring within the columnstore index. If we applied a columnstore index to our Customers.Address table, you would still find 999,706 entries in the index for the StateProvinceID column, it would just take much less space due to compression. A significant improvement would have been to simply store the 51 unique values, a count for the number of occurrences, and a map back to the location of the row in the table for each of the unique values. But, the column based storage with the increased compression still provides a pretty good benefit.

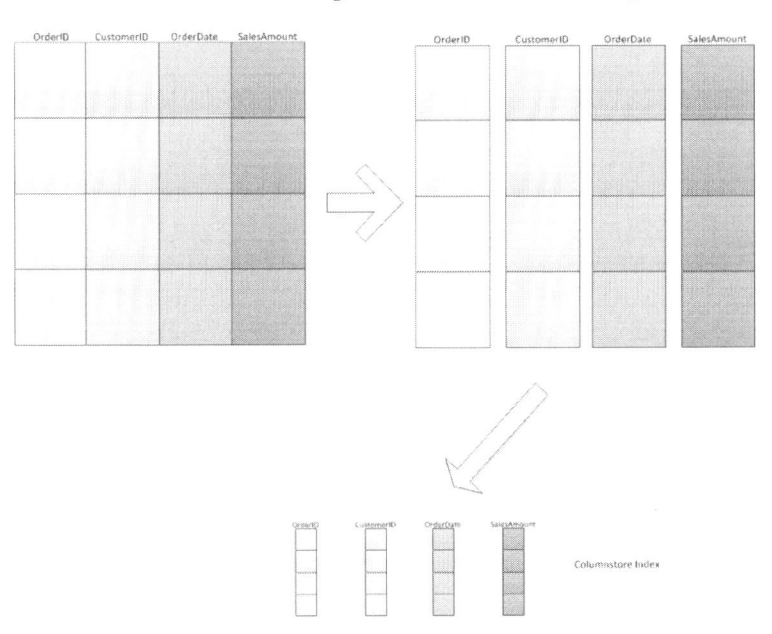

Figure 12-7 Columnstore index structure

Columnstore Restrictions

Columnstore indexes are a type of nonclustered index, but have a much different internal structure and follow a different set of rules from other nonclustered indexes. The 16 column limit for nonclustered indexes does not apply, but cannot contain more than 1024 columns. A columnstore index also cannot include a column with the following data types: BINARY, VARBINARY, VARCHAR(MAX), NVARCHAR(MAX), UNIQUEIDENTIFIER, ROWVERSION, TIMESTAMP, DECIMAL/NUMERIC with a precision larger than 18 digits, DATETIMEOFFSET with a scale larger than 2, XML, and CLR data types including HIERARCHYID, GEOMETRY, and

GEOGRAPHY.

In addition to the data type and column limitations, a columnstore index cannot be unique, include a sparse column, be defined as a primary key, act as a foreign key, changed using ALTER INDEX, specify a sort order, include a column defined for FILESTREAM, or contain included columns. You also can't create a columnstore index on a table using row or page compression, replication, change tracking, change data capture, or FILESTREAM.

The biggest restriction is that a table with a columnstore index defined cannot be modified. You cannot run an INSERT, UPDATE, or DELETE statement against a table which has a columnstore index defined. If you have to modify data in the table, you have to first drop the columnstore index. This means that a table with a columnstore index defined is effectively read only, although creating a columnstore index is not a way to mark a table as read only. While you can't change the contents of a table with a columnstore index, you can defrag all of the rest of the indexes on the table, except the columnstore index.

Columnstore Index Processing

The limited explanation of the columnstore index supplied above was good enough to get you to the basics of what is going on. But, columnstore indexes apply several more principles than just optimizing the storage.

The most basic principle I had drilled into my head when I first started developing applications was to do the most possible with the least amount of code. Of course, this was when we had the unfathomable 8K of RAM. For many reading this, yes, there was an era where applications ran very happily and did a lot of critical tasks with a tiny fraction of the memory as you have available in the computer chip in your vacuum cleaner responsible for managing the On/Off switch. Not only did you pay attention to every character in your code, you paid attention to the total number of instructions that were needed to accomplish a task.

As machines got much larger and new generations of developers starting building applications, this basic principle was forgotten. Now building applications usually means I find a bunch of off the shelf components, wire them together, add business logic on top, and deploy the application. The off the shelf components try to cram every possible feature and configuration option that someone could ever want. Along the way, they acquire more and more code and more and more layers in the code. This occurs, because "maintainability" starts overriding performance considerations. I would be willing to bet that most developers would be horrified by the actual number of commands their applications are executing in order to perform even trivial tasks. They don't have to worry about it, because processors keep getting faster and those disk drives where all of the interesting data sits are really slow. Meaning that the time difference it took to pull stuff off disk compared to the time to compute on a processor was so large, no one noticed all of the extra instructions. They also don't usually have to worry about it, because they can just buy a bigger server or spread their code across multiple servers. However, there comes a point when you simply can't do that.

SQL Server used to be able to get away with executing code paths that resulted in many more instructions than were really needed and balancing maintainability and code reuse with performance because the processors could run so much faster than the disk drives could serve up data. SQL Server has finally hit a point where you can't simply throw a bigger server at it or buy faster disk drives. The hardware has finally caught up to the point where the processing bottleneck has moved to the processor. There is only one way to improve performance once the bottleneck is the processor – run less code.

There are two places where you can optimize the code for retrieving data. You can process with fewer instructions and you can do more with instructions you already have loaded. You see the second piece almost every day in assembly line processing, which also isn't a new concept. The first known example of assembly line processing can be found in bread baking in ancient Rome. The simple idea is to have numerous people contribute a small task (set of instructions) to an overall finished product. Each person only performs a single task, so they don't have to constantly switch between tasks and tools. This makes each individual step much faster thereby allowing you to produce more bread in a single day than would be possible for a single person performing all of the individual pieces. Translated to computer code, you load up one set of instructions and use the same set of instructions as many times as possible before needing to switch to a different set of instructions.

How this plays into modern computer chip architecture can be seen in Figure 12-8, which shows a basic diagram of the processor cache on a 10 core Intel Xeon E7-4870. Level 1 cache is the faster memory on a server and is split in half. One half is allocated to data and the other half to instructions for the processor core to execute against the data. If you have to constantly switch instruction sets, you are throwing the existing instructions off level 1 cache to load another set before the CPU can continue processing. With each step up the stack, the memory gets larger while also getting slower. So, Level 1 cache is the fastest you can go, Level 2 is at least an order of magnitude slower, Level 3 cache is at least an order of magnitude slower yet, and main memory moves at a glacial pace in comparison to the processor cache. If you can structure your code such that the instructions load once for a query and stay loaded while the entire set of data streams through, you can eliminate a lot of waiting as instructions are swapped on and off L1 cache.

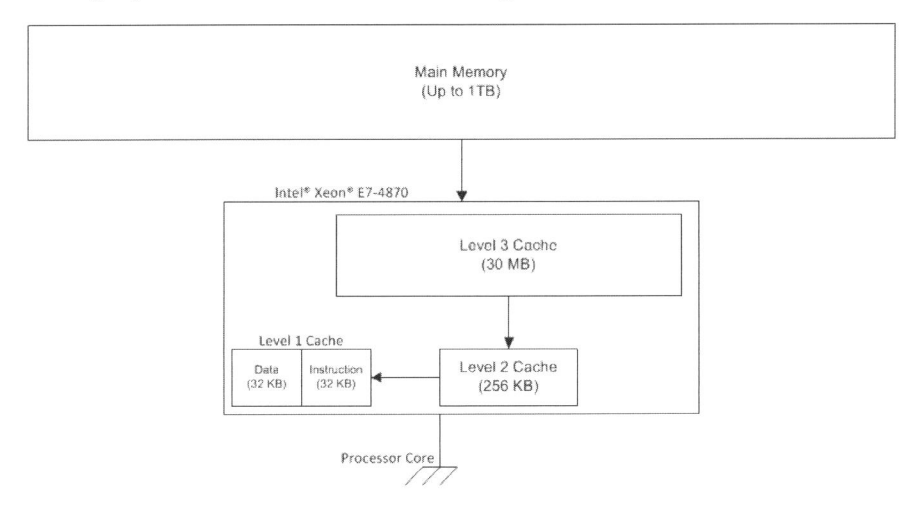

Figure 12-8 Basic Processor Cache Architecture

I don't write processor code or data retrieval code inside a database engine, so this basic explanation of how SQL Server was processing a query and how it was changed is courtesy of

Conor Cunningham who works on the core storage engine team. Any mistakes in the explanation are my own.

The basic processing of a query is to retrieve a row, check if it matches the filter criteria, and then add then row to the result set being accumulated. In Conor's basic example, these three functions are called Project, Filter, and Table Scan. SQL Server started out on the top of the stack with Project. Project was asked to get a row, but the method had no ability to perform this function so it passed the request down the stack to Filter. Filter also didn't have an ability to perform this function, so the request was passed down to the Table Scan operator. Table Scan retrieved the first row and pushed it back up to the Filter method which determined that the row didn't meet the criteria so it was thrown away. Bubble back up to Project with a miss which was then told to get another row. Back to Filter to call Table Scan to push the next row back up and determine that it also didn't match, throw row away, return back up the stack, call all the way back down. Repeat this process until you can hit the end of the rows in the table(s) you are querying.

If each of the instruction sets for Project, Filter, and Table Scan were between greater than 16KB and less than 32KB, it would mean each call to a function both on the way down the stack as well as on the way back up the stack would require throwing the instructions for the parent method off the L1 cache so that the instructions for the child could be loaded. Progress on the actual work you wanted performed would have to wait each time this happened.

What the core engine team did was realize that calling down the stack wastes a LOT of time. If you simply flipped it upside down, you would get a lot closer to the assembly line approach to retrieving data. Now you could start by loading Table Scan into L1 cache and having it run over and over and over again, retrieving rows until the 32KB of the data side of L1 cache is filled. Then that entire batch could be pushed to L2 cache and Table Scan could go back to retrieving rows. This could continue until Table Scan reached the end of the tables in your query. This would cause Filter to then load into L1 cache and begin to operate on the rows retrieved; cycling through the entire set in 32KB batches. Once Filter reached the end, Project could be loaded to return the results. You have a lot fewer cache misses and the processor can spend more time cycling through your data instead of waiting on instructions to load.

If you managed to squeeze the code for the Table Scan and Filter operators enough to allow them to both fit in L1 cache, then you could speed up the process even more because you would be streaming rows into the 32KB L1 Data cache until you filled it with rows matching the filter before the batch was pushed up to L2 cache. In order to accomplish this, the query processor team had to build new capabilities into the Query Processor which are referred to as Batch Mode. When queries run in Batch Mode, they are optimized to process sets of data at a time before moving on to the next step which coupled with the way data is organized in a column store index causes a dramatic drop in retrieval time for certain types of aggregate queries.

Processing Blocks

If you'll recall from Chapter 5, I didn't quite jump up and down about using the minimum sized data type necessary to store your data. Now, I'm jumping up and down, waving my arms, and yelling. Yes, "disk is virtually unlimited". Yes, memory is getting cheaper and you can put a lot more memory into a machine. Now that you understand just how large the data cache is on a processor core, in order to return a result the data has to move through the 32KB available in the

L1 cache, and the size of the L1 cache hasn't gotten much bigger in several year, you should have a much better appreciation as to why something as simple as an extra 1 byte can limit the scalability of an application.

With that basic understanding, let's drive down into the processor core to understand how you can take maximum advantage in this processing logic…with the way you define your data. Going from 32 bit to 64 bit was a really big deal. What did that really mean? The smallest block you see in figure 12-8 is 32KB with the overall size of the L1 cache at 64KB. 64 bit doesn't have anything to do with the memory structures. 64 bit defines the "width" of the processing channel on a CPU core. While L1 cache is 32KB in size, the maximum amount of information that a CPU core can operate on is 64 bits. We'll ignore the set of instructions to the CPU which tell it what to do at the moment, because the size of that code is known only to the SQL Server team and you can't do anything about it. You can control the data. A BIGINT is 8 bytes in size or 64 bits. That means it exactly fits the CPU register or it takes exactly 1 CPU cycle to deal with the BIGINT. BUT, what if you defined the BIGINT as NULL? You'll recall from Chapter 6 that this adds 1 more bit to that BIGINT. Now it consumes 65 bits, which is larger than the CPU register. You now require 2 CPU cycles to process that same BIGINT. Put another way, a nullable BIGINT is twice as slow as a not null BIGINT. What if you used a BIGINT when all you needed was an INT or a SMALLINT?

As I've said many times before and continue to say, this kind of attention to your data definitions simply does not matter. The databases are so small in comparison to the processing available that no one would ever know you are wasting CPU cycles. However, you never know when that application with a tiny database will turn into something where you have to churn millions, billions, or trillions of rows of data. When you have to process large amounts of data, every wasted CPU cycle adds up to poor performance and dissatisfied users.

It's taken us over 500 pages to get to the understanding of why every piece of code you execute and every byte you consume is so important in the performance and ultimately the success of any application you build. Hopefully, you will apply this knowledge to make very simple changes in the initial design which can have far ranging effects.

Character data

Character data is one of the most variable blocks of data you will store. Not only are there an infinite number of values within a business domain, the size of the data varies widely. Columnstore indexes work around this wide variability as well as the large possible size using one of the more common techniques in database design – the lookup table. When a columnstore index is built on character data, the unique values are loaded into a lookup table, also known as a dictionary, assigned an integer value, and then the integer value is used to represent the string within the index. The dictionary undergoes the same compression found in the rest of the columnstore index. The Query Processor operates on the integer values stored within the index and then substitutes the character values back into the result set as one of the final steps in the query process.

Creating a Columnstore Index

The syntax for creating a columnstore index is very simple. The generic syntax is as follows:

```
CREATE [ NONCLUSTERED ] COLUMNSTORE INDEX index_name
    ON <object> ( column  [ ,...n ] )
    [ WITH ( <column_index_option> [ ,...n ] ) ]
    [ ON {{ partition_scheme_name ( column_name ) } | filegroup_name | "default"}][
;  ]
```

Instead of including an example at this point, we will reserve the creation of a columnstore index for Chapter 14 where we can discuss how it can work with the partitioning feature to allow modifications to the table.

Summary

Indexes are used to improve the performance of queries. There is no other reason for an index to exist. At a very basic level, indexes are simple, elegant structures which allow you to search vast amounts of data with only a very small number of operations. At the heart of every index is a set of statistics which builds a histogram based on sampling data that helps the Query Optimizer decide whether to utilize an index to satisfy a query.

Chapter 13
Full-Text Indexes

> **Setup:** Please run the Chapter 13 Setup script in the companion files prior to starting the exercises in this chapter to ensure that your databases are at the correct starting point. Every exercise in this book assumes that you have created the c:\ChampionValleyPress\Data and c:\ChampionValleyPress\Log folders, contained databases are enabled, and this is the location of all of the data, log, and filestream files which will be used for this book. If you have chosen a different path, you will need to adjust the paths listed accordingly. Every setup script also assumes that you have enabled FILESTREAM access for the instance. When executing commands, it is assumed that you will change context to the appropriate database since understanding the contents of each database in this book is the same skill you will need for working with your databases. All scripts also assume you are using a default instance.

In Chapter 12, you learned about almost every index available. Each of the indexes you learned about could be added to a table to improve query performance, but you could run the same query without an index in place. All of the indexes covered so far are only indirectly visible to an application. You can detect a performance improvement, but you can't prove that an index is the cause of the improvement.

Full-text indexes are a special purpose index designed for querying semi-structured data. Unlike other indexes, full-text indexes enable capabilities in a SELECT statement which would not otherwise be possible. You know, by the code you are running, that you are taking advantage of a full-text index.

In this chapter, we will finish off our discussion of indexes by showing you how to search large quantities of character based data regardless of whether you are searching some kind of comment column in a table or a library of documents stored within the FileTable feature.

> **Note:** You can full-text index rows in a table as well as entire documents stored using either the FileTable or FILESTREAM features. In full-text indexing, we refer to both of these sets of data as a document. A single row in a table will be called a document as will a file store in a FileTable.

"Unstructured" Data

Anyone who knows me knows that I don't like imprecise or misleading definitions. I've fallen into the trap in the past and probably will in the future, but I try to get back out of the quagmire as soon as I realize the error. The explanation of what full-text indexes do for you almost always starts with "unstructured" data. Everyone is expected to simply know what the person is saying and almost everyone just nods with everyone in this "insider knowledge" way. Anyone who knows me also knows that I call this "baffling people with bullshit". Just about anyone working in IT has seen this kind of thing before. You're in a room with a bunch of people trying to solve some problem. One of the people in the room has already decided that their way is the only way, because they are smarter, more experienced, or somehow better than everyone else. (By the way, where I grew up, we call these people A**h***s.) Suddenly in the middle of the discussion this person starts in with this rambling explanation laced with acronyms, technobabble, and politically stilted language. As they drone on, the eyes start glazing over and the heads start nodding. No one in the room has the slightest idea what they are talking about, but it "sounds smart", so I should just nod my head in this knowing way, because I want to be part of the crowd, feel superior, and don't want to be the one to admit that I don't have the slightest clue what this person is saying.

This is the problem with "unstructured" data. You hear the term thrown around a lot and you always see a lot of heads nodding. But, ask one of them to precisely define unstructured data and you either get a blank stare or a bunch of BS. The second part is actually the most accurate. "Unstructured" data is complete and utter BS. It is a complete and absolute impossibility.

I used to throw "unstructured" data, into every discussion on full-text indexes. Where I finally caught a clue was in having to deal with "Big Data". (BTW, if you want to make my skin crawl, say Big Data or The Cloud which are two of the biggest pieces of marketing BS every perpetuated on the IT industry.) What do "unstructured" data, "Big Data", and "The Cloud" have to do with each other? They are all complete marketing vapor designed with exactly one purpose – to sell you stuff you don't need by changing the terminology to something that sounds so complicated, scary, and important that you need to have some expensive consultant come in and do it for you.

What is "unstructured" data? Dictionary.com defines "unstructured" as "without formal structure or systematic organization". So, unstructured data is data that doesn't have a formal structure. What does it mean to not have a structure? It means that I can basically put things anywhere I want to. When asked for examples, the first thing that people think of is a document. Are you really sure a document is unstructured? Would it even be possible for you to read a document that has no structure? A document such as the one you are reading right now? This document isn't unstructured. It has a table of contents, chapters, sections, and paragraphs. Paragraphs are composed of one or more sentences and sentences are composed of one or more words. *to the sentences Could rules supposed read didn't language? it structure according follow of grammar follow which the sentence this you English are if to all the* (Could you read this sentence if it didn't follow the structure which all sentences are supposed to follow according to the grammar rules of the English language?).

Sentences have a varying length, but all sentences have a structure, regardless of language, otherwise we couldn't understand them. Put very simply, language has structure.

One of the more novel examples offered for unstructured data is the white noise you can encounter in audio or video streams. To most people, there is no structure or pattern. To a physicist or mathematician, they can produce an equation or series or equations to duplicate the pattern of white noise you are seeing/hearing. So, even "white noise" has a structure.

Somewhere in every pitch for Big Data is something about the ability to store and search large volumes of unstructured data. Somewhere in almost every explanation of full-text indexing is creating an ability to search unstructured data. But, in order for us to understand it, doesn't it have to have a structure? In order for us to store it or index it, doesn't it have to have a structure? That leads us to – in order for it to even BE data, does it have to have SOME kind of structure even if you might not know how to articulate what that structure is? Unstructured data is a complete contradiction. You might not understand the structure, but data cannot exist without a structure. When you store the data, you impose an additional structure around it. I could simply take this document you are reading, which was written using Microsoft Word, and store it on a file system on a computer somewhere. My structured language acquired an additional structure dictated by the WordML specification and in order to store it, the WordML had an additional structure imposed on it in order to produce a file which could be stored and retrieved from a computer. If I move this document into a FileTable, it acquires yet another structure. Based on the reaction I've gotten over the last couple of years when I bring this subject up, at least one of you is spluttering and turning purple at this point.

Let's take this a step further. Sentences can, theoretically, have an unlimited length and still be a valid sentence. But, if you really think about it, is it even a sentence if the length is unlimited? In order to be a sentence, you have to terminate the sentence with a punctuation mark. If the length is unlimited, it means the sentence is still being written, which by definition means that it isn't yet a sentence. Is a line stretching to infinity really a line? More important to our purposes as database professionals, can you store a sentence which is still being written? Can you even use data that doesn't have a structure? Do I even have to understand the details of the structure in order to use the data? I use files every day. I move them around, make copies of them, change their names, and do all kinds of other things with them, but I have no idea what the structure is which makes it a file. As an author, I use Microsoft Word every day, but I don't have the slightest clue what the XML structure is which is imposed by Word for everything that I write.

The best term that I have to describe what a full-text index provides is a means to index semi-structured, sentence based data. Semi-structured means that there IS a structure, but the structure can be manipulated from one row to the next. Every row still obeys a single, overarching structure. Full-text indexes are designed to allow you to search written language. Full-text indexes don't search numbers, dates, binary strings, or even single words. You wouldn't apply a full-text index to a person's name, address, or a product name. You might apply a full-text search to a product description column if you cared about finding individual words or phrases across a group of products.

Full-text Catalogs

The first step in building a full text index is to create a storage container. Prior to SQL Server 2008, full-text indexes were stored outside the database and the full-text catalog provided the mapping to the external storage. Beginning with SQL Server 2008, full-text indexes are stored inside the database and the catalog is not associated to any filegroup. The full-text catalog simply defines a virtual container to manage full-text indexes. Each full text catalog contains one or more full text indexes, but a full-text index can only belong to a single catalog.

The generic syntax for creating a full text catalog is:

```
CREATE FULLTEXT CATALOG catalog_name
    [WITH ACCENT_SENSITIVITY = {ON|OFF}]
    [AS DEFAULT] [AUTHORIZATION owner_name ]
```

Many languages have accent marks which change the sound and/or the meaning of words. ACCENT_SENSITIVITY tells SQL Server whether to consider or ignore accent marks when building or querying a full-text index assigned to the catalog. Since the accent sensitivity affects how words are treated when the index is built, changing the accent sensitivity requires you to rebuild all full-text indexes associated to the catalog.

The DEFAULT property of a full-text catalog works the same as the DEFAULT option for a filegroup. If you do not specify a catalog name when creating a full-text index, the index will be created within the catalog that is marked as the default.

The owner of the full-text catalog is specified by the AUTORIZATION option.

Full-text Indexes

You can create full-text indexes on columns which are used to store semi-structured data. These would be CHAR/VARCHAR, XML, and VARBINARY(MAX) data types. The VARBINARY(MAX) columns are those you use with the FILESTREAM feature or the column containing the actual file within a FileTable.

Parsers

Building a full-text index on an XML column might sound a little strange. When you full-text index an XML document, the indexing engine uses the attribute markers to determine the boundaries of the data, but does not include any of the structural elements in the index. The indexing engine will also only index data that is a string data type, ignoring numbers, dates, times, and encoded binary data. As part of building a full-text index on an XML column, the engine loads an XML parser to perform the task of understanding the XML structure.

VARBINARY(MAX) presents the most interesting case for full text indexing. Prior to SQL Server 2008, if you wanted to full-text index the contents of a document, you had to extract the text, load it into a column, and then build a full-text index on that column. If the contents of the document changed, you had to repeat the extract and load process again. With the FILESTREAM capability introduced in SQL Server 2008 and extended to FileTable in SQL Server 2012, SQL Server can now directly manipulate and manage files. The full-text engine has been enhanced to take these files into account and allows you to directly build a full-text index without any of the extract/load process. The files are indexed in place and when the contents of the file change, the full-text index can be automatically updated with the changes. Just like an XML column, in order to full-text index files, the engine needs to employ specialized assemblies which have been designed for a variety of file types. The file types are specified by including an additional column which specifies the default extension for the file such as .xls, .doc, .ppt, or .pdf. SQL Server then reads the type column and loads the appropriate parser to handle the file. SQL Server 2012 ships with fifty-five filters that allow processing of a variety of document types such as HTML, Word, PowerPoint, and Excel. It does not ship with a PDF parser, but one is freely available for download from Adobe. You'll see how to load and use a 3rd party parser when we get to the semantic search capabilities at the end of this chapter.

Helper Services

Now that we've established that unstructured data does not exist and that full-text indexes are designed to index written language, we have a second problem that the indexing engine has to overcome. Every written language has grammar rules, but grammar rules are unique to each language. English, Chinese, Spanish, German, Klingon, and Elvish have different rules. If you have a computer apply English grammar rules to German, it won't even be able to figure out where one word ends and another one begins.

Word Breaker

To solve this problem, the full-text indexing engine uses helper services such as word breakers and stemmers that are specific to each language to build indexes.

The first step in building a full-text index is to gather a list of words within the data being indexed. Word breakers are the helper service designed to locate breaks between words so that the engine knows what it needs to index.

Stemmer

Working in conjunction with a word breaker is a second helper service called a stemmer. Verbs in many languages have multiple forms referred to as tense. One of the interesting things that a full-text index can do is handle verb conjugations within a search so that things like run, ran, and running can all be found. The stemmer is responsible for finding the verbs within each language and applying stemming rules. When you full-text index a column, you specify the language to use for the word breaker and stemmer.

Languages are not uniform throughout the world. For example, there is a slightly different version of French spoken in France, Canada, and Belgium just as there is a different version of Spanish spoken in Spain and Mexico. SQL Server refers to these dialects of a language as subgroups. Not all subgroups have word breakers and stemmers. In these cases, the major group language should be used. For example, the French word breaker/stemmer can be applied to French, Canadian French, and Belgium French. Remember that the full-text index engine is not trying to understand the meaning of a language, only to find the words within each language and inflectional forms of verbs.

Stop Words

Every language is decorated with common words that we really don't care to have in our indexes. Indexing the word "the" would be almost useless for English since you will find the word "the" is in a large percentage of sentences. Your organization also has words that you don't care to index. A repository of documents at Microsoft probably has the word "Microsoft" at least once on every document, making a search on that term worthless. The words that you don't care to index were previously called noise words. Since calling certain words noise hurt their feelings, they are now called stop words. SQL Server has a standard list of stop words for each language included in the word breaker. For example, *the*, *a*, and *an* would be considered stop words for the English language, whereas *le*, *la*, *les*, and *l'* would be stop words for the French language. You can add additional words by configuring a stop list for the full-text index. Stop words are removed by the word breaker prior to passing the parsed list to the stemmer and are never included in the index.

A stop word has two components, the word and the language identifier. Stop words are applied by the word breaker on a language by language basis, so the word breaker can ignore any stop words which do not match the language definition of the full-text index. It also means that if you have a word which is common to multiple languages, you need to add the same word for each language you will be indexing. For example, if you are indexing a table of product descriptions which all have Champion Valley Pens in the description within a table that stores the description in 15 different languages, each language in a different column, you would have to specify Champion Valley Pens 15 times with each one defined for a different language. You add stop words for the indexer to consider by creating a stop list and adding words to the list. The stop list can then be associated to one or more full-text indexes, but each full-text index can only have a single stop list.

You create a stop list by using the CREATE FULLTEXT STOPLIST as follows:

```
CREATE FULLTEXT STOPLIST stoplist_name
[ FROM { [ database_name.]source_stoplist_name } | SYSTEM STOPLIST ]
[ AUTHORIZATION owner_name ];
```

The most basic command creates an empty stop list. You can also pre-populate a stop list from an existing stop list or from the default stop list.

Once the stop list is created, you manipulate the contents of the stop list by using the ALTER FULLTEXT STOPLIST command.

```
ALTER FULLTEXT STOPLIST stoplist_name
{ ADD [N] 'stopword' LANGUAGE language_term
  | DROP {'stopword' LANGUAGE language_term | ALL LANGUAGE language_term | ALL};
```

The ADD clause is where you add words for each language. The combination of a stop word and language is required to be unique within a stop list. The DROP clause allows you to remove one or more stop words. You can drop a single stop word, all stop words for a specified language, or all stop words in the stop list. The entries in a stop list are more accurately referred to as a term. You can have entries which are a single word or multiple words. You can also include full-text tokens. The only limitation is that the stop list term cannot exceed 64 characters.

Stop lists are applied when the indexer is populating a full-text index. If you add a stop word, the indexer will not go back through the index and remove the word from existing index entries. Likewise, dropping a stop word does not prompt the indexer to load any occurrences of that word into existing index entries. In order to bring existing index entries in line with stop list updates, you have to either force a change to a row or initiate a full crawl of the index.

Languages

You can find the list of languages supported by the full-text engine by querying sys.fulltext_languages. This will return an ID for the language along with a description. For example, 1033 is for US English and 2057 is for British English. The ID of the language, found in the LCID column is the value that you specify for the LANGUAGE option of any full-text command.

Exercise 1: Creating a Full-Text StopList

In preparation for indexing product descriptions and documentation for customer searching, the company wants to configure a stop list for words likely to be found on almost every document.

1. Execute the following code against the ChampionValleyPens database to create a full-text stop list.
    ```
    CREATE FULLTEXT STOPLIST ProductsStopList FROM SYSTEM STOPLIST;
    ```
2. Execute the following code to add Champion Valley Pens to the stop list.
    ```
    ALTER FULLTEXT STOPLIST ProductsStopList
        ADD 'Champion Valley Pens' LANGUAGE 'English';
    ```
3. Repeat steps 1 and 2 to create and populate the same stop list for the ChampionValleyPensDocs database.
4. Execute the following query to view the stop lists present in the database.
    ```
    SELECT * FROM sys.fulltext_stoplists
    ```
5. Execute the following query to review the stop words in the stop list you just created.
    ```
    SELECT * FROM sys.fulltext_stopwords WHERE language = 'English'
    ```

> Warning: One of the mistakes that many people make when creating a full-text stop list is assuming that your stop list is added on top of the system stop list. A full-text index only applies a single stop list. If you do not specify a stop list, the system stop list is used. If you specify a custom stop list, then the indexing process will use your custom stop list instead of the system stop list. If you want all of the default stop words to be considered PLUS your custom additions, then you need to create your stop list initially populated from the system stop list and then add your customizations.

Creating a Full-Text Index

You are only allowed to create one full-text index per table, but you can index more than one column in the table.

The generic syntax for creating a full text index is:

```
CREATE FULLTEXT INDEX ON table_name
    [ ( { column_name
            [ TYPE COLUMN type_column_name ]
            [ LANGUAGE language_term ]
            [ STATISTICAL_SEMANTICS ] } [ ,...n] ) ]
    KEY INDEX index_name
    [ ON <catalog_filegroup_option> ]
    [ WITH [ ( ] <with_option> [ ,...n] [ ) ] ][;]
<catalog_filegroup_option>::=
 {fulltext_catalog_name}
<with_option>::=
    { CHANGE_TRACKING [ = ] { MANUAL | AUTO | OFF [, NO POPULATION ] } }
    | STOPLIST [ = ] { OFF | SYSTEM | stoplist_name }
    | SEARCH PROPERTY LIST [ = ] property_list_name }
```

The TYPE COLUMN parameter is used with a VARBINARY(MAX) column to designates the filter type that the full text index engine should utilize to parse the file. The LANGUAGE parameter allows you to specify the language of the data being indexed. Just as you saw with the creation of primary and secondary XML indexes, a full-text index requires a primary key on the table. The primary key for a table with a full-text index can only have a single column. The KEY INDEX parameter specifies the name of the primary key. When the full-text index is built, the primary key is migrated into the index to link the row to the corresponding piece of the full-text index.

The initial population of a full-text index can be quite resource intensive, especially if you index a FileTable containing hundreds, thousands, or even millions of documents. You can specify the NO POPULATION option which will allow the full-text index to be created, but the index will not be populated. This allows you to shift the population of the index to a time when more resources are available and the population will have a lower impact to other requests.

Language, Word Breakers, and Stemmers

The single full-text index per table restriction isn't a problem for a single language database, but poses a design challenge for multi-lingual databases. Word breakers, stemmers, and stop lists are language specific, so how do you apply a full-text index to a column which contains multiple languages?

There are two basic methods to handling multiple languages. The first method stores all of the languages in a single column and specifies the most complicated language to use with the full-text index. This method works reasonably well when all of the languages are from the same language family such as French, Spanish, English, and German. However, when you have languages from multiple families such as Chinese, Japanese, German, and Arabic, you need to split the languages into separate columns so that you can apply the appropriate language to each one. Splitting languages across columns also means you need to query each of the columns in order to find data.

The language specification is a key component in building an effective full text index. While you could simply use a single word breaker for all of your data, when the data spans multiple languages, you can have unexpected results. For example, the English language breaks words with a space whereas languages such as German and French can combine words together. If a word breaker only recognized white space between words as breaks, the full text index would only meet your needs if all data stored was English.

The language specification is used to control the specific word breaker and stemmer loaded by the full text indexing engine. The selected word breaker and stemmer will be the same for the entire full text index and cannot dynamically change based on a type column like you can apply to a VARBINARY(MAX) column. However, you do not have to split column data based on each specific language. While words may differ, many languages can be grouped into a small set of general language families and each word breaker has the ability to handle words that span a narrow group of languages.

For example, you might be storing data that spans various Western European languages such as English, German, French, and Spanish. You could utilize a single language to index the column which would appropriately break the words for the index. When you have data spanning languages, you should specify a language setting for the most complicated language. For example, the German word breaker can also break English, Spanish, and French whereas the English word breaker would have trouble with some of the language elements of German.

When the languages vary widely such as storing Arabic, Chinese, English, and Icelandic you should split the data into separate columns based on language otherwise you will not be able to validly break all words and build a full text index that behaves as you expect.

SQL Server 2008 ships with 50 language specific word breakers/stemmers. Support is also included for 3rd party word breakers/stemmers to be registered and used within SQL Server. For example, Turkish, Danish, and Polish are 3rd party word breakers that ship with SQL Server 2008.

Word breakers locate and tokenize word boundaries within text. The full text index then aggregates each token to build distribution statistics for searching. Additionally, word breakers recognize proximity within the data set and build the proximity into the full text statistics. The ability to search based on word proximity is a unique characteristic of full text indexes that allow for compound search criteria that take into account the relationship of words.

Stemmers are used to allow a full text index to search on all inflectional forms of a search term. For example: drive, drove, driven, and driving. Stemming is language specific. While you could employ a German word breaker to tokenize English, the German stemmer cannot process English.

The resulting index contains each token, the primary key for the row, the position of the token within the column, and some additional information to track stems and relationships between tokens.

Populate Full Text Indexes

Populating a full-text index is referred to as performing a crawl. Crawls can be kicked off manually or automatically and for either a full or incremental crawl. A full crawl is done when the index in initially populated and subsequent updates are usually done with incremental crawls.

You can also stop, pause, or resume population of an index in order to control resource utilization when making large volumes of changes to a full text index. This is especially useful when you have created the full-text index with the NO POPULATION option. In the case of an extremely large volume of documents needing to be indexed, you can start population of the index, pause the population several hours later to allow other requests to utilize resources, then resume the population a day later when resources are available again. In some cases, you might need to slowly populate a full-text index over the course of several days using the pause and resume capabilities.

You manually populate a full-text index by using the ALTER FULLTEXT INDEX command with the following syntax:

```
ALTER FULLTEXT INDEX ON table_name
   { ENABLE
   | DISABLE
   | SET CHANGE_TRACKING [ = ] { MANUAL | AUTO | OFF }
   | ADD ( column_name
       [ TYPE COLUMN type_column_name ]
       [ LANGUAGE language_term ]
       [ STATISTICAL_SEMANTICS ] [,...n] )
       [ WITH NO POPULATION ]
   | ALTER COLUMN column_name
       { ADD | DROP } STATISTICAL_SEMANTICS
       [ WITH NO POPULATION ]
   | DROP ( column_name [,...n] )
       [ WITH NO POPULATION ]
   | START { FULL | INCREMENTAL | UPDATE } POPULATION
   | {STOP | PAUSE | RESUME } POPULATION
   | SET STOPLIST [ = ] { OFF| SYSTEM | stoplist_name }
       [ WITH NO POPULATION ]
   | SET SEARCH PROPERTY LIST [ = ] { OFF | property_list_name }
       [ WITH NO POPULATION ] }[;]
```

The portions of the ALTER FULLTEXT INDEX command which are relevant to index population are the START and STOP sections. When you start an index crawl, you can specify FULL, INCREMENTAL, and UPDATE. When you do a FULL crawl, you are doing a complete rebuild of the full-text index. An UPDATE crawl processes any changes since the last time the index was populated and requires that CHANGE_TRACKING = MANUAL be set for the index. You can still perform an incremental update of the index without change tracking being enabled, but you have to have a timestamp column present on the table. If you have a timestamp column present, you can issue an INCREMENTAL crawl which will process all changes since the last index population even if CHANGE_TRACKING is set to OFF. If CHANGE_TRACKING is set to AUTO, you wouldn't utilize the START clause since changes would be automatically indexed.

You can control the processing of the index by using the STOP, PAUSE, and RESUME POPULATION options. When you stop population, the index crawl halts, but does not affect auto change tracking or a background update process. PAUSE and RESUME are used with full populations and do not have an effect on INCREMENTAL or UPDATE crawls.

Change Tracking

The CHANGE_TRACKING option determines whether incremental changes to an indexed column are tracked. When you specify either MANUAL or AUTO, SQL Server maintains a list of changes to the indexed data. MANUAL means that while changes to the underlying column are tracked, you are responsible for periodically initiating a crawl to propagate the changes into the full text index. If you set CHANGE_TRACKING to AUTO, SQL Server will automatically update the full-text index as the data is modified. Automatically maintaining a relational index is a synchronous process, meaning your DML statement does not complete until the changes to both the data and any indexes have committed. Population of a full-text index occurs asynchronously. Your data change will commit and then a short time later the full-text index will reflect the change. This behavior is by design, because the indexing engine has a lot more work to perform through the word breakers, stop lists, stemmers, and filters than occurs with any other index. All of these libraries mean there will always be a significant amount of latency in building a full-text index, so the entire process is moved outside of transaction boundaries.

You can also disable change tracking by setting the CHANGE_TRACKING option to OFF. In this case, the only way to get any updates into the index is to perform a full crawl and completely repopulate the index. While this may be useful in cases where you are loading a large volume of new data which has to be indexed, most full-text indexes should be incrementally populated either manually or automatically.

Build Process

When SQL Server initiates a crawl, whether automatically due to a change or manually via a scheduled job or direct command execution, the full-text indexer manages a workflow amongst several components. The first stage is to enlist the protocol handler to retrieve data from the columns you are indexing. The data being retrieved is passed to a filter daemon. The filter daemon is the core process which enlists the word breakers, stemmers, and stop lists to tokenize the content into a set of index fragments. The final piece of the process takes all of the index fragments and writes them into a single full-text index. The consolidation process is referred to as a master merge. That's the technobabble explanation of what is going on.

The process described in more understandable terms is that the index process calls a piece of code responsible for retrieving data. Each row of data that is retrieved is broken into individual words, verbs are conjugated, and stop words are thrown out. When a row is done being broken apart, it is set aside as this thing called an index fragment. The indexer then repeats the process on the next row until it reaches the end of the table. Once it reaches the end, it takes all of the pieces and stuffs them into the full-text index. If this is the initial build of the index, the fragments are just smashed into a single list of words. If this is an update to an existing index, then each fragment is inserted into the index in the appropriate location.

Unlike changes to other indexes, the master merge does not block queries. You can continue to query the full-text index, but you will only receive the results which match the contents of the index at the time your query ran.

Custom Filters

SQL Server ships with the ability to index 50 different document types. You can also add 3rd party filters. For example, you probably have PDF documents which you would like to index, but SQL Server does not ship with a PDF filter for the full-text engine.

In order to register a 3rd party filter, you have to first install the filter on the machine hosting your SQL Server instance. Once installed, the path to the filter dll needs to be added to the system path in order to be recognized. Following the path modification, you have to reload resources and restart the SQL Server instance.

Exercise 2: Loading a PDF Filter

Champion Valley Pens wants to index all of the PDF documents for its products. The following exercise will walk you through downloading and configuring the PDF filter from Adobe.

1. Open a browser and go to http://www.adobe.com/support/downloads/thankyou.jsp?ftpID=4025&fileID=3941

2. Download the Adobe PDF iFilter 9 for 64-bit platforms

3. Once downloaded, open the zip file, run the installation routine, follow the prompts, and don't change the installation path.

4. Once the installation completes, click the start button, right click Computer, and select Properties. Alternatively, you can open the control panel and select System.

5. Select Advanced System Settings and click the Environment Variables button.

6. In the System variables section, select the Path item and click the Edit button.

7. Scroll to the far right of the variable value, type a semi-colon followed by C:\Program Files\Adobe\Adobe PDF iFilter 9 for 64-bit platforms\bin. *__Be EXTREMELY careful when you are editing this variable. Do not remove any existing value from the Path variable. This is a semi-colon delimited list, so make sure you have entered a semi-colon prior to inputting the path specified above. Double check, triple check, and check at least one more time to make sure you have appended this value to the end of the list and did NOT overwrite anything else which was already there. You will cause all kinds of problems on your machine if you get this step wrong.__*

8. After you've checked this again, click OK to close the Path editor, OK again to close the environment variables dialog, OK to close the System Properties, and then close the System screen.

9. Execute the following code to load the resources and verify code signatures.
    ```
    EXEC sp_fulltext_service 'load_os_resources', 1;
    EXEC sp_fulltext_service 'verify_signature', 0;
    ```

10. Restart your SQL Server instance by right clicking the instance name in the Object Explorer and selecting Restart.

11. Once the instance has restarted, execute the following code.
    ```
    SELECT * FROM sys.fulltext_document_types WHERE document_type LIKE '%pdf%';
    ```

12. If you followed the instructions above, you should see a single row returned telling you that the Adobe PDF filter has been loaded and can be used by the full-text engine.

13. One of the more interesting omissions from SQL Server 2012 is support for all of the new Microsoft Office document types. Just like the Adobe download, these are available as a separate download.

14. Download the Office 2012 filter pack at http://www.microsoft.com/en-us/download/details.aspx?id=17062 and run the installer.

15. Execute the following code to load the resources and verify code signatures.

    ```
    EXEC sp_fulltext_service 'load_os_resources', 1;
    EXEC sp_fulltext_service 'verify_signature', 0;
    ```

16. Restart your SQL Server instance by right clicking the instance name in the Object Explorer and selecting Restart.

17. Once the instance has restarted, execute the following code to verify that the new filters have been installed. You will also find Zip, OneNote, Visio, Publisher, and Open Document filters.

    ```
    SELECT * FROM sys.fulltext_document_types WHERE document_type IN
    ('.docx','.pptx','.xlsx');
    ```

Property Lists

In addition to the content, some file types have a set of properties such as author, title, and keywords. Prior to SQL Server 2012, all of the document properties were just treated as part of the file and indexed like any other word. This made a search for documents by a particular author, keyword, or other property extremely difficult. SQL Server 2012 added capabilities to the document filters to separate document properties from the document content.

When you define a full-text index on a set of documents by indexing the VARBINARY(MAX) column in a FileTable or one configured with the FILESTREAM attribute, you can now choose whether to index document properties or ignore them. If you choose to index document properties, you can specify the properties that you want to index.

Not all filters return document properties. For example, an XML or text file does not have any properties, so the XML and text filters ignore the property specification of the index, but Word and Excel filters do return document properties.

Property searching is configured the same way as stop lists. You create a search property list and then alter the list to add one or more properties. The syntax to create a property list is:

```
CREATE SEARCH PROPERTY LIST new_list_name
   [ FROM [ database_name. ] source_list_name ]
   [ AUTHORIZATION owner_name ];
```

Just as with a stop list, you can create an empty search property list or create one from an existing search property list.

Defining the search properties is a little more complicated. You can't just add something like the Author to the list. You are asking the filters to pull out what is essentially a programming element for the file, so you have to specifically identify the property. Just as the filters for each document type are registered, the available properties for each filter are also registered with the SQL Server instance. A document property has three elements – unique identifier of the property set, the identifier of the property within the set, and the name of the property. Yes, this means you are digging through reference material to find GUIDs and IDs and there isn't a single place to find this information. For example, F29F85E0-4FF9-1068-AB91-08002B27B3D9 with an ID of 2 is the title property while an ID of 4 is the author property for documents created using Microsoft software.

You can get document properties for Microsoft software by searching the published Windows properties list found at http://msdn.microsoft.com/library/dd561977.aspx. Of course, you have to actually know or guess the property name to find it.

Another method which works for all file types is to use the filtdump.exe utility from the Windows SDK. You have to first download and install the Windows SDK for whichever operating system version you are running. Once you install the SDK, you can run the filtdump.exe to return a list of document properties. For example, on my 64 bit Windows 7 machine I would run the following command to retrieve properties for Microsoft Word. You need to either use an existing file or preferably create an empty file of the type you want. The reason why an empty file is preferable is because filtdump.exe will return the entire contents of the file you specify, making it very difficult to find the properties within all of the rest of the information.

```
C:\Program Files\Microsoft SDKs\Windows\v7.1\Bin\x64\filtdump.exe c:\data\test.docx
```

This would dump piles and piles of output to the screen that you have to comb through. A better way, although the output is even uglier is to pipe the output to a file as follows:

```
C:\Program Files\Microsoft SDKs\Windows\v7.1\Bin\x64\filtdump.exe c:\data\test.docx
>>c:\data\test.txt
```

When you open the output file, everything will be smashed together in quite a mess. What you are looking for is sections like the following:

```
CHUNK: -----------------------------------------------------------
Attribute = {F29F85E0-4FF9-1068-AB91-08002B27B3D9}\2 (System.Title)
idChunk = 1
BreakType = 3 (Paragraph)
Flags (chunkstate) =   (Value)
Locale = 0 (0x0)
IdChunkSource = 1
cwcStartSource = 0
cwcLenSource = 0
VALUE: -----------------------------------------------------------
Type = 31 (0x1f), VT_LPWSTR
Value = "This is a title"
```

The Attribute row is where all the information you need is located. The GUID is the GUID that you need for the search property list. The number following the \ after the GUID is the ID of the property within the property set. The value in parenthesis, System.Title, is the name of the property within the property set.

You then find the properties you want to index and add them to the search property list by using ALTER SEARCH PROPERTY LIST with the following syntax:

```
ALTER SEARCH PROPERTY LIST list_name
{ADD 'property_name'
    WITH
        (   PROPERTY_SET_GUID = 'property_set_guid'
          , PROPERTY_INT_ID = property_int_id
        [ , PROPERTY_DESCRIPTION = 'property_description' ] )
   | DROP 'property_name' };
```

Exercise 3: Creating a Search Property List

When searching documents, document properties should be searchable separately from the contents of the document. Champion Valley Pens wants to enable property searches for the Title and Author properties of documents which are allowed to be stored as either .docx or .pdf files.

1. Execute the following code against the ChampionValleyPens database to create a search property list.

   ```
   CREATE SEARCH PROPERTY LIST DocumentProperties;
   ```

2. Execute the following code to add the Title and Author properties.

   ```
   ALTER SEARCH PROPERTY LIST DocumentProperties
       ADD 'Title'
      WITH ( PROPERTY_SET_GUID = 'F29F85E0-4FF9-1068-AB91-08002B27B3D9',
   PROPERTY_INT_ID = 2,
           PROPERTY_DESCRIPTION = 'System.Title - Title property of a document.' );
   ALTER SEARCH PROPERTY LIST DocumentProperties
       ADD 'Author'
      WITH ( PROPERTY_SET_GUID = 'F29F85E0-4FF9-1068-AB91-08002B27B3D9',
   PROPERTY_INT_ID = 4,
           PROPERTY_DESCRIPTION = 'System.Author - Author property of a document.' );
   ```

3. Repeat steps 1 and 2 against the ChampionValleyPensDocs database.

The document properties above work for both Adobe and Microsoft documents, because both companies use the same document property standards. When you load a custom filter, you will want to use the filtdump utility to determine the GUID and ID for the properties you are interested in and add any which do not use the same identifiers as you have in your search property lists.

Exercise 4: Creating a Full-Text Index

Champion Valley Pens wants to allow customers to search on product descriptions in order to find related products as an extension to the hard coded links currently being created.

1. Execute the following code against the ChampionValleyPens database to create a full-text catalog for the product description indexes.

   ```
   CREATE FULLTEXT CATALOG ProductDescriptions AS DEFAULT;
   ```

2. Execute the following code to index the XML ProductDescription.

   ```
   CREATE FULLTEXT INDEX ON ChampionValleyPens.Products.Product (ProductDescription LANGUAGE 1033)
   KEY INDEX pk_Product ON ProductDescriptions
   WITH STOPLIST = ProductsStopList, CHANGE_TRACKING AUTO;
   ```

3. Execute the following code to index the Description column in the Products.SKU table.

   ```
   CREATE FULLTEXT INDEX ON ChampionValleyPens.Products.SKU (Description LANGUAGE 1033)
   KEY INDEX pk_SKU ON ProductDescriptions
   WITH STOPLIST = ProductsStopList, CHANGE_TRACKING AUTO;
   ```

Querying Full-Text Indexes

SQL Server 2012 provides four commands to query full text data: CONTAINS, FREETEXT, CONTAINSTABLE, and FREETEXTTABLE. CONTAINS and FREETEXT return a true/false value while CONTAINSTABLE and FREETEXTTABLE return a result set.

Querying a full-text index involves many of the processes used to build the index. The word or words which you are querying have to be run through a word breaker, stemmer, and stop lists. Just like the index build, this tokenizes the search term. The tokens are then compared to the available distribution statistics for the full-text index in order to determine the optimal query path to satisfy the request.

FREETEXT

The most basic form of a full-text search use the FREETEXT command with the following generic syntax:

```
FREETEXT ( { column_name | (column_list) | * }
         , 'freetext_string' [ , LANGUAGE language_term ] )
```

An example of a FREETEXT query is:

```
SELECT SKU, Description
FROM Products.SKU
WHERE FREETEXT(Description,N'kit');
```

Just as you can specify a language which dictates the word breaker and stemmer applied to a column in an index, a LANGUAGE parameter can be passed to each full-text query command that specifies the word breaker, stemmer, and stop list applied to the search term. While you can use a different language for a search term than we used to build the full-text index, you may get variances in your results. For example, if you used a 1033 (US English) language to build an index on a column containing German text along with 1031 (German) for the FREETEXT query, you probably won't find all of the results you are looking for since the English word breaker will have problems with the way words are compounded in the German language and an English stemmer doesn't have any idea how to conjugate German verbs. In the end, this is still a computer which is looking for a match to an input pattern. You can score points in a game of horseshoes, but SQL Server won't return results that are "close" to what you asked for.

> **Warning:** Something which is commonly overlooked is the data type of the search terms used in full-text search. Full-text indexes are Unicode. All search parameters are Unicode. This might seem like a trivial point, until you try to do a full-text search across 1000s or millions of rows of data and you see abysmal performance. When you send a non-Unicode search term, SQL Server has to perform a data type conversion to Unicode based on the collation settings of your connection. In essence, this creates a calculation, which to the query optimizer means an indeterminate value. In every one of these cases, the Query Optimizer will not use the full-text index as a filtering source for the query but will instead process all other tables in the query before scanning the full-text index. For those of you reading query plans, which will be covered in detail in the next book, this means you will see a cost estimate of 10,000 for the full-text index. You should ensure that you are always using Unicode search terms to avoid this performance bottleneck.

If you want a result set instead of a simple true/false, you can use FREETEXTTABLE. The returned result set has additional information that ranks the results in accordance to how close the match was to the original search term. The generic syntax for FREETEXTTABLE is:

```
FREETEXTTABLE (table , { column_name | (column_list) | * }
    , 'freetext_string'
  [ ,LANGUAGE language_term ]
  [ ,top_n_by_rank ] )
```

You can express the same query from above with FREETEXTTABLE is as follows:

```
SELECT a.SKU, a.Description, b.*
FROM Products.SKU a INNER JOIN
    FREETEXTTABLE(Products.SKU,Description,N'kit') b ON a.SKU = b.[Key];
```

CONTAINS

FREETEXT/FREETEXTTABLE only provide prefix match search capabilities. For example, if you search for pen, FREETEXT/FREETEXTTABLE will return documents which contain pen, pens, and pencil. Sometimes you want quite a bit more flexibility as well as more control in your search. CONTAINS/CONTAINSTABLE provide an extremely flexible search capability. You can search inflectional forms, exact match, prefix searches, employ a thesaurus, do word proximity searches, and specify weighting factors in a list of search terms as just a few examples.

The generic syntax for CONTAINS is:

```
CONTAINS (
    { column_name | ( column_list ) | * | PROPERTY ( { column_name },
'property_name' ) }
    , '<contains_search_condition>' [ , LANGUAGE language_term ] )
```

```
<contains_search_condition> ::=
   { <simple_term> | <prefix_term> | <generation_term> | <generic_proximity_term>
    | <custom_proximity_term> | <weighted_term> } |
   { ( <contains_search_condition> ) [ { <AND> | <AND NOT> | <OR> } ]
        <contains_search_condition> [ ...n ] }
<simple_term> ::=
        { word | "phrase" }
<prefix term> ::=
   { "word*" | "phrase*" }
<generation_term> ::=
    FORMSOF ( { INFLECTIONAL | THESAURUS } , <simple_term> [ ,...n ] )
<generic_proximity_term> ::=
    { <simple_term> | <prefix_term> } {{{ NEAR | ~ } { <simple_term> | <prefix_term> }
  [...n ]}
<custom_proximity_term> ::=
    NEAR ( {{ <simple_term> | <prefix_term> } [ ,...n ] | ( {<simple_term> |
<prefix_term>} [,...n ])
        [, <maximum_distance> [, <match_order> ] ] })

        <maximum_distance> ::= { integer | MAX }
        <match_order> ::= { TRUE | FALSE }

<weighted_term> ::=
    ISABOUT ({ { <simple_term> | <prefix_term> | <generation_term> | <proximity_term>}
        [ WEIGHT ( weight_value ) ] } [ ,...n ] )
```

Exact Match Searches

Search terms can be used for either exact matches or as prefixes. The following query returns the products with an exact match on the word "bike". While the query looks almost exactly equal to the FREETEXT version, the CONTAINS query will return four fewer rows due to the exact matching:

```
SELECT SKU, Description
FROM Products.SKU
WHERE CONTAINS(Description,N'kit');
```

Wildcard Searches

To make CONTAINS behave the same as FREETEXT, you would specify a basic wildcard search as follows (note the double quotes within the single quotes):

```
SELECT SKU, Description
FROM Products.SKU
WHERE CONTAINS(Description,N'"kit*"');
```

With CONTAINS, you have to explicitly specify that you want to perform prefix searching, which would include word prefixes, but FREETEXT defaults to prefix searching.

Word Forms

To search for word variants, you can utilize the FORMSOF, INFLECTIONAL, and THESAURUS options. INFLECTIONAL causes the full text engine to consider word stems. For example, searching on inflectional forms of "ride" will also produce "rode", "ridden", "riding"," etc.

The THESAURUS produces synonyms for the search term. An example of searching on word variants is as follows:

```
SELECT SKU, Description
FROM Products.SKU
WHERE CONTAINS(Description,N' FORMSOF (INFLECTIONAL,plate) ');
```

Thesaurus Files

A thesaurus is used to find synonyms for words. For example, the word happy can be replaced with joyful, cheerful, and merry as these are synonyms. A thesaurus for full-text indexing performs the same basic function. When you apply a thesaurus, full text queries can retrieve rows that match the search argument along with synonyms of a search argument. As you have probably guessed by now, a thesaurus is specific to a language. Unlike all of the other full-text objects, the thesaurus for each language is an XML file stored in the FTDATA directory. FREETEXT and FREETEXTTABLE will automatically use a thesaurus while you have to specify the FORMSOF THESAURUS option for CONTAINS and CONTAINSTABLE queries.

A thesaurus can contain expansion sets or replacement sets. When you define a replacement, the term or terms specified are replaced within the search argument prior to the word breaker tokenizing the argument list. An expansion set defines a set of terms that are used to expand upon a search argument. When an expansion set is used, a row is returned if a match is found on any term within the expansion set.

The basic structure of a thesaurus file is:

```
<XML ID="Microsoft Search Thesaurus">
<!-- Commented out
    <thesaurus xmlns="x-schema:tsSchema.xml">
    <diacritics_sensitive>0</diacritics_sensitive>
        <expansion>
            <sub>Internet Explorer</sub>
            <sub>IE</sub>
            <sub>IE5</sub>
        </expansion>
        <replacement>
            <pat>NT5</pat>
            <pat>W2K</pat>
            <sub>Windows 2000</sub>
        </replacement>
        <expansion>
            <sub>run</sub>
            <sub>jog</sub>
        </expansion>
    </thesaurus>
-->
</XML>
```

The diacritics setting specifies whether the thesaurus is accent sensitive. A value of 0 tells the word breaker to ignore diacritics while a value of 1 causes the word breaker to obey the diacritic marks.

A replacement set has two components, a pattern to match and a substitution value. If you specify an empty substitution, the engine will return an empty result set when it encounters any of the defined patterns,

A thesaurus file exists for each supported language. All thesaurus files are XML files stored in the FTDATA directory underneath your default SQL Server installation path. It would be nice if the thesaurus files which ship with SQL Server had already been populated with accepted synonyms for each language, like the system stop list is already populated. However, each thesaurus file is empty and it is up to you to populate the file based on the example provided which is shown above. In addition to the thesaurus files being empty, the files have names that leave a lot of people scratching their heads. The name of the thesaurus file does not match the LANGUAGE parameter you use within full-text indexing and it also doesn't match the language ID. Prior to the Sharepoint team documenting the languages corresponding to each thesaurus file, you had to use a lot of trial and error along with asking questions. Now you just go out to http://technet.microsoft.com/en-us/library/dd361734%28v=office.14%29.aspx#Section5 to look up the name of the thesaurus file for the language you are using. For example tseng.xml is the thesaurus file for English which has an ID of 1033 while tsenu.xml is the thesaurus file for British English which has an ID of 2057.

Exercise 5: Creating a Thesaurus

Many of the products sold by Champion Valley Pens are plated in a variety of precious metals or coated with multiple colors of Chinese lacquer. To facilitate searching, a customer should be able to pull products with any type of precious metal plating when specifying a single type of metal. You will need to create a thesaurus in order to enable this capability.

1. Run the following query and verify that you get an empty result set.

    ```
    SELECT SKU, Description
    FROM Products.SKU
    WHERE CONTAINS(Description,N' FORMSOF (THESAURUS,metal) ');
    ```

2. Locate the FTDATA directory for your instance which should be in the same location as the data files for your system databases. On my machine which used the default locations this is C:\Program Files\Microsoft SQL Server\MSSQL11.MSSQLSERVER\MSSQL\FTData.

3. Right click tsenu.xml and open it in Notepad.

4. Replace the contents of the file with the following definition:

    ```xml
    <XML ID="Microsoft Search Thesaurus">
        <thesaurus xmlns="x-schema:tsSchema.xml">
    <diacritics_sensitive>0</diacritics_sensitive>
            <expansion>
                <sub>metal</sub>
                <sub>precious metal</sub>
                <sub>gold</sub>
                <sub>24k gold</sub>
                <sub>silver</sub>
                <sub>platinum</sub>
                <sub>rhodium</sub>
            </expansion>
        </thesaurus>
    </XML>
    ```

5. Save the file, close it, and return to a query window in SSMS.

6. Execute the following code to load the updated thesaurus file.
   ```
   USE ChampionValleyPens;
   EXEC sys.sp_fulltext_load_thesaurus_file 1033;
   ```

7. Run the CONTAINS query again and verify that you are now getting 5 rows even though the word *metal* does not appear in any of the descriptions.
   ```
   SELECT SKU, Description
   FROM Products.SKU
   WHERE CONTAINS(Description,N' FORMSOF (THESAURUS,metal) ');
   ```

Proximity Searches

Being able to search for a specific word, inflectional forms of a word, or apply a thesaurus search to a word are nice, but the search is limited to a single word. You can perform compound searches, but with the capabilities we've covered so far, you are still doing single word searches without any intelligence behind sentence structure. The NEAR keyword allows you to bring in sentence semantics to search for words based on location within the index. By using CONTAINSTABLE, you can retrieve a ranking value. As the words get closer together, the rank value increases.

The following query applies the thesaurus to show how multiple search criteria can be combined to return all rows where any of the synonyms for metal exist as well as where *Gold* is near *pen*.

```
SELECT a.SKU, a.Description, b.*
FROM Products.SKU a INNER JOIN
    CONTAINSTABLE(Products.SKU, Description,
        N'FORMSOF (THESAURUS,metal) AND NEAR(Gold,pen)') b ON a.SKU = b.[Key]
ORDER BY b.[Rank];
```

Rank and *Key* need to be enclosed in square brackets, because they are reserved words. The NEAR function says to return any rows where both *Gold* and *pen* exist and rank them according to proximity. The two words could appear anywhere or in any order as long as both appear. If you wanted to limit the results to cases where the words were a certain distance away from each other, you can add a distance value to the NEAR function. The following query only returns rows where *Gold* and *pen* are within 5 words of each other.

```
SELECT a.SKU, a.Description, b.*
FROM Products.SKU a INNER JOIN
    CONTAINSTABLE(Products.SKU, Description,
        N'FORMSOF (THESAURUS,metal) AND NEAR((Gold,pen),5)') b ON a.SKU = b.[Key]
ORDER BY b.[Rank];
```

If you want to enforce an order on the terms, you can apply a 3rd parameter to the NEAR function. The following example says to find all cases where *Gold* is within 5 words of *pen*, but *Gold* has to come before *pen*.

```
SELECT a.SKU, a.Description, b.*
FROM Products.SKU a INNER JOIN
    CONTAINSTABLE(Products.SKU, Description,
        N'FORMSOF (THESAURUS,metal) AND NEAR((Gold,pen),5,TRUE)') b ON a.SKU = b.[Key]
ORDER BY b.[Rank];
```

Weighted Results

One of the things that you've heard about since search engines became popular, even spawning an entire series of commercials, is "the algorithm". Search engines live and die by the algorithms which rank search results. While the algorithms used by search engines are a bit more complicated, at their core is a set of weighting factors which cause one entry to be ranked higher than another. Full-text search has the same weighting capability with the ISABOUT function.

You can specify weighting factors between 0 and 1 for a set of words which will cause results to be ranked higher based on the number of matches as well as the factor applied to each match. The following example returns the top 5 matches based on the rank which is derived using the specified weighting factors.

```
SELECT a.SKU, a.Description, b.*
FROM Products.SKU a INNER JOIN
    CONTAINSTABLE(Products.SKU, Description,
        N'ISABOUT (heirloom WEIGHT (.8), Rhodium WEIGHT (.6),
        gold WEIGHT (.2) , fountain WEIGHT (.5))', 5) b ON a.SKU = b.[Key]
ORDER BY b.[Rank] DESC;
```

Monitoring Index Population

Since you can't retrieve information for a document until it has been indexed, one of the most important things for an administrator to understand is the population status of an index. You retrieve this information by querying sys.fulltext_indexes, sys.dm_fts_index_population, sys.dm_fts_outstanding_batches, and sys.dm_fts_population_ranges.

Sys.fulltext_indexes displays the basic configuration information about each full-text index in a database such as the table associated to the index, change tracking options, stop list, and search property list. The most important pieces of information for monitoring are the crawl_start_time and crawl_end_date. This allows you to determine if a crawl has recently started and when the last time a crawl completed.

Sys.dm_fts_index_population displays the population status for all full-text indexes within the instance, so you will want to limit the results to the database ID you are interested in. The most important column is the status column and its corresponding status_description column which tell you the current population state for each index. The most common states are 3, 5, and 7. You will see the index with a status = 3 when all documents have been indexed and there is no more work to do. A status = 5 means that a crawl is currently running. A status = 7 means that the indexer has completed a batch and is performing a master merge into the full-text index.

When the index population has a status of either 3 or 5, the outstanding_batch_count column will tell you how many more batches still need to be processed by the indexing engine. You will also see rows in sys.dm_fts_outstanding_batches and sys.dm_fts_population_ranges which provide more detail on each batch currently being processed.

Contents of a Full-Text Index

Full-text indexes are stored on pages, just like all other data, but the information is stored in a binary format which isn't readable unless you care to parse binary strings. Unlike clustered and nonclustered indexes, the raw information on a page for full-text indexes doesn't provide any knowledge you can use to design better systems. However, viewing the contents of a full-text index can be extremely useful.

By querying sys.dm_fts_index_keywords, you can return a list of all of the words which have been indexed for the table and how many times each word appears within the index.

```
SELECT * FROM
sys.dm_fts_index_keywords(DB_ID('ChampionValleyPens'),OBJECT_ID('Products.SKU'));
```

You can break this down even more by returning the list of words in the index for each document which returns a count of each term within the document.

```
SELECT * FROM
sys.dm_fts_index_keywords_by_document(DB_ID('ChampionValleyPens'),OBJECT_ID('Products.SKU'))
WHERE display_term <> 'END OF FILE'
ORDER BY document_id;
```

The word list and the number of times each term occurs might be interesting to put into a book, but what good does it do in the real world application you have to produce?

One of the things you find companies wanting to do is understand customer perceptions. One of the ways this information is gathered is through feedback forms where customers can post feedback for the company as a whole or for individual products. Many web retailers simply append these customer reviews to the product list, after filtering out any reviews for offensive language. But, as a customer, can you really do anything with 8,000 feedback comments? What if you could distil all of the comments for a product in a way which makes the overall sentiments immediately apparent? One of the most powerful ways to "get the general idea" about something is to use a word cloud. This takes all of the words and puts them into a basic word picture where the size of a word is relative to the number of times in which it occurs. Once complete, a simple glance tells you what the general theme of the content is.

In order to build these word clouds, software vendors have to build word breakers which are language specific, tokenize each term found in a document, throw out common words they don't care about, count the number of times it occurs, and then perform a visual layout of the results. The full-text engine doesn't handle the visual layout, but it does handle everything else. Instead of building all of this yourself, all you have to do is build a program to perform the visual layout. You then apply a full-text index to the data and use sys.dm_fts_index_keywords as the data source.

If you want to allow a user to interactively drill into the word cloud, you can allow them to click a word, use sys.dm_fts_index_keywords_by_document to find all documents with the clicked word, and display a new word cloud containing just that subset of documents. If you want them to be able to drill back to the original row in the table, you can use sp_fulltext_keymappings to retrieve the relationship between the primary key value in your table and the internal document ID used by the full-text index.

The following code retrieves the key mapping for the Products.SKU table.

```
DECLARE @table INT = OBJECT_ID('Products.SKU');
EXEC sp_fulltext_keymappings @table;
```

Semantic Search

One of the "holy grails" within the computer world is to build a program capable of understanding language. Not just locating words, but to actually understand the meaning and intent, semantics, behind spoken and written language.

New in SQL Server 2012 is a semantic search capability which attempts to apply statistical analysis to the full-text search engine so that you can search for similarities between documents. While it is called semantic search, the SQL Server engine does not understand language semantics any better than a machine can translate from one language to another, as of the writing of this book. What machines are very good at doing is counting the occurrence of words, the distance between words, the relationship between repeating patterns of words, and coming up with an answer that appears to give you a basic idea of what a document is about. Just as it is quite simple to fool the Google search algorithm given enough websites spread around the globe, you can very easily fool the semantic search engine. But, we don't build business solutions to fool an algorithm.

The goal of the semantic search engine is to allow you to index a set of documents and then run queries which can find related content. Basically, given a document on whales, find me all of the other documents within the index which are similar to the document specified. The engine does this by comparing the key phrases computed using the semantic statistics and returning documents with a score similar to the reference document.

There will be someone with their hopes up on the fact that key phrases are being compared, just like someone has their hopes up that you are actually comparing the meaning of words. If I mention whale enough times in this chapter, you'll find a full-text search chapter come up when you search for documents similar to a reference document on blue whales. The engine does not understand the meaning of documents; no matter how many times Microsoft wants to state it in their documentation. The engine doesn't actually understand phrases either. The semantic search engine is limited to single words and the similarity indexes are computed and compared based on single words. The semantic engine doesn't even have the flexibility found within the full-text engine as it treats each word precisely as it is. Singular and plural forms are different words and it has no ability to use stemmers to consider verb conjugation or a thesaurus. With those limitations in mind, we're ready to embark on semantic search.

Configuring Semantic Search

The semantic algorithms were packaged in a separate database to allow for future updates to the algorithms without needing to install a patch or service pack to SQL Server. While you can retrieve the semantic database from your SQL Server installation media, I would recommend downloading it to ensure you get the most recent version.

You download the semantic search database from http://www.microsoft.com/en-us/download/details.aspx?id=29069. Once downloaded, you can run the installer to unpack the database files, move the files to the same location as the rest of your databases, and then attach the database to your instance. While you can use any name you want for the database, I would very strongly recommend not changing the name.

After the database is attached, you have to register the database using the following command:

```
EXEC sp_fulltext_semantic_register_language_statistics_db @dbname = N'semanticsdb';
```

You can verify that the database has been successfully registered by querying sys.fulltext_semantic_language_statistics_database.

Exercise 6: Enabling Semantic Search

Champion Valley Pens wants to allow customers to search product manuals using regular full-text capabilities as well as semantic search. The Human Resources department also wants to search their library of employee documents.

1. Open a browser and download the semantic search database from http://www.microsoft.com/en-us/download/details.aspx?id=29069.

2. Run the installer to unpack the database files and place them in the same location as the rest of your system databases.

3. Attach the database.

4. Execute the following query to register the semantic statistics database.
    ```
    EXEC sp_fulltext_semantic_register_language_statistics_db @dbname = N'semanticsdb';
    ```

5. Run the following query to verify that the database is registered.
    ```
    SELECT * FROM sys.fulltext_semantic_language_statistics_database;
    ```

6. Execute the following code to create full-text catalogs for the documents in the ChampionValleyPensDocs database.
    ```
    CREATE FULLTEXT CATALOG ProductManuals AS DEFAULT;
    CREATE FULLTEXT CATALOG EmployeeDocuments AS DEFAULT;
    ```

7. Execute the following code to index the Product manuals.
    ```
    CREATE FULLTEXT INDEX ON ChampionValleyPensDocs.Products.ProductDocument
    (file_stream
        TYPE COLUMN file_type
        LANGUAGE 1033
        Statistical_Semantics)
    KEY INDEX PK__ProductD__5A5B77D569EDD851 ON ProductManuals
    WITH STOPLIST = ProductsStopList, CHANGE_TRACKING AUTO;
    ```

8. Execute the following code to index the employee documents.

```
CREATE FULLTEXT INDEX ON ChampionValleyPensDocs.HumanResources.EmployeeDocument
(file_stream
    TYPE COLUMN file_type
    LANGUAGE 1033
    Statistical_Semantics)
KEY INDEX PK__Employee__5A5B77D502DFD323 ON EmployeeDocuments
WITH STOPLIST = ProductsStopList, CHANGE_TRACKING AUTO;
```

9. Execute the following code to add semantic search capabilities to the product description full-text indexes.

```
ALTER FULLTEXT INDEX ON ChampionValleyPens.Products.Product
    ALTER COLUMN ProductDescription
        ADD Statistical_Semantics;
ALTER FULLTEXT INDEX ON ChampionValleyPens.Products.SKU
    ALTER COLUMN Description
        ADD Statistical_Semantics;
```

> **Note:** There comes a time in every project, when the "gold plating" has to stop and the project has to be delivered to the customer. That customer is you and the project is this book you are reading. The sample databases are based on a real business named Champion Valley Pens that sells many of the products you find within the data. Pieces of the product descriptions such as the quantum finish and many of the product configurations do not actually exist. All of this data was created while this book was being written and I didn't have a team to do the work for me like happens with AdventureWorks. That is where updates and the companion website come in. It allows me to release the book and at a later date come back in and fill the database in with more complete data giving you more querying options. It also allows me to write a more extensive set of documents for the FileTable feature. The product manuals are one of these items. When this book initially ships, there aren't any product manuals. If you subscribe to our update notifications, you will be notified when I've written product manuals which you can load to play with the full-text index created in the exercise above. If you want to use your own documents, feel free to dump anything into the FileTable you want to see how the indexing performs.

Semantic Searches

Once you have the full-text indexes built with semantic search capability, you can start querying the documents. In the exercise above, you added semantic search capability to the two full-text indexes in the ChampionValleyPens database. You also created full-text indexes on two of the FileTables we created back in Chapter 5. Data is data is data. It doesn't matter if it is a piece of text stored in a column within one of your tables or a bunch of text in a file, it is all just data. With the inclusion of the TYPE COLUMN option, we enabled SQL Server to full-text index the documents stored using FileTable and the file_type column told the indexing engine which document filter to load so that the contents of the document could be parsed.

If you want to retrieve a list of the top key phrases along with the semantic similarity score for each document, you can query the semantickeyphrasetable function as shown below.

```
SELECT name, document_key, keyphrase, score
FROM semantickeyphrasetable(HumanResources.EmployeeDocument, *)
INNER JOIN HumanResources.EmployeeDocument ON path_locator = document_key
ORDER BY name, score DESC;
```

The function takes three arguments – the name of the table, the column/columns to search, and the key of the document you want to return. The key is optional and corresponds to the index key used when creating the full-text index.

You can limit the results to a single document by specifying the 3rd parameter as shown below.

```
DECLARE @Title AS NVARCHAR(1000);
DECLARE @DocID AS HIERARCHYID;
SET     @Title = 'Beth J Meeks.pdf';
SELECT @DocID = path_locator FROM HumanResources.EmployeeDocument WHERE name = @Title;
SELECT name, document_key, keyphrase, score
FROM semantickeyphrasetable(HumanResources.EmployeeDocument, *, @DocID)
INNER JOIN HumanResources.EmployeeDocument ON path_locator = document_key
ORDER BY name, score DESC;
```

Finding similar documents is done by using the semanticsimilaritytable function which takes 3 parameters – table to query, column/columns, and the key of the document to compare to. The query below returns the documents similar to the Beth Meeks W4 tax form.

```
DECLARE @Title AS NVARCHAR(1000);
DECLARE @DocID AS HIERARCHYID;
SET @Title = 'Beth J Meeks.pdf';
SELECT @DocID = path_locator FROM HumanResources.EmployeeDocument WHERE name = @Title;

SELECT @Title AS SourceTitle, name AS MatchedTitle, stream_id, score
FROM semanticsimilaritytable(HumanResources.EmployeeDocument , *, @DocID)
INNER JOIN HumanResources.EmployeeDocument ON path_locator = matched_document_key
ORDER BY score DESC;
```

It shouldn't be a surprise that the list of similar documents were also W4 forms since these government tax documents contain a large amount of standard text. This gives you a baseline to start investigating the results when you try different documents, especially the Word documents which are resumes.

It's nice that SQL Server returned a list of related documents along with a score. How did the engine determine the matches? The semanticsimilaritydetailstable function allows you to compare two documents and returns a list of key phrases that were used to determine the similarity score.

The query below compares the Beth Meeks and James Proctor PDF documents.

```sql
DECLARE @SourceTitle AS NVARCHAR(1000);
DECLARE @MatchedTitle AS NVARCHAR(1000);
DECLARE @SourceDocID AS HIERARCHYID;
DECLARE @MatchedDocID AS HIERARCHYID;

SET     @SourceTitle = 'Beth J Meeks.pdf';
SET @MatchedTitle = 'James A Proctor.pdf';

SELECT @SourceDocID = path_locator
FROM HumanResources.EmployeeDocument
WHERE name = @SourceTitle;

SELECT @MatchedDocID = path_locator
FROM HumanResources.EmployeeDocument
WHERE name = @MatchedTitle;

SELECT @SourceTitle AS SourceTitle, @MatchedTitle AS MatchedTitle, keyphrase, score
FROM semanticsimilaritydetailstable
        (HumanResources.EmployeeDocument, file_stream, @SourceDocID, file_stream,
         @MatchedDocID)
ORDER BY score DESC;
```

Summary

Indexes are simple structures, with far reaching consequences. The full-text engine extends SQL Server capabilities for searching text data. You can perform proximity searches, weight results, and basically create a simplified search engine without any fancy programming. Just create a FileTable, load all of your company's documents, create a full-text index, and start searching. If you want to find similar documents, all you have to do is load up the semantic statistics. By spending almost 20% of this book on indexes, you should have a good idea that while simple in concept, indexes are an extremely important object for your applications.

Chapter 14
Partitioning

> **Setup:** Please run the Chapter 14 Setup script in the companion files prior to starting the exercises in this chapter to ensure that your databases are at the correct starting point. Every exercise in this book assumes that you have created the c:\ChampionValleyPress\Data and c:\ChampionValleyPress\Log folders, contained databases are enabled, and this is the location of all of the data, log, and filestream files which will be used for this book. If you have chosen a different path, you will need to adjust the paths listed accordingly. Every setup script also assumes that you have enabled FILESTREAM access for the instance. When executing commands, it is assumed that you will change context to the appropriate database since understanding the contents of each database in this book is the same skill you will need for working with your databases. All scripts also assume you are using a default instance.

Through several chapters, I've carefully navigated around the topic of partitioning. We talked about storing tables and indexes on filegroups and we've looked at the internal storage structures behind tables and indexes. If you were paying attention to the functions we discussed for retrieving some of the storage information, you would have noted that an option was "conveniently" ignored. The reason that partitioning has been ignored so far is that it doesn't significantly affect how your databases work or how you interact with them, but it does make the discussion of storage structure a lot messier.

Partitioning was introduced in SQL Server 2005 to deal with a very specific problem which arises with large data sets and manipulation of large blocks of data. The two specific scenarios addressed were the need to delete large volumes of data from a table and the need to insert large volumes of data into a table. We'll discuss some additional things you can take advantage of with partitioning in the next book "SQL Server 2012 Database Programming", but anything that partitioning delivers beyond the mass insert and delete is a bonus.

Prior to SQL Server 2005, the storage boundary for any object which contained data was a filegroup. Neither a table, nor an index could be stored on more than one filegroup. Partitioning allows you to associate more than one filegroup to a storage structure called a partition scheme and then specify the partition scheme in the ON clause for a table or index. This allows the table or index to be split across multiple filegroups.

The process for partitioning a table or index is as follows:

1. Create a partition function

2. Create a partition scheme mapped to a partition function

3. Create the table or index ON the partition scheme

Partition Functions

Partitioning doesn't simply allow you to group more than one filegroup to a partition scheme and then have SQL Server randomly spread the data across multiple filegroups. You specify the way in which the data will be split and distributed across the filegroups. The distribution is defined by boundary points specified in a partition function.

Since a partition function is used to define how data is stored, it has to map the entire range of data values without any gaps. Every partition will contain a set of values defined by the boundary points. Unlike distribution statistics, boundary points can't simply be a convenient value to split the data into buckets, because each partition has to be stored in a single filegroup. Partitions are not allowed to span filegroup. When defining a partition function, you specify which partition each boundary point belongs to by specifying RANGE LEFT or RANGE RIGHT.

An example of a partition function is:

```
CREATE PARTITION FUNCTION pfn_OrderHeader (DATE)
AS RANGE LEFT
FOR VALUES ('12/31/2001','12/31/2002','12/31/2003','12/31/2004');
```

Each partition function requires a name and data type. The data type defines the range of values for the function. The data type for a partition function can be any native SQL Server data type, except VARBINARY(MAX), TIMESTAMP, XML, and (N)VARCHAR(MAX). T-SQL user-defined data types and CLR data types such as HIERARCHYID, GEOMETRY, and GEOGRAPHY are also not allowed.

The FOR VALUES clause is used to specify the boundary points for the partition function. The partition function maps the entire range of possible values and it is helpful to think of those values being written in a line from left to right. RANGE LEFT means the boundary point will be included in the left partition. RANGE RIGHT means the boundary point will be included in the right partition. Figure 14-1 shows how the partition function above lays out.

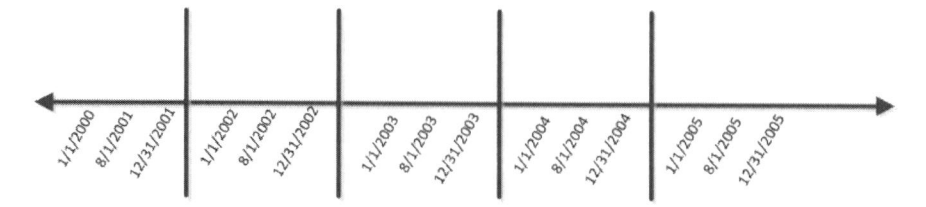

Figure 14-1 Visual representation of pfn_OrderHeader

You cannot specify duplicate boundary points since that would be the equivalent of duplicating a block of data. NULLs are always stored in the leftmost partition unless you explicitly specify NULL as a boundary point and use the RANGE RIGHT syntax.

The partitions formed by the boundary points are numbered from left to right beginning with 1 as shown in Figure 14-2.

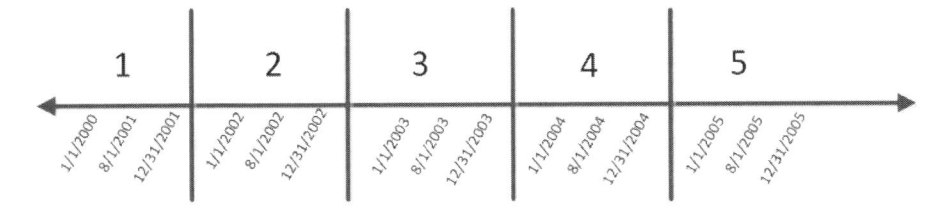

Figure 14-2 Partition numbering

Since the entire range of values is always mapped, the number of partitions created is always one more than the number of boundary points. You can create up to 15,000 partitions, which means you can specify a maximum of 14,999 boundary points.

Partition Schemes

Once a partition function is created, you can create a partition scheme to map the boundary points to storage. The generic syntax for creating a partition scheme is:

```
CREATE PARTITION SCHEME partition_scheme_name
AS PARTITION partition_function_name
[ ALL ] TO ( { file_group_name | [ PRIMARY ] } [ ,...n ] )
```

You have to specify at least 1 filegroup, but it is most common to specify as many filegroups as you have partitions so that each partition is stored in a separate filegroup. However, you can use a single filegroup to store all partitions.

The following are examples of partition schemes:

```
CREATE PARTITION SCHEME ps_OrderHeader
AS PARTITION pfn_OrderHeader TO (FG1, FG2, FG3, FG4, FG5);

CREATE PARTITION SCHEME ps_OrderHeader
AS PARTITION pfn_OrderHeader TO (FG1, FG1, FG2, FG2, FG3);

CREATE PARTITION SCHEME ps_OrderHeader
AS PARTITION pfn_OrderHeader ALL TO (FG1);
```

The AS PARTITION clause specifies the partition function that will be mapped to the partition scheme. The TO clause specifies the list of filegroups that are included in the partition scheme. All filegroups specified have to exist in the database prior to creation of the partition scheme.

There is a basic rule for the number of filegroups specified in a partition scheme. When the partition scheme is created, you must either specify the ALL keyword with a single filegroup or you have to specify the same number of filegroups as you have partitions. This is necessary, because SQL Server matches filegroups to partitions in the order defined within the partition scheme. If the partition scheme defines more than one filegroup, but does not have enough filegroups to store each partition, SQL Server wouldn't have any place to store the left over partitions. Since the engine won't throw away data, it has to have someplace to put each partition.

Figure 14-3 shows how the partition function and the partition scheme are mapped together.

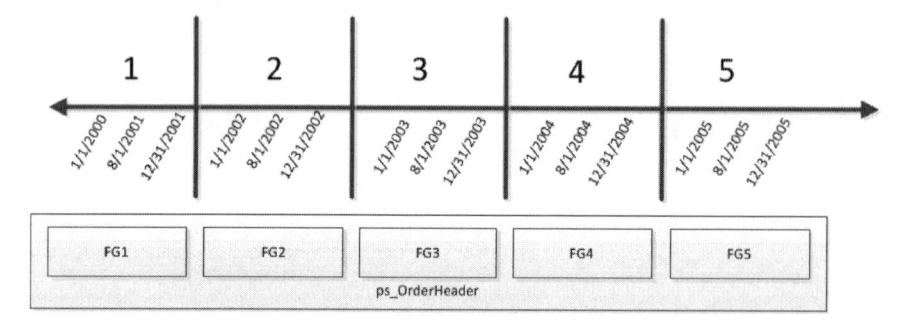

Figure 14-3 Partition function mapped to a partition scheme

Partitioning Tables and Indexes

Creating a partitioned table or index is quite simple once you have the partition scheme created. When you create tables or indexes, one of the options is to specify where to store the data. A partition scheme is just another definition of storage. Therefore, any place you can specify a filegroup, you can specify a partition scheme.

You can partition based on any column in a table or index as long as it meets the data type restrictions. In the chapter on indexing, we covered how you can index a computed column. One of the restrictions on indexing a computed column was that the computation needed to be deterministic. Determinism is required, because it is quite difficult to store a piece of data that changes every time you calculate it. So, it should come as no surprise that partitioning requires the computed column to be deterministic. Partitioning also doesn't allow a table to be partitioned based on a function. It has to be partitioned on a single column which contains data, so a computed column used for partitioning must also be persisted.

Creating a Partitioned Table

You can partition on a column with an imprecise data type such as REAL, but again, each piece of data must go in one and only one partition and the partition cannot change if you move the database to a server with different processor architecture. If you are using a column with an imprecise data type, the column must also be persisted.

An example of a partitioned table is as follows:

```
CREATE TABLE Orders.OrderHeader
(OrderID         INT         IDENTITY(1,1),
CustomerID       INT         NOT NULL,
AddressID        INT         NOT NULL,
OrderDate        DATE        NOT NULL CONSTRAINT df_CurrentDate DEFAULT (GETDATE()),
OrderTime        TIME        NOT NULL CONSTRAINT df_CurrentTime DEFAULT (GETDATE()),
OrderSubTotal    MONEY       NOT NULL CONSTRAINT ck_OrderSubTotalGreaterThanZero
                                               CHECK (OrderSubTotal > 0),
SalesTax         MONEY       NOT NULL CONSTRAINT df_SalesTax DEFAULT (0),
                             CONSTRAINT ck_SalesTaxNotNegative CHECK (SalesTax >=0),
ShippingAmount   MONEY       NOT NULL CONSTRAINT ck_ShippingAmountNotNegative
                                               CHECK (ShippingAmount >= 0),
OrderTotal       AS OrderSubTotal + SalesTax + ShippingAmount PERSISTED,
CONSTRAINT pk_orderheader PRIMARY KEY (OrderDate, OrderID))
ON ps_OrderHeader(OrderDate);
```

The CREATE TABLE statement is the same statement you used in Chapter 5 to create the Orders.OrderHeader table. The two important pieces for partitioning are the PRIMARY KEY clause and the ON clause.

It looks quite strange to have the primary key on both the OrderDate and the OrderID, especially when the OrderID is the only column required to make a row unique in the table. The reason OrderDate is part of the primary key is because the partitioning column is required to be included in any unique index; either primary key, unique constraint, or unique index.

The ON clause is where the partition scheme is applied to the table. You specify the partition scheme to apply along with the column used to partition the table or index. Up until this point, the partition function and partition scheme were abstract objects. When applied to the ON clause, the data in the table or index is partitioned according to the partition function. In this case, orders dated 12/31/2001 and prior belong to partition 1 which corresponds to FG1. Orders dated between 1/1/2002 and 12/31/2002 belong to partition 2 and are stored in FG2. This is how you can have the data in a table or index span filegroups.

The column specified for the partitioning key must match the data type and length of the partition function. You couldn't specify a VARCHAR(20) for the partition function and then use a VARCHAR(10) as the partitioning key just as you can't use a BIGINT for the partition function and partition using an INT column.

Below is another example of the same table being partitioned which shows you how to apply a partition function to a unique constraint.

```
CREATE TABLE Orders.OrderHeader
    (OrderID         INT        IDENTITY(1,1),
    CustomerID       INT        NOT NULL,
    AddressID        INT        NOT NULL,
    OrderDate        DATE       NOT NULL CONSTRAINT df_CurrentDate DEFAULT (GETDATE())
              CONSTRAINT uc_OrderDate UNIQUE CLUSTERED ON ps_OrderHeader(OrderDate),
    OrderTime        TIME       NOT NULL CONSTRAINT df_CurrentTime DEFAULT (GETDATE()),
    OrderSubTotal    MONEY      NOT NULL CONSTRAINT ck_OrderSubTotalGreaterThanZero
                                                        CHECK (OrderSubTotal > 0),
    SalesTax         MONEY      NOT NULL CONSTRAINT df_SalesTax DEFAULT (0),
                                CONSTRAINT ck_SalesTaxNotNegative CHECK (SalesTax >=0),
    ShippingAmount   MONEY      NOT NULL CONSTRAINT ck_ShippingAmountNotNegative
                                                        CHECK (ShippingAmount >= 0),
    OrderTotal       AS OrderSubTotal + SalesTax + ShippingAmount PERSISTED,
    CONSTRAINT pk_OrderHeader PRIMARY KEY NONCLUSTERED (OrderDate, OrderID)
        ON ps_OrderHeader2(OrderID))
ON ps_OrderHeader(OrderDate);
```

In this case, I've made the PRIMARY KEY nonclustered while adding a clustered, unique constraint to the OrderDate column. This syntax looks really weird, so take a minute to look at it.

SQL Server implements primary key and unique constraints as indexes. Indexes can be partitioned just as tables are partitioned and with the exception of the clustered index, can be partitioned using a different partition scheme. What the syntax above does is creates a unique, clustered index on the OrderDate column, placing the index on the ps_OrderHeader partition scheme. The nonclustered primary key is implemented as a unique nonclustered index and stored on the ps_OrderHeader2 partition scheme.

The ON clause at the end applies to the table and is irrelevant. If I had specified a partition scheme which was different from the unique constraint, SQL Server would have ignored the table's ON clause. The leaf level of a clustered index is the table, so it is impossible to place the table on a different partition scheme than the clustered index. This should also tell you that the way to move the table to a different partition scheme is to drop and recreate the clustered index on the partition scheme you want to move the table to.

Creating a Partitioned Index

An index is partitioned by specifying a partition scheme in the ON clause as shown in the example below:

```
CREATE NONCLUSTERED INDEX in_OrderHeader_CustomerID
    ON Orders.orderHeader(CustomerID)
ON ps_OrderHeader(OrderDate);
GO
```

The first thing you'll notice is the messy syntax. The first ON clause specified the table/column(s) which define the index. The second ON clause specifies the storage for the index. The partitioning column for the index also does not have to be defined in the first ON clause. If you remember from chapter 12, a nonclustered index can have an INCLUDE clause. If the partitioning column is not part of the nonclustered index definition, SQL Server will automatically add the partitioning column to an INCLUDE clause. This places the partition key on the leaf level of the index so that SQL Server can split the index structure according to the partition function. If you are partitioning a clustered index on a column which is not part of the index definition, SQL Server doesn't do anything, because the leaf level of the clustered index already contains the partitioning column.

When I first started teaching partitioning way back in the Beta 1 cycle of SQL Server 2005, I had someone ask me how to partition a table with a column which wasn't in the table to be partitioned. That caused a bit of head scratching as to why you would even want to do something like that. But, the question was reasonable, although impossible to accomplish. Say you wanted to partition the Orders.OrderHeader table on the OrderDate and place each year in a separate filegroup. You then wanted to partition the Orders.OrderDetail table which does not contain an OrderDate so that the details for each order are stored in the same filegroup with the corresponding OrderHeader rows. Now think about what SQL Server would have to do if this were allowed. In order to partition Orders.OrderDetail, SQL Server would have to query the entire contents of Orders.OrderHeader and use that to retrieve the set of OrderIDs for each OrderDate, and then use the OrderIDs to partition the table. Every modification to either Orders.OrderHeader or Orders.OrderDetail would incur this same query overhead. That's a tremendous amount of work just between two tables. What if you then wanted to take this a 3rd level down with the Orders.Shipment table? At some point, the entire platform would simply melt with the amount of work required to maintain the structure. SQL Server requires the partitioning column to be part of the table, and for indexes the partitioning column has to be part of the table the index is being created on.

Exercise 1: Partitioning Tables

In order to maintain reasonable performance and reduce the footprint of the orders database, management at Champion Valley Pens has decided that they only want to keep the current plus last 2 fiscal years of order data online. (The fiscal year runs from January 1 through December 31.) The DBAs have decided that they need to partition the Orders.OrderHeader, Orders.OrderDetail, and Orders.Shipment tables to meet this requirement without impacting the ability of customers to place orders. (We're going to assume that it is 2003 for the purpose of the exercises in this chapter.)

1. The DBAs have decided that they will initially create partitions for the first 4 years; each partition will contain an entire year of data and each yearly partition of the three tables will be stored in the same filegroup. Execute the following code to add 5 new filegroups to the ChampionValleyPens database.

    ```
    ALTER DATABASE ChampionValleyPens
        ADD FILEGROUP FG1;
    ALTER DATABASE ChampionValleyPens
        ADD FILEGROUP FG2;
    ALTER DATABASE ChampionValleyPens
        ADD FILEGROUP FG3;
    ALTER DATABASE ChampionValleyPens
        ADD FILEGROUP FG4;
    ALTER DATABASE ChampionValleyPens
        ADD FILEGROUP FG5;
    ```

2. Execute the following code to add 1 file to each of the filegroups.

```
ALTER DATABASE ChampionValleyPens
  ADD FILE
  (NAME= 'ChampionValleyPens1',
   FILENAME = 'C:\ChampionValleyPress\Data\ChampionValleyPens1.ndf',
   SIZE = 20MB, MAXSIZE = UNLIMITED, FILEGROWTH=20MB)
  TO FILEGROUP FG1;
ALTER DATABASE ChampionValleyPens
  ADD FILE
  (NAME= 'ChampionValleyPens2',
   FILENAME = 'C:\ChampionValleyPress\Data\ChampionValleyPens2.ndf',
   SIZE = 20MB, MAXSIZE = UNLIMITED, FILEGROWTH=20MB)
  TO FILEGROUP FG2;
ALTER DATABASE ChampionValleyPens
  ADD FILE
  (NAME= 'ChampionValleyPens3',
   FILENAME = 'C:\ChampionValleyPress\Data\ChampionValleyPens3.ndf',
   SIZE = 20MB, MAXSIZE = UNLIMITED, FILEGROWTH=20MB)
  TO FILEGROUP FG3;
ALTER DATABASE ChampionValleyPens
  ADD FILE
  (NAME= 'ChampionValleyPens4',
   FILENAME = 'C:\ChampionValleyPress\Data\ChampionValleyPens4.ndf',
   SIZE = 20MB, MAXSIZE = UNLIMITED, FILEGROWTH=20MB)
  TO FILEGROUP FG4;
ALTER DATABASE ChampionValleyPens
  ADD FILE
  (NAME= 'ChampionValleyPens5',
   FILENAME = 'C:\ChampionValleyPress\Data\ChampionValleyPens5.ndf',
   SIZE = 20MB, MAXSIZE = UNLIMITED, FILEGROWTH=20MB)
  TO FILEGROUP FG5;
```

3. Execute the following code to create the partition functions for the three tables.

```
CREATE PARTITION FUNCTION pfn_OrderHeader (DATE)
AS RANGE LEFT
FOR VALUES ('12/31/2001','12/31/2002','12/31/2003','12/31/2004');
CREATE PARTITION FUNCTION pfn_OrderDetail (DATE)
AS RANGE LEFT
FOR VALUES ('12/31/2001','12/31/2002','12/31/2003','12/31/2004');
CREATE PARTITION FUNCTION pfn_OrderShipment (DATE)
AS RANGE LEFT
FOR VALUES ('12/31/2001','12/31/2002','12/31/2003','12/31/2004');
```

4. Execute the following code to create the partition scheme for the three tables.

```
CREATE PARTITION SCHEME ps_OrderHeader
AS PARTITION pfn_OrderHeader TO (FG1, FG2, FG3, FG4, FG5);
CREATE PARTITION SCHEME ps_OrderDetail
AS PARTITION pfn_OrderDetail TO (FG1, FG2, FG3, FG4, FG5);
CREATE PARTITION SCHEME ps_OrderShipment
AS PARTITION pfn_OrderShipment TO (FG1, FG2, FG3, FG4, FG5);
```

5. In order to partition these three tables on the OrderDate, we're going to have to modify the primary key of all three tables, add the OrderDate column to Orders.OrderDetail and Orders.Shipment, and then set the partition scheme for the table. The first step will be to drop the foreign keys between the three tables. Execute the following code to drop the foreign keys.

    ```
    ALTER TABLE Orders.OrderDetail
        DROP CONSTRAINT fk_OrderHeaderToOrderDetailOnOrderID;
    ALTER TABLE Orders.Shipment
        DROP CONSTRAINT fk_OrderHeaderToShipmentOnOrderID;
    --Don't forget foreign keys to the Orders.ShipmentXrefOrderDetail table
    ALTER TABLE Orders.ShipmentXrefOrderDetail
        DROP CONSTRAINT fk_OrderDetailToShipmentXRefOrderDetailOnOrderDetailID;
    ALTER TABLE Orders.ShipmentXrefOrderDetail
        DROP CONSTRAINT fk_ShipmentToShipmentXRefOrderDetailOnShipmentID;
    ```

6. Each of the primary keys are clustered and changing the primary key definition and moving it to a new storage structure requires dropping and recreating the primary key. Execute the following code to drop all of the nonclustered indexes so that we don't have to incur the overhead of removing the clustering key to replace it with a RID and then having to take the RID back out and replace it with the new clustering key.

    ```
    DROP INDEX ifn_OrderDate ON Orders.OrderHeader;
    DROP INDEX in_OrderTotal ON Orders.OrderHeader;
    DROP INDEX in_SKU ON Orders.OrderDetail;
    DROP INDEX ifn_ShipDate ON Orders.Shipment;
    ```

7. Now add the OrderDate column to Orders.OrderDetail and Orders.Shipment. Since we need to populate the column with the appropriate values, the column needs to be nullable to begin with as it shouldn't have a default constraint assigned to it.

    ```
    ALTER TABLE Orders.OrderDetail
        ADD OrderDate    DATE    NULL;
    ALTER TABLE Orders.Shipment
        ADD OrderDate    DATE    NULL;
    ```

8. Execute the following code to populate the OrderDate column.

    ```
    UPDATE a
    SET a.OrderDate = b.OrderDate
    FROM Orders.OrderDetail a INNER JOIN Orders.OrderHeader b ON a.OrderID = b.OrderID;

    UPDATE a
    SET a.OrderDate = b.OrderDate
    FROM Orders.Shipment a INNER JOIN Orders.OrderHeader b ON a.OrderID = b.OrderID;
    ```

9. Execute the following code to change the nullability of the OrderDate column so that it can be added to the primary key.

    ```
    ALTER TABLE Orders.OrderDetail
        ALTER COLUMN OrderDate    DATE    NOT NULL;
    ALTER TABLE Orders.Shipment
        ALTER COLUMN OrderDate    DATE    NOT NULL;
    ```

10. Execute the following code to drop the primary key on all three tables.

    ```
    ALTER TABLE Orders.OrderHeader
        DROP CONSTRAINT pk_OrderHeader;
    ALTER TABLE Orders.OrderDetail
        DROP CONSTRAINT pk_OrderDetail;
    ALTER TABLE Orders.Shipment
        DROP CONSTRAINT pk_Shipment;
    ```

11. Execute the following code to recreate the primary key and partition the table on the appropriate partition scheme.

    ```
    ALTER TABLE Orders.OrderHeader
        ADD CONSTRAINT pk_OrderHeader PRIMARY KEY CLUSTERED (OrderDate, OrderID)
        ON ps_OrderHeader(OrderDate);
    ALTER TABLE Orders.OrderDetail
        ADD CONSTRAINT pk_OrderDetail PRIMARY KEY CLUSTERED (OrderDate, OrderDetailID)
        ON ps_OrderDetail(OrderDate);
    ALTER TABLE Orders.Shipment
        ADD CONSTRAINT pk_Shipment PRIMARY KEY CLUSTERED (OrderDate, ShipmentID)
        ON ps_OrderShipment(OrderDate);
    ```

12. Execute the following code to put the foreign keys back in place. Remember that you need an updated definition since you now have a two column primary key, you have a 2 column foreign key. Your columns in the FOREIGN KEY and REFERENCES clause must be in the same order as the primary key in the Orders.OrderHeader table.

    ```
    ALTER TABLE Orders.OrderDetail
      ADD CONSTRAINT fk_OrderHeaderToOrderDetailOnOrderID FOREIGN KEY(OrderDate,OrderID)
        REFERENCES Orders.OrderHeader (OrderDate,OrderID);
    ALTER TABLE Orders.Shipment
      ADD CONSTRAINT fk_OrderHeaderToShipmentOnOrderID FOREIGN KEY(OrderDate,OrderID)
        REFERENCES Orders.OrderHeader (OrderDate,OrderID);
    ```

13. Finally, recreate the nonclustered indexes by executing the following code. When we create the indexes, we'll partition the indexes to match the table.

    ```
    CREATE NONCLUSTERED INDEX ifn_OrderDate ON Orders.OrderHeader (OrderDate)
    WHERE (OrderDate>='20020115')
    ON ps_OrderHeader(OrderDate);
    CREATE NONCLUSTERED INDEX in_OrderTotal ON Orders.OrderHeader (OrderTotal)
    ON ps_OrderHeader(OrderDate);
    CREATE NONCLUSTERED INDEX in_SKU ON Orders.OrderDetail (SKU)
    ON ps_OrderDetail(OrderDate);
    CREATE NONCLUSTERED INDEX ifn_ShipDate ON Orders.Shipment (ShipDate)
    WHERE (ShipDate>='20020115')
    ON ps_OrderShipment(OrderDate);
    ```

14. Take a deep breath and celebrate. That was a lot of work. You can also celebrate the fact that you just went through one of the more complicated tasks a DBA has to perform and you probably have a piece of knowledge that more than half of the SQL Server DBAs do not.

As you can see from the steps above, it would have been much easier if we would have simply partitioned the table when it was initially created in Chapter 5. But, in order to partition the table way back in Chapter 5, you would have had to understand a lot more about how a database works and how data is stored, something which was explained in subsequent chapters. It also would have made for an extremely boring example. ☺

You should take the time to carefully review all of the steps we went through to move three existing tables filled with data to a partitioning scheme. The steps above should also leave you with a few questions that basically boil down to "why did you do THAT"? Some of the very fine points in the process above will be explained in detail in the following sections, particularly around steps 3, 4, and 13.

Querying Partitioned Tables

The wonderful thing about partitioning a table or an index is that it does not require you to change anything. Partitioning interacts at the storage level, splitting the table or index into storage fragments. It has no effect on the syntax of any command that accesses a table or an index.

Many of the functions we've worked with throughout this book allow you to specify a partition number, but the partition number is always optional. You can run the same command against a partitioned or non-partitioned table without any changes. One interesting item is that you can specify a partition number = 1 for a non-partitioned table and get results back. This is because, in effect, **every** table is partitioned. Instead of having to design 2 storage methodologies – one for partitioned tables and one for non-partitioned tables, the SQL Server team chose to setup the storage engine such that every table will have at least 1 partition. So, for a non-partitioned table or index, every row is stored in partition 1 which is mapped to the filegroup you specified for the table/index storage.

However, when you partition a table, you do have access to a system function called $PARTITION. The $partition function is an overloaded function which accepts either a value or a column name.

For example, if you wanted to know which partition number a certain value belonged to, you could run the following query:

```
SELECT $PARTITION.pfn_OrderHeader ('10/22/2001') ;
SELECT $PARTITION.pfn_OrderHeader ('10/22/2002') ;
```

You specify the partition function you want to query along with the value you are looking for. The value must be either of the same data type as the partition function or possible to implicitly convert to the partition function's data type.

You can use it with a column name to retrieve the partition number of each row as shown in the query below:

```
SELECT $PARTITION.pfn_OrderHeader(OrderDate) AS Partition,
COUNT(*) AS NumberOfRows
FROM Orders.OrderHeader
GROUP BY $PARTITION.pfn_OrderHeader(OrderDate)
ORDER BY Partition;
```

This query reports that the Orders.OrderHeader table has 7364 rows in partition 1 and 724 rows in partition 2. The way this works is that the value in the OrderDate column is handed to the $PARTITION function which then returns the partition number. All we've done with this query is then group by the partition number and return a count for each partition.

Finally, you can use $PARTITION to retrieve all values in a given partition as shown below:

```
SELECT * FROM Orders.OrderHeader
WHERE $PARTITION.pfn_OrderHeader(OrderDate) = 2;
```

Managing Partitions

Once a table or index is partitioned, data will be placed in the appropriate partition by the storage engine. For some tables or indexes, the initial definition you provide for the partition function won't need to change, but for others you will need to add, remove, or both add and remove boundary points from the partition function. This is accomplished with the SPLIT and MERGE commands.

Next Used

NEXT USED is a property of a filegroup within a partition scheme which designates the filegroup which will receive the next partition which is created. This property is automatically set when the partition scheme is created. If the partition scheme was created using the ALL option to send all of the partitions to a single filegroup, then the single filegroup will be assigned the NEXT USED property. If the partition scheme was created such that the number of filegroups exceeds the number of partitions, the first unassigned filegroup will be assigned the NEXT USED property. If the number of filegroups matches the number of partitions, it will depend upon whether you created the partition function as either LEFT or RIGHT. Of course, you can also alter the partition scheme and set the NEXT USED explicitly. So, how can you possibly know what the NEXT USED filegroup is going to be?

I first started working with partitioning almost 11 years ago. In that time, I've repeatedly asked for a simple way to get information about how the boundary points mapped to each filegroup underneath a partition scheme along with the filegroup marked with the NEXT USED property. Unfortunately, Microsoft still hasn't given us the one DMV which would show us the details behind partitioning of each object in a database. So, I had to do it the hard way. You get to do it the easy way…copy the following, **really** nasty query, and use it.

You get all of the information about how objects are partitioned using the following query:

```sql
WITH Main_CTE (SchemaName, TableName, IndexName, PartitionScheme, PartitionSchemeID,
PartitionFunctionID, RangeType, FileGroupName, LogicalFileName, PhysicalFileName,
PartitionNumber, NumRows, DestDataSpaceID, ContainerID)
AS (SELECT DISTINCT SCHEMA_NAME(tbl.schema_id) SchemaName, tbl.name TableName,
        CASE WHEN idx.is_primary_key = 1 THEN 'Primary Key' ELSE idx.name END IndexName,
        CASE WHEN 'PS'=dsidx.type THEN dsidx.name ELSE N'' END PartitionScheme,
        ps.data_space_id AS PartitionSchemeID, ps.function_id PartitionFunctionID,
        CASE WHEN pf.boundary_value_on_right = 1 THEN 'RIGHT' ELSE 'LEFT' END RangeType,
        fg.name FileGroupName, df.name LogicalFileName, df.physical_name PhysicalFileName,
        p.partition_number, p.rows, dds.data_space_id, a.container_id
    FROM sys.tables tbl INNER JOIN sys.indexes idx ON idx.object_id = tbl.object_id
        INNER JOIN sys.data_spaces dsidx ON dsidx.data_space_id = idx.data_space_id
        INNER JOIN sys.partition_schemes ps ON dsidx.name = ps.name
        INNER JOIN sys.destination_data_spaces dds
                                            ON ps.data_space_id = dds.partition_scheme_id
        LEFT JOIN sys.allocation_units a ON a.data_space_id = dds.data_space_id
        INNER JOIN sys.partitions p ON idx.object_id = p.object_id
                                                         AND idx.index_id = p.index_id
            AND (p.hobt_id = a.container_id OR a.container_id IS NULL)
        INNER JOIN sys.filegroups fg ON dds.data_space_id = fg.data_space_id
        INNER JOIN sys.database_files df ON fg.data_space_id = df.data_space_id
        INNER JOIN sys.partition_functions pf ON ps.function_id = pf.function_id
    WHERE dsidx.type = 'PS'),
Part_CTE (function_id, BoundaryValue, partition_id)
AS (SELECT a.function_id, b.value BoundaryValue,
        CASE WHEN a.boundary_value_on_right = 0 THEN b.boundary_id ELSE b.boundary_id + 1 END
    FROM sys.partition_functions a INNER JOIN sys.partition_range_values b
                                                ON a.function_id = b.function_id),
Space_CTE(SchemaName, TableName, IndexName, PartitionScheme, FileGroupName, PartitionNumber,
NumRows, RangeType, BoundaryValue, LogicalFileName, PhysicalFileName)
AS
(SELECT DISTINCT main.SchemaName, main.TableName, main.IndexName, main.PartitionScheme,
main.FileGroupName, NULL PartitionNumber, NULL NumRows, NULL RangeType, NULL BoundaryValue,
main.LogicalFileName, main.PhysicalFileName
FROM Main_CTE main LEFT JOIN Part_CTE AS part ON main.PartitionFunctionID = part.function_id
        AND main.PartitionNumber = part.partition_id
WHERE main.ContainerID IS NULL
UNION
SELECT DISTINCT main.SchemaName, main.TableName, main.IndexName, main.PartitionScheme,
main.FileGroupName, main.PartitionNumber, main.NumRows, main.RangeType, part.BoundaryValue,
main.LogicalFileName, main.PhysicalFileName
FROM Main_CTE main LEFT JOIN Part_CTE AS part ON main.PartitionFunctionID = part.function_id
        AND main.PartitionNumber = part.partition_id
WHERE main.ContainerID IS NOT NULL)

SELECT s.SchemaName, s.TableName, s.IndexName, s.PartitionScheme, s.FileGroupName,
s.PartitionNumber, s.NumRows, s.RangeType, s.BoundaryValue, s.LogicalFileName,
s.PhysicalFileName,
    CASE WHEN s.FileGroupName = (SELECT TOP 1 fg.name
                                FROM sys.partition_schemes ps
                                    INNER JOIN sys.destination_data_spaces dds
                                            ON dds.partition_scheme_id = ps.data_space_id
                                    INNER JOIN sys.filegroups fg
                                            ON fg.data_space_id = dds.data_space_id
                                    LEFT JOIN sys.partition_range_values prv
                                            ON prv.boundary_id = dds.destination_id
                                            AND prv.function_id = ps.function_id
                                WHERE ps.name = s.PartitionScheme
                                ORDER BY dds.destination_id DESC)
        THEN 'NextUsed' ELSE '' END AS NextUsed
FROM Space_CTE s;
```

Any questions about whether you can write or understand really large SELECT statements? Thought you had a reasonable handle on how space was allocated internally? This query will actually explain how all of the storage pieces are tracked within the database catalog. To understand what this monstrosity does, let's break it down into pieces.

The first piece, Main_CTE, is really just an all-purpose space allocation query tailored to partitioned objects. If you wanted all objects, not just the partitioned objects, all you have to use are sys.indexes, sys.partitions, sys.allocation_units, and sys.objects (instead of sys.tables).

```sql
WITH Main_CTE (SchemaName, TableName, IndexName, PartitionScheme, PartitionSchemeID,
    PartitionFunctionID, RangeType, FileGroupName, LogicalFileName, PhysicalFileName,
    PartitionNumber, NumRows, DestDataSpaceID, ContainerID)
AS (SELECT DISTINCT SCHEMA_NAME(tbl.schema_id) SchemaName, tbl.name TableName,
    CASE WHEN idx.is_primary_key = 1 THEN 'Primary Key' ELSE idx.name END IndexName,
    CASE WHEN 'PS'=dsidx.type THEN dsidx.name ELSE N'' END PartitionScheme,
    ps.data_space_id AS PartitionSchemeID, ps.function_id PartitionFunctionID,
    CASE WHEN pf.boundary_value_on_right = 1 THEN 'RIGHT' ELSE 'LEFT' END RangeType,
    fg.name FileGroupName, df.name LogicalFileName, df.physical_name PhysicalFileName,
    p.partition_number, p.rows, dds.data_space_id, a.container_id
    FROM sys.tables tbl INNER JOIN sys.indexes idx ON idx.object_id = tbl.object_id
        INNER JOIN sys.data_spaces dsidx ON dsidx.data_space_id = idx.data_space_id
        INNER JOIN sys.partition_schemes ps ON dsidx.name = ps.name
        INNER JOIN sys.destination_data_spaces dds
                                    ON ps.data_space_id = dds.partition_scheme_id
        LEFT JOIN sys.allocation_units a ON a.data_space_id = dds.data_space_id
        INNER JOIN sys.partitions p ON idx.object_id = p.object_id
                                    AND idx.index_id = p.index_id
            AND (p.hobt_id = a.container_id OR a.container_id IS NULL)
        INNER JOIN sys.filegroups fg ON dds.data_space_id = fg.data_space_id
        INNER JOIN sys.database_files df ON fg.data_space_id = df.data_space_id
        INNER JOIN sys.partition_functions pf ON ps.function_id = pf.function_id
    WHERE dsidx.type = 'PS')
```

Each object which consumes space has to be stored somewhere. The "somewhere" is called a data space and identified by a data_space_id. When you bring partitioning into the picture, you have to map the partition scheme storage object to a data space. This is the destination data space. In order to retrieve information about a partition related to the partition scheme, you have to join the destination data space through the allocation units and then on to sys.partitions. The destination data space is also used to get to the file and filegroup definitions underneath the partition scheme. I would encourage you to spend quite a bit of time playing with this query and the contents of the DMVs referenced in the FROM clause to understand how space is tracked in the database's metadata.

The second piece is a little bit easier. It just pulls the boundary value for each partition of each partition function.

```sql
Part_CTE (function_id, BoundaryValue, partition_id)
AS (SELECT a.function_id, b.value BoundaryValue,
    CASE WHEN a.boundary_value_on_right = 0 THEN b.boundary_id ELSE b.boundary_id + 1 END
    FROM sys.partition_functions a INNER JOIN sys.partition_range_values b
                                    ON a.function_id = b.function_id)
```

The third piece takes the basic space utilization and pulls all of the partitioning information together. The rows where the container_id from sys.allocation_units is NULL are the either the "end" filegroup in the partition scheme or the filegroup marked NEXT USED. The "end" filegroup would be the filegroup containing the far right side of a RANGE RIGHT partition function or the far left side of a RANGE LEFT partition function. Where the container_id is not NULL, the container holds a partition boundary point.

All that is left is to return the desired result set with the last piece of the query.

```
SELECT s.SchemaName, s.TableName, s.IndexName, s.PartitionScheme, s.FileGroupName,
s.PartitionNumber, s.NumRows, s.RangeType, s.BoundaryValue, s.LogicalFileName,
s.PhysicalFileName,
    CASE WHEN s.FileGroupName = (SELECT TOP 1 fg.name
                                  FROM sys.partition_schemes ps
                                    INNER JOIN sys.destination_data_spaces dds
                                        ON dds.partition_scheme_id = ps.data_space_id
                                    INNER JOIN sys.filegroups fg
                                        ON fg.data_space_id = dds.data_space_id
                                    LEFT JOIN sys.partition_range_values prv
                                        ON prv.boundary_id = dds.destination_id
                                       AND prv.function_id = ps.function_id
                                  WHERE ps.name = s.PartitionScheme
                                  ORDER BY dds.destination_id DESC)
         THEN 'NextUsed' ELSE '' END AS NextUsed
FROM Space_CTE s;
```

The important piece of this query is the TOP 1 query which retrieves the highest numbered destination data space.

You can explicitly set the NEXT USED property by using ALTER PARTITION SCHEME as follows:

```
ALTER PARTITION SCHEME pfn_OrderHeader NEXT USED FG5;
```

What does this all really mean? You can either figure out what the next used filegroup is the hard way by trying to wrap your head around the query above or you can apply the Mr. Harshbarger rule which boils down to finding the easy way. What is the easy way? Every time you have to perform a SPLIT or MERGE operation, you execute ALTER PARTITION SCHEME to explicitly set the next used filegroup and never worry about running this obnoxiously huge and convoluted query.

Split and Merge

The SPLIT operator adds a new boundary point to a partition function. MERGE removes a boundary point from a partition function. The general syntax is as follows:

```
ALTER PARTITION FUNCTION partition_function_name()
{SPLIT RANGE ( boundary_value )
  | MERGE RANGE ( boundary_value ) } [ ; ]
```

You can add or remove a boundary point with each operation. If you need to add or remove multiple boundary points, you have to execute ALTER PARTITION FUNCTION once for each boundary point.

SPLIT and MERGE operate on a partition function.

You must be very careful when using the SPLIT and MERGE operators. You are either adding or removing an entire partition from the partition function.

Merge

A partition can only exist in a single filegroup. So, what happens if you have partition 1 stored in FG1, partition 2 stored in FG2, and you remove the boundary point between these two partitions forming a single partition? The data for the single partition cannot remain located in FG1 or FG2. So, SQL Server has to either move all of the data in FG2 to FG1 or move all of the data from FG1 into FG2. The big question is which operation is performed. The answer that many people expect to hear is that SQL Server determines which move is less expensive and selects that operation. Unfortunately, it does not work that way. When you perform the merge, you are basically destroying one partition within the definition. The surviving partition is the one which gets all of the data. Refer to Figure 14-3 below for the example which follows:

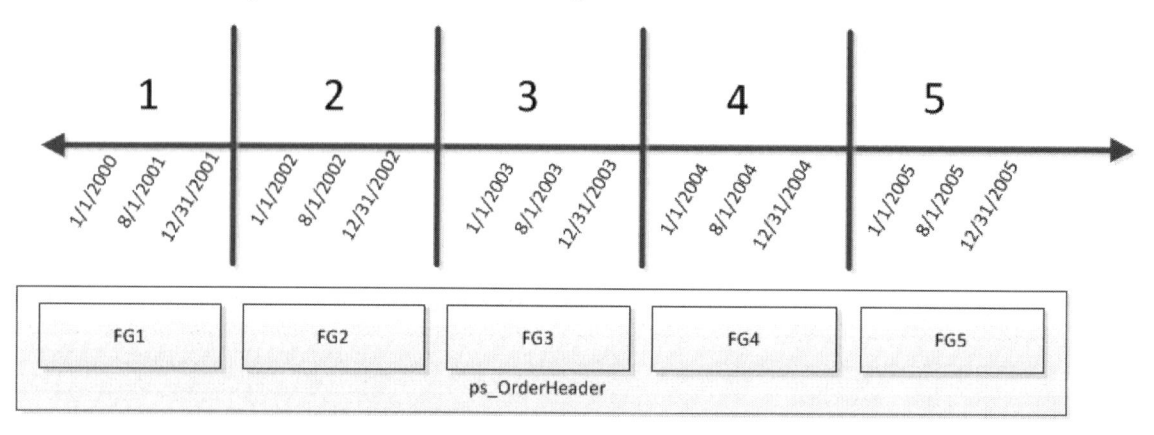

Figure 14-3 Partition function mapped to a partition scheme

The boundary separating partition 1 from partition 2 is 12/31/2001. Since this was defined as RANGE LEFT, the boundary point 12/31/2001 belongs to partition 1. If we remove the 12/31/2001 boundary point by executing the following code, the question is whether all of the data will be stored in FG1 or FG2.

```
ALTER PARTITION FUNCTION pfn_OrderHeader() MERGE RANGE ('12/31/2001');
```

By removing the boundary point at 12/31/2001, we are destroying what is currently partition 1 since the boundary point being removed belongs to partition 1. The surviving partition is partition 2. Therefore, all of the data currently in FG1 will be moved to FG2 when the 12/31/2001 boundary point is removed. The last step of the merge process is to renumber the partitions beginning at 1, so the partition in FG2 becomes partition 1, FG3 becomes partition 2, etc. If we had defined the partition function as RANGE RIGHT, the all of the data in FG2 would have been copied into FG1.

If a merge operation causes a filegroup to no longer contain a partition, the filegroup is also removed from the partition scheme as long as the filegroup is not marked NEXT USED.

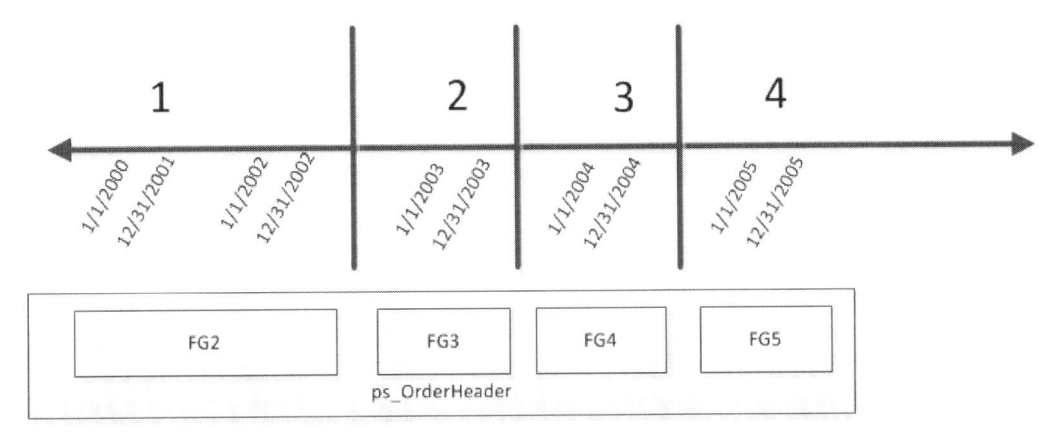

Figure 14-4 Merging a range

Split

If we split a partition which contains data, then the data corresponding to the newly created partition will be moved to the filegroup marked as NEXT USED. Extending the example of above, when we created the ps_OrderHeader partition scheme, it had as many filegroups as partitions. We haven't explicitly set NEXT USED, so the next used filegroup is still set to the default of the last filegroup, which would be FG5.

If we perform the opposite operation by splitting partition 1 by re-introducing the 12/31/2001 boundary point, the question now becomes where is the data?

```
ALTER PARTITION FUNCTION pfn_OrderHeader() SPLIT RANGE ('12/31/2001');
```

When we put the boundary point back in, you might be thinking that the data in 2002 is the newly created partition and all of 2002's data will be moved to FG5 (next used). That isn't the case. The data from -∞ to 12/31/2001 defines the newly created partition. This causes all of 2001's data to move to FG5.

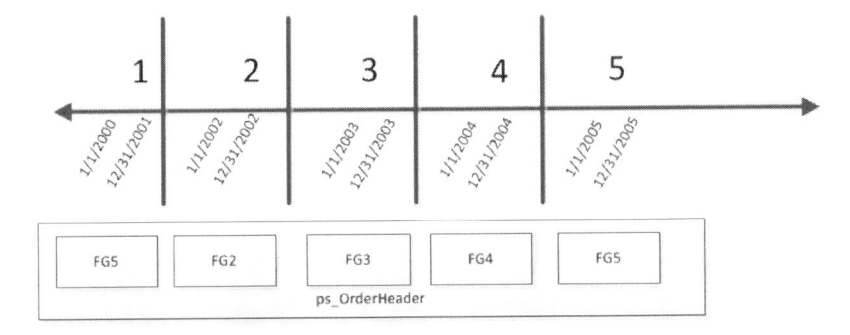

Figure 14-5 Splitting a range

The tables we are working with in the ChampionValleyPens database do not contain very many rows. What would happen if you split a range containing billions of rows of data and caused several million or billion rows to be moved from one filegroup to another? This is why it is critical to understand which partition is being created or destroyed when you alter a partition function. Sometimes splitting or merging a range which causes data to be moved is unavoidable. However, if at all possible, you want to perform your SPLIT and MERGE operations using boundary points which cause an empty partition to be created so that SQL Server does not have to move any data.

This brings us back to steps 3 and 4 in Exercise 1. We created what appear to be duplicate partition functions and schemes. We could have easily created one partition function mapped to a single partition scheme and then partitioned all three tables to the same partition scheme. Now picture what would happen if you had to perform a SPLIT or MERGE causing data to move. The SPLIT and MERGE happen to the partition function. Every table using the partition function would be affected and in this case instead of having just one table with data moving, you would have 3. This is why you will always see me create a different partition function and partition scheme for every table I need to partition. Then if I need to SPLIT or MERGE, I only affect a single table at a time. You also saw me use a generic naming convention for filegroup names. This is because I will generally reuse filegroups instead of dropping them once they no longer contain a partition.

Altering a Partition Scheme

Filegroups can be added to an existing partition scheme in order to create more storage space for a partitioned table. The general syntax is as follows:

```
ALTER PARTITION SCHEME partition_scheme_name
NEXT USED [ filegroup_name ] [ ; ]
```

We already discussed using ALTER PARTITION SCHEME to set the next used filegroup. ALTER PARTITION SCHEME is also used to add a new filegroup to the partition scheme. In order to add a new filegroup to a partition scheme, you have to set the NEXT USED property on the filegroup.

Exercise 2: Splitting and Merging ranges

In the following exercise, we will add several new partitions to the Orders.OrderHeader, Orders.OrderDetail, and Orders.Shipment tables in expectation of loading data through 12/31/2008. We will follow the same convention used where each partition is in a separate filegroup and the three tables are partitioned the same way.

1. Execute the following code to add filegroups for 2006 through 2008.

```
ALTER DATABASE ChampionValleyPens
    ADD FILEGROUP FG6;
ALTER DATABASE ChampionValleyPens
    ADD FILEGROUP FG7;
ALTER DATABASE ChampionValleyPens
    ADD FILEGROUP FG8;
ALTER DATABASE ChampionValleyPens
    ADD FILEGROUP FG9;
```

2. Execute the following code to add 1 file to each of the filegroups.

   ```
   ALTER DATABASE ChampionValleyPens
     ADD FILE
     (NAME= 'ChampionValleyPens6',
      FILENAME = 'C:\ChampionValleyPress\Data\ChampionValleyPens6.ndf',
      SIZE = 20MB, MAXSIZE = UNLIMITED, FILEGROWTH=20MB)
     TO FILEGROUP FG6;
   ALTER DATABASE ChampionValleyPens
     ADD FILE
     (NAME= 'ChampionValleyPens7',
      FILENAME = 'C:\ChampionValleyPress\Data\ChampionValleyPens7.ndf',
      SIZE = 20MB, MAXSIZE = UNLIMITED, FILEGROWTH=20MB)
     TO FILEGROUP FG7;
   ALTER DATABASE ChampionValleyPens
     ADD FILE
     (NAME= 'ChampionValleyPens8',
      FILENAME = 'C:\ChampionValleyPress\Data\ChampionValleyPens8.ndf',
      SIZE = 20MB, MAXSIZE = UNLIMITED, FILEGROWTH=20MB)
     TO FILEGROUP FG8;
   ALTER DATABASE ChampionValleyPens
     ADD FILE
     (NAME= 'ChampionValleyPens9',
      FILENAME = 'C:\ChampionValleyPress\Data\ChampionValleyPens9.ndf',
      SIZE = 20MB, MAXSIZE = UNLIMITED, FILEGROWTH=20MB)
     TO FILEGROUP FG9;
   ```

3. Execute the following code to introduce the 12/31/2005 boundary point.

   ```
   ALTER PARTITION SCHEME ps_OrderHeader NEXT USED FG5;
   ALTER PARTITION SCHEME ps_OrderDetail NEXT USED FG5;
   ALTER PARTITION SCHEME ps_OrderShipment NEXT USED FG5;
   ALTER PARTITION FUNCTION pfn_OrderHeader() SPLIT RANGE ('12/31/2005');
   ALTER PARTITION FUNCTION pfn_OrderDetail() SPLIT RANGE ('12/31/2005');
   ALTER PARTITION FUNCTION pfn_OrderShipment() SPLIT RANGE ('12/31/2005');
   ```

4. Execute the following code to introduce the 12/31/2006 boundary point.

   ```
   ALTER PARTITION SCHEME ps_OrderHeader NEXT USED FG6;
   ALTER PARTITION SCHEME ps_OrderDetail NEXT USED FG6;
   ALTER PARTITION SCHEME ps_OrderShipment NEXT USED FG6;
   ALTER PARTITION FUNCTION pfn_OrderHeader() SPLIT RANGE ('12/31/2006');
   ALTER PARTITION FUNCTION pfn_OrderDetail() SPLIT RANGE ('12/31/2006');
   ALTER PARTITION FUNCTION pfn_OrderShipment() SPLIT RANGE ('12/31/2006');
   ```

5. Execute the following code to introduce the 12/31/2007 boundary point.

   ```
   ALTER PARTITION SCHEME ps_OrderHeader NEXT USED FG7;
   ALTER PARTITION SCHEME ps_OrderDetail NEXT USED FG7;
   ALTER PARTITION SCHEME ps_OrderShipment NEXT USED FG7;
   ALTER PARTITION FUNCTION pfn_OrderHeader() SPLIT RANGE ('12/31/2007');
   ALTER PARTITION FUNCTION pfn_OrderDetail() SPLIT RANGE ('12/31/2007');
   ALTER PARTITION FUNCTION pfn_OrderShipment() SPLIT RANGE ('12/31/2007');
   ```

6. Execute the following code to introduce the 12/31/2008 boundary point.
   ```
   ALTER PARTITION SCHEME ps_OrderHeader NEXT USED FG8;
   ALTER PARTITION SCHEME ps_OrderDetail NEXT USED FG8;
   ALTER PARTITION SCHEME ps_OrderShipment NEXT USED FG8;
   ALTER PARTITION FUNCTION pfn_OrderHeader() SPLIT RANGE ('12/31/2008');
   ALTER PARTITION FUNCTION pfn_OrderDetail() SPLIT RANGE ('12/31/2008');
   ALTER PARTITION FUNCTION pfn_OrderShipment() SPLIT RANGE ('12/31/2008');
   ```
7. Execute the following code to leave each partition scheme pointing to the next empty filegroup to be used.
   ```
   ALTER PARTITION SCHEME ps_OrderHeader NEXT USED FG9;
   ALTER PARTITION SCHEME ps_OrderDetail NEXT USED FG9;
   ALTER PARTITION SCHEME ps_OrderShipment NEXT USED FG9;
   ```
8. Go back to the partitioning monstrosity query above to review the changes to the partitioning layout for the three tables.

Index Alignment

You can partition a table and its indexes using different partition schemes and functions. The only restriction is that the clustered index has to be partitioned the same as the table, because the leaf level of a clustered index is the table. If a table and all of its indexes are partitioned utilizing the same partition function, they are said to be aligned. If a table and all of its indexes utilize the same partition function and the same partition scheme, the storage is aligned as well.

By aligning the storage, rows in a table along with the indexes dependent upon the rows are stored in the same filegroups. If you look at a storage aligned index, you will find that all of the rows for a partition within the index correspond to the same set of rows in the table for the same partition. By storage aligning the indexes and table, you can use one of the most powerful tools for loading and archiving data – SWITCH.

Switch Operator

To understand the effect of storage alignment, we'll take a step back to chapter 6 with our doubly linked list as shown in Figure 14-6.

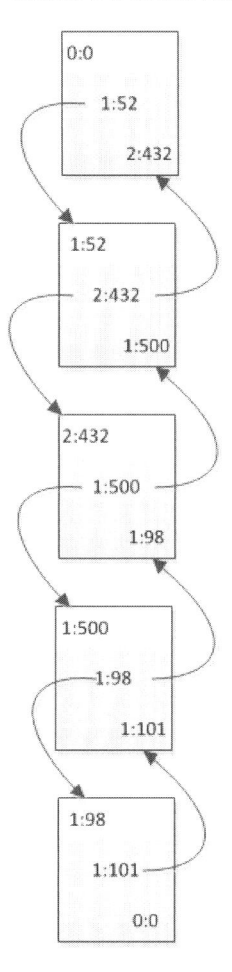

14-6 Doubly linked list

The first page in an object will not have a previous page, therefore the entry will be set to 0:0. The last page of the object does not have a next page entry, so the value will be set to 0:0. When a value of 0:0 for the next page is located, SQL Server does not have to read any further. That means the 0:0 entries define the first and last pages of the table. As soon as SQL Server hits a next page ID of 0:0, it stops reading.

When a table is partitioned, the data is physically sorted, split into partitions, and stored in filegroups. Partition 1 will contain the first page in the page chain and the highest numbered partition will contain the last page in the page chain. What that means is all you really have to do is go into the page chain at any point and set the next page ID to 0:0 and all of the pages which were part of the table "disappear" since SQL Server will never read past 0:0. The change made is a very simple and very fast metadata operation which causes anything downstream from the page being modified to get chopped off the table.

The opposite also applies. If you had a long stack of pages in a doubly linked list and wanted to append the entire stack to the end of a table, all you would have to do is find the last page in the table and change the next page ID from 0:0 to the page ID of the first page in the stack as well as change the previous page ID in the stack from 0:0 to the last page in the table. Suddenly, the entire stack of pages is part of the table, accomplished with two metadata writes.

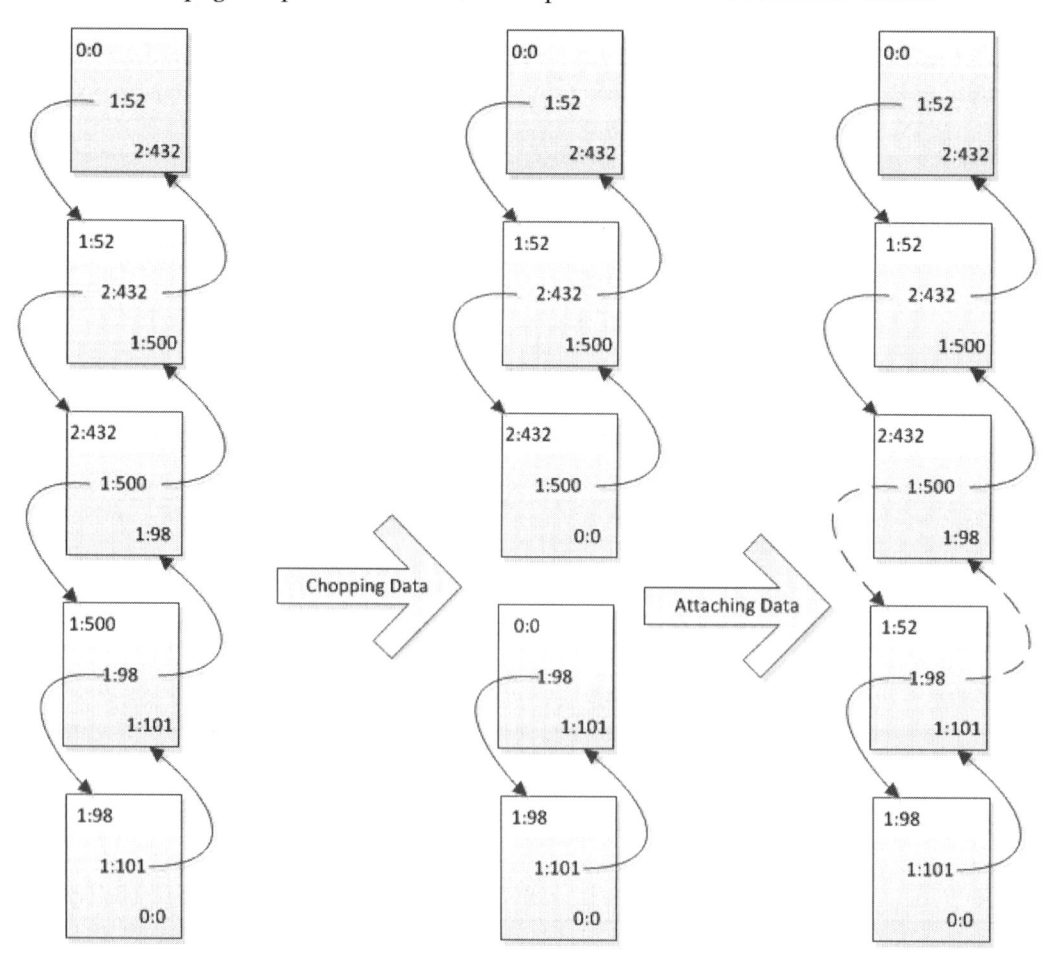

Figure 14-7 Removing or Adding data to a table

You can't simply throw pages away and you can't magically build a stack of pages outside of a table structure. What you can do is create a second table with the same definition as the partitioned table and then move an entire partition between the two tables.

Swapping partitions between two tables is done by the SWITCH operator and is only possible if the following conditions are met:

- Source and target tables must have the same structure. Same column definitions as well as all of the indexes being the same.
- The table and indexes for the source and target tables must be storage aligned.
- Data cannot be moved from one filegroup to another.
- Two partitions with data cannot be exchanged, which means the target partition must be empty.
- The source or target table cannot be participating in replication.
- The source or target tables cannot have full text indexes or a FILESTREAM data type defined.

The reason for all of the restrictions on SWITCH is because it was designed with one primary requirement – to be perfectly scalable. Perfectly scalable means the performance of SWITCH is not dependent on the amount of data being moved. In order to be perfectly scalable, SWITCH must be constrained to performing a metadata only operation. It cannot read data pages or write data pages. All of the data being moved has to be present in the same filegroup so that all SWITCH has to do is manipulate page pointers.

Change Tracking

Both Change Tracking and Change Data Capture log changes to a table. SWITCH performs a metadata only operation which cannot be logged by either Change Tracking or Change Data Capture. Therefore, you cannot use the SWITCH operator if the table is configured for either Change Tracking or Change Data Capture.

Columnstore Indexes

In chapter 12, I told you that when a columnstore index is created on a table, the table becomes read only. INSERT, UPDATE, DELETE, and MERGE statements will fail. However, that was only a piece of the story. You can modify a table that has a columnstore index, but you have to do it using the SWITCH operator.

While you can perform a SWITCH, the SPLIT and MERGE commands are not allowed when the table has a columnstore index.

Exercise 3: Moving data using SWITCH

In the following exercise, we'll build a simple demo database for you to play with all of the partitioning features, including SWITCH. We will be archiving a year's worth of data.

1. Run the following code to create the PartitionTest database.

    ```
    CREATE DATABASE PartitionTest
    CONTAINMENT = NONE
    ON  PRIMARY
    (NAME = N'PartitionTest', FILENAME =
    N'C:\ChampionValleyPress\Data\PartitionTest.mdf' ,
                                    SIZE = 10MB , MAXSIZE = UNLIMITED,
    FILEGROWTH = 10MB ),
    FILEGROUP FG1
    (NAME = N'PartitionTest1', FILENAME =
    N'C:\ChampionValleyPress\Data\PartitionTest1.ndf' ,
                                    SIZE = 10MB , MAXSIZE = UNLIMITED,
    FILEGROWTH = 10MB ),
    FILEGROUP FG2
    (NAME = N'PartitionTest2', FILENAME =
    N'C:\ChampionValleyPress\Data\PartitionTest2.ndf' ,
                                    SIZE = 10MB , MAXSIZE = UNLIMITED,
    FILEGROWTH = 10MB ),
    FILEGROUP FG3
    (NAME = N'PartitionTest3', FILENAME =
    N'C:\ChampionValleyPress\Data\PartitionTest3.ndf',
                                    SIZE = 10MB , MAXSIZE = UNLIMITED,
    FILEGROWTH = 10MB )
    LOG ON
    (NAME = N'PartitionTestLog', FILENAME =
    N'C:\ChampionValleyPress\Log\PartitionTest.ldf',
                                    SIZE = 10MB , MAXSIZE = UNLIMITED ,
    FILEGROWTH = 10%);
    ```

2. Run the following code to change context to the PartitionTest database and created the partition function and partition scheme we will be using.

    ```
    USE PartitionTest;
    GO


    CREATE PARTITION FUNCTION pfn_Orders (DATE)
    AS RANGE RIGHT FOR VALUES ('1/1/2005','1/1/2006');
    CREATE PARTITION SCHEME ps_Orders
    AS PARTITION pfn_Orders TO (FG1, FG2, FG3);
    ```

3. Execute the following code to create the Orders.Orders table.

    ```
    CREATE SCHEMA Orders AUTHORIZATION dbo;
    GO

    CREATE TABLE Orders.Orders
    (OrderID     INT      IDENTITY(1,1),
    OrderDate    DATE     NOT NULL,
    OrderAmount  MONEY    NOT NULL
    CONSTRAINT pk_Orders PRIMARY KEY CLUSTERED (OrderDate,OrderID))
    ON ps_Orders(OrderDate);
    ```

4. Execute the following code to populate the table with some sample data.

```
SET NOCOUNT ON;
DECLARE @month  INT = 1,
        @day    INT = 1,
        @year   INT = 2005;

WHILE @year < 2007
BEGIN
    WHILE @month <= 12
    BEGIN
        WHILE @day <= 28
        BEGIN
            INSERT Orders.Orders (OrderDate, OrderAmount)
            SELECT CAST(@month AS VARCHAR(2)) + '/' + CAST(@day AS VARCHAR(2)) + '/'
                  + CAST(@year AS VARCHAR(4)), @day * 20;

            SET @day = @day + 1;
        END;

        SET @day = 1;
        SET @month = @month + 1;
    END;

    SET @day = 1;
    SET @month = 1;
    SET @year = @year + 1;
END;
```

5. Execute the following code to create the columnstore index.

```
CREATE NONCLUSTERED COLUMNSTORE INDEX ics_Orders
ON Orders.Orders (OrderDate, OrderAmount)
ON ps_Orders(OrderDate);
```

6. Execute the following code to create the archive table and then review the contents of each table.

```
CREATE TABLE Orders.OrdersArchive
(OrderID     INT     NOT NULL,
OrderDate    DATE    NOT NULL,
OrderAmount  MONEY   NOT NULL
CONSTRAINT pk_OrdersArchive PRIMARY KEY CLUSTERED (OrderDate,OrderID))
ON FG2;
GO

SELECT * FROM Orders.Orders;
SELECT * FROM Orders.OrdersArchive;
```

7. Execute the following code to move the 2005 data from the Orders.Orders table to the Orders.OrdersArchive table.

```
ALTER TABLE Orders.Orders
SWITCH PARTITION 2 TO Orders.OrdersArchive;
```

8. Review the contents of each table following the SWITCH operation.

```
SELECT * FROM Orders.Orders;
SELECT * FROM Orders.OrdersArchive;
```

Summary

You can store tables and indexes on two types of storage structures; filegroups and partition schemes. When you store a table or index on a filegroup the entire contents of the table/index must reside on the single filegroup. A partition scheme creates an alternative storage structure which can allow you to store a table/index on multiple filegroups, but each partition must still be located on a single filegroup underneath the partition scheme.

The reason that partitioning was introduced in SQL Server 2005 was to enable the ability to quickly move large quantities of data into and out of tables. You could load large volumes of data offline where users were not impacted by locks being acquired. Once the data was staged you could then use the SWITCH operator to move the entire set of data into the table where it would become visible for users to query without having to take out locks. You could also purge or archive large volumes of data without needing the locks associated with a DELETE operation. You can simply SWITCH an entire partition out of the table and once removed you could either drop the archive table, removing all of the data, or you could perform additional operations to move the data to a permanent archive without impacting users.

Index

ACID properties, 139

Aggregate functions, 119, 174, 185, 213, 214, 215, 216, 219, 223, 229, 234, 241, 242, 245, 248, 251, 252, 253, 254, 255, 256, 257, 258, 269, 277, 295, 406, 410

Aggregates
  AVG(), 213, 248, 253, 257, 262, 279, 295
  CEILING(), 184
  COUNT(), 184, 185, 198, 211, 212, 213, 214, 215, 216, 217, 218, 219, 220, 221, 222, 225, 228, 248, 249, 260, 261, 262, 367, 451
  MAX(), 114, 115, 213, 225, 228, 233, 236, 237, 248, 259, 262, 295
  MIN(), 184, 213, 215, 220, 221, 236, 237, 238, 248, 249, 259, 262, 295
  Running, 253
  SUM(), 184, 213, 214, 215, 216, 217, 218, 219, 220, 221, 222, 228, 229, 238, 239, 241, 242, 243, 245, 248, 249, 250, 251, 252, 253, 254, 255, 256, 257, 258, 260, 261, 263, 264, 265, 266, 277, 278, 279, 280, 366

Alias, 120, 171, 172, 173, 201, 221, 222, 224, 235, 242, 244, 246, 252, 275, 346, 350

ALTER DATABASE, 25, 26, 28, 75, 126, 127, 131, 132, 149, 155, 159, 160, 447, 448, 458, 459

ALTER TABLE, 54, 55, 56, 75, 123, 124, 126, 127, 211, 329, 349, 356, 391, 449, 450, 465

ANSI SQL Standard, 36, 37, 52, 138, 166, 192, 223, 290, 337

APPLY Operator, 244, 245
  Cross Apply, 244, 245, 246, 278, 279

arc, elliptic, 284, 302, 303

ArcGIS, 307

asterisk (*)
  SELECT statement, 43, 71, 92, 93, 94, 95, 104, 108, 111, 116, 124, 131, 136, 137, 150, 154, 159, 160, 161, 162, 163, 168, 193, 194, 195, 209, 210, 224, 228, 236, 237, 308, 309, 317, 322, 328, 329, 330, 369, 380, 384, 392, 393, 398, 399, 419, 424, 425, 435, 437, 452, 465

AVG() function, 166, 174, 213, 248, 249, 253, 257, 262, 279, 295, 365, 366, 367, 368, 375, 376

Books Online, 10

Bounding box, 354

B-tree, 85, 313, 314, 315, 325, 337, 338, 339, 357, 362, 376, 377, 378, 380, 387, 394, 403

B-Trees, 315

BufferWithCurves() function, 294

Bulk Copy Program (BCP), 8, 106, 107, 108, 109, 140, 210, 376, 393

BULK INSERT, 8, 106, 109, 110, 140, 210, 376, 393

CASE expression, 10, 187, 188, 206, 226, 241, 242, 243, 262, 278, 383, 384, 453, 454, 455

CAST function, 41, 99, 174, 175, 176, 178, 181, 184, 225, 465

Catalog views, 18, 19, 24, 25, 26, 28, 31, 71, 78, 103, 104, 128, 312, 339, 356, 397, 401, 405, 406, 415, 416, 419, 428, 452, 453

CELLS_PER_OBJECT, 352, 353, 356

Change Data Capture, 125, 127, 129, 130, 131, 134, 145, 408

Change Tracking, 125, 126, 127, 128, 129, 130, 131, 134, 145, 408, 422, 423, 434

CHANGETABLE function, 127, 128

Character Data Types, 38

Circular Strings, 284

Clustered Indexes, 325

COALESCE function, 178, 179, 180, 196

Collations, 5, 6

Column names, 50, 59, 92, 119, 122, 169, 171, 185, 201, 215, 221, 231, 236, 242, 243, 244, 246, 346, 398, 401, 451

Column Properties, 5, 7, 8, 20, 23, 28, 29, 58, 59, 60, 61, 62, 63, 64, 65, 66, 71, 73, 74, 75, 86, 91, 93, 94, 95, 96, 100, 123, 124, 135, 166, 230, 281, 312, 316, 317, 408, 413, 416, 425, 441, 445, 446, 463, 464

Column set, 65, 66, 70, 86, 173, 224

Comment, 102, 173, 175, 176, 178, 179, 180, 181, 182, 184, 185, 205, 212, 213, 216, 217, 219, 221, 231, 238, 240, 243, 247, 249, 250, 254, 255, 256, 258, 267, 290, 292, 426, 431, 449

Common Language Runtime (CLR), 24, 45, 100, 281, 286, 287, 407, 442

Common Table Expression (CTE), 11, 235, 236, 237, 238, 239, 242, 244, 245, 246, 247, 251, 252, 253, 254, 255, 256, 257, 258, 259, 260, 261, 262, 263, 264, 265, 266, 267, 268, 277, 279, 280, 309, 355, 398, 399, 453, 454, 455

   Recursive, 11, 239

Common Table Expressions (CTEs), 240

Compound Curves, 285

Compression, 7, 12, 87, 88, 89, 319

Computed Column, 7, 13, 66, 335, 336

Constraints, 57

   Check, 6, 55
   Default, 103
   Foreign Key, 6, 8, 51, 96, 122, 210
   Primary Key, 6, 13, 50, 51, 52, 54, 55, 56, 57, 58, 59, 66, 71, 72, 75, 116, 123, 124, 158, 354, 356, 384, 445, 446, 450, 453, 454, 464, 465
   Unique, 7, 10, 12, 14, 46, 56, 211, 212, 315, 322, 326, 334, 382

Contained Database, 27, 28, 29, 72, 91, 127, 135, 166, 230, 281, 312, 413, 441

Contained Databases, 27

Contains function, 15, 23, 428, 429, 430, 431, 432, 433

Conversion functions, 176

Convert function, 174, 175, 176, 178, 183, 225

Correlated subquery, 207, 208, 209, 210, 228, 233, 238

Count function, 166, 174, 184, 185, 198, 211, 212, 213, 214, 215, 216, 217, 218, 219, 220, 221, 222, 225, 228, 248, 249, 260, 261, 262, 367, 451

CREATE PARTITION FUNCTION, 442, 448, 464

CREATE PARTITION SCHEME, 443, 448, 464

CREATE PRIMARY XML INDEX, 343

CREATE SELECTIVE XML INDEX, 344, 345, 346, 347, 349

CREATE SPATIAL INDEX, 356

CREATE TABLE, 48, 49, 50, 51, 52, 54, 55, 56, 57, 58, 59, 60, 66, 71, 72, 73, 75, 94, 95, 116, 123, 124, 136, 137, 158, 168, 194, 195, 247, 322, 328, 384, 392, 445, 446, 464, 465

Creating Databases, 28

CROSS JOIN, 10, 206, 244, 264, 309, 328

CUBE, 218

Cunningham, Conor, 410

CURRENT_TIMESTAMP, 180

Curved Polygons, 285

CurveToLineWithTolerance() function, 298

Data Definition Language, 48, 49, 91, 98, 139, 164, 331, 391

Data integrity, 6, 8, 51, 96, 122, 210

Data Manipulation, 134

   Hierarchies, 103
   Identity, 95

Data Manipulation Language, 48, 91, 92, 120, 122, 151, 235, 340, 383, 422

Data Modeling, 33

Data Modification Tables, 119

Data Types

   Binary, 42, 49, 51, 52, 59, 60, 62, 83, 84, 85, 126, 272, 348, 391, 392, 407, 416, 420, 425, 442
   Character, 36, 37, 38, 42, 49, 51, 52, 54, 55, 57, 58, 59, 66, 72, 82, 83, 84, 85, 94, 95, 99,

100, 116, 123, 124, 158, 175, 177, 178, 180, 181, 185, 194, 195, 203, 225, 230, 247, 275, 276, 329, 343, 347, 384, 391, 392, 407, 416, 439, 440, 442, 445, 465

Date and Time, 40, 41, 42, 51, 52, 55, 56, 59, 66, 71, 99, 123, 124, 145, 177, 178, 179, 180, 181, 182, 183, 184, 225, 259, 373, 407, 442, 445, 446, 448, 449, 464, 465

HIERARCHYID, 63

Numeric, 38, 39, 41, 47, 49, 50, 51, 52, 54, 55, 56, 57, 58, 59, 66, 71, 75, 82, 88, 94, 95, 99, 100, 116, 123, 124, 136, 137, 158, 172, 177, 178, 179, 180, 183, 184, 203, 230, 247, 249, 266, 295, 316, 322, 328, 337, 384, 392, 407, 411, 427, 436, 444, 445, 446, 464, 465

ROWVERSION, 6, 46, 407

Spatial, 45, 46, 64, 100, 281, 287, 290, 292, 293, 294, 295, 296, 306, 310, 355, 356, 407, 442

UNIQUEIDENTIFIER, 6, 46, 64, 75, 82, 407

XML, 6, 11, 13, 42, 43, 63, 65, 66, 67, 70, 83, 84, 100, 175, 269, 270, 271, 272, 273, 274, 275, 276, 280, 340, 341, 342, 343, 344, 345, 346, 347, 348, 349, 350, 354, 377, 385, 391, 397, 407, 415, 416, 420, 425, 428, 431, 432, 442

Database Allocation, 77

Database Context, 25

Database Design, 32

Database Internals, 5, 2, 105

Database Structure

Database File, 5, 19

Filegroups, 18

FILESTREAM, 5, 7, 8, 20, 23, 28, 29, 59, 60, 61, 62, 63, 64, 73, 74, 75, 91, 135, 166, 230, 281, 312, 317, 408, 413, 416, 425, 441, 463

FileTable, 8, 22, 71, 73, 74, 75, 110, 198, 272, 413, 415, 416, 420, 425, 438, 440

Transaction Log, 5, 20, 106

Date and Time, 187

Date and Time Data Types, 41

DATE function, 373

DATEADD function, 182, 183, 184, 225, 236, 237, 238, 253

DATEDIFF function, 182, 184, 225, 236, 237, 238, 259

DATENAME function, 182, 241, 242, 243

DATEPART function, 182

DAY function, 182

DBCC PAGE, 79

DBCC SHRINKDATABASE, 26

Deadlock, 153

Deadlocks, 154

DECLARE statement, 39, 41, 99, 100, 102, 112, 114, 115, 116, 131, 177, 178, 179, 180, 185, 287, 290, 292, 293, 294, 295, 296, 306, 310, 355, 436, 439, 440, 465

DEFAULT property, 18

DELETE, 116, 117, 118, 119, 120, 121, 122, 125, 126, 127, 132, 155, 162, 234, 235, 332, 376, 380, 381, 382, 383, 393, 408, 463, 466

DENSE_RANK(), 11, 258, 262, 263

Derived Tables, 222

Designing Tables, 76

Detach database, 27

Determinism, 174

Deterministic functions, 173, 174, 259, 336, 337, 444

directed graph, 44

Dirty reads, 382

Dirty Reads, 145

DML

Delete, 116, 117, 118, 119, 120, 121, 122, 125, 126, 127, 132, 155, 162, 234, 235, 332, 376, 380, 381, 382, 383, 393, 408, 463, 466

INSERT, 92, 93, 94, 95, 96, 101, 102, 103, 104, 109, 112, 113, 116, 117, 119, 120, 121, 122, 124, 125, 126, 131, 136, 137, 140, 155, 158, 194, 195, 210, 234, 235, 247, 319, 322, 328,

332, 376, 377, 381, 382, 383, 384, 388, 392, 408, 463, 465

Update, 111, 112, 113, 114, 115, 116, 117, 119, 120, 121, 122, 124, 125, 126, 127, 132, 151, 153, 154, 155, 159, 160, 161, 162, 163, 234, 329, 332, 373, 375, 376, 382, 383, 384, 385, 388, 408, 422, 449, 463

doubly linked list, 79

DROP TABLE, 75, 117, 328, 380, 384, 393

Duplicate Keys, 322

Dynamic file growth, 19

edges, 44

ellipsoid, 304, 306, 351

EPSG (European Petroleum Survey Group), 303, 305

ESRI, 307

EXCEPT, 233

Exclusive Locks, 139, 140, 143, 145, 147, 148, 151, 152, 154, 165, 379

exist() method, 276, 344

EXISTS predicate, 209, 210, 228, 236, 237

FileTables, 74

Fill Factor, 319

filtered indexes, 337, 338, 374, 385, 398

FIPS code, 308

Fixed Length Rows, 83

FOR XML AUTO, 271, 272

FOR XML RAW, 272, 273, 274

Foreign Keys, 54, 56, 75, 116, 123, 124, 450

forwarding pointers, 328, 330, 333

FROM clause, 9, 43, 71, 92, 93, 94, 95, 102, 104, 108, 110, 111, 112, 114, 115, 116, 117, 122, 124, 125, 127, 131, 132, 136, 137, 150, 151, 154, 158, 159, 160, 161, 162, 163, 167, 168, 169, 170, 171, 172, 173, 175, 177, 178, 179, 185, 187, 188, 189, 190, 191, 192, 193, 194, 195, 196, 201, 202, 203, 204, 205, 206, 207, 208, 209, 210, 211, 212, 213, 214, 215, 216, 217, 218, 219, 220, 221, 222, 223, 224, 225, 226, 227, 228, 229, 231, 232, 233, 234, 235, 236, 237, 238, 239, 241, 242, 243, 244, 245, 246, 248, 249, 250, 251, 252, 253, 254, 255, 256, 257, 258, 259, 260, 261, 262, 263, 264, 265, 266, 267, 269, 271, 272, 273, 274, 275, 276, 277, 278, 279, 280, 308, 309, 310, 317, 322, 328, 329, 330, 333, 335, 342, 343, 355, 369, 373, 380, 381, 383, 384, 392, 393, 398, 399, 418, 419, 424, 425, 428, 429, 430, 431, 432, 433, 434, 435, 437, 439, 440, 449, 451, 452, 453, 454, 455, 465

FROM Clause, 171

FULL OUTER JOIN, 204, 205

GEOGRAPHY data type, 45, 46, 64, 100, 281, 287, 306, 310, 355, 356, 408, 442

GEOMETRY data type, 45, 46, 64, 100, 281, 287, 290, 292, 293, 294, 295, 296, 306, 356, 407, 442

GeometryCollection, 285

GETDATE() function, 41, 56, 59, 66, 71, 180, 181, 182, 183, 184, 225, 234, 445, 446

GETUTCDATE() function, 180

Globally unique identifiers, 46, 64, 426, 427

graph theory, 43

Graphs, 43

Grid Cells, 350, 351, 352, 353, 354, 355, 356

GROUP BY, 10, 167, 213, 214, 215, 216, 217, 218, 219, 220, 221, 222, 223, 228, 229, 231, 232, 236, 237, 238, 239, 241, 242, 243, 245, 248, 250, 251, 252, 253, 254, 257, 258, 259, 260, 261, 262, 263, 264, 265, 266, 268, 269, 278, 279, 280, 451

Grouping, 10, 167, 213, 214, 215, 216, 217, 218, 219, 220, 221, 222, 223, 228, 229, 231, 232, 236, 237, 238, 239, 241, 242, 243, 245, 248, 249, 250, 251, 252, 253, 254, 257, 258, 259, 260, 261, 262, 263, 264, 265, 266, 268, 269, 278, 279, 280, 451

Grouping sets, 220

GROUPING SETS, 218, 219, 220, 249

HAVING clause, 221

Heap, 90, 320, 325, 326, 327, 328, 330, 331, 376, 377, 378, 379, 380, 381, 402

HIERARCHYID, 45

Histogram, 359, 360, 361, 362, 363, 364, 365, 366, 367, 368, 369, 370, 371, 372, 375, 376, 399, 400, 412

IDENTITY, 58

indegree, 44

Index
    Defragmentation, 389, 390, 392, 393, 403, 408

Indexes, 412
    Clustered, 322
    Disable, 127, 422
    Filtered, 337, 338, 374, 385, 398
    Fragmentation, 328, 330, 333
    Page splits, 157, 318, 319, 377, 378, 381, 387, 388, 389
    Pages, 85, 313, 314, 315, 316, 317, 318, 319, 325, 326, 327, 331, 338, 339, 377, 378, 385, 391, 392, 393, 400, 401, 402, 403, 446, 460
    Spatial, 356

Indexs
    Columnstore, 412, 465
    Nonclustered, 335, 336, 338, 339, 340, 392, 396, 400, 446, 450, 465

INNER JOIN, 10, 158, 202, 203, 204, 205, 206, 209, 211, 212, 213, 214, 215, 216, 217, 218, 219, 220, 221, 222, 227, 229, 232, 234, 235, 236, 237, 238, 239, 241, 242, 243, 245, 251, 253, 257, 258, 263, 266, 271, 272, 273, 274, 277, 278, 279, 280, 373, 398, 399, 429, 433, 434, 439, 449, 453, 454, 455

INSERT, 92, 93, 94, 95, 96, 101, 102, 103, 104, 109, 112, 113, 116, 117, 119, 120, 121, 122, 124, 125, 126, 131, 136, 137, 140, 155, 158, 194, 195, 210, 234, 235, 247, 319, 322, 328, 332, 376, 377, 381, 382, 383, 384, 388, 392, 408, 463, 465

Intent lock, 149, 150

intent shared lock, 150, 151

Intermediate level page, 85, 313, 314, 318, 319, 331, 377, 385, 392, 400

INTERSECT, 11, 167, 230, 232, 233, 234

IS NOT NULL, 196, 228, 246, 453

IS NULL, 196, 205, 227, 453, 454

ISDATE(), 181

Isolation levels, 150, 151, 153, 154, 160, 162, 163

Joins, 212
    Cross, 10, 206, 244, 264, 309, 328
    Inner, 10, 158, 202, 203, 204, 205, 206, 209, 211, 212, 213, 214, 215, 216, 217, 218, 219, 220, 221, 222, 227, 229, 232, 234, 235, 236, 237, 238, 239, 241, 242, 243, 245, 251, 253, 257, 258, 263, 266, 271, 272, 273, 274, 277, 278, 279, 280, 373, 398, 399, 429, 433, 434, 439, 449, 453, 454, 455
    Outer, 10, 204, 205, 208, 209, 215, 227, 233, 234

Leaf level page, 85, 313, 314, 315, 316, 317, 318, 319, 325, 326, 327, 331, 338, 339, 377, 378, 385, 391, 392, 393, 400, 401, 402, 403, 446, 460

Left Hand Rule, 305

LEFT OUTER JOIN, 204, 205

Left-hand rule, 305

Line strings, 287, 291, 292, 293, 306, 308

Lines, 287, 291, 292, 293, 306, 308

Lock Escalation, 143

Locks
    Deadlock, 153
    Exclusive, 139, 140, 143, 145, 147, 148, 151, 152, 154, 165, 379
    Intent, 149, 150
    Intent Shared, 150, 151
    Lock structures, 142
    Lock types, 141
    Schema, 331, 391
    Schema Modification, 140, 147
    Shared, 139, 140, 142, 147, 148, 149, 150, 151, 152, 154, 391
    Update, 140

Log sequence number, 20, 130, 132, 133, 134

Longitude, 45, 302, 303, 304, 305

Lost Updates, 146

MakeValid(), 294, 295

Many to Many Relationships, 58

Mass Loading Data, 111

Median, 261

MERGE, 120, 121, 122, 123, 124, 125, 134, 376, 383, 384, 385, 452, 455, 456, 458, 463

Microsoft Help Viewer, 10

Missing indexes, 397, 398, 399

MONTH function, 182, 234, 254, 255, 256, 257, 279

Morten Nielsen, 307

Naming Conventions, 6, 34

National Transportation Atlas, 306

nodes(), 344

Nonclustered Indexes, 331

Nondeterministic functions, 173, 174, 337

Nonrepeatable Reads, 146

NTILE(), 11, 258, 259, 260, 261, 262, 267, 268

NULL, 48

NULLs, 180

Numeric Data Types, 40

OGC, Open Geospatial Consortium, 285, 287, 288, 289, 290, 291, 294

OPENQUERY, 174

OPENROWSET, 174

OPENXML, 174

ORDER BY, 189

ORDER BY clause, 166, 188, 189, 190, 199, 204, 205, 208, 209, 211, 212, 213, 215, 216, 219, 223, 224, 225, 227, 228, 229, 230, 231, 233, 236, 237, 238, 239, 241, 242, 243, 244, 245, 251, 252, 253, 254, 255, 256, 257, 258, 259, 260, 261, 262, 263, 264, 265, 266, 267, 269, 277, 278, 279, 280, 328, 334, 355, 396, 433, 434, 435, 439, 440, 451, 453, 455

outdegree, 44

OUTER JOIN, 10, 204, 205, 206, 208, 209, 215, 233, 234

OUTPUT clause, 119, 120, 122, 124, 125

OVER clause, 223, 248, 249, 250, 251, 252, 253, 254, 255, 256, 257, 258, 259, 260, 261, 262, 263, 265, 266, 267, 268, 269, 279, 280, 328

PAD_INDEX, 319

Page splits, 157, 318, 319, 377, 378, 381, 387, 388, 389

PARSE() method, 176

PARTITION BY operator, 254, 255, 256, 257, 258, 262, 266, 267, 269, 279, 280

Partitioning
  Schemes, 443, 448, 464
Patitioning
  Functions, 442, 448, 454, 456, 464

Persisted columns, 66, 116, 445, 446

Pessimistic concurrency model, 135, 154

Phantom Reads, 146

PIVOT operator, 11, 235, 241, 242, 243, 244, 277

Points, 287, 288, 290, 291, 292, 294, 309, 310

Polygons, 292, 293, 294, 295, 296

PRIMARY KEY constraints, 50, 51, 52, 54, 55, 56, 57, 58, 59, 66, 71, 72, 75, 116, 123, 124, 158, 356, 384, 445, 446, 450, 464, 465

Prime Meridian, 304, 305

Query Optimizer, 13, 357, 358, 360, 362, 366, 369, 370, 371, 372, 373, 375, 378, 382, 385, 386, 387, 393, 394, 397, 398, 400, 402, 403, 412, 429

query() method, 275, 276, 344

RANGE LEFT, 442, 448, 454, 456

RANGE RIGHT, 442, 454, 456, 464

RANK(), 11, 258, 262, 263, 264, 267, 280

Ranking functions, 11, 258, 259, 260, 261, 262, 263, 264, 267, 268, 280, 328

READ COMMITTED, 151, 153, 154

Index 473

READ SERIALIZABLE, 149

READ UNCOMMITTED, 382

Reduce() function, 298

REPEATABLE READ, 150, 151

Restricted Length Data, 84

RID, 150, 326, 327, 330, 331, 332, 338, 382, 391, 395, 449

RIGHT OUTER JOIN, 204, 206, 215, 227

ROLLBACK transaction, 136, 137, 147, 148, 151

ROLLUP, 217

Root page, 85, 319, 331, 377, 378

Row Constructors, 235

Row Versioning, 165

ROW_NUMBER(), 11, 258, 259, 260, 261, 262, 263, 328

Schema, 35

schema lock, 331, 391

Schemas, 35, 43, 140, 144, 348

Security

    Authentication, 5, 6, 9

SELECT, 8, 39, 41, 43, 71, 91, 92, 93, 94, 95, 99, 100, 101, 102, 104, 108, 111, 112, 114, 115, 116, 120, 121, 122, 124, 125, 126, 127, 131, 134, 136, 137, 150, 151, 154, 158, 159, 160, 161, 162, 163, 164, 166, 167, 168, 169, 170, 171, 172, 173, 174, 175, 176, 177, 178, 179, 180, 181, 182, 183, 184, 185, 186, 187, 188, 189, 190, 191, 192, 193, 194, 195, 196, 200, 201, 202, 203, 204, 205, 206, 207, 208, 209, 210, 211, 212, 213, 214, 215, 216, 217, 218, 219, 220, 221, 222, 223, 224, 225, 226, 227, 228, 229, 230, 231, 232, 233, 234, 235, 236, 237, 238, 239, 241, 242, 243, 244, 245, 246, 248, 249, 250, 251, 252, 253, 254, 255, 256, 257, 258, 259, 260, 261, 262, 263, 264, 265, 266, 267, 270, 271, 272, 273, 274, 275, 276, 277, 278, 279, 280, 281, 287, 290, 292, 293, 294, 295, 296, 306, 308, 309, 310, 311, 317, 322, 323, 328, 329, 330, 332, 342, 343, 355, 369, 373, 380, 382, 384, 392, 393, 394, 395, 398, 399, 400, 401, 413, 419, 424, 425, 428, 429, 430, 431, 432, 433, 434, 435, 437, 439, 440, 451, 452, 453, 454, 455, 465

    SELECT INTO, 8, 39, 41, 43, 71, 91, 92, 93, 94, 95, 99, 100, 101, 102, 104, 108, 111, 112, 114, 115, 116, 120, 121, 122, 124, 125, 126, 127, 131, 134, 136, 137, 150, 151, 154, 158, 159, 160, 161, 162, 163, 164, 166, 167, 168, 169, 170, 171, 172, 173, 174, 175, 176, 177, 178, 179, 180, 181, 182, 183, 184, 185, 186, 187, 188, 189, 190, 191, 192, 193, 194, 195, 196, 200, 201, 202, 203, 204, 205, 206, 207, 208, 209, 210, 211, 212, 213, 214, 215, 216, 217, 218, 219, 220, 221, 222, 223, 224, 225, 226, 227, 228, 229, 230, 231, 232, 233, 234, 235, 236, 237, 238, 239, 241, 242, 243, 244, 245, 246, 248, 249, 250, 251, 252, 253, 254, 255, 256, 257, 258, 259, 260, 261, 262, 263, 264, 265, 266, 267, 270, 271, 272, 273, 274, 275, 276, 277, 278, 279, 280, 281, 287, 290, 292, 293, 294, 295, 296, 306, 308, 309, 310, 317, 322, 323, 328, 329, 330, 332, 342, 343, 355, 369, 373, 380, 382, 384, 392, 393, 394, 395, 398, 399, 400, 401, 413, 419, 424, 425, 428, 429, 430, 431, 432, 433, 434, 435, 437, 439, 440, 451, 452, 453, 454, 455, 465

Sequence gaps, 259

Service Accounts, 5

Set Operators, 234, 246

Shape files, 307

Shape2SQL, 307

shared lock, 139, 140, 142, 147, 148, 149, 150, 151, 152, 154, 391

Slots, 81

SNAPSHOT, 153, 155, 159, 160, 162, 163

Sparse columns, 7, 64, 65, 66, 86, 316

Spatial, 46

    Boundaries, 286

    Data Types, 45, 46, 64, 100, 281, 287, 290, 292, 293, 294, 295, 296, 306, 310, 355, 356, 407, 442

    Left-hand rule, 305

    Methods, 294, 295

Spatial Data, 311
Spatial Reference Systems, 305
SQL Server 2012 Editions, 5
SQL Server Instances, 6
SQL Server Tools, 16
    Configuration Manager, 5, 11, 12, 60, 131, 132
    Database Engine Tuning Advisor, 5, 16
    Distributed Replay, 5, 7, 8, 16
    Management Studio, 5, 13, 14, 15, 16, 22, 23, 25, 62, 67, 123, 168, 169, 170, 173, 272, 275, 308, 432
    Profiler, 5, 15, 16
SRID, Spatial Reference Identifier, 303, 304
Starbucks, 307
STArea() function, 291, 292
STAsText() function, 288, 290, 309
STBoundary() function, 291
STBuffer() function, 294, 298, 300, 310, 355
STContains() function, 296, 300, 355
STConvexHull() function, 310
STCrosses() function, 297
STCurveN() function, 291
STCurveToLine() function, 298
STDifference() function, 296, 298
STDimension() function, 291
STDistance() function, 298, 310, 355
STEquals() function, 299, 355
STExteriorRing() function, 291, 300
STGeometryN() function, 290
STGeometryType() function, 290
STInteriorRingN() function, 291
STIntersection() function, 295
STIntersects() function, 296, 298, 309, 355
STIsClosed() function, 291
STIsEmpty() function, 291
STIsRing() function, 291
STIsSimple() function, 291
STIsValid() function, 294
STLength() function, 293, 306
STNumCurves() function, 291
STNumGeometries() function, 291
STNumInteriorRing() function, 291
STNumPoints() function, 291
Storage Internals
    Extent, 253, 254
    Large Objects, 6, 7, 37, 84, 88, 89, 90, 391
    Page, 7, 12, 14, 38, 78, 80, 88, 89, 158, 318, 377, 394
    Row, 82
    Slot, 324, 329, 330
Storage Metadata, 90
STOverlaps() function, 297, 355
STPointN() function, 291
STRelate() function, 300
String functions
    UPPER(), 184
STSymDifference() function, 296
STTouches() function, 296
STUnion() function, 295, 296, 298
STWithin() function, 294, 296, 355
Subqueries
    Correlated, 207, 208, 209, 210, 228, 233, 238
SWITCHOFFSET function, 181
sys.dm_db_index_operational_stats, 402
sys.dm_db_index_physical_stats, 316, 317, 322, 323, 326, 328, 329, 390, 392, 393, 399, 402, 403
sys.dm_db_index_usage_stats, 402, 403
sys.dm_db_missing_index_details, 397, 398, 399
sys.sp_cdc_enable_db, 129, 131
sys.spatial_reference_systems, 303, 304

System Database, 5, 12, 15, 16, 24, 25, 27, 32, 42, 43, 63, 68, 71, 72, 106, 126, 127, 129, 133, 134, 135, 148, 155, 156, 157, 159, 160, 165, 199, 204, 212, 214, 215, 247, 256, 302, 320, 405, 423, 434

System Databases, 25

Tables

   FileTable, 8, 22, 71, 73, 74, 75, 110, 198, 272, 413, 415, 416, 420, 425, 438, 440

   Temporary, 116

TABLESAMPLE, 191

tempdb, 5, 25, 71, 72, 148, 155, 156, 157, 165, 214, 215, 256, 320

Temporary Tables, 73

Terminators, 123

Tessellation, 350, 351, 352, 353, 354, 355, 356

Texas, 308

TIGER/Line, 306

TIME data type, 40, 41, 51, 52, 55, 56, 59, 66, 71, 180, 181, 182, 183, 445, 446

TIMEOUT clause, 144

TODATETIMEOFFSET function, 181

TOP operator, 190

Tracking Changes, 134

Transaction, 165

Transaction Isolation Levels, 149

Transactions

   Committing, 136, 137, 150, 161, 163, 380, 381

   Isolation Level, 149, 150, 151, 153, 154, 155, 159, 160, 162, 163, 382

   Rollback, 136, 137, 147, 148, 151

   Starting, 136, 137, 150, 151, 153, 154, 160, 161, 162, 163, 164, 380, 381

tree, 44

TRUNCATE, 118

Unicode Data, 37

UNION ALL operator, 231, 232, 239, 277UNION operator, 11, 167, 230, 231, 232, 239, 265, 277, 453

UNPIVOT operator, 11, 235, 242, 243, 244, 246, 278

Unrestricted Length Data, 85

UPDATE, 111, 112, 113, 114, 115, 116, 117, 119, 120, 121, 122, 124, 125, 126, 127, 132, 151, 153, 154, 155, 159, 160, 161, 162, 163, 234, 329, 332, 373, 375, 376, 382, 383, 384, 385, 388, 408, 422, 449, 463

update lock, 140

UPPER(), 184

Variable Length Rows, 83

Variables, 100, 178

WGS 84, World Geodetic System of 1984, 304

WHERE clause, 196

Wildcards, 195

Window functions, 223, 248, 249, 250, 251, 252, 253, 254, 255, 256, 257, 258, 259, 260, 261, 262, 263, 265, 266, 267, 268, 269, 279, 280, 328

Window Functions, 269

WKB, Well known binary, 287, 288, 290

WKT, Well known text, 287, 288, 290, 299

XML

   Attribute Centric, 271, 272, 273, 274

   Methods, 275, 276, 344

   Output Options, 271, 272, 273, 274, 275

   Typed, 43, 67, 270, 275, 341, 347, 348, 349

XML Index

   Selective, 344, 345, 346, 347, 349

XML Methods

   exists(), 276, 344

XMLSCHEMA, 272, 273, 274, 275

YEAR function, 182, 213, 214, 215, 216, 217, 218, 219, 220, 221, 222, 229, 234, 241, 242, 243, 254, 255, 256, 257, 266, 279

Made in the USA
San Bernardino, CA
15 December 2013